THIRD EDITION

# Financial Decision Making

THIRD EDITION

# Financial Decision Making
## Concepts, Problems, & Cases

John J. Hampton
*Seton Hall University*

RESTON PUBLISHING COMPANY, INC.
*A Prentice-Hall Company*
Reston, Virginia

**Library of Congress Cataloging in Publication Data**

Hampton, John J.
　Financial decision making.

　1. Corporations—Finance.　I. Title.
HG4026.H27　1983　658.1'5　82-21619
ISBN 0-8359-2012-7

© 1983 by Reston Publishing Company, Inc.
*A Prentice-Hall Company*
Reston, Virginia

1　3　5　7　9　10　8　6　4　2

PRINTED IN THE UNITED STATES OF AMERICA

To Malissa, Dean and Kirk—*three nice people*

# Contents

**Preface**   xiii

PART I

## The Foundation   1

### 1   Overview of Financial Management   3

Environment of the Firm 3   Nature of Finance 5   Fields of Finance 6   Objectives of the Firm 8   Goals of Financial Management 12   Functions of Financial Management 14   Finance Tools 18   Organization of the Finance Function 21   Financial Management of the Corporation 24   Impact of Data-Processing Systems 25

KEY TERMS 27   STUDY QUESTIONS 27

### 2   Financial Securities and Markets   29

Forms of Business Organization 30   Debt Versus Equity Securities 33   Capital Structure 41   Markets for Corporate Securities 45

KEY TERMS 50   STUDY QUESTIONS 50   PROBLEMS 51

HARRISON INDUSTRIES CASE: *Basic Planning*   52

SMITH AND ASSOCIATES CASE: *Financing Alternatives*   54

### 3   A Review of Financial Accounting   57

Overview 57   Double-Entry Accounting 63

KEY TERMS 71   STUDY QUESTIONS 71   PROBLEMS 72

FREEMAN SOLVENTS CASE: *Managerial Accounting*   75

vii

PART II

# The Firm and Its Operations    83

## 4  Financial Statements    85

Funds and Working Capital 86    Balance Sheet 87    Income Statement 95    Flow-of-Funds Statement 100    Uses of Financial Statements 105    Developing a Flow-of-Funds Statement 106
KEY TERMS 114    STUDY QUESTIONS 115    PROBLEMS 115
CHAMPION SPORTS CASE: *Analyzing Financial Statements    118*

## 5  Financial Analysis    121

Liquidity Ratios 125    Profitability Ratios 132    Ownership Ratios 141
KEY TERMS 149    STUDY QUESTIONS 150    PROBLEMS 150
DONLAN AND PENK CASE: *Financial Analysis    152*
WINNING RACQUETS CASE: *Analyzing Financial Statements    155*
GLENWAY COMPANY CASE: *Analysis of Financial Data    158*

## 6  Profit Planning    161

Financial Planning 161    Break-Even and Profit-Volume Analysis 164    Marginal Analysis 170    Future Earnings Per Share 173
KEY TERMS 179    STUDY QUESTIONS 179    PROBLEMS 180
THE SEN-LIGHT COMPANY CASE: *Marginal Analysis    181*
BALTIMORE POLYMERS COMPANY CASE: *Future Earnings per Share    183*
DAVIDSON PLASTICS CASE: *Profit Planning With Inflation    185*
DUTCH COUNTRY MANUFACTURING CASE: *Profit Planning    191*

## 7  Leverage    194

Return-on-Investment Leverage 194    Marginal-Analysis Leverage 198    Financial Leverage 203    Weaknesses of Profit Planning 207
KEY TERMS 208    STUDY QUESTIONS 209    PROBLEMS 209
DALTON COMPANY CASE: *Leverage    211*
GILBERT VERSUS GRANT CASE: *Which Is Better Manager?    214*

PART III

# Working-Capital Management    217

## 8  Working-Capital and Cash Management    219

Working-Capital Policies 220    Managing Working Capital 223    Cash and Near-Cash Assets 225    How Large a Cash Balance is Needed? 229    Forecasting Cash Flow 232    Cash Management—An Application 234    Managing Disbursements and Collections 237
KEY TERMS 244    STUDY QUESTIONS 244    PROBLEMS 245
CALCO ELECTRONICS COMPANY CASE: *Cash-Flow Forecasting    246*

**9   Management of Receivables and Inventory   248**

Nature of Receivables 248   Costs of Maintaining Receivables 251   Factors Affecting Size of Receivables 253   Policies for Managing Accounts Receivable 254   Receivables Management—The Profit Decision 258   Establishing Credit Limits 263   Nature of Inventories 270   Benefits of Holding Inventories 271   Risks and Costs Associated with Inventories 273   Inventory Management—Minimizing Costs 275   Inventory-Management System 277

KEY TERMS 283   STUDY QUESTIONS 283   PROBLEMS 284
ELKHART SUPPLY AND HARDWARE COMPANY CASE: *Management of Receivables   287*
TEXAS ELECTRONICS COMPANY CASE: *Credit Limits   291*
NORTH JERSEY CARPET COMPANY CASE: *Credit Decision   295*
WESTERN OUTFITTERS CASE: *Management of Inventories   303*


**10   Economics of Working Capital   305**

Time Value of Money 305   Compound or Present Value Tables 309   Present and Compound Value Calculators 310   Effective Cost of Working-Capital Decisions 316
KEY TERMS 320   STUDY QUESTIONS 321   PROBLEMS 321
LARSON MANUFACTURING CASE: *Economics of Credit   322*


**11   Investing Excess Cash   326**

Return on Treasury Bills 326   Rates of Return on Interest-Bearing Bonds 330
Certificates of Deposit Versus Commercial Paper 333   Identifying Sources of Risk 335
KEY TERMS 343   STUDY QUESTIONS 343   PROBLEMS 343
DUNN INDUSTRIES CASE: *Short-Term Investing   345*


PART IV
# Investment Policy   347

**12   Capital Budgeting   349**

Nature of Capital Budgeting 350   Cash Flows 354   Time Value of Money 363
Calculating the Cash-Flow Stream 367   Evaluation of Investment Returns 374
KEY TERMS 384   STUDY QUESTIONS 384   PROBLEMS 385
DARNELL CASE: *Capital Budgeting   388*
BALMOR CORPORATION CASE: *Capital Budgeting   390*


**13   Risk and Required Return   395**

Capital Asset Theory 396   Weighted Average Required Return 402   Calculation of Overall Required Return 410   How Should We Determine Required Return? 415
STUDY QUESTIONS 418   PROBLEMS 418
ARNOLD ATHLETIC SUPPLIES CASE: *Required Return   420*
GENERAL TRANSPORT CASE: *Required Return   423*

## 14   Valuation of the Firm   428

Concept of Value 428   Value of Debt or Fixed Return Securities 435   Value of Common Stock 436   The Gordon Model 440   Comparative Approaches to Valuation 445
KEY TERMS 447   STUDY QUESTIONS 448   PROBLEMS 448
PANAMA PRINTING COMPANY CASE: *Valuation   450*
MARSHALL INVESTMENT CASE: *Security Valuation   454*

## 15   Mergers and Acquisitions   457

Measures of Corporate Growth 457   Forms of Business Combinations 460   Factors Affecting External Growth 464   Pyramiding 469   Takeover Strategies 475   Accounting for Mergers and Acquisitions 486
KEY TERMS 491   STUDY QUESTIONS 492   PROBLEMS 492
INTERNATIONAL TELECOMMUNICATIONS CASE: *Acquisition   494*

## PART V
# Financing Decisions   501

## 16   Sources of Short- and Intermediate-Term Financing   503

Short-Term Financing 503   Financing Secured by Receivables 515   Intermediate-Term Financing 522
KEY TERMS 525   STUDY QUESTIONS 525   PROBLEMS 526
LARSON MANUFACTURING CASE II: *Factoring Decision   528*
OCEANVIEW CONDOMINIUMS: *Intermediate-Term Financing   533*

## 17   Long-Term Financing Decisions   544

Convertible Securities 544   Warrants 547   Long-Term Project Financing 549   Effective Cost of Long-Term Debt 551
KEY TERMS 558   STUDY QUESTIONS 558   PROBLEMS 558
LAWRENCE MANUFACTURING COMPANY CASE: *Project Financing   560*
ACORN INDUSTRIAL APPLICATIONS CASE: *Comparing Long-Term Financing   562*

## 18   Lease-Buy Decisions   565

Introduction to Leasing 565   Issues Related to Leasing Decisions 569   Leasing Forms 573   Installment Financing 575   Factors in Lease-Buy Decisions 579   Comparing Leasing versus Buying 583
KEY TERMS 589   STUDY QUESTIONS 589   PROBLEMS 590
LEVINE SHOES CASE: *Lease-Buy Decision   592*
BENNING HOTELS CASE: *Lease-Buy Decision   595*

**19   Dividend Policies and Decisions   597**

Nature of Dividend Decisions 597   Factors Affecting Dividend Decisions 599
Alternative Forms of Dividends 602   Developing Dividend Policies 608
KEY TERMS 609   STUDY QUESTIONS 610   PROBLEMS 610
DRYDEN INVESTING COMPANY CASE: *Dividend Policies   611*


**Bibliography   615**
**Index   637**

# Preface

A third edition of a finance book published in 1983 is no small task. The availability of financial calculators and low-cost computing capability has changed the world forever for the financial manager. This edition of *Financial Decision Making* reflects those changes which, incidentally, are so substantial that we considered changing the name of the book and not making it a third edition at all.

The difficulty with calculators and computers is to ensure that the reader masters the basic principles of finance during the learning process. If a book moves directly to the techniques without adequately developing the logic, the reader may become a technician rather than an analyst or manager. Careful attention has been paid to balancing the new calculating tools with the fundamentals of finance.

The third edition of *Financial Decision Making* reflects several changes of note to the reader:

1. *A Return to Basics.* The book has been reorganized to emphasize the foundations of finance. A chapter to review accounting has been added for readers whose accounting skills have been diminished by the passage of time. A number of other changes have been incorporated to firmly implant the principles of the discipline.
2. *Expanded Working Capital Coverage.* The high cost of money and increasing uncertainty in the business environment in the 1980s has brought working capital management to the fore for financial managers. New techniques for handling cash, receivables, and inventory have been developed and implemented by companies. The enlarged coverage of cash and receivables management is designed to better prepare the reader for a career in finance.

**3.** *Full Integration of Financial Calculators.*  If the reader understands the role of time value of money, a finance book may be deemed successful. But when that reader enters the financial area of a company, most of the calculations are actually done with computers or financial calculators. This edition continues to illustrate the principles in terms of formulas and tables but also includes a full coverage of time value techniques using calculators with built-in formulas for the time value of money.

In spite of the substantial changes, the third edition of *Financial Decision Making* continues its stress on the analytical aspects of problem solving. The chapters develop step-by-step approaches to guide the reader from basic concepts to increasingly sophisticated analyses. The materials have been revised in response to the comments of a number of readers and reviewers. I would like to convey my appreciation to the students and professors who were kind enough to offer constructive criticisms as well as suggestions for improvement.

Many people contributed to the refinements and changes in this edition. I particularly thank Henry Arnold, M. Cozzini, C. Wagner, and D. Condon. While space does not permit mentioning so many others, they deserve thanks if this edition better meets the reader's needs.

The Foreword to the first edition noted that "Very few things are as exciting as financial management in large organizations that are working to make it through the 1970s." Looking back, financial management almost seemed calm in the 1970s compared to the world of computers and variable interest rates in the 1980s. The challenges are more exciting than ever. As you read these pages, I hope you will see why.

BERNARDSVILLE, N.J.                                                                J.J.H.

PART I

# The Foundation

Overview of Financial Management
Financial Securities and Markets
A Review of Financial Accounting

# 1

# Overview of Financial Management

## ENVIRONMENT OF THE FIRM

The modern industrial or service firm must conduct its business in a rapidly changing and highly competitive environment. A premium is placed on the ability to react quickly and correctly to constantly changing market conditions. Management must be concerned with all aspects of the firm's operations, including production of goods and delivery of services, sales and marketing activities, and supporting functions, such as personnel, training, and data processing. To handle these responsibilities, most firms make extensive use of financial data and reports.

The traditional role of the financial manager involved accurate record keeping, preparation of reports on the company's status and performance, and managing cash so that the firm could pay its bills on time. In this role, financial managers were called upon only when their specialty was needed. For example, when the firm ran short of cash, the financial manager was responsible for locating and obtaining additional funds.

Over time, the role of the financial manager has changed considerably. As of the early 1980s, the financial manager had transcended the traditional role of preparing reports and raising external funds. As businesses became larger and more complex, finance assumed the responsibility of dealing with the problems and decisions associated with managing the firm's assets. The financial manager is involved with the total amount of capital employed by the firm, with the allocation of funds to differing projects and activities, and with the measurement of the results of each allocation. In this framework, the financial manager needs a broad range of skills, a strong grasp of the nature and scope of the finance function, and an understanding of how the firm operates in its particular marketplace.

Today's financial manager deals with a variety of developments that affect the firm's liquidity and profitability, including:

1. High financing costs identified with risk-bearing investments in a capital-intensive environment
2. Diversification by firms into differing businesses, markets, and product lines
3. High rates of inflation that significantly affect planning and forecasting the firm's operations
4. Emphasis on growth, with its requirements for new sources of funds and improved uses of existing funds
5. High rates of change in technology, with an accompanying need for expenditures on research and development
6. Speedy dissemination of information, employing high-speed computers and nationwide and worldwide networks for transmitting financial and operating data

As we enter the mid-1980s, financial management is an exciting and challenging area in managing large organizations. *Financial Decision Making* is primarily concerned with developing the skills needed to make correct decisions in a fast-moving and technologically complex corporate environment. It is organized with a focus on the problems facing the firm and will assist managers in answering pertinent questions dealing with the firm and its competitive performance. Examples of these issues are:

1. Which new proposals for employing capital should be accepted by the firm?
2. What steps can be taken to increase the value of the firm's common stock?
3. How much working capital will be needed to support the company's operations?
4. Where should the firm go to raise long-term capital, and how much will it cost?
5. Should the firm declare dividends on its common stock, and, if so, how large a dividend should be declared?

CHAPTER 1

# NATURE OF FINANCE

Finance is a specialized, functional field found under the general classi-fication of business administration. The term *finance* can be defined as the management of the flows of money through an organization, whether it be a corporation, school, bank, or government agency. Finance concerns itself with the actual flows of money, as well as any claims against money.

Finance, or financial management, is an applied field of business administration. Principles developed by financial managers or borrowed from accounting, economics, or other fields are applied to the problems of managing money. Finance has its own theories and principles but is fundamentally concerned with applications.

As a business discipline, finance can be carefully differentiated from both accounting and economics. *Accounting* is concerned with the record-ing, reporting, and measuring of business transactions. Using a widely accepted double-entry bookkeeping system, accounting provides data on an organization's activities. The data may be historical, as in the case of last year's balance sheet, or they may be a forecast of future operations, as in the case of next year's operating budget. Finance uses the informa-tion provided by the accounting system to make decisions to help orga-nizations achieve their objectives. Stated briefly, accounting is a data-collection process dealing with accurate recording and reporting; finance is a managerial or decision-making process.

Although accountants and financial managers perform different tasks, careers in the two areas frequently overlap. It is not unusual, for example, for a young person to study accounting and then take a position as an accountant. This may be in a corporate setting or with a firm of *certified public accountants*. In mastering the discipline, the accountant will become aware of the financial problems facing the firm or clients. Increas-ingly, the accountant will advise on courses of action contemplated by the firm. After a number of years, the accountant may have become a fi-nancial analyst or manager, no longer doing any accounting on a day-to-day basis. When studying finance, one should recognize its close, natural relationship, as well as the differences, with accounting.

In a similar manner, finance can also be differentiated from *econom-ics*. Economics is concerned with analyzing the allocation of resources in a society. It studies transactions among people involving goods and serv-ices with or without the exchange of money. It is interested in supply and demand, costs and profits, and production and consumption. The broad and highly developed field of economics is closely related to other social sciences, such as sociology, political science, and psychology. Economics may be conveniently divided into two major categories.

1. *Microeconomics* is basically a body of theory that studies how businesses make decisions about pricing and production in different kinds of markets and under differing assumptions. Also called *price theory* or *theory of the firm,* microeconomics tries to explain how rational persons make business decisions.
2. *Macroeconomics,* which is the study of the overall economic situation of a nation or group of nations, attempts to relate such factors as production and consumption into a meaningful view of national economies. It uses definitions such as *gross national product (GNP)* to measure the level of economic activity and has developed fairly sophisticated means for forecasting.

The field of finance rests heavily on the work of economists and uses many economic tools. It begins with the theories and assumptions developed in microeconomics and attempts to apply them in order to explain the workings of a modern business firm. It borrows forecasting and other models from macroeconomics and tests them against current situations in order to predict the results from varying courses of action considered by the firm. Finance is less concerned with theory than is economics. Financial analysts forecast for the individual firm; economists forecast for the industry and the overall level of economic activity.

## FIELDS OF FINANCE

The academic discipline of financial management may be viewed as being made up of five specialized fields. In each field, the financial manager is dealing with the management of money and claims against money. Distinctions arise because different organizations pursue different objectives and do not face the same basic set of problems. There are five generally recognized areas of finance:

1. *Public Finance.* Federal, state, and local governments handle large sums of money, which are received from many sources and must be utilized in accordance with detailed policies and procedures. Governments have the authority to tax and otherwise raise funds and must dispense funds according to legislative and other limitations. Also, governments do not conduct their activities to

achieve the same goals as private organizations. Businesses try to make profits, whereas a government attempts to accomplish social or economic objectives. As a result of these and other differences, a specialized field of public finance has emerged to deal with governmental financial matters.

2. *Securities and Investment Analysis.* Purchases of stocks, bonds, and other securities involve analysis and techniques that are highly specialized. An investor must study the legal and investment characteristics of each type of security, measure the degree of risk involved with each investment, and forecast probable performance in the market. Usually this analysis occurs without the investor having any direct control over the firm or institution represented by the security. The field of investment analysis deals with these matters and attempts to develop techniques to help the investor reduce the risk and increase the likely return from the purchase of selected securities.

3. *International Finance.* When money crosses international boundaries, individuals, businesses, and governments must deal with special kinds of problems. Each country has its own national currency; thus, a citizen of the United States must convert dollars to French francs before being able to purchase goods or services in Paris. Most governments have imposed restrictions on the exchange of currencies, and these may affect business transactions. Governments may be facing financial difficulties, such as balance-of-payments deficits, or may be dealing with economic problems, such as inflation or high levels of unemployment. In these cases, they may require detailed accounting for the flows of funds or may allow only certain types of international transactions. The study of flows of funds between individuals and organizations across national borders and the development of methods of handling the flows more efficiently are properly within the scope of international finance.

4. *Institutional Finance.* A nation's economic structure contains a number of financial institutions, such as banks, insurance companies, pension funds, and credit unions. These institutions gather money from individual savers and accumulate sufficient amounts for efficient investment. Without these institutions, funds would not be readily available to finance business transactions, the purchase of private homes and commercial facilities, and the variety of other activities that require substantial amounts of capital. Institutional finance deals with issues of cap-

ital formation and the organizations that perform the financing function of the economy.

5. *Financial Management.* Individual businesses face problems dealing with the acquisition of funds to carry on their activities and with the determination of optimum methods of employing the funds. In a competitive marketplace, businesses must actively manage their funds to achieve their goals. Many tools and techniques have been developed to assist financial managers to recommend proper courses of action. These tools help the manager determine which sources offer the lowest cost of funds and which activities will provide the greatest return on invested capital. Financial management is the field of greatest concern to the corporate financial officers and will be the major thrust of the approach that we will use in studying finance.

An overview of the five fields of finance is given in Figure 1–1.

## OBJECTIVES OF THE FIRM

A successful business enterprise often uses a goal-oriented financial structure. The financial manager performs certain tasks or functions that help to achieve the goals of the finance department. These goals in turn help the firm achieve its overall operating objectives. The firm should ensure that the actions of all operating units, including finance, are helping it to achieve its stated or understood objectives.

| Public Finance | Securities and Investment Analysis |
|---|---|
| Used in federal, state, and local government. Examines taxes and other revenues. Pursues nonprofit goals. | Used by individual and institutional investors. Measures risk in securities transactions. Measures likely return. |
| Institutional Finance | International Finance |
| Examines banks, insurance companies, and pension funds. Studies saving and capital formation. | Studies economic transactions among nations and individuals internationally. Concerned with flows among countries. |
| Financial Management | |
| Studies financial problems in individual firms.   Seeks sources of low-cost funds.   Seeks profitable business activities. | |

**Figure 1–1**   Various Fields of Finance.

The starting point for developing a goal-oriented financial structure is the defining of workable goals for the firm as a whole. Although they may be stated in general terms, properly defined and understood objectives are the key to successfully moving the firm to a future, desired position. Since business firms are profit-seeking organizations, their objectives are frequently expressed in terms of money. Two primary objectives are commonly encountered: maximization of profits and maximization of wealth.

## MAXIMIZATION OF PROFITS

The first frequently stated goal of the firm is to maximize profits. Many businessmen believe that as long as they are earning as much as possible while holding down costs, they are achieving this goal. Profit maximization has the benefit of being a simple and straightforward statement of purpose. It is easily understood as a rational goal for a business; it focuses the firm's efforts toward making money.

Profit maximization is widely professed, but in fact the concept has several weaknesses:

1. *It Is Vague.* The problem is the definition of the term *profits.* Profits in the short run may be quite different from profits in the long run. If a firm continues to operate a piece of machinery without proper maintenance, it may be able to lower this year's operating expenditures. This will increase profits. But the firm will pay for the short-run saving in future years, when the machine is no longer capable of operating because of prior neglect. Clearly, maximizing profits does not mean neglecting the long-term picture in favor of short-term considerations.

2. *It Ignores Timing.* Because money received today has a higher value than money received next year, a profit-seeking organization must consider the timing of cash flows and profits. If a firm is maximizing profits, does it select a 3-year project with a 20 percent return or a 5-year project with a 17 percent return? The 17 percent project may result in greater total profits if the firm could not immediately reinvest its profits when they were received from the 3-year project.

3. *It Overlooks Quality Aspects of Future Activities.* Businesses do not carry on their activities solely with an eye to achieving the highest possible profits. Some businesses have placed a high value on the growth of sales and are willing to accept lower profits in or-

der to gain the stability provided by a large volume of sales. Other businesses recognize that diversifying their activities into different products or markets strengthens the firm, even though it may result in short-term declines in profits. Other firms use a portion of their profits to achieve social goals or to make contributions to society. It is widely observed that nonprofit factors influence the determination of corporate goals, even in firms professing to maximize profits.

## MAXIMIZATION OF WEALTH

The second frequently encountered objective of a firm is to maximize the value of the firm over the long run. This goal may also be stated as the maximization of wealth, with *wealth* defined as the net present worth of the firm. Rather than focusing directly on profits, this goal emphasizes the impact of profits on the current market value of the firm's securities, notably its common stock. Naturally, there is a correlation between the present worth of a firm and its value over the long run. If the firm will be highly valuable for the foreseeable future, it has a high current value. The reverse would be true for a firm with poor prospects.

The maximization-of-wealth objective is linked to the long-term profits of the firm. A simple calculation that links current value with long-term profits is given in Figure 1–2.

As an example, if a firm expects a net income after taxes of $150,000 per year for many years, the firm would have a present worth of $1 million to an investor who was considering purchasing the firm and who desires a 15 percent return on the money invested ($150,000/.15 = $1 mil-

---

Formula

$$CS_{mkt} = \frac{\text{Net Income}}{E(Rtn)_{req}}$$

where $CS_{mkt}$ =   current market value of the firm's common stock, expressed in dollars.

Net Income =   annual net income after taxes forecast for the firm over the long term.

$E(Rtn)_{req}$ =   expected return that is required by investors before they will purchase and hold the firm's common stock.

---

**Figure 1–2**   Current Value of Common Stock of a Firm Expressed as a Function of Future Earnings and Required Return.

lion). If the firm expected a $225,000 profit each year, we would expect the firm to have a higher present value. By applying the formula, we can see that the firm's present worth would increase to $1.5 million ($225,000/.15).

> **Example:** The Borden Company has 12 million shares of common stock outstanding. Its net income after taxes is $54 million, and this level should continue indefinitely. Investors who purchase Borden stock require a 12.5 percent return on their investment. What is the total value of Borden's common stock? the value on a per share basis?
>
> **Answer:** $432 million at $36 per share as follows:

$$CS_{mkt} = \frac{54,000,000}{.125} = \$432,000,000$$

$$MktPr = \text{market price per share} = \frac{432,000,000}{12,000,000}$$

$$= \$36$$

Maximization of wealth implies other factors in addition to profits. Long-run value is affected by the firm's growth, the amount of risk offered to investors, the price of its stock, and the dividend that it pays. As a general guideline, a firm that is maximizing wealth must do the following:

1. *Avoid High Levels of Risk.* If a firm is taking a long-term perspective on its business operations, it must avoid unnecessary or high levels of risk. Projects that promise exceptionally high profits with relatively high degrees of risk are not accepted. Accepting these projects over the long run means that a single major failure might jeopardize the firm's continued operation.
2. *Pay Dividends.* Dividends are payments from the firm to the stockholders who own the firm. Dividends must be consistent with the firm's and stockholders' needs. During the firm's early, high-growth years, dividends may be small or may take the form of stock to allow the firm to conserve its cash. As the firm reaches maturity and needs to retain less cash to finance its expansion, it will be able to pay out a larger share of profits as div-

idends. By paying consistent, reasonable dividends, the firm helps attract investors seeking dividends, which maintains the market value of the stock and keeps up its present worth.

3. *Seek Growth.* As a firm increases sales and develops new markets for its products, it protects itself against a business setback that might drive it from the marketplace. A large, stable, and diversified volume of sales provides a cushion for the firm against economic recessions, changes in consumer preferences, or other reductions in demand for the firm's products. For this reason, firms taking a maximization-of-wealth approach are continually seeking growth in sales and earnings.

4. *Maintain Market Price of Stock.* The value of the firm's common stock in the marketplace is a matter of primary concern to a management pursuing a goal of wealth maximization. It is the price of the common stock that is, in effect, being maximized. A company's management can take a number of positive steps to maintain the market price of the stock at reasonable levels. By taking time to explain company actions, the managers can encourage individuals to invest in the firm's stock, thus creating a demand for the stock. By seeking sound investments, the firm will appear to be a wise investment choice over the long term. These and other actions can help to draw attention to the firm and keep the present worth of its stock at high levels.

Maximization of wealth is more useful than maximization of profits as a statement of the objective of most business firms. It properly points out that the profit factor should be considered from a long-term point of view. At the same time, it balances this single factor with related goals such as growth, stability, risk avoidance, and the market price of the firm's stock.

## GOALS OF FINANCIAL MANAGEMENT

In the pursuit of maximum wealth, financial management interprets the firm's primary goal into more immediate goals. This is true of other operating areas as well as finance. The marketing area might identify goals such as increasing sales or successfully entering new markets. The production area might establish goals of reducing manufacturing expenses or speeding the production process. By reaching their own functional area goals, these departments help the firm achieve the overall wealth maximization goal.

A number of classifications can be used to define the specific goals of financial management. We will discuss two of these approaches.

## PROFIT-RISK APPROACH TO FINANCIAL GOALS

The first classification scheme recognizes that finance deals with creating the proper framework to maximize profits at a given level of risk. In pursuing this balance, the firm must develop controls over flows of funds while allowing sufficient flexibility to respond to changes in the operating environment. This classification method identifies four goals:

1. *Maximize Profits.* Finance should strive for a high level of primarily long-term and secondarily short-term corporate profits.
2. *Minimize Risk.* Finance should always seek courses of action that avoid unnecessary risks and anticipate problem areas and ways of overcoming difficulties.
3. *Maintain Control.* Funds flowing in and out of the firm must be constantly monitored to assure that they are safeguarded and properly utilized. The financial reporting system must be designed to provide timely and accurate pictures of the firm's activities. Errors or weaknesses should be located and corrected without undue delay.
4. *Achieve Flexibility.* The firm should always be prepared to deal with an uncertain future. Flexibility is gained by careful management of funds and activities. If the firm has located sufficient sources of funds in advance of needs, it will be flexible when money is required. If it identifies and analyzes a variety of potential projects, it will have flexibility in determining its courses of action. Finance attempts to be as flexible as possible in providing the funds or data needed to support the production and marketing areas of the firm.

## LIQUIDITY-PROFITABILITY APPROACH TO FINANCIAL GOALS

A second classification states that the financial manager has two goals to achieve. The first is *liquidity*, which means that the firm has adequate cash on hand to meet its obligations at all times. Stated another way, the firm can pay all its bills when due and have sufficient cash to take unanticipated discounts for large cash purchases. In addition, the firm must have a certain level above its expected needs to act as a reserve to meet emergencies. The second goal is *profitability*. We have already discussed the meaning of profitability, which requires the firm's operations to yield a long-term profit for the stockholders as part of the overall goal of maximizing the present value of the common stock.

These two classification schemes are similar and overlapping. Under the risk-profit approach, an element in minimizing risk is the achieving of liquidity. In the same way, achieving liquidity under the liquidity-profitability approach requires the minimization of risk and the maintenance of control in the firm's activities. Whatever the classifying scheme, the financial manager must understand the goals of the firm and the goals of the finance function. Only then can the manager take steps to achieve both sets of goals properly.

## FUNCTIONS OF FINANCIAL MANAGEMENT

In the context of achieving the goals stated previously, financial managers perform tasks in several areas. We will refer to these as the functional areas of finance and use two approaches to identify the functions that must be performed. One classification system links the functions to the twin goals of liquidity and profitability. Each task is linked with the goal of liquidity, profitability, or both. The second classification method focuses on what is being managed—assets or funds. With this method, a distinction is made between the decision-making aspects of finance and the specialized advisory role of the financial manager.

### FUNCTIONS LEADING TO LIQUIDITY

In seeking sufficient liquidity to carry out the firm's activities, the financial manager performs tasks such as the following:

1. *Forecasting Cash Flows.* Successful day-to-day operations require the firm to be able to pay its bills promptly. This is largely a matter of matching cash inflows against outflows. The firm must be able to forecast the sources and timing of inflows from customers and use them to pay its creditors and suppliers.
2. *Raising Funds.* The firm receives its financing from a variety of sources. At different times some sources will be more desirable than others. A possible source of funds may not, at a given time, have sufficient funds available to meet the firm's needs, or the funds may be prohibitively expensive. The financial manager must identify the amount of funds available from each source

and the periods when the funds will be needed; then the manager must take steps to ensure that the funds will actually be available and committed to the firm. As an example, the manager may decide to sell additional shares of the firm's stock in order to raise money. When a firm issues new common stock, it generally uses the services of an investment banker. The banker helps the firm to find sufficient purchasers for all the new shares at a fair price to the firm. If the issue is not properly timed, it may fail to raise the money needed by the firm.

3. *Managing the Flow of Internal Funds.* A large firm has a number of different bank accounts for various operating divisions or for special purposes. The money that flows among these internal accounts should be carefully monitored. Frequently, a firm has excess cash in one bank account when it has a need for cash elsewhere in the firm. By continuously checking on the cash levels in the headquarter's and each operating division's accounts, the manager can achieve a high degree of liquidity with minimum external borrowing. Shortages and the costs associated with short-term borrowing are reasons to control the use and distribution of the firm's money aggressively.

## FUNCTIONS LEADING TO PROFITABILITY

In seeking profits for the firm, the financial manager can be a full member of the corporate management structure. In this role, the manager provides specific input into the decision-making process, based on financial training and actions. With respect to profitability, some of the specific functions are the following:

1. *Cost Control.* Most large corporations have detailed cost-accounting systems to monitor expenditures in the operational areas of the firm. Data are fed into the system on a daily basis and computer-processed; reports containing important information on activities are printed. Because of supervising the accounting and reporting functions, the financial manager is in a position to monitor and measure the amounts of money spent or committed by the company. Possibly the first person to recognize rising costs for supplies or production processes, the manager can then make recommendations to bring costs back under control.

2. *Pricing.* Some of the most important decisions made by the firm

involve the prices established for its products, product lines, and services. The philosophy and approach to the pricing policy are critical elements in the company's marketing effort, image, and sales level. Determination of the appropriate price should be a joint decision of the marketing and finance managers. The marketing manager provides information on how differing prices will affect demand in the market and the firm's competitive position. The financial manager can supply important information about costs, changes in costs at varying levels of production, and the profit margins needed to carry on the business successfully. In effect, finance provides tools to analyze profit requirements in pricing decisions and contributes to the formulation of pricing policies.

3. *Forecasting Profits.* The financial manager is usually responsible for gathering and analyzing the relevant data and making forecasts of profit levels. To estimate profits from future sales, the firm must be aware of current costs, likely increases in costs, and likely changes in the ability of the firm to sell its products at established or planned selling prices. Many variables affect these items; finance must receive cost inputs from purchasing and production and sales inputs from marketing. Once costs and sales are forecast, the data must be arranged in a financial format to calculate the expected profit. In the same way, before funds are committed to new projects, the expected profits must be determined and evaluated. Will the profits justify the initial expenditure?

4. *Measuring Required Return.* Every time a firm invests its capital, it must make a risk-return decision. Is the level of return offered by the project adequate for the level of risk therein? The *required return* is the rate of return that must be expected from a proposal before it can be accepted. It is sometimes called the *cost of capital.* Determining the firm's required return or cost of capital is a profitability function.

## MANAGEMENT FUNCTIONS

In performing the many functions leading to liquidity and profitability, the financial manager operates in two distinct roles. One role is a manager, a decision maker, a participant on the corporate team trying to maximize the value of the firm over the long run. The other role is a specialized staff officer, an expert on financial matters and money markets, an individual with specific knowledge and skills in the area of money management.

These two roles are recognized in the two categories of functions performed by the financial manager. These are managing assets and managing funds.

## MANAGING ASSETS

*Assets* are the resources by which the firm is able to conduct business. The term *assets* includes buildings, machinery, vehicles, inventory, money, and other resources owned or leased by the firm. A firm's assets must be carefully managed and a number of decisions must be made concerning their use.

The function of asset management recognizes the decision-making role of the financial manager. Finance personnel meet with other officers of the firm and participate in making decisions affecting the current and future utilization of the firm's resources. As an example, these managers may discuss the total amount of assets needed by the firm to carry out its operations. They will determine the composition or mix of assets that will help the firm best achieve its goals. They will identify ways to use existing assets more effectively and reduce waste and unneeded expenses.

This decision-making role crosses liquidity and profitability lines. Converting idle equipment to cash improves liquidity. Reducing costs improves profitability.

## MANAGING FUNDS

*Funds* may be viewed as the liquid assets of the firm. The term *funds* includes cash held by the firm, money borrowed by the firm, and money gained from purchasers of common and preferred stock.

In the management of funds, the financial manager acts as a specialized staff officer to the president of the company. The manager is responsible for having sufficient funds for the firm to conduct its business and to pay its bills and must locate money to finance receivables and inventories, make arrangements for the purchase of assets, and identify sources of long-term financing. Cash must be available to pay dividends declared by the board of directors.

The management of funds has both liquidity and profitability aspects. If the firm's funds are inadequate, the firm may default on the pay-

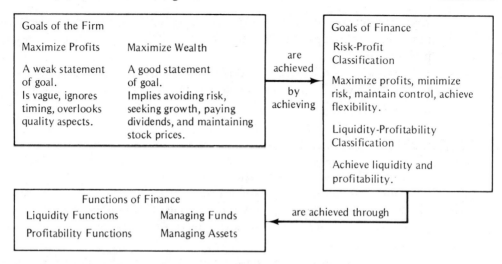

**Figure 1-3** Relationship Between Goals of the Firm and Functions of Finance.

ment of bills, interest on its debt, or repayment of the principal when a loan is due. If the firm does not carefully choose its financing methods, it may pay excessive interest costs with a subsequent decline in profits.

An overview of how the goals of the firm are achieved through goals and functions of finance is presented in Figure 1-3.

## FINANCE TOOLS

However they are defined, the functions of financial management involve the use of tools to achieve the objectives of the firm. Because the functions are interrelated, they are usually performed together in the striving for goals. If the firm's problems are approached in a systematic manner using the appropriate analytical tools, competent decision making will result.

### WHAT IS A FINANCIAL TOOL?

A *financial tool* is any logical method or technique that can be employed in the hands of a skilled analyst to accomplish the following goals:

1. *Measure the Effectiveness of Actions.* Most managers recognize the difficulty in measuring the effectiveness of the firm's actions and

decisions. For example, the firm may have accepted a project that eventually earned $100,000. Was it successful? Should it have earned $200,000? The application of relevant tools can help provide the answer.

2. *Measure the Validity of Decisions.* Equally difficult are assessments of the validity of a firm's decisions to accept or reject projects. When evaluating mutually exclusive proposals, management must finally select one and reject the others. Will it be the right one? Would another course of action better achieve the company's goal? Although these questions can never be completely answered, financial tools help reduce the uncertainty in this kind of decision making.

### HOW ARE FINANCIAL TOOLS USED?

The use of the tools of financial management begins and ends with the objectives of the firm. In the absence of goals, financial analysis has limited utility at best. To say that a firm earned $2 a share, and thus to use a tool called earnings per share, is meaningless in the absence of other information. If the objective were $1.75 per share, the analysis shows that the firm did better than it expected. If the goal were $4.20 per share, it did not even achieve one-half its objective. This is an obvious example that applies in more complicated analysis—the results must be compared with the objective before the tool has validity.

In line with the firm's objectives, tools help managers solve problems. They do not make the manager's decision. The most sophisticated computer application of financial techniques does no more than accept the variables proposed by the analyst and process them according to the analyst's specifications. The result may be either of the following:

1. *Proper Conversion.* When financial tools are used properly, the result is a conversion of *data*—bits and pieces of fact and knowledge—*to information*—data arranged in some manner useful for decision making.

2. *Improper Conversion.* When improperly handled, tools convert random bits and pieces of knowledge to formatted bits and pieces that are worthless for logical decision making.

The difference between useless data and useful information results from the manager's skill in applying the tool. In this context, one should remember that the tool does not determine the value of its results. Properly used, however, financial tools aid in gaining information for problem solving.

### PROBLEM-SOLVING PROCESS

Financial tools should be applied in a logical, overall problem-solving process. It is the manager's job to find a systematic manner of developing valid information from available data. A common six-step process may be outlined as follows:

1. *Gather Relevant Data.* Knowledge of a firm's activities can be obtained from many sources. Production workers, engineers, salesmen, analysts, managers, and secretaries can provide valuable data. Company reports from the marketing, personnel, accounting, and other departments can contain material that is already prepared for computer processing, if this is desirable. The financial manager should make every effort to determine the location of useful data and the methods to collect them rapidly and accurately.

2. *Select Appropriate Tools.* Finance has developed an array of tools that can be applied to the processing of data. The financial manager must have knowledge of the available techniques and must be able to choose the correct tool for the problems at hand.

3. *Process the Data.* Depending on the amount and complexity of the data, the processing may be done by hand, calculator, or computer. Care must be taken throughout the processing to ensure that the tools properly accept and accurately handle the supplied data.

4. *Examine the Information.* The final phase of processing produces information to be used by the manager. It should be formatted to allow a grasp of the pertinent aspects of the problem. The information should be carefully evaluated. Is it useful? Can it be applied to the problem at hand?

5. *Identify Alternative Courses of Action.* With accurate and timely information, the manager can distinguish different courses of action that will solve the problem facing the firm. Each alternative must be identified, its strengths and weaknesses determined, and its likely success evaluated in terms of achieving the goal or solving the problem.

**6.** *Select One Alternative.* The final step in financial problem solving is to select a single course of action and begin its implementation.

## ORGANIZATION OF THE FINANCE FUNCTION

Top management should be very concerned with the structure and organization of the department responsible for carrying out the functions of finance. Much is at stake. If the firm is given conflicting information, it will have difficulty in identifying suitable courses of action. If financial data are missing or inaccurate, serious problems may not be detected in time for corrective action. The roles of different finance personnel should be clearly defined to avoid conflicts and overlapping of responsibilities.

### FACTORS AFFECTING FINANCIAL STRUCTURE

Large corporations differ widely in the organization of their finance activities, for which there are several reasons:

1. *Varying Needs.* Depending on the nature of the business, size of the firm, and kinds of financing of operations, firms have different financial needs. Manufacturing firms require large amounts of capital to purchase the fixed assets needed for production. These firms require detailed accounting of raw materials, processing of goods, and final inventories. Companies whose major outputs are services have limited concern with the financing of production activities. They may be interested instead in developing a financial system to account for individuals' time spent with each customer and services provided. These different needs help determine the financial organization.
2. *Capabilities of Financial Officers.* The training, skills, and natural abilities of the personnel working on financial problems have an important influence on the structure of the finance functions. If a firm has several highly capable financial managers, they may work in a structure that utilizes their talents to the fullest extent possible. If the managers are less capable, the firm may choose an organization that places less stress on individual personalities and instead emphasizes routine accounting and financial reporting.
3. *Financial Philosophy of the Firm.* Firms vary from the very traditional to the very modern in their approaches to financial management. Some firms make extensive use of computers; other

firms employ mechanical systems of record keeping. Some firms do limited planning; others make extensive use of financial data to forecast conditions. These considerations affect the organization of the finance area.

## TITLES OF FINANCIAL MANAGERS

A variety of titles are used in American business to identify the key financial managers. Although there is no complete agreement, many firms designate three major financial positions in their corporate structure. One position is reserved for the top financial officer with responsibilities over all financial activities. Reporting to that person are two financial officers with their main responsibilities separated along the lines of functional areas: asset management and funds management.

A classification system that is emerging in large corporations uses three titles to identify these three managers:

1. *Vice-President Finance.* This title is reserved for the main financial officer who reports directly to the president of the company. In many cases, a firm has a finance committee formed from top management and members of the board of directors. In these cases, the vice-president finance normally serves as a member of the committee and may report directly to it.

   The vice-president finance has both line and staff responsibilities and is accountable for all the firm's financial activities, including control of funds, decision making, management, and planning. This officer works closely with other members of the top-management team in formulating policies, making decisions, and advising the board of directors. The vice-president finance supervises a staff including the treasurer and controller, who work together closely to monitor the financial impact of operations of other departments.

2. *Treasurer.* The functions related to the management of funds come under the scope of the treasurer. The principal responsibilities include managing the firm's cash flow, forecasting financial needs, maintaining relations with financial institutions, and such operational duties as borrowing, spending, transferring, and safeguarding funds.

3. *Controller.* The functions related to the management and control of assets come under the scope of the controller. This person is responsible for such areas as profit planning, capital spending,

cost measurement, and control, financial studies, and the operational duties involved with corporate accounting and payroll functions.

## DISTINGUISHING BETWEEN THE CONTROLLER AND TREASURER

The distinction between the functional areas of the controller and treasurer has occurred within the past 20 or so years for most firms. Originally, *treasurer* was the title given to the chief financial officer of the firm. Since World War II, the field of *controllership*, particularly with respect to developments in budgeting and financial reporting, became recognized as a distinct functional area. Firms began to identify the controller as the chief accounting officer who gathered data, prepared management reports, and monitored the accounting functions of the firm. The treasurer became the chief financial officer with responsibilities in the area of funds management. A logical development was to create a new top financial position to supervise both activities—the vice-president finance.

Many firms still maintain that the controller is the chief accounting officer, whereas the treasurer is the chief financial officer, both working for a member of the top management group called the vice-president finance. In a sense, this is an unfortunate and outdated distinction, since both positions are concerned with financial matters. The controller is usually an accountant and is thoroughly familiar with accounting matters. Still, the job demands applying the tools of finance to the accounting data to facilitate financial decision making. The controller moves beyond the accounting area into the activities of finance and participates in such tasks as planning, budgeting, and forecasting. Rather than make the distinction between chief financial and chief accounting officer, it is more accurate to distinguish the two positions as the *manager of funds* and the *manager of assets*.

## ADVANCEMENT FOR FINANCIAL OFFICERS

Because of a grasp of problems in many areas of the firm, the vice-president finance is in a particularly good position to be considered for the presidency of the firm when a vacancy occurs. This is especially the case for firms experiencing financial difficulties. The *Harvard Business Review* occasionally reports the percentage of presidents of major firms from various fields. The magazine consistently reports that 15 to 20 percent of corporate presidents spent more than 50 percent of their pre-presidential careers in the finance area.

Individuals may enter the finance field through a variety of entry-level positions. Positions are available in accounting, credit analysis, cash management, and inventory management. Persons who demonstrate the ability to use data to make correct decisions will find finance a challenging and rewarding field.

Finance is a field that should prove particularly attractive to women, members of minority groups, or other individuals who fear that they will not receive full opportunities for advancement. In finance, promotions and additional responsibilities are given to persons who demonstrate high levels of performance. Virtually all business firms value employees who make important contributions to liquidity and profitability. Finance offers real opportunities for persons who seek rewards and recognition through on-the-job performance.

### FINANCE IN THE CORPORATE STRUCTURE

Figures 1–4 and 1–5 give examples of how a firm might be organized with respect to the finance function. Figure 1–4 shows the relationship of the finance area to the other major functional areas of a firm. Figure 1–5 shows the internal organization of the department reporting to the vice-president finance. These organizational charts are highly simplified models. Actual organizational charts vary greatly and contain much greater detail.

## FINANCIAL MANAGEMENT OF THE CORPORATION

The modern financial manager is involved in the broad range of decision making within the corporation. As a foundation, a knowledge of financial markets and financial statements is required. These are used in a frame-

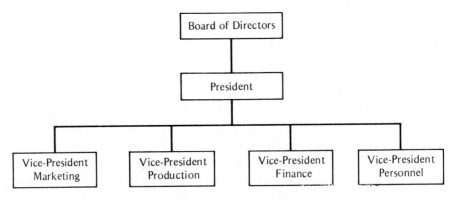

**Figure 1–4**   Sample Organizational Structure of a Firm.

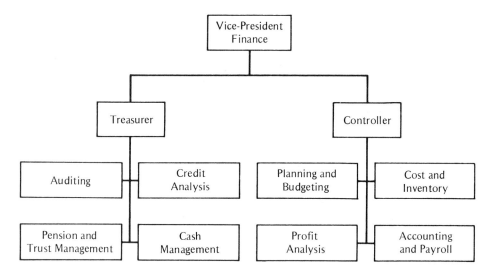

**Figure 1–5**  Sample Organizational Structure of a Financial Department.

work of the theory of risk and return and the time value of money as analytical tools for measuring and forecasting the firm's activities. Decisions may be viewed as either short-term or long-term in nature. The management of near-term assets considers the sources of short-term funds and brings the financial manager into decisions on cash levels, receivables, and inventory. It also requires planning that covers this year's operating revenues and expenses and deals with leverage concepts in the firm's operations and financing. The management of long-term assets builds upon sources of long-term funds and covers issues related to dividend policy, investment policy, cost of capital, and the firm's capital structure. Decisions are also made in related areas, including such issues as the valuation of the firm and mergers and acquisitions.

A graphic overview of financial management of the modern corporation is given in Figure 1–6.

## IMPACT OF DATA-PROCESSING SYSTEMS

From the point of view of decision making, the major impact of the 1970s and 1980s involves changes in the area of electronic data processing. Two developments are of most interest to the financial analyst:

1. *Microprocessors.* Many corporations, businesses, and other organizations own or lease microprocessors, small computers that can

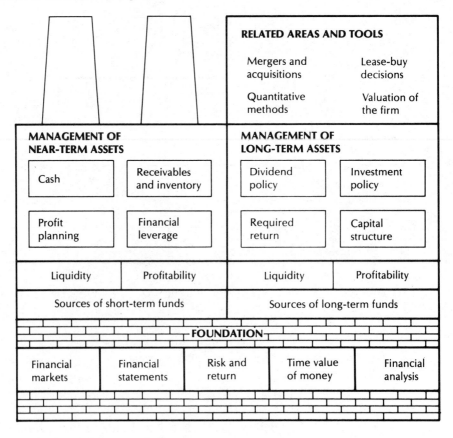

**Figure 1–6**   Financial Management of the Corporation.

store, process and retrieve data. Examples of microprocessors are financial calculators, such as those manufactured by Hewlett-Packard and Texas Instruments, and small computers, such as those manufactured by IBM, Radio Shack, Apple, Wang, and others. A user can enter data into the computer using a keyboard, can manipulate the numbers while viewing them on a television-type screen called a *cathode ray tube* (CRT), and can print the final result to be studied by other analysts. The availability of such units to process relatively large volumes of data offers considerable assistance to an analyst working with a complex financial calculation.

2. *Computer Networks.* A second development of the 1970s and 1980s involves the *computer network,* which is defined as a linkage of a

computer and a number of remote devices, called *terminals,* that allow a user to have access to the computer. Using a terminal next to a desk, an analyst can "talk" to the computer. Data stored in the computer can be updated, processed, and retrieved, either on a screen or as printed copy, in a few minutes without requiring the analyst to leave the desk. A computer network allows an analyst to work with massive amounts of data stored in a large computer even though the computer may be located in another area, building, or city.

While the developments in computer technology have significantly enhanced the capabilities of the financial analyst, the fundamental financial principles have not changed. Companies and organizations still need people who know how to set up a problem and solve it. As an aid to decision making, the computer is a useful tool that should be mastered early in the career of any serious student of finance. At the same time, the computer accepts none of the burden of correctly formatting and analyzing financial situations. This book incorporates financial calculators and computer technology and uses them in a framework of financial analysis.

## KEY TERMS

| | | |
|---|---|---|
| *accounting* | *EDP* | *microprocessor* |
| *assets* | *finance* | *profitability* |
| *certified public accountant* | *financial tool* | *public finance* |
| *computer network* | *funds* | *securities and investment* |
| *controller* | *institutional finance* | *analysis* |
| *cost of capital* | *international finance* | *terminal* |
| *CRT* | *liquidity* | *treasurer* |
| *economics* | *maximization of wealth* | *vice-president finance* |

## STUDY QUESTIONS

1. How do we define *finance*?
2. What are some of the challenges facing the modern financial manager?
3. What are the differences among accounting, economics, and finance?
4. How does public finance differ from financial management?
5. How does securities and investment analysis differ from institutional finance?
6. Why is maximizing wealth a better goal than maximizing profits?
7. When has the firm achieved liquidity and profitability?

8. What are some financial functions that help achieve liquidity? profitability?
9. What does it mean to *manage assets*? *manage funds*?
10. How do financial tools relate to data and information?
11. What is the relationship between tools and decision making?
12. Why do different firms organize their finance activities differently?
13. What are the main functions of the three top financial managers?
14. Why is the controller more than just the chief accounting officer?
15. A firm has earnings of $3 with a 10 percent return on investment desired by investors. What is its current market value?
16. What two recent developments in electronic data processing have had an effect in financial decision making?

# 2

# Financial Securities and Markets

Financial decisions are made in the overall operating and financial environment of the individual firm. In this chapter, we will cover some of these environmental considerations. First we will examine the forms of business organization that can be used to conduct the business. Then, we will review the differing securities that the firm can use to raise its capital. Next we will discuss the capital structure of the firm and considerations that affect the mix of debt and equity securities. Finally we will examine the markets for corporate securities.

As indicated, the role of securities is an important emphasis in this chapter. Before going further, let us define the term. A *financial security* is a legal instrument that represents either an ownership or a creditor claim on a company. Two basic kinds of securities are of concern to the financial manager. A *debt security* arises when a firm borrows money. The firm incurs a liability to repay the amount of money borrowed at some future maturity date. In addition, the firm must pay interest—usually in periodic payments—in return for the right to use the creditor's money. An *equity security* represents ownership in the firm. People who purchase equity securities are entitled to different rights and conditions from the firm's creditors. The exact ownership rights are usually agreed to in advance and may be written in the organizational agreement.

## FORMS OF BUSINESS ORGANIZATION

The exact kinds of securities used in a business venture depend to a large degree on the form of organization selected by the owners. In the United States, there are three basic forms of business organization: the sole proprietorship, the partnership, and the corporation. Each of these is discussed briefly in the following sections.

### SOLE PROPRIETORSHIP

A *sole proprietorship* is a firm owned by a single person who holds the ownership rights to all the assets and who is responsible for all the firm's debts. The single owner receives all the profits from the firm or must suffer any losses. Two aspects of sole proprietorships are noteworthy.

1. *It Is the Easiest Business Form to Establish.* In most cases, an individual begins a sole proprietorship by simply starting up operations. No financial security is required as proof of ownership. The only securities arising from a sole proprietorship are debt securities in the event that the owner borrows money.
2. *It Is the Most Common Form of Business Organization.* Sole proprietorships account for well over half the business in the country. Most sole proprietorships are small operations. Thus, this form is less important than the corporation in terms of business activity. The corporate form is much more prominent in terms of sales, assets, profits, and contributions to the national economy.

### PARTNERSHIP

A *partnership* is a business activity carried on by two or more persons who intend to share the resulting profits or losses. Although a partnership can be formed almost as easily as a sole proprietorship, it is wise to draw up a written agreement to avoid conflicts over such matters as the responsibilities of individual partners or the means for sharing profits. Two types of partnerships should be noted:

1. *General Partnership.* Under this agreement, all partners are liable for the debts of the business. This is the most common form of partnership agreement.
2. *Limited Partnership.* Under this agreement, a partnership has one or more general partners. Other individuals may be designated

as limited partners, whose liability is limited to the amount stipulated in the agreement. The limited partner normally does not
share in the management of the business but shares in the profits
to the extent specified in the agreement.

Although partnerships involve written agreements in most cases,
the agreement is not treated as a financial security. The partnership
agreement is viewed as a legal contract rather than as a security evidencing ownership of a business.

**CORPORATION**

A *corporation* is a legal entity created under the law and empowered to
own assets, to incur liabilities, and to engage in business operations. The
classic definition of the corporation was written by Chief Justice Marshall
in 1819:

> A corporation is an artificial being, invisible, intangible, and existing
> only in contemplation of the law. Being a mere creature of law, it
> possesses only those properties which the character of its creation
> confers upon it, either expressly, or as incidental to its very exist-
> ence. [*Dartmouth College* v. *Woodward*, 4 Wheaton (1819)]

Several characteristics of the corporate form are important:

1. *It Is Formed under the Laws of a Specific State.* The incorporators
   must select a state and then file a *certificate of incorporation* with
   the appropriate state agency. This includes such information as
   the name of the corporation, its purposes, the amount of stock
   authorized, and the location of the main office. After the certificate and any required fees are accepted by the state, a *charter* is
   issued. The incorporators take the charter, which spells out the
   relationship between the corporation and the state, and then
   adopt a set of *bylaws* to regulate the internal management of the
   firm. Once this is done, the corporation is ready to begin business operations.
2. *It Exists Apart from Its Owners.* A corporation is not a group of
   people who have formed a business; it is a separate business entity. Ownership is represented by equity securities. If an individual holding an ownership interest should die, the shares of stock
   pass to the heirs or estate in accordance with the law. The operations of the corporation will probably not be affected.

3. *It Is Advantageous for Large Business Operations.* The corporate form is especially suited for large, complex business activities. The advantages of this form are discussed in the next section.

### ADVANTAGES OF THE CORPORATE FORM

The corporate form of business enterprise is employed by most large firms because it offers three major advantages over sole proprietorship or partnership:

1. *Limited Liability.* Both sole proprietors and general partners are personally liable for the debts of their businesses. If the business fails and cannot pay its debts, the creditors can force the owners to sell their homes or other assets to fulfill the business obligations. This is not true under the corporate form. Once an owner has fully paid for whatever shares being purchased, the owner has no further liability to the firm or to the creditors of the firm. This protection against unlimited liability allows strangers to invest in the common stock of a corporation without fear of losing their personal assets.

2. *Perpetual Existence.* Corporations may be granted a perpetual charter or a 20- or-more-year charter, which can be easily renewed. This allows the corporation to conduct its business indefinitely as long as it is sufficiently profitable to avoid bankruptcy. This is an advantage over sole proprietorships, which cease at the death or retirement of the owner, and partnerships, which are legally dissolved upon the withdrawal, death, or bankruptcy of one of the partners.

3. *Ease of Transferring Ownership.* Because the ownership of a corporation is represented by shares of stock, a portion or all of the ownership can be easily transferred by the sale of stock. In noting this advantage, we must distinguish between two types of corporations:
    a. *Closed corporation* is the term used to describe a small, family-owned corporation in which most of the owners are tied together along either family or friendship lines. These account for approximately 99 percent of all corporations. The owners of a closed corporation experience difficulties in finding buyers for their shares of stock.
    b. *Publicly traded corporations* represent the largest corporations and account for the great bulk of all corporate assets. The

shares of over 5,000 such companies are listed on the different stock exchanges or are quoted in the over-the-counter market. Shares of stock in these large companies have an extremely high degree of transferability. Incorporation represents a significant advantage over other business forms for these firms.

The three forms of business organization are compared in Figure 2–1.

## DEBT VERSUS EQUITY SECURITIES

To start a corporation, the owners must arrange financing. In some cases, the owners have adequate cash for the business needs. They then purchase shares of stock in return for cash, and the firm begins operations. If the owners decide to arrange additional financing, they have two choices: (1) to seek additional owners who will also purchase shares of stock or (2) to borrow money from creditors, thus creating debt securities.

Both debt and equity securities are used in most corporations. The three major financial securities are bonds, preferred stock, and common stock. Each will be discussed in turn.

**Figure 2–1**  Characteristics of the Three Forms of Business Organizations.

**CORPORATE BONDS**

A *corporate bond* is a security representing a long-term promise to pay a certain sum of money at a certain time or over the course of the loan, with a fixed rate of interest payable to the holder of the bond. The specific promises and details of the issue are written in the *bond indenture,* the agreement between the corporation and the bondholders. Corporate bonds are normally issued in denominations of $1,000, and interest may be paid annually or semiannually.

The following are some of the classifications used to identify the differing characteristics of corporate bonds:

1. *Secured versus Unsecured Bonds.* A *debenture* is a bond backed or secured only by the general credit of the corporation. It is the most widely used debt security of American corporations. Although a debenture is not secured by specific assets, its holders have a claim to the corporation's assets if the interest and principal payments are not made. In some cases, the bond debenture specifies that the claim to assets is secondary to the claims of other bondholders. Such a bond is called a *subordinated debenture.* Some bonds are secured by specific assets. A *mortgage bond* is secured by a mortgage lien on a piece of property or on a building. A *collateral trust bond* is secured by collateral, such as stocks or bonds held by a trustee. An *equipment trust bond* is secured by a piece of machinery or equipment, such as a locomotive, whose title is deposited with a trustee.

2. *Bond Maturity.* Bonds have a fixed maturity specified in the bond indenture. A *serial bond* issue has portions that mature in small amounts at periodic intervals. As an example, bonds numbered 1 to 100 may mature in 1995, 101 to 200 may mature in 1998, and so on. A *sinking fund bond* issue requires the corporation to set aside money at regular intervals, usually payable to a trustee, so that sufficient funds accrue to repay the principal at maturity. This technique increases the chances that the firm has sufficient funds set aside to redeem the issue when the time arrives. The setting aside of money at intervals for the gradual payment of a debt is called *amortization.*

3. *Ownership. Bearer bonds* or *coupon bonds* are owned by the person who has physical possession of them, just as a dollar bill is owned by its bearer. These bonds are said to be highly *negotiable* in that they are easily transferred or sold to other parties. These bonds have coupons attached to them, which represent the in-

terest payments on specified dates. To receive interest, the bearer presents the coupon to the agent of the corporation, normally a bank. *Registered bonds* require that the owner's name be listed on the books of the corporation or its agent. When such a bond is sold, the agent must be notified. Interest payments are mailed by check to the registered owner. A registered bond, although somewhat less negotiable than a bearer bond, offers the owner a high degree of safety from theft.

4. *Special Features.* Bonds may be classified by the special features associated with them such as the following:

   a. Interest on *income bonds* does not have to be paid unless the firm earns sufficient income to cover the interest payment. Income bonds are usually issued in connection with the reorganization of a financially troubled firm.

   b. *Convertible bonds* can be converted into common stock or another security of the same corporation at a stated price, under stated conditions, at the option of the holder. When the bond is issued, the conversion price will be higher than the current price. The market price may rise above the conversion price. This will increase the value of the bond and make it attractive to convert it into stock. In return for this attractive feature, a convertible bond normally requires the firm to pay less interest than would be paid for a comparable nonconvertible bond.

   c. *Attached warrants* used to increase the attractiveness of a bond issue permit the bondholder to buy shares of common stock during a stated time period and at a given price. If the warrants are *detachable,* they may be separated from the bonds and sold as separate securities. Such warrants are often listed for trading on the major exchanges.

   d. *Callable bonds* contain a provision in the bond indenture that allows the corporation to retire the issue at a fixed price prior to maturity. The *call price* is normally slightly above par. Most bonds have a call feature, and usually the bondholders are given the option of converting the bond into common stock during the period between the *call* and the retirement date.

## EXAMPLES INVOLVING CORPORATE BONDS

**Example:** A firm issues a bond that is not secured by specific assets. The bond has a provision in the indenture that other bonds have a first priority on the firm's assets in the event of liquidation of the firm. What kind of bond is this?

**Answer:** A subordinated debenture.

**Example:** A $1,000 bond can be converted into 30 shares of common stock at any time prior to 1991. Stock is selling for $28 per share. If the bond were converted and the stock were immediately sold, how much would the bondholder gain or lose (assume a $20 cost for the transactions)?

**Answer:** The bondholder would receive 30 shares of stock worth $28 each, or $840 worth of stock. When the stock is sold, he would receive $840 − $20, or $820, a loss of $180 from the $1,000 value of the bond.

**Example:** In the previous problem, at what selling price of the stock would the bondholder neither gain nor lose?

**Answer:** When the value of 30 shares is $1,020, he neither gains nor loses: $1,020/30 = $34 per share selling price.

**Example:** A bondholder has a $1,000 bond convertible into 50 shares of a firm's stock. The stock is selling for $25. The bond has been called at $1,050. If he converts the bond and sells the stock, he will have a $25 commission to pay. Allowing the bond to be called has no transaction cost. Which alternative yields the most money?

**Answer:** Allowing the call brings in $1,050. Converting yields 50 shares times $25 = $1,250 − $25 transaction costs = $1,225. Converting the bond yields $175 more than allowing the call.

**Example:** A bond has 20 detachable warrants that allow a person to buy 20 total shares of common stock at $10 per share. The stock is selling for $15. It costs $20 to cash in the warrants. Approximately what value would the warrants have if they were detached and sold?

**Answer:** With the warrants, an investor can save $5 per share for 20 shares, or $100; $100 minus the $20 transaction costs means that the warrants should be worth approximately $80.

## PREFERRED STOCK

Although preferred stock is a form of equity security, it combines features of both debt and common stock. Some of the most important features are the following:

1. *Preference to Dividends.* Dividends may be declared on preferred stock after the firm has paid its operating expenses, covered its interest charges, and paid the applicable taxes. The preferred stock has preference over common stock when dividends are distributed. The actual payment of the dividend is discretionary and must be declared by the board of directors. If the board declines to declare a dividend, it is declining to *share the profits of the firm with the shareholders.* Thus, the omission of a dividend is not the same as the default on a debt, since the dividend is not a fixed obligation of the firm. Whenever dividends are declared, the preferred stockholders must receive their dividend before a dividend can be paid to common stockholders.

2. *Preference to Assets.* In the event of liquidation of the firm, the preferred shareholders occupy a middle ground between creditors and common shareholders. A bond is a senior security in the sense that its claims to assets are senior to the claims of the preferred and common stockholders. After the assets are liquidated, the bondholders are paid first. If any money is left, the preferred shareholders are paid second. If money is still remaining, it is shared by the holders of the junior security, the common shareholders. Just as the bondholders can only receive assets equal to the face value of the debt, so the preferred shareholders can only receive assets equal to the par value of the stock. For $100 par preferred stock, the maximum settlement in a liquidation is $100 per share.

3. *Basically a Fixed Return.* The maximum return on preferred stock is usually limited to the stated dividend. Thus, a 12 percent, $100 par issue will return no more than $12 per share per year. In some cases the preferred stock contains a *participating* feature that allows the holder to share in earnings above some specific point. As an example, a participating feature may state that, if the common stock dividend is greater than $2 per share, the preferred stockholders will share equally in the additional dividends. Although preferred stock may have this feature, the great majority of issues are nonparticipating and result basically in a fixed return for the preferred shareholder.

4. *Indefinite Life.* Most preferred stock issues have no stated maturity. At the same time, most issues have a *call feature* similar to corporate bonds. This allows the firm to retire an issue should the firm decide that the preferred stock has become too expensive or has otherwise outlived its usefulness.

5. *Usually Nonvoting.* Most preferred stock does not contain provi-

sions to allow its holders to vote or have other voices in the management of the firm. Sometimes an exception is stated in the stock certificate. For example, the preferred shareholders may become entitled to vote should the firm miss a specified number of consecutive dividends. Other provisions for voting are also occasionally found, but for the most part preferred stock is nonvoting.

6. *Cumulative Dividends.* Most preferred stocks have a cumulative feature that requires unpaid dividends in any one year to be carried forward to the next. When this happens, the preferred dividends are said to be *in arrears*. The dividends accumulated in arrears must be paid before the corporation is allowed to pay any dividends on common stock. If this feature is not present, the stock is noncumulative.

7. *Miscellaneous Features.* Preferred stock can have other features similar to bonds. The stock certificate can provide that the preferred stock be convertible into common stock at the option of the holder. The issue may provide for a sinking fund to allow the orderly retirement of the stock over a period of time or at the end of a certain time period. The number and type of other features that can be incorporated into a preferred stock issue are limited only by the market situation and needs of the firm.

## COMMON STOCK

*Common stock* is a security representing the residual ownership of a corporation. It guarantees only the right to participate in sharing the earnings of the firm if the firm is profitable. Common shareholders usually have the additional right to vote at stockholders meetings on issues affecting fundamental policies of the corporation. Also, the shareholders have the right to elect the members of the board of directors, the right to inspect the firm's books (only for the legitimate purpose of evaluating the performance of management), and the right to obtain a list of the names and addresses of other shareholders.

An exception to these rights may occur if the firm issues more than one class of common stock. In this situation, the firm is said to have *classified common stock*, which is often divided into two classes normally designated as class A and class B. The holders of one class do not have the right to vote on corporate matters except in specified situations. In return for giving up this right, the shareholders receive first rights to common dividends. The other class has all the rights of common shareholders, unless somehow restricted by provisions in the stock certificate.

The firm's common shareholders are entitled to receive dividends, if and when they are declared by the board of directors. *Dividends* are a share of the profits, which are distributed among all the outstanding shares of common stock. The dividend varies with the performance of the company and the amount of cash available. If the firm needs the cash for expansion or if business is poor, the dividend may be omitted or a non-cash dividend may be declared. Basically, there are three types of dividends:

1. *Cash Dividends.* These are the most common form and are expressed in terms of dollars per share. Thus, if a firm declares a dividend of $4 per share, a shareholder with 100 shares receives a check for $400 as the share of the cash dividends.
2. *Stock Dividends.* These occur when the board votes to give each shareholder additional stock on a percentage basis. A 5 percent stock dividend gives 5 shares of the company's stock to an investor holding 100 shares when the dividend is declared. Stock dividends are less desirable than cash but may be more desirable than no dividend at all, particularly if the market does not drop the price of the common stock in response to the dividend.
3. *Property Dividends.* These are very rare but may result in the distribution of bonds, preferred stock, stock of other companies, other securities, or merchandise. An example of a merchandise dividend might be the distribution of small bottles of perfume by the company manufacturing the perfume.

Common stockholders have other rights. They may transfer their ownership by selling their stock without the consent of the corporation. They are entitled to share in the proceeds of a liquidation, but they have the last claim on assets after the liabilities, bondholders, and preferred stockholders have been paid. They have the right to maintain their share of earnings and assets by purchasing proportionate amounts of future stock offerings, unless such right has been waived. This is called a *preemptive right.*

### EXAMPLES INVOLVING COMMON AND PREFERRED STOCK

**Example:** An investor holds 300 shares of $100 par preferred stock with a 9 percent dividend. The investor paid $80 per share for the stock. How much does the stockholder receive in dividends?

**Answer:** $2,700 annually ($9 dividend times 300 shares). The dividend is calculated on the par value of the stock, not on the price paid by the holder.

**Example:** A 10 percent cumulative preferred stock has not paid dividends in 2 years. In year 3, the firm declared dividends on both preferred and common stock. An investor has 100 shares of the preferred stock. How much does the stockholder receive in dividends ($100 par)?

**Answer:** $3,000. The cumulative stock was in arrears by $20 per share. The current preferred dividend of $10 is also due before the common shareholders can receive dividends. The firm must declare a $30 dividend per share of preferred, and the holder of 100 shares would receive $3,000.

**Example:** A firm has been liquidated and the assets sold. After paying the creditors, the firm has $7 million to distribute among the preferred and common shareholders. The firm has outstanding 50,000 shares of 13 percent, $100 par preferred stock and 100,000 shares of $1 par common stock. How much will each shareholder receive?

**Answer:** Since the preferred stock has preference to assets, the preferred shareholders receive full payment before the common shareholders receive any money. At $100 per share, it takes $5 million to pay off the preferred stock ($100 × 50,000 shares). The remaining $2 million is divided among the 100,000 common shares at $20 per share ($2,000,000/100,000 = $20). Each preferred shareholder receives $100, and each common shareholder receives $20.

**Example:** A firm has declared a 10 percent stock dividend. The firm's stock sells for $20 per share. If the market price does not change in response to the stock dividend, how much additional value would be gained by a shareholder who originally had 200 shares?

**Answer:** The shareholder would have 20 additional shares (200 × 10 percent) worth $20 per share, or $400 more market value.

**Example:** A firm has declared a 20 percent stock dividend. The firm's stock sold for $50 before the dividend but dropped to $45 after the dividend. If an investor had 100 shares, how much would be gained or lost in market value?

**Answer:** The old value was 100 shares times $50, or $5,000. The new value is 120 shares times $45, or $5,400. The investor gains $400.

**Example:** A shareholder owns 500 of the 6,000 outstanding shares of a small company. The company has decided to issue 2,000 new shares. How many of these shares does the shareholder have the right to purchase?

**Answer:** The shareholder's preemptive right allows maintaining a proportionate share of ownership in the firm. Before the new issue, the shareholder had 500/6,000, or 8.33 percent, of the firm; .0833 times 2,000 shares is 167 shares. The shareholder has the right to purchase a minimum of 167 shares (and could probably purchase more if wanted, the firm agreed, and some shares were left after all shareholders exercised their preemptive rights).

# CAPITAL STRUCTURE

*Capital structure* is the composition of debt and equity securities that comprise a firm's financing of its assets. Both debt and equity securities are used in most large corporations. The choice of the amount of debt and equity is made after a comparison of certain characteristics of each kind of security, of internal factors related to the firm's operations, and of external factors that can affect the firm. These will be discussed in turn.

## SECURITY CHARACTERISTICS THAT AFFECT CAPITAL STRUCTURE

Security characteristics that affect the firm's capital structure fall under four classifications:

1. *Ownership Rights.* The issuance of new securities involves the question of extending the ownership rights to the new security holders. Creditors exercise no ownership control during routine periods of operation. In some cases, the debt agreement might place restrictions on management activities, such as the prohibition of paying dividends, should cash fall below a certain level. The holders of preferred stock may or may not have any ownership rights, depending on whether the stock is voting or nonvot-

ing. New holders of common stock, except for class A nonvoting stock, receive immediate and full ownership rights.

If the shareholders do not wish to share their ownership rights with new investors, the firm will attempt to use debt or preferred-stock financing rather than common-stock financing. The firm's ability to use these financing means may be limited by other factors; as a general rule, ownership rights accompany the residual owners—common shareholders—rather than the preferred owners or creditors.

2. *Repayment Requirements.* Debt matures and must be repaid according to the conditions in the bond indenture or other agreement. Preferred stock ordinarily has no maturity date, although it usually has a call feature that allows its retirement. Common stock involves no repayment requirements. If the firm does not wish to face specific repayment requirements, preferred or common stock is preferable to debt.

3. *Claim on Assets.* The bondholders have the first claim on assets in the event of liquidation, the preferred shareholders the next claim, and the common shareholders the residual claim. If the firm does not want to give new investors a priority claim on assets, common stock is desirable.

4. *Claim on Profits.* Interest must be paid on bonds regardless of the level of profits. Although bondholders have no right to share in profits, they have a legally enforceable right to the payment of the stipulated interest. The preferred shareholders have the first right to share in the profits but only up to a specified limit. The common shareholders have the absolute right to share in the profits of the firm. If the firm wants to restrict the right of new investors to share in the firm's profits, debt or preferred stock is desirable.

The characteristics that affect a firm's capital structure are presented in Table 2–1.

### INTERNAL FACTORS THAT AFFECT CAPITAL STRUCTURE

*Internal factors* are those considerations within the firm that have a bearing on the kinds and amounts of securities in the capital structure, such as the following:

1. *Matching Fluctuating Needs against Short-Term Sources.* A firm may have a busy season just before Christmas and may need extra

**TABLE 2–1**   Security Characteristics That Affect Capital Structure.

|  | Bonds | Preferred Stock | Common Stock |
|---|---|---|---|
| Ownership rights | None, in most cases. | None, unless voting. | Full rights. |
| Repayment requirements | Full requirement; must be repaid. | None, but may be callable. | None. |
| Claim on assets | A senior security, first claim. | Senior to common stock, a second claim. | A junior security, last claim. |
| Claim on profits | None, but interest must be paid first. | First claim, but only up to specified amount. | Full claim on residual profits. |

money during October, November, and December to conduct its business. Since the need is only for three months each year, it would be expensive to use long-term financing that requires interest or dividends on an annual basis. For fluctuating needs, the firm would probably reject debt and equity securities and prefer a short-term loan from a bank.

2. *Degree of Risk.* The more debt a firm has, the larger the interest payments and the greater the chance of inability to make the payments, with consequent bankruptcy. Equity securities need not be repaid and dividends need not be declared. Thus, equity securities reduce risk; debt securities increase risk.

3. *Increasing Owners' Profits.* If the firm can borrow at 11 percent and earn 16 percent with the money, all profits above the 11 percent interest will be distributed to the owners (after taxes are paid, of course). The ability to increase the owners' return without increasing their investment is an argument for debt financing. This is thoroughly discussed under the topic of leverage.

4. *Surrendering Operational Control.* In some cases, a firm is unable to sell bonds without agreeing to allow the bondholders to exercise certain operational controls, such as selecting a member of the board of directors if interest payments are not made on time. At the same time, the sale of common stock brings new voting investors into the firm and dilutes the control of the existing shareholders. The possible loss of operational control is a factor influencing the financing mix.

5. *Future Flexibility.* A firm is expected to maintain a balanced mix-

ture of debt and equity securities. Excessive debt reduces the firm's ability to borrow and hence reduces flexibility. The need to maintain a balance to ensure flexibility of financing alternatives affects the capital structure.

Table 2–2 shows the internal factors that affect the use of the three principal financial securities.

### EXTERNAL FACTORS THAT AFFECT CAPITAL STRUCTURE

*External factors* are those considerations outside the firm that have a bearing on the composition of debt and equity securities such as the following:

1. *General Level of Business Activity.* If the overall level of business activity is rising, most firms need money to expand their operations. The need for additional long-term funds brings a firm to the money markets for either debt or equity funds. On the other hand, a decline in business activity may allow a firm to cut back its operations and use its cash to retire debt or equity securities.

**TABLE 2–2**   Internal Factors That Affect Capital Structure.

|  | *Bonds* | *Preferred Stock* | *Common Stock* |
|---|---|---|---|
| Matching fluctuating needs against short-term sources | Not useful, a long-term security. | Not useful, a long-term security. | Not useful, a long-term security. |
| Degree of risk | Payments required, risk increased. | Payments not required, low risk. | Payments not required, low risk. |
| Increasing owners' profits | All profits above interest go to owners. | All profits above fixed dividends go to owners. | All profits shared equally by existing and new shareholders. |
| Surrendering operational control | No control, except restrictions or default. | Control only if voting rights granted. | New shareholders gain voice, except classified A nonvoting stock. |
| Future flexibility | Excessive debt restricts borrowing. | Increases flexibility. | Increases flexibility. |

2. *Level of Interest Rates.* Interest rates on bonds fluctuate in the market in response to supply-and-demand factors. If interest rates become excessive, firms delay debt financing, switch to short-term financing until long-term debt can be offered at lower rates, or switch to equity securities.

3. *Level of Stock Prices.* When firms issue new common stock, they hope to receive as much money as possible from each share. When stock prices are depressed, the firm does not offer common stock. If stock prices are high, the firm can raise relatively large amounts of money by issuing relatively few shares.

4. *Availability of Funds in the Markets.* Money and capital markets in the United States are a constantly changing, complex phenomenon. At times money is plentiful and any reasonably priced debt or equity offering can be sold. At other times, money is scarce and offerings fail to sell out. The availability of funds affects the firm's ability to offer debt and equity securities.

5. *Tax Policy on Interest and Dividends.* At present, interest is paid on debt prior to the calculation of the corporate income tax. Dividends are declared after the tax calculation. This tax policy makes the payment of dividends more costly than the payment of interest and has severely reduced the number of issues of preferred stock in recent years.

## MARKETS FOR CORPORATE SECURITIES

Bonds, preferred stock, and common stock are traded in carefully regulated money and capital markets. These markets may be studied in detail under topics such as money and banking, capital markets, or investments and security analysis. For our purposes, we will provide a brief overview of the markets for the three types of corporate securities.

### PRIMARY MARKETS

A *primary issue* is the offering of stocks or bonds that have never been previously issued. The offering may be made in two ways:

1. *Direct Placement.* A bond or stock issue may be placed directly with the individuals or company who will own the securities. A firm may agree, for example, to place $10 million with four life insurance companies that will hold the bonds and collect the interest as it comes due. The agreement can be worked out directly

between the corporation and a representative of the insurance companies.

2. *Underwritten Placement.* An offering may be made by a corporation through an *investment banker*, a principal who acts as the middleman between the issuer and the public. In this role, the investment banker is an *underwriter* of the offering, who brings together a group of other investment bankers to *underwrite* or purchase the entire offering. Once the underwriting syndicate has made the purchase, it will resell the securities to a variety of individuals and institutions through the mechanisms of the over-the-counter market.

## SECONDARY MARKETS

Securities that have been previously issued are traded in the different *secondary markets*, which include the organized exchanges and the over-the-counter market. The trading is aided by dealers and brokers:

1. *Dealers. Dealers* act as principals and buy for their own accounts and sell securities from their own inventories.
2. *Brokers. Brokers* do not buy or sell from their own inventory of securities. They act as agents for others and receive a commission for assisting a transaction.

The same firm or individual may act as either a broker or a dealer at different times and in different transactions in the secondary markets, as long as disclosing this capacity to the customer.

## OVER-THE-COUNTER MARKET

The *over-the-counter market* is an informally organized grouping of brokers and dealers from all over the country. It handles both primary issues and secondary transactions and is the largest securities market, in terms of both the number and dollar volume of securities traded. It handles all corporate securities and virtually all government bonds.

The over-the-counter market is a *negotiated* market, because prices are established by individual bargaining between buyers and sellers. Normally, a customer works through a broker to locate a dealer who is always prepared either to buy or sell a certain stock or bond. These dealers *make a market* for the specific security.

As an example, let us consider the dealer who makes a market for the common stock of Hardwicke Company. This dealer always carries an inventory of Hardwicke stock and quotes prices for buying or selling the stock. The dealer may quote a *bid* price of 8 and an *ask* price of 8 1/4. This means a willingness to buy Hardwicke shares at $8 in lots of 100 shares or to sell shares at $8.25 in lots of 100 shares. The customer's broker may call the dealer making the market and bargain or negotiate in an attempt to get a better price.

Most brokers and dealers in the over-the-counter market operate with the assistance of a computerized information system called the National Association of Securities Dealers Automated Quotation System (NASDAQ). This electronic hookup of thousands of brokers across the country allows current price quotations to be displayed on request on a terminal in the office of an individual broker. Participants in this sytem are members of the National Association of Securities Dealers, an organization that regulates the over-the-counter market and promotes fair dealings between dealers or brokers and customers. Violations of the association's rules or practices may result in disciplinary action or loss of membership.

The over-the-counter market has become an increasingly important factor in securities transactions as a result of developments in electronic data processing. By one estimate, over 90 percent of all bonds are traded in this market. In addition, about 30 percent of the dollar volume of stock transactions occur over the counter. The activity in this market is reflected in daily quote listings of bid and ask prices that appear in periodicals such as the *Wall Street Journal.*

## NEW YORK STOCK EXCHANGE

In addition to the over-the-counter market, corporate securities can be traded on the various stock exchanges. A *stock exchange* is a central location where members may buy or sell securities. Stocks and bonds may be listed by companies seeking greater marketability of the stock and greater liquidity for shareholders, who may, through their brokers, bring the stocks to the exchange to be traded.

The New York Stock Exchange is the largest in the country and accounts for the majority of dollar value and number of shares of stock traded on all U.S. exchanges. Historically, the exchange is traced to a group of businessmen who began trading securities on Wall Street in the 1790s. Stocks and bonds can be traded on the floor of the New York Stock Exchange only by members. There are over 1,300 members, each of whom must own a *seat,* which represents membership. Only individuals may own seats, but the individual may be associated with others in a corporation or partnership.

## AMERICAN STOCK EXCHANGE

The American Stock Exchange is the second largest in the country. It is located near the New York Stock Exchange in New York City. Firms may not list their securities on both the New York and American Exchanges but may list securities on one of these as well as on other exchanges outside New York City.

The American Stock Exchange is smaller in size than the New York Stock Exchange, with approximately 500 seats. Unlike the New York Stock Exchange, the American Stock Exchange allows trading in both listed and unlisted securities. The companies represented in the trading are generally smaller than those on the New York Stock Exchange and usually trade at lower prices, with most shares in the range of $50 or less.

## OTHER STOCK EXCHANGES

Less than 10 percent of the securities traded on organized exchanges are traded at a variety of regional and local exchanges. The exchanges are located in cities in different parts of the country and include the Midwest Stock Exchange in Chicago and the Pacific Coast Stock Exchange in California. The importance of these exchanges has diminished owing to two factors:

1. *Nationwide Communications.* The availability of rapid communications between the New York and American Exchanges and the rest of the country has resulted in ease of trading on the major exchanges.
2. *Organization of Over-the-Counter Market.* The NASD's successful efforts to organize and computerize the over-the-counter market have diminished the need for local exchanges to trade strictly local securities.

Figure 2–2 provides an overview of the U.S. market for corporate securities.

## REGULATION OF THE SECURITIES MARKET

The securities markets in the United States are carefully regulated to ensure that individual investors are treated honestly and fairly. The 1929

**Figure 2–2**  Markets for Bonds, Preferred Stock, and Common Stock.

crash of the stock market had been preceded by a widespread manipulation of stock prices and misrepresentation of financial data. Following the crash, the federal government took steps to correct the situation. An investigation led to a number of federal security laws and the creation of the Securities and Exchange Commission (SEC) in 1934.

The SEC administers the Securities Act of 1933. This act has two objectives:

1. *To Make Financial Data Public.* The act requires firms to provide investors with financial and other information concerning the securities offered for public sale. If a firm will not disclose the required information, the bonds, preferred stock, or common stock cannot be sold publicly.
2. *To Prohibit Fraud.* The act prohibits misrepresentation, dishonesty, or fraud connected with any offering of stocks and bonds.

The SEC is also responsible for administering a variety of other securities acts and regulations. All new issues by corporations must be registered with the SEC. Those offerings that fail to meet the requirements of the applicable laws do not receive an effective registration statement and may not be issued to the public.

A number of states have laws regulating the sale of corporate securities. Some states, such as New York, Illinois, and California, have relatively strict laws; other states are more lenient. These laws generally apply to securities that are either too small in volume to be included under federal regulations or to securities exempt from registration under the rules of SEC.

The organized exchanges have regulations for listed stocks. The New York Stock Exchange has adopted extensive regulations for its stocks and bonds. The other exchanges have less severe rules.

The NASD has a set of rules and regulations governing behavior in the over-the-counter market. Failure to comply with these rules can bring penalties such as censure, fines, suspension, or expulsion from the organization.

## KEY TERMS

amortization
bearer bonds
bond indenture
broker
callable bond
capital structure
classified common stock
collateral trust bond
convertible bond
corporate bond
corporation
coupon bonds
cumulative dividends
dealer
debenture

detachable warrants
direct placement
dividends
equipment trust bonds
financial security
income bonds
investment banker
mortgage bond
National Association of
    Security Dealers
    (NASD)
over-the-counter market
partnership
preemptive right

primary issue
primary market
registered bond
secondary market
Securities and Exchange
    Commission (SEC)
serial bonds
sinking fund
sole proprietorship
stock exchange
stock split
subordinated debenture
underwriter
warrant

## STUDY QUESTIONS

1. What are two important facts related to sole proprietorship?
2. What is the difference between a limited and general partnership?
3. What is a corporation? a certificate of incorporation? a charter? bylaws?
4. Why is the corporate form highly desirable for large business organizations?
5. What are two types of corporations?
6. What is the difference between a bond indenture and a debenture?
7. What are some examples of secured bonds?
8. If a bond is a subordinated, callable debenture with detachable warrants, what characteristics does it have?
9. What are some characteristics associated with a registered convertible income bond?
10. What is the difference between a serial bond and a sinking fund bond? Which one uses amortization?
11. Why is one class of stock called preferred stock? How does it differ from common stock? How is it the same as common stock?
12. What is common stock? classified common stock?

13. What are three types of dividends?
14. What is the preemptive right?
15. What is a firm's capital structure? How do the characteristics of different securities affect it?
16. What is the difference between internal and external factors that affect capital structure? What are some examples of each?
17. What are primary issues? secondary markets? Give examples of each.
18. What is the difference between a dealer and broker?
19. What is the difference between a direct placement and an underwritten placement?
20. What is the over-the-counter market? Why is it a negotiated market? What is a bid price? an ask price? What does it mean to make a market?
21. What is a stock exchange? Which ones are important?
22. How are the securities industry and trading regulated?

## PROBLEMS

1. A $1,000 bond can be converted into 20 shares of common stock at any time prior to 1991. The stock is selling for $54 per share and the transaction cost is $20. If the bond were immediately converted, would the bondholder gain or lose? How much?
2. A $1,000 bond has been called at $1,050. The bondholder has the option of accepting the call or converting the bond into 40 shares of common stock, currently selling at an unknown price. If the holder converts, a $25 cost is involved. At what price of the stock would the bondholder be indifferent to converting or accepting the call?
3. A bond has 10 detachable warrants that allow the holder to buy 10 shares of common stock at $45 per share. The stock is selling for $60. It costs $30 to cash in the warrants. Approximately what value would the warrants have if they were detached and sold?
4. A 9 percent cumulative preferred stock has not paid dividends in 3 years. In the 4th year, the firm declared dividends on both preferred and common stock. An investor has 200 shares of the preferred. How much was received in dividends ($100 par)?
5. A firm has been dissolved and its assets have been sold for $12 million. The firm had debt of $4 million, 70,000 shares of $100 par preferred stock outstanding, and 200,000 shares of $1 par common stock outstanding. How much will each common shareholder receive?
6. A firm has declared a 12 percent stock dividend. The firm's stock is selling for $40. If the market price does not change in response to the stock dividend, how much value is gained by an investor holding 100 shares?

# HARRISON INDUSTRIES CASE
# Basic Planning

*This case can help the reader develop an approach to structuring a case solution. It requires a logical approach to solving a general financial problem.*

Harrison Industries has been manufacturing fireworks at a small facility just outside Greensboro, North Carolina. The firm is known for the high level of quality control in its production process and is generally respected by distributors in states where fireworks are legal. Its selling market is fairly well defined; it has the capacity to produce 600,000 cases annually, with peak consumption in the summer. The firm is fairly confident that all of next year's production can be sold for $5 a case.

On September 1, the company has $2,250,000 in cash. The firm has a policy against borrowing to finance its production, a policy first established by William Harrison, owner of the firm. Mr. Harrison keeps a tight rein on the firm's cash and invests any excess cash in treasury bonds, which are paying a 10 percent return and involve no risk of default.

The firm's production cycle revolves around the seasonal nature of the fireworks business. Production begins right after Labor Day and runs through May. The firm's sales occur in February through May; the firm closes from June 1 to Labor Day, when its employees return to farming. During this time, Mr. Harrison visits his grandchildren in New Jersey and Pennsylvania. As a result of this scheduling, the firm pays all its expenses between September and May and receives all its revenues from its distributors within 6 weeks after the Fourth of July. The customers send their checks directly to Wachovia National Bank, where the money is deposited in Harrison's account.

Mr. Harrison is the only full-time employee of his company, and he and his family hold all the common stock. Thus, the company's only costs are directly related to the production of fireworks. The costs are affected by the law of variable proportions, depending on the production level. The first 100,000 cases cost $4.00 each; the second 100,000 cases, $4.25 each; the third 100,000 cases, $4.50 each; the fourth 100,000 cases, $4.75 each; the fifth 100,000 cases, $5.00 each; the sixth 100,000 cases, $5.25 each. As an example, the total of 200,000 cases would be $400,000 plus $425,000, or $825,000.

### HARRISON INDUSTRIES INC.—Income Statement
#### (August 31, Fiscal Year Just Ended)

| | |
|---|---:|
| Revenues from operations | $1,375,000 |
| Revenues from interest on government bonds | 105,000 |
| Total revenues | $1,480,000 |
| Operating expenses | 1,160,000 |
| Earnings before taxes | 320,000 |
| Taxes | 128,000 |
| Net income after taxes | $   192,000 |

Harrison Industries is a corporation and pays a 40 percent tax on income. Because of the paperwork involved, Mr. Harrison will only invest his excess cash on September 1 in 1-year treasury bonds. He will not invest for shorter periods.

### Questions

1. What production level maximizes total profits?
2. How does this level affect long-term prospects for wealth maximization?

# SMITH AND ASSOCIATES CASE
# Financing Alternatives

*This case provides the opportunity to match financing alternatives with the needs of different companies. It allows the reader to demonstrate a familiarity with different types of securities.*

Gary Thomas was finishing some weekend reports on a Friday afternoon in the downtown offices of the investment banking firm of Smith and Associates. Bob Arrighi, a partner in the firm, had not been in the New York office since Monday. He was on a trip through Pennsylvania, visiting five potential clients that were considering the flotation of securities with the assistance of Smith and Associates. Wednesday Bob had called the office and told Gary's secretary that he would cable his recommendations Friday afternoon. Gary was waiting for the call.

Gary knew that Bob would be recommending types of securities for each of the five clients to meet their individual needs. He also knew Bob wanted him to call each of the clients with a recommendation prior to 5 P.M. to allow the clients to consider the recommendations over the weekend. Gary was prepared to make these calls as soon as the cable arrived. At 3 P.M. a secretary handed Gary the following telegram:

> Gary Thomas, Smith and Associates STOP Taking advantage of offer to go skiing in Poconos STOP Recommendations as follows: (1) common stock, (2) preferred stock, (3) debt with warrants, (4) convertible bonds, (5) callable debentures. STOP See you Wednesday STOP Bob Arrighi

As Gary picked up the phone to make the first call, he suddenly realized that the potential clients were not matched with the investment alternatives. In Bob's office, Gary found folders on each of the five firms seeking financing. In the front of each folder were some handwritten notes that Bob had made Monday before leaving. Gary read each of the notes in turn:

> *APT, Inc.* Needs $8 million now and $4 million in 4 years. Packaging firm with high growth rate in tristate area. Common stock trades over the counter. Stock is depressed but should rise in year to 18

months. Willing to accept any type of security. Good management. Expects moderate growth. New machinery should increase profits substantially. Recently retired $7 million in debt. Has virtually no debt remaining except short-term obligations.

*Medford Enterprises.* Needs $15 million. Crusty management. Stock price depressed but expected to improve. Excellent growth and profits forecast in the next year. Low debt-equity ratio, as firm has record of retiring debt prior to maturity. Retains bulk of earnings and pays low dividends. Management not interested in surrendering voting control to outsiders. Money to be used to finance machinery for plumbing supplies.

*Woltersdorf Brothers, Inc.* Needs $25 million to expand cabinet and woodworking business. Started as family business but has 1,300 employees, $45 million in sales, and is traded over the counter. Seeks additional shareholders but not willing to sell stock at discount. Cannot raise more than $10 million with straight debt. Fair management. Good growth prospects. Very good earnings. Should spark investor interest. Banks would be willing to lend money for short-term needs.

*Massachusetts Energy Systems.* The firm is well respected by liberal investing community near Boston area. Sound growth company. Stock selling for $15 per share. Management would like to sell common stock at $20 or more. Willing to use debt to raise $25 million, but this is second choice. Financing gimmicks and chance to turn quick profit on investment would appeal to those likely to invest in this company.

*Pagano Industries.* Needs $20 million. Manufacturers boat canvas covers and needs funds to expand operations. Needs long-term money. Closely held ownership reluctant to surrender control. Cannot issue debt without permission of bondholders and First National Bank of Philadelphia. Relatively low debt-equity ratio. Relatively high profits. Good prospects for growth. Strong management with minor weaknesses in sales area.

As Gary was looking over the folders, Bob Arrighi's secretary entered the office. Gary said, "Did Bob leave any other materials here Monday except for these notes?"

She responded, "No, that's it, but I think those notes should be useful. Bob called early this morning and said that he verified the facts in the folders. He also said he learned nothing new on the trip and he sort of indicated that he wasted his week. Except, of course, that he was invited to go skiing at the company lodge up there."

Gary pondered the situation. He could always wait until next week, when he could be sure that he had the right recommendations for each client. But this could be harmful to the firm and the chances for doing the business on all these accounts. On the other hand, he did have five specific recommendations and some of the considerations that outlined each client's needs and situation. If he could determine which firm matched each recommendation, he could still call the firms by 5 P.M. and meet the original deadline. Gary decided to return to his office and match each firm with the appropriate financing.

## Question

1. Which type of financing is appropriate to each firm?

# 3

# A Review of Financial Accounting

*Financial accounting* is a system of keeping business records so as to explain what is happening in the business. The goal of accounting is to develop records that (1) identify individual commercial transactions, (2) allow the preparation of summarized financial statements that show significant information about a business or organization, and (3) can be used to improve business decision making. To a large degree, accounting is the language of corporations, banks, and other business entities. An understanding of financial accounting is an essential prerequisite to making effective decisions in the area of finance.

In this chapter, we will review the basic principles and structure of financial accounting. The rules of accounting and different categories of accounts will be covered first. Then the basic techniques of double-entry accounting will be examined along with examples of debit and credit transactions. Finally, the raw accounting data will be converted into the financial statements published by the business.

## OVERVIEW

The field of accounting can be divided into four major areas:

1. Financial Accounting. Recording transactions and preparing reports and financial statements that can be used by management,

owners, creditors, government agencies, and others to understand what is happening in the business or nonprofit organization.

2. Managerial Accounting. Also called *budgeting*, this involves planning for the future. Accounting data are prepared on an expected, or *pro forma*, basis; that is, the firm is forecasting business
activity. After a financial plan, called a *budget*, is developed, the
firm attempts to follow the plan and achieve the results. The
process of developing such plans and comparing actual results
with pro forma estimates is covered in the area of managerial
accounting.

3. Cost Accounting. This area covers techniques for determining
the costs of a business and developing methods for controlling
those costs. Particular attention is given to computing the cost of
an individual product or service in situations where thousands
or even millions of such products or services are sold. As an example, when Ford Motor Company wants to manufacture a new
car, it must incur large capital costs in advance, train thousands
of workers on a new assembly line, stock millions of components
and parts, and finally begin production. What does it cost to produce the first car? the one-millionth car? These questions are answered in the area of cost accounting.

4. Auditing. An *audit* may be defined as an examination of accounting or financial records to determine whether a company, bank,
or other organization is meeting certain rules or standards. Auditing is the field that develops standards for audits and provides
the people to conduct audits. An auditor may work for a company and conduct an *internal audit*, ensuring that established accounting procedures and management instructions are being followed throughout a company. An auditor may work for an
outside accounting firm and conduct an *external audit* to verify
accounting and financial records to creditors, stockholders, or
the government.

This chapter will deal with the fundamentals of financial accounting
as a first step toward managerial accounting. The techniques of recording
transactions correctly must be understood before an analyst can use accounting data to develop budgets and financial plans. Similarly, an ability
to analyze a firm's liquidity and profitability position requires a basic
knowledge of the assumptions and methodology of financial accounting.

## GENERALLY ACCEPTED ACCOUNTING PRINCIPLES

A *principle* is a fundamental law or rule upon which other rules and practices are formed. Over the years, the profession of accounting has developed a number of *generally accepted accounting principles* that must be followed in recording transactions and preparing financial statements. These principles have been accepted by professional groups such as the American Institute of Certified Public Accountants (AICPA), the Financial Accounting Standards Board (FASB), and the American Accounting Association (AAA).

Some of the most important of the generally accepted accounting principles follow:

1. **Business Entity.** When accounting transactions are recorded, every business or organization is treated as a separate entity. A sole proprietorship has business records separate from the owner's personal records just as a corporation has records separate from its shareholders.

2. **Going Concern.** A *going concern* is a business that is expected to operate for an indefinite period of time. This principle is followed in preparing accounting records unless there is evidence that the business is experiencing difficulties and may cease operating.

3. **Cost Basis.** All expenses are recorded at actual cost as determined by the amount of cash involved or the market value of the transaction. If a machine is purchased for $100,000, the accounting records reflect this value even though the firm's management may feel that the machine "is worth $150,000."

4. **Accrual Basis.** The economic effects of all transactions are recognized during the time period in which they occur. Under an accrual system, revenues are recognized (accrued) at the point of sale even though cash may be received later. Similarly, expenses are recognized when the obligations are created, not necessarily when they are paid. Revenues resulting from credit sales that have not yet been paid are recorded as receivables. Expenses that have been incurred but not paid are recorded as payables. In a small percentage of cases, businesses may operate on a *cash basis,* where transactions are not recognized until the cash is collected or paid. This situation is relatively rare and will not be considered in this chapter.

**5.** Current Dollars. A *current dollar* is a unit of money that is not adjusted during a period of inflation; therefore, its purchasing power fluctuates over a period of time. A *constant dollar* is a unit of money mathematically calculated so that it has the same purchasing power at all times even though price levels may be changing. Stated differently, it is a future dollar with the same purchasing power as today's dollar. In recording accounting transactions, firms use current dollars. In periods of high inflation, this can distort the economic effects of some transactions. At the same time, it provides a stability to the records since all transactions are measured in the same absolute unit—the dollar.

**Example:** A firm buys a building for $150,000 and sells it in 3 years for $250,000. During the 3 years, the purchasing power of the dollar has dropped 60 percent. What is the gain in current dollars? in constant dollars?

**Answer:** $100,000 in current dollars (250,000 − 150,000). No gain in constant dollars. The $250,000 has the purchasing power of 60 percent when compared to the original dollars. Its purchasing power is $150,000 (250,000 × .60). Therefore, there is no gain.

To show the effects of inflation, many firms publish *price-level-adjusted financial statements,* where current dollars are converted to constant dollars. This is in addition to the traditional current dollar statements. Most accountants prefer the traditional statements and believe that current dollars are a better basis for publishing accounting data. We will follow this trend and consider only those statements prepared in current dollars.

## CATEGORIES OF ACCOUNTS

In financial accounting, five categories of accounts may be identified:

**1.** Asset Account. An *asset* is any resource that allows a firm to conduct its business. A *tangible asset* has a physical existence, as in the case of cash or a machine. An *intangible asset* has no physical existence. Its value is derived from the fact that the firm has the right to use it. Examples include patents on products and copyrights on books. In developing financial records, assets are typically divided into three areas:

**a.** *Current assets.* All assets that will be converted into cash within the current accounting period or within the next year as a result of the ordinary operations of the business.

**b.** *Fixed assets.* Resources that the firm will use to generate revenues. These assets will not be converted into cash in the current accounting period unless they are damaged, become obsolete, or are otherwise replaced.

**c.** *Intangible assets.* Resources that do not represent physical property or securities.

2. Liability Account. A *liability* is a debt of the business. These are normally divided into three areas:

   **a.** *Current liabilities.* Debts of the firm that must be paid during the current accounting period, normally 1 year.

   **b.** *Long-term liabilities.* Debts of the firm that will not be paid during the next year.

   **c.** *Obligations under capital leases.* Also called a *financial lease,* a *capital lease* is a long-term agreement to rent an asset under terms so that the agreement cannot be canceled by either party. The economic consequence of such an agreement is the same as though the company had borrowed money and purchased the asset. The obligations under such leases are shown in the financial records of the firm.

3. Equity Account. *Equity* is a term used to represent the ownership rights in a company. The term *capital* is used to represent ownership rights in a bank. In a corporation, three major types of equity accounts may be identified:

   **a.** *Preferred stock.* An equity security that is given a preference over other stock of a corporation with respect to dividends and return of the stockholder's investment if the firm is liquidated.

   **b.** *Common stock.* A security representing the residual ownership of a corporation.

   **c.** *Retained earnings.* The ownership rights that occur because the firm has retained income earned in prior periods and has reinvested such income.

4. Revenue Account. A *revenue* is an inflow of assets, not limited to cash, in exchange for goods sold or services rendered. The term *sales* is commonly used in place of the term *revenues.* Two types of revenue accounts are commonly found:

   **a.** *Operating revenues.* Inflows from sales of goods or performance of services in the firm's main operating areas.

     **b.** *Other income.* Inflows from investments or other sources not considered part of the firm's normal operations.

5. Expense Account. An *expense* is the consumption of any asset while conducting the business of the firm. It may be represented by the payment of cash for materials, labor, or other costs associated with goods sold or services rendered. It may be represented by the wearing out of assets during the process of conducting business. Four types of expense accounts are commonly identified:

     **a.** *Cash expenses.* Costs that must be paid in cash shortly after they are incurred.

     **b.** *Noncash expenses.* Costs that reflect the decline in the value of assets that are consumed during the course of business.

     **c.** *Interest charges.* When the firm borrows money, it must pay interest on the debt. The interest payments are an expense of the business.

     **d.** *Taxes, other than income taxes.* A cash expense that firms must pay state, local, real estate, sales, and other taxes.

## BALANCE SHEET EQUATION

A *balance sheet* is a financial statement that shows the financial position of a firm as of a specific date, usually at the close of the last day in a month or accounting period. It shows how the resources of the firm (assets) are provided by capital from creditors (liabilities) and owners (equity). It provides a snapshot, if you will, of the firm's financial position at the close of an accounting period.

As its name implies, the two sides of the balance sheet must always balance. The assets on the left must equal the total of the liabilities and equity on the right. This may be expressed:

$$\text{assets} = \text{liabilities} + \text{equity}$$

## INCOME STATEMENT FORMULA

An *income statement* is a report of the firm's activities during a given accounting period, normally 1 year. Also called the *profit and loss statement* or *statement of earnings,* it shows revenues and expenses of a firm, the effect of corporate income taxes, and the net income. The relationships on the income statement can be expressed by the formula:

$$\text{revenues} - \text{expenses} - \text{taxes} = \text{net income}$$

This completes our overview of the basic concepts of financial accounting. Now we will begin to develop the basic techniques of double-entry accounting in order to review the basic mechanics of developing financial statements.

## DOUBLE-ENTRY ACCOUNTING

The term *double-entry accounting* refers to a system of keeping a firm's financial records whereby each transaction affects two or more accounts with equal debits and credits. A *debit* is an entry on the left-hand side of an account; a *credit* is an entry on a right-hand side of an account. The double-entry system, developed by Italian merchants in the 13th century, is largely unchanged today. Two entries for each transaction and the need for financial records to balance at the end of the accounting period offer protection against errors. Whether the system is manual or computerized, double-entry accounting is the main record-keeping system in use today.

### THE T-ACCOUNT

The mechanics of double-entry accounting may be illustrated using a *T-account*, which may be defined as the simplest form of bookkeeping account. A title is placed above the account, and debit and credit entries are entered on the left and right side respectively. The account looks like the letter T, as follows:

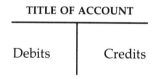

A basic concept of double-entry accounting is that debits and credits must be equal. A second basic concept is that an asset account is increased by a debit entry. From these two fundamental ideas, we can develop the mechanics of the system. For example, if an asset is increased by a debit, it must be decreased by a credit. Similarly, if the firm borrows an asset, thus incurring a liability, and debits the asset account to reflect the new asset, it must credit the liability account to reflect the new debt. This means that liabilities increase with a credit entry. Following this logic and applying it to the balance sheet equation, we get increases and decreases in T-accounts as follows:

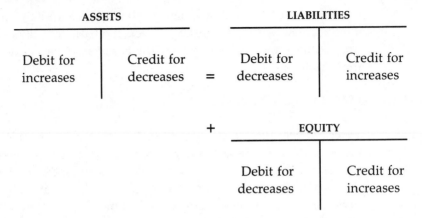

Similarly, we can develop increases and decreases in the income statement accounts. If an asset increases because the firm earns a revenue, a debit entry increases the asset account and a credit entry must increase the revenue account. If an expense of the business decreases cash (a credit entry to the cash account), the expense must be recorded with a debit entry (an increase in expenses). Following this logic with the income statement formula, we get increases and decreases in T-accounts as follows:

| REVENUES | | EXPENSES | |
| --- | --- | --- | --- |
| Debit for decreases. | Credit for increases. | Debit for increases. | Credit for decreases. |

| INCOME TAXES | | NET INCOME | |
| --- | --- | --- | --- |
| Debit for increases. | Credit for decreases. | Debit indicates loss for period. | Credit indicates income for period. |

## PROCESSING SOME OPENING TRANSACTIONS

In order to indicate the basic mechanics of the double-entry approach, let us develop some transactions to open a business. Suppose some individuals get together to open a business. Common stock is sold for $2 million and preferred stock for $500,000. The money is placed in a checking account. The transactions, in thousands of dollars, are:

| CASH | | PREF. STOCK | | COMMON STOCK | |
|---|---|---|---|---|---|
| 2,500 | | | 500 | | 2,000 |

Suppose that the business purchases machinery at a cost of $1.3 million, a building for $600,000, and land for $250,000. A $500,000 mortgage is taken on the building and $650,000 is borrowed from a bank on a long-term note. The balance is paid in cash. The entries are:

| CASH | | MACHINERY | | BUILDING | | LAND | |
|---|---|---|---|---|---|---|---|
| 2,500 | | 1,300 | | 600 | | 250 | |
| | 1,000 | | | | | | |

| MORTGAGE | | L-T BANK NOTE | |
|---|---|---|---|
| | 500 | | 650 |

In this example, $2.5 million was already in cash. The new transactions have total debits of $2,150,000 and total credits of $2,150,000.

The next transaction occurs when the firm pays $100,000 for 3 years' insurance on the building and machinery and pays $200,000 to license the right to manufacture a product. The transactions are:

| CASH | | PREPD. INSUR. | | LICENSES | |
|---|---|---|---|---|---|
| 2,500 | | | | | |
| | 1,000 | 100 | | 200 | |
| | 300 | | | | |

New debits and credits balance at $300,000.

Another transaction occurs when the firm purchases materials to sell in its business. Items worth $400,000 are purchased for resale, $250,000 on short-term credit and $150,000 with money borrowed short-term from a bank. The entries are:

| INVENTORIES | ACCTS. PAYABLE | S-T BANK NOTE |
|---|---|---|
| 400 | 250 | 150 |

Our final opening transaction involves investing the firm's excess cash. The firm decides to keep $50,000 in the checking account and invest the balance in short-term marketable securities. The transaction is:

| CASH | MKT. SECS. |
|---|---|
| 2,500 | |
| | 1,000 | |
| | 300 | |
| | 1,150 | 1,150 |

After these opening transactions, we can summarize the financial position of the firm using the balance sheet equation. We will show the debit balances in the asset accounts and the credit balances in the liability and equity accounts. The balances are:

| *Assets* | | *Liabilities + Equity* | |
|---|---|---|---|
| Cash | $    50,000 | Accts. payable | $  250,000 |
| Mkt. secs. | 1,150,000 | S-T bank note | 150,000 |
| Inventories | 400,000 | L-T bank note | 650,000 |
| Ppd. insur. | 100,000 | Mortgage | 500,000 |
| Machinery | 1,300,000 | Pref. stock | 500,000 |
| Building | 600,000 | Common stock | 2,000,000 |
| Land | 250,000 | | |
| Licenses | 200,000 | | |
| Total Debits | $4,050,000 | Total Credits | $4,050,000 |

In our example, after processing the opening transactions and calculating the balances in the T-accounts, our entries balance at $4,050,000 in the balance sheet equation. The fact that the accounts balance is a good indication that we have not made any mistakes in recording our transactions.

## PROCESSING INCOME TRANSACTIONS

Now that the business is open and ready for business, we can record the entries in the first accounting period. Normally, hundreds or thousands of entries are recorded in any period. This explains the convenience of computerized accounting systems. In our example, we will use only summary transactions to minimize the level of detail.

During the first period, the firm had revenues of $1.6 million, of which $1.3 million was received in cash. The entries are:

| CASH | RECEIVABLES | REVENUES |
|------|-------------|----------|
| 50 | | |
| 1,300 | 300 | 1,600 |

The firm had $850,000 of labor expenses, of which $800,000 was paid in cash:

| CASH | WAGES PAYABLE | LABOR EXPENSE |
|------|---------------|---------------|
| 50 | | |
| 1,300 | | |
| 800 | 50 | 850 |

During the period, the firm sold inventories of $250,000:

| INVENTORIES | MATERIALS EXPENSE |
|-------------|-------------------|
| 400 | |
| 250 | 250 |

Although it prepaid 3 years of insurance, $30,000 of the insurance benefit was used up in the period:

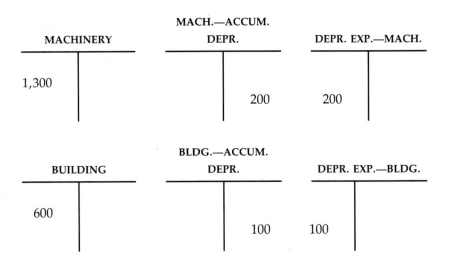

The firm was allowed to take a noncash expense on its machinery and building. This expense is called *depreciation*. To reflect the accumulation of depreciation, we create a new account beside each asset account. This is called an *asset contra account*, or *accumulated depreciation*. The transactions for $200,000 of depreciation on the machinery and $100,000 on the building are:

The firm paid $225,000 in interest on its debts:

Finally, the firm had to repay portions of the principal amount of its debt. It repaid the entire short-term bank note and paid off $60,000 of the long-term note and $80,000 of the mortgage. The entries are:

| CASH | | S-T BANK NOTE | | L-T BANK NOTE | | MORTGAGE | |
|---|---|---|---|---|---|---|---|
| 50 |  |  | 150 |  | 650 |  | 500 |
| 1,300 |  |  |  |  |  |  |  |
|  | 800 |  |  |  |  |  |  |
|  | 225 |  |  |  |  |  |  |
|  | 290 | 150 |  | 60 |  | 80 |  |

These entries completed the business transactions for the firm. The ending balances in all its accounts, identified as debits or credits, are

|  | Debits | Credits |
|---|---|---|
| Cash | 35 |  |
| Marketable securities | 1,150 |  |
| Receivables | 300 |  |
| Inventories | 150 |  |
| Prepaid insurance | 70 |  |
| Machinery | 1,300 |  |
| Accum. depr.—machinery |  | 200 |
| Building | 600 |  |
| Accum. depr.—building |  | 100 |
| Land | 250 |  |
| Licenses | 200 |  |
| Accounts payable |  | 250 |
| Wages payable |  | 50 |
| Short-term bank note |  | 0 |
| Long-term bank note |  | 590 |
| Mortgage |  | 420 |
| Preferred stock |  | 500 |
| Common stock |  | 2,000 |
| Revenues |  | 1,600 |
| Labor expense | 850 |  |
| Materials expense | 250 |  |
| Insurance expense | 30 |  |
| Depr. exp.—machinery | 200 |  |
| Depr. exp.—building | 100 |  |
| Interest expense | 225 |  |
| Totals | 5,710 | 5,710 |

## CLOSING THE ACCOUNTS

By listing all the accounts so that we can see debits and credits, we have prepared a *trial balance*. When a trial balance has an equal number of dollars in the debit and credit columns, the accountant assumes that the transactions were recorded correctly and no mathematical mistakes exist. It is now possible to *close the accounts,* which consists of separating balance sheet and income statement accounts. When we do this for our data, we get:

|  | Income Statement | | Balance Sheet | |
|---|---|---|---|---|
|  | *Debit* | *Credit* | *Debit* | *Credit* |
| Cash |  |  | 35 |  |
| Mkt. secs. |  |  | 1,150 |  |
| Receivables |  |  | 300 |  |
| Inventories |  |  | 150 |  |
| Prepaid insur. |  |  | 70 |  |
| Machinery |  |  | 1,300 |  |
| Accum. depr. |  |  |  | 200 |
| Building |  |  | 600 |  |
| Accum. depr. |  |  |  | 100 |
| Land |  |  | 250 |  |
| Licenses |  |  | 200 |  |
| Accounts payable |  |  |  | 250 |
| Wages payable |  |  |  | 50 |
| S-T bank note |  |  |  | 0 |
| L-T bank note |  |  |  | 590 |
| Mortgage |  |  |  | 420 |
| Pref. stock |  |  |  | 500 |
| Common stock |  |  |  | 2,000 |
| Revenues |  | 1,600 |  |  |
| Labor expense | 850 |  |  |  |
| Materials expense | 250 |  |  |  |
| Insurance expense | 30 |  |  |  |
| Depr. exp.—mach | 200 |  |  |  |
| Depr. exp.—bldg | 100 |  |  |  |
| Interest exp. | 225 |  |  |  |
| **Totals** | 1,655 | 1,600 | 4,055 | 4,110 |

At this point, we have an apparent problem. The balance sheet does not balance. We have debits of $4,055,000 and credits of $4,110,000. The difference is $55,000. This is the same difference found in the debit and credit columns on the income statement. In fact, the firm had revenues of $1.6 million and expenses of $1,655,000, a loss of $55,000 for the first accounting period. The final step in closing the accounts is to balance both sets of columns with the entry:

|  | Income Statement | | Balance Sheet | |
|  | Debit | Credit | Debit | Credit |
| --- | --- | --- | --- | --- |
| Totals | 1,655 | 1,600 | 4,055 | 4,110 |
| Net loss |  | 55 | 55 |  |
| Balance | 1,655 | 1,655 | 4,110 | 4,110 |

To close the books completely, the firm's equity would have to be reduced by the amount of the loss and a $55,000 loss would be reported on the income statement. The ending equity balance would be $2,000,000 − 50,000, or $1,950,000.

## KEY TERMS

accrual basis
accumulated depreciation
asset
asset contra account
auditing
balance sheet
budget
business entity
capital
capital lease
cash basis
cash expense
close the accounts
common stock
constant dollars
cost accounting
cost basis
credit
current asset

current dollar
current liability
debit
depreciation
double-entry accounting
equity
expense
external audit
financial accounting
financial lease
fixed asset
generally accepted
    accounting principle
going concern
income statement
intangible asset
interest charge
internal audit
long-term liability

managerial accounting
noncash expense
operating revenue
other income
preferred stock
price-level-adjusted financial
    statement
principle
profit and loss statement
pro forma
retained earnings
revenue
sales
statement of earnings
T-account
tangible asset
taxes
trial balance

## STUDY QUESTIONS

1. What are the four major areas of accounting? What is done in each area?
2. What is a generally accepted accounting principle? What are some examples of such principles?
3. What are the five categories of accounts?
4. What is the balance sheet equation? the income statement formula?
5. What is double-entry accounting? a debit? credit? a T-account?
6. How do we increase each of the five major categories of accounts?

## PROBLEMS

1. A business opens with $450,000 of common stock purchased by six shareholders, $50,000 of preferred stock purchased by three shareholders, and $300,000 of long-term bank financing. Eighty percent of the initial financing is invested in marketable securities. The balance is placed in a checking account. Show the debit and credit entries to start the business.

2. A company finances $750,000 of machinery with 25 percent in cash, 50 percent mortgage on the asset, and 25 percent from a second mortgage held by a bank. Account for the transaction, showing debits and credits.

3. A firm finances $1.6 million of inventories by payables (35 percent), cash (40 percent), and a short-term bank loan for the balance. Show the transactions.

4. A firm has annual revenues of $3.6 million and collects cash for 85 percent of the amount. Show the accounting for the transaction.

5. A firm has a labor expense of $510,000, of which 90 percent is paid in cash. Its expense for goods sold is $600,000, which represents materials removed from its inventory. It also has an insurance expense of $25,000 but this was prepaid last year. Show the debits and credits for these transactions.

6. A machine had depreciation of $30,000 during the year. The original cost of the machine was $150,000. Accumulated depreciation already was $40,000 before the year. Show the starting T-account balances and debits and credits for this transaction.

7. A firm paid a bank $550,000—$420,000 representing interest on a bank loan and the balance to repay principal. Show the debits and credits for this transaction.

8. A firm begins operations early this year with $1.5 million in common stock and $300,000 of preferred stock sold for cash to shareholders. It purchased plant and equipment for $2.1 million and land for $300,000, financing the purchases with long-term notes of $1,190,000, a mortgage of $575,000, and cash for the balance. It purchased $1,420,000 of inventory, creating payables of $430,000, signing short-term notes for $250,000, and giving cash for the balance. Revenues for the year were $1,960,000, with $1,320,000 in cash and the balance in receivables. The materials expense from inventory was $505,000. An insurance expense was $15,000, with $5,000 of the amount coming from prepaid expenses. This was possible because the company prepaid $25,000 of expenses at the start of the period. A depreciation expense of $400,000 was taken during the period. The company paid $150,000 for royalties in the year. Labor expenses were $735,000, with all but $100,000 paid in cash. The company used cash to pay interest charges of $285,000, mortgage principal reduction of $50,000, and $150,000 of long-term notes. During the period, the company invested $390,000 of its cash in short-term marketable securities.

   Prepare the debits and credits for these transactions. Prepare the trial balance. Close the accounts to a balance sheet and income statement.

# Managerial Accounting

*This case tests the reader's understanding of basic accounting concepts and financial statements. Provided with certain data, the reader is asked to prepare an income statement, balance sheet, and flow-of-funds statement.*

Freeman Solvents has two things going for it—a barrel-sized canister and a large international bank. The canister is the invention of Charles Freeman, a petroleum engineer who wanted to escape a life in the oil fields or on off-shore rigs. His opportunity came when he developed a new process for cleaning oil and grit off machinery parts used in drilling rigs and other applications. Combining powerful solvents with a brushing and agitating action, Charlie's canister is a hot item in the energy boom areas from Texas to Montana, in western Canada, and the North Slope of Alaska. From his manufacturing plant located just west of Dallas, Charlie and his 48 employees produce 600 to 800 canisters a year with rapidly rising sales to customers in the United States, Canada, Northern Europe, and the Middle East.

Freeman Solvents got its start with some major assistance from Republic Bank in Dallas. The bank located a group of Texas and Oklahoma businessmen who purchased 40 percent of the common stock. Within 2 years, Freeman Solvents was actively traded through the National Association of Securities Dealers Automated Quotation system (NASDAQ), a computerized linkage of brokers throughout the country. Republic Bank also assisted Charlie in locating mortgage financing for a manufacturing facility near the Dallas-Fort Worth airport. Finally, the bank provided over $300,000 of initial working-capital financing and continues to be a major supplier of funds to the company.

Paul Bressler has handled the Freeman account for almost 2 years and has developed a strong personal relationship with Charlie Freeman. On the second Tuesday of each month, the two men lunch together and discuss business. Paul was somewhat surprised when Charlie came to the November luncheon with a set of accounting records. He knew that Charlie had sharply increased Freeman's borrowings in October and he also knew that Freeman Solvents was nearing its $750,000 limit on the line. But he did not expect Charlie to bring records with him to discuss the matter.

After eating, Charlie took out some papers and said, "You probably are curious as to what happened in October. Well, I don't really know. We sold 66 units at just over $6,500 apiece. We completed 81 units in production that passed all the quality control tests. We held our costs in line with forecasts and had fairly good control of overtime all month. Still, up went our line of credit by $80,000. I don't know what to say."

The two men talked for awhile before Charlie referred to the records that he had brought. Charlie said, "Even though Joe, my accountant, did not finish preparing the monthly financial statements, we can probably find the answer here. Unfortunately, Joe is sick—nothing serious, but he may be out for the rest of the week. I figured that I had better bring you what I got just in case I need to ask you to raise the limit on the $750,000 credit line."

After glancing at the records, Paul suggested that Charlie let him take the books, find out what happened, and get back to Charlie with the bank's observations and comments. That night Paul took the materials on Freeman Solvents home with him. After dinner, he began to work on them. He made some notes on how to prepare a cost of goods sold schedule, as shown in Figure 3–1. It had been some years since he studied accounting and he felt more comfortable using an overview to guide him through the calculation of cost of goods sold. Surely this had to be

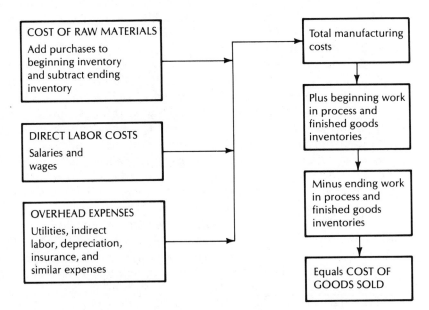

**Figure 3–1**  Preparing the Cost of Goods Sold.

useful in determining what was happening. While thumbing through his accounting book, he took note of two other processes. The first dealt with the accounting steps for closing cost of goods sold to the income summary account, as shown in Figure 3–2. The second was a T-account procedure for handling credit purchases, as shown in Figure 3–3.

As he reviewed the materials, he thought of the irony of the process. One of the reasons that he chose banking was to avoid accounting. Here he was, a lending officer needing to sort out accounting data to help

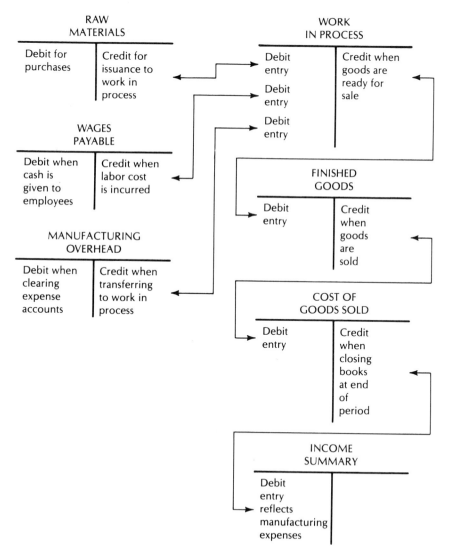

**Figure 3–2**   Accounting for the Cost of Goods Sold.

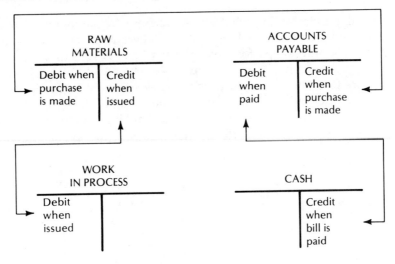

**Figure 3-3**   Accounting for Credit Purchases.

out a client and see if the bank were in any trouble on it outstanding loan.

As he worked with the data on Freeman Solvents, Paul Bressler tried to remember some of the principles of cost accounting. He knew that *manufacturing costs* were the total expenses for a period to cover the transformation of raw materials into finished products that can be sold. Three major components of manufacturing costs can be identified:

1. Direct Materials. The steel, wood, electric circuits, transistors, plastic components, or any other materials that become an integral part of the finished product and can be conveniently traced to the product.
2. Direct Labor. The salaries, benefits, or contractual charges for assembly line workers, carpenters, machine operators, and others who process the raw materials and convert them into finished products.
3. Manufacturing Overhead. All the other costs of production. This category includes heat, electricity, maintenance, property taxes, insurance, depreciation, and all other expenses of the factory. It also includes indirect materials, which is defined as glue, nails, paper, or other items that cannot easily be traced to specific products. Similarly, it includes indirect labor, which is defined as the labor costs of supervisors, janitors, security guards, and other individuals who do not work on specific products.

To reflect the expenses in the manufacturing overhead account, Paul knew that a two-step process was needed. First, expenses had to be debited to individual expense accounts. Second, the accounts had to be closed to the overhead account. He diagrammed the process, as shown in Figure 3–4.

Once he remembered some of the steps for examining the firm's books, he began to work with specific accounts for Freeman Solvents. He started with the data from the beginning of October, as summarized in Figure 3–5. He then worked carefully through the individual accounts to determine the changes in account balances. These are summarized in Figure 3–6. Finally, he prepared a worksheet of T-accounts that he could use to figure out what happened in October. These are given in Figure 3–7 on pages 80–81.

At this point, Paul was ready to develop the financial statements and prepare the bank's comments for presentation to Charlie Freeman.

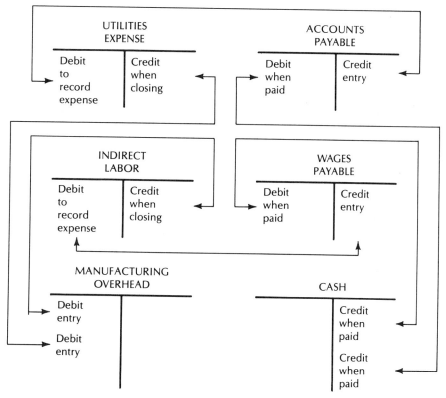

**Figure 3–4**  Accounting for Manufacturing Overhead Transactions.

1. Freeman has prepaid expenses of $7,000.
2. In the bank $6,000 is in a checking account and $35,000 is invested in the Fidelity Capital Fund, a money market fund that allows withdrawals upon 1 day's notice.
3. Suppliers are owed $330,000 for inventory items purchased during the preceding 104 days.
4. The company has $72,000 worth of steel, plastics, and other raw materials.
5. The equity accounts reflect 220,000 shares of common stock at $1 par, additional contributed capital of $400,000, and retained earnings of $655,000.
6. Buildings and fixtures have an original cost of $1,125,000 with $325,000 of accumulated depreciation.
7. The outstanding loan balance exercised against the bank line of credit is $616,000.
8. Equipment has an original cost of $1,720,000 with $620,000 of accumulated depreciation.
9. The finished goods inventory totals $68,000.
10. The balance on the mortgage is $740,000.
11. The firms owns land that originally cost $300,000.
12. The work-in-process inventory is $47,000.
13. Wages payable are $22,000.
14. The accounts receivable balance is $580,000.
15. Taxes payable are $32,000.

**Figure 3–5**  Summary of "T" Accounts for Freeman Solvents.

## Required

1. Prepare a cost-of-goods-sold schedule for Freeman Solvents for the month of October.
2. Prepare the income statement.
3. Prepare a comparative balance sheet as of September 30 and October 31.
4. Prepare a summary of cash inflows and outflows for October.
5. Prepare the bank's comments for Charlie Freeman.

1. Wages payable had net debit entries of $5,000.
2. Raw materials purchases were $187,500 and transfers of materials to work in process totaled $152,500.
3. Additional drawdowns on the line of credit raised the outstanding balance by $89,300.
4. Utilities expenses were $21,500 and local taxes were $3,000.
5. No dividends were declared or paid.
6. Transfers from work in process to finished goods totaled $125,500.
7. Accounts payable had net debit entries of $25,000.
8. Depreciation for the month was $10,000 on the building and fixtures and $11,000 on equipment.
9. Direct labor costs for production were $71,000 and indirect labor costs were $32,500.
10. Insurance expenses of $6,000 and miscellaneous expenses of $15,000 were incurred in support of manufacturing activities.
11. The ending finished goods inventory was $103,000.
12. General and administrative expenses were $54,000, not including $19,000 interest on the mortgage and bank loan.
13. The balances in prepaid expenses and mortgage accounts declined by $1,000 each.
14. No buildings, fixtures, equipment, or land was sold or purchased during the month.
15. Accounts receivable increased by 9.483 percent during the month.
16. Taxes payable declined by $5,000 during the month.
17. No common stock was issued or retired.
18. Federal income taxes totaled $29,800.
19. Machinery rental charges were $16,000 for the month.
20. Sales and other income totaled $430,000.
21. Manufacturing overhead was used as the clearing account for utilities, machinery rental, indirect labor, insurance, depreciation, local taxes, and miscellaneous expenses.

**Figure 3–6**   Summary of Changes in Account Balances During October.

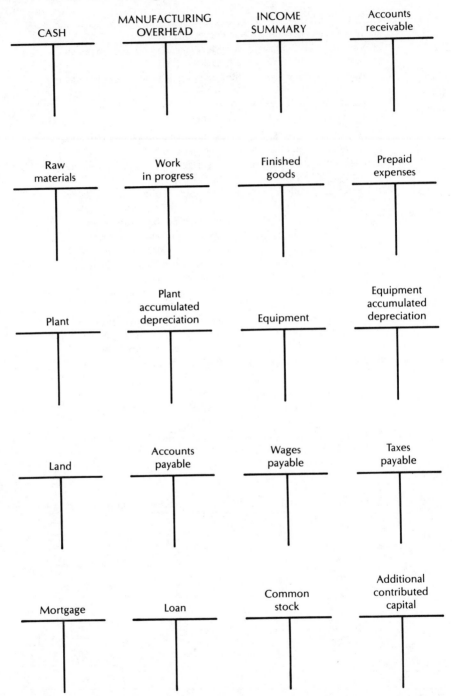

**Figure 3–7** Worksheet of "T" Accounts for Freeman Solvents.

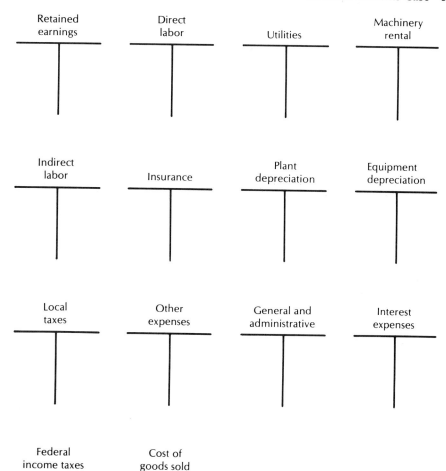

**Figure 3–7** *Continued.*

PART II

# The Firm and Its Operations

Financial Statements
Financial Analysis
Profit Planning
Leverage

# 4
# Financial Statements

Building upon a base of financial accounting, we are now ready to examine the major characteristics of the firm's financial statements. Different statements are prepared with different purposes in mind; even the same statement varies when prepared by two different managers or firms. Knowing the purposes and characteristics of each kind of statement, the analyst can use the statements to gain a great deal of information concerning the status of a company.

A *financial statement* is a collection of data organized according to logical and consistent accounting procedures. Its purpose is to convey an understanding of some financial aspects of a business firm. It may show a position at a moment in time, as in the case of a balance sheet, or may reveal a series of activities over a given period of time, as in the case of an income statement. Financial statements are the major means employed by firms to present their financial situation to stockholders, creditors, and the general public. The majority of firms include extensive financial statements in their annual reports, which receive wide distribution.

The proper preparation and use of financial statements requires the financial manager to define and distinguish among certain terms. To avoid any misunderstandings that may arise from imprecise terminology, we will carefully define terms as we examine different financial statements.

## FUNDS AND WORKING CAPITAL

The terms *funds* is commonly used with a number of meanings, ranging from the broad to the very restricted. Some managers use the term *funds* to refer to all financial resources held by a firm. In this usage, all the firm's assets—both fixed and current—would be forms of funds. A more specific definition limits funds to current assets, those assets usually converted into cash within the next 12 months. With this definition, funds would include cash, marketable securities, accounts receivable, and inventories. Fixed assets, such as property, plant, and equipment, would be omitted. Still another definition identifies funds as the difference between current assets and current liabilities. A firm's current liabilities are those debts that must be paid during the next year. With this usage, only the excess of current assets over current liabilities is considered as funds. The most restricted usage of the term equates funds with the firm's cash.

The term *working capital* is closely related to the term funds and has two common meanings. It is used to mean current assets or current assets minus current liabilities.

To avoid confusion arising from misunderstandings in the usage of terms, financial managers should always question the meaning of a term. When a colleague uses the term *funds*, the manager should ask what is meant by the term. For our purposes, we define these terms precisely:

1. *Cash.* When we mean currency, money deposited in a bank, or money held in highly liquid money market investments (a cash equivalent), we will use the term *cash*. The term *marketable securities* will be used for short-term investments that do not mature in the next week or so.
2. *Funds or Working Capital.* These two terms will be used synonymously to refer to a firm's current assets.
3. *Current Assets minus Current Liabilities.* The difference between current assets and short-term debts will be defined as *net working capital*. This reflects an important measure of a firm's liquidity. Net working capital is the excess cash, receivables, and inventory held by the firm above the level of short-term obligations.
4. *All Financial Resources.* The term *assets* will be reserved for discussions of the firm's total financial resources.

These distinctions become important as we discuss such matters as liquidity, profitability, and the management of working capital. The firm must be able to analyze precisely its liquid assets, the assets that provide funds during periods of stress. If for some reason a firm experiences a shortage of cash, it must concern itself with questions of liquidity, possibly at the expense of profit.

The distinction between income and working capital or funds is quite important to the financial manager (Figure 4–1). The firm cannot pay its bills with income or profit. Bills must be paid in cash. A high level of income is important as an indicator that the firm can generate sufficient working capital for its liquidity needs. But if the firm were to invest its cash in new machinery or land, it might lack the funds to meet its current obligations. A reverse situation may be true with a low level of income. Although the firm is not profitable, it may be able to acquire funds through borrowing, floating stock, or selling fixed assets. Because income and funds have different meanings and implications for the firm, the financial manager must monitor both profits and liquidity as measured by the firm's income from operations, and the level and changes of working capital.

## BALANCE SHEET

The balance sheet is the first of three major financial statements discussed in this chapter. The others are the income statement and the flow-of-funds statement. Although a variety of other statements may be included in a firm's annual report, these three financial statements are of prime importance in analyzing a firm's liquidity and profitability from financial data.

As covered in Chapter 3, the *balance sheet* shows the assets, liabilities, and equity for the firm as of the last day of the accounting period. In effect, it matches resources (assets) with sources (liabilities and equity). It is commonly presented in two columns that illustrate the relationship between assets and the sources of those assets. The assets or resources of

| Terms Defined | Relationship between Income and Funds |
|---|---|
| Cash = cash | Firms cannot pay bills with income. |
| Current assets = liquid assets = funds = working capital | Funds may be generated by income. |
| Net working capital = current assets − current liabilities | Funds may be generated by other means. |
| Assets = total resources | Funds are liquidity matter. |
|  | Income is profit matter |

**Figure 4–1**  Funds or Working Capital and Income.

the firm are displayed in the left-hand column and the sources of those assets in the right-hand column. In this sense, the assets are balanced by the sources (debt and equity) of the assets. It should be carefully noted that no resources are contained in the equity accounts such as common stock or retained earnings. These are balancing accounts showing sources of assets and do not represent bank balances.

Each of the three major categories on the balance sheet is divided into subsections on most balance sheets. Many different accounts can be listed, depending upon such factors as the nature of the firm's business, the kind of assets owned, and the sources of its assets. Some representative, and important, accounts are described next.

**ASSETS**

*Current assets* is a subsection that contains all assets to be converted into cash within the current accounting period or within the next year, through the ordinary operations of the business (Figure 4–2). It includes the following:

1. *Cash and Cash Equivalents.* The money held in bank accounts, cash registers, petty cash, money market funds, and highly liquid investments.
2. *Marketable Securities.* Stocks or bonds of other firms or government agencies that the firm has purchased. These securities will pay a return either in the form of interest or dividends. In addition, they are relatively liquid and can be quickly converted to cash if the firm needs money.
3. *Receivables.* When a firm makes a sale on credit, it gains the right to collect money from the purchaser. This is shown on the balance sheet as an account receivable. If the firm has a credit policy that goods must be paid for in 30 days from the date of purchase—a policy of *net* 30—the bulk of the receivables will be converted to cash in the next 30 days. If the firm is experiencing liq-

| Marketable Securities | Accounts Receivable | Inventories |
|---|---|---|
| The securities of another firm. Pay a return. Easily convertible to cash. | Very liquid. Converted to cash in less than 60 days. May be used as collateral for short-term borrowing. | Goods held for resale. Least liquid of current assets. Two steps away from cash. |

**Figure 4–2** Characteristics of Current Assets.

uidity problems, the receivables can be used as collateral (security) for a bank loan. Because the receivables will usually become cash in a relatively short time (few firms have credit terms longer than 30 to 60 days), they are considered liquid assets.

4. *Inventories.* These are goods held by the firm for eventual resale. Portions of the inventories may be raw materials, goods tied up in the production process, or finished goods ready to be sold. Inventories are carried at their cost on the balance sheet. They are considered the least liquid of the current assets because they are two steps away from cash. First, they must be sold (which creates a receivable) and, second, the receivable must be collected.

*Fixed assets* is the subsection that contains the assets used by the firm to generate revenues. These assets will not be converted into cash in the current accounting period unless they are damaged, become obsolete, or are otherwise replaced. Four representative accounts are:

1. *Plant and Equipment at Cost.* This account includes the physical assets owned by the firm. Buildings, machinery, and other equipment are recorded at cost and are adjusted by the depreciation recorded each year.

2. *Accumulated Depreciation.* The total amount of depreciation charged to the plant and equipment. This item represents an *asset contra* account, which normally has a credit balance, and is shown on the balance sheet with an amount in parentheses.

3. *Real Estate.* This account lists the property owned by the firm. Since land does not wear out with use (as does machinery), this account may not be accompanied by an accumulated depreciation account.

4. *Other Fixed Assets.* Long-term assets not covered in the first three accounts.

We should note that plant and equipment may be shown on a balance sheet using either of two conventional formats. One method shows both the total cost of the plant and equipment and the total of the accumulated depreciation charged against the account. For a machine costing $150,000 with 3 years' depreciation of $20,000 per year, the balance sheet would show the entry in Figure 4–3a. The second method shows only the net value of the machinery as in Figure 4–3b. In both cases, the net or book value of the machinery is $90,000.

| a. | b. |
|---|---|
| Machinery                                          $150,000 | Machinery (at cost less accumulated |
| Less accumulated depreciation      ($60,000) | depreciation)                                          $90,000 |

**Figure 4–3**   Two Methods of Showing Plant and Equipment on a Balance Sheet.

The first method by separating cost and total depreciation provides more information to the analyst. The net book value alone may conceal outdated plant and equipment. As an example, consider two firms with a book value for machinery of $750,000. Firms A and B show the machinery on their respective balance sheets as follows:

Machinery (cost – accumulated depreciation)* $750,000

If a person did not notice the asterisk (which probably indicates that the amount of accumulated depreciation is listed in a footnote), it would appear that the firms have the same kind of fixed assets. But suppose the firms showed the machinery as follows:

|  | Firm A | Firm B |
|---|---|---|
| Machinery (at cost) | $3,000,000 | $1,000,000 |
| Less accumulated depreciation | ($2,250,000) | ($250,000) |

From this information, we see that firm A has a great deal more machinery, but it is probably quite old since it has been depreciated to 25 percent of its original cost. Firm B has less machinery, but it is apparently much newer since it has been depreciated to only 75 percent of its original cost. Knowing the relative age and amount of machinery might be very useful to a financial analyst studying a balance sheet.

## LIABILITIES

*Liabilities* are debts of the firm. They represent sources of assets since the firm either borrows the money listed as liabilities or makes use of certain assets that have not yet been paid for. Liabilities are divided into current and long-term.

*Current liabilities* are the debts of the firm that must be paid during the current accounting period, normally 1 year. Examples are the following:

1. *Accounts Payable.* When a firm makes purchases on credit, it incurs an obligation to pay for the goods according to the terms given by the seller. Until the cash is paid for the goods, the obligation to pay is recorded in an accounts-payable account.
2. *Short-Term Notes Payable.* If the firm owes money against promissory notes that mature during the next year, the debt should be shown in this account. If a note is due in the future but not in the next year, it is recorded in a long-term account.
3. *Other Payables.* At the end of the accounting period, the firm may owe money to miscellaneous parties. These are listed here. Examples are wages payable and tax liabilities to federal, state, or local governments.

*Long-term liabilities* are the firm's debts that will not be paid off during the next year. Examples are the following:

1. *Long-Term Secured Financing.* This covers mortgages and notes where a building or other fixed assets are pledged as specific collateral for the debt.
2. *Long-Term Unsecured Financing.* This consists largely of notes and bonds. *Notes payable* are promissory notes with maturities in excess of 1 year. When the note enters its final year, it will be transferred to a current-liabilities account.

    Bonds are a major source of long-term financing for many firms. Bonds are usually sold *(floated)* to the general public in the form of debentures. A *debenture* is a general obligation of the firm and is not secured by specific physical assets. Frequently, the balance sheet lists all major bond offerings currently outstanding and the interest owed on the bonds on an annual basis.

## EQUITY

*Equity* represents the ownership rights in a company and arises from several sources. Owners purchase the preferred or common stock either through an initial offering or through later sales by the firm, or the firm retains a portion of its profits and reinvests them in the firm. Equity does not represent money held by the firm but does show the sources of assets and approximately what portion of the assets is financed by the owners and retention of earnings. Types of equity include:

1. *Preferred Stock.* This account reflects the amount of preferred stock outstanding, if any. The dollar amount of the account is

usually equal to the number of shares outstanding times the par value of the stock. If a firm has 100,000 shares of $100 par preferred stock outstanding, the account shows $10 million as a balance.

2. *Common Stock.* This account shows the capital contributed by the owners of the firm to purchase the stock of the firm. The dollar amount of this account is usually equal to the number of outstanding shares of stock times the par or stated value of the stock. Thus, if a firm has 1 million outstanding shares of $50 par stock, the common stock account shows $50 million as a balance.

3. *Contributed Capital in Excess of Par.* Also called *premium* or *surplus,* this account records money given to the firm by its owners for stock purchased in excess of the par or stated value of the stock. If the shareholders purchase 1 million shares of $50 par stock for $75 per share, the firm would record $50 in the common stock account and the remaining $25 million in this account.

4. *Retained Earnings.* This account shows the dollar value of ownership rights that result from the firm's retention of past income. Each year, if the firm makes a profit, it might wish to pay cash dividends (payments from profits) to its owners. If it does not declare dividends equal to its entire net income after taxes, the firm is retaining a portion of the aftertax profits to finance future growth. By keeping some of the profits, the firm is able to purchase new assets without having to borrow or sell additional stock.

The *book value* of the common stock is the total of the common stock, contributed capital in excess of par, and retained earnings accounts. That is, a portion of the retained earnings must be considered in addition to the contributed capital accounts. If a firm has $50 million in the common-stock account, $25 million in contributed capital in excess of par, and $25 million in retained earnings, each of its 1 million shares has a book value of $100  [($50,000,000 + $25,000,000 + 25,000,000)/1,000,000 = $100]. In effect, this book value indicates that each share of common stock should be credited with contributing $100 to finance the firm's assets.

### BALANCE-SHEET ACCOUNTS—TITLES AND ARRANGEMENTS

Individual balance sheets vary considerably and may or may not show accounts with the titles just listed. Even when the account does appear, it may be called by another title. For example, contributed capital in excess of par may be called *surplus* or *premium on common stock*. Whatever the title, the analyst should be thoroughly acquainted with the kinds of accounts appearing on the balance sheet.

An important characteristic of the balance sheet is that the items are recorded in a specific order, normally from most liquid to least liquid or vice versa. Assets, for example, would be listed in order of liquidity or nearness to cash. Cash, the most liquid asset, would come first; marketable securities, slightly less liquid, come second, and so on through the highly illiquid plant and equipment. Liabilities, on the other hand, may be listed in the approximate order of repayment. The most urgent debts (those to be paid first) would be listed first. The long-term debt, a low-urgency obligation, would be listed near the end of the liabilities section. In the equity section, the common stock that was issued to start the business would be listed first. The retained earnings, which accrued after the business was in operation, would be listed last.

## LIMITATIONS OF THE BALANCE SHEET

Although it provides useful information, the balance sheet has its limitations. It does not show the events or activities that resulted in the balances in each of the accounts, or the accounting techniques used to prepare them. Many accounting methods are standard, but some variance is permitted, which could greatly change the amounts reported in certain accounts. Another weakness is that the analyst preparing the balance sheet may make improper assumptions either mistakenly or to distort the *picture* shown on the balance sheet. Assumptions as to when obligations have been incurred or when revenues have accrued can have marked effects on the final figures on the balance sheet.

## USES OF THE BALANCE SHEET

The major use of the balance sheet as a financial tool is as a statement of a firm's financial condition at a given point in time. It shows balances in permanent accounts and the results of all the accounting transactions since the first day of operation. It lists the accounting (not market) value of the firm's assets and shows the portion of the assets financed by debt and equity.

When used in conjunction with an income statement and other financial data, the balance sheet provides valuable information on the firm. Financial ratios can be developed to gain an insight into the liquidity and profitability aspects of the business. This is particularly true because most

| Logical Order of Balance-Sheet Accounts—May Be | Limits on Balance-Sheet Uses |
|---|---|
| Assets—in order of nearness to cash. | No explanation of how balances occurred. |
| Liabilities—in order of nearness to repayment. | Accounting techniques may vary. |
| Equity—contributed capital before retained earnings. | Not all assumptions are known. |

**Figure 4–4**  Order of Accounts and Limitations on the Use of the Balance Sheet.

balance sheets are comparative. A *comparative balance sheet* displays the current balances and the prior year's balances for each account in two columns. This allows the analyst to compare the beginning and end-of-year positions and to measure the changes in each account during the course of the year.

If properly prepared and certified by an independent auditor (a certified public accountant), the balance sheet can be used as a reasonably accurate picture of a firm's financial position at a moment in time.

The order of accounts and limitations of a balance sheet are summarized in Figure 4–4.

| CHILDS COMPANY, INC.—Balance Sheet (December 31, 1984). | | | | | |
|---|---|---|---|---|---|
| *Assets* | 1984 | 1983 | *Liabilities and Equity* | 1984 | 1983 |
| Current assets | | | Current liabilities | | |
| Cash | $ 45,000 | $ 30,000 | Accts. payable | $ 60,000 | $ 52,000 |
| Accts. receivable | 60,000 | 50,000 | | | |
| Inventories | 81,000 | 63,000 | Long-term debt | | |
| | | | Mortgage (7%) | 50,000 | 60,000 |
| Equipment | 155,000 | 115,000 | | | |
| Less accum. deprec. | (55,000) | (40,000) | Common stock ($25 par) | 150,000 | 90,000 |
| | | | Premium on stock | 10,000 | — |
| Land | 45,000 | 30,000 | Retained earnings | 61,000 | 46,000 |
| Total assets | $331,000 | $248,000 | Total | $331,000 | $248,000 |

Answer the following questions on the Childs Company balance sheet before proceeding to the next section.

1. What are the total liabilities of the Childs Company at the end of 1984?

2. What is the net value of the firm's equipment at the end of 1983?
3. What is the minimum amount of new equipment purchased by the firm in 1984?
4. What percentage of the firm's assets are fixed assets at the end of 1984?
5. How much did current liabilities increase during 1984?
6. How many shares of stock are outstanding at the end of 1984?
7. What percentage of the firm's assets are financed by borrowing at the end of 1984?
8. (Tough bonus question) How many shares of stock were sold during 1984 and how much did the company receive for each share?

## INCOME STATEMENT

The *income statement,* which was also covered in Chapter 3, is a report of a firm's activities during a given accounting period. Firms often publish income statements showing the results of each quarter and the full accounting year. It shows the revenues and expenses of the firm, the effect of interest and taxes, and the net income for the period. It may be called by other titles, such as the *profit-and-loss statement* or the *statement of earnings.*

Whereas the balance sheet offers a view of the firm at a moment in time, the income statement summarizes the profitability of operations over a period of time. It is an accounting device designed to show stockholders and creditors whether the firm is making money. It can also be used as a tool to identify the factors that affect the degree of profitability.

The income statement is prepared according to generally accepted accounting procedures. The various accounts on the books of the firm are carefully defined and then placed in a specified format on the statement. Most large firms hire a certified public accountant at the end of the fiscal period to certify the accuracy of the firm's financial statements. When this is done, we can usually rely on the accuracy of the profit picture presented on the income statement.

### SAMPLE INCOME STATEMENT

The following income statement for the Donaldson Company illustrates a format suitable for presentation to the stockholders in a firm's annual report. It begins with the firm's revenues, deducts expenses and taxes, and shows the income or loss. From this statement we can discover certain items of interest to potential creditors or owners of the company. For example, we see that the firm had a profit after taxes in 1983, but it had a loss in 1984. This indicates that the firm is experiencing difficulty. If we check the net sales, we see that sales dropped by approximately 50 percent between 1983 and 1984. This appears to be the major factor affecting the reversal from a profit to a loss.

| DONALDSON COMPANY—Income Statement (December 31, 1984). | | |
|---|---|---|
| | *1984* | *1983* |
| Net sales | $9,570 | $14,740 |
| Cost of sales and operating expenses | | |
| Cost of products sold including delivery expenses | 8,670 | 10,790 |
| General and administrative expenses | 940 | 1,000 |
| Interest charges | 260 | 200 |
| Total cost of sales | 9,870 | 11,990 |
| Earnings (losses) before taxes | (300) | 2,750 |
| Federal taxes on income | 0 | 1,100 |
| Net income | $(300) | $ 1,650 |

## REVENUES, SALES, AND NET SALES

The *revenues* from the firm's operations and investments are the first item to appear on the income statement. As a general rule, these revenues are reported using one of four approaches:

1. *Sales.* This term is used interchangeably with revenues for most companies and refers to a firm's net sales for the period.
2. *Net Sales.* This term refers to the difference between the firm's gross sales and any returns or discounts. Every time an item is sold, the firm's books record a sale. If the item is later returned, the value of the item must be deducted from the gross sales for the period. Similarly, on credit sales the firm may offer a lower price for prompt payment. If the customer takes the discount, the dollar value of the discount must be deducted from gross sales.

   **Example:** A firm has $200,000 of sales in June. Items sold for $3,000 are returned; prompt payments give customers $1,500 in discounts. What is the net sales figure for the firm in June?

**Answer:** $195,500. The calculation is: $200,000 gross sales minus $3,000 returns minus $1,500 discounts equals $195,500.

3. *Revenues.* Although many firms use this term synonymously with sales, a firm may have revenues from other sources. For example, a firm may own securities and may receive interest or dividends from them. A firm may wish to identify this revenue separately from sales in an account such as revenue from investments or other income.
4. *Cash and Credit Sales.* Many firms, particularly retail operations such as department stores, have significant cash sales. These firms may identify cash and credit sales separately. If this is not done, analysts generally assume that all or virtually all sales are made on credit.

## CHARGES AGAINST INCOME ON THE INCOME STATEMENT

The Donaldson Company income statement uses a format that combines all the firm's costs into three major categories, as follows:

1. *Cost of Goods Sold.* This category represents an accounting allocation of the costs of raw materials, labor, overhead, and other expenses that can be matched against the goods sold by the firm. It contains a mixture of fixed and variable costs.
2. *General and Administrative Expenses.* These expenses are incurred in support of the firm's nonproduction activities and include marketing expenses, salaries of corporate staff personnel, and other miscellaneous expenses. These costs also represent a mixture of fixed and variable costs.
3. *Interest.* The fixed charges paid by the firm on the money that it borrows are reported here. Unlike the first two categories, this is not an operating expense; rather it is related to the financial structure of the firm. This is a large expense for firms with considerable debt; it is relatively small for firms with mostly equity financing.

The fourth charge against income on the Donaldson Company statement is federal taxes against the firm's income. Although federal tax payments do not represent an expense, they are included on the statement to allow the firm to report its net income after taxes.

### INCOME STATEMENT—MANAGEMENT FORMAT

For management purposes, the analyst should modify the income statement to separate each major type of cost and taxes. When this is done, two new items appear that are not part of the Donaldson Company statement:

1. *Gross Margin.* The amount of profit that the firm realizes as a result of the difference between the cost of goods sold (direct production costs) and the receipts from sales.
2. *Operating Income (EBIT).* The beforetax income after all operating expenses have been deducted from total revenues. This is also called *earnings before interest and taxes.*

**DONALDSON AND COMPANY—Income Statement–Management Format.**

|  |  | 1984 | 1983 |  |
|---|---|---|---|---|
|  | Total revenues | $9,570 | $14,470 | Operating effects |
|  | Cost of goods sold | 8,670 | 10,790 |  |
|  | Gross margin | 900 | 3,950 |  |
| Four | Administrative expenses | 940 | 1,000 |  |
| profit | Operating income (EBIT) | (40) | 2,950 |  |
| measures | Interest charges | 260 | 200 | Financing effects |
|  | Earnings before taxes (EBT) | (300) | 2,750 |  |
|  | Federal income taxes | 0 | 1,100 | Tax effects |
|  | Net income | $ (300) | $ 1,650 |  |

With the format shown in the income statement, the analyst is able to focus on four distinct measures of profit. Gross profit margin is a direct measure of the profit from sales. Operating income is the profit from operations. Earnings before taxes contains both operating factors and the cost of financing the firm's debt. Net income is the final profit after all expenses and taxes have been paid.

### INCOME STATEMENT—MARGINAL-ANALYSIS FORMAT

Another approach to preparing the income statement breaks out operating expenses into fixed and variable costs. These costs replace the cost of goods sold and operating expenses on the income statement. Three new items appear on the statement:

1. *Variable Costs.* These are those costs that vary in direct proportion to changes in the volume of production. This category contains the bulk of the expenses found in cost of goods sold and also contains some general and administrative expenses.
2. *Fixed Costs.* These are constant charges that do not vary with the level of production. Most general and administrative expenses are fixed costs, as are some charges in cost of goods sold.
3. *Marginal Contribution.* This is the profit measure calculated as the difference between total sales and total variable costs. This is the profit available to the firm to cover fixed costs, interest, and taxes and to provide a net income after taxes. As we will see, marginal contribution may be calculated in total, as is the case on the income statement, or on a per-unit basis, in which case it is the difference between the selling price per unit and the variable cost per unit.

When the expenses on the income statement are divided into variable and fixed costs, we are using a technique called *marginal analysis.* This format allows the analyst to develop relationships between the level of sales and the expenses incurred to make the sales. By definition, the fixed costs will not change with differing levels of output. If the level of fixed costs is high, the firm must generate a large volume of sales to cover them. If the level is low, the firm has less difficulty covering them. In either case, the firm must cover fixed costs with its marginal contribution. Marginal analysis helps the analyst to focus on marginal contribution—a key measure of profit that must first cover fixed costs and then interest and taxes, and finally provide a profit to shareholders.

**DONALDSON AND COMPANY—**

**Income Statement—Marginal-Analysis Format.**

|  |  | 1984 | 1983 |  |
|---|---|---|---|---|
|  | Total revenues | $9,570 | $14,740 |  |
| A new | Variable costs | 6,590 | 8,530 | Two different |
| profit——— | Marginal contribution | 2,980 | 6,210 | ———categories of |
| measure | Fixed costs | 3,020 | 3,260 | operating expenses |
|  | Operating income (EBIT) | (40) | 2,950 |  |
|  | Interest charges | 260 | 200 |  |
|  | Earnings before taxes (EBT) | (300) | 2,750 |  |
|  | Federal income taxes | 0 | 1,100 |  |
|  | Net income | $ (300) | $ 1,650 |  |

## FLOW-OF-FUNDS STATEMENT

A third important financial statement is the *flow-of-funds* or *sources-and-uses-of funds* statement. This statement shows the movement of funds into the firm's current-asset accounts from external sources such as stockholders, creditors, and customers. It also shows the movement of funds to meet the firm's obligations, retire stock, or pay dividends. The movements are shown for a specific period of time, normally the same time period as the firm's income statement.

Figure 4–5 shows the sources supplying funds to the firm's working-capital pool and the uses removing funds from the pool. The *working-capital pool* consists of all the current accounts of the firm. In a sense, the

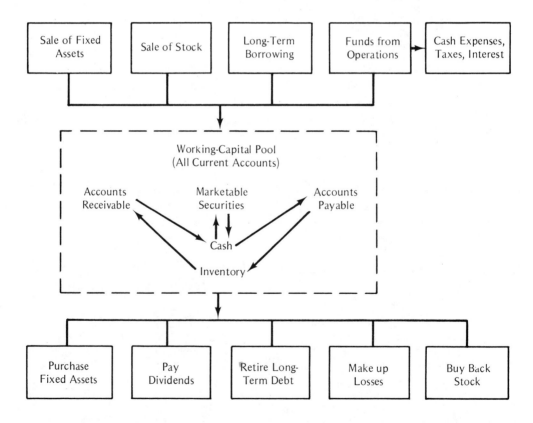

**Figure 4–5**   Sources and Uses of Funds and the Working-Capital Pool.

pool is a measure of net working capital. Only transactions that affect noncurrent accounts may be classified as sources or uses of funds.

> **Example:** A firm takes out a 6-month note and uses the money to increase inventory. Will this transaction affect the size of the working-capital pool? Will it be shown on the flow-of-funds statement?

> **Answer:** Since the working-capital pool is a measure of net working capital, increasing a current liability to finance the increase of a current asset does not affect the overall size of the pool. It will not be shown on the flow-of-funds statement because only transactions that affect noncurrent accounts may be classified as sources or uses of funds.

## FUNDS FROM OPERATIONS

The firm may gain funds from a number of sources. Over a long period of time, the most important source is *funds from operations.* Essentially, these funds come from the everyday business of the firm. To calculate the amount of funds from operations, we can use two different calculations:

1. *Net Income plus Noncash Expenses.* Funds from operations may be calculated by adding back any noncash expenses (primarily depreciation) to the reported net income after taxes. This is a mechanical operation that correctly reflects the fact that depreciation and other noncash expenses shield a portion of the firm's sales. This means that they appear on the income statement as expenses and thus reduce net income. In fact, no funds were needed for the noncash expenses. Funds are used when a piece of equipment is purchased, not when it is depreciated. The purchase would be treated as a use of funds; the depreciation is added back to net income to get the inflow of funds from operations.
2. *Sales minus Cash Expenses.* The second method begins with sales and deducts all cash expenses or changes in funds. Only operating expenses, interest, and taxes are deducted in the calculation of funds from operations.

Table 4–1 shows the two methods of calculating the funds from operations.

**TABLE 4-1.**  Two Methods of Determining the Funds from Operations.

|  | Cash Basis | Accounting Basis |
|---|---|---|
| Sales | $100,000 | $100,000 |
| Less cash expenses | − 60,000 | − 60,000 |
| Less noncash expenses (depreciation) |  | − 8,000 |
| Earnings before interest and taxes |  | 32,000 |
| Cash remaining | 40,000 |  |
| Less interest payments | − 10,000 | − 10,000 |
| Less taxes | − 10,120 | − 10,120 |
| Net income |  | 11,880 |
| Cash remaining | 19,880 |  |
| Add back noncash expenses |  | + 8,000 |
| Funds from operations | $ 19,880 | $ 19,880 |

## OTHER SOURCES OF FUNDS

Three other sources of funds are important to most firms:

1. *Sale of Stock.* Whenever the firm issues additional shares of stock, it receives funds. The receipts are recorded in the cash account, and the source is shown in equity accounts under contributed capital.
2. *Long-Term Borrowing.* Whenever a firm borrows through the use of bonds, mortgages, or other long-term means, the sources are reflected in the long-term liabilities accounts.
3. *Sale of Fixed Assets.* If the firm sells a portion of its fixed assets, the funds are treated separately from funds from operations.

## USES OF FUNDS

A firm may apply its funds in a number of areas. A portion of the funds is expended for operations. This is included in the calculation of funds from operations and not identified as a separate use of funds. The uses are the following:

1. Purchase Fixed Assets. As already noted, it is a use of funds when plant, equipment, or land is purchased, not when they are depreciated.

**KING TRUCKING COMPANY—Flow-of-Funds Statement**
**(December 31, 1984).**

|  | 1984 | 1983 |
|---|---|---|
| Sources of funds |  |  |
| Net income from operations | $148,262 | $127,065 |
| Noncash expenses, including depreciation | 107,296 | 92,297 |
| Total funds from operations | 255,558 | 219,362 |
| Proceeds from long-term borrowing | 92,621 | 41,832 |
| Sale of property | 6,101 | 1,499 |
| Sale of common stock | 2,112 | 1,804 |
| Total sources of funds | $356,392 | $264,497 |
| Application of funds |  |  |
| Expenditures for property and equipment | $234,511 | $174,408 |
| Miscellaneous investments | 4,728 | 3,215 |
| Payment of cash dividends | 50,924 | 48,107 |
| Funds held by trustee for plant construction | 975 | 45,378 |
| Total application of funds | $291,138 | $271,108 |
| Increase (decrease) in net working capital | $ 65,254 | $( 6,611) |

2. Pay off Liabilities or Retire Stock. When long-term debt reaches maturity, the firm must pay it off with available funds. If the firm wishes to reduce the amount of outstanding stock, it uses funds to repurchase the stock.
3. Declare Cash Dividends. If the firm is profitable and pays dividends to its stockholders, the declaration of cash dividends is a use of funds.
4. Make up Losses. If the firm is not profitable, it must apply funds to make up its losses until it does become profitable.

### SAMPLE FLOW-OF-FUNDS STATEMENT

The flow-of-funds statement for the King Trucking Company shows the sources and application of funds for 1983 and 1984. The difference between sources and uses is shown as an increase or decrease in net working capital. If the firm has more funds coming in than going out, net working capital increases, because current assets increase more quickly or decrease less quickly than current liabilities. When uses are greater than sources, the reverse is true.

Most corporations print a flow-of-funds statement as part of their annual reports. If not, the analyst can develop one from the balance sheet, income statement, and accompanying notes to the annual report. Because of the variety of styles of financial statements and the differing accounting procedures used by corporations, the development of a flow-of-funds statement requires a thorough grasp of the relationship among accounts.

## THREE FORMATS OF STATEMENTS MEASURING FLOWS

The flow of cash and funds through an organization is commonly measured using three basic formats:

1. *Measuring Changes in Net Working Capital.* This format is illustrated by the preceding examples. The statement has three major categories: sources, uses, and changes in net working capital.
2. *Balancing Sources and Uses.* A second format contains only two categories: sources and uses. The sources must equal the uses. In this format, the changes in the current accounts are considered either sources or uses. The rules are the following:
   a. *Sources* are decreases in current assets and increases in current liabilities. When the firm reduces a current-asset account, it is viewed as a source of funds. An increase in a current-liability account is treated in the same manner as a long-term liability increase.
   b. *Uses* are increases in current assets and decreases in current liabilities.
   This format is less useful to the financial manager than one that measures changes in net working capital. For accounting purposes, sources may be viewed as balancing uses. For financial purposes, this is not true. When a firm increases its cash account, for example, it is not using funds. Rather, it is holding funds to make them available when needed. Changes in net working capital reflect liquidity, an important use of fund statements. The balancing of sources and uses makes it more difficult to measure changes in liquidity.
3. *Measuring Changes in Cash.* This format has three categories: sources, uses, and changes in the cash balance. This format considers the current accounts as part of the sources and uses profile, but cash is excluded. It treats changes in current accounts in the same manner as the format balancing sources and uses. This statement, usually called a cash-flow statement, is useful for focusing on the most liquid of current assets—the cash account. It is more restricted in scope than the statement that measures changes in net working capital.

**TABLE 4–2.**   Examples of Three Formats for Flow Statements.

| (a) Net Working Capital Format (does not itemize current accounts) | | (b) Sources Equal Uses Format (itemizes current accounts) | | (c) Cash-Flow Format (separates changes in cash) | |
|---|---|---|---|---|---|
| Sources | | Sources | | Sources | |
| Net income | $ 50,000 | Net income | $ 50,000 | Net income | $ 50,000 |
| Depreciation | 30,000 | Depreciation | 30,000 | Depreciation | 30,000 |
| Funds fr. opera. | 80,000 | Funds fr. opera. | 80,000 | Funds fr. opera. | 80,000 |
| Sale of bonds | 60,000 | Sale of bonds | 60,000 | Sale of bonds | 60,000 |
| Sale of machinery | 40,000 | Sale of machinery | 40,000 | Sale of machinery | 40,000 |
| | | Inc. wages pay. | 10,000 | Inc. wages pay. | 10,000 |
| | | Dec. accts. rec. | 15,000 | Dec. accts. rec. | 15,000 |
| Total sources | $180,000 | Total sources | $205,000 | Total sources | $205,000 |
| | | | | | |
| Uses | | Uses | | Uses | |
| Dividends | $ 30,000 | Dividends | $ 30,000 | Dividends | $ 30,000 |
| Retire bonds | 65,000 | Retire bonds | 65,000 | Retire bonds | 65,000 |
| | | Dec. accts. pay. | 50,000 | Dec. accts. pay. | 50,000 |
| | | Inc. cash | 60,000 | | |
| Total uses | $ 95,000 | Total uses | $205,000 | Total uses | $145,000 |
| | | | | | |
| Inc. net work cap. | $ 85,000 | | | Inc. cash | $ 60,000 |

Of the three common formats, the most useful for financial purposes is the format illustrated in Table 4–2, column a. With some exceptions, the best measure of liquidity is given by measuring changes in net working capital. The cash-flow format in Table 4–2, column c, is also useful. Table 4–2, column b, is a balancing format and requires the analyst to prepare calculations to measure changes in the firm's liquidity.

## USES OF FINANCIAL STATEMENTS

Financial statements are major tools in understanding what happens to the firm's money as the firm pursues its business activities. When used together, the balance sheet, income statement, and flow-of-funds statement offer valuable insights into the firm's efforts to achieve liquidity and profitability.

Financial statements have two major uses in financial analysis. First, they are used to present a *historical record* of the firm's financial development. When compiled over a number of years, a trained analyst can determine important financial factors that have influenced the growth and current status of the firm. Second, they are used to *forecast a course of action* for the firm. A pro forma financial statement is prepared for a future period. It is the financial manager's estimate of the firm's future performance.

Perhaps the most valuable use of financial statements is to gain an understanding of how funds flow through the organization. Figure 4–6 is a representation of the internal and external flow of funds. In analyzing this figure, note that the flows are continuous. In a complex business organization, funds are in constant use and movement throughout the firm.

## DEVELOPING A FLOW-OF-FUNDS STATEMENT

Most small businesses have accountants who prepare balance sheets and income statements at yearend. However, in many cases these statements do not answer important questions concerning where the firm received and spent its funds. For example, it is common to hear a businessman state, "Our income statement shows a profit of $150,000 after taxes, yet

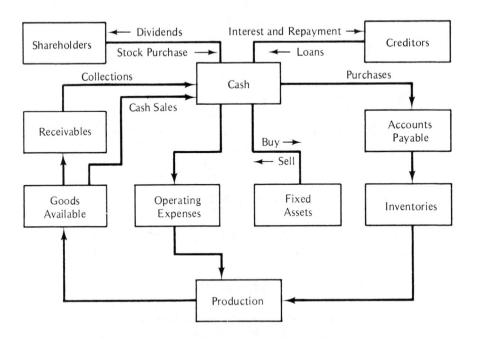

**Figure 4–6**   Flow of Funds Through a Firm.

I have no money in the bank. How can that be?" The easiest way to answer that question is to take the firm's balance sheet and income statement and use them to prepare a flow-of-funds statement.

Several basic accounting techniques are needed to develop a flow-
of-funds statement from other financial statements. These will be illustrated using the data on the Packard Company. Note that our example
provides a comparative balance sheet—the current and prior years' balances are displayed—and a current income statement. The major steps
for developing a flow-of-funds statement are illustrated next.

### PACKARD COMPANY—Balance Sheet (December 31, 1984).

|  | 1984 | 1983 |  | 1984 | 1983 |
|---|---|---|---|---|---|
| Cash | $ 40,000 | $ 100,000 | Accts. payable | $ 90,000 | $ 40,000 |
| Mkt. secs. | 20,000 | 70,000 | Taxes payable | 30,000 | 20,000 |
| Accts. rec. | 150,000 | 140,000 | Mortgage (5%) | 120,000 | 130,000 |
| Inventories | 300,000 | 250,000 | Bonds (6%) | 350,000 | 220,000 |
| Plant and equip. | 900,000 | 600,000 | Common stock | 200,000 | 150,000 |
| Less acc. depr. | (250,000) | (200,000) | Premium | 120,000 | 50,000 |
| Misc. invest. | 70,000 | 70,000 | Retain. earn. | 630,000 | 730,000 |
| Land | 310,000 | 310,000 |  | $1,540,000 | $1,340,000 |
|  | $1,540,000 | $1,340,000 |  |  |  |

NOTE: The firm purchased $400,000 in equipment in 1984.

### PACKARD COMPANY—INCOME STATEMENT
### (period ending December 31, 1984).

| Sales | $750,000 |  |
|---|---|---|
| Misc. investments | 2,000 | $752,000 |
| Production costs | $470,000 |  |
| Depreciation | 80,000 |  |
| General expenses | 234,000 |  |
| Interest | 28,000 | 812,000 |
| Net income (loss) |  | $ (60,000) |

## FUNDS FROM OPERATIONS

Funds from operations are the total of net income and noncash expenses.
Packard had a net loss, and this $60,000 is a use rather than a source. The
depreciation shielded a source of $80,000. Both figures are given on the
income statement.

**CHANGES IN PLANT AND EQUIPMENT**

The plant and equipment account can help identify both a source and use of funds, as follows:

1. *Purchase of Plant and Equipment Is a Use.* If the firm buys new plant or equipment, the expenditure is recorded as a use of funds. The new equipment is normally recorded at cost. Since Packard's plant and equipment balance rose from $600,000 to $900,000, the firm must have purchased a minimum of $300,000 of new equipment. The footnote reveals that it actually purchased $400,000, representing a $400,000 use of funds.

2. *Sale of Plant and Equipment Is a Source.* When a firm sells used equipment, the money that it receives is a source of funds. To reflect this source, the firm has a *writeoff* of the asset and its accumulated depreciation. A *net sale* of a fixed asset is defined as the removal of the asset and associated accumulated depreciation from the firm's books and may be calculated by the formula.

$$\frac{\text{net sale of}}{\text{equipment}} = \frac{\text{fixed asset}}{\text{written off}} - \frac{\text{accumulated depreciation}}{\text{written off}}$$

Table 4–3 shows the calculation of the net sale for Packard. From the table and from the purchases on the balance sheet, we can determine that the plant and equipment account reveals a $400,000 use of funds and a $70,000 source of funds, both of which appear on the flow-of-funds statement.

**TABLE 4–3.**   Net Sale of Equipment for Packard.

| Fixed Assets Sold | | Accumulated Depreciation on Sold Equip. | |
|---|---|---|---|
| 1983 plant and equip. | $   600,000 | 1983 accum. depr. | $200,000 |
| 1984 purchases | 400,000 | 1984 depreciation | 80,000 |
| Total | $1,000,000 | Total | $280,000 |
| Less ending P&E | 900,000 | 1984 ending depr. | 250,000 |
| Sale of equip. | $   100,000 | Depr. on sale | $  30,000 |

$$\underset{\$100,000}{\text{equipment sale}} - \underset{\$30,000}{\text{accum. depr. on sold equipment}} = \underset{\substack{= \$70,000 \text{ source} \\ \text{of funds}}}{\text{net sale}}$$

If we had net sales of fixed assets, the formula is:

net fixed     net decrease     amount of
assets    =  in plant,    −   annual
sold          equipment       depreciation

**Example:** A firm has accounts as follows. What was the net flow of funds represented by these accounts if 1986 depreciation was $150,000?

|  | 1986 | 1985 |
|---|---|---|
| Plant, equipment | $4,500 | $4,750 |
| Less accum. depr. | (1,600) | (1,500) |

**Answer:** A source of $200,000 is represented by the net sale of fixed assets. The net change from 1985 to 1986 may be shown:

|  | 1986 | 1985 |
|---|---|---|
| Plant, equipment (net) | $2,900 | $3,250 |

The decline was $350 ($3,250 − $2,900) showing a net sale. The effect on cash flow is the decline less the 1986 depreciation, or $200 as follows:

net fixed assets sold $= 350 - 150 = 200$

**Example:** A firm has net plant and equipment of $410,000 in 1984 and $475,000 in 1985. Its 1985 depreciation was $60,000. What was the effect on flow of funds?

**Answer:** $125,000 use of funds. It purchased assets equal to the increase in the account plus the amount of annual depreciation, or

net fixed assets purchased $= 65,000 + 60,000 = \$125,000$

In using this technique to measure the flow of funds, we might raise a question. What happens if the firm sells assets so that it realizes a gain or loss on the sale? Does such a sale affect the determination of the flow of funds? The answer is yes but the analyst does not have to worry about the gain or loss since it is picked up elsewhere. To illustrate what is happening, let us consider the three possible situations when a firm sells a fixed asset and we are comparing the cash received against the book value of the asset.

1. *Selling Price Can Equal the Book Value.* A firm may have a machine that cost $50,000 with accumulated depreciation of $30,000 and a book value of $20,000. If the firm receives $20,000 for the machine, the book value ($50,000 – $30,000) is equal to the cash received; thus, a source of $20,000 is reflected when the asset is written off.

2. *Selling Price Can Exceed the Book Value.* When this happens, the firm receives more cash than the accounting value of the machine. If the firm had received $25,000 for the $20,000–book-value machine, the source would be $25,000. What happens to the extra $5,000? Since it is a gain on the sale of assets, it is taxable and is reflected as income on the income statement. Thus, the first $20,000 is reflected as a source in the equipment account change, and the net gain is reflected after taxes on the income statement. The $20,000 may correctly be identified as a source of funds from the sale of assets; the excess is correctly shown as part of the net income on the income statement.

3. *Selling Price Can Be Less than the Book Value.* When this happens, the firm receives less cash than the accounting value of the machine. If the firm had received only $15,000 for the $20,000–book-value machine, the source would be $15,000. What happens to the $5,000 difference between the cash received and the book value? It is a loss on the sale of assets and is picked up as a non-cash expense on the income statement. It shields another $5,000 in addition to depreciation and thus increases the total source to $20,000. The $20,000 may be correctly listed as a source of funds as long as the funds from operations does not include the non-cash expense *loss on the sale of capital equipment.*

In all three situations, the firm's $20,000 net change in plant and equipment can be validly and accurately used as a source of funds from the sale of fixed assets.

**Example:** A firm's balance sheet shows the following:

|                   | 1983  | 1982  |
|-------------------|-------|-------|
| Machinery         | 700   | 500   |
| Less acc. depr.   | (300) | (280) |

The footnotes tell us that the firm bought $300,000 of new equipment and wrote off equipment with an accumulated depreciation of

$50,000. How much machinery at cost did the firm write off? What is the firm's annual depreciation?

**Answer:** The firm wrote off $100,000 of equipment at cost. It bought $300,000, but its machinery account only went up by $200,000. The balance was written off. The firm had $70,000 in depreciation. If it had not written off any accumulated depreciation, the new total would be $280,000 + $70,000 = $350,000. Since $50,000 was written off, it is $350,000 − $50,000, or $300,000.

|     MACHINERY     |       |       |     ACC. DEPR.     |       |       |
|-------------------|-------|-------|-------------------|-------|-------|
| 500               |       |       |                   |       | 280   |
| 300               |       |       |                   |       | 70    |
|                   |       | 100   | 50                |       |       |
| 700               |       |       |                   |       | 300   |

**Example:** A firm's balance sheet shows the following:

|                    | 1984  | 1983  |
|--------------------|-------|-------|
| Machinery          | 260   | 300   |
| Less acc. depr.    | (90)  | (100) |

The footnotes tell us the firm bought no new equipment and wrote off old equipment with an accumulated depreciation of $30,000. How much machinery at cost did the firm write off? What is the firm's annual depreciation?

**Answer:** The firm wrote off $40,000 of equipment ($300,000 − $260,000). The firm's annual depreciation is $20,000. It wrote off $30,000, reducing accumulated depreciation from $100,000 to $70,000. Then the $20,000 annual depreciation increased the accumulated depreciation to $90,000.

|     MACHINERY     |       |       |     ACC. DEPR.     |       |       |
|-------------------|-------|-------|-------------------|-------|-------|
| 300               |       |       |                   |       | 100   |
|                   |       | 40    |                   |       | 20    |
|                   |       |       | 30                |       |       |
| 260               |       |       |                   |       | 90    |

**Example:** A firm's balance sheet shows the following:

|              | 1983  | 1982  |
|--------------|-------|-------|
| Machinery    | 400   | 250   |
| Less acc. depr. | (120) | (100) |

The firm's net income for 1983 is $50,000. It wrote off $80,000 of machinery with accumulated depreciation of $10,000. What are the firm's funds from operations? uses of funds to purchase machinery?

**Answer:** The firm had $30,000 depreciation since it wrote off $10,000 but still increased accumulated depreciation by $20,000. This $30,000 plus $50,000 net income equals $80,000 funds from operations. The firm wrote off $80,000 of machinery but still had an increase of $150,000, from $250,000 to $400,000. It must have purchased $150,000 plus $80,000, or $230,000 of machinery.

```
        MACHINERY                    ACC. DEPR.

    250      │                            │    100
    230      │                            │     30
             │    80            10        │
    ─ ─ ─ ─ ─┼─ ─ ─ ─          ─ ─ ─ ─ ─ ─┼─ ─ ─ ─
    400      │                            │    120
             │                            │
```

## CHANGES IN LONG-TERM LIABILITIES

If the firm increases its liabilities, it has borrowed money and is provided with a source of funds. Paying off debt is a use of funds. For the Packard Company, $10,000 of funds was used to reduce the mortgage. Bonds increased from $220,000 to $350,000, indicating a source of funds of $130,000.

## CHANGES IN CONTRIBUTED CAPITAL

The common-stock and premium accounts represent capital contributed by the owners of the firm through purchases of stock. Their total increase of $120,000 indicates that the firm sold stock for this amount, thus realizing a source of funds.

**Example:** If the Packard Company has $5 par common stock, how many shares did it sell in 1984?

**Answer:** 10,000 shares were issued. The $50,000 increase in the common stock account is divided by the par value to get the number of shares issued. It received $12 per share. The total increase in common stock and premium of $120,000 is divided by 10,000 shares.

## CHANGES IN RETAINED EARNINGS

This account is affected by two items:*

1. *Net Income or a Loss.* If the firm has a net income, the retained earnings account increases when the books are closed. A loss, on the other hand, decreases the retained earnings account.
2. *Dividends.* If the firm declares cash dividends, the outflow of cash is a use of funds, which decreases the retained earnings account.

In effect, the retained earnings account reflects the sources of funds from net income or the uses of funds to cover a loss or pay dividends. The fundamental relationship may be expressed in a formula as follows:

$$\text{change in retained earnings} = \text{net income} - \text{dividends}$$

For the flow-of-funds statement, we do not need the retained earnings account to calculate net income. This can be taken from the income statement and is already considered in the funds from operations. We can use the formula to calculate the dividends declared. For Packard, the change in retained earnings is $630,000 to $730,000, or a decrease of $100,000. The loss accounts for $60,000 of this drop. The remainder results because the firm declared $40,000 in cash dividends during the year.

**Example:** A firm has a 1986 retained earnings balance of $600,000 and a 1987 balance of $550,000. It paid dividends of $20,000. What was its 1987 net income?

**Answer:** A loss of $30,000. The decrease of $50,000 in retained earnings from 1986 to 1987 is accounted for by a $20,000 dividend and a $30,000 loss.

---

*Be sure to check the footnotes for possible accounting adjustments in retained earnings. Occasionally, auditors require the firm to make adjustments for past periods that affect this account.

PACKARD COMPANY FLOW-OF-FUNDS STATEMENT

Since the flow-of-funds statement measures the changes in net working capital (defined as current assets minus current liabilities), it is not necessary to record any movements of funds solely within the current accounts. The movements from current to noncurrent accounts and vice versa would result in the following statement for the Packard Company:

**PACKARD COMPANY—Flow-of-Funds Statement**
**(Period Ending December 31, 1984).**

| Sources of Funds | | Uses of Funds | | Changes in |
|---|---|---|---|---|
| Depreciation | $ 80,000 | Net loss | $ 60,000 | net working |
| Sale of bonds | 130,000 | Cash dividends | 40,000 | capital |
| Sale of stock | 120,000 | Additions to | | |
| Sale of equip. | 70,000 | plant and equip. | 400,000 | |
| | | Mortgage reduc. | 10,000 | |
| | $400,000 | | $510,000 | ($110,000) |

The Packard Company experienced a $110,000 decrease in net working capital according to the statement that we prepared. To check this figure, we can use the comparative balance-sheet current accounts. First, we find the total net working capital for 1984. From this figure we subtract the net working capital for 1983. The difference is, in fact, $110,000.

| Total Working Capital (Net) 1984 | | Total Working Capital (Net) 1983 | | Difference |
|---|---|---|---|---|
| Current assets | $510,000 | Current assets | $560,000 | |
| Current liabilities | 120,000 | Current liabilities | 60,000 | |
| Net working capital | $390,000 | Net working capital | $500,000 | −$110,000 |

## KEY TERMS

| | | |
|---|---|---|
| accounts payable | common stock | debenture |
| accumulated depreciation | comparative balance sheet | equity |
| asset | contributed capital in excess | financial statements |
| asset contra account | of par | fixed assets |
| balance sheet | cost of goods sold | fixed costs |
| book value | current assets | floated |
| cash and cash equivalents | current liabilities | flow of funds |

| funds from operations | marketable securities | receivables |
| gross margin | net sales | retained earnings |
| historical record | net working capital | revenues |
| income statement | plant and equipment | sales |
| inventories | preferred stock | short-term notes payable |
| liabilities | premium or surplus | statement of earnings |
| long-term liabilities | pro forma | variable costs |
| marginal analysis | profit and loss statement | working capital |
| marginal contribution | real estate | working-capital pool |

## STUDY QUESTIONS

1. Distinguish among funds, working capital, net working capital, and income.
2. Arrange the following accounts in balance-sheet order: accounts receivable, accounts payable, cash, notes payable, equipment, retained earnings, inventories, common stock, land, long-term debt.
3. How does the balance sheet show the source of resources for a firm?
4. Why does a firm purchase marketable securities?
5. Why are accounts receivable considered more liquid than inventories?
6. What are two ways to show depreciable assets on a balance sheet?
7. What are the differences among the three major types of equity accounts?
8. What are some limitations on the use of balance sheets?
9. Where and how is a loss shown on an income statement?
10. On the income statement, where would the salaries to salesmen be shown?
11. How does interest differ as an expense from cost of goods sold and administrative expenses?
12. If a firm has sales of $350,000, a marginal contribution of $100,000, and an operating income of $40,000, what are the firm's variable costs? fixed costs?
13. Why is *marginal contribution* an important profit concept?
14. A firm has an operating income (EBIT) of $750,000, sales of $3.5 million, and fixed costs of $1,250,000. It pays 7 percent interest on $2 million debt. Prepare an income statement.
15. What is the most important source of funds for a firm and how is it calculated?
16. If a firm has depreciation of $12,350 and a net income of $25,000, what are its total funds from operations?
17. A firm has depreciation of $55,000 and a net loss of $32,000. What are its total funds from operations?

## PROBLEMS

1. A firm has the following amounts in the plant and equipment account:

|  | 1983 | 1982 |
| --- | --- | --- |
| Plant & equip. | $7,400 | $6,700 |
| less acc. depr. | (850) | (700) |

   **a.** How much new equipment did the firm buy as a minimum in 1983?
   **b.** How much depreciation did it have in 1983 if it wrote off $80 in accumulated depreciation?
2. A firm had a net income of $4.2 million and paid dividends of $2.5 million. How much did retained earnings change?
3. A firm had a loss of $275,000 and paid dividends of $520,000. How much did retained earnings change?
4. A firm has four asset accounts: cash, $20,000; accounts receivable, $65,000; inventory, $53,000; plant and equipment, $175,000. It has two current liability accounts: accounts payable, $15,000; notes payable, $8,000. It has one long-term debt account: an $85,000 mortgage. Its common-stock account has $45,000. How much does it have in retained earnings?

In 1983, Liken Company had the following activities and changes:
1. net income, $75,000
2. purchase of new machinery, $60,000
3. floated a 12 percent bond, $35,000
4. depreciation expenses, $23,000
5. paid $43,000 dividends
6. had increases in accounts receivable, $7,000; inventory, $12,000; accounts payable $18,000
7. no changes in wages payable

| LIKENS COMPANY—1982 Balance Sheet | |
|---|---:|
| Cash | $ 25,000 |
| Accounts receivable | 40,000 |
| Inventory | 110,000 |
| Plant & equipment | 175,000 |
| | $350,000 |
| | |
| Accounts payable | $ 30,000 |
| Wages payable | 15,000 |
| Bonds (10%) | 125,000 |
| Equity | 180,000 |
| | $350,000 |

5. Prepare a 1983 balance sheet for Likens Company.
6. Prepare a 1983 flow-of-funds statement showing the change in net working capital for the Liken Company.
7. Use the comparative balance sheet to calculate the change in net working capital. Does your answer agree with the flow-of-funds statement from problem 6?

In 1983, Barth Industries had the following activities and changes:
1. net income, $80,000
2. sold old machinery, $35,000
3. retired a bond, $27,000
4. depreciation expense, $56,000

5. paid $95,000 dividends
6. had decrease in accounts receivable, $25,000; inventory $20,000; increases in accounts payable, $35,000; wages payable, $12,000

**BARTH INDUSTRIES—1982 Balance Sheet**

| | |
|---|---:|
| Cash | $ 52,000 |
| Accounts receivable | 93,000 |
| Inventory | 250,000 |
| Plant & equipment | 410,000 |
| | $805,000 |
| | |
| Accounts payable | $ 78,000 |
| Wages payable | 30,000 |
| Bonds (10%) | 326,000 |
| Equity | 371,000 |
| | $805,000 |

8. Prepare a 1983 balance sheet for Barth Industries.
9. Prepare a 1983 flow-of-funds statement showing the change in net working capital for Barth Industries.
10. Use the comparative balance sheet to calculate the change in net working capital. Does your answer agree with the flow-of-funds statement from problem 9?

**SIMMONS COMPANY—Balance Sheet & Income Statement (000s)**

| | 1983 | 1982 | | 1983 | 1982 |
|---|---:|---:|---|---:|---:|
| Cash | $ 220 | $ 275 | Accts. pay. | $ 295 | $ 310 |
| Accts. rec. | 165 | 175 | Bonds (10%) | 385 | 415 |
| Inv. | 275 | 300 | C.S. ($1 par) | 150 | 100 |
| P&E | 800 | 650 | Premium | 245 | 215 |
| (less acc. depr.) | (75) | (50) | Ret. Earn. | 310 | 310 |
| | $1,385 | $1,350 | | $1,385 | $1,350 |

| | |
|---|---:|
| Sales | $1,650 |
| Cost of goods sold | 1,000 |
| Admin. expenses | 300 |
| Interest | 40 |
| Fed. income taxes | 124 |
| Net income | $ 186 |

**Note:** 1983 depreciation = $80
Purchase P&E 225

11. Prepare a 1983 flow-of-funds statement for the Simmons Company. Does it agree with the actual changes in net working capital?

# Analyzing Financial Statements

*This case develops the skill to assemble a flow-of-funds statement from a balance sheet and information that can be made into an income statement. It also covers the development of an ending balance sheet.*

Anderson Ltd. is a growing sporting goods manufacturer located near Toronto, Canada. The company was founded 14 years ago by Lawrence Anderson after he left his position as a track coach on the Canadian Olympics team to enter private business. Over the years, Anderson expanded the firm's activities into the manufacture of custom-made uniforms, as well as a diverse line of sporting goods. In January 1985, the firm had a number of large contracts to supply college and professional teams in eastern Canada and the northeastern United States with athletic equipment and uniforms.

Anderson Ltd. did well in 1984. The firm reported a net income of $4.5 million; Lawrence Anderson felt that the firm was positioned for a period of steady growth. The firm had approximately $32 million in assets, a strong equity position, and prospects to sign several sizable contracts with colleges and school systems. Anderson's strong competitive position was a factor that encouraged Champion Sports to propose a joint venture. Rick Sinck, the president of Champion Sports, presented a proposal for the two firms to work together on a line of football helmets that would reduce the frequency and severity of head injuries. Rick presented some figures that were very attractive and indicated considerable growth and profit prospects for both firms in the U.S. and Canadian markets. Lawrence expressed an interest in pursuing the proposal and told Rick that he would send him additional information on Anderson Ltd.

After Rick left, Lawrence called in Frank Collazo, a planning analyst in the accounting department. "Frank," he said, "we're giving serious thought to a venture with Champion Sports. Send the firm some information on our company—you know, a balance sheet and income statement. I expect that it will be sending us the same information. Here's what I would like you to do. Run some figures on the expected performance of Champion Sports for 1985. I need to know what you think it will do. As a matter of fact, put it in the form of a balance sheet, income statement, and flow-of-funds statement. The firm knows that we're doing this analysis and will cooperate fully."

Frank returned to his office and began the process of checking on Champion Sports. He got out the loose-leaf from an investment service and learned that Champion Sports was forecasting 1985 sales of $215 million. It was obviously a big operation. If historical trends continued, Champion would probably have total operating expenses of $150 million in 1985. This would include about $22 million in depreciation. After reviewing these numbers, Frank called Champion's accounting department. After a few calls, he learned that the company had plans to purchase $35 million of new manufacturing equipment in 1985. This would partly be financed by the sale of a warehouse. The cost accountant at Champion estimated that the warehouse could be sold for $33 million. It was carried on the books at a $45 million original cost and had $20 million of accumulated depreciation charged to it. Another item of information was that the firm would probably have 1985 interest charges of $11 million on its interest-bearing debt.

After gathering some related information, Frank made a call directly to the office of Rick Sinck. Rick assured him that Champion Sports had no plans to change from the level of its 1984 dividend payment, which was $20 million. Sinck also pointed out that Champion Sports would pay off $8 million in bonds during 1985. This would be more than offset by an increase in its secured financing and a sale of common stock. The mortgage would probably rise by $15 million, and Champion hoped to sell 200,000 shares of common stock to net $60 a share. The proceeds of these new financings would be used to purchase $6 million of real estate and a $21 million manufacturing facility on the land.

Frank needed just a little more information on the liquidity of Champion Sports. He called a staff accountant at Champion and got several estimates for 1985: inventory would increase by $7 million; accounts payable, by $5 million; and the current portion of long-term debt, by $3 million. Receivables would probably drop by about $4 million. The accountant also sent Frank a 1984 balance sheet, which arrived in 3 days. An attached note indicated that Champion Sports had an effective tax rate of 40 percent on its earning before taxes.

## CHAMPION SPORTS INC.—Position Statement (preliminary in 000s).
### December 31, 1984

| | | | |
|---|---|---|---|
| Cash and short-term holdings | $  8,000 | Trade and accounts payable | $ 10,000 |
| Accounts receivable | 30,000 | Current portion of long-term debt | 11,000 |
| Inventories | 55,000 | | |
| Plant and equipment (basis: original cost or market, whichever lower) | 200,000 | Mortgages and secured borrowing | 35,000 |
| | | Bonds and long-term unsecured debt | 22,000 |
| Less accumulated depreciation | (125,000) | Common stock ($1 par) | 5,000 |
| | | Additional paid-in capital | 40,000 |
| Land and real estate | 15,000 | Retained earnings | 60,000 |
| | $183,000 | | $183,000 |

## Required:

Prepare the 1985 balance sheet, income statement, and flow-of-funds statement for Champion Sports, using the information located by Frank Collazo. Use a comparative statement format for the balance sheet.

# 5
# Financial Analysis

*Financial analysis* is the process of determining the significant operating and financial characteristics of a firm from accounting data and financial statements. The goal of such analysis is to determine the efficiency and performance of the firm's management, as reflected in the financial records and reports. The analyst is attempting to measure the firm's liquidity, profitability, and other indications that business is conducted in a rational and orderly way. If a firm does not achieve financial norms for its industry or relationships among data that seem reasonable, the analysts note the deviations. The burden of explaining the apparent problems may then be placed upon management.

In this chapter, we will develop ratio analysis as the primary tool for examining the firm's financial position and performance. We will recognize two viewpoints in receiving and evaluating financial data:

1. *External Analysis.* This is performed by outsiders to the firm, such as creditors, stockholders, or investment analysts. It makes use of existing financial statements and involves limited access to confidential information on a firm.
2. *Internal Analysis.* This is performed by the corporate finance and accounting departments and is more detailed than external analysis. These departments have available more detailed and current information than available to outsiders. They are able to prepare pro forma, or future, statements and are able to produce a

more accurate and timely analysis of the firm's strengths and weaknesses.

## SEPARATING CAUSES AND SYMPTOMS OF PROBLEMS

Financial analysis is used primarily to gain insights into operating and financial problems confronting the firm. With respect to these problems, we must be careful to distinguish between the cause of the problem and a symptom of it. A *cause* is an event that produces a result or effect; in our case the result is a problem. A *symptom* is a visible indicator that a problem exists. The firm may observe symptoms, such as a low level of profits, but it must deal with causes of problems, such as high costs. If it does not deal with the problem cause, the firm will probably not be able to correct the problem.

As we will see in this chapter, financial ratios are used to locate symptoms of problems. Once the symptoms have been located, the financial analyst must determine the cause of any problem. Then he must find a solution for it. Examples of symptoms, causes, and solutions of problems are given in Table 5–1.

## FINANCIAL RATIOS

A *ratio* may be defined as a fixed relationship in degree or number between two numbers. In finance, ratios are used to point out relationships that are not obvious from the raw data. Some uses of ratios are the following:

1. *To Compare Different Companies in the Same Industry.* Ratios can highlight the factors associated with successful and unsuccessful firms. They can reveal strong firms and weak firms, overvalued and undervalued firms.
2. *To Compare Different Industries.* Every industry has its own unique set of operating and financial characteristics. These can be identified with the aid of ratios.
3. *To Compare Performance in Different Time Periods.* Over a period of years, a firm or an industry develops certain norms that may indicate future success or failure. If relationships change in a firm's data over different time periods, the ratios may provide clues on trends and future problems.

From all the financial accounts on the balance sheet, income statement, and flow-of-funds statement, it is possible to formulate countless

**TABLE 5–1.**   Symptoms, Causes, and Solutions for Problems Revealed by
Financial Ratios.

| Symptom | Problem | Solution |
|---|---|---|
| Abnormal liquidity ratio | Inadequate cash | Raise additional funds. |
| | Excessive receivables | Restrict terms of trade; institute a more aggressive collection policy. |
| | Excessive inventory | Improve inventory management. |
| | Excessive current liabilities | Obtain additional long-term financing. |
| Abnormal profitability ratio | High production costs | Institute cost-cutting measures. |
| | Idle assets | Sell excess or obsolete assets. |
| | Inadequate sales | Increase size and quality of sales force; improve advertising. |
| | Inadequate selling price | Raise it. |
| | High administrative expenses | Reduce them. |
| | Excessive interest payments | Seek lower-cost debt financing; seek equity financing. |

ratios. To be successful in financial analysis, the analyst must select only
those ratios that provide significant information about a firm's situation.

## USERS OF RATIOS

Different analysts desire different kinds of ratios, depending largely on
who the analyst is and why the firm is being evaluated. Some users of
ratios are the following:

1. *Short-Term Creditors.* These persons hold obligations that will
   soon mature, and they are concerned with the firm's ability to
   pay its bills promptly. In the short run, the amount of liquid assets determines the ability to pay off current liabilities. These
   persons are interested in liquidity.
2. *Long-Term Creditors.* These persons hold bonds or mortgages

against the firm and are interested in current payments of interest and eventual repayment of principal. The firm must be sufficiently liquid in the short term and have adequate profits for the long term. These persons examine liquidity and profitability.

3. *Stockholders.* In addition to liquidity and profitability, the owners of the firm are concerned about the policies of the firm that affect the market price of the firm's stock. Without liquidity, the firm could not pay cash dividends. Without profits, the firm would not be able to declare dividends. With poor policies, the common stock would trade at low prices in the market.

## COMPARATIVE RATIOS

Ratios are most effectively used when compared to industry averages or norms for similar firms. A *comparative ratio* is defined as a fixed relationship between numbers that is derived from industry averages or other data that can provide a benchmark for evaluating an individual firm. As an example, if an industry average shows a ratio of 6/1 and an individual firm has a ratio of 8/1, we can say that, on a comparative basis, the firm exceeds the industry average.

Comparative ratios are provided by a number of organizations. Dun and Bradstreet is probably the most widely known organization providing such ratios. It provides data on different ratios showing business activity for some 125 business categories under the general headings of manufacturing and construction industries, wholesalers, and retailers. A second source of ratios is Robert Morris Associates, which is a national organization of bank lending officers. This association compiles and publishes averages based upon financial statements received by commercial banks in connection with business loans made by the banks. Other sources of comparative ratios are individual commercial banks, industry trade associations, and the Federal Trade Commission.

## KINDS OF RATIOS

Financial ratios may be classified a number of ways. One classification scheme uses three major categories:

1. *Liquidity Ratios.* These examine the adequacy of funds, the solvency of the firm, and the firm's ability to pay its obligations when due.
2. *Profitability Ratios.* These measure the efficiency of the firm's activities and its ability to generate profits.

3. *Ownership Ratios.* These are generally linked directly or indirectly to profits and liquidity. They assist the stockholder in evaluating the firm's activities and policies that affect the market price of the common stock.

# LIQUIDITY RATIOS

A firm's ability to pay its debts can be measured partly through the use of liquidity ratios. Short-term liquidity involves the relationship between current assets and current liabilities. If a firm has sufficient net working capital (the excess of current assets over current liabilities), it is deemed to have sufficient liquidity. Two ratios are commonly used to measure liquidity directly: the current ratio and the quick ratio, or acid test.

## CURRENT RATIO AND QUICK RATIO, OR ACID TEST

The *current ratio* is a ratio of the firm's total current assets to its total current liabilities. A low ratio is an indicator that a firm may not be able to pay its future bills on time, particularly if conditions change, causing a slowdown in cash collections. A high ratio may indicate an excessive amount of current assets and management's failure to utilize the firm's resources properly. To determine whether this ratio is high, low, or just right, the analyst should consider such factors as the firm's past history, goals, and the current ratios of similar companies. As a general rule, a 2/1 ratio is considered acceptable for most firms.

The *quick ratio,* or *acid test,* is a more stringent measure of liquidity than the current ratio because inventories, which are the least liquid of current assets, are excluded from the ratio. The quick ratio may be calculated two ways:

$$\frac{\text{cash} + \text{marketable securities} + \text{accounts receivable}}{\text{current liabilities}}$$

or

$$\frac{\text{current assets} - \text{inventories}}{\text{current liabilities}}$$

Inventories require a two-step process in order to be converted into cash. They must be sold, converted into receivables (with the markup), and collected. The acid test is so named because it shows the ability of a firm to pay its obligations without relying on the sale and collection of its inventories.

As a guideline, a 1/1 quick ratio has traditionally been deemed adequate for most firms. A higher ratio may have several meanings. It could indicate that the firm has excessive cash or receivables, both signs of lax management. It could indicate that the firm is too cautiously ensuring sufficient liquidity. A low ratio is usually an indication of possible difficulties in the prompt payment of future bills.

## RECEIVABLES RATIOS

Two ratios are used to measure the liquidity of a firm's account receivables:

$$\text{accounts receivable turnover} = \frac{\text{sales}}{\text{accounts receivable}}$$

$$\text{average collection period} = \frac{\text{accounts receivable}}{\text{daily sales}}$$

The *accounts receivable turnover* is a comparison of the size of the firm's sales and the size of its uncollected bills from customers. If the firm is having difficulty collecting its money, it has a large receivables balance and a low ratio. If it has a strict credit policy and aggressive collection procedures, it has a low receivables balance and a high ratio. The *average collection period* compares the receivables balance with the daily sales required to produce the balance. If the firm has $1,000 of sales each day and a receivables balance of $50,000, it took 50 days to accumulate the receivables (a highly simplified statement). More importantly, if neither sales nor receivables change, the firm needs 50 days to collect the $50,000 currently held as receivables. This is why the ratio reflects the average collection period.

Several techniques are available to help the manager analyze the significance of the receivables turnover and average collection period.

1. *Make Comparisons with Other Firms in the Industry.* Since conditions concerning the terms of trade and selling practices are usually similar throughout an industry, this comparison can indicate whether the firm is lax or strict in its collection and sales policies.
2. *Compare Ratios with the Terms of Trade.* The terms of trade are a very important factor in analyzing receivables. To illustrate, let us compare two firms with average collection periods of 44 days. Firm A has terms 2/10 net 30 (indicating that the firm gives a 2 percent discount for payment on its receivables within 10 days

and expects full payment in 30 days). For this firm, a collection period of 44 days means that a number of receivables are still uncollected on the final due date of 30 days. Firm B has terms of 2/10 net 60. For this firm, a period of 44 days means that collections are probably well within the 60-day period. Without further information, we could conclude that firm B is doing a better job of collecting its receivables than firm A.

3. *Use Only Net Credit Sales.* Sales figures may include both cash and credit sales. Since only credit sales become receivables, a more accurate turnover is given if only credit sales are used in the ratio. The same is true for the average collection period.

4. *Use Average Receivables Figures.* If the analyst takes the beginning and ending receivables balance and divides by 2, the average receivables balance may give a more accurate picture of turnover and collections than a single ending figure. A monthly view (add all the ending monthly balances and divide by 12) might be even more accurate. The averaging technique makes sense for firms whose ending receivables balance is not a normal figure.

5. *Avoid Cyclical Figures.* The analyst must always beware of applying ratio analysis to firms operating in industries with cyclical sales. The busy season will distort the ratios in one direction; the quiet season, in the other. Even the average of the busy and quiet periods may not be useful. It would be better to develop two sets of ratios: the turnover and collection period during (1) the busy period and (2) the quiet period.

## INVENTORY TURNOVER

The liquidity of a firm's inventory may be calculated by dividing the cost of goods sold by the firm's inventory:

$$\text{inventory turnover} = \frac{\text{cost of goods sold}}{\text{inventory}}$$

The cost of goods sold is for the period being studied, normally 1 year. Two factors are important in calculating this ratio:

1. *Physical Turnover of Inventory Is Measured.* The sales figure includes a markup for profit. Thus, a $50 sale may turn over only $30 of inventory. The cost of goods sold in this case would be $30 and would measure actual movement of inventory.

2. *Average Inventory May Be Used.* The inventory may be calculated using an average figure in a manner similar to averaging accounts receivable.

The significance of inventory turnover is that it helps the analyst measure the adequacy of goods available to sell compared to the actual sales. In this context, the carrying of inventory involves two risks:

1. *Running out of Goods to Sell.* In some industries, customers place orders and are willing to wait for production and delivery of the goods. In most industries, running out of stock means a loss of sales. When a customer immediately needs an item that the firm does not stock, it will be purchased elsewhere with a consequent loss of profit for the firm. If this happens repeatedly, it can be very costly.
2. *Excessive Carrying Charges due to Excessive Inventory.* Maintaining inventory requires the firm to make expenditures for storing the goods, protecting them from theft or breakage, and handling them. If the firm maintains unneeded inventory, it is paying for unnecessary warehouse space, insuring goods that it need not hold, and incurring other costs that can be a financial burden on the firm.

Because the manager must compromise between running out of goods to sell and investing in excessive inventory, either a high or low ratio may be an indication of poor management, as follows.

1. *High Turnover May Indicate Future Shortages.* A high inventory turnover results when the firm maintains extremely low stocks of goods or raw materials. The low level of finished goods may indicate that the firm will suffer a loss of sales due to an inability to deliver goods promptly. The low level of raw materials could cause shutdowns of the firm's production line, resulting in higher costs.
2. *Low Turnover May Indicate Overstocking of Inventory.* A low inventory turnover results from excessive inventory being carried by the firm. The firm may be incurring high costs from overstocking finished goods or raw materials. At the same time, the firm may be carrying obsolete goods in its inventory.

Different firms turn over their inventories at markedly different rates. A firm that has many items at varying stages of production might be expected to have a relatively low turnover. If the inventory contains only a few fast-moving items, a high turnover would be expected. The analyst should remember that high and low turnovers are relative terms. The current turnover must be compared to previous periods or to some industry norms before it is designated as high, low, or normal. The nature of the business should also be considered in analyzing the appropriateness of the size and turnover of the inventory.

**ALTERNATIVE CALCULATION OF INVENTORY TURNOVER**

An alternative calculation of inventory turnover divides the firm's sales by its inventory:

$$\text{inventory turnover} = \frac{\text{sales}}{\text{inventory}}$$

This differs from the first formula by the markup for profit that the firm receives when it sells an item of inventory. Because the sales figure is generally higher than the cost of goods sold figure, the alternative calculation gives a higher turnover than the calculation using the cost of goods sold.

The reader might ask, "Which calculation is more useful as a measure of the liquidity of a firm's inventory?" The answer is that the two calculations measure different things but either may be useful. The calculation with the cost of goods sold measures the physical turnover of the inventory and is useful to identify a sluggish inventory situation or a situation where inadequate inventory is stocked. The calculation with sales measures the dollars generated from the inventory in the normal course of business. It measures liquidity if the firm continues to sell its inventory at its normal markup.

**Example:** A firm sells 1,000 units of a product at $10 per unit during a 1-year period. The cost of each unit is $6. The firm's inventory is 100 units. What is the inventory turnover in units? the turnover of dollars?

$$\frac{\text{turnover of}}{\text{physical inventory}} = \frac{\text{cost of goods sold}}{\text{inventory}} = \frac{6,000}{600} = 10/1$$

$$\frac{\text{turnover of}}{\text{dollar value}} = \frac{\text{sales}}{\text{inventory}} = \frac{10,000}{600} = 16.67/1$$

In using comparative ratios, the analyst must be aware of which calculation is being used, so that a valid comparison is made. Dun and Bradstreet, for example, regularly publishes the turnover of sales to inventory. In order to have figures that can be correctly compared with Dun and Bradstreet figures, the analyst must use the sales-to-inventory method of calculation.

## ANALYZING LIQUIDITY

The cash, receivables, and inventory ratios should be used together to gain an overall grasp on the liquidity of the firm. We shall analyze each area and draw conclusions on the liquidity of Syntex, Inc., using the balance sheet and income statement provided.

The current ratio and quick ratio are as follows:

$$\text{current ratio} = \frac{\text{cash} + \text{marketable securities} + \text{accounts receivable} + \text{inventory}}{\text{accounts payable} + \text{other payables}}$$

$$= \frac{7,000 + 21,000 + 60,000 + 75,000}{55,000 + 12,000} = \frac{163,000}{67,000} = 2.4/1 \text{ for } 1984$$

$$\text{quick ratio} = \frac{\text{cash} + \text{marketable securities} + \text{accounts receivable}}{\text{accounts payable} + \text{other payables}}$$

$$= \frac{7,000 + 21,000 + 60,000}{55,000 + 12,000} = \frac{88,000}{67,000} = 1.3/1 \text{ for } 1984$$

### SYNTEX, INC.—Balance Sheet (Year Ending December 31, 1984).

|  | 1984 | 1983 |  | 1984 | 1983 |
|---|---|---|---|---|---|
| Current assets |  |  | Current liabilities |  |  |
| Cash and equivalents | $ 7,000 | $ 10,000 | Accts. payable | $ 55,000 | $ 25,000 |
| Mkt. securities | 21,000 | 23,000 | Other payables | 12,000 | 7,000 |
| Accts. receivable | 60,000 | 45,000 |  |  |  |
| Inventories | 75,000 | 62,000 | Mortgage | 70,000 | 75,000 |
|  |  |  | Unsecured long-term financing | 80,000 | 90,000 |
| Fixed assets |  |  | Equity |  |  |
| Machinery (less acc. depr.) | 80,000 | 75,000 | Preferred stock | 20,000 | 20,000 |
| Plant (less acc. depr.) | 166,000 | 110,000 | Common stock | 60,000 | 60,000 |
| Land | 60,000 | 60,000 | Excess over par | 25,000 | 25,000 |
|  |  |  | Retained earnings | 147,000 | 83,000 |
| Total assets | $469,000 | $385,000 | Total | $469,000 | $385,000 |

**SYNTEX, INC.—Income Statement (Year Ending December 31, 1984).**

|  | 1984 | 1983 |
|---|---|---|
| Net sales and other revenues | $495,000 | $370,000 |
| Cost of goods sold | 225,000 | 165,000 |
| Gross margin | 270,000 | 205,000 |
| Administrative expenses | 115,000 | 85,000 |
| Operating income | 155,000 | 120,000 |
| Interest paid | 21,000 | 23,000 |
| Earnings before taxes | 134,000 | 97,000 |
| Federal income taxes | 53,600 | 38,800 |
| Earnings after taxes | 80,400 | 58,200 |
| Preferred stock dividends | 3,000 | 3,000 |
| Net income | $ 77,400 | $ 55,200 |

Syntex, Inc. has a current ratio of 2.4/1, which exceeds the 2/1 guideline. Its acid test is 1.3/1, which exceeds the 1/1 guideline. Since both ratios are higher than the norms, the company appears to be sufficiently liquid. To check this conclusion, we can compare the 1984 ratios with 1983. In 1983, Syntex, Inc. had ratios of

*Current Ratio, 1983*

$$\frac{10+23+45+62}{25+7} = \frac{140}{32} = 4.4/1$$

*Quick Ratio, 1983*

$$\frac{10+23+45}{25+7} = \frac{78}{32} = 2.4/1$$

Between 1983 and 1984, the current ratio dropped from 4.4 to 2.4; the quick ratio dropped from 2.4 to 1.3. From this information, we can conclude that the firm is less liquid in 1984 than in 1983. Although the 1984 figures may still be adequate, the analyst may wish to investigate the reasons for the drop in both ratios.

To check the liquidity of accounts receivable, we can calculate the 1983 and 1984 turnover and collection period:

Accounts Receivable Turnover

*1984*

$$\frac{495}{60} = 8.2 \text{ times}$$

*1983*

$$\frac{370}{45} = 8.2 \text{ times}$$

Average Collection Period

*1984*

$$\frac{60,000}{495,000/360 \text{ days}} = \frac{60}{1.38} = 44 \text{ days}$$

*1983*

$$\frac{45{,}000}{370{,}000/360\ \text{days}} = \frac{45}{1.03} = 44\ \text{days}$$

Both ratios have remained steady at 8.2 and 44 days, respectively, indicating no deterioration in the receivables liquidity. (*Note:* To check the mathematics of our calculation, we can multiply the turnover times the collection period to see if we get approximately 360 days; $8.2 \times 44 = 360.8$ days. This reveals the relationship between the two ratios. A turnover of 8.2 is the same as waiting 44 days to collect the amount of accounts receivable shown on the balance sheet.)

To check the liquidity of the inventory, we can perform three calculations (*Note:* We will use the cost of goods sold in the calculation):

*1984*
*inventory*
*turnover*

*1983 inventory*
*turnover*

$$\frac{225{,}000}{75{,}000} = 3/1 \qquad\qquad \frac{165{,}000}{62{,}000} = 2.7/1$$

*Turnover using average inventory*

$$\frac{225{,}000}{1/2\ (75{,}000 + 62{,}000)} = 3.3/1$$

From this overall liquidity analysis, we can conclude that the receivables and inventory ratios show little change in liquidity, and the current ratio and quick ratio show a possible deterioration. The analyst would make efforts to learn more about the company but first would examine the balance sheet to see why the ratios changed. The major cause of the change seems to be the large increase in accounts payable from 25,000 to 55,000. Although increases in receivables and inventories accompany the increase in payables, the analyst should inquire as to the cause of the payables rise.

## PROFITABILITY RATIOS

Basically, there are two major categories of profitability ratios:

1. *Profits in Relation to Sales.* It is important from a profit standpoint that the firm be able to generate adequate profit on each unit of

sales. If sales lack a sufficient margin of profit, it is difficult for the firm to cover its fixed costs and fixed charges on debt and to earn a profit for shareholders.

2. *Profits in Relation to Assets.* It is similarly important that profit be compared to the capital invested by owners and creditors. If the firm cannot produce a satisfactory profit on its asset base, it may be misusing the assets.

In addition to these two categories, the analyst links the profit ratios through a ratio of sales to assets. An important factor in the firm's ability to produce profits is the relationship between the level of sales and the level of assets required to attain the sales. The relationships among sales, assets, and profits are examined as profitability ratios.

## PROFIT MARGIN

The firm's profit margin is calculated by dividing operating income by sales:

$$\text{profit margin} = \frac{\text{operating income}}{\text{sales}}$$

Both figures are normally taken from the income statement. The significance of this ratio is that it helps measure the relationship between sales and operating profits. If the profit margin is inadequate, the firm cannot achieve satisfactory returns for its investors.

The profit margin is an indicator of the ability of the firm to withstand adverse conditions, which may arise from several sources, such as the following:

1. *Falling Prices.* If the general price level in the marketplace experiences a decline, does the firm have a sufficient margin to drop its price and still show a profit on individual sales?

2. *Rising Costs.* If the firm is caught in a period of rising costs when it cannot raise its prices, will the firm continue to be profitable?

3. *Declining Sales.* Can the firm withstand unexpected drops in sales and still show a profit?

Similarly, the profit margin may be used as an indicator of possible success under favorable conditions, such as the following:

1. *Rising Prices.* If the firm is able to raise its prices, how quickly will profits rise?
2. *Lowered Costs.* If supplies and materials decline in price, what profits can be expected?
3. *Increasing Sales.* If the firm is able to gain large increases in sales without price or cost effects, what would be the profit forecast?

## GROSS PROFIT MARGIN

A second ratio that links sales and profits is the gross profit margin, which is calculated by dividing the gross margin by sales. This ratio shows the profits relative to sales after the direct production costs are deducted. It may be used as an indicator of the efficiency of the production operation and the relation between production costs and selling price:

$$\text{gross profit margin} = \frac{\text{sales} - \text{cost of goods sold}}{\text{sales}}$$

The difference between profit margin and gross profit margin lies in the general and administrative expenses. These are included in the profit margin; thus the profit margin presents a total operations picture. They are excluded from the more narrow profit measure of gross profit margin.

## ASSET TURNOVER

The asset turnover is calculated by dividing sales by the firm's assets:

$$\text{asset turnover} = \frac{\text{sales}}{\text{total assets}} \qquad \text{or} \qquad \frac{\text{sales}}{\text{operating assets}}$$

It highlights the amount of assets that the firm used to produce its total sales. The ability to produce a large volume of sales on a small asset base is an important part of the firm's profit picture. Idle or improperly used assets increase the firm's need for costly financing and the expenses for maintenance and upkeep. By achieving a high asset turnover, a firm reduces costs and increases the eventual profit to its owners.

In the calculation of asset turnover, assets may be defined three ways:

1. *Total Assets.* The most common usage of assets involves the total assets reported on the balance sheet. This is basically the book

value of current fixed assets. It is the most common asset measure since it is the most readily available, appearing in the firm's
annual report.

2. *Operating Assets.* A more accurate measure of the assets used to
   generate a given volume of sales is the actual operating assets.
   The analyst might eliminate excess current assets, capital tied up
   in expansion activities, or other assets not used in the firm's operations in order to produce the reported EBIT. The difficulty in
   using operating assets is identifying them. If the firm is constructing a $25-million factory, this may be noted in the annual
   report. Since it is not operating yet, it can be eliminated from the
   total assets. But there may be other unused assets, and this may
   not be known.

3. *Total Assets plus Estimated Value of Leased Assets.* When a firm
   leases plant or equipment, it is earning a return on an asset that
   is not shown on the balance sheet. When comparing different
   firms, the approximate value of each firm's assets should be reflected. If an airline is leasing a $20-million jet plane, it should be
   included as a portion of the assets in the calculation of asset
   turnover.

As a general rule, external analysis uses total assets, with or without
an estimate of the value of leased assets. Internal analysis should use operating assets and should consider the value of leased assets.

## RETURN ON INVESTMENT

Individually, the profit margin and the asset turnover have certain weaknesses. The profit margin ignores the money invested by the firm to earn
the profit. On the other hand, the asset turnover does not consider the
profits made on the use of the assets. To overcome these individual
weaknesses, the two ratios may be combined to form a return on investment (ROI).

Return on investment may be calculated in two ways:

1. *EBIT Divided by Assets.* The firm's return on investment is a ratio
   of its operating income to the assets used to produce the income.

2. *Asset Turnover Times Profit Margin.* The size of a firm's return on
   investment is a function of the margin of profit on sales and the
   amount of sales generated on the asset base. A formula for return on investment is:

$$\text{profit margin} \times \text{asset turnover} = \text{return on investment}$$

$$\frac{\text{EBIT}}{\text{sales}} \times \frac{\text{sales}}{\text{assets}} = \frac{\text{EBIT}}{\text{assets}} = \frac{\text{return on}}{\text{investment}}$$

As illustrated in the formula, when the multiplication is performed, the sales in the denominator of the profit margin and the sales in the numerator of the asset turnover cancel out, leaving EBIT/assets. The *DuPont chart*, so called because it was first used by the DuPont Company, shows the factors producing return on investment (Figure 5–1).

The return on investment is the key indicator of profitability for a firm. It matches operating profits with the assets available to earn a return. Firms that are efficiently using their assets have a relatively high return. Less efficient firms have a lower return. As we will see, the return on investment is a very important concept in profit planning.

## RETURN ON EQUITY

The return on equity (ROE) is an important profit indicator to shareholders of the firm. It is calculated by the formula

$$\frac{\text{net income}}{\text{total equity}} = \text{return on equity}$$

This ratio indicates the degree to which the firm is able to convert operating income into an aftertax income that eventually can be claimed by shareholders. Stated differently, ROE is used to measure the aftertax profits that accrue to the common shareholders since preferred stock dividends, if any, are subtracted before arriving at net income. This is a use-

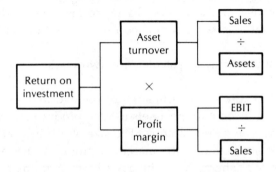

**Figure 5–1**  DuPont Chart.

ful ratio for analyzing the ability of the firm's management to realize an adequate return on the capital invested by the owners of the firm.

## EARNING POWER

Earning power is calculated by dividing net income by total assets. It is a measure of the aftertax return achieved by the company compared to the firm's resources. It links aftertax profits to the book value of the assets. If a firm is using its assets efficiently, it has a high earning power when compared with similar firms.

Earning power may be viewed as the firm's aftertax return on investment. Many managers use the term *return on investment* when they are relating net income to assets. For clarity and precision, we use *return on investment* to mean EBIT/assets and *earning power* to mean net income/assets.

When others use the term *return on investment*, the analyst should always ask what the person means.

The three major ratios linking profits to resources are given in Table 5–2.

## TIMES INTEREST EARNED

A useful measure of profit that does not link return to resources is the times interest earned ratio. It is calculated by dividing the firm's operating income by the interest that it must pay on its debt:

$$\text{times interest earned} = \frac{\text{operating income}}{\text{interest}}$$

It relates operating profits to the fixed charges created by the firm's borrowing.

---

**TABLE 5–2.** Comparing Three Major Ratios Linking Profits and Resources.

| Return on Investment (ROI): EBIT/Assets | Return on Equity (ROE): Net Income/Equity | Earning Power (EP): Net Income/Assets |
|---|---|---|
| Measures ability of management to earn a return on resources. | Measures ability of firm to convert operating profits into aftertax return for common shareholders. | Measures efficiency of firm in achieving an aftertax return on resources. Also called aftertax ROI. |

---

The times interest earned ratio provides an indication of the margin of safety between financial obligations and the net income. A firm may have an operating profit but may face difficulty in making excessive interest payments. If it is confronted by a drop in operating profits, it may be unable to meet its debt obligations. In either case, its net income will decline or vanish. A satisfactory guideline for this ratio is that EBIT should be 5 to 7 times interest charges. Thus, a firm could experience an 80 to 86 percent drop in EBIT and still cover interest payments.

**Example:** A firm has a times interest earned ratio of 3/1. What percentage drop can it sustain in operating income and still meet its interest payments?

**Answer:** 67 percent drop. The operating income can decrease to one-third its current level.

### ANALYZING PROFITABILITY

Many factors influence a firm's profitability. Each factor in turn affects the profitability ratios. In analyzing a firm's profitability from ratio analysis, we must recognize the interrelationships of factors. Figure 5–2 identifies factors and shows which ratios help explain other ratios.

In using Figure 5–2, note the cumulative effect of the individual factors. Every factor affects earning power, even though none leads to it directly. For example, high production costs, which affect gross profit margin, have an effect through the profit margin, return on investment,

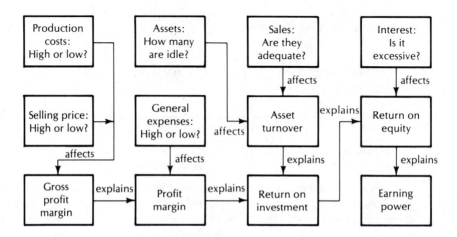

**Figure 5–2**   Factors Affecting Profit and Interrelation of Profitability Ratios.

return on equity, and finally earning power. One ratio explains another because the factors that affect it also affect the others.

**APPLICATION OF PROFITABILITY ANALYSIS**

As an example of profitability analysis, we will use the Syntex, Inc. data. The *profit margins* are

$$1984 \quad \frac{155,000}{495,000} = 31\% \qquad 1983 \quad \frac{120,000}{370,000} = 32\%$$

As a guideline, a profit margin of 15 to 25 percent is considered satisfactory. If firms similar to Syntex have profit margins in this range, Syntex is realizing a higher profit on sales than its competition.

Syntex's *gross profit margins* are

$$1984 \quad \frac{270,000}{495,000} = 55\% \qquad 1983 \quad \frac{205,000}{370,000} = 55\%$$

This compares to a profit margin of 31 to 32 percent. Since the gross profit margin does not consider general and administrative expenses in the numerator of the fraction and hence covers fewer costs, the gross profit margin is always a larger percentage than the profit margin. As a general guideline, a gross profit margin of 35 to 50 percent is satisfactory.

The asset turnovers for Syntex are

$$1984 \quad \frac{495,000}{469,000} = 1.06 \text{ times} \qquad 1983 \quad \frac{370,000}{385,000} = .96 \text{ times}$$

Note that these ratios do not mean that that firm is selling its operating assets. Rather, the dollar volume of Syntex's sales was 5 percent larger in 1984 and 4 percent smaller in 1983 than the dollar value of the firm's assets as shown on the balance sheet. A turnover of 1 to 2 times is considered satisfactory for most industrial firms.

The returns on investment for Syntex are

$$1984 \quad \frac{155,000}{469,000} = 33\% \qquad 1983 \quad \frac{120,000}{385,000} = 31\%$$

This may also be calculated by multiplying the profit margin by the asset turnover.

**1984**   $(31\%)\,(1.05)=33\%$      **1983**   $(32\%)\,(.96)=31\%$

As a guideline, we expect mature firms to have returns on investment in a range of 25 to 40 percent. Syntex is within this range.

Syntex has returns on equity as follows:

$$1984 \quad \frac{77,400}{60,000+25,000+147,000} = \frac{77,400}{232,000} = 33.4\%$$

$$1983 \quad \frac{55,200}{60,000+25,000+83,000} = \frac{55,200}{168,000} = 32.9\%$$

The return on equity is usually lower than the return on investment for a mature industrial firm. This is the case because ROE is an aftertax measure of profit, and corporate taxes are a large percentage of the firm's earnings before taxes. In some cases, however, the ROE exceeds ROI. This occurs if the firm is using a significant portion of debt to finance its assets and the debt cost is much lower than the return on investment. As a guideline, a satisfactory return on equity is 70 to 90 percent of return on investment. For example, if ROI is 30 percent, ROE should be 21 to 27 percent. Syntex has a high ROE each year and appears to be very successful in converting operating income into net income.

Syntex's earning power for each year is:

$$1984 \quad \frac{77,400}{469,000} = 16.5\% \qquad 1983 \quad \frac{55,200}{385,000} = 14.3\%$$

A satisfactory earning power would be 12 to 16 percent. Syntex is at the top of this range and improved from 1983 to 1984.

Syntex's times interest earned ratios are:

$$1984 \quad \frac{155,000}{21,000} = 7.4 \text{ times} \qquad 1983 \quad \frac{120,000}{23,000} = 5.2 \text{ times}$$

These ratios are within the guideline of 5 to 7 times. In 1984 Syntex could experience an 86 percent drop in EBIT (a drop of $134,000) and still be able to cover its fixed charges on debt.

After calculating the profit ratios for Syntex, the analyst prepares a matrix such as Table 5–3. This allows a comparison of the expected ratios and the actual figures for the company being examined. If any of the ratios fail to meet the guidelines, the analyst considers the factors in Figure

**TABLE 5–3.**   Comparison Matrix Showing Guidelines and Actual Ratios.

| Profitability Ratio | Guideline | Syntex Actual | |
|---|---|---|---|
| | | 1984 | 1983 |
| Gross profit margin | 30–50% | 55% | 55% |
| Profit margin | 15–25% | 31% | 32% |
| Asset turnover | 1–2 times | 1.06 times | .96 times |
| Return on investment | 25–40% | 33% | 31% |
| Return on equity | 70–90% of ROI | 33.4% (101% of ROI) | 32.9% (106% of ROI) |
| Earning power | 12–16% | 16.5% | 14.3% |
| Times interest earned | 5–7 times | 7.4 times | 5.2 times |

5–2 and traces the ratios to the causes of the inadequate performance. For example, the return on investment might be low and the cause may be a low selling price, idle assets, high production costs, inadequate sales, high administrative expenses, or a combination of these factors. Table 5–3 indicates that Syntex meets the profit guidelines established by the analyst.

## OWNERSHIP RATIOS

Ownership ratios assist the stockholder in analyzing present and future investment in a company. Stockholders are interested in the way certain variables affect the value of their holdings. The ratios compare the value of the investment with factors such as debt, dividends, earnings, and the market price of the stock. By understanding the profitability and liquidity ratios, the owner gains insights into the soundness of the firm's business activities. By investigating ownership ratios, the stockholder is able to analyze the likely future market value of the stock.

In this section, we will analyze three major groupings of ownership ratios:

1. *Earnings Ratios.* These provide information on the earnings of the firm and how earnings affect the price of common stock. The earnings ratios are earnings per share, price-earnings ratio, and capitalization rate.
2. *Capital Structure Ratios.* A firm's *capital structure* is the relation of debt to equity as sources of the firm's assets. The two ratios that reflect capital structure are the debt-equity ratio and the debt-asset ratio.

3. *Dividend Ratios.* These provide measures of the adequacy of dividend payments. The two ratios are dividend payout and dividend yield.

## EARNINGS PER SHARE (EPS)

Stockholders are concerned about the earnings that will eventually be available to pay them dividends or that are used to expand their interest in the firm because the firm retains the earnings. These earnings may be expressed on a per-share basis. Earnings per share is calculated by dividing net income by the number of shares outstanding. Shares authorized but not issued, or authorized, issued, and repurchased *(treasury stock)*, are omitted from the calculation.

A year-by-year comparison of earnings per share can be very informative to the investor. As an example, an investor is considering the purchase of a large bloc of shares of either firm A or B. Each stock will sell for $40 per share. The earnings trend for the two firms is as follows:

|            | 1979 | 1980 | 1981 | 1982 | 1983 | 1984 |
|------------|------|------|------|------|------|------|
| Firm A EPS | 1.23 | 1.42 | 1.65 | 1.87 | 2.15 | 2.45 |
| Firm B EPS | 2.55 | 2.98 | 2.06 | 2.24 | 2.03 | 2.45 |

In the last year the two firms have identical earnings per share. Firm A began at a low EPS but has steadily progressed and has doubled EPS in 5 years. Firm B has held steady in EPS and has displayed wide fluctuations over the 5 years. The trends of the two earnings streams appear to forecast a brighter future for firm A than firm B.

## PRICE-EARNINGS RATIO

The price-earnings ratio (P/E) is calculated by dividing earnings per share into the market price of the stock (MktPr/EPS). It is the most important measure of value used by investors in the marketplace. Many investors consider no other factor prior to making purchases.

The P/E ratio is used as a *going-concern* method of valuing stock. As long as the firm is a viable business entity, its real (or going-concern) value is reflected in its profits. The P/E ratio considers aftertax profits and market price, and links earnings per share to activity in the market. If a stock has a low P/E multiple, for example, 4/1, it may be viewed as an undervalued stock. If the ratio is 20/1, it may be considered overvalued.

The P/E ratio may be used several ways:

1. *To Determine Expected Market Value of a Stock.* Within any given industry, there is usually a wide variation in the P/E multiples for the firms. One firm may trade at 6/1, while another trades at 10/1. If the firms are somewhat similar, the P/E ratio may help to identify the undervalued and overvalued stocks. For example, if we expect a firm to have a 9/1 multiple because other firms have this multiple, and if the firm has an EPS of $3, we can say the stock has a value of (9/1) ($3), or $27. This is an example of using a normal P/E multiple to calculate an expected market value. Note that the actual market price may be higher or lower than $27. If it is lower, we may be buying an undervalued stock. If it is higher, we may be avoiding an overvalued stock.

2. *To Determine Future Market Value of a Stock.* If the stock is purchased for $27 and has $3 EPS, what will it be worth in 5 years when EPS is $7? If the P/E ratio stays approximately 9/1, the stock will be worth (9/1) ($7), or $63. If EPS only goes to $4, it will be worth (9/1) ($4), or $36.

3. *To Determine Capitalization Rate of a Stock.* The P/E ratio may be used to measure the rate of return investors demand before they purchase a stock. The reciprocal of the P/E ratio is EPS/MktPr and gives this return. If the stock has $3 EPS and sells for $27, the marketplace demands that the stock return 3/27, or 11 percent. This is the stock's *capitalization rate* (see Table 5–4). An 11 percent capitalization rate means that the firm earns 11 percent on the value of the common stock. If investors did not require this return, they would pay more for the stock and the rate of return or capitalization rate would drop.

## CAPITAL STRUCTURE RATIOS

Two ratios are important in analyzing the relationship between the debt and equity components of the firm's capital structure:

1. *Debt-Equity Ratio.* This is calculated by dividing the total debt by the total equity.

**TABLE 5–4.**   Price-Earnings Ratios Expressed as Capitalization Rates.

| Price-earnings ratio | 5/1 | 8/1 | 10/1 | 12.5/1 | 15/1 | 20/1 | 25/1 | 30/1 | 35/1 | 40/1 |
|---|---|---|---|---|---|---|---|---|---|---|
| Capitalization rate | 20% | 12.5% | 10% | 8% | 6.67% | 5% | 4% | 3.33% | 2.9% | 2.5% |

**2.** *Debt-Asset Ratio.* This is calculated by dividing the total debt by the total assets.

These ratios show how much of the firm's assets are financed by debt and equity and give important information about prospects for future financing. If a firm has excessive debt, it will experience difficulty in locating additional debt financing. The firm will be able to borrow only at high interest rates, if at all. On the other hand, if the ratio is low (virtually no debt), it may indicate a failure to use relatively lower cost borrowed funds to raise the return earned on the common stock.

Analysts differ on whether short-term debt should be included in the capital structure ratios. One group reasons that accounts payable and similar short-term items allow a temporary use of assets (notably inventory) but are not really a form of borrowing to finance the firm's resources. In other words, current liabilities are not a permanent part of the capital employed by the firm. For our purposes, current liabilities are included in the debt-equity and debt-asset ratios. Our reasoning is that careful management of the short-term debt accounts allows the firm to take advantage of inexpensive (and frequently free) funds that it would otherwise have to borrow at higher rates. Also, short-term debt represents obligations of the firm. If capital structure ratios measure a degree of financial risk by showing how much the firm owes, they should reflect all debt owed by the firm.

There are three major uses of capital structure ratios:

1. *To Identify Sources of Funds.* The firm finances all its resources from debt or equity sources. The amount of resources from each source is shown by these ratios.
2. *To Measure Financing Risk.* One measure of the degree of risk resulting from debt financing is provided by these ratios. If the firm has been increasing the percentage of debt in its capital structure over a period of time, this may indicate an increase in risk for its shareholders.
3. *To Forecast Borrowing Prospects.* If the firm is considering expansion and needs to raise additional money, the capital structure ratios offer an indication of whether debt funds will be available. If the ratios are too high, the firm may not be able to borrow.

As a general guideline, the debt should not exceed 50 percent of the total sources of funds. It should be less than 50 percent for a firm in a risky business that produces wide swings in operating income. Thus, a

**TABLE 5–5.** Comparison of Capital Structure Ratios.

| If the Debt-Equity Ratio Is: | Then the Debt-Asset Ratio Is: | And the Percentage of Total Assets Financed by Debt Is: |
| --- | --- | --- |
| 0 | 0 | 0 |
| .2/1 | .167/1 | 16.7 |
| .4/1 | .286/1 | 28.6 |
| .6/1 | .375/1 | 37.5 |
| .8/1 | .444/1 | 44.4 |
| 1.0/1 | .50/1 | 50.0 |
| 1.5/1 | .60/1 | 60.0 |
| 2.0/1 | .67/1 | 66.7 |
| 5.0/1 | .83/1 | 83.3 |

debt-equity ratio of 1/1 or a debt-asset ratio of .5/1 should be maximum for industrial firms. Table 5–5 offers a comparison of the two ratios at different levels.

**BOOK VALUE PER SHARE**

The book value of a firm's common stock is calculated by dividing the stockholders' equity by the number of shares outstanding. This ownership ratio is somewhat related to the capital structure ratios, since it measures the accounting value of a portion of the firm's assets—the portion financed by the owners.

Book value is the reflection of the accounting records of the firm rather than a strong measure of the real value of the firm's assets. If two otherwise identical firms used different depreciation schedules, the book value of their assets would be different. Historically, the book value has resulted from the use of conservative accounting techniques and has been lower than the market value of the stock. For this reason, it is of limited value as an ownership ratio. Three valid uses of book value may be identified:

1. *Liquidation Value.* When a firm is experiencing liquidity or profitability problems, it may consider selling its assets, paying off its debts, and distributing the remaining money, if any, to its shareholders. In cases of possible liquidation, the book value gives an indication of the amount that can be distributed to shareholders. If the firm can sell its assets for, say, 80 percent of the recorded

asset value, and it pays its debt at 100 percent of value, the remainder is available for common shareholders. Normally, a firm with a high book value per share has more remaining for shareholders than a firm with a low book value per share.

2. *Market Price near Book Value.* In many cases, an interesting phenomenon occurs when a firm's market price nears its book value. Investors note that the firm's assets do support a certain price (book value) and do not allow the market price to drop below that price. In effect, the book value becomes a support level for the price of the common stock. In some cases, it may become a rallying point, and investor demand will begin to push up the price of the stock. Analysts and investors take notice of the low market price in relation to book value and begin to purchase the apparently undervalued stock.

3. *Legal Proceedings.* In certain legal or tax proceedings, book value may have a use. It may become the taxable base for taxes on securities.

## DIVIDEND RATIOS

The common stockholder is very concerned about the position taken by the firm with respect to the payment of cash dividends. If the firm is paying insufficient dividends, the stock is not attractive to investors desiring some current income from their investment. If it pays excessive dividends, it may not be retaining adequate funds to finance future growth.

To pay consistent and adequate dividends, the firm must be liquid and profitable. Without liquidity, the firm cannot locate the cash needed to pay the dividends. Without profits, the firm does not have sufficient retained earnings to make dividend declarations. Firms cannot declare dividends if the balance in their retained-earnings accounts is not at least as large as the amount of the dividend. A more important factor is that, without profits, the firm does not have the resources to pay the dividends.

Two dividend ratios are particularly important:

1. *Dividend Payout* (DPS/EPS). This is a ratio of dividends per share to earnings per share. It tells what percentage of the firm's earnings is being paid to the common shareholder in the form of dividends. The percentage not paid out is retained for the firm's future needs.

2. *Dividend Yield* (DPS/MktPr). This is a ratio of dividends per share

to the market price per share. It gives the current return to the investor as a percentage of his investment. It is of interest to potential shareholders who are considering purchasing the firm's stock and who desire dividends as a source of income.

Guidelines for these two ratios vary widely. Firms often attempt to pay approximately 50 percent of their earnings as dividends. If the firm needs funds to support its operations, it might allow the dividends to decline in relation to earnings. If the firm lacks opportunities to use funds generated by retained earnings, it might allow the dividends to increase in relation to earnings. In either case, consistency of dividend payment would be important to investors, so that changes would be gradual.

The dividend yield to a stockholder ranges from 0 to 10 or 12 percent. No dividend yield exists for a firm that does not declare dividends. High-growth firms may declare dividends, but the yield may only be 2 or 3 percent. For mature industrial firms, the yield may be 7 or 8 percent. When stock prices are depressed or for utilities or similar firms, the yield may reach 10 to 12 percent.

## ANALYZING OWNERSHIP RATIOS

Using the data from Syntex, Inc., an analyst has prepared Table 5–6, showing the ratios for the company and the analyst's estimate of normal ratios for this kind of firm.

From Table 5–6 an analyst might draw the following conclusions about Syntex.

1. *It Offers a Low Return.* The high price-earnings ratio results in a low capitalization rate. Since this is a measure of the profit earned by the firm compared to the price of the stock, it indicates that the firm is near the bottom of the expected range for return on a shareholder's investment. The price of the stock is less likely to increase while Syntex is near the top of its normal P/E range of 5 to 10/1.

2. *It Has a Reasonable Capital Structure.* The debt-equity and debt-asset ratios are close to the norm.

3. *It Does Not Offer Satisfactory Current Income.* The dividend ratios indicate that Syntex is retaining its earnings rather than paying expected cash dividends to its shareholders. The dividend payout is approximately half the norm, and the dividend yield is even lower.

**TABLE 5–6.**   Worksheet of Ownership Ratio for Syntex, Inc.

| Ratio | Syntex, 1984 | Syntex, 1983 | Norms |
|---|---|---|---|
| **Earnings ratios** | | | |
| Earnings per share[a] | 77,400/40,000 = $1.94 | 55,200/40,000 = $1.38 | none |
| Price-earnings[b] | 17/1.94 = 8.8/1 | 15/1.38 = 10.9/1 | 5–10/1 |
| Capitalization rate | 1.94/17 = 11.4% | 1.38/15 = 9.2% | 10–20% |
| | | | |
| **Capital structure** | | | |
| Debt-equity | 217,000/252,000 = .86/1 | 197,000/188,000 = 1.05/1 | 1/1 |
| Debt-asset | 217,000/469,000 = .46/1 | 197,000/385,000 = .51/1 | .5/1 |
| Book value | 232/40 = $5.80 share | 168/40 = $4.20 share | none |
| | | | |
| **Dividend ratios[c]** | | | |
| Dividends per share | 16,000/40,000 = $.40 | 14,000/40,000 = $.35 | none |
| Dividend payout | .40/1.94 = 20.6% | .35/1.38 = 25.4% | 40% |
| Dividend yield | .40/17 = 2.3% | .35/15 = 2.3% | 7–8% |

[a]Syntex has 40,000 shares outstanding.
[b]Syntex's market price is $17 at the end of 1984 and $15 at the end of 1983.
[c]Syntex paid a $16,000 dividend in 1984 and a $14,000 dividend in 1983.

From a potential owner's point of view, we might conclude that Syntex is a reasonable-return, financially balanced firm that offers long-term prospects for increases in market price rather than payments of cash as current income. With a high profit and high retention of earnings, the firm may be expected to grow rapidly, with eventual increase in the price of its stock. Since the other ratios reveal that the firm is liquid and profitable, our external analysis indicates that it offers a good buy for the long-term investor who is not seeking current income.

## DETERMINING FINANCIAL NORMS

One of the most difficult aspects of financial analysis involves the determination of the appropriate norms against which an individual firm may be judged. At least five guidelines may be used:

1. *Industry Norms.* A firm may be compared against the financial ratios of other firms in the same industry. This is only partially satisfactory in most cases because industry norms vary widely from the strongest to the weakest firm in the grouping. Frequently, an average for the industry offers little utility because the spread is

so wide. The analyst can use industry norms to see how the firm compares to other individual firms. For example, if the firm is second highest in profit in a 10-firm industry, it is relatively profitable.

2. *Similar Firms.* If we compare the firm with similar firms in other industries, we often gain a better insight into the financial condition. For example, if we are examining a growth firm in a non-growth industry, it makes sense to compare it with other growth firms in other industries.

3. *Historical Trends.* We can compare a firm with itself—or rather with its own performance over a period of time. It is a good sign if the firm is maintaining or increasing its profits, and a bad sign if its liquidity is dropping.

4. *Future Expectations.* Economists and analysts make efforts to forecast conditions. These expectations can be used as norms to compare firms today. For example, in 3 years an analyst may expect a surge of investor confidence and hence an increase in the normal price-earnings ratios. How does this affect the individual firm being evaluated?

5. *Common Sense.* This is the catchall guideline that is so frequently ignored. If all else fails, the analyst can use subjective judgment and reason. For example, a 2 percent return on investment can never be a norm because it is too low for rational investors. At the same time, a 60 percent ROI is too high. Common sense tells us that 30 percent is more reasonable as a norm.

In conclusion, we might urge the analyst to do the following to conduct a proper financial analysis:

1. Use liquidity, profitability, and ownership ratios together to gain a single, overall view of a firm.
2. Determine the norms using a combination of the five preceding guidelines.
3. Perform further investigation to explain any deviations from the norms.

## KEY TERMS

| | | |
|---|---|---|
| accounts receivable turnover | dividend payout | internal analysis |
| acid test | dividend yield | inventory turnover |
| asset turnover | Dun and Bradstreet | norms |
| average collection period | DuPont chart | price-earnings ratio |
| book value per share | earning power | profit margin |
| capitalization rate | earnings available to the | quick ratio |
| capital structure ratios | common shareholder | ratio |
| comparative ratio | earnings per share | return on equity |
| current ratio | external analysis | return on investment |
| debt-asset ratio | financial analysis | terms of trade |
| debt-equity ratio | gross profit margin | times interest earned |

## STUDY QUESTIONS

1. How are financial ratios classified?
2. What are some sources of comparative ratios?
3. What is the difference between the current ratio and acid test?
4. What is the difference between the two methods of calculating inventory turnover?
5. Why do we distinguish between profit margin and gross profit margin?
6. Why is asset turnover considered a profitability ratio?
7. What is the difference between the uses of ROI and ROE?
8. What is the difference between dividend payout and dividend yield?

## PROBLEMS

1. If a firm has sales of $750,000 and average accounts receivable of $93,750, what is its accounts-receivable turnover? average collection period?
2. A firm has sales of $225,000, a cost of goods sold of $150,000, and an inventory of $55,000. What is its inventory turnover?
3. A firm has cash of $7,000, receivables of $45,000, and inventories of $62,000. It has no other current assets. How much can it have in current liabilities and retain a 3/1 current ratio?
4. A firm has $80,000 in inventory and $150,000 of cost of goods sold. Management has set a 2/1 goal for inventory turnover. How much is the inventory over or under the amount that would give this 2/1 ratio?
5. A firm has a profit margin of 12 percent and an asset turnover of 3. What is its ROI?
6. The firm in question 5 has an EBIT of $180,000 and assets of $500,000. What are its sales?
7. A firm has sales of $3,750,000, cost of goods sold of $2,100,000 and administrative expenses of $650,000. What are the gross profit margin and profit margin?

8.  A firm has an EBIT of $235,000, interest charges of $12,000, taxes of $89,200, total assets of $1.1 million, and total liabilities of $300,000. What is its ROE?

9.  A firm has an operating income of $660,000 and pays 9 percent interest on a total debt of $3 million. What is its times interest earned?

10. A firm has a times interest earned ratio of 9/1. What percentage of drop in EBIT would result in a zero EBT?

11. A firm has a net income of $135,000 and 50,000 shares outstanding, selling at a market price of $32.50. What is the firm's P/E ratio?

12. A firm has a P/E ratio of 8/1. What rate of return do investors demand on this stock?

13. A firm has current liabilities of $125,000, a mortgage of $200,000 and unsecured long-term debt of $225,000. Its total equity is $650,000. What is its debt-equity ratio? debt-asset ratio?

14. A firm has a net income of $300,000 and pays cash dividends of $120,000 on its 60,000 shares of outstanding stock at a time when the stock is selling for $25. What is the dividend yield? dividend payout?

15. Questions 13 and 14 concern the same firm. What is its book value per share?

16. A firm has a capitalization rate of 12 percent. What is its P/E ratio?

17. What are the values of accounts-receivable turnover and average collection period when sales are $4.2 million and accounts receivable are $600,000?

18. A firm has an EBIT of $170,000 and $500,000 in debt at 10 percent. What is its times interest earned ratio?

19. In 1985 a firm has a net income of $840,000 and 200,000 shares outstanding. The stock price is $42. What is the P/E ratio?

20. A firm has $26,000 in current liabilities, $85,000 long-term debt, and total equity of $124,000. What is the debt-equity ratio? debt-asset ratio?

21. A firm's stock is selling for $18 per share. It has a 1984 EPS of $5 and paid a $2 dividend. What is the dividend payout? dividend yield?

22. A share of stock sells for $30 and its capitalization rate is 15 percent. If the capitalization rate drops to 10 percent, will the price go up or down? How much will it be?

# DONLAN AND PENK CASE
# Financial Analysis

*This case tests skills in evaluating the levels of liquidity and profit-
ability for a company. Financial ratios are used to compare a company
with industry standards.*

Donlan and Penk is a small manufacturer of plumbing supplies located in
Toronto, Canada. It is in a highly competitive industry and therefore
must maintain an aggressive marketing posture to survive.

The firm's board of directors will meet in a few days to elect a new
president. Robert Donlan, the son of an original founder of the firm, is
the choice of a majority of the board for the presidency. Bob has been the
vice-president for sales and marketing and has spent much of the last 4
years visiting distributors in the eastern provinces. He has recently
turned over the marketing job to Rick Watson and is preparing to accept
the presidency.

Robert Donlan is concerned about the future of Donlan and Penk.
Although sales rose slightly between 1982 and 1983, aftertax profits declined substantially. Robert has gathered recent financial statements and
a table of industry averages and has decided to use ratio analysis to identify potential trouble areas. He also wants to be able to explain to the
board why profits have declined.

In addition to the data given, Robert learned that the firm's stock
sold for $18 a share at the end of 1982 and $22 a share at the end of 1983.
As he began his work, he noticed that for some reason the accounting
department had omitted the number of shares outstanding and the 1983
dividends from the working papers provided to him.

## Questions

1. What is the number of shares outstanding? How much did Donlan
   and Penk pay in cash dividends in 1983?
2. Is Donlan and Penk a strong firm in this industry?

3. Do any of its ratios indicate possible problem areas?
4. Do the changes in ratios from 1982 to 1983 offer evidence that the firm is growing stronger or weaker? Which ratios give this information?

*Plumbing-Supply Industry Averages*
*for Financial Ratios*

| | |
|---|---|
| Current ratio | 1.8 / 1 |
| Acid test | 1.0 / 1 |
| Accounts-receivable turnover | 12 / 1 |
| Inventory turnover | 5 / 1 |
| Profit margin | 16% |
| Gross profit margin | 30% |
| Asset turnover | 1.3 / 1 |
| Return on investment | 25% |
| Return on equity | 10% |
| Times interest earned | 12 |
| Price-earnings ratio | 21 |
| Book value | none |
| Debt-equity ratio | .55 / 1 |
| Debt-asset ratio | .30 / 1 |
| Dividend payout | 25% |
| Dividend yield | 3% |

**DONLAN AND PENK LTD.—Income Statement (000s)**

| | 1983 | | 1982 | |
|---|---|---|---|---|
| Sales | 74,500 | | 70,000 | |
| Income from investments | 500 | | 500 | |
| Total revenues | | 75,000 | | 70,500 |
| Beginning inventory | 6,000 | | 6,500 | |
| Total manufacturing costs | 49,000 | | 42,000 | |
| Less ending inventory | (11,000) | | (6,000) | |
| Cost of goods sold | | 44,000 | | 42,500 |
| Gross profit | | 31,000 | | 28,000 |
| General and admin. expenses | | 15,500 | | 11,000 |
| Operating income | | 15,500 | | 17,000 |
| Interest expenses | | 840 | | 1,050 |
| Earnings before taxes | | 14,660 | | 15,950 |
| Federal income taxes (40%) | | 5,864 | | 6,380 |
| Net income after taxes | | 8,796 | | 9,570 |
| Dividends declared and paid | | | | 4,500 |

## DONLAN AND PENK LTD.—Balance Sheet (000s)

|                                | 1983   |        | 1982   |        |
|--------------------------------|--------|--------|--------|--------|
| Cash                           | 2,280  |        | 2,157  |        |
| Marketable securities          | 1,400  |        | 1,500  |        |
| Accounts receivable            | 4,500  |        | 2,500  |        |
| Inventories                    | 11,000 |        | 6,000  |        |
| Total current assets           |        | 19,180 |        | 12,157 |
| Plant and equipment            |        |        |        |        |
| (less acc. dep.)               | 22,000 |        | 18,000 |        |
| Land                           | 9,000  |        | 9,000  |        |
| Total fixed assets             |        | 31,000 |        | 27,000 |
| Total assets                   |        | 50,180 |        | 39,157 |
|                                |        |        |        |        |
| Accounts payable               | 4,500  |        | 1,100  |        |
| Notes payable                  | 7,200  |        | 3,000  |        |
| Accrued liabilities            | 1,300  |        | 1,000  |        |
| Total current liabilities      |        | 13,000 |        | 5,100  |
| First mortgage (10%)           | 4,200  |        | 4,200  |        |
| Second mortgage (12%)          | —      |        | 2,000  |        |
| Bond (10%)                     | 4,200  |        | 3,900  |        |
| Total long-term liabilities    |        | 8,400  |        | 10,100 |
| Common stock ($1 par)          | 10,000 |        | 10,000 |        |
| Capital in excess of par       | 3,000  |        | 3,000  |        |
| Retained earnings              | 15,780 |        | 10,957 |        |
| Total equity                   |        | 28,780 |        | 23,957 |
| Total liabilities and equity   |        | 50,180 |        | 39,157 |

# WINNING RACQUETS CASE
## Analyzing Financial Statements

*This case tests skills in developing financial statements and analyzing liquidity and profitability of a company. Financial ratios are used to compare the company with norms for the industry.*

Aaron Williams, a loan officer for the Metropolitan Commercial Bank, was sitting in the office of Karen Morris, the bank's executive vice-president in charge of commercial lending, on February 18, 1986.

Karen explained to Aaron that Winning Racquets, a long-time customer of the bank, had recently asked that its unsecured line of credit be extended from $9 million to $12 million to allow the firm to raise its notes payable from the current level of $8.2 million. In her discussion with the president of Winning Racquets, Inc., Karen Morris learned that the company plans to request a first mortgage on a new building in order to establish a racquetball club and health spa. The building will consist of 24 racquetball courts, 12 tennis courts, an indoor and outdoor pool, a gymnasium, a pro shop, and a restaurant. In addition, solar panels will be used in the construction of the building to capitalize on heat-saving techniques. The architect's plan for the building indicates that it will cost $24 million, and Winning Racquets would request an 80 percent mortgage. Naturally, Metropolitan Commercial Bank would be the lead bank in providing the mortgage financing. The construction is scheduled to begin within 4 months.

Karen explained some of the background on Winning Racquets and its relationship with the bank. The company was founded in 1959 by Scott Winfield and has been a successful manufacturer of tennis equipment. The company's product line originally consisted of wooden tennis racquets, with first-year sales just over $55,000. However, the quality and construction of the racquets produced rapid success and by 1965 the company diversified into aluminum racquets, tennis balls, and tennis apparel. In the late 1970s, Winning Racquets expanded again to capitalize on the racquetball industry, which was forecast to surpass the enthusiasm for tennis. Sales grew rapidly to over $69 million in 1985. The company's aftertax profits have also risen rapidly and are expected to reach

$6.5 million in the following year. Metropolitan Commercial Bank had excellent relations with Winning Racquets and would like to continue to work with the firm as it finances its expansion and growth. However, before increasing the line of credit or making a mortgage loan, the bank plans to investigate the firm's plans and financial position thoroughly. Karen indicated that she would visit Winning Racquets' offices within 2 weeks to discuss the request.

Karen gave Aaron a folder containing the balance sheet, income statement, and other information on Winning Racquets and other manufacturers of tennis and racquetball equipment. She asked Aaron to analyze this financial information and to prepare a report on the financial status of the company. The information is needed by March 2 for her visit with Scott Winfield.

Aaron returned to his office and reviewed the contents of the folder immediately. He saw the comparative balance sheets and income statements for 1983 to 1985. He also noted the table of ratios for the sporting goods manufacturers for 1985.

Aaron decided to use these items to prepare a flow-of-funds statement for 1985 and to develop liquidity and profitability ratios for the company. He would then take this data and compare them against the industry standards and use the results to prepare a report.

**Standard Ratios, Sporting Good Manufacturers, 1985**

|  | 1st Quartile | Median | 3rd Quartile |
|---|---|---|---|
| Current ratio | 4.9 | 3.5 | 2.7 |
| Acid test | 2.6 | 1.7 | 1.3 |
| Receivables turnover | 10/1 | 8/1 | 6/1 |
| Inventory turnover | 4.2 | 3.1 | 2.5 |
| Profit margin | 8.4% | 4.5% | 2.6% |
| Asset turnover | 3.0 | 2.4 | 2.0 |
| Return on investment | 25.2% | 10.8% | 5.2% |
| Return on equity | 34% | 16.2% | 10.7% |
| Earning power | 12.6% | 7.4% | 3.1% |
| Times interest earned | 6.2 | 3.5 | 2.1 |
| Price-earnings ratio | 25/1 | 20/1 | 15/1 |
| Debt-equity ratio | 35% | 69% | 108% |
| Dividend payout | 34% | 20% | 15% |

**WINNING RACQUETS, INC.—Balance Sheet (000s)**

|  | 1985 | 1984 | 1983 |
|---|---|---|---|
| Cash | 5,330 | $ 4,372 | $10,810 |
| Accounts receivable | 8,160 | 6,660 | 6,360 |
| Inventories | 14,840 | 12,140 | 11,240 |
| Plant & equipment (at cost) | 89,800 | 84,200 | 73,700 |
| Less accumulated depreciation | (42,310) | (38,710) | (35,710) |
| Total assets | 75,820 | 68,662 | 66,400 |
|  |  |  |  |
| Accounts payable | $ 3,000 | $ 2,700 | $ 2,400 |
| Notes payable—bank | 8,200 | 4,600 | 3,400 |
| Other current liabilities | 5,900 | 3,800 | 3,500 |
| Mortgage (11%) | 17,060 | 17,660 | 18,260 |
| Common stock | 29,700 | 29,700 | 29,700 |
| Retained earnings | 11,960 | 10,202 | 9,140 |
| Total liabilities & equity | 75,820 | 68,662 | 66,400 |

**WINNING RACQUETS, INC.—Income Statement (000s)**

|  | 1985 | 1984 | 1983 |
|---|---|---|---|
| Net sales | $69,360 | $63,060 | $58,560 |
| Cost of goods sold | 53,890 | 49,390 | 46,390 |
| Gross margin | 15,470 | 13,670 | 12,170 |
| General and administrative expenses | 6,037 | 5,700 | 5,400 |
| Earnings before interest & taxes | 9,433 | 7,970 | 6,770 |
| Interest expense | 2,003 | 1,700 | 1,770 |
| Earnings before taxes | 7,430 | 6,270 | 5,000 |
| Federal income taxes (40%) | 2,972 | 2,508 | 2.000 |
| Net income after taxes | 4,458 | 3,762 | 3,000 |
| Dividends declared and paid | $ 2,700 | $ 2,700 | $ 2,100 |

## Questions

1. Develop the financial statement and ratios for 1985.
2. What recommendation would you make to Karen Morris?

# Analysis of Financial Data

*This case is designed to allow the reader to combine skills in two areas:
(1) the use of ratios and (2) preparing financial statements. Knowledge in both areas is needed to prepare the balance sheet and income
statement.*

Nichole Anderson has been working for the Richland Bank and Trust
Company since she graduated from high school. During the first 4 years,
she was a part-time teller while attending the University of Pennsylvania.
After graduating magna cum laude in business administration, she was
asked to enter the credit analysis training program. For the first 8 months
she worked closely with loan officers and analysts, learning to analyze
and forecast the financial conditions of current and prospective borrowers. In addition, she was taught the fundamentals of predicting trends in
the money market.

After training, she was assigned as a junior analyst in the commercial loan department, where her superiors felt that she made very competent lending decisions. She spent 2 years in this department and was
promoted to an analyst position in the international lending division. Nichole worked in this department for 3 years while attending night school
for her master's degree in business administration. Four months after
graduating, she was promoted to assistant vice-president in the commercial lending department. After a 4-week seminar to orient her into her
position, Nichole was assigned her first customer, Glenway Company
Incorporated.

Glenway Company is a family-run business and has been so for four
generations. Its president is Glenn Wayne IV, the great-grandson of the
founder. Glenway is a key manufacturer of recreational vehicles, but the
company has not grown spectacularly in recent years because of economic conditions. Many people have been reluctant to buy these vehicles
as a result of sharp increases in the price of gas, the threat of fuel shortages, high interest rates on borrowed money, and the problem of overcrowding of campgrounds. Despite these setbacks, Glenway held its own
and even slightly increased sales and profits in recent years. To Nichole,
this appeared to be an easy account. She was pleased to have received it.

Nichole called the company and made an appointment with Mr. Wayne for October 25. When the day came, she arrived promptly at 9:00 a.m. and was escorted into his office. She was not prepared for Glenn Wayne's initial comments. After brief formalities, he said, "I'm a very busy man and have absolutely no reason to waste your time or mine, Miss Anderson or Mrs. Anderson or whatever the case may be. I am not in favor of this women's lib business, where females supposedly can do the jobs of men better. In fact, I am in opposition to you handling Glenway, a matter that I have discussed with your president. He assured me that you have the skills to handle my account and asked me to give you a chance. I do not like it, but a chance you shall have. I have no intentions of waiting until you make a serious mistake that will hurt my business. I have informed your boss that, if you cannot handle what I am about to give you, I intend to ask for another account officer. So, let's learn immediately whether you know your stuff. Here's an envelope with some information on Glenway. If you can prepare my balance sheet and income statement for next year, and if you do it exactly right, maybe you have good skills and only maybe you can keep this account. If you can't do them both, you're out and I will go to another bank if Richland will not assign a competent man to handle the account. I will have no incompetents handling my account."

After making his statement, Glenn Wayne handed Nichole a sealed envelope. After taking the envelope, she replied, "First of all, Mr. Wayne, it's Ms. Anderson. My personal situation is not relevant to my ability to manage this account. Second of all, Glenway is fortunate to have a competent banker to handle this account. Third of all, you will have your balance sheet and income statement on your desk the first thing Monday morning. If anyone can do it, I can do it. I look forward to working with you on this account."

As she left the office, Nichole realized that the account could be trouble. Driving to the office, she thought of numerous responses that she could have given to Mr. Wayne. However, she had never encountered such an aggressive attitude before and was not prepared to deal with it. She finally decided that her actual response was not that bad, provided she could handle the financial data in the envelope. When she returned to the bank she opened the envelope and read the following:

1. At year's end, we will have 625,000 shares of common stock outstanding, at $1 par.
2. Using cost of goods sold, our inventory turnover will be 17.5385/1.
3. We will have beforetax earnings of $3.75 million. The tax rate is 40 percent.
4. Asset turnover will be 3/1.
5. Interest charges of $1,125,000 will be paid during the year.

6. Total assets will be $12.5 million.
7. The current ratio will be 1.6667/1
8. Gross profit margin will be 24 percent.
9. The debt-equity ratio will be 1.2222/1.
10. Accounts-receivable turnover will be 33⅓ times.
11. Current liabilities will equal 15 percent of total assets, with payables equal to $1,125,000.
12. The balance sheet will have 13 total accounts:

| | |
|---|---|
| cash | accumulated depreciation |
| payables | long-term bank notes |
| retained earnings | receivables |
| mortgage | common stock |
| plant & equipment | inventories |
| premium | land |
| other current liabilities | |

13. Land will be recorded at 20 percent of the net value of our fixed assets.
14. Retained earnings will be the same dollar value as total current assets.
15. We will have $5 million in long-term debt: 40 percent of it in unsecured bank notes and the balance in mortgages.
16. Accumulated depreciation will be $1.5 million.

   After looking at the data, Nichole suspected that this would not be such a difficult task. However, she realized she would be getting home quite late. She sat down at her desk, opened a can of soda, turned on the computer terminal, and began working to prepare the balance sheet and income statement.

**Required:**

Prepare the balance sheet and income statement with accounts rounded to the nearest thousand dollars.

# 6

# Profit Planning

## FINANCIAL PLANNING

A major role of the financial manager lies in setting corporate goals and the policies to achieve them. The major departments, including marketing, production, personnel, and finance, participate in the activity of determining the firm's direction and courses of action. This involves the management of resources and decision making both in the near and long term.

*Planning* is the specific process of setting goals and developing ways to reach them. Stated another way, planning represents the firm's efforts to predict events and be prepared to deal with them. In many firms, the task of planning is coordinated by a department of one or more persons designated as the corporate planning department, long-range planning department, or budgeting department. Whatever the title, these individuals are responsible for receiving inputs from sales, production, finance, and other operating areas of the company. By coordinating the process of planning, management assures that the differing departments are working toward the same goals and taking actions consistent with the overall objectives of the firm.

In this chapter, we will examine the basic principles of profit planning. We will look at break-even analysis and profit-volume analysis, two tools for managing assets in the near term. We will also cover marginal analysis as a technique for forecasting operating results with the aid of the income statement. We will conclude with a method for estimating the value of the firm's common stock, using the technique of future earnings per share. All of these techniques are designed to assist the firm in managing its assets over the next accounting period, normally a single year.

## PLANNING PROCESS

As a general rule, the firm's formal planning process involves the efforts of many operating and financial managers. Once plans are agreed upon by the operating units, they are usually presented to the management committee or chief operating officer of the firm. At this level they are challenged and either approved with possible modifications or returned to the operating units for further analysis. The final plans, whether short- or long-term, become the blueprint for the firm's operations.

Planning basically involves two major areas for analysis:

1. *External Factors.* The starting point in the planning process is the operating environment of the firm. The planner evaluates the outlook for the economy as a whole. Will the firm be operating during a period of economic growth and expansion? Will the next 1 to 3 years be a period of recession and stagnation? As part of the total environment, the firm considers the expected level of activity in its industry and possible changes in the market for its products. Is the industry anticipating growth or decline? Does the firm have a stable market for its products? Is the firm's competition gaining or losing strength? Thus, the analysis of external factors considers both the overall economy and the individual industry as a framework for the next operating periods.

2. *Internal Factors.* Some factors are internal in the sense that they are under the control of the firm. For example, such items as cash levels, kind and amount of inventories, and nature of the fixed assets are operating elements that can be varied by the firm. This is not true for the external factors, such as a national recession or an industry decline.

## CONTROLLABLE INTERNAL FACTORS

The most developed portion of the firm's short- and long-term plans deals with internal factors and stresses:

1. *Market Demand for the Product Line or Services.* The firm can decide, after a careful evaluation of the external factors, what mix

of products or services it will offer in the marketplace. If the firm produces its existing product line, what sales are likely? If it changes or modifies its products, will sales increase or decrease? These kinds of questions are analyzed in this part of the plan.

2. *Future Costs.* A firm may have a number of opportunities to reduce the costs of its products in future periods. The purchase of new and more modern equipment may increase fixed costs while reducing variable costs. Should the equipment be purchased? Better scheduling or planning may help minimize production or administrative expenses. High-cost areas in the firm may be examined to see how economies could be achieved.

3. *Sources of Funds.* As the firm plans expenditures, it analyzes the funds available to finance its activities. If sufficient funds are not predicted, steps are taken to locate money as needed at reasonable costs.

These factors are internal only in the sense that the firm has the ability to influence them to a greater or lesser degree. The firm cannot have very much impact on the overall level of economic activity for the entire nation, but it can affect the demand for its product by more aggressive advertising or changes in product pricing or design. It cannot control inflation, but it can take actions to reduce costs. It cannot make money available in the economy, but it can find institutions and individuals who will make funds available for its needs.

## BENEFITS OF PLANNING

As a result of the planning process, the firm realizes a number of benefits:

1. *Anticipation of Problems and Opportunities.* Planning involves people at different levels in the organization and forces them to think ahead. This encourages managers on varying levels to anticipate possible problems and to attempt to identify potential opportunities.

2. *Coordination of Actions.* Because they are involved in planning discussions with others in management positions, managers begin to coordinate courses of action. Frequently, early coordination facilitates the achievement of company goals by increasing communication and reducing potential conflicts. The very process of setting goals and subgoals gives the different operating areas a

common focus and encourages everyone to pursue compatible courses of action.

3. *Assistance in Control.* Plans may be used as tools to help managers control their areas of operation. A detailed plan gives departments and divisions specific goals to pursue and means to achieve the goals. As the firm conducts its operations, managers can watch for variations from the plan that indicate a need for tighter supervision and control.

4. *Providing Standards of Performance.* A comparison of the plan with actual performance during the planning period can be used to provide a standard of achievement. Did the company reach the goals outlined in the plan? If not, why not? Did certain areas perform exceptionally well? Answers to such questions help the firm evaluate its own performance during a recent operating period.

## BUDGET

A *budget* is the result of financial planning. Stated simply, a budget is a formal plan expressed in dollars. The process of financial planning is frequently called *budgeting;* it makes use of pro forma financial statements. Balance sheets, income statements, fund-flow statements, and other formal statements may be incorporated in the firm's budgets.

In addition to these statements, the manager has several specific analytical tools available to assist in planning and budgeting. These tools can increase the accuracy of forecasts of sales and costs and thus can increase the reliability and validity of the financial statements. Several of these tools will be discussed.

## BREAK-EVEN AND PROFIT-VOLUME ANALYSIS

A fundamental profit-planning tool involves the determination of the likely profits at different levels of production. To develop the necessary calculations, the financial manager builds on the basic tool of break-even analysis and expands it through profit-volume analysis.

*Break-even analysis* is used to determine the level of operations at which a firm neither makes a profit nor loses money. At this level, the firm operates at a zero profit level, or *break-even point.* Break-even analysis makes use of fixed costs, variable costs, and revenues and may be used graphically or mathematically.

**GRAPHIC APPROACH TO BREAK-EVEN ANALYSIS**

The graphic approach to break-even analysis plots dollars on the vertical axis and units on the horizontal axis, as shown in Figure 6–1. The costs that are included in the analysis are:

1. *Fixed costs* remain the same at all levels of production. An example would be the rent paid on a building. Graphically the fixed costs (FC) would be a horizontal line.
2. *Variable costs* change directly with the number of units produced. At zero units of production, the firm incurs no variable costs. As production rises, the variable costs rise proportionately. Two aspects of variable costs are important and should be noted:
   a. *Variable Costs Plotted as Total Costs.* If the variable costs are plotted from the zero point on the graph, they reflect only the variable costs of production. It is more common, however, to plot them from the left-hand side of the fixed-costs line. When this is done, the line represents total operating costs and shows the slope of the variable costs. This is the total costs line in the figure.
   b. *Variable Costs as Constant Costs.* It is traditional to plot unit var-

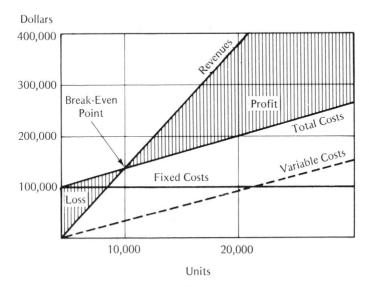

**Figure 6–1**  Break-Even Analysis.

iable costs using a straight line. This implies that unit variable costs are *constant costs;* that is, they are the same at all levels of production. If the first unit costs $3, the second also costs $3, and so on until the last. In fact, variable costs are not constant. The first units are very expensive until setup costs are absorbed. Then the bulk of production is approximately constant until the production begins to bottleneck at some high level of production. At high levels, when overtime must be paid or machines must be run for excessively long periods without time for maintenance, variable costs rise, and production is expensive on a per-unit basis.

For our purposes, variable costs are treated as constant costs. This assumes that the firm is operating in a range of efficient production, where costs are relatively linear. This issue is discussed shortly in the section on nonlinear break-even analysis.

*Revenues,* or sales, are needed to complete the picture of the break-even analysis. The total revenues (TR) are plotted diagonally, beginning at unit zero, and the slope of the line rises more quickly than the total costs. This is true because the firm (we hope!) will receive more revenues per unit of production than the variable cost of producing each unit.

This completes the profit picture for the firm. The break-even point occurs at the crossing of the revenue and total cost lines. Above this production level, the firm will be profitable. Below it, the firm will incur a loss. Note that the profits are measured in the triangle above the break-even point and losses below the break-even point, in each case in the areas defined by the revenue and total cost lines.

### MATHEMATICAL APPROACH TO BREAK-EVEN ANALYSIS

The break-even point may be calculated using mathematical techniques. Two approaches are common and are shown in Figure 6–2. As examples of the use of these formulas to solve for the break-even point, firm A has fixed costs of $50,000, a selling price of $2, and variable costs of $1. Firm B has fixed costs of $300,000 and a marginal contribution of 30 percent. What are the break-even points in units and dollars?

*Firm A*

$$U = \frac{50,000}{2-1} = 50,000 \text{ units}$$

*Firm B*

$$\$ \text{ sales} = \frac{\$300,000}{.30} = \$1,000,000$$

$$\$ \text{ sales} = \quad (50,000)\ (\$2SP) = \$100,000$$

$1,000,000/SP = $ break-even in units. Cannot be solved because selling price is not given.

**(a) In Terms of Units Sold**

$$U = \frac{FC}{SP - VC}$$

where
  U = units sold at
    break-even point
FC = fixed costs
 SP = selling price per unit
VC = variable cost per unit

**(b) In Terms of the Dollar Sales Volume**

$$\$ \text{ Sales} = \frac{FC}{MC\%}$$

where
$ Sales = dollar sales volume at
    break-even point
MC% = marginal contribution
    as a % of selling price;
    calculated by
$$\frac{SP - VC}{SP}$$

**Figure 6–2**   Two Formulas for Deriving the Break-Even Point.

NONLINEAR BREAK-EVEN ANALYSIS

Break-even analysis generally assumes that linear or straight-line relation-ships exist for revenues and costs at different operating levels. This is not the case. In most manufacturing and service environments, costs rise rap-idly at low levels of sales, then level off in a range of efficient production, and finally rise steeply as the firm nears full capacity. Similarly, revenues may rise more quickly at low sales levels but then level off as the firm offers price reductions to achieve high volume in certain markets.

Figure 6–3 illustrates nonlinear break-even relationships. Note that two break-even points exist, and a point is designated for the maximum profit from operations. This differs from linear break-even analysis, where a single break-even point can be located and profits grow indefi-nitely once the break-even point is reached. With nonlinear break-even analysis, the firm strives for an optimum output in a range of efficient production.

Although nonlinear analysis is theoretically superior, linear analysis is more commonly used in industrial settings. This is appropriate in most cases since firms are usually dealing with decisions that involve relatively constant unit variable costs. In these situations, the firm is planning only for operations in the range where production is efficient, that is, where setup costs are overcome but below levels where bottlenecks occur. Since

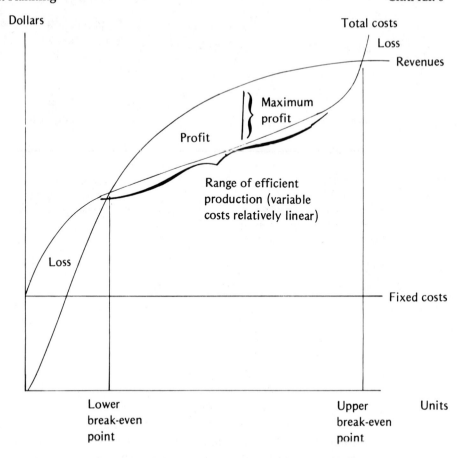

**Figure 6–3**  Nonlinear Break-Even Diagram Showing Range of Efficient Production.

production in this efficient range involves fairly constant costs, the calculations are quite accurate, and realistic decisions are reached.

### PROFIT-VOLUME ANALYSIS

A modification of the break-even formula results in a tool that relates profits to sales at different operating levels. By writing the break-even formulas so that fixed costs are replaced by both fixed costs and profits, the manager can solve for sales volumes needed to produce desired profit levels. The general form of the formulas would be:

$$\$ \text{ sales} = \frac{FC + \text{profit}}{MC\%} = \begin{array}{l} \text{dollar sales needed to achieve a desired} \\ \text{profit} \end{array}$$

$$U \quad = \frac{FC + \text{profit}}{SP - VC} = \text{unit sales needed to achieve a desired profit}$$

These formulas recognize the fundamental relationship between sales and profits: *The excess of sales over costs, or marginal contribution, is the direct profit from operations.* This excess may be used to cover fixed costs that are not related to the volume of sales or operations. It is also available to cover any financing charges—such as interest on a mortgage—to pay federal income taxes, and to provide a profit to shareholders. Note that both formulas use marginal contribution, in the first case directly on a percentage basis and in the second case as the difference between selling price and variable costs.

The profit-volume formulas may be applied to different measures of profit. The basic meaning of *profit* in the formula is EBIT. But EBIT may be broken out to reflect two other profit measures, as follows:

$$EBIT = \text{interest} + EBT \qquad EBIT = \text{interest} + \text{taxes} + NIAT$$

Table 6–1 shows the breakout of the three profit measures and the formulas used to solve for each. Although they solve for different profits, in effect the formulas in the table represent break-even calculations at desired profit levels.

To illustrate the use of these formulas, consider a firm that has a selling price of $6, unit variable costs of $4, fixed costs of $100,000, debt of $300,000 at 10 percent, and a 40 percent tax rate.

**TABLE 6–1.**   Profit-Volume Formulas for Three Desired Profits.

| *Desired Profit* | *Dollar Sales Formula* | *Unit Sales Formula* |
|---|---|---|
| EBIT | $\$ \text{ sales} = \dfrac{FC + EBIT}{MC\%}$ | $U = \dfrac{FC + EBIT}{SP - VC}$ |
| EBT | $\$ \text{ sales} = \dfrac{FC + \text{interest} + EBT}{MC\%}$ | $U = \dfrac{FC + \text{interest} + EBT}{SP - VC}$ |
| Net Income | $\$ \text{ sales} = \dfrac{FC + \text{interest} + \text{taxes} + NIAT}{MC\%}$ | $U = \dfrac{FC + \text{interest} + \text{taxes} + NIAT}{SP - VC}$ |

**Example 1:** If the firm desires an EBIT of $200,000, what level of sales must it achieve?

**Answer:** $ sales $= \dfrac{100,000+200,000}{(6-4)/6} = \dfrac{300,000}{33\frac{1}{3}\%} = \$900,000$

$$U = \dfrac{100,000+200,000}{6-4} = \dfrac{300,000}{2} = 150,000 \text{ units}$$

**Example 2:** If the firm desires an EBT of $250,000, what level of sales must it achieve?

**Answer:** $ sales $= \dfrac{100,000+30,000+250,000}{33\frac{1}{3}\%} = \$1,140,000$

$$U = \dfrac{380,000}{6-4} = 190,000 \text{ units}$$

**Example 3:** If the firm desires a net income of $300,000, what level of sales must be achieved?

**Answer:** Taxes will be $[300,000/(1-.40)] = \$200,000$.

$ sales $= \dfrac{100,000+30,000+200,000+300,000}{33\frac{1}{3}\%} = \dfrac{630,000}{33\frac{1}{3}\%}$

$= \$1,890,000$

$$U = \dfrac{630,000}{6-4} = 315,000 \text{ units}$$

## MARGINAL ANALYSIS

We have already been introduced to marginal analysis, which was defined as breaking down an income statement into fixed and variable costs. The formulas for profit-volume analysis use the concept of marginal analysis, because they define costs and profits using fixed and variable costs. In this section, we will work directly with the income statement to show how marginal analysis helps the manager forecast the effect of differing selling prices, costs, and sales levels on the firm's net income.

VARYING THE LEVEL OF SALES

Holding the selling price and unit variable costs constant, a financial analyst may wish to forecast profits at varying sales levels. Suppose a firm wants to know its income if it sells 100,000, 150,000, or 200,000 units. If it has a selling price of $5 per unit, unit variable costs of $3 per unit, fixed costs of $220,000, and debt of $200,000 at 12 percent, marginal analysis provides three different net incomes, as shown in Table 6–2: a loss of $44,000 or net incomes of $33,600 and $93,600. If the firm sells only 100,000 units, it will be operating below its break-even point and will incur a loss. Since it will make a profit at 150,000 units, the break-even point lies between 100,000 and 150,000 units, or B/E = 220,000/(5 − 3) = 110,000 units.

VARYING PRICES RESULTING IN VARYING SALES

In most cases, a firm considers several possible prices for a new product about to enter the marketplace. An established product also is frequently evaluated with respect to the appropriateness of its selling price. Different prices usually result in different levels of unit sales, with lower prices bringing more unit sales. The additional sales may or may not result in additional profits. In finance we want to determine whether a lower sales price is beneficial in terms of profit. To illustrate how marginal analysis helps in this determination, from our previous example, assume that the

**TABLE 6–2.**  Marginal Analysis to Analyze the Effect of Varying Sales Level and Changes in Net Income.

|  | If We Sell: | | |
|---|---|---|---|
|  | 100,000 units | 150,000 units | 200,000 units |
| Total revenues ($5 each) | $500,000 | $750,000 | $1,000,000 |
| Variable costs ($3 each) | 300,000 | 450,000 | 600,000 |
| Marginal contribution | 200,000 | 300,000 | 400,000 |
| Fixed costs | 220,000 | 220,000 | 220,000 |
| EBIT | (20,000) | 80,000 | 180,000 |
| Interest expenses | 24,000 | 24,000 | 24,000 |
| EBT | (44,000) | 56,000 | 156,000 |
| Taxes (.40) | 0 | 22,400 | 62,400 |
| Net income or (loss) | ($ 44,000) | $ 33,600 | $  93,600 |

firm believes that it will sell only 100,000 units at $5. The marketing manager has predicted that it could sell 75,000 units if it raised the price to $6.50, or it could sell 125,000 units if it dropped the price to $4.50. Which price should the firm establish?

Table 6–3 shows a profit only with the $6.50 price; the other two choices result in losses.

Using the language of economics, we could explain the differing profits in Table 6–3 in terms of elasticities of demand. From a financial point of view, it is sufficient to note that lowering the price to $4.50 lowers profits even though it increases sales. Increasing the price to $6.50 lowers sales, but the increased marginal contribution results in increased profits. If the firm is willing to accept a decline in sales, the $6.50 price should be established.

## VARYING CONTROLLABLE COSTS

In many cases, a firm has some control over the relationship between fixed and variable costs. For example, a firm may be operating at a given level of fixed and variable costs. If the firm invests in more modern equipment, it would incur increased fixed costs for such items as maintenance, depreciation, and insurance. But the greater efficiency of the new machinery might have the positive effect of lowering variable costs. If the firm has sufficient production so that the reduced variable costs provide savings greater than the increased costs, the firm would have higher profits by purchasing the equipment.

Using the preceding example in which the firm sells 75,000 units at

**TABLE 6–3.**   Marginal Analysis to Analyze How Varying Prices Affect Net Income.

|  | If We Sell: | | |
|---|---|---|---|
|  | 100,000 units at $5 | 75,000 units at $6.50 | 125,000 units at $4.50 |
| Total revenues | $500,000 | $487,500 | $562,500 |
| Variable costs | 300,000 | 225,000 | 375,000 |
| Fixed costs | 220,000 | 220,000 | 220,000 |
| EBIT | (20,000) | 42,500 | (32,500) |
| Interest | 24,000 | 24,000 | 24,000 |
| Taxes (.40) | 0 | 7,400 | 0 |
| Net income or (loss) | ($ 44,000) | $ 11,100 | $( 56,500) |

**TABLE 6–4.**    Effect of Variable- and Fixed-Cost Changes.

| | 75,000 Units at $6.50 with: | |
| --- | --- | --- |
| | *VC = $3 and FC = $220,000* | *VC = $2.50 and FC = $245,000* |
| Total revenues | $487,500 | $487,500 |
| Variable costs | 225,000 | 187,500 |
| Fixed costs | 220,000 | 245,000 |
| Interest | 24,000 | 24,000 |
| EBT | 18,500 | 31,000 |
| Taxes (.40) | 7,400 | 12,400 |
| NIAT | $ 11,100 | $ 18,600 |

$6.50, assume that the firm can lower its variable costs to $2.50 from $3 by accepting an increase in its fixed costs of $25,000. Comparing the two choices, we get the results shown in Table 6–4. From this use of marginal analysis, we can forecast high profits as a result of purchasing the new equipment.

The major factor affecting the degree of profit with each choice is the forecast level of sales. If the firm's sales fall short of the 75,000 predicted, the alternative with higher variable costs and lower fixed costs results in the most profit or the least loss. In the preceding example, if the firm is able to sell only 30,000 units, the marginal analysis in Table 6–5 shows that the new equipment results in a $10,000 greater loss due to the additional fixed costs.

## FUTURE EARNINGS PER SHARE

In financial planning, it is very important that the firm consider the effect of different courses of action on the value of the stock. If the firm takes

**TABLE 6–5.**    Effect of Sales Shortages on Net Income.

| | 30,000 Units at $6.50 with: | |
| --- | --- | --- |
| | *VC = $3 and FC = $220,000* | *VC = $2.50 and FC = $245,000* |
| Total revenues | $195,000 | $195,000 |
| Variable costs | 90,000 | 75,000 |
| Fixed costs | 220,000 | 245,000 |
| Interest | 24,000 | 24,000 |
| (Loss) | ($139,000) | ($149,000) |

actions that cause a decline in the market price of the common stock, management may be criticized by angry shareholders. A valuable tool for analyzing the future market price of the stock is the calculation of future earnings per share.

## WHY FUTURE EARNINGS PER SHARE ARE CRITICAL

In profit planning, two measures of corporate profits are especially important:

1. *Return on Investment (ROI).* This is an operating indicator of profits and a key measure of the success of the firm's management. If this ratio is high, the firm is generating sufficient sales on its asset base and is making sufficient profit margins on its sales. The use of ROI allows a financial manager to make comparisons of the operating profits of different firms or of the same firm in different time periods.
2. *Earnings per Share (EPS).* This is a market indicator of profits and the most important profit measure for stockholders and other individuals outside the firm. If the earnings continue to increase on a per-share basis, the firm is judged to be increasingly successful. On the other hand, a drop in earnings per share is viewed as a symptom of problems.

Given the important role of earnings per share in the eyes of shareholders and the investing public, the firm must be particularly conscious of actions that will affect the reported earnings. For this reason, profit planning focuses on how different alternatives will affect the future earnings per share reported by the firm.

## COMPARING FUTURE EVENTS AT THE MARGIN

The technique of forecasting future earnings per share measures the effect of each decision at the margin. That is, the technique recognizes that the firm will have some future earnings per share without any decisions being required. The firm is operating, and, should it continue its operations without major changes, it will achieve some level of earnings. When the firm considers new investments, the revenues and expenses associated with the investments will change the projected earnings. To determine the effect of each project, the firm does the following:

1. *Project EPS with No New Projects.* The analyst estimates the sales and expenses for the next period in the absence of any new investment.

2. *Project Each Separate Proposal's Effect on EPS.* The analyst begins with the first proposal and forecasts EPS on a combined basis. If the EPS are higher with the proposal than without it, the analyst knows that the proposal helps increase EPS. If the EPS are lower with the proposal, the analyst knows the proposal weakens future profitability.

Comparing future events at the margin means that each proposed investment is evaluated separately to see how it will affect the firm's sales and profits. If, for example, two projects were combined, the undesirable effects of one project might be obscured by the desirable effects of the other. This is avoided by individually combining each new proposal with the existing operations.

## NORMAL PRICE-EARNINGS MULTIPLE

A *normal price-earnings multiple* is the ratio expected when a firm is realizing a satisfactory return on its capital, and the stock market is not disturbed by unusual psychological or economic factors. It may be determined by analyzing historical data, similar firms and industry norms or by common sense. If, for example, a firm's stock sells at a 12/1 multiple this year, we may expect it to continue to sell at this multiple. If the firm maintains this *norm* and its EPS rise from $2 to $3, the market price of the stock rises from $24 to $36. To analyze likely future market prices, we forecast *future earnings per share* and multiply EPS by normal P/E.

> **Example:** A firm is considering accepting project A. Without the project, its EPS next year will be $2.15. With the project, EPS will be $2.35. Its normal P/E is 10/1. What will be its market value next year with and without the project?
>
> **Answer:** ($2.35) (10) = $23.50 with the project. ($2.15) (10) = $21.50 without the project.

## FORECASTING SALES AND EBIT

To use the future-earnings-per-share approach to profit planning, we begin with a forecast of sales next period without any new investments.

Marginal analysis is then used to calculate the EBIT. Next each separate investment possibility is analyzed with respect to future sales and EBIT. A separate income statement is prepared showing the combined results of the firm's planned activities plus the project. Thus, in Table 6–6, the second column shows the combined sales of the firm if it accepts project A. If the Property Management Corporation accepts no new projects, it will have sales of $12 million. If it accepts project A, sales will be $27 million ($12 million by itself and $15 million contributed by A). If it accepts B and rejects A, the combined sales will be $52 million ($40 million of which contributed by B).

**TABLE 6–6.**   Example of Future Earnings per Share Calculation with Property Management Corporation.

|  | PMC Alone | PMC & Project A | | | PMC & Project B | | |
|---|---|---|---|---|---|---|---|
|  |  | 14.5% Bank Debt | 16% Pref. Stock | Common Stock | 14.5% Bank Debt | 16% Pref. Stock | Common Stock |
| Forecasted sales | 12,000 | 27,000 | 27,000 | 27,000 | 52,000 | 52,000 | 52,000 |
| Forecasted EBIT | 4,600 | 8,600 | 8,600 | 8,600 | 10,600 | 10,600 | 10,600 |
| Current interest (10,000 × .095) | 950 | 950 | 950 | 950 | 950 | 950 | 950 |
| New interest (10,000 × .145) |  | 1,450 |  |  |  |  |  |
| (50,000 × .145) |  |  |  |  | 7,250 |  |  |
| Earnings before taxes | 3,650 | 6,200 | 7,650 | 7,650 | 2,400 | 9,650 | 9,650 |
| Less taxes (.40) | 1,460 | 2,480 | 3,060 | 3,060 | 960 | 3,860 | 3,860 |
| Earnings after taxes | 2,190 | 3,720 | 4,590 | 4,590 | 1,440 | 5,790 | 5,790 |
| Preferred stock dividends (10,000 × .16) |  |  | 1,600 |  |  |  |  |
| (50,000 × .16) |  |  |  |  |  | 8,000 |  |
| Net income | 2,190 | 3,720 | 2,990 | 4,590 | 1,440 | (2,210) | 5,790 |
| Divided by comm. stock original shares | 500 | 500 | 500 |  | 500 | 500 |  |
| (500 + 10,000/20) |  |  |  | 1,000 |  |  |  |
| (500 + 50,000/20) |  |  |  |  |  |  | 3,000 |
| Earnings per share | $4.38 | $7.44 | $5.98 | $4.59 | $2.88 | ($4.42) | $1.93 |
| Times likely P/E multiple | 7/1 | 6/1 | 7/1 | 8/1 | 6/1 | 7/1 | 8/1 |
| Expected market price | $31 | $45 | $42 | $37 | $17 | — | $15 |

## CALCULATING THE FINANCING CHARGES

For a firm to invest in new major projects, it must have the capital available. The method that it uses to raise funds will affect the earnings per share. Four major financing choices are possible:

1. *Internal Funds.* If the firm has an adequate cash flow, it may retain a large sum of funds from operations. These can be used to finance new investments. If this means is used, future EPS should rise because internal funds have no financing charge nor do they require the issuance of additional shares of stock.
2. *Debt Financing.* If a firm borrows to raise money to finance the project, it will have interest payments to make. These are shown on the income statement and will affect the EPS. If the firm earns more on the project than it pays in financing charges, EPS will increase. If it earns less, EPS will decrease.
3. *Preferred-Stock Financing.* If this method is used to raise funds, the dividends payable to preferred shareholders will affect EPS. With a 40 percent tax rate, the firm must earn more than 1.67 percent on the project for every 1 percent of dividends in order to increase EPS. Why is this so? If $1.67 is earned, taxes will be (1.67) (.40), or $.67. Thus, $1 remains for preferred dividends. If it makes less than this 1.67/1 ratio, EPS will decrease, because the firm must pay taxes on EBT before declaring dividends to preferred shareholders.
4. *Common-Stock Financing.* This method involves no additional charges for the new project, but net income must be divided among a larger number of shares than previously. If the new project is not as profitable as the firm's existing projects, EPS will decrease. This drop resulting from the acceptance of less-profitable projects than current is called *dilution of earnings* and generally is not viewed favorably by shareholders, who expect EPS to increase. If the new project is more profitable than existing operations, EPS will increase.

## CALCULATING FUTURE MARKET PRICE

Once all the financing charges are calculated, the income statement is completed down to the net income, which is then divided by the shares outstanding to get future EPS. This is multiplied by the normal P/E ratio, and the expected future market price is obtained. Needless to say, the firm normally prefers the projects and financing method that offer the highest future value to the firm.

### OTHER FACTORS RELATED TO FUTURE EPS

It should be noted that the firm does not limit its decision solely to future EPS, since such factors as the following affect future market price:

1. *Risk from High Levels of Debt.* Borrowing is less costly than pre-ferred-stock financing and avoids the dilution of earnings asso-ciated with common-stock financing. But debt involves more risk than equity financing. If interest payments are not made, the firm may face unpleasant consequences, including bankruptcy. This danger is increased if the firm uses variable rate debt in a period of low interest rates and then must pay more interest when rates rise. The market value of the stock will drop if the firm makes excessive use of debt funds and incurs a high level of risk as a result.

2. *Growth.* The future-EPS technique makes a projection only 1 year into the future. Long-term growth will be a different factor than next year's earnings, and the expected growth characteristics of a proposal will affect the firm's future market value aside from the likely profits.

3. *Difficulties in Implementing Proposals.* In some cases, a firm will not want to accept a profitable project that may cause complications for its other operations. The proposal may be highly complicated and may require extensive time from key operating personnel, time that will be taken from other areas. The project may cause the firm to receive adverse publicity or to experience other diffi-culties that make it undesirable. These difficulties can affect the market price of the firm's stock and will influence acceptance of a project.

4. *Risk from Uncertain Ventures or Unstable Returns.* Any proposal contains the risk that the firm will be unable to achieve the pro-jected returns. This risk may arise from changes in the general level of economic activity, the entry of strong competitors into a firm's primary market, or other factors. The degree of business risk and the expected stability of returns are factors that affect the decision to accept or reject proposals.

**PROPERTY MANAGEMENT CORPORATION—A SOLVED EXAMPLE**

To illustrate the calculation of future EPS, let us consider Property Management Corporation. The firm forecasts next year's sales at $12 million and an EBIT of $4.6 million. It has $10 million in debt at a cost that should average 9.5 percent. It has 500,000 shares of outstanding common stock. The corporation is evaluating two new investments. Project A should generate sales of $15 million and an EBIT of $4 million next year. To invest in this project, the firm must raise $10 million. Project B would have likely sales of $40 million and an EBIT of $6 million next year. Its cost is $50 million. Both projects should produce sales well into the future.

Property Management Corporation can raise funds three ways. Seven-year bank financing can be arranged at a variable rate that should average 14.5 percent annually for the 7 years. Preferred stock can be sold with an indicated dividend of 16 percent. Common stock can be sold to yield $20 a share. In each case, the costs include the commissions paid to the investment banker so that issuance fees need not be included in the calculations.

Property Management Corporation has traditionally sold for a 7/1 P/E multiple. If it finances either project with debt, this might drop to 6/1. With common stock financing, it might rise to 8/1.

Table 6–6 shows the calculation of future EPS and market price. It reveals significant differences in the effects of each method of financing. With any financing method, project B produces poor results. Project A, on the other hand, gives favorable earnings and market prices with all 3 methods. On balance, the debt or preferred stock methods give the best results with a final decision to be reached after considering all factors.

## KEY TERMS

| | | |
|---|---|---|
| break-even analysis | long-range planning | normal price-earnings ratio |
| budgeting | marginal contribution as a | planning |
| constant costs | percentage | profit-volume analysis |
| dilution of earnings | nonlinear break-even | |
| future earnings per share | analysis | |

## STUDY QUESTIONS

1. What does the process of planning represent?
2. What are the two major areas of planning analysis? Give examples of each.

3. What are the three controllable internal factors?
4. What are the four benefits that a firm realizes from planning?
5. What costs are included in break-even analysis?
6. Where does the break-even point occur in a graphic representation of break-even analysis? Where are the profits measured?
7. What is the difference between linear and nonlinear break-even analysis? Which is superior? more commonly used?
8. What is the fundamental relationship between sales and profits?
9. What is marginal analysis? How does a manager use it?
10. What are two measures of corporate profits? What do they indicate?
11. What two things should a firm do when it is considering new investments?
12. How is a normal price-earnings multiple determined? How is it used?
13. What are the four steps used in the future EPS approach to profit planning?

## PROBLEMS

1. A firm can sell 3.5 million units at $4. Its variable costs are $2.50 and fixed costs are $2,250,000. What is the break-even point in both units and dollars?
2. How much fixed costs can the firm in problem 1 have and break even at its projected sales goal?
3. A firm has fixed costs of $12 million, a selling price of $200 per unit, and a marginal contribution of 30 percent. What is the break-even point in both units and dollars?
4. A firm has fixed costs of $6 million, a marginal contribution of 25 percent, and variable costs of $7.50 per unit. What is its break-even point in units?
5. If the firm in problem 4 desires an operating income of $14 million, how many units and dollars must it have in sales?
6. A firm has fixed costs of $75,000, debt of $150,000 at 12 percent, a selling price of $8 per unit, and variable costs of $4 per unit. How many sales in dollars must it have to achieve an EBT of $150,000?
7. If the firm in problem 6 has a 40 percent tax rate, how many units must it sell to have a net income of $162,000?
8. If the firm in problem 6 can sell 600,000 units, how much of a rise could it have in its debt at 12 percent and still have an EBT of $150,000?
9. If the firm in problem 6 can sell 700,000 units, how much of a rise could it have in its debt at 12 percent and still have a net income of $200,000?
10. A firm can sell 600,000 units at $12 each and 400,000 units at $15 each. It has variable costs of $7 per unit, fixed costs of $1 million, and interest of $200,000. Which selling price yields the highest net income?
11. If the firm in problem 10 can lower variable costs to $5 per unit by purchasing new equipment that will increase fixed costs to $1.5 million, should it purchase the equipment?
12. If a firm accepts a project, it will have a 15 percent rise in EPS, currently at $4. Its normal P/E multiple is 6/1. What will be the future EPS and future market price?

# THE SEN-LIGHT COMPANY CASE
## Marginal Analysis

*This case tests the reader's skills in evaluation using marginal analysis. It exposes the reader to varying prices and costs and the results of these variations.*

The Sen-Light Company is an exclusive manufacturer of sensor executive desk lamps. The firm's manufacturing plant is centrally located in a large midwestern state with access to a variety of transportation facilities, making product distribution less costly. The lamps, ranging from simple elegance to the most ornate, offer optional features such as a special sensor switch that allows them to move freely, yet be easily turned on or off. Lamps and lighting fixtures of the Sen-Light Company are available in a variety of sizes, styles, and colors to suit the discriminating executive who wants to add a touch of individuality to an office or den.

The Sen-Light Company's wide range of prices, reputation for quality, exclusive patented feature, durability, and superior craftsmanship have resulted in sustained success for the owners. In 1983, the firm sold 210,000 units of its basic sensor desk lamps at a market price of $22.75. For 1984, the firm anticipates a volume of sales of 230,000 units at the reduced price of $22.00. The increased demand for the sensor lamps will allow Sen-Light to use its plant facility to capacity, thus reducing cost. This reduction in cost will allow Sen-Light to pass the savings to customers in 1984 and still increase profits.

The firm's president, Nick Stoner, has made plans to continue the growth of the company by shipping the lamps to wholesalers in the eastern area. He has arranged to meet with wholesalers from New York, Connecticut, and Pennsylvania on December 18, 1983 to discuss other measures to improve the level of sales and profits for the Sen-Light Company in 1984.

During the meeting in December, Danielle Harris, the vice-president of marketing, recommended lowering the prices of the basic model of sensor desk lamps further in the following year to increase the volume of sales. She had data showing that 290,000 units could probably be sold at $21.50 and 330,000 units could be sold at $20.75. It is expected that this action would result in an increased share of the market for Sen-Light.

Ron Carlsen, vice-president of production, opposed Danielle's price-cutting suggestion and focused on an entirely different way to reduce expenses. Ron's plan was to offer an incentive bonus to its distributers for the volume of sales reached. By automating several manufacturing processes, the result would be a reduction of the variable costs of the basic lamps from $18.00 to $17.00 per unit. Ron emphasized that this decrease in variable cost would be offset by a rise in fixed production and depreciation of $52,500 annually. The improvements would cost approximately $300,000 but would be worthwhile for numerous production and financial reasons, which Ron discussed thoroughly at the meeting.

Nick Stoner realized that Sen-Light would have no difficulty in obtaining manufacturer's financing to cover the $300,000 capital improvement. The interest rate on the financing would be 12 percent. Sen-Light has accounts payable of $40,000, other current liabilities of $83,950, and a long-term debt of $375,000, on which it pays 8 percent annual interest. Although the company does not have excessive debts outstanding, Nick feels that the recommendations from Danielle and Ron should be evaluated thoroughly in terms of the firm's reported profits since any drop in profits would be subject to close skepticism by the major stockholders who control the board of directors and who are overly conscious of the firm's reported earnings.

### Required

1. Which selling price would yield the highest net income after taxes in 1984?
2. Would the acquisition of new machinery increase or decrease the firm's net income after taxes in 1984?
3. Which alternatives would you recommend?

# Future Earnings per Share

*This case allows the reader to apply the concept of future EPS in evaluating a course of action in terms of its effect on the market value of the firm's common stock.*

Baltimore Polymers Company (BPC) is a medium-sized producer of chemicals and vinyl coating used in a variety of industrial processes. The company's main facilities are located in an industrial park in East Baltimore, a central site on a rail line linking the firm with its major customers on the east coast.

Last year the firm recorded over $150 million in sales, showed a net income of $25 million, and concluded a very successful year. For the coming year, the firm expects a 10 percent improvement in sales and operating income figures.

The firm's management committee, consisting of the president and the vice-presidents for production, marketing, and finance, will be meeting in 2 weeks to discuss a major new activity for the next year. Baltimore Polymers Company has been invited to bid on a long-term contract to produce a line of plastics for a large chemical company in Wilmington, Delaware. It appears that the firm can easily get the $60 million contract, which should yield an additional $18 million in operating income. These figures are for next year only, and the firm estimates even higher sales and profits in future years.

Bob Mrozinski, vice-president for finance, has been studying the financial data related to the new line of plastics. The production manager knows of a small plastics company located about 3 miles from BPC's facilities. The plastics company has all the equipment needed to produce the new line of plastics; the company is for sale for $105 million. This price represents largely the value of the assets, since the company has lost its only large contract. Bob has discussed the purchase of this plastics

183

company with a local real estate agent and has decided that it is available for $90 million.

Bob figures that BPC has sufficient working capital to add the new plastics line but does not have the cash to buy the $90 million of machinery and equipment needed to begin production. Discussion with a representative of a large Baltimore bank reveals that BPC can borrow $40 million through a 13 percent mortgage on its main facilities. A mortgage company has indicated that it would help finance the plastics machinery with a $50 million, 13.5 percent mortgage. Bob is considering these choices but knows that BPC has traditionally kept its debt-asset ratio below 40 percent. He would not want to borrow if the additional debt caused the ratio to exceed 40 percent.

Bob discussed equity financing with BPC's investment banker on a recent trip to New York City. He learned that the firm could probably issue up to $100 million in 14 percent preferred stock or class A common stock. If the common stock were offered, it could net $21 per share to BPC. Bob called New York and confirmed that these options were still open to the firm.

In making decisions on new investments, Bob believes in the validity of the future-earnings-per-share technique. He knows that BPC has traditionally traded at a 7/1 price-earnings multiple, and he expects that this will hold. Thus, if a new project increases future earnings per share, it will increase the value of the firm to its shareholders.

## Required

1. Using the future-earnings-per-share approach, perform the analysis needed to decide whether to accept the plastics project.
2. Prepare a written recommendation that Bob Mrozinski can bring to the meeting of the management committee, including a recommendation on the financing method, if the project is acceptable.

**BALTIMORE POLYMERS COMPANY, INC.—Recent Year's Balance Sheet**

| | | | |
|---|---|---|---|
| Cash | $ 13,126,700 | Current liabilities | $ 20,114,700 |
| Receivables | 26,932,100 | Long-term debt (15%) | 50,000,000 |
| Inventories | 20,971,100 | Common stock ($1 par) | 8,000,000 |
| Fixed assets | 159,073,400 | Retained earnings | 141,988,600 |
| | $220,103,300 | | $220,103,300 |

| BALTIMORE POLYMERS COMPANY, INC.—Recent Year's Income Statement | |
|---|---|
| Sales | $154,545,500 |
| Cost of goods sold | 82,304,500 |
| Gross margin | $ 72,241,000 |
| Administrative costs | 17,695,500 |
| Operating income | $ 54,545,500 |
| Interest | 9,500,000 |
| Earnings before taxes | 45,045,500 |
| Federal income taxes | 18,018,200 |
| Net income | $ 27,027,300 |
| | |
| Earnings per share | $3.38 |
| Dividends per share | $1.50 |

# DAVIDSON PLASTICS CASE
# Profit Planning With Inflation

*This case employs the profit-planning techniques but adds the element of changing cost and price levels to the analysis.*

Art Pulis had seen it all in his 11 years at Davidson Plastics. After finishing his chemistry degree at Arizona State, he began as a bench chemist in the Tucson manufacturing plant. Five years later he was working in manufacturing accounting. Four months ago, he was named general manager of the new Specialty Plastics Division, which he opened with 17 employees in Wickenburg, Arizona.

If Art had a single weakness, it was in the area of profit planning. He had no problem with the numbers if the task were to document historical activities. But the preparation of pro forma statements was more difficult. He particularly felt lost when dealing with the impact of inflation on a company's operations. Two years ago, he had seen Davidson's entire forecast collapse when price levels took off. He was determined that the profit plans for his division would consider the impact of changing price and cost levels.

Now it was time for him to submit his division profit plan for the next fiscal year. To prepare himself for this task, he recently attended an American Management Association seminar in San Francisco, where a 2-hour session was devoted to profit planning under conditions of inflation. He reviewed his notes from that session:

> In dealing with the relationship between sales and operating income, we must recognize that different items will be responsive to inflation at different rates. For example, we may be able to raise the selling price on our finished goods by only 4 percent at a time when the cost of producing the goods has risen by 10 percent. Also, within the area of costs, wages may be rising at one rate while raw materials are rising at a different rate. To handle these differences, use a different calculation for each line item on the income statement, that is, for sales, wages, raw materials, general and administrative expenses, and other accounts.
>
> A key element of the analysis is identifying how each item will respond to changes in the sales level as well as the price level. Wages, for example, may increase when sales rise and also when price levels rise. Maintenance, on the other hand, may be fixed so that it does not rise with a rise in sales, but it may rise with increases in price levels.
>
> To account for both the sales change and price change, consider the use of a *period-to-period formula* for each income statement item. Sample formulas are:
>
> $$\text{sales}_{t+1} = (\text{sales}_t)(1 + G_{\text{sales}})(1 + \text{infla})$$
>
> where
>
> $\text{sales}_{t+1} =$ the sales in period $t+1$
>
> $G_{\text{sales}} =$ the percentage growth rate of sales in the absence of changes in price levels
>
> infla $=$ the percentage rate of increase or decrease in the selling prices for the firm's goods
>
> $$\text{exp (var)}_{t+1} = [\text{exp (var)}_t][1 + G_{\text{sales}}][1 + \text{infla}]$$

where

$$\exp\ (var)_{t+1} = \text{a cost or expense that will vary with sales in period } t+1$$

$$\text{infla} = \text{the rate of inflation appropriate to the expense item for period } t+1$$

$$\exp\ (fix)_{t+1} = [\exp\ (fix)_t][1+\text{infla}]$$

where

$$\exp\ (fix)_{t+1} = \text{a fixed cost or expense in period } t+1$$

**Example:** A firm has sales of $150,000, variable costs of $70,000, and fixed costs of $50,000. Next year, sales will grow by 10 percent in terms of units sold. The rate of inflation will be 12 percent on the selling price of goods sold and 8 percent on costs. What will be next period's operating income?

**Answer:** $47,640

| | | |
|---|---|---:|
| $sales_{t+1} = 150,000 \times 1.10 \times 1.12 =$ | | $184,800 |
| $\exp\ (var)_{t+1} = 70,000 \times 1.10 \times 1.08 =$ | | $-83,160$ |
| $\exp\ (fix)_{t+1} = 50,000 \times 1.08 =$ | | $\underline{-54,000}$ |
| Operating income | | $ 47,640 |

Art Pulis was glad that he had the foresight to copy the example for using the formulas. He was also wise to take a note of the difference between the annual and average rates of inflation. When using the formulas, he knew that the *inflation factor* must be the average rate of price change for the period. This may be only one-half the actual change in value from the start to the end of the period. For example, if a watch cost $100 on January 1 and $110 on December 31, the price change during the year would be 10 percent [(110−100)/100] but the average price of all watches sold over the course of the year would be $105 [(100+110)/2]. Thus, the average inflation factor would be 5 percent, when figuring sales change from the price level on January 1.

A firm's inflation factor is based upon the changes in the cost of its goods or services. It is calculated as a weighted average. As an example, Art had taken notes for a firm with three costs and a different rate of inflation applying to each. The annual expense for each of the three costs in the example and the rate of inflation that would apply was given as:

| Cost Item | Annual Cost with No Inflation | Forecast Rate of Inflation |
|---|---|---|
| 1 | 100 | 8 percent |
| 2 | 150 | 10 percent |
| 3 | 200 | 12 percent |
| Total cost | $450 | |

The inflation factor for this firm would be 5.2 percent:

$$\left(\frac{100}{450}\right)\ \left(1+\frac{.08}{2}\right)+\left(\frac{150}{450}\right)\ \left(1+\frac{.10}{2}\right)+\left(\frac{200}{450}\right)\ \left(1+\frac{.12}{2}\right)$$

$$= .2311 + .3500 + .4711 = 1.052$$

This formula weights each cost by the total costs and converts the annual rate of inflation to the average rate for each item.

The inflation factor can be used in two places. First, it can be multiplied (along with 1) times the forecasted revenues to get the revenues with inflation if the firm raises prices to keep up with rising costs. Second, it can be multipled with 1 against the starting selling price to get the average selling price with inflation. The formulas are:

$$\frac{\text{forecast revenues}}{\text{without inflation}} \times (1+\text{infla}) = \frac{\text{forecast revenues}}{\text{with inflation}}$$

and

$$\frac{\text{starting}}{\text{selling}} \times (1+\text{infla}) = \frac{\text{Average selling price to}}{\text{keep up with the rate}}$$
$$\text{price} \qquad \qquad \text{of inflation on costs}$$

Art was ready to begin on his profit plan for next year. He had already estimated next year's operating costs in the absence of inflation, as shown in the table. His plant could produce at 100 percent capacity, if needed, and generate 110,000 molding assemblies, with some custom work required on approximately 35 percent of the units. Davidson Plastics' marketing department indicated that it would need about 77,000 assemblies next year, and Art would work with that figure. The marketing director at Davidson was forecasting an average price per assembly of $34, a price that could rise with cost inflation with no detrimental effect on sales. Art felt that his division could support this level of production with the assets shown in the balance sheet for his division, approximately $2 million of total assets.

A few things were missing from Art's data. One was the cost of debt. The payables, of course, would have no cost, but the debt had a variable rate tied to the prime rate. He estimated that his short- and long-term borrowings would have an average cost of 17 percent for the year.

**Next Year's Operating Costs, Specialty Plastics Division, Based on Percentages of Total Capacity**

*110,000 units = 100 percent*

|  | PRODUCTION LEVEL | | |
|---|---|---|---|
|  | *60%* | *80%* | *100%* |
| **Direct Costs** (000s) | | | |
| Salaries, wages | $ 210 | $ 280 | $ 335 |
| Materials | 345 | 465 | 575 |
| Cash overhead | 40 | 40 | 40 |
| Asset cost recovery (depreciation) | 360 | 360 | 360 |
|  | 955 | 1,145 | 1,310 |
| **Indirect Costs** (000s) | | | |
| Salaries, benefits | 180 | 180 | 180 |
| Selling expenses | 105 | 125 | 145 |
| Maintenance | 40 | 60 | 80 |
| Insurance | 60 | 80 | 100 |
| Other | 20 | 40 | 55 |
|  | 405 | 485 | 560 |
| **Total Costs** (000s) | $1,360 | $1,630 | $1,870 |

**Beginning Balance Sheet, Specialty Plastics Division, Start of Next Year (000s)**

| | | | |
|---|---|---|---|
| Cash & equivalents | $ 70 | Payables | $ 50 |
| Receivables | 380 | Short-term debt | 350 |
| Inventories | 150 | Long-term debt | 750 |
| Fixed assets at cost | 2,700 | Equity | 950 |
| Accum. depreciation | (1,200) | | |
| | $2,100 | | $2,100 |

Another missing item was the inflation rates on the costs. After talking with Davidson's controller, he forecasts annual inflation as follows for each item:

| Expense Item | Jan. 1–Dec. 31 Rate of Inflation |
|---|---|
| Salaries, wages | 12% |
| Materials | 6 |
| Cash overhead | 6 |
| Depreciation | 0 |
| Selling expenses | 6 |
| Maintenance, insurance, other | 6 |

Each of these rates reflected annual cost changes, with the average change being half the annual change.

Art was ready to prepare his division's budget for the next year. He wanted his numbers to reflect the rates of inflation on operating costs. He also wanted to assume that he would raise the price of the molding assemblies so that his revenues would rise by the rate of inflation on his costs. This would produce a larger earnings before taxes than would be achieved in the absence of inflation. When his budget was forwarded to Davidson's headquarters, he would clearly indicate his assumptions on inflation.

### Required

1. What will the earnings be before taxes for the division in the absence of inflation?
2. What is the weighted average inflation factor for the division's operating and financial expenses?
3. During the year, how much must the selling price be raised in order for EBT to rise by the amount of the inflation factor?

# DUTCH COUNTRY MANUFACTURING CASE
# Profit Planning

*This case tests the reader's ability to make planning decisions in terms of maximizing profits. The reader must also develop a pro forma income statement.*

The Dutch Country Manufacturing Company is a small, family-owned manufacturer of household ornaments and novelty items. It was founded in British Columbia in 1925 by Jules de Fries, an immigrant from Rotterdam. The present facility employs 14 people in a small plant 30 miles north of Vancouver. Peter de Fries, the grandson of the founder, is the principal owner of the business and conducts the day-to-day operations. Most of the planning and profit decisions are shared with his sister Karyn, who spends 4 days a week at the plant.

In recent years, the de Fries have severely reduced the variety of products available from their firm. In an effort to achieve volume, they have concentrated on the craze for antique-style ornaments that has been sweeping Canada and the United States. The firm's products are ordered from catalogues found in a variety of stores and specialty shops in western Canada and some parts of the western and southern United States.

Two years ago, the de Fries decided to concentrate on producing three fairly popular items:

1. An accessory kit fo fireplaces. The kit contains three cast-iron tools plus a holder.
2. "Rustic" candlesticks—a matched pair of frontier-style bronze candlesticks.
3. "Pioneer" doorknockers—a bronze, western-style doorknocker.

Since specializing in these three items, the firm has dropped the many custom items previously produced. This has not hurt business, as the three items are selling well. Karyn has projected sales for each item on a unit basis for the next fiscal year. The firm should be able to sell 6,000 accessory kits, 5,000 pairs of candlesticks, and 6,000 doorknockers.

These figures represent the maximum demand for each item at Karyn's planned selling prices, and the firm should be close to these figures.

In order to achieve the projected sales figures, the firm must operate at 77 percent capacity. The 6,000 accessory kits will require 45 percent of the firm's productive capacity, while the candlesticks and doorknockers will require 16 percent each.

Karyn has projected next year's income statement, which includes a breakdown by product areas, as follows:

**DUTCH COUNTRY MANUFACTURING COMPANY LTD.**
**—Pro Forma Income Statement**

|  | Total Figures | Fireplace Kits | Candlesticks | Doorknockers |
|---|---|---|---|---|
| Sales | $600,000 | $360,000 | $150,000 | $90,000 |
| Variable costs |  |  |  |  |
| Raw materials | 260,000 | 140,000 | 75,000 | 45,000 |
| Labor | 140,000 | 90,000 | 20,000 | 30,000 |
| Marginal contribution | 200,000 | 130,000 | 55,000 | 15,000 |
| Fixed costs |  |  |  |  |
| Manufacturing | 70,000 | 42,000 | 17,500 | 10,500 |
| Sales | 30,000 | 18,000 | 7,500 | 4,500 |
| Administrative | 40,000 | 24,000 | 10,000 | 6,000 |
| EBIT and EBT[a] | $ 60,000 | $ 46,000 | $ 20,000 | $( 6,000) |

[a]Firm has no debt and pays no taxes. All taxes are paid by individual members of the family.

To achieve her projected income statement, Karyn applied basic cost-accounting techniques. The manufacturing costs would include depreciation on the firm's machinery, repairs and maintenance, insurance, taxes, and the production foreman's salary and benefits. Sales costs are basically the salary and expenses of an office clerk who deals with retail customers and distributes by mail or phone. Advertising and promotion are included at a $5,000 figure. The administrative fixed costs cover items needed to run the company with a major item being the costs involved with providing information and materials in support of catalogue operations. These fixed costs were allocated to the products on the basis of a ratio of fixed costs to total sales. For example, Karyn noted that fireplace kits will make up 60 percent of the total sales; thus she allocated 60 percent of the fixed costs to fireplace kits.

In an effort to use 100 percent of capacity, Karyn has considered lowering the price of the three products. At a $50 selling price, 8,000 pairs of candlesticks could probably be sold. At $12, 7,000 doorknockers could be sold. At $25, 1,000 pairs of candlesticks could probably be sold.

Another alternative to use the excess capacity would be to produce a fourth product. The firm once sold "Ye Old Lantern" kits and did fairly well with this item. The firm could probably sell 3,000 lanterns at a $25 selling price. The raw materials would cost about $8 and the labor $4 per lantern kit. Karyn has estimated that producing 200 of the lanterns would use 1 percent of the firm's productive capacity.

Peter and Karyn both feel that the firm should operate to maximize profits next year. Peter has often remarked during planning sessions, "In these uncertain times, we must produce for profit if we are to survive."

## Required

1. What should the firm produce and what should the selling price be for each item in order to maximize next year's profits?
2. Prepare an income statement showing the pro forma figures from your recommendation.

# 7

# Leverage

In the area of profit planning, the firm seeks ways to conduct its operations to increase the amount of profit that reaches the bottom line, or the line showing net income after taxes. To achieve aftertax profits, considerable attention is given to different kinds of leverage. A general dictionary definition of the term *leverage* would refer to an increased means of accomplishing some purpose. In some cases, as with lifting heavy objects, leverage allows us to accomplish things not otherwise possible at a given level of effort. This concept is valid in running a company. The financial manager can identify many different types of leverage. In most cases, the effects are reversible, so that the leverage may be favorable or unfavorable.

In this chapter, we will bring together the different concepts of leverage in the planning process of the firm. Each concept will link a measure of profit, such as return on investment or earnings before taxes, with another area of the firm's operating or financial situation. Each type of leverage will be analyzed to determine what it measures and what it shows with respect to the firm's operations or financing. As we will see, each type of leverage may be used as a tool of financial planning to provide insights into specific areas of the firm's anticipated profits.

## RETURN-ON-INVESTMENT LEVERAGE

It has already been noted that return on investment (ROI) is the prime indicator of management's efficiency in achieving profit from operations.

194

As the DuPont chart illustrated, ROI is the product of two factors: asset turnover and profit margin. If either of these ratios can be increased, ROI will be increased to a greater degree, as shown in Table 7–1.

## ASSET-TURNOVER SIDE OF ROI LEVERAGE

The term *asset leverage* is frequently used to refer to the asset-turnover aspects of ROI leverage. It is the tool that links the firm's return on investment with its degree of efficiency in employing assets. It is important for two reasons.

1. *Similar Profit Margins Are Common.* When comparing firms producing similar products for similar markets, we might expect them to have the same approximate profit margins. This recognizes that their costs will be about the same and they will be forced by market factors to establish equal selling prices for the goods. In this situation, it is difficult to increase ROI by increasing profit margin; thus the employment of assets becomes very important.
2. *Asset Turnover Reflects Efficiency.* The ability to generate a large volume of sales on a small asset base is a measure of a firm's operating efficiency. Firms with excessive idle assets tend to be poorly managed and are sluggish in their operating characteristics. Aggressive, profit-minded firms strive for a rapid turnover in order to gain the benefits of asset leverage on ROI.

Asset turnover is the tool that we use to monitor the employment of assets on a comparative basis. If a firm has a relatively high asset turnover compared to other firms, we say that it has a high degree of asset leverage. If low, it has a low degree of asset leverge. Note that a firm cannot have absolute high or low asset leverage; it has a relative high or low leverage. Examples of asset leverage are given in Figure 7–1.

**TABLE 7–1.**  Using Asset Turnover or Profit Margin to Produce ROI Leverage.

|  | Original | If Profit Margin Increases by 1 Percentage Point | If Asset Turnover Increases by 1 Time |
|---|---|---|---|
| Profit margin | .06 | .07 | .06 |
| Asset turnover | × 3 | × 3 | × 4 |
| Return on investment | .18 | .21 | .24 |

| (a) | (b) |
|-----|-----|
| Company A has a higher ROI because of a higher degree of asset leverage. | Both companies increase their profit margins by 2% due to changes in their markets. Company A widens the difference in ROIs because of asset leverage. |

(a)

Company A has a higher ROI because of a higher degree of asset leverage.

|        | Profit margin | x | Asset turnover | = ROI |
|--------|--------|---|--------|------|
| Co. A  | 5%     | x | 4      | 20%  |
| Co. B  | 6%     |   | 3      | 18%  |

(b)

Both companies increase their profit margins by 2% due to changes in their markets. Company A widens the difference in ROIs because of asset leverage.

|        | PM | x | AT | = ROI |
|--------|----|---|----|------|
| Co. A  | 7% | x | 4  | 28%  |
| Co. B  | 8% |   | 3  | 24%  |

Figure 7–1  Two Examples of Asset Leverage.

### PROFIT-MARGIN SIDE OF ROI LEVERAGE

Although similar firms tend to have similar profit margins, careful cost control can increase profit margin with a levering effect on ROI. Some major areas where cost control is possible are the following:

1. *Production.* The process of producing goods involves a variety of costs, including manufacturing facilities and equipment, maintenance, labor, and losses due to equipment not properly operating.
2. *Selling Expenses.* In addition to salaries and salesmen's expenses, advertising and sales-support activities cost money. The firm tries to identify essential items and minimize others as a part of cost control.
3. *Distribution.* The movement of goods from the factory to warehouses and on to the customer involves many handling and inspecting steps. These should be examined to see if all are necessary and if more streamlined distribution channels would reduce costs.
4. *Administrative Expenses.* The firm's miscellaneous and general expenses should be frequently reviewed to ensure that all are needed in the conduct of the daily business.

### LEVERING ROI THROUGH TIGHTER MANAGEMENT

Figure 7–2 shows an example of how the control of costs can help a firm to lever its ROI. Small reductions in the size of operating assets combined with small decreases in operating costs can have significant effects. Care-

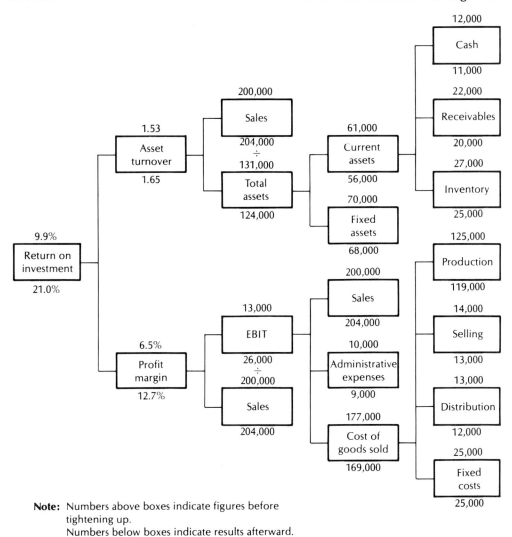

**Note:** Numbers above boxes indicate figures before tightening up.
Numbers below boxes indicate results afterward.

**Figure 7–2**   Levering Return on Investment Through Tighter Management.

ful planning can help the firm achieve the lower costs, which result in better use of assets and higher reported profits.

In the figure, the numbers above the boxes reflect the original estimates by the firm in its operating budget. The numbers below the boxes show the revised plan after efforts were made to find areas to economize. The change in ROI from 9.9 to 21 percent is significant.

## MARGINAL-ANALYSIS LEVERAGE

Three kinds of leverage are identified with the marginal-analysis approach to profit planning. Each relates a profit measure to another aspect of the firm's operating or financial situation. We will examine each in turn.

### OPERATING LEVERAGE

*Operating leverage* exists when changes in revenues produce greater changes in EBIT. Several important points should be noted about operating leverage:

1. *Related to Fixed Costs.* The degree of operating leverage is related to the fixed costs of the firm. If the firm has relatively large fixed costs, much of its marginal contribution (revenues minus variable costs) must be applied to cover fixed costs. Once the break-even point is reached (revenues = fixed + variable costs), all the marginal contribution becomes EBIT.
2. *Greatest Leverage near Break-Even Point.* After the firm reaches its break-even point, small percentage increases in sales cause larger percentage increases in EBIT. In the same manner, a small drop in sales erases the entire EBIT if the firm is near its break-even point.

**Example:** A firm has a marginal contribution of $5 per unit and sells one unit of an item above the break-even point. EBIT is $5. If the firm sells a second unit, what happens to EBIT?

**Answer:** It doubles to $10, a 100 percent rise in EBIT with a far smaller percent rise in revenues.

The degree of operating leverage at any single sales volume can be calculated from a ratio of marginal contribution to EBIT. If the marginal contribution is $900,000 and the EBIT is $450,000, the operating leverage is 900/450, or 2/1. Thus, any percentage increase in sales results in twice that percentage increase in EBIT. Figure 7–3 shows two formulas for calculating operating leverage and gives an example of a calculation and check.

Note that the rise in sales in the figure produces a new degree of operating leverage at 150,000 units. Another rise in sales will be accom-

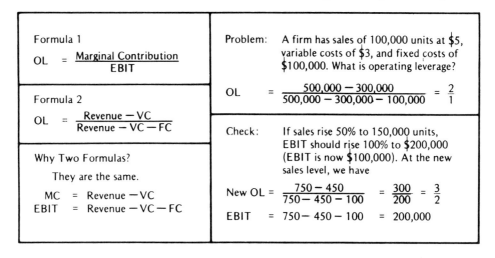

**Figure 7–3**  Calculation of Operating Leverage.

panied by only 1½ times as large an increase in operating income. Operating leverage decreases with each increase in sales above the breakeven point, because fixed costs become relatively smaller compared to revenues and variable costs.

## SIGNIFICANCE OF OPERATING LEVERAGE

What does operating leverage tell the financial manager? It tells the impact of changes in sales on operating income. If a firm has a high degree of operating leverage, small changes in sales have large effects on EBIT. If the change is a small rise in sales, profits will rise dramatically. But if the change is a small decline in forecast sales, EBIT may be wiped out and a loss may be reported.

As a general rule, firms do not like to operate under conditions of a high degree of operating leverage. This is a high-risk situation in which a small drop in sales can be excessively damaging to the firm's efforts to achieve profitability. The firm prefers to operate sufficiently above breakeven to avoid the danger of a fluctuation in sales and profits.

## INTEREST-CHARGES LEVERAGE

*Interest-charges leverage* (sometimes called *financial leverage*) exists whenever a firm has debt that requires the payment of interest. It gives us a measure of the degree to which changes in operating income will affect

EBT. It makes use of the same principle as operating leverage with a formula as follows:

$$\text{interest-charges leverage} = \frac{\text{revenue} - \text{VC} - \text{FC}}{\text{revenue} - \text{VC} - \text{FC} - \text{int}} = \frac{\text{EBIT}}{\text{EBT}}$$

In our previous example, if the firm had annual interest payments of $25,000, its interest-charges leverage at 100,000 units of sales would be

$$\text{interest-charges leverage} = \frac{500 - 300 - 100}{500 - 300 - 100 - 25} = \frac{100}{75} = \frac{1.33}{1} \text{ or } 1\frac{1}{3} \text{ times}$$

This means that any percentage increase in EBIT would be accompanied by a 1⅓ percentage increase in EBT. If EBIT rises by 100 percent (a rise to $200,000), EBT would rise by 133 percent (from $75,000 to $175,000). The new level of interest-charges leverage would be 200/175, or 1.14/1. As with operating leverage, interest-charges leverage also decreases with increases in EBIT.

Interest-charges leverage is more commonly called *financial leverage* in financial literature. This is confusing because there are two different leverage concepts identified by the term *financial leverage*. To avoid this confusion, we will always call the ratio of EBIT/EBT by the name *interest-charges leverage*.

### COMBINED LEVERAGE

*Combined leverage* is used to compare changes in revenues with changes in EBT and also changes in net income. As the name implies, it combines the effects of operating and interest-charges leverage. It may be calculated in two ways:

1. *A Ratio of Marginal Contribution to EBT.* This may be done with either the MC/EBT or (revenue − VC)/(revenue − VC − FC − int) formulas.
2. *Operating Leverage Times Interest-Charges Leverage.* Thus, if the operating leverage is 2/1 and the interest-charges leverage is 3/1, the combined leverage is 6/1.

In the preceding example, at 100,000 units the combined leverage would be 2/1 times 1.33 (OL × IChL = 2.66/1). This means that any change in sales will produce 2.66 times that percentage of change in EBT. The combined leverage for the example may also be calculated from the formula:

$$\frac{\text{combined}}{\text{leverage}} = \frac{\text{MC}}{\text{EBT}} = \frac{\text{revenue} - \text{VC}}{\text{revenue} - \text{VC} - \text{FC} - \text{int}}$$

$$= \frac{500 - 300}{500 - 300 - 100 - 25} = \frac{200{,}000}{75{,}000} = 2.66 \text{ times}$$

Table 7–2 gives the formulas and some of the important characteristics of each of the marginal-analysis leverages.

## TWO QUESTIONS ON MARGINAL-ANALYSIS LEVERAGE CONCEPTS

1. *Why Can Changes in Revenues Be Measured Directly Even Though Operating Leverage and Combined Leverage Use Marginal Contribution, Not Sales?* With constant costs assumed in the range of op-

**TABLE 7–2.**   Characteristics of the Three Kinds of Leverage Using Marginal Analysis.

| *Operating Leverage* | | | |
|---|---|---|---|
| $\dfrac{\text{revenue} - \text{VC}}{\text{revenue} - \text{VC} - \text{FC}} = \dfrac{\text{MC}}{\text{EBIT}}$ | Isolates fixed costs | Compares changes in revenues to changes in EBIT by formula: (O.L.) (% change) = % change in sales      in EBIT |

| *Interest-Charges Leverage* | | |
|---|---|---|
| $\dfrac{\text{revenue} - \text{VC} - \text{FC}}{\text{revenue} - \text{VC} - \text{FC} - \text{int}} = \dfrac{\text{EBIT}}{\text{EBT}}$ | Isolates interest | Compares changes in EBIT to changes in EBT formula: (IChL) (% change) = % change in EBIT      in EBT |

| *Combined Leverage* | | |
|---|---|---|
| $\dfrac{\text{revenue} - \text{VC}}{\text{revenue} - \text{VC} - \text{FC} - \text{int}} = \dfrac{\text{MC}}{\text{EBT}}$ | Isolates both fixed costs and interest | Compares changes in revenues to changes in EBT and net income by formula: (C.L.) (% change) = % change in sales      in EBT or net income |

erations, the relationship between revenues and variable costs does not change on a unit basis. Therefore, each additional unit of sales produces a unit of marginal contribution. With marginal contribution and sales locked in a fixed relationship, we can deal directly with changes in sales in order to see leverage effects.

2. *Does Leverage Work When Sales Are Decreasing as Well as Increasing?* Yes, with the single exception of net income effects when losses occur. If, for example, operating leverage were 2/1, a drop of 50 percent in sales would erase EBIT. If combined leverage were 4/1, a 25 percent drop in sales would erase earnings before taxes and net income. But with a larger drop in sales, we can use the combined leverage to estimate only the new level of EBT, not net income. This is true because of the fact that tax effects cease once EBT reaches zero. This situation is demonstrated in one of the following examples.

**Example:** A firm has sales of $2 million, variable costs of $1.4 million, fixed costs of $400,000, debt of $1 million at 10 percent, and a 40 percent tax rate. What are its operating and interest charges and combined leverages?

**Answer:**

$$\text{Operating leverage} = \frac{2{,}000 - 1{,}400}{2{,}000 - 1{,}400 - 400} = \frac{600}{200} = 3/1$$

$$\text{Interest-charges leverage} = \frac{200}{200 - 100} = \frac{200}{100} = 2/1$$

$$\text{Combined leverage} = \quad 600/100 \quad = \quad 6/1$$

**Example:** If the preceding firm wants to double its EBIT, how much of a rise in sales would be needed on a percentage basis?

**Answer:** The formula is:

$$\left(\begin{array}{c}\text{operating}\\\text{leverage}\end{array}\right)\left(\begin{array}{c}\text{percent change}\\\text{in sales}\end{array}\right) = \left(\begin{array}{c}\text{percent change}\\\text{in EBIT}\end{array}\right)$$

$$(3/1)\,(\%\ \text{sales}) = 100\%$$

$$\%\ \text{sales} = \frac{100\%}{3} = .3333 \text{ rise in sales to get a 100 percent rise in EBIT.}$$

**Example:** if the preceding firm had a 20 percent rise in sales, what percentage rise would it have in EBIT? EBT? net income?

**Answer:** 3/1 times 20 percent, or a 60 percent rise in EBIT. 6/1 times 20 percent, or a 120 percent rise in EBT and net income.

**Example:** If the preceding firm had a 50 percent decline in sales, what percentage drop would it have in EBIT? EBT? net income?

**Answer:** 3/1 times 50 percent, or a 150 percent drop in EBIT. The firm would show an operating loss. 6/1 times 50 percent, or a 300 percent drop in EBT. The firm would show a loss. As we can see, the drop in net income exceeds 300 percent because the income tax calculation ceases once EBT reaches 0.

|  | *Present* | *With 20% Rise in Sales* | *With 50% Decline in Sales* |
|---|---|---|---|
| Sales | $2,000 | $2,400 | $1,000 |
| Variable costs | 1,400 | 1,680 | 700 |
| Marginal contribution | 600 | 720 | 300 |
| Fixed costs | 400 | 400 | 400 |
| EBIT (loss) | 200 | 320 (60% rise) | (100) (150% drop) |
| Interest | 100 | 100 | 100 |
| EBT | 100 | 220 (120% rise) | (200) (300% drop) |
| Federal income taxes (.40) | 40 | 88 | 0 |
| Net Income (loss) | $ 60 | $ 132 (120% rise) | (200) (430% drop) |

## FINANCIAL LEVERAGE

As has already been pointed out, two types of leverage are commonly called by a single term. The most widely accepted usage of *financial leverage* refers to a situation in which both of the following exist:

1. *Limited Cost Securities.* A firm must be financing a portion of its assets by using debt, preferred stock, or some other security with a limited cost to the firm. It can be fixed or variable rate securities, but the return to the holder must be limited.
2. *ROI Is Not Equal to Cost of the Limited-Cost Securities.* The firm's ROI must not be equal to the percentage of interest or dividend being paid on the limited-cost security.

## THREE POSSIBLE SITUATIONS WITH DEBT

The sole criterion for determining whether a firm has financial leverage with its debt involves a comparison of the firm's ROI with the average interest rate. Three situations are possible.

1. *ROI Is Greater than the Interest Rate.* If the ROI exceeds the interest rate, the firm is making money as a result of borrowing. It may be making 15 percent on its assets but is only paying 10 percent to its creditors. The extra 5 percentage points will be divided between the government (in the form of federal income taxes) and the shareholders. In this situation, it makes sense to borrow. When ROI exceeds interest rate, we say that the firm has *favorable financial leverage.* Another common term to describe this situation is to say that the firm is *trading on the equity.*
2. *ROI Equals Interest Rate.* In this situation, the firm is earning on the money exactly what it pays for the use of the money. It neither makes sense nor is totally objectionable to borrow in this position unless other factors are considered.
3. *ROI Is Less than Interest Rate.* When this happens, the firm is borrowing and then losing money on the use of the funds. It does not make sense to borrow, conduct operations, and then make less than the cost of the borrowed money. This situation is called *unfavorable financial leverage.*

## IMPORTANCE OF FINANCIAL LEVERAGE

Many financial managers would argue that financial leverage is the most important of the leverage concepts. It finds particular application in capital-structure management. A firm's *capital structure* is the relation between the debt and equity securities that make up the firm's financing of its assets. A firm with no debt is said to have an all-equity capital structure. Since most firms have capital structures with both debt and equity elements, the financial manager is highly concerned with the effects of borrowing. If a firm is making money on its borrowing (has favorable financial leverage), the shareholders are realizing higher earnings per share than in the absence of debt.

## CAPITAL-STRUCTURE MANAGEMENT—FIRST EXAMPLE

To demonstrate the effect of financial leverage in a firm's capital structure, consider four firms with $500,000 of assets. All four firms earn a 12 percent return on investment. Each firm has sold common stock for $10 a share. Firm A sold $500,000 of stock while firms B, C, and D sold $300,000 of stock. Firms B, C, and D borrowed the remaining $200,000 at different interest rates. Firm B borrowed at 8 percent and, with the 12 percent return on investment, has favorable financial leverage. Firm C borrowed at 12 percent and has neither favorable nor unfavorable leverage. Firm D borrowed at 16 percent and has unfavorable financial leverage. Financial data for each firm are given in Table 7–3.

Analyzing each situation in turn, we can see the effects of financial leverage. Even though the stock sold for $10 and a 12 percent ROI is present for each firm, the aftertax earnings and EPS varied. Firm A, with no debt, earns $.72 per share (a 7.2 percent aftertax return). This is also the situation for firm C, the firm that borrows at the same interest rate as its ROI. But firm B, the firm that borrows at less than its ROI, levers its profits to $.88 by paying only 8 percent to the creditors, who provide 40 percent of the assets ($200,000 of $500,000). Firm D has the reverse effect from Firm B. Firm D is paying 16 percent interest, which is more than its ROI. This firm must use a portion of the profits otherwise designated for the shareholders in order to pay its creditors.

This example shows that it is logical for a firm to borrow, up to reasonable amounts, if it can earn a higher return on the borrowing than it pays for the money. Similarly, a firm should not borrow if it cannot earn more than the cost of the money.

**TABLE 7–3.** Four Firms with Identical Operating Incomes and Different Capital Structures, Illustrating the Effects of Financial Leverage.

|  | Firm A | Firm B | Firm C | Firm D |
|---|---|---|---|---|
|  |  | Financial Leverage with Interest Rate of: | | |
|  |  | 8%<br>Favorable | 12%<br>No leverage | 16%<br>Unfavorable |
| Equity | $500,000 | $300,000 | $300,000 | $300,000 |
| Debt | 0 | 200,000 | 200,000 | 200,000 |
| Total assets | 500,000 | 500,000 | 500,000 | 500,000 |
| EBIT (ROI = 12%) | 60,000 | 60,000 | 60,000 | 60,000 |
| Interest | 0 | 16,000 | 24,000 | 32,000 |
| EBT | 60,000 | 44,000 | 36,000 | 28,000 |
| Taxes (.40) | 24,000 | 17,600 | 14,400 | 11,200 |
| Net income | $ 36,000 | $ 26,400 | $ 21,600 | $ 16,800 |
| Divided by shares outstanding | ÷ 50,000 | ÷ 30,000 | ÷ 30,000 | ÷ 30,000 |
| Earnings per share | $.72 | $.88 | $.72 | $.56 |

CAPITAL-STRUCTURE MANAGEMENT—SECOND EXAMPLE

A second way to analyze financial leverage is to consider the effects of differing profit levels with each situation. A firm is not guaranteed a 12 percent ROI, and management may consider the effects of achieving a lower or higher return. In the preceding situations with firms A, B, C, and D, we may evaluate how differing ROIs will affect EPS for each firm. Table 7–4 shows the EPS for each firm with four different ROIs.

**TABLE 7–4.** Measuring the Impact of Changes in ROI on Changes in EPS for Four Firms with Differing Capital Structures.

|            | Firm A<br>EPS | Firm B<br>EPS | Firm C<br>EPS | Firm D<br>EPS |
|------------|--------|--------|--------|--------|
| (18% ROI)  | $1.08  | $1.48  | $1.32  | $1.16  |
| (12% ROI)  | .72    | .88    | .72    | .56    |
| ( 6% ROI)  | .36    | .28    | .12    | (.07)  |
| ( 0% ROI)  | 0      | (.53)  | (.80)  | (1.07) |

The table illustrates the general pattern of effects for levered firms. When the ROI is high, the firms with favorable financial leverage report the highest earnings. Similarly, when ROI drops, the firms with the largest interest payments report the largest losses or smallest earnings. The firm with no debt has lower earnings in high-profit periods and higher earnings in low-profit periods than firms with debt. This can be seen more clearly in Figure 7–4.

FINANCIAL LEVERAGE WITH PREFERRED STOCK

When calculating whether preferred stock offers a firm favorable financial leverage, a modification of the formula is necessary. The preferred dividends are declared after the payment of federal income taxes on the corporation. This means that the ROI must be greater than the combined taxes and dividends for the leverage to be favorable. The formula is

$$ROI > \frac{dividend}{1 - tax\ rate}$$

If, for example, the preferred stock carried a 15 percent coupon on $100 par value, the ROI must exceed $.15/ (1 - .40) = .25$ percent (assumes 40 percent taxes) for the leverage to be favorable.

**Example:** A firm is considering a 13 percent preferred-stock offering and has a 40 percent corporate tax rate. Above what ROI will the firm have favorable financial leverage?

**Answer:** 21.67 percent. The calculation is $.13/(1-.40) = .2167$

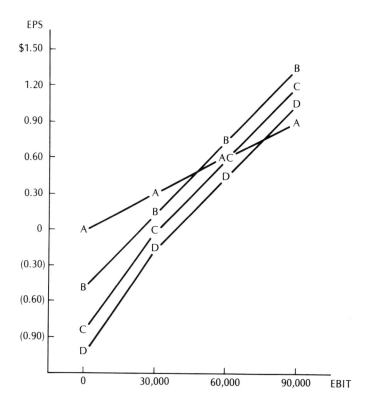

**Figure 7–4**   EBIT/EPS Analysis.

## WEAKNESSES OF PROFIT PLANNING

The future-earnings-per-share approach to profit planning and the different leverage concepts are highly useful to firms with stock outstanding in the hands of public investors or institutions. External analysts are very concerned with reported profits and capital structure, and this influences the market price of the firm's stock.

In spite of the value of these techniques, they have weaknesses, which will be briefly described.

## SHORT-TERM OUTLOOK

Because of the many factors involved, future earnings per share are usually projected only 1 or 2 years in advance. It is assumed that the situation will remain the same after this period. In fact, it is more accurate to use a technique that projects the entire life of a new investment, as will be done under the topic of capital budgeting.

## IMPROPERLY HANDLED DEPRECIATION

Depreciation and the other noncash expenses serve to reduce the net income and future earnings per share. Actually, these expenses shield a portion of the revenues from sales and provide a cash inflow to the firm. The larger the noncash expense, the more desirable the project on a cash-flow basis but not on an accounting basis.

This problem is partly handled by the firm's accountants who prepare the annual reports. Although the firm takes advantage of accelerated cost recovery to maximize cash flow, straight-line depreciation is reported in the stockholders' literature so as not to understate profits.

## ASSETS AT BOOK, NOT MARKET, VALUE

In profit-planning techniques, for consistency, the firm's assets are recorded at book value rather than at actual market value. Since all firms use the same general depreciation or cost recovery schedules and record assets at cost, comparisons can be made. If every firm made an estimate of the current market value of its assets, wide discrepancies would exist between firms with similar assets.

The effect of listing assets at book value in most cases is to overstate ROI and the turnover on the use of the assets. Completely depreciated machinery shows a return on zero assets, whereas no asset can exceed its actual cost. This is not a serious problem but should be noted by the financial manager.

## KEY TERMS

asset leverage
capital structure
combined leverage
favorable financial leverage
financial leverage

interest-charges leverage
leverage
marginal-analysis-leverage
    concepts
operating leverage

return on investment
    leverage
trading on the equity
unfavorable financial
    leverage

## STUDY QUESTIONS

1. What are the two aspects to ROI leverage? Which is more important? why?
2. What can be done to increase profit margins? turnover?
3. What is the significance of operating leverage? interest-charges leverage? combined leverage?
4. When does a firm have financial leverage?
5. When is it favorable? unfavorable?
6. What are some weaknesses of profit planning?

## PROBLEMS

1. A firm has sales of $5.25 million, a profit margin of 11 percent, and an ROI of 26 percent. A second firm has an EBIT of $950,000, an asset turnover of 2.5, and an ROI of 18 percent. Which firm has the highest degree of asset leverage?

Use the following information to answer problems 2–9. If you do not have adequate information to answer any questions, state what you are missing.

| | |
|---|---|
| Sales | $9.25 million |
| Variable costs | $5.5 million |
| Fixed costs | $1.1 million |
| Debt | $6 million at 10 percent average cost |
| Equity | $7.2 million |

2. What is the firm's ROI?
3. Does it have favorable financial leverage? How do you know?
4. If it is in an industry with an asset turnover of 2.3, does it have a high or low asset leverage?
5. What are its operating, interest-charges, and combined leverages?
6. What are its earnings per share?
7. If sales drop to $6 million, what will happen to the firm's EBIT? What will be the new EBIT?
8. How much would the firm's sales have to decline in order for the earnings before taxes to be equal to zero?
9. If EBIT doubles, what will be the new level of EBT?

Use the following data to solve problems 10–13.

| | |
|---|---|
| Sales | 230,000 units |
| Selling price per unit | $17 |
| Fixed costs | $310,000 |
| Variable cost per unit | $12 |
| Debt | $400,000 at 11 percent average cost |
| Equity | 25,000 shares with a market price of $60 per share. |

10. What are the operating, interest-charges, and combined leverages?
11. Does the firm have favorable financial leverage? why?

12. If the firm is in an industry with an asset turnover of 1.75, does it have a high or low degree of asset leverage?
13. Assume that another firm has the same book value per share, the same ROI, the same total assets as this firm, and no debt. Does the all-equity firm have a greater or lesser EPS than the above firm? why? (Use tax rate of 40 percent.)
14. Which firm has a better earnings per share? why?
15. At what level of interest would the two firms have the same EPS?

# DALTON COMPANY CASE
# Leverage

*This case provides the reader with the opportunity to apply different concepts of leverage to the planning process of the firm.*

Dalton Company is an important producer of swimming pools and associated objects for the pool and patio. The firm is located in an urban area outside Baltimore. The firm's primary markets are hardware and discount stores located in five northeastern states. Dalton's products reach its markets mostly by truck, although some rail is also utilized.

Most of Dalton's financial planning is done by Don McLean, vice-president of finance. Don has recently prepared financial statements estimating next year's operating results. He estimates that the firm will earn just over $900,000 in the current year on sales of $9 million and is forecasting sales of $12 million next year. It is likely that variable costs will remain at approximately the same percentage of sales next year as this year. Fixed costs will probably rise 15 percent next year.

Dalton has been investigating the addition of a number of new product lines to be sold through its existing distribution channels. Two items have been of particular interest. The first would involve the production and sale of chaise lounges for use around swimming pools. The product would be aimed at commercial users, such as motels, but could be sold through hardware and discount stores as a residential product. The second new item would be a patio umbrella. The umbrella would be a large, 10-rib, multicolored canvas with fringe and would be aimed at the residential market. Both products would fit in with Dalton's existing product line and neither would require any increase in net working capital.

In his analysis of the new-product proposals, Don McLean recognized that the firm will have to build new facilities to produce each product. The lounges would require an investment of $3.5 million which would include the purchase and installation of manufacturing and packaging machinery. The umbrellas, although a relatively simple concept, would require an investment of $5 million for efficient production. For both products, it would take less than 90 days to install the major equipment. This means that production could begin by January 1.

Thomas Malar, the firm's vice-president of sales, has prepared sales estimates for the two products. He forecasts $3 million in sales for the lounges and $4.2 million in sales for the umbrellas on an annual basis. The report from the cost-accounting department estimates variable costs of two-thirds of the sales value for the lounge unit and 61 percent for the umbrellas. Fixed costs would be $300,000 and $550,000, respectively.

To finance the new projects, Don has been working with Dalton's investment bankers in Baltimore. At a recent meeting, Don was told that the firm could raise money from two sources under current market conditions. First, it could borrow on a 10-year note at 13 percent for either or both of the projects in an amount not to exceed $9.5 million. Second, the investment bankers felt confident that they could underwrite a preferred-stock issue with a 9 percent dividend up to a dollar amount of $6 million. The issue would have to be cumulative with respect to dividends. Common-stock financing would not be a possibility at present.

## Questions

1. Without the new proposals what would be Dalton's operating, interest charges, and combined leverage next year? Would Dalton have favorable financial leverage?
2. How does the acceptance of each project affect the differing leverages? asset leverage?
3. With each financing alternative, does Dalton's future earnings per share increase or decrease? why?

**DALTON COMPANY—Balance Sheet**
**(Projected through Dec. 31 this year)**

| | |
|---|---:|
| Cash | $ 325,000 |
| Accounts receivables | 850,000 |
| Inventory | 500,000 |
| Fixed assets | 7,650,000 |
| | $9,325,000 |
| | |
| Current liabilities | $ 600,000 |
| Long-term debt (10%) | 3,700,000 |
| Common stock ($3 par) | 1,500,000 |
| Retained earnings | 3,525,000 |
| | $9,325,000 |

**DALTON COMPANY—Income Statement**
**(Projected through Dec. 31 this year)**

| | |
|---|---:|
| Sales | $9,000,000 |
| Variable costs | 6,030,000 |
| Marginal contribution | 2,970,000 |
| Fixed costs | 1,043,480 |
| EBIT | 1,926,520 |
| Interest | 370,000 |
| EBT | 1,556,520 |
| Taxes (40%) | 622,608 |
| Net Income | $  933,912 |

Figures for industry comparisons:
Normal asset turnover 1.5/1
Normal profit margin 18%

# Which Is Better Managed?

*This case provides the reader with the opportunity to analyze two firms with respect to their degrees of leverage and how this affects their operations.*

Jack LeSabre is a senior commercial loan officer with the North Carolina National Bank in Charlotte, North Carolina. Approximately 60 percent of Jack's accounts are in the thriving textile industry of North and South Carolina; over the years, Jack has compiled extensive data on the proper management of firms in the textile industry. He has published several articles in business and trade journals and frequently receives calls from out of state, particularly New York City, for advice or comment on the financing of textile transactions.

As a result of his background, it was not surprising that Harry Gilbert and George Grant brought their problem to Jack. Harry Gilbert is the principal owner of Gilbert Industries, a medium-sized producer of specialty fabrics. Gilbert Industries is the primary employer in a small town 32 miles from Charlotte and has, on occasion, borrowed money from North Carolina National. George Grant is the president and major stockholder in Grant and Sanford Incorporated, a cotton-processing firm known locally as G&S. George has worked extensively with Jack LeSabre, since G&S is one of Jack's accounts.

"We have a problem," George began, "and we believe you're the guy who can help us resolve it."

"That's right," added Harry. "We're thinking about combining our operations but we can't get over an initial hurdle. It's pretty obvious to me that G&S is not managed nearly as well as Gilbert Industries, but I'm having difficulty proving it to George. As a matter of fact, George feels that G&S is better run than Gilbert. We want you to decide, to tell us which company is better run. Then I think we can work out an arrangement to combine the operations."

Although Jack tried to convince the two men that he could not decide which company is better run, Harry and George insisted that Jack was the most qualified person to comment on the management of the two firms. Jack finally agreed to analyze each man's claims and provide a judgment on the merit of each position. As the two men talked, Jack made a series of notes on the major points presented for each firm. The notepad is reproduced as follows:

1.  Next year Gilbert will have higher earnings per share, $2.50 to $1.50.
2.  Next year Gilbert will have $6 million in current assets compared to $7 million for G&S.
3.  Next year, G&S's EBIT will be double that of Gilbert and G&S's net income will be 80 percent higher than Gilbert's.
4.  Gilbert has $18 million in equity compared to $13 million for G&S. Harry claims that this is lower cost equity, because Gilbert has only 1 million shares of common stock outstanding compared to G&S's 3 million shares.
5.  Gilbert has total debt of $10 million compared to G&S's debt of $22 million. Harry claims this means that Gilbert has less risk than G&S.
6.  Gilbert will pay $500,000 in interest next year compared to G&S's $2 million. Harry claims that Gilbert's debt cost is only 11 percent compared to 14 percent for G&S, another indicator of good management for Gilbert.
7.  G&S will have higher sales next year, $32 million compared to $24.5 million for Gilbert. G&S will have variable costs of $11 million compared to the $18 million costs for Gilbert. George pointed out that variable costs are 34.375 percent of sales for G&S but are over 73 percent for Gilbert, a clear sign of Gilbert's weak management.
8.  Harry countered the variable-costs argument by pointing out that Gilbert has only $1 million in fixed costs compared to $10 million for G&S.
9.  Harry concluded that Gilbert's stock sells for a higher price since both firms have been trading at a 10/1 price-earnings multiple and Gilbert has higher earnings.

The two men left the office after agreeing that they would return in 3 days to learn what Jack thought of each firm. Jack sat down and prepared a list of questions to answer on the firms. As Jack began the list, he remembered the final words of Harry Gilbert.

> We both agree on one thing. We would never want to join with a firm that could not stand a drop in sales and still be able to cover interest payments. As a general rule, we would want to be

able to sustain a 20 percent drop in sales for 3 consecutive years (20 percent each year) and still be able to cover interest on debt. If a firm could not do that, it would have hard times in a field as turbulent as textiles.

## Questions

1. Prepare the balance sheet for each company.
2. Prepare next year's income statement for Gilbert Industries and G&S Incorporated and a combined statement for the two firms.
3. Using leverage ratios, which firm has the most risk that a drop in sales will cause a greater drop in profits?
4. What percentage drop in sales will erase net income for each firm? What percentage drop in sales will erase EBIT?
5. Which firm qualifies under the general guideline that it sustain a 20 percent annual drop in sales for 3 years and still cover its interest payments from current profits?
6. Which firm makes the best use of favorable financial leverage?
7. How much of each firm's earnings per share is due to favorable financial leverage?
8. If the two firms combine, how much of the combined net income would be contributed by each of the old firms?
9. Which firm is better managed?

## PART III

# Working-Capital Management

Working-Capital and Cash Management
Management of Receivables and Inventory
Economics of Working Capital
Investing Excess Cash

# 8

# Working-Capital and Cash Management

One of the most important areas in the day-to-day management of the firm deals with the management of *working capital,* which is defined as all the short-term assets used in daily operations. These consist primarily of cash, marketable securities, accounts receivable, and inventory. The balances in these accounts can be highly volatile as they respond quickly to changes in the firm's operating environment. The effective management of working capital requires both medium-term planning and immediate reactions to changes in forecasts and conditions.

*Net working capital* may be defined as the difference between current assets (working capital) and current liabilities. It is a measure of *liquidity,* which is defined as the adequacy of near-term cash to meet the firm's obligations. A highly liquid firm has sufficient cash to pay its bills at all times. An illiquid firm is unable to pay its bills when due.

*Working-capital management* is the functional area of finance that covers all the current accounts of the firm. It is concerned with the adequacy of current assets as well as the level of risk posed by current liabilities. It is a discipline that seeks proper policies for managing current assets and liabilities and practical techniques for maximizing the benefits from managing working capital.

In this chapter, we will examine policies for the management of a firm's short-term assets and liabilities. We will look at the nature of working capital and issues affecting it. Then we will discuss policies for managing cash and assets that have the characteristics of cash. We will examine cash forecasting and techniques for estimating the amounts and timing of future cash flows. Finally we will cover concepts for managing the firm's disbursements of cash and collections on receivables.

## WORKING-CAPITAL POLICIES

*Current assets* may be defined as assets that are usually converted into cash in the ordinary course of business within the current accounting cycle, or 1 year. Thus, they are cash or near-cash resources. The value represented by these assets *circulates* among several balance-sheet accounts. Cash is used to purchase raw materials and pay the labor and other manufacturing costs to produce goods, which are then carried as inventories. When the inventories are sold, accounts receivable are created. The collection of the receivables brings cash into the firm, and the process starts again, as shown in Figure 8–1.

The firm's working capital may be viewed as being comprised of two components:

1. *Permanent Working Capital.* These assets are required on a continuing basis over the entire year. It represents the amount of cash, receivables, and inventory maintained as a minimum to carry on operations at any time.
2. *Variable Working Capital.* This represents additional assets required at certain times during the year. Added inventory must be maintained to support peak selling periods. Receivables will increase and must be financed after a period of high sales. Extra cash may be needed to pay for increased supplies preceding high activity.

Figure 8–2 graphically displays permanent and variable working-capital needs for a firm whose level of business is growing. The level of

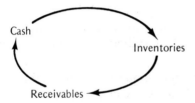

**Figure 8–1** Circulating Nature of Current Assets.

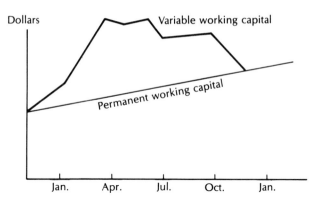

**Figure 8–2**   Permanent and Variable Working Capital.

working capital is higher in the summer than in the winter, reflecting a cyclical business activity.

## GOALS OF WORKING CAPITAL POLICIES

The firm's policies for managing its working capital should be designed to achieve three goals:

1. *Adequate Liquidity.* If a firm lacks sufficient cash to pay its bills when due, it will experience continuing problems. The most important goal is to achieve adequate liquidity for the conduct of day-to-day operations.

2. *Minimization of Risk.* In selecting its sources of financing, payables and other short-term liabilities may involve relatively low costs. The firm must ensure that these near-term obligations do not become excessive compared to the current assets on hand to pay them. The matching of assets and liabilities among current accounts is a task of minimizing the risk of being unable to pay bills and other obligations.

3. *Contribute to Maximizing Firm Value.* The firm holds working capital for the same purpose as it holds any other assets, that is, to help maximize the present value of common stock and value of the firm. It should not hold idle current assets any more than it should have idle fixed assets. The investment of excess cash, minimizing of inventories, speedy collection of receivables, and

elimination of unnecessary and costly short-term financing all contribute to maximizing the value of the firm.

## FACTORS AFFECTING THE NEED FOR WORKING CAPITAL

A firm's requirements for working capital are mainly determined by four factors:

1. *Sales Volume.* This is the most important factor affecting the size and components of working capital. A firm maintains current assets because they are needed to support the operational activities that culminate in sales. Over time, a firm will keep a fairly steady rate of current assets to annual sales. For most manufacturing firms, this ratio is 20 and 40 percent (current assets/sales). A firm realizing a steady level of sales operates with a fairly constant level of cash, receivables, and inventory, if properly managed. Firms experiencing growth in sales require additional permanent working capital. If sales are declining, a reduction in permanent working capital would be expected.

2. *Seasonal and Cyclical Factors.* Most firms experience seasonal fluctuations in the demand for their products and services. These variations in sales affect the level of working capital. Similarly, the overall economy undergoes business and financial cycles. In a recession, a firm's sales may temporarily decline, thus reducing the need for inventories and the level of receivables. In a period of high interest rates, customers may be slow in paying their bills, a fact that will cause an increase in receivables.

3. *Changes in Technology.* Technological developments, particularly related to the production process, can have sharp impacts on the need for working capital. If the firm purchases new equipment that processes raw materials at a faster rate than previously, the permanent need for inventory may be changed. If the faster processing requires more raw materials for efficient production runs, the permanent inventory will increase. If the machine can use less expensive raw materials, the inventory needs may be reduced.

4. *Policies of the Firm.* Many of the firm's policies affect the levels of permanent and variable working capital. If the firm changes its credit policy from net 30 to net 60, additional funds may be permanently tied up in receivables. If it changes production policies, inventory requirements may be permanently or temporarily af-

fected. If it changes its safety level of cash on hand, permanent working capital may increase or decrease. If the level of cash is linked to the level of sales, variable working capital may be affected.

## MANAGING WORKING CAPITAL

The management of current assets basically involves two processes:

1. *Forecasting Needed Funds.* Changes in the firm's operations can have almost immediate effects on the working capital needed. For example, if suppliers increase the price of raw materials, more money will be tied up in inventories than previously. Even if the firm can increase the price for its final product, it will need additional working capital to support its sales efforts. An alert manager will observe operating activities and estimate the level of working capital required for future periods.
2. *Acquiring Funds.* Once the needs have been estimated, the manager must acquire the necessary funds from the best source, for the lowest cost, and for the time period involved.

The effective management of working capital is the primary means of achieving the firm's goal of adequate liquidity. It is, after all, the working capital—cash, marketable securities, receivables, and inventory—that will be available in the near term to pay bills and meet obligations. It is the net working capital—excess of current assets over net current liabilities—that helps measure the degree of protection against problems that might cause a shortage of funds.

Managing working capital requires a number of actions, including the following:

1. *Monitoring Levels of Cash, Receivables, and Inventory.* On a daily or weekly basis, the manager should know how much funds are tied up in each of the current-asset accounts. Questions should be asked. Are the amounts in each account appropriate? How do the balances compare to previous balances? to the firm's standards? to industry norms? Any deviations from expectations should be investigated.
2. *Knowing Percentage of Funds in Current Accounts.* Working capital represents a large investment for most firms. Some 30 to 60 percent of a firm's total assets are tied up in current accounts. The

manager should be aware of the relationship between current and fixed assets and any changes in the percentage of funds in current accounts.

3. *Recording Time Spent Managing Current Accounts.* Although estimates vary, somewhere between one-third and two-thirds of the financial manager's time is spent managing the working capital. A knowledge of how much time each member of the finance department spends with current accounts can offer an insight into the effectiveness of working-capital management.

## HOW MUCH WORKING CAPITAL IS NEEDED?

To determine the amount of working capital needed by the firm, a number of factors may be included in the analysis, such as the following:

1. *Size of the Firm.* It may be argued that a firm's size, either in assets or sales, affects its need for working capital. A small firm may use extra current assets as a cushion against cash-flow interruptions. Small firms have cash inflows from fewer sources than larger firms and hence are more affected by the failures of a few customers to pay on time. Larger firms with many sources of funds may need less working capital as compared to total assets or sales.

2. *Activities of Firm.* If a firm must stock a heavy volume of inventory or sell on relatively easy credit terms (net 75, for example), it has greater needs for working capital than firms providing services or making cash sales.

3. *Availability of Credit.* A firm with readily available credit from banks can get by with less working capital than a firm without such credit.

4. *Attitude toward Profits.* Since all funds have a cost, a relatively large amount of current assets tends to reduce a firm's profit. Some firms want extra working capital and are willing to suffer small costs. Other firms maintain an absolute minimum of working capital at all times in order to gain the full profits from operations.

5. *Attitude toward Risk.* The greater the amount of capital, particularly cash and marketable securities, the lower the risk of liquidity problems. Firms that do not wish to incur even slight risks of liquidity deficiencies may keep extra cash. Other firms accept the risks to earn profits and may not always keep adequate cash to pay bills on time.

Most firms seek to maintain sufficient working capital to meet their needs for liquidity without tying up unnecessary funds. In striving for this goal, many firm's emphasize the minimizing of risk from inadequate liquidity. If the firm has sufficient financing for its cash, receivables, and inventory needs, management can concentrate its efforts on achieving a return. Still, the primary goal of working-capital management is to avoid the risks from inadequate liquidity.

One goal of working-capital management deals with earning a return for the firm. In this context, interest-rate levels affect the amount of working capital that a firm will hold. When interest levels are high, the firm is encouraged to reduce levels of cash, receivables, and inventory. This will minimize financing costs for working capital and will allow the firm to invest its cash for a relatively high return. On the other hand, a drop in interest rates may produce a relaxing of working-capital policies. With lower interest charges, the firm may be willing to maintain higher levels of working capital.

Whatever the level of interest rates, the firm must maintain adequate levels of working capital to efficiently conduct its business. Inadequate working capital produces a high risk of liquidity problems. At the same time, inadequate levels of working capital demand considerable amounts of management time and attention. This has the effect of diverting attention from the firm's operations and usually produces a drop in profits. By maintaining sufficient funds, the firm is properly balancing its efforts to achieve a return without accepting unnecessary risks.

## CASH AND NEAR-CASH ASSETS

Once the firm has developed policies for the overall management of working capital, it can turn its attention to the three primary assets that provide liquidity: cash, receivables, and inventory. In this chapter, we will cover cash management; in the next chapter, receivables and inventory are covered.

In a financial sense, the term *cash* refers to all money items and sources that are immediately available to help pay a firm's bills. On the balance sheet, cash assets may be shown as cash, cash equivalents, or marketable securities. It is increasingly the practice to consider highly liquid short-term securities as an alternative form of cash. This is the case because most government and corporate securities can be liquidated in a matter of hours or minutes through a telephone call. The treasurer's office simply calls the bank or broker in the morning, and cash is available for disbursement by midday.

Three securities are widely used as short-term investments and alternative forms of cash. Each security offers different characteristics that make it suitable for different firms. These securities are described in turn.

## TREASURY BILLS

A *treasury bill* is an unconditional promise by the U.S. Treasury to pay to the holder of the bill a specified amount at maturity. Treasury bills are issued for short periods of time, normally 3, 6, or 12 months. Maturities on these bills are spaced 1 week apart, so that the financial manager can purchase the bills that will mature at approximately the same time as his forecast need for cash.

Two characteristics of treasury bills should be noted:

1. *Non-Interest-Bearing.* Treasury bills are sold at a discount on a bid basis, mainly to securities dealers and large commercial banks, who resell them to individuals and firms. For example, a bank may purchase a $10,000 face-value bill for $9,625 and immediately resell it to a firm for $9,675. If the firm holds the bill for a full 12 months, the Treasury will redeem the bill for $10,000. The difference between the $10,000 face value and the $9,675 discount price is the profit to the firm for holding the security.
2. *Most Secure and Liquid Marketable Security.* Treasury bills are the most secure and liquid kind of marketable security. With respect to security, the U.S. government guarantees their redemption. With respect to liquidity, there is a large, active market for the bills; they can be quickly and easily sold prior to maturity if the firm runs short on cash.

Closely related to treasury bills are treasury notes and bonds. These are issued for a longer period of time than bills and are interest-bearing. As notes and bonds near their maturities, they are similar to bills in the yield that they offer to the investor. They are frequently purchased in lieu of treasury bills.

## COMMERCIAL AND FINANCE PAPER

*Commercial paper* refers to short-term, unsecured promissory notes of large nonfinancial corporations. *Finance paper* refers to similar notes from finance companies. These notes are issued by firms needing cash for periods of 30 to 270 days. They are purchased by individuals or other firms with excess cash that have a desire to earn a higher yield than available from treasury bills. In return for the higher yield the firm accepts slightly greater risk and less liquidity.

Commercial paper is normally purchased through a bank or securities dealer, while the bulk of finance paper is purchased directly from finance companies. In both cases, the paper is often held to maturity, since a limited secondary market exists to transfer paper. In some cases, finance companies honor requests to buy back their paper, usually charging a fee for this service.

Commercial and finance paper have grown in importance over the years. At one time, conservative managements insisted that treasurers limit their short-term investments to treasury securities. The excellent repayment record and higher yields of paper from large, stable companies has encouraged firms to become more active in the paper market.

## NEGOTIABLE CERTIFICATES OF DEPOSIT

*A certificate of deposit (CD)* is a receipt for a time deposit at a bank or other financial institution. The bank agrees to pay the bearer the amount of the deposit plus a stipulated amount of interest at maturity. The certificates of *prime* banks (the nation's largest and strongest banks) have been very popular with financial managers for two reasons:

1. *Secure, High Yields.* Certificates of deposit are very secure investments with slightly higher yields than treasury bills, yields that are competitive with those on commercial and finance paper.
2. *Highly Liquid.* Unlike commercial paper, there is a large and active secondary market for certificates of deposit; they can be quickly sold before maturity, if desired.

In recent years, there have been many developments in the markets for certificates of deposit. The kinds and characteristics of certificates of deposit may be expected to change as banks compete with increasing sophistication for their share of funds in the nation's money markets.

## OTHER MARKETABLE SECURITIES

In addition to the three most popular securities for short-term investment of excess cash, a number of other securities are available to the corporate treasurer. Some of these are:

1. *Treasury Notes.* These securities are virtually identical to treasury bills with two exceptions. First, they have longer maturities since they are issued for periods of 1 to 7 years. The longer maturities do not eliminate them from consideration as short-term investments. This is true because they can be sold at any time in a relatively large secondary market. The second difference between treasury notes and bills involves the method of achieving a return. Bills are discounted from face value when sold; notes are interest-bearing.

2. *Federal Agency Issues.* A number of U.S. government agencies issue securities to finance their activities. These include the Federal Home Loan Bank, Federal National Mortgage Association (Fannie Mae), Government National Mortgage Association (Ginnie Mae), Federal Housing Administration, and Federal Land Banks. Unlike treasury securities, not all these issues are guaranteed by the U.S. government and may not be part of the public debt. Thus, they must be viewed as being somewhat more risky than treasury issues; consequently they offer slightly higher yields than comparable treasury securities. Although not all are guaranteed by the government, they are very secure investments. They also can be actively sold in secondary markets through securities dealers, as the case with treasury issues, and they have been gaining in popularity in recent years. The majority of government agency securities are issued with maturities of 1 year or less, but some issues are available with maturities of 10 years or more.

3. *Money Market Funds.* A money market fund is a professionally managed company that invests in marketable securities, such as those already mentioned. Instead of purchasing the security directly, an investor can purchase shares or interests in these funds. The yields to the investor will approximate the yields on the securities purchased by the fund. Because of a high degree of liquidity, competitive returns, and low transactions costs, money market funds have become an increasingly attractive investing vehicle for excess cash.

4. *Banker's Acceptances.* A banker's acceptance is an instrument used primarily to finance international trade. A draft is drawn by a company or individual ordering a commercial bank to pay some amount of money to the holder at some specified future date. When the order is accepted by the bank, it becomes an obligation of the bank. It can then be purchased at some discount from face

value and held as a marketable security. Maturities on banker's acceptances are usually from 30 days to 6 months, and a secondary market exists to trade them.

5. *Repurchase Agreements.* These involve the sale of securities by a dealer, bank, or other institution to a company with an accompanying agreement that the dealer will repurchase the securities at a stipulated price at a specified date. Called *REPOs,* these arrangements are widely used to provide a return from the investment of money for a short period of time, normally one day. The agreement could, as an example, be used to invest money over a weekend so that the funds do not sit idle in the bank for the 72 hours. In a repurchase agreement, the treasurer would invest temporarily idle cash and the dealer would obtain short-term funds.

## HOW LARGE A CASH BALANCE IS NEEDED?

The size of a firm's cash balance depends basically upon the three major reasons for liquidity. From the economist J. M. Keynes, we have learned that the firm's major needs for cash are the following:

1. *Transactions Needs.* A firm needs cash to carry out the day-to-day functions of the business. Just as the firm's level of operations affects working-capital requirements, it affects the need for cash. If the volume of sales increases, cash will be received from customers and will be expended for materials and wages in larger amounts. Adequate cash to cover these and other transactions allows the firm to pay its bills on time.

2. *Contingency Needs.* If the firm could perfectly forecast its needs for cash, it would not have to be concerned with unexpected occurrences or emergencies that require cash. Because this is not possible, the firm must be prepared for contingencies. If suddenly a major customer does not pay its bill, the cash inflows will be reduced below the forecasted level. The firm must have money to pay its own bills until the customer's check arrives. A supplier may be having difficulties and may be forced to eliminate the firm's credit purchases. The unanticipated elimination of credit may mean that the firm must pay cash to buy raw materials, a contingency need related to cash outflows.

3. *Opportunity Needs.* These involve the chance to profit from having cash available. For example, a supplier may have several can-

cellations of orders and may wish to move a large unwanted inventory of raw materials from his warehouse. If the supplier offers a large discount for cash purchasing of the materials, the firm will have the opportunity to realize a substantial savings on its purchases and, hence, additional profits from the sale of the finished goods.

In addition to these needs for cash, several important factors may be identified as affecting the size of the cash balance maintained by the firm.

### AVAILABILITY OF SHORT-TERM CREDIT

To avoid holding unnecessarily large balances of cash for contingency or opportunity needs, most firms attempt to make arrangements to borrow money in case of unexpected needs. One useful agreement between the firm and its bank is the *line of credit*, a formal or informal agreement for a bank to provide credit if requested. The bank may agree, for example, to supply up to $100,000 on 72-hour notice for maturities of 30 days to 1 year. The loan would be charged at the prevailing interest rate for its corporate customers whenever the request is made. With such an arrangement, the firm normally pays a slightly higher rate of interest than on long-term debt but has to pay interest only during the period that the money is actually used. Because a line of credit allows a firm to rely upon an already approved loan for unexpected needs, it reduces the size of the balance needed in cash and cash equivalents.

### MONEY MARKET RATES

The *money market* consists of the institutions and individuals who lend or borrow money as part of the normal course of business activity. The interest charged on any loan is affected by a number of factors, including the size of the loan and the credit rating of the borrower. Two factors have the greatest effect on interest rates. First, the availability of money is a key factor. If money is plentiful in the economic system compared to companies or individuals who need money, interest rates tend to drop. If money is scarce, interest rates are higher. Second, the policies of the Federal Reserve System influence interest rates. The Federal Reserve is responsible for managing the money supply in the United States. In order to achieve specific economic goals, the Fed may take specific steps to influence interest rates. Thus, interest rates may be rising when money is plentiful or falling when money is scarce.

How does the level of interest rates—high or low—affect the size of the cash balance maintained by a firm? If money will bring only a low return in the money markets, a firm may choose not to invest it. Since the loss of profit is small, it may not be worth the trouble to make the loan. Thus, the firm keeps excess cash in its checking account; this has the effect of increasing cash balances. On the other hand, if interest rates are very high, every extra dollar will be invested. High money-market rates attract funds from firms that otherwise would not invest for the short term.

## VARIATIONS IN CASH FLOWS

In addition to contingency needs, some firms experience wide fluctuations in cash flows as a routine matter. If a firm requires its customers to pay their bills on the 10th day of the month, it will receive a much larger cash inflow at that time than at other times during the month. This firm will have a larger average cash balance than a firm that collects its receivables throughout the month. If the city experiences a storm that delays mail for several days near the 10th of the month, the firm may be unable to meet its own obligations due at the same time. Another example is a firm whose main customers are small businesses with cash problems. This firm will experience many delays in payment. Some months the cash will arrive as expected. Other months, the firms will be slow to pay.

As a general rule, a firm with steady inflows and outflows can maintain a fairly uniform cash balance. The balance is also lower than for firms with widely fluctuating flows. The firm can more accurately predict its cash balances and has fewer difficulties with cash management.

## COMPENSATING BALANCES

If a firm has borrowed money from a bank, the loan agreement may require the firm to maintain a minimum balance of cash in its checking account. This is called a *compensating balance*. In effect, this requires the firm to use the services of the bank making the loan and gives the bank a guaranteed deposit of money on which it pays no interest. Another reason for a compensating balance is that the bank is expected to provide for certain *free* services for the firm. The interest-free deposit is the bank's compensation for its advice and assistance.

A requirement to maintain a minimum cash balance increases the amount of cash that the firm must hold. It may be argued that this does not, in fact, increase the firm's liquidity. Since the firm cannot write checks on the compensating balance, it does not really have liquidity from the funds.

## FORECASTING CASH FLOW

Once the financial manager has identified the firm's policies on cash-flow management, he must face the problem of predicting the amounts and timing of future inflows and outlays of cash. This is a difficult process for most firms because cash flows are affected by many factors and may involve numerous accounts, operating divisions, or even subsidiaries. But the stakes are high. The failure to prepare for the proper level of cash poses three risks to the company:

1. *Default.* The failure to pay interest or principal payments on a firm's borrowings is a *default*, a situation that may result in legal actions by the firm's creditors.
2. *Overdue Bills.* The failure to pay short-term obligations, such as payables, is less serious than default on loans but may result in a lowering of the firm's credit rating in the business community. This may be accompanied by higher interest rates when the firm applies for loans or may cause creditors to refuse to ship supplies on credit.
3. *Lost Savings on Purchases.* Inadequate cash may cause the firm to lose opportunities to make special cash purchases or to take generous trade discounts on purchases of goods.

In attempting to minimize these risks, the firm pursues the twin goals of cash forecasting, namely:

1. *Liquidity.* By predicting cash surpluses or shortages, the firm achieves liquidity—sufficient money in the bank to pay debts as they come due.
2. *Profitability.* Accurate cash forecasting achieves profits by allowing the firm to take profitable discounts on purchases, invest surplus funds, or reduce the costs of maintaining idle cash balances.

### CASH-FLOW FORECAST

A useful tool to deal with the forecasting aspect of cash-flow management is the *cash-flow forecast*. This is a schedule over time of cash inflows and outlays. Several characteristics of this tool are important:

1. *Focuses on Receipts and Payments.* The cash-flow forecast ignores profits or losses, sales, and costs as such. It concentrates on the cash receipts, regardless of when the sales were made. Thus, cash sales would be included, as would the collections on the accounts receivable, which were created by credit sales. With respect to debts of the firm, only the cash payments are included. The creation of liabilities does not involve a flow of cash and is omitted.

2. *Noncash Expenses Excluded.* It should be obvious that, since noncash expenses such as depreciation involve no payments, they are not considered in a cash-flow forecast. Cash payments to purchase machinery would be included.

3. *Joint Effort of Several Departments.* Although the cash-flow forecast is prepared under the direction of the financial manager, it represents a joint effort of several operating departments. The sales prediction, and indirectly the collections on receivables, is provided by the marketing personnel. The production expenses are calculated with production-department managers and cost accountants. Other departments are involved to the degree that they are responsible for receiving or disbursing cash.

## IMPORTANCE OF TIMING

Cash-flow forecasting is characterized by lags, which are delays between an action and the cash flow that results from the action. To illustrate the lags with respect to inflows and outlays, consider the following:

|  | *June 26* | *July 2* | *July 9* | *July 16* | *July 19* | *Aug 2* |
|---|---|---|---|---|---|---|
| Action | Sale, 30,000 net 20 | Purchase, 16,000 net 30 | Purchase, 24,000 net 10 |  |  |  |
| Cash Flow |  |  |  | +30,000 | −24,000 | −16,000 |

In this example, the credit sale on June 26 with trade terms of net 20 brings an inflow (indicated by the plus sign) on July 16. The two purchases result in outflows (indicated by the minus signs) on future dates that are appropriate to the credit terms.

In preparing cash-flow forecasts, it is particularly important to check the timing of flows and to identify all the lags. If, for example, the firm knows that a certain percentage of receivables is not collected on time, it should not expect the cash from 100 percent of receivables within the period specified by the terms of trade. If it does not consider lags properly, cash shortages may needlessly occur.

## CASH MANAGEMENT—AN APPLICATION

Earlier in this chapter, we noted that two processes were required in managing current assets: forecasting the needed funds and acquiring the funds. To illustrate these processes with cash management, we will use the example of the Copyrite Printing Company.

### SITUATION

The Copyrite Printing Company will start the second half of the calendar year with $3,000 in its bank account and $5,000 in the United Money Market Fund run by a local investment banker. Its cash sales and other income should be fairly steady over the next 6 months, as shown in the forecast in Table 8–1. Its collections on receivables are another matter. As a result of the summer business slump, Copyrite closes down for the last 2 weeks in July and 1st week of August. Collections fluctuate to reflect this period of inactivity. Wages and salaries, on the other hand, do not fluctuate, an arrangement that provides steady income to employees during the vacation period. Rent, utilities, and operating expenses are also relatively constant. Purchases of supplies and payments on payables reflect the closing. Materials and supplies must be replenished in the summer, and high cash outlays are incurred, as shown in the forecast. Overall, the table shows the cash pattern forecast by Copyrite for a 6-month period.

### PREPARING THE CASH-FLOW FORECAST

How did the forecast in the table develop? The financial manager began with the $8,000 of cash and equivalent on July 1, developed the inflows and outlays for July, and calculated the ending cash balance of $17,300. This amount was brought forward to the top of the August column and the process was repeated. Parentheses indicate negative cash balances at the end of September and October. By December, the firm is forecasting a positive cash balance once again.

**TABLE 8–1.**   Cash-Flow Forecast, 6-Month Period, Copyrite Printing Company.

| | *July* | *August* | *Sept.* | *Oct.* | *Nov.* | *Dec.* |
|---|---|---|---|---|---|---|
| **Cash on hand,** first of month | $ 8,000 | $17,300 | $ 5,100 | $(11,100) | $(2,300) | $ 7,500 |
| **Inflows** | | | | | | |
| Cash sales | 2,000 | 2,000 | 2,000 | 2,000 | 2,000 | 2,000 |
| Collections on receivables | 27,000 | 16,000 | 16,000 | 30,000 | 30,000 | 30,000 |
| Other income | 3,000 | 3,000 | 2,000 | 2,000 | 3,000 | 3,000 |
| Cash available | 40,000 | 38,300 | 25,100 | 22,900 | 32,700 | 42,500 |
| **Outlays** | | | | | | |
| Wages | 7,500 | 7,500 | 7,500 | 7,500 | 7,500 | 7,500 |
| Taxes, FICA | 1,500 | 1,500 | 1,500 | 1,500 | 1,500 | 1,500 |
| Supplies, payables | 11,500 | 22,000 | 25,000 | 14,000 | 14,000 | 12,000 |
| Rent, utilities | 1,200 | 1,200 | 1,200 | 1,200 | 1,200 | 1,200 |
| Other operating expenses | 1,000 | 1,000 | 1,000 | 1,000 | 1,000 | 1,000 |
| Cash outlays | 22,700 | 33,200 | 36,200 | 25,200 | 25,200 | 23,200 |
| **Cash on hand,** end of month | $17,300 | $ 5,100 | $(11,100) | $(2,300) | $ 7,500 | $19,300 |

## CALCULATING THE CASH SHORTAGES

Once the forecast has been prepared, the analyst can evaluate the firm's position. An important part of the evaluation deals with the adequacy of cash. A *safety level* may be defined as the minimum amount of cash needed to conduct the firm's business properly. It is the amount of cash and equivalents (not tied up in compensating balances) that the firm always has available to meet transactions, contingencies, and opportunity needs. In comparing cash on hand with the safety level, four conditions are possible:

1. *Surplus.* If the firm forecasts cash above the safety level as being available, the firm has a surplus. No additional cash is needed, and the manager may have the opportunity to invest excess cash when the time arrives.

2. *Optimum.* If the firm has approximately the same amount of cash forecast as the safety level, no additional cash is required. The term *approximately* has different meanings to different analysts but might be defined as a cash balance within 5 to 10 percent of the safety level.

3. *Shortage.* If the firm has a positive cash balance (it is not forecasting running out) but the balance is below the safety level, the firm has a shortage. The manager must make plans to cover the shortage.

4. *Deficit.* If the firm forecasts a negative cash balance, it cannot make all its planned payments. The manager must make plans for cash to cover the deficit as well as the shortage below the safety level.

How does the firm determine the safety level? In fact, there are two safety levels to consider:

1. *Operating Safety Level.* The firm needs cash or cash equivalents to conduct its business in an uncertain operating environment. The amount needed is determined by common sense and experience. In the case of Copyrite Printing, let us assume that the firm establishes a safety level of $10,000.

2. *Backup Safety Level.* In addition to the operating safety level, the firm needs protection against large fluctuations in cash flows. This is, in effect, a margin of safety in case of a large and unexpected problem or profit opportunity. The backup safety margin is usually obtained by holding marketable securities or by arranging a line of credit with a bank or financial institution. The volatility of the firm's business is the primary factor affecting the size of a backup safety level. With large cash fluctuations, a large backup source of cash is needed; with small fluctuations, a smaller backup is needed. For Copyrite, let us assume that a $20,000 backup safety level is adequate.

Table 8–2 shows the situation for Copyrite with the assumed safety levels. The firm faces operating shortages in August, September, October, and November and backup shortages in all 6 months. To remedy this

**TABLE 8–2.**   Surplus or Shortage Calculation, Copyrite Printing Company.

|  | July | August | Sept. | Oct. | Nov. | Dec. |
|---|---|---|---|---|---|---|
| Cash on hand, end of month | $17,300 | $ 5,100 | $(11,100) | $( 2,300) | $ 7,500 | $19,300 |
| Operating safety level | 10,000 | 10,000 | 10,000 | 10,000 | 10,000 | 10,000 |
| Operating surplus or shortage | 7,300 | (4,900) | (21,100) | (12,300) | (2,500) | 9,300 |
| Backup safety level | 20,000 | 20,000 | 20,000 | 20,000 | 20,000 | 20,000 |
| Backup surplus or shortage | $(12,700) | $(24,900) | $(41,100) | $(32,300) | $(22,500) | $(10,700) |

lack of liquidity, the firm should attempt to arrange a line of credit with its bank. It should inform the bank that approximately $20,000 of the line would be used in the summer to cover the operating shortage in September and another $20,000 would serve as a backup source of funds. Therefore, a total line of $40,000 would be requested.

Based on these numbers, the firm would probably borrow $20,000 at some point in August and repay it in November. The treasurer normally plans a little extra borrowing to avoid bothering the bank with a series of small loans and repayments. Any excess cash would, of course, be invested in the firm's money market fund until needed.

This example ties together the total scope of the cash-management function. With the aid of the cash-flow forecast, the financial manager is better able to identify future needs for cash. This does not mean that errors in projections will not be made. Rather, it means that the manager has attempted to determine the operating needs of the firm in the next period in order to prepare to deal with any likely cash shortages.

## MANAGING DISBURSEMENTS AND COLLECTIONS

The firm's system of cash management employs a combination of instruments, techniques, and services with a goal of achieving an efficient use of corporate funds. In this section, we will examine the major elements of a cash management system.

GOALS

In developing its overall system of cash management, the company's primary goal is to enhance the use of funds. Generally, this requires developing methods to speed up collections, to avoid unnecessary or early disbursements, and to minimize idle balances. A related goal is to minimize the operating costs of the system. A well-designed program of cash management should provide a greater return than the cost incurred for its operation. A final goal is to routinize the steps in the cash program and minimize the time and involvement of the company's management in dealing with recurring actions and procedures.

FLOAT

The term *float* is used to refer to the periods that affect cash as it moves through the different stages of the collection process. Four kinds of float, which are identified in Figure 8–3, can be identified:

1. *Billing Float.* An invoice is the formal document that a seller prepares and sends to a purchaser as the payment request for goods sold or services provided. The time between the sale and the mailing of the invoice is the *billing float*.
2. *Mail Float.* This is the time when a check is being processed by the post office, messenger service, or other means of delivery.

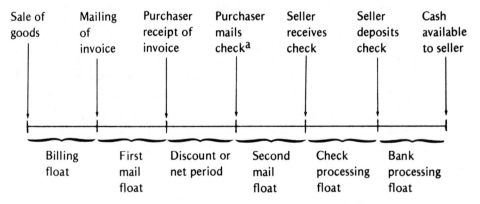

a Deliberate purchaser delays in making payments are omitted in this discussion.

**Figure 8–3** Differing Stages and Kinds of Float in Collection Process.

3. *Check-Processing Float.* This is the time required for the seller to sort, record, and deposit the check after it has arrived in the company's mailroom.

4. *Bank-Processing Float.* This is the time from the deposit of the check to the crediting of funds in the seller's account.

## CONTROL OF FLOAT

Control is the timely receipt and effective use of information on the status of the firm's cash receipts, disbursements, and balances. It requires complete and timely reporting on the varying aspects of the system to allow up-to-date monitoring of cash requirements. It also permits the firm to exploit opportunities that may arise in order to avoid shortages or problems that can be avoided. We will examine several different approaches to controlling the firm's float.

### Reporting System

A multidivision firm can conduct the bulk of its cash movements directly in its subsidiaries while receiving reports from the differing banks. A *depository bank* is one that receives the firm's cash; a *disbursing bank* is one that the firm uses for paying its bills. Commonly, these are the same bank for a subsidiary. These banks handle the firm's cash and should provide status reports either to the corporate headquarters or to the individual subsidiaries. This arrangement is shown in Figure 8-4. As a general statement, this figure shows a relatively unsophisticated approach to a cash-control system.

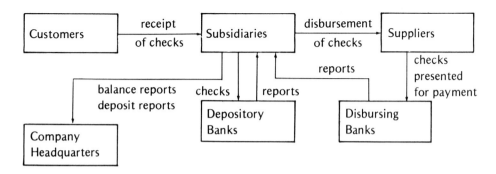

**Figure 8-4**  Regular Cash Management System for Company with Several Operating Units or Subsidiaries.

### Lockbox System for Collections

A *lockbox* is a post office box under the control of a bank. The bank providing the lockbox service collects the mail and deposits the checks directly into the firm's account. The bank then sends a copy of the checks along with letters or other materials in the envelopes to the company's accounting department. A lockbox system is shown in Figure 8–5.

The lockbox is the most widely used service for accelerating the collection of receivables. A lockbox system reduces the mail float because lockboxes can be established at different geographical locations and thus reduce mailing time. It eliminates the check-processing float completely because the firm does not record the checks until after they have been deposited. To ensure that check-processing time is minimized, some banks offering lockbox services pick up and process mail on a continuing basis and process checks on a 24-hour basis.

The lockbox bank frequently provides services related to the acceleration of cash flows. For example, the bank may send automated information on a computer tape that can be handled directly by the firm's computer. As another service, a bank could use optical scanning equipment to read invoices enclosed with checks. The invoice information can then be forwarded to the firm on tape for direct processing and updating of receivables files.

A final service of the lockbox bank is the *wire transfer,* which is the fastest way to transfer cash between banks. With a wire transfer, the cash

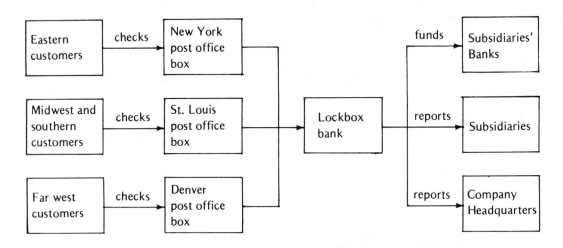

**Figure 8–5**   Model of a Lockbox System with Three Lockboxes.

is available immediately to the firm in the receiving bank. Two wire systems are available. The Federal Reserve System has established the *fed wire* to assist in the movement of funds between member banks. *The bank wire* system is a private service that banks can use to transfer cash, report securities transactions, or exchange credit information.

## Concentration Banking

*Concentration banking* is a system of centralizing corporate cash in order to control the firm's funds and minimize idle cash balances. Under this system, a *concentration bank* is designated to receive funds from lockboxes or any of the subsidiaries' depository banks. Wire transfer can be made automatically, according to instructions given by the firm. The concentration bank reports available balances daily so that the firm's treasurer can take maximum advantage of investment opportunities.

A second method of concentration banking employs a *depository transfer check* (DTC), which is a nonnegotiable demand deposit instrument used to transfer money from one bank account to another. The DTC can be paper or electronic; that is, it can be transmitted in the form of paper like other checks or it can be sent electronically. Unlike a wire, which is sent immediately during the day, the DTC is sent so that it arrives either at night or the next day.

Rapid processing can be achieved by using a DTC system. After the operating unit makes its deposit in a local bank or customers send checks to lockboxes, the amount of the deposit is telephoned to a central point such as the headquarter's accounting department or a data collection agency. When all deposit amounts are known, the totals are transmitted to the concentration bank, where depository transfer checks are prepared and processed for collection.

The choice between a wire or mail transfer in a concentration cash system depends upon two factors: the dollars involved and the cost of overnight money. The firm can determine whether to wire or use a DTC to transfer money by calculating the break-even point between the two alternatives. The formula is:

$$(\text{wire cost} - \text{DTC cost}) = (\text{cash balance}) \left( \frac{\text{annual money cost}}{365 \text{ days}} \right)$$

The use of this formula can be illustrated with an example. Suppose a firm can use wire transfer at $8 per wire or DTC transfer at $1 per DTC. Further assume that it can invest funds overnight in a money market fund to yield 13 percent. The break-even balance where it makes no difference whether wire or DTC is used would be:

$$(\$8 - \$1) = (\text{cash balance}) (.13/365) = \$19,654$$

For balances above this amount, the firm should wire the funds. For balances below $19,654, a DTC should be used to transfer funds.

The relationship between wire and DTC transfers can be expressed graphically using a form of break-even analysis. This is nothing more than using the preceding formula and calculating different break-even cash balances. Figure 8–6 shows the break-even graph when wire transfer costs $8 and a DTC costs $1. At an 8 percent overnight interest rate, amounts above $32,000 should be wired; at a 14 percent overnight rate, amounts above $18,000 should be wired.

## DISBURSEMENTS

The preceding discussion on lockboxes and concentration banking focused primarily on collections. Efficient disbursements are also a key element of total cash management. Most firms desire to maintain their reputations and good relations with suppliers by disbursing funds in a timely and accurate fashion. At the same time, a disbursement system

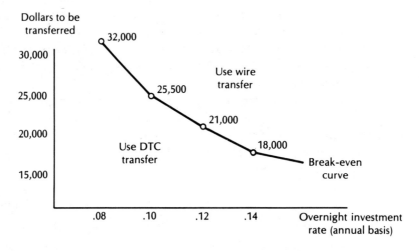

**Figure 8–6**  Break-Even Graph for DTC Versus Wire Transfer When Wires Cost $8 Each and DTC's Cost $1 Each.

should have a low operating cost, provide accurate management reports, and extend disbursement float where practical and reasonable.

### Zero-Balance Account Disbursing

A number of banks offer a *zero-balance account (ZBA)* service that allows the writing of checks against individual operating accounts containing no funds. The checks clear through regular banking channels and are then presented for collection. At the close of business, the bank automatically transfers funds from the company's concentration of master account to the different operating accounts in order to return each operating account to a zero balance.

A ZBA system offers a number of benefits to the firm. No idle cash balances are maintained in the various disbursement accounts. Also, the bank normally provides computerized reports to the firm's accounting department so that the treasurer can monitor cash balances on a daily basis and make the appropriate investment and cash-allocation decisions. Thus, ZBA offers decentralized disbursements with centralized control.

### Remote Disbursing

A second approach to extending disbursement float uses *remote disbursing,* where checks are drawn on banks in areas that do not receive frequent clearing service from the Federal Reserve. This system can include a zero-balance account feature so that the firm is not tying up funds before the checks are presented for payment. Remote disbursing creates some problems for the Federal Reserve System in its efforts to manage the money supply and is generally discouraged by the Fed and some banks. In spite of the discouragement, many firms continued to use some form of remote or controlled disbursement.

### Electronic Funds Transfer (EFT)

Increasingly, cash management systems will use *electronic funds transfer* techniques, whereby transactions are recorded on magnetic tape and cleared directly through an automated clearinghouse. This will eliminate the need to print checks, will minimize float, and will significantly reduce paperwork and related expenses. At the same time, banks expect that EFT systems will improve recordkeeping while minimizing processing errors.

## KEY TERMS

| | | |
|---|---|---|
| banker's acceptance | disbursing bank | remote disbursing |
| billing float | electronic funds transfer | repurchase agreement |
| cash-flow forecast | (EFT) | safety level |
| certificate of deposit | financial paper | shortage |
| commercial paper | float | surplus |
| compensating balance | line of credit | transactions need |
| concentration bank | lockbox | treasury bills |
| contingency need | mail float | treasury notes |
| default | money market | wire transfer |
| deficit | opportunity need | zero-balance account (ZBA) |
| depository bank | optimum cash balance | |
| depository transfer check | | |
| (DTC) | | |

## STUDY QUESTIONS

1. Why do we distinguish between permanent and variable working capital?
2. What are the goals of working-capital policies?
3. What is the most important factor affecting working capital? What are some other factors?
4. What two processes are accomplished in the management of working capital?
5. What are some factors that influence the amount of working capital needed by a firm?
6. Why might a financial manager invest in treasury bills rather than commercial paper or certificates of deposit? why commercial paper? why certificates of deposit? What are some other available marketable securities?
7. What are three cash needs faced by firms? What does each mean?
8. How does a line of credit help reduce the need for cash balances?
9. How do money market rates affect the size of the cash balance?
10. Do compensating balances increase the liquidity of the firm?
11. What is the difference between default and the failure to pay overdue bills?
12. What is the goal of cash-flow forecasting?
13. What kinds of transactions are the primary concern of cash-flow forecasts?
14. What is the difference between a shortage and a deficit? How does each compare to a surplus?
15. What is a safety level? What are two different types of safety levels?
16. What is float? What are some different kinds of float?
17. What is a lockbox system? concentration banking? a depository transfer check? a zero-balance account? remote disbursing? electronic funds transfer?

## PROBLEMS

1. The Cozzini and Wagner Company had sales of $95,000 in December. It expects sales of $70,000 in January. Sales levels should increase by 15 percent per month over the next 5 months. Cash sales will be 35 percent of total sales, the remainder collected in the following month. Other cash income is expected to be 5 percent of monthly sales. Wages and salaries will be constant at $35,000. Taxes will be 20 percent of wages and salaries. Rent, utilities, and operating expenses are constant at $4,000, $3,000, and $8,000 per month, respectively. Supplies purchased will be 50 percent of sales. The firm has $10,000 in its bank account and $25,000 in a money market fund. Prepare a 6-month cash flow forecast.

2. If the firm in problem 1 had an operating safety level of $10,000, what would be the operating surplus or shortage for each month? Suppose this firm also had a $20,000 backup safety level. What would be the backup surplus or shortage?

3. Suppose C & M Inc. can use wire transfers at $10 per wire or DTC transfers at $2 per DTC. Further assume that it can invest funds overnight in a money market fund to yield 15 percent. At what amount should the firm wire funds?

# CALCO ELECTRONICS COMPANY CASE
# Cash-Flow Forecasting

*This case tests the reader's ability to develop a basic cash-flow forecast for a firm and prepare a recommendation for backup financing over a 90-day period.*

A leading producer of electronic equipment and a major contender in minicomputers and calculators is Calco Electronics Company. The company, located in an industrial park in Akron, is one of the leading distributors of electronic instruments to large corporations. The company's business has been growing rapidly in recent years despite increased competition. The primary reasons for increased growth are technological improvements that have increased production capacity, an aggressive marketing effort, and a reputation for quality products and excellent service.

Matt Cooper, a financial analyst for the company, has been assigned the task of preparing a quarterly cash-flow forecast for the first quarter of 1985. After checking with marketing, he has received a monthly breakdown of actual and forecast sales for 1984 and 1985 as follows:

| *Actual Sales (1984)* | | *Forecast Sales (1985)* | |
|---|---|---|---|
| September | $4,500,000 | January | $5,500,000 |
| October | 4,500,000 | February | 6,000,000 |
| November | 5,000,000 | March | 6,500,000 |
| December | 5,500,000 | April | 7,000,000 |
| | | May | 7,800,000 |

Matt obtained information on the expected cash receipts and disbursements from the firm's accounting records. Over the past 3 years, Calco Electronics has averaged cash sales at 15 percent of the firm's total sales. The remaining 85 percent of sales become receivables. Sixty percent of these receivables are collected in the 1st month after the sale. Thirty-five percent are collected in the 2nd month after the sale. The remaining 5 percent are collected in the 3rd month after sale. The firm incurs a negligible bad-debt loss.

In addition, Calco Electronics has scheduled the sale of common stock to a large group of investors for April 1, 1985. This large group of investors has agreed to purchase $2 million worth of stock. However, the percentage of total stock represented by this $2 million will not be decided by the company until early January 1985.

Calco Electronics' cost of goods sold averages 63 percent of sales. The records indicate that 35 percent of this cost is paid during the month of the sale. Another 60 percent is paid in the month following the sale. The remaining 5 percent represents noncash expenses such as depreciation.

Matt Cooper has found that the firm expects general and administrative expenses of $750,000 per month plus 15 percent of sales. These are all cash expenses and are paid during the month of the sales.

In addition to recurring expenses, Matt is aware of additional requirements for cash in the next year. Calco Electronics is required to make a quarterly interest payment on $12.5 million of outstanding bonds that carry a 12 percent coupon. This payment is made in March. At the same time the firm is required to make a sinking-fund payment of $3 million as a part of a program to retire a bond. Matt has been informed that the final payment of $1 million on new machinery is due February 15, 1985.

Three additional disbursements are expected by Calco Electronics. The firm must make a monthly income tax deposit with the Internal Revenue Service. These should average $46,000 a month during 1985, reflecting a $6,000 increase from the previous year. Payment on a bank note of $1.2 million is planned in February. Also, if the firm declares its expected dividend, a $750,000 dividend payment will be made on March 31, 1985.

After gathering all the data, Matt Cooper has checked the cash situation with the company's accounting department and has learned that the cash balance as of December 31, 1984 should be approximately $1.2 million. Matt has decided that Calco Electronics Company should maintain a $2 million safety level throughout the first quarter of 1985, such cash to be invested in marketable securities with maturities of 2 weeks or less.

## Required

Prepare the cash-flow forecast for the first quarter of 1985. If the firm must borrow, make a recommendation on the size of the backup line of credit that should be arranged with a bank.

# 9

# Management of
# Receivables and Inventory

In addition to the management of cash and marketable securities, the financial manager must be concerned with two other important areas of working capital. First, sales made on credit involve the creation of receivables that must be converted to cash. Since the cash is not firmly in hand until the money is collected, receivables represent an exposure that must be analyzed and managed. Second, in order to have goods to sell, the firm must maintain inventories. Until the goods are sold, they also represent an exposure that must be managed.

In this chapter, we will examine the major principles of receivables and inventory management. We will begin with policies and techniques for managing receivables. Next we will discuss approaches to establishing credit limits. Then we will cover the benefits, risks and costs of holding inventories. Finally we will develop the components of an inventory management system.

## NATURE OF RECEIVABLES

*Receivables* are asset accounts representing amounts owed to the firm as a result of the sale of goods or services in the ordinary course of business. The value of these claims is carried on the balance sheet under titles such as *accounts receivable, trade receivables,* or *customer receivables.*

Accounts receivable play a major role in the conduct of business for most firms. The great majority of companies do not demand immediate cash payment when they sell goods to their regular, creditworthy customers. This is true both for firms engaging in retail trade and firms that sell primarily to other businesses. Because of this practice, most sales require the firm to carry a receivable for a customer for 10 to 60 days. Thus, receivables represent a significant current asset that must be financed on a continuing basis.

Most credit sales are made on *open account*, which means that no formal note is needed to recognize the debt. The only documents evidencing the sale are a purchase order, shipping invoice, and perhaps a billing statement. The open account facilitates the transaction of business and reduces the paperwork required for a credit sale.

Two major exceptions to the open account should be noted:

1. *Revolving-Charge Plan.* The charge-card phenomenon has become very popular for financing purchases of a variety of consumer items. American Express, Visa, MasterCard, and similar plans require an individual to provide detailed background information and a signed request for credit on demand. If the application is approved, a card is issued; it allows the individual to make credit purchases by showing the card and signing a draft. In a sense, the draft becomes a formal note acknowledging the debt.

   Firms that use revolving charge plans are able to collect the cash rapidly for their credit sales from the bank that provides the plan. The bank accepts the risk of nonpayment in most cases. In return for the rapid payment and transfer of risk of nonpayment, the firm pays a service charge to the bank of 2 to 6 percent.

2. *Financing of Consumer Durables.* Consumer durables are major items such as automobiles and appliances sold to individuals for their personal use. Since these items involve large sums of money compared to other individual purchases, the purchaser normally signs a formal note to finance them. By signing the note, the purchaser is allowed to pay for the items over a period of months or years. The note spells out the terms of payment, the interest charges, and the right of the holder of the note to reclaim the asset if payments are interrupted or halted. Normally the note is not carried as a receivable but is discounted to a financial institution. The institution holds the note and gives the firm cash for the sale of the item.

## PURPOSE OF RECEIVABLES

Every commitment of financial resources in a firm is expected to contribute to the goal of maximizing the present value of the firm in the marketplace. The commitment of funds to accounts receivable is no exception. In support of this objective, we can identify three goals of maintaining receivables (Figure 9–1):

1. *To Achieve Growth in Sales.* If a firm permits sales on credit, it usually can sell more goods than if it insisted on immediate cash payment. Many customers are not prepared to pay cash when they purchase. They prefer to write a check at a later time rather than carry a checkbook with them. They may want the bill to be sent to their accounting department, where it will be processed. In other cases, the purchase order may be transmitted over the telephone with instructions to send the goods and to bill for payment. Finally, many firms do not have the available cash to make immediate payment upon the receipt of goods. They must wait until they resell the goods before they have money to pay for them. Because of these and other factors, fewer sales could be expected if a firm eliminated its credit policies.

2. *To Increase Profits.* If the direct result of maintaining receivables is to increase sales, an indirect result is that the additional sales normally result in higher profits for the firm. This is the case when the marginal contribution or gross margin is greater than the additional costs associated with administering the credit policy. If the firm does not realize higher profits from its credit policy and receivables, it should consider an all-cash sales program.

3. *To Meet Competition.* As a defensive measure, most firms establish credit policies similar to the policies of competitors. It is a common practice in American business for the terms of trade to be identical throughout an industry, with wide variances in practices from one industry to another. In the same area, textiles may be purchased on terms of 2/10 EOM (a 2 percent discount if payment is made by the 10th day of the next month), whereas sta-

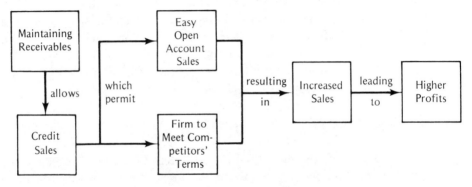

**Figure 9–1**  Flowchart Showing the Purpose of Maintaining Receivables.

tionery supplies carry terms of net 30. By adapting its terms of trade to the industry norms, a firm avoids the loss of sales from customers who would buy elsewhere if they did not receive the expected credit.

All three goals have a single purpose—to generate a larger flow of operating revenue, and hence profit, than possible without a commitment of funds to accounts receivable.

## COSTS OF MAINTAINING RECEIVABLES

As with all assets and operations, the willingness to allow credit sales involves certain costs. With respect to receivables, we can identify four major costs to the firm:

1. *Financing the Receivables.* Carrying accounts receivable ties up a portion of the firm's financial resources. These resources must be financed from one of three sources: (1) past profits retained in the business, (2) contributed capital from the owners, or (3) debt provided by creditors. In each of these cases, the firm incurs a cost for the use of the funds.

2. *Administrative Expenses.* To keep records on credit sales and payments, the firm accepts additional expenses. For example, it may hire a receivables bookkeeper, provide an adding machine and supplies, and allocate office space for a working area and files. In addition, most firms conduct investigations of potential credit customers to determine their creditworthiness. These and other expenses, such as telephone charges and postage, constitute the administrative costs of maintaining receivables.

3. *Collection Costs.* When an individual or company does not pay its bills on time, the firm must take additional steps to increase the chances for eventual payment. Such actions require the firm to incur collection costs. Money will initially be spent to prepare and mail reminders that the payment is overdue. If these are not successful, the firm may hire personnel or collection agencies to visit the delinquent customer and demand payment.

4. *Bad-Debt Losses.* After making serious efforts to collect on overdue accounts, the firm may be forced to give up. If a customer declares bankruptcy, no payment may be forthcoming. If the customer leaves the city or state, it may be too costly to trace him and demand payment. In these cases, the firm is forced to accept a bad-debt loss on the account. Most firms expect to incur bad-

debt losses in the normal course of business. High-risk customers may be the major source of these losses, but occasionally
a sound firm unexpectedly runs into liquidity problems and
eventually enters bankruptcy. These losses are properly viewed
as a cost of administering a credit policy.

## CALCULATING THE FINANCING COSTS FOR RECEIVABLES

When a firm is evaluating different credit policies, it must consider the
cost of financing additional receivables or the benefit from freeing funds
tied up in receivables. Two costs are commonly used:

1. *Cost of Debt.* If a firm reduces its receivables, the savings may be
   used to reduce debt. If it increases receivables, it may borrow to
   finance the addition. Thus, it appears logical to use the debt cost
   as the financing cost for receivables.
2. *Opportunity Cost of Funds.* When a firm frees or ties up funds, it
   gains or loses an investment opportunity. This is the correct cost
   of funds tied up in receivables. If the firm only considers the
   debt costs, it fails to recognize the impact on the firm of increasing or decreasing total debt. To avoid this shortcoming, the analyst should use the opportunity cost of funds in receivables
   decisions.

## CALCULATING CHANGES IN ADMINISTRATIVE EXPENSES

Collection costs and bad-debt losses are two components of administrative expenses affected by changes in the level of receivables. Techniques
for estimating likely changes in administrative expenses are as follows:

1. *Changes in Collection Costs.* The costs of collecting delinquent accounts are usually a fairly constant percentage of the total receivables. If receivables change by a fixed percentage, collection costs
   will change by a similar percentage. For example, a firm may
   have collection costs of $5,000 when its receivables are $80,000.
   This is a ratio of 5/80, or 6.25 percent. If the firm adopts a policy
   that increases receivables to $120,000, the collection costs would
   be expected to be (.0625)($120,000), or $7,500.

   The relationship between collection costs and receivables
   usually holds even though firms may be making sales to riskier
   customers when they change the terms of trade to attract more
   customers. It might be argued that the collection cost should be

higher with sales to customers with lower credit ratings. Two factors oppose this argument: (1) the higher costs are offset to some degree by economies that accrue with the larger collection activities; (2) the firm makes some efforts to hold collection costs in line with previous expenditures.

2. *Changes in Bad-Debt Losses.* If a firm increases credit sales by a fixed percentage, bad-debt losses will increase by a larger percentage in most cases. The amount of increase should be estimated by the marketing and finance managers most familiar with the firm's situation. For example, a firm may estimate $3,000 bad-debt losses on credit sales of $500,000. If its sales double as the result of a change in the terms of trade, bad-debt losses should increase by more than double, perhaps to $7,000.

3. *Changes in Miscellaneous Administrative Expenses.* The remaining administrative expenses change only slightly compared to the changes in sales and receivables. Additional bookkeeping is required for increases in sales, but to a smaller degree. As a guideline, changes in miscellaneous expenses are 5 to 10 percent of the percentage of change in receivables.

## FACTORS AFFECTING SIZE OF RECEIVABLES

We have already noted that the firm's receivables are a major component of its current assets. The approximate size of the receivables is determined by a number of factors. Three primary factors are the level of credit sales, the credit policies established by the firm, and the terms of trade.

### LEVEL OF SALES

The first major factor in determining the volume of receivables is the level of the firm's credit sales. Since the terms of trade are similar in most industries, one firm in the industry with a large volume of sales may have a larger level of receivables than a firm with a small volume of sales.

Sales levels can be used to forecast changes in receivables. If a firm predicts an increase of 20 percent in its credit sales for the next period, it will probably also experience a 20 percent increase in receivables.

### CREDIT POLICIES

The philosophy behind the firm's policies on extending credit determines the amount of risk that it is willing to undertake in its sales activities. If the firm has a relatively lax credit policy, it will experience a higher level of receivables than a firm with a more rigid policy. This is true for two reasons:

1. *Strong Customers Will Be Less Careful.* A lax credit policy encourages firms to settle their accounts without haste. Companies that otherwise pay their bills on time are not overly concerned if they are a few days late in paying bills to a firm that seems to accept slow payments as normal.
2. *Weak Customers Will Default.* With pressure to pay, weak firms are more prompt in payment. In the absence of this pressure, defaults on payments are more common. A number of firms may delay for long periods and then declare bankruptcy, resulting in bad-debt losses.

In establishing its credit policies, the firm tries to find a satisfactory middle ground between the excessive collection costs that accompany a highly aggressive policy and the excessive defaults and bad debts that accompany a lax policy.

### TERMS OF TRADE

The size of the receivables balance is closely related to the firm's credit terms. If, for example, a firm changes its credit terms from net 15 to net 30—a 100 percent increase—it could expect a 100 percent increase in the size of its receivables. Customers that previously had waited 15 days to pay their bills would take advantage of the new situation and wait an additional 15 days. Similarly, if the firm changed from net 30 to 2/10 net 30, many customers would take advantage of the 2 percent discount for prompt payment and would pay in 10 instead of 30 days. This would cost the firm the 2 percent discount but would reduce the volume of receivables.

## POLICIES FOR MANAGING ACCOUNTS RECEIVABLE

The firm should establish its receivables policies after carefully considering both the benefits and costs of different policies. Three major factors should be analyzed:

1. *Profits.* The firm should investigate different possibilities and forecast the effect of each on its future profits. The cost of funds tied up in receivables, collection costs, bad-debt losses, and

money lost with discounts for early payment should be compared with additional sales or losses of sales as a result of each proposed policy. These factors may be compared using an income statement in the marginal-analysis format. This is explained later.

2.  *Growth in Sales.* Sometimes firms are willing to accept short-term setbacks with respect to profits if a new policy enables the firm to increase its sales significantly. A firm may adopt a certain policy to gain a foothold in a previously closed market. Because growth is so important aside from profits, it should be viewed as a separate factor in determining receivables policies.

3.  *Possible Problems.* In spite of increased sales and profits, some policies may be accompanied by obvious and annoying problems. For example, by relaxing its credit terms, the firm may gain new customers. But if the firm's management must be concerned with collection policies and bad debts on a continuing basis, the firm might not be able to focus on its goals of increasing sales and reducing costs through other means. In such a case, the firm may choose to maintain tight credit with the intention of building sales without changing its terms of trade.

In any case, the final decision should be made after forecasting profits, considering the impact of the new policies on growth of sales, and evaluating the difficulties that will accompany the new policies. If a firm feels that the disadvantages of a liberal credit policy outweigh increased profits and sales, the policy should be rejected. If growth is important, policies that encourage expansion into new markets will be sought. If profits are the main concern, policies will be found to promote the chances for long-term profits.

## USE OF RATIOS

To help determine whether the firm is too strict or too lax in its receivables policies, the firm can compare its accounts-receivable turnover and average collection period with the same ratios for the industry as a whole or with ratios for similar firms. If the ratios differ significantly from other norms, it may be a sign of a poor or inappropriate policy. Further investigation should be undertaken.

## AGING OF ACCOUNTS RECEIVABLE

Another method of analyzing the appropriateness of receivables policies involves the use of an *aging of accounts.* An *aging schedule* is a tabular classification of receivables showing the length of time the accounts have been outstanding. The schedule may present the accounts by dollar amount percentage breakdown, or both, as in Table 9–1.

The table shows a firm that has a $600,000 balance of receivables on January 1. By checking the ledger cards for the accounts receivable, the financial manager discovered that $300,000 represented sales made in December, $150,000 sales in November, $100,000 in October, $20,000 in September, and $30,000 prior to September. Using $600,000 as 100 percent, the aging schedule displays the dollar amounts outstanding by month of sale and the percentage outstanding.

To use the aging schedule in the table properly, we must know the credit terms of the firm. If the terms for the firm were 2/10 net 30, 50 percent of the receivables would be current, 25 percent would be up to 1 month overdue, 17 percent up to 2 months overdue, and 8 percent more than 2 months overdue. With 50 percent of its receivables overdue, it would appear that the firm is lax in collecting its receivables. If on the other hand, the terms of trade were net 60, only 25 percent would be overdue—those from October and earlier. A 25 percent overdue figure still indicates problems. In either of these cases, the firm should review its credit and collection policies.

### RISK-CLASS APPROACH

To routinize the decision to extend credit, many firms use a *risk-class approach* to the approval of credit sales. The firm establishes a certain number of risk classes ranging from the strongest and most-established customers to the weakest firms. A separate credit policy is developed for each class. When a customer first applies for credit, the customer is investigated and placed into one of the classes. This eliminates the need to make a separate decision on extending credit each time the customer wants to make a purchase. Table 9–2 shows risk classes, a description of

**TABLE 9–1.**  Aging Schedule of Accounts Receivable.

|  | Receivables Balance on January 1 | Dec. | Representing Sales Made In Nov. | Oct. | Sept. | pre-Sept. |
|---|---|---|---|---|---|---|
| Dollar amount (000s) | $600 | 300 | 150 | 100 | 20 | 30 |
| Percentage of total | 100% | 50 | 25 | 17 | 3 | 5 |
|  |  | Current with terms of net 30 | Overdue with terms of net 30 |  |  |  |

**TABLE 9–2.**   Risk-Class Approach to Receivables Management.

| Risk Class | Description of Firm | Credit Policy |
|---|---|---|
| 1 | Large firms whose financial position and past record indicate virtually no risk. | Open credit up to certain limit without approval required. |
| 2 | Financially sound firms not supported by a detailed past record. | Open credit with approval for purchases in excess of certain amounts up to a specified limit. |
| 3 | Solid firms with past records that indicate some risk. | Limited credit line with frequent checks. |
| 4 | Not-too-solid firms that require close watching. | Restricted credit. |
| 5 | High-risk, weak firms. | No credit. |

the type of firm in each class, and a brief statement of the applicable credit policy.

As an example of the application of the risk-class approach, consider a firm in risk class 2 from the table. The firm is a relatively new customer and was placed in class 2 after a complete credit check. The credit limit for individual orders has been set at $70,000, and the outstanding balance has been limited to $225,000. The ledger card for receivables for this customer is as follows:

Acme Company—Accounts Receivable

| Date | Item | Charges | Payments | Balance Due |
|---|---|---|---|---|
| Jan. 20 | Invoice 963522 | $45,000 | | $140,000 |
| Jan. 23 | Invoice 963641 | 50,000 | | 190,000 |
| Jan. 25 | Invoice 963698 | 12,000 | | 202,000 |
| Jan. 25 | | | $30,000 | 172,000 |
| Jan. 28 | Invoice 963811 | 40,000 | | 212,000 |

On January 30, a purchase order is received from Acme for goods totaling $80,000. What does the firm do?

The accounting clerk compares the order with the file on Acme and discovers that the order exceeds the $70,000 single-purchase limit authorized for the firm. A check of the ledger card reveals that the order will place the total receivables balance above the $225,000 limit. The order is brought to the financial manager, who can take several possible actions:

1. *Raise the Limits.* The financial manager may decide that this firm deserves new credit limits. Since the original limits were imposed, the firm may have demonstrated that it pays its bills promptly. The credit limits can be raised and the firm considered for possible movement to risk class 1.

2. *Investigate Further.* The manager may wish to call the Acme Company and inquire about the order. Did it know that the order was larger than the limits? Does it want to be considered for higher limits? Will it supply information if needed to raise the limits? If the investigation reveals the credit should be extended, new credit limits may be set.

3. *Deny the Request.* If the financial manager has information that the request should not be granted, the purchase order will be returned with an explanation of why it was not filled. The manager may suggest that it be divided into two separate orders and be submitted after the balance is reduced.

## RECEIVABLES MANAGEMENT—THE PROFIT DECISION

In evaluating different proposals for credit or receivables policies, a major factor is the effect of each on the firm's profits. To analyze this effect, the firm prepares a pro forma income statement for each policy proposal. As an example of this technique, consider a firm that has a present policy of net 30 and is contemplating four possible policies: (1) no credit, (2) 2/10 net 30, (3) 2/10 net 60, and (4) net 60. A step-by-step approach will be used to analyze this decision.

### FORECASTING SALES WITH EACH ALTERNATIVE

The sales forecast is the first and perhaps most important step in preparing the income statement. If not reasonable, the forecast will distort all the following figures, including the final profit estimate.

The marketing department works closely with the finance department to forecast the likely level of sales with each alternative. In our example, the managers feel that the firm can achieve $3 million in sales if 30-day credit is offered. If the terms are extended to 60 days, an additional $500,000 is expected in sales. Many of these sales will be made to customers experiencing liquidity problems, and a high level of bad-debt losses would be expected. If no credit were offered, the marketing manager estimates a drop in sales to $2 million. This is based on detailed knowledge of the market, the prospective customers, and the fact that some of the firm's products are not available from other sources. Without credit, the marketing manager also feels that most customers would not be happy, because they are used to having time to receive and inspect the goods before preparing a check for payment.

## DETERMINING COSTS OF GOODS SOLD

The approximate percentage of the cost of goods sold to the sales volume is available from the cost-accounting department in most cases. At each sales level the percentage will drop because certain fixed costs such as depreciation will already be covered. In our example, the firm's cost of goods sold is estimated as follows:

1. *At $2 Million Sales Level.* Past data indicate that the cost of goods sold is approximately 60 percent of sales at this level.
2. *At $3 Million Sales Level.* The cost accountant estimates that this is the full production capacity for one shift. The efficient utilization of plant and equipment will drop the cost of goods sold to 55 percent of sales.
3. *At $3.5 Million Sales Level.* This level will require overtime work and higher maintenance costs on the machinery. The cost accountant estimates that the cost of goods sold will return to a figure of 60 percent of sales.

Using the cost of goods sold instead of variable costs is a modification of the marginal-analysis technique described earlier. If variable costs are readily obtainable, they may be used. The cost of goods sold and administrative cost breakdown are used because these figures are usually known or more easily estimated by the cost accountant for different sales levels.

## FORECASTING ADMINISTRATIVE COSTS, COLLECTION COSTS, BAD-DEBT LOSSES

The manager estimates $500,000 in administrative costs with any of the proposed credit policies. With the present policy, a part-time collection department is maintained. This costs approximately $100,000 per year, including the occasional use of outside collectors. If the terms of trade are extended to 60 days, a full-time collection effort, costing approximately $220,000, will be needed. With no credit terms, no collection costs would be incurred.

Estimating bad-debt losses involves a judgment by the credit manager based on past data. With terms of 30 days, bad debts should be something less than 2 percent of sales, or $50,000. At 60-day terms of trade, bad debts may be as high as 4 percent of sales, or $140,000.

## FORECASTING DISCOUNTS TAKEN

Since two of the possible policies involve discounts for payment within 10 days, the firm must estimate the number of customers who will take the discount. Past data and the experience of other firms in the industry may be used. Although difficult to estimate, at some point the credit manager forecasts a percentage of customers who will take the discount. The percentage is expressed in terms of the dollar value of sales, not the number of customers.

Once this percentage is forecast, the following formula is used to calculate discounts taken:

$$\text{discounts taken} = \left( \begin{array}{c} \% \text{ customers who will} \\ \text{pay in discount period} \end{array} \right) (\% \text{ discount}) \left( \begin{array}{c} \text{annual} \\ \text{sales} \end{array} \right)$$

If it is estimated that 70 percent of a firm's customers will take the discount and the terms are 2/10 net 30, a firm with $3 million in sales will have discounts taken of (.70)(.02)($3,000,000) = $42,000.

With terms of 2/10 net 60, it would be expected that a smaller percentage of customers would take the discount than at 2/10 net 30 because some customers would prefer the extra 30 days' use of the funds rather than the discount. If sales are $3.5 million and 50 percent of the customers take the discount of 2 percent, the discounts taken will be (.50)(.02)($3,500,000), or $35,000.

## FORECASTING THE AVERAGE COLLECTION PERIOD

In calculating the average collection period, we recognize that a portion of the customers will take the discount and a portion will not. Those taking the discount will pay in the discount period plus a few days. Of those not taking the discount, some will pay in the *net* period and some will be late. Most firms include a factor for late payments by customers.

Data from credit managers indicate that firms have become generally lax about paying on time, a trend accelerated by the high cost of money in the early 1980s. Although collection experience varies by industry, the relationship between required payment terms and actual cash receipts can be approximated from Table 9–3.

**TABLE 9–3.**   Terms of Trade and Actual Practices, as Reported by Credit Managers.

| Terms of Trade | Average Collection Period in Actual Practice |
|---|---|
| 2/10 | 18 to 22 days |
| net 15 | 22 to 26 days |
| net 30 | 47 to 53 days |
| 2/10 net 30 | 28 to 32 days |
| net 60 | 80 to 90 days |
| 2/10 net 60 | 60 to 70 days |

Slowness of payment is partly the result of lax collection practices and partly a fact of life in U.S. business today. In our examples, we will use the data in the table. In actual practice, a firm would use its experience to estimate the average collection period under different terms of trade.

### FORECASTING AVERAGE SIZE OF ACCOUNTS RECEIVABLE

If a firm has a steady level of sales throughout the year, we can forecast the average size of its receivables using a modification of a formula from ratio analysis. The modification is shown in Figure 9–2.

Using the guidelines in Table 9–3 and the formula in Figure 9–2 for the firm in our example, we get the average receivables balances as shown in Table 9–4.

### CALCULATING MARGINAL COST OF FUNDS TIED UP IN RECEIVABLES

The firm's income statement already includes a certain level of receivables financed from the various sources of funds. The new level of receivables

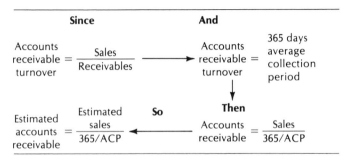

**Figure 9–2**   Estimating the Average Size of Accounts Receivables.

**TABLE 9–4.**   Estimated Receivables with Each Credit Policy.

| Terms of Trade | Average Collection Period from Table | Estimated Accounts Receivable Sales/(365/ACP) |
|---|---|---|
| 2/10 net 30 | 30 days | $\dfrac{\$3{,}000{,}000}{365/30} = \$247{,}000$ |
| net 30 | 50 days | $\dfrac{3{,}000{,}000}{365/50} = 411{,}000$ |
| 2/10 net 60 | 65 days | $\dfrac{3{,}500{,}000}{365/65} = 623{,}000$ |
| net 60 | 85 days | $\dfrac{3{,}500{,}000}{365/85} = 815{,}000$ |

calculated in the previous step will involve greater or lesser costs of tying up funds in receivables. The firm has $750,000 in debt financed at 14 percent. This is part of the financing for the $300,000 receivables with the net 30 terms. The cost of changing the level of receivables can be added to the $105,000 in existing interest if receivables are increased; the savings from reducing receivables can be decreased from $105,000.

To solve for the marginal cost of funds tied up in receivables, we must be given an opportunity cost of funds. Let us assume that it is 17 percent. With this rate, Table 9–5 shows the marginal benefit or cost with each proposed policy.

### ORGANIZING THE CALCULATION USING MARGINAL ANALYSIS

The final step involves organizing this data in an income statement. Table 9–6 is the statement based on our example.

**TABLE 9–5.**   Savings or Added Cost with Each New Policy On Terms of Trade.

| Terms of Trade | New Level of Receivables | | Original Level of Receivables | | Funds Freed or Tied up | | Opportunity Costs | | Savings or Added Cost |
|---|---|---|---|---|---|---|---|---|---|
| no credit | $ 0 | − | $411,000 | = | $−411,000 | × | .17 | = | $69,870 savings |
| 2/10 net 30 | 247,000 | − | 411,000 | = | −164,000 | × | .17 | = | 27,880 savings |
| 2/10 net 60 | 623,000 | − | 411,000 | = | +212,000 | × | .17 | = | 36,040 added cost |
| net 60 | 815,000 | − | 411,000 | = | +404,000 | × | .17 | = | 68,680 added cost |

**TABLE 9–6.**  Net Income Comparisons for 5 Credit Policies (000s).

|  | Net 30 | No Credit | 2/10 Net 30 | 2/10 Net 60 | Net 60 |
|---|---|---|---|---|---|
| Forecast sales | $3,000 | $2,000 | $3,000 | $3,500 | $3,500 |
| Cost of goods sold (either 55% or 60%) | 1,650 | 1,200 | 1,650 | 2,100 | 2,100 |
| Gross margin | 1,350 | 800 | 1,350 | 1,400 | 1,400 |
| Steady administrative expenses | 500 | 500 | 500 | 500 | 500 |
| Collection costs | 100 | 0 | 100 | 220 | 220 |
| Bad-debt losses | 50 | 0 | 50 | 140 | 140 |
| Discounts taken | 0 | 0 | 42 | 35 | 0 |
| Forecast operating income (EBIT) | 700 | 300 | 658 | 505 | 540 |
| Present interest on debt | − 105 | − 105 | − 105 | − 105 | − 105 |
| Savings or added cost on receivables | 0 | + 70 | + 28 | − 36 | − 69 |
| Forecast earnings before taxes | 595 | 265 | 581 | 364 | 366 |
| Taxes (40%) | 238 | 106 | 232 | 146 | 146 |
| Forecast net income | $ 357 | $ 159 | $ 349 | $ 218 | $ 220 |

**PROFIT DECISIONS**

The profits forecast in the table for the different credit policies indicate that the net 30 alternative will yield the most profit. It is closely followed by 2/10 net 30; the other alternatives are considerably less profitable. Based on the profit aspects of receivables management, one of the two choices (net 30 or 2/10 net 30) is preferable to the others.

Before the final decision is made, the profit forecasts will be compared with the growth prospects and the likelihood of additional problems. It is only after taking this total viewpoint that a decision should be made.

## ESTABLISHING CREDIT LIMITS

A major decision area in working-capital management is the establishment of credit limits for differing customers of the firm. In this section, we will examine techniques for dealing with two aspects of setting limits: (1) how to deal with numerous small accounts, where credit information is limited or where the sales level is too low to justify detailed evaluation of the customer's credit and (2) larger accounts, where a balance sheet and income statement are available.

HANDLING NUMEROUS SMALL ACCOUNTS

Many firms operate in industries where sales are divided among thousands of customers with average unit sales of $25 to $1,000. In this environment, the credit department lacks financial statements on most customers. An even greater problem is that it lacks the time to perform more than a cursory analysis of firms that are applying for credit. The credit manager may check with Dun and Bradstreet or a similar credit agency but, in most cases, the extension of credit is almost automatic.

These accounts are probably best handled with an overall credit policy that strives for a good balance between cash at risk and first-year profit. The exact policy varies with individual industries, but a simple rule of thumb might be that the first-year profit on an account should equal or exceed the maximum cash at risk at any one time.

As an example of following this credit policy, let us consider a firm selling products with a 20 percent profit margin. The credit department has received an application for credit with a limit up to $5,000. The potential customer is expected to purchase goods worth $30,000 annually if the credit is approved. On the basis of this information, the credit department calculates the first-year profit and cash at risk as follows:

| First-year Profit | | Cash at Risk | |
|---|---|---|---|
| Sales | $30,000 | Credit limit | $5,000 |
| Cost of sales (80%) | 24,000 | Less profit (20% margin) | 1,000 |
| First-year profit | $6,000 | Cash at risk | $4,000 |

In this example, the first-year profit exceeds the cash at risk, and therefore the credit application falls within the established policy.

The preceding approach will not be acceptable to many credit departments. It makes no attempt to come to grips with the basic creditworthiness of the customer. As a practical matter, it is both difficult and expensive to monitor the creditworthiness of hundreds or thousands of small accounts. The firm must recognize that the price of doing business using this policy will be moderate collection costs and bad debts. If, however, the collection costs and bad debts represent a dollar value of 5 to 10 percent of sales, the firm will earn a profit on these customers.

One additional guideline can be used in conjunction with this policy to reduce exposure further. The firm can set a policy that no credit will be extended to firms that have not been in business a minimum period, say 3 years. Since a large portion of businesses fail in the first 3 years, the firm will avoid this high risk from sales to new and untested firms.

## CREDIT LIMITS FOR LARGE ACCOUNTS

A totally different approach should be taken for establishing the credit limit for a large account. The first step is to require a credit application from the potential customer that contains a balance sheet and income statement for a recent period. In the discussion that follows, we shall use the financial data for Polwin Inc. to illustrate the process of evaluating the application and establishing the credit limit. The data are found in Tables 9–7 and 9–8.

**TABLE 9–7.**   Polwin Inc.—Balance Sheet (000s).

|  | This Year | | Last Year | |
|---|---|---|---|---|
| Cash | $    100 | | $     80 | |
| Marketable securities | 120 | | 120 | |
| Accounts receivable | 350 | | 200 | |
| Inventories | 580 | | 300 | |
| Total current assets | | $1,150 | | $  700 |
| Plant and equipment (less acc. depr.) | 1,500 | | 1,400 | |
| Land | 750 | | 750 | |
| Total fixed assets | | 2,250 | | 2,150 |
| Total assets | | $3,400 | | $2,850 |
| Accounts payable | 300 | | 60 | |
| Notes payable | 600 | | 220 | |
| Accrued liabilities | 100 | | 70 | |
| Total current liabilities | | 1,000 | | 350 |
| First mortgage | 200 | | 300 | |
| Second mortgage | — | | 200 | |
| Long-term bank notes | 300 | | 300 | |
| Total long-term liabilities | | 500 | | 800 |
| Common stock ($1 par) | 600 | | 600 | |
| Capital in excess of par | 400 | | 400 | |
| Retained earnings | 900 | | 700 | |
| Total equity | | 1,900 | | 1,700 |
| Total liabilities and equity | | $3,400 | | $2,850 |

**TABLE 9–8.** Polwin Inc.—Income Statement (000s).

|  | This Year |  | Last Year |  |
|---|---|---|---|---|
| Sales | $5,980 |  | $5,780 |  |
| Income from investments | 20 |  | 20 |  |
|    Total revenues |  | $6,000 |  | $5,800 |
|  |  |  |  |  |
| Beginning inventory | 300 |  | 400 |  |
| Total manufacturing costs | 4,200 |  | 3,200 |  |
| Less ending inventory | (580) |  | (300) |  |
|    Cost of goods sold |  | 3,920 |  | 3,300 |
|  |  |  |  |  |
| Gross profit |  | $2,080 |  | $2,500 |
| General and administrative expenses |  | 950 |  | 750 |
|  |  |  |  |  |
|    Operating income |  | $1,130 |  | $1,750 |
| Interest expense |  | 160 |  | 162 |
|    Earnings before taxes |  | $ 970 |  | $1,588 |
| Federal income taxes |  | 388 |  | 635 |
|    Net income after taxes |  | $ 582 |  | $ 953 |
|    Dividends declared and paid |  |  |  | 250 |

## Step 1. Maximum Credit Extended to Any One Customer

The first step in processing a credit application is to acknowledge the maximum credit that the firm is willing to extend to any one customer. The firm usually desires to limit its exposure to a single customer, no matter how creditworthy the customer may be. In our example, let us assume that our own firm will not grant credit in excess of $100,000 to any customer.

## Step 2. Two Broad Guidelines—Net Worth and Net Working Capital

Before beginning a detailed financial analysis, the credit analyst should check the financial statements for adequacy of net worth and net working capital. *Net worth* is defined as the equity on the balance sheet. *Net working capital* is defined as the excess of current assets over current liabilities. The firm should establish broad guidelines for comparing credit limits to both items. For example, the firm might want to limit credit to 10 percent of net worth and 20 percent of net working capital. If these broad guidelines are used, the analyst can make a quick check to determine the initial limits on Polwin's credit, as shown in Table 9–9. Using the lesser of the two guidelines in the table, Polwin qualifies for a $30,000 maximum credit limit.

## Step 3. Stable Liquidity Test

Since we have a balance sheet with two years' financial data, we can evaluate whether Polwin has sufficient liquidity to pay its bills on time. Four liquidity ratios can be used to overview the potential customer's cash and near-cash position:

### LIQUIDITY OVERVIEW—POLWIN INC.

| Ratio | Calculation of Ratio | This Year | Last Year |
|---|---|---|---|
| Current ratio | $\dfrac{\text{Current assets}}{\text{Current liabilities}}$ | $\dfrac{1,150}{1,000}=1.15$ | $\dfrac{700}{350}=2.00$ |
| Acid test | $\dfrac{\text{Current assets}-\text{inventory}}{\text{Current liabilities}}$ | $\dfrac{570}{1,000}=.57$ | $\dfrac{400}{350}=1.14$ |
| Accounts receivables turnover | $\dfrac{\text{Sales}}{\text{Receivables}}$ | $\dfrac{5,980}{350}=17\text{ times}$ | $\dfrac{5,780}{200}=29\text{ times}$ |
| Inventory turnover | $\dfrac{\text{Sales}}{\text{Inventory}}$ | $\dfrac{5,980}{580}=10.3\text{ times}$ | $\dfrac{5,780}{300}=19.3\text{ times}$ |
| | $\dfrac{\text{Cost of goods sold}}{\text{Inventory}}$ | $\dfrac{3,920}{580}=6.7\text{ times}$ | $\dfrac{3,300}{300}=11\text{ times}$ |

**TABLE 9–9.** Net Worth and Net Working Capital Guidelines.

| 10% of Net Worth Guidelines | | 20% of Net Working Capital Guideline | |
|---|---|---|---|
| Net worth from balance sheet | $1,900,000 | Current assets | $1,150,000 |
| | | Minus current liabilities | 1,000,000 |
| | | Net working capital | 150,000 |
| Times 10 percent factor | × .10 | Times 20 percent factor | × .20 |
| Maximum credit | $  190,000 | Maximum credit | $    30,000 |

Two tests of the liquidity position can be made. First, how does Polwin compare to average figures for the industry? Suppose the industry averages are:

| | |
|---|---|
| Current ratio | 1.8 |
| Acid test | 1.1 |
| Receivables turnover | 10    times |
| Inventory turnover | |
| With sales | 11    times |
| With cost of goods sold | 7    times |

Polwin basically meets or exceeds the averages for last year but is below the current-ratio and acid-test averages for this year.

Second, does the year-to-year comparison show that liquidity is strengthening, holding steady, or deteriorating? It appears that a major deterioration has occurred from one year to the next.

At this point, the analyst should return to the original balance sheet to determine what has caused the liquidity decline. The major problem appears to be the rise in current liabilities from $350,000 to $1 million. The analyst should make a note to ask the reason for this rise. The firm may have increased accounts payable to take advantage of low-cost trade credit and its current notes payable may have risen as a prelude to a long-term commercial bank financing that has not yet been completed. The firm may be unable to obtain long-term financing, and the heavy use of short-term financing may indicate that it is a serious credit risk.

## Step 4. Stable Profitability Test

Combining the balance sheet and income statement, we can use ratios to check the profitability of Polwin as follows:

### PROFITABILITY OVERVIEW—POLWIN INC.

| Ratio | Calculation of Ratio | This Year | Last Year |
|---|---|---|---|
| Profit margin | $\dfrac{\text{Operating income (EBIT)}}{\text{Sales}}$ | $\dfrac{1{,}130}{5{,}980} = .19$ | $\dfrac{1{,}750}{5{,}780} = .30$ |
| Return on investment | $\dfrac{\text{Operating income (EBIT)}}{\text{Assets}}$ | $\dfrac{1{,}130}{3{,}400} = .33$ | $\dfrac{1{,}750}{2{,}850} = .61$ |
| Return on equity | $\dfrac{\text{Net income}}{\text{Equity}}$ | $\dfrac{582}{1{,}900} = .31$ | $\dfrac{953}{1{,}700} = .56$ |

We now make the same two tests as for liquidity. First, assume that industry averages are:

| | |
|---|---|
| Profit margin | .15 |
| Return on investment | .20 |
| Return on equity | .09 |

We can conclude that Polwin is relatively profitable compared to the industry average. Second, the year-to-year test indicates a declining profitability. Going back to the financial statements, two factors appear to account for much of the decline. There was a sharp rise in cost of goods sold from $3,300,000 to $3,920,000 on a sales rise of only $200,000. Also, general and administrative expenses rose sharply from $750,000 to $950,000. The firm should be asked about these cost rises.

## Step 5. Liquidation Coverage

The next step is to determine whether Polwin has sufficient asset value to cover its liabilities in the event of forced liquidation. Even though we will extend credit only to firms that are likely to continue operations indefinitely, a liquidation coverage offers a view of the worst possible situation.

Assets can be sold at some fraction of their balance-sheet value. In some cases, as with land, the assets may be grossly undervalued compared to actual market values. In other cases, as with inventory, the reported value may far exceed the liquidation value in the event of a distress liquidation. Each firm will determine its own liquidation percentages. We will use 100 percent for cash, marketable securities, and land; 90 percent for receivables; 60 percent for inventory; and 40 percent for fixed assets. The result of the analysis for Polwin is given in Table 9–10. It thus appears, given our percentages of assumed realizable value of the assets in a distress situation, that Polwin would be able to cover all its liabilities in the event of a liquidation.

## Step 6. Gathering the Additional Information

The credit analyst must now get answers to the questions raised in the preceding liquidity and profitability analysis. The analyst also performs

**TABLE 9–10.**   Net Liquidation Value of Polwin.

| Category of Asset | Dollar Value for Polwin Inc. | Appropriate Percent | Assumed Realizable Value |
|---|---|---|---|
| Cash | $ 100,000 | 100 | $ 100,000 |
| Marketable securities | 120,000 | 100 | 120,000 |
| Receivables | 350,000 | 90 | 315,000 |
| Inventory | 580,000 | 60 | 348,000 |
| Plant and equipment | 1,500,000 | 40 | 600,000 |
| Land | 750,000 | 100 | 750,000 |
| Liquidation value of assets | | | $2,233,000 |
| Less 100 percent of liabilities | | | 1,500,000 |
| Net liquidation value | | | $ 733,000 |

such tasks as checking the credit rating of the firm with the appropriate credit agencies and calls the references listed in the credit application. If all appears satisfactory when this process is completed, the final step must be taken.

**Step 7. Establishing the Credit Limit**

In our preceding analysis, the restricting factor was $30,000, which represents 20 percent of net working capital in step 2. This appears to be reasonable as an initial credit limit. If this limit is not acceptable to Polwin's needs, the credit analyst should work with the sales manager, the credit manager, and other interested persons to determine whether an exception to policy should be made and a larger limit established.

## NATURE OF INVENTORIES

The second major topic of this chapter deals with the firm's efforts to manage its inventories. *Inventory* may be defined as the goods held for eventual resale by the firm. As such, inventories are a vital element in the efforts of the firm to achieve desired sales levels. Depending upon the nature of the industry and firm, inventories may be durable or nondurable, perishable or nonperishable, valuable or inexpensive. Whatever the nature of the inventories, the accounting process is careful to distinguish goods held for resale from other current assets, such as office supplies or furniture, which are not sold but are used to help the firm conduct its business. In this section, we will examine the basic nature of inventories.

## KINDS OF INVENTORIES

Three types of inventories may be identified:

1. *Raw Materials.* These are goods that have not yet been committed to production in a manufacturing firm. Raw materials range from iron ore awaiting processing into steel to electronic components to be incorporated into stereo amplifiers.
2. *Goods in Process.* This category includes those materials that have been committed to the production process but have not been completed. Goods in process include such items as components and subassemblies that are not yet ready to be sold.
3. *Finished Goods.* These are completed products awaiting sale. In a manufacturing firm, they are the final output of the production process. For retail firms and wholesalers, they are usually referred to as the *merchandise inventory.*

Many firms tie up considerable financial resources in each of the three types of inventories. Income tax data from the Internal Revenue Service show that inventories average approximately 20 percent of a manufacturing firm's total assets. For retail firms, the figure is closer to 30 percent. These percentages indicate that, for most product-oriented firms, investment in inventory is an important commitment of funds.

## BENEFITS OF HOLDING INVENTORIES

As shown in Figure 9–3, by holding inventories the firm is able to separate the processes of purchasing, producing, and selling. If firms were not willing to hold adequate raw materials and finished goods, purchasing would take place only when immediate production and sales were anticipated. When a customer signed a purchase agreement, the firm would not be able to offer rapid delivery. When the firm scheduled production runs, it would achieve none of the economies that longer runs provide. Inventories are used to provide cushions so that the purchasing, production, and sales functions can proceed at their own optimum paces.

In achieving the separation of these functions, the firm realizes a number of specific benefits:

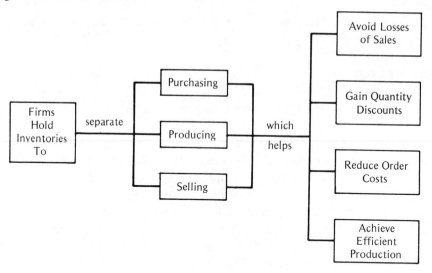

**Figure 9–3**   Why Firms Hold Inventories.

1. *Avoiding Losses of Sales:* If the firm does not have goods available for sale, it will lose sales. Customers requiring immediate delivery will purchase their goods from the firm's competitors, and others will decide that they do not need the goods after all, if they must wait for delivery. The ability of the firm to give quick service and to provide prompt delivery is closely tied to the proper management of inventory.

2. *Gaining Quantity Discounts.* If a firm is willing to maintain large inventories in selected product lines, it may be able to make bulk purchases of goods at large discounts. Suppliers frequently offer a greatly reduced price if the firm orders double or triple its normal requirement. By paying less for its goods, the firm can increase profits, as long as the costs of maintaining the inventories are less than the amount of the discount. For example, if the cost of storing an item for the extra time is estimated at $1 and the discount is $3, the firm benefits by $2 per unit from the quantity discount.

3. *Reducing Order Costs.* Every time a firm places an order, it incurs certain costs. Forms must be typed, checked, approved, and mailed. When goods arrive, they must be accepted, inspected, and counted. The invoice must be checked with the goods and then sent to the accounting department so that the supplier can be paid. The variable costs associated with individual orders can

be reduced if the firm places a few large rather than numerous small orders.

4. *Achieving Efficient Production Runs.* Once an assembly line or piece of machinery is prepared to receive certain raw materials and perform selected production operations, a *setup* cost has been incurred. This cost must be absorbed in the subsequent production run. If the setup cost is $200 and the run produces 200 units, the cost is $1 per unit. A longer run of 2,000 units would reduce the setup cost to $.10 per unit. Inventories assist the firm in making sufficiently long runs to achieve efficient production. If the firm had to change setups frequently, it would experience high unit costs of production.

Adequate inventories also protect against shortages that would delay or halt production. If the firm has scheduled a long run and begins production, only to discover a shortage of a vital raw material, the production may be halted at considerable cost to the firm.

## RISKS AND COSTS ASSOCIATED WITH INVENTORIES

When a firm holds goods for future sale, it exposes itself to a number of risks and costs. The effective management of inventory involves a trade-off between having too little and too much inventory. In achieving this tradeoff, the financial manager should realize that risks and costs may be closely related. Some costs, such as the purchase price of the goods, involve little risk and may be calculated in advance with some accuracy. Other costs, such as damage to the goods in the warehouse, are incurred only when a risk materializes. Because risks may be viewed as possible future costs, we will include them as cost items in the following discussion.

The benefits of holding inventory have already been discussed; basically it helps to reduce risks, hold down costs, and increase revenues. To examine inventory from the cost side, we will identify five categories of costs. The first three are direct costs, the costs immediately connected to buying and holding goods. The last two are *indirect costs,* the losses of revenues that vary with differing inventory management decisions.

The five costs of holding inventories are the following:

1. *Materials Costs.* These are the costs of purchasing the goods plus transportation and handling. This may be calculated by adding

the purchase price (less any discounts), the delivery charges, and the sales tax (if any).

2. *Order Costs.* These are the variable costs of placing an order for the goods. Each separate shipment involves certain expenses connected with requesting and receiving materials. Examples of these costs are the typing of the order and the inspection of the goods after they arrive. The fewer the orders, the lower the order cost will be for the firm.

3. *Carrying Costs.* These are the expenses of storing goods. Once the goods have been accepted, they become part of the firm's inventories. The following are examples of different kinds of carrying costs:

   a. *Storage Costs.* The firm must provide for storage space, usually through the operation of a warehouse or supply room. The firm must employ workers to move, clean, count, record, and protect the goods. All of these activities dealing with the physical holding of the goods are considered storage costs.

   b. *Insurance.* In spite of the best precautions, firms must protect themselves against such hazards as fire or accidents in the warehouse. Larger amounts of inventory require larger amounts of insurance. The insurance premiums represent a carrying cost on inventory.

   c. *Obsolescence and Spoilage.* When firms hold goods, they expose themselves to the possibility that the goods will not be salable when the time arrives. Obsolescence is the cost of being unable to sell goods because of current market factors deriving from changes in styles, tastes, or other factors. If a product is no longer wanted, the firm must sell it at a fraction of its value or destroy it. Spoilage occurs when a product is not salable because of deterioration during storage, such as foods that rot, plants that die, garments that are attacked by moths, candles that discolor, or chemicals that decompose.

   d. *Damage or Theft.* Although a firm makes every effort to protect goods against damage and safeguard items against pilferage, goods are damaged and stolen. A portion of these expenses are not covered by insurance and are losses to the firm. In some businesses, particularly retail stores and firms producing luxury products such as alcoholic beverages, damage and theft may constitute major carrying costs.

4. *Cost of Funds Tied up in Inventory.* Whenever a firm commits its resources to inventory, it is using funds that otherwise might be

available for other purposes. A portion of the inventory is financed by trade credit from suppliers and involves no cost. If the firm buys clothing on terms of net 30, the clothing may be sold before the firm must pay its supplier. The balance of the inventory must be financed from the firm's general funds and involves a cost. If the firm is considering an expansion of inventory and plans to borrow to obtain funds, the firm will have to pay interest on the additional debt. If the firm finances additional inventory through the sale of common stock, an opportunity cost is involved. The firm has lost the use of funds for other, profit-making purposes. Whatever the source of funds, inventory has a cost in terms of financial resources; excess inventory represents an unneeded cost.

5. *Cost of Running out of Goods.* Whenever a firm incurs shortages of products, it incurs costs. If the firm is unable to fill an order, it risks losing a sale. If the firm runs out of raw materials, it may force a costly shutdown of the production process. Adequate inventory helps reduce additional costs and lost revenues due to shortages.

## INVENTORY MANAGEMENT—MINIMIZING COSTS

The goal of effective inventory management is to minimize the total costs—direct and indirect—that are associated with holding inventories. The analyst estimates the different expenses with varying inventory levels and chooses the level with the lowest total cost. In Figure 9–4, this occurs at 30,000 units of inventory.

In the figure, we can see the rising slope to carrying costs as the level of inventory is increased. We also can see the declining order costs with higher inventory levels. The lowest total cost considers both the carrying costs and ordering costs. To complete the picture from the figure, we would need to include lost opportunity costs, that is, the cost of shortages. When the firm lacks inventory at critical times, it can produce lost sales and production delays. These considerations must be included in any analysis seeking to minimize costs in inventory management.

### MANAGE THE IMPORTANT ITEMS

In using the computer to minimize the costs of holding inventories, the major emphasis is on items considered important to the firm's operations. Not all inventory items deserve careful management. If a firm can

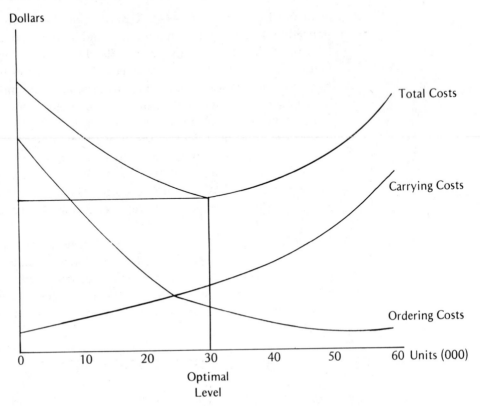

Figure 9–4   Minimizing Total Costs with Inventory Management.

run out of an item without losing a sale or disappointing a customer, it may waste money in keeping a close watch on the item. If the item accounts for relatively few sales in terms of dollars, the firm may spend more managing it than it returns in profits. The types of inventory items that might be considered important to a firm include the following:

1. *High-Cost Items.* If a firm is holding relatively expensive and valuable inventory, such as a jeweler or a firm making certain kinds of electronic components, the loss of a single item can be very costly. These items must be closely managed to prevent theft, breakage, or other loss.

2. *High-Volume or High-Profit Items.* If inventory is important because it accounts for a high volume of sales, it should be managed carefully. The same is true if the item has a high profit margin, and a shortage would be costly in terms of lost profits.

3. *Bottleneck Items.* In a production process, certain items are needed for many of the firm's finished goods. If these items are not available, production may be forced to shut down. As an example, an electronics firm may use the same transistor in a number of its components. If this single transistor were not available, most of the firm's production would be stopped. This bottleneck at a certain point in the production process could prove very costly.

## INVENTORY-MANAGEMENT SYSTEM

To manage its inventories effectively, a firm should use a systems approach to inventory management. A systems approach considers in a single model all the factors that affect the inventory. The model, called a *system*, may have any number of subsystems tied together to achieve a single goal. In the case of inventory systems, the goal is to minimize costs.

A system for effective inventory management involves three subsystems: economic order quantity, reorder point, and stock level. The computer brings these subsystems together to assist the financial manager in making inventory decisions. Each subsystem will be discussed in turn, and then all will be brought together into a single system.

### ECONOMIC-ORDER-QUANTITY SUBSYSTEM

The *economic order quantity (EOQ)* refers to the order size that will result in the lowest total of order and carrying costs for an item of inventory. If a firm places unnecessary orders, it will incur unneeded order costs. If it places too few orders, it must maintain large stocks of goods and will have excessive carrying costs. By calculating an economic order quantity, the firm identifies the number of units to order that results in the lowest total of these two costs.

A number of mathematical models are available to calculate the economic order quantity. Generally, they minimize a cost function, as shown in Figure 9–4. Numerous models exist, as the field of inventory management is highly developed and can be studied in college programs such as operations research and production management. Without getting into highly refined decision models, we can illustrate the concept of economic order quantity with a basic mathematical model. As with all models, we must carefully spell out the limitations and restrictions on its use. For our model, the constraints and assumptions follow.

1. *Demand Is Known.* Although it is difficult to predict accurately the firm's level of sales for individual items, the marketing manager must provide a sales forecast. Using past data and future plans, a reasonably accurate prediction of demand can often be made. This is expressed in units sold per year.

2. *Sales Occur at a Constant Rate.* This model may be used for goods that are sold in relatively constant amounts throughout the year. A more complicated model is needed for firms whose sales fluctuate in response to seasonal or other cyclical factors.

3. *Costs of Running out of Goods Are Ignored.* Costs associated with shortages, delays, or lost sales are not considered. These costs are considered in the determination of safety level in the reorder-point subsystem.

4. *Safety Stock Level Is Not Considered.* The safety stock level is the minimum level of inventory that the firm wishes to hold as a protection against running out. Since the firm must always be above this level, the EOQ formula need not consider the costs of maintaining the safety stock level.

The basic formula for calculating economic order quantity under these conditions is derived using calculus. We will not derive it but rather will give it as follows:

$$\text{EOQ} = \sqrt{\frac{(2)\,(U)\,(OC)}{(CC\%)\,(PP)}}$$

where 2 = mathematical factor that occurs during the deriving of the formula

  U = units sold per year, a forecast provided by the marketing department

  OC = cost of placing each order for more inventory, provided by cost accounting

  CC% = inventory carrying costs expressed as a percentage of the average value of the inventory, an estimate usually provided by cost accounting

  PP = purchase price for each unit of inventory, supplied by the purchasing department

As an example of the use of this formula, a firm anticipates 50,000 units of annual sales of a product that costs the firm $10. The cost of placing an order is $10, and the carrying costs have been estimated by cost accounting as 10 percent of the inventory value. The economic order quantity is

$$EOQ = \sqrt{\frac{(2)\ (50,000)\ (10)}{(10\%)\ (10)}} = \sqrt{\frac{1,000,000}{1}} = 1,000 \text{ units}$$

Thus, the firm should order 1,000 units if it places an order to minimize total order costs.

**Example:** A firm has forecast sales of 1,250,000 units of a product in the next 12 months. Each order would cost the firm $10. The firm pays $20 per unit for the product and estimates that inventory carrying costs are 20 percent of the inventory value. What is the economic order quantity for this product?

**Answer:** 2,500 units. The formula is:

$$EOQ = \sqrt{\frac{(2)\ (1,250,000)\ (10)}{(20\%)\ (20)}} = \sqrt{\frac{25,000,000}{4}} = 2,500 \text{ units}$$

**REORDER-POINT SUBSYSTEM**

An important question in any inventory-management system is, "When should an order be placed so that the firm does not run out of goods?" The answer, expressed in terms of units of inventory, is provided by the reorder-point subsystem.

The *reorder point* is the level of inventory at which the firm places an order in the amount of the economic order quantity. If the firm places the order when the inventory reaches the reorder point, the new goods will arrive before the firm runs out of goods to sell.

In designing a reorder-point subsystem, three items of information are needed as inputs to the subsystem:

1. *Usage Rate.* This is the rate per day at which the item is consumed in production or sold to customers. It is expressed in units. It may be calculated by dividing annual sales by 365 days. If the sales are 50,000 units, the usage rate is 50,000/365, or 137 units per day.

   A more complicated analysis may be used with computer-based reorder-point subsystems. The usage rate can be adjusted to reflect seasonal or cyclical factors and will result in differing reorder points at different times in the year.

2. *Lead Time.* This is the amount of time between placing an order and receiving the goods. This information is usually provided by the purchasing department. The time to allow for an order to arrive may be estimated from a check of the company's records and the time taken in the past for different suppliers to fill orders.

3. *Safety Stock Level.* This minimum level of inventory may be expressed in terms of several days' sales. The level can be calculated by multiplying the usage rate times the number of days that the firm wants to hold as a protection against shortages. As an example, the firm may wish to hold sufficient inventory for 15 days of production in the event its order for raw materials does not arrive on time. In this case, the safety stock level is 15 days, and it is calculated in terms of units of inventory by multiplying 15 times the daily usage rate.

   Determining the number of days of safety stock to hold involves a complex number of variables. Some questions that must be answered are the following:

   a. How much variation exists in the usage rate, and how likely is it that the firm will run out of the goods?

   b. How much does it cost in terms of lost revenues and profits if the firm runs out for 1 day? 2 days? 1 week?

   c. At what point are the carrying costs higher than the lost revenues due to shortages?

Mathematical models exist to assist the inventory manager in dealing with these issues. These models are beyond the scope of this chapter. We will assume that such models are used when appropriate to estimate the number of days of safety stock needed for a product.

To calculate the reorder point, the following formula is used:

$$\text{reorder point} = \left(\begin{array}{c}\text{usage} \\ \text{rate}\end{array}\right)\left(\begin{array}{c}\text{lead} \\ \text{time}\end{array} + \begin{array}{c}\text{days of} \\ \text{safety}\end{array}\right)$$

As an example of the use of this formula, consider a firm with a usage rate of 137 units per day, a lead time of 6 days, and a safety stock desired of 20 days of sales. The reorder point is

$$137\,(6+20) = 3{,}562 \text{ units}$$

In this case, the firm would place an order for the economic order quantity when the inventory gets down to 3,562 units.

**Example:** A firm expects annual sales of 9,125 units, desires to maintain a 12-day safety stock level, and has an 8-day lead time for orders. What is the reorder point for the firm?

**Answer:** 500 units. The formula is

9125/365 days = 25 units daily usage
25 (8 + 12) = 500 units

## STOCK-LEVEL SUBSYSTEM

This stock-level subsystem keeps track of the goods held by the firm, the issuance of goods, and the arrival of orders. It is made up of the records accounting for the goods in stock. Thus, the stock level subsystem maintains records of the current level of inventory. For any period of time, the current level is calculated by taking the beginning inventory, adding the inventory received, and subtracting the cost of goods sold. Whenever this

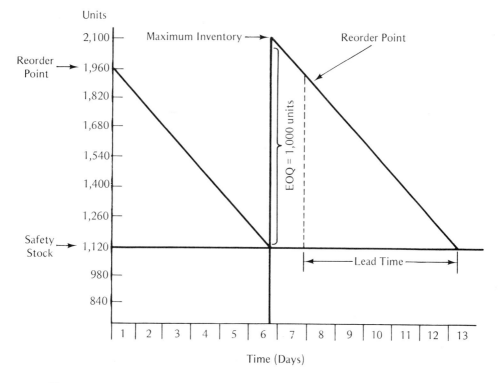

**Figure 9–5** Inventory-Management System.

subsystem reports that an item is at or below the reorder-point level, the firm will begin to place an order for the item.

## TOTAL SYSTEM

The three subsystems are tied together in a single inventory-management system. This may be illustrated graphically by charting units of inventory on one axis and time on the other. Figure 9–5 shows a system for an item with a reorder point of 1,960 units, a safety stock level of 1,120 units, and an economic order quantity of 1,000 units. The firm reorders at 1,960 units and continues to use its inventory until 1,120 units, when the order of 1,000 units arrives to return the inventory to 2,120 units.

The inventory-management system can also be illustrated in terms of the three subsystems that comprise it. Figure 9–6 ties each subsystem together and shows the three items of information needed for the deci-

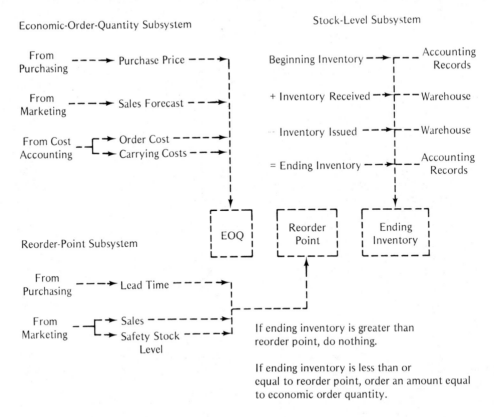

**Figure 9–6**   Three Subsystems of the Inventory-Management System.

sion to order additional inventory. The computer or analyst compares the level of the ending inventory with the reorder point for the items. If the ending inventory is less than the reorder point, an order should be placed for the economic order quantity.

## KEY TERMS

| | | |
|---|---|---|
| aging of accounts receivable | funds tied up in receivables | net worth |
| aging schedule | high-cost items | open account |
| bad-debt losses | high-volume or high-profit | order costs |
| bottleneck items |    items | receivables |
| carrying costs | indirect inventory costs | reorder point |
| collection costs | inventory | revolving charge plan |
| credit limit | inventory management | risk-class approach |
| days of safety |    system | safety stock level |
| direct inventory costs | lead time | setup costs |
| discounts taken | materials cost | stock-level subsystem |
| economic order quantity | net period | terms of trade |
| funds tied up in inventory | net working capital | usage rate |

## STUDY QUESTIONS

1. What is the role of accounts receivable in a firm's operation?
2. What is an open account? Is it widely used?
3. What are three reasons firms maintain receivables?
4. What are the major costs of allowing credit sales?
5. What two costs may be used in calculating the financing costs for receivables?
6. What are collection costs? bad-debt losses?
7. What three factors affect the size of a firm's receivables?
8. What are the three major items to be included in any decision to change a firm's credit policies?
9. How do ratios help a firm determine whether its credit policies are lax or strict?
10. Describe an aging schedule for receivables.
11. What is the purpose of a risk-class approach to receivables management?
12. How does a firm forecast sales with each possible credit policy?
13. Who determines the likely cost of goods sold at differing sales levels? How is it done?
14. Why is it important to forecast each of the following—(a) collection costs, (b) bad-debt losses, (c) discounts taken, and (d) cost of funds tied up in receivables—in estimating the future profits from different credit policies?
15. Why is a marginal-analysis format useful in making profit decisions on different credit policies?

16. What is one approach to handling numerous small accounts when making the credit decision? Should the same approach be used for large accounts?
17. What are two broad guidelines for establishing credit limits? How do we check for liquidity and profitability? Why do we also include liquidation coverage?
18. How does inventory differ from other items sold by the firm?
19. What are three types of inventories?
20. Why do firms hold inventories?
21. What is the relationship between risk and cost with respect to inventories?
22. What are the five major costs of holding inventories?
23. What are some examples of carrying costs?
24. What is the major goal of effective inventory management?
25. What kinds of items are managed in an effective inventory-management system?
26. What are the major assumptions of the basic EOQ model? How do these assumptions affect the usefulness of the model?
27. How does a firm calculate the reorder point for an item of inventory?
28. What is the goal of the stock-level subsystem? the reorder-point subsystem? the EOQ subsystem?
29. What items of information are supplied by the purchasing department with respect to an inventory-management system? by marketing? by cost accounting? by the warehouse?

## PROBLEMS

1. A firm has $500,000 in receivables on July 1. The sales represented by this amount were made as follows: $200,000 in June, $150,000 in May, $100,000 in April, and the remainder prior to April. If the terms are 2/10 net 30, what percentage is overdue?
2. For the firm in problem 1, if the terms are net 60, what percentage is overdue?
3. For the firm in problem 1, if the percentage of overdue receivables is 50 and the firm gives a 1 percent discount for payment in 20 days, what are the likely credit terms?
4. A firm has sales of $2.5 million with terms of net 30. If the firm changes to net 60, it is estimated that sales will change by 20 percent. Will the sales increase or decrease and why? What will the new level of sales be?
5. For the firm in problem 4, the cost of goods sold is 60 percent at the initial level and should be 55 percent at the second level with the new credit policy. In dollars, what would the cost of goods sold at each level be?
6. A firm expects sales of $1.2 million, and 60 percent of its customers will take the discount on terms of 2/10 net 30. Assume the average collection period is 20.4 days. What are the following—(a) discounts taken, and (b) average size of accounts receivable?

7. A firm expects sales of $4 million on terms of 2/10 net 40, and 40 percent of its customers will take the discount. Assume the average collection period is 32.8 days. What are the following—(a) discounts taken and (b) average receivables balance?

8. A firm is considering offering additional credit that will increase sales by $110,000 and will change net income from $80,000 to $75,000. Should the firm extend the credit?

9. For the firm in problem 6, if its cost of debt is 9 percent, what is the cost of funds tied up in receivables?

10. For a firm with an average receivables balance of $400,000, and a cost of debt of 12 percent, what is the cost of funds tied up in receivables?

11. A firm has credit sales of $250,000 and an earnings before interest and taxes of $45,000. Administrative costs are $55,000, of which $2,000 represents bad-debt losses and $4,000 is collection costs. The firm has $100,000 in debt at a cost of 5 percent. The firm is considering changing its credit policy from net 15 to net 30. It expects a 20 percent increase in sales as a result of the relaxed terms of trade. It also expects a 2 percent increase in miscellaneous administrative costs, a doubling of collection costs, and a tripling of bad-debt losses. The cost of financing the additional receivables will be 8 percent. Cost of goods sold will not change as a percentage of sales.

   Assume a 40 percent tax rate. Use Table 9–3 to determine average collection period of accounts receivables. (a) What is the likely current and new accounts receivables balance? (b) What will the forecast net income be with each policy?

12. A firm is considering changing its credit policy from net 15 to 2/10 net 30. Its sales should increase from $500,000 to $700,000; its cost of goods sold will go from 55 to 50 percent of sales. Miscellaneous administrative costs will remain steady at $40,000, but collection costs will increase from $20,000 to $30,000 and bad-debt losses will go from 5 to 10 percent of its average accounts receivables. Forty percent of the customers are expected to take the discount. The firm has debt of $200,000 at 6 percent, which includes the financing costs for the funds tied up in receivables. If the balance in receivables increases or decreases with the new policy, the extra cost of funds tied up will be calculated at the 10 percent estimated cost of the firm's new debt.

   Use Table 9–3 to determine the average collection period of accounts receivables. Assume a 40 percent tax rate. (a) What is the likely receivables balance with each policy? (b) What will the forecast net income be with each policy?

13. A firm expects sales of 600,000 units purchased by the firm for $10 per unit. The order cost is $30 and the firm's carrying cost as a percentage of the inventory value has been estimated at 20 percent. What is the economic order quantity?

14. A firm has sales of 200,000 units, which are sold at a constant rate throughout the year. The firm's EOQ has been calculated at 30,000 units, the safety stock level is 15 days, and the lead time for orders is 10 days. What is the reorder point for the firm?

15. A firm expects sales of 20,000 units, which cost the firm $2 per unit. It has a

policy of 20 days as a safety stock level and has estimated that carrying costs are 25 percent of inventory value. The firm's order costs are $32 and the lead time for orders is 10 days. What is the reorder point for the firm, and how many units should the firm order?

16. Diagram the system in problem 15 using the graph illustrated by Figure 9–5.
17. Diagram the system in problem 15 using the format in Figure 9–6. Replace words with numbers wherever possible.
18. A firm selling products with a 40 percent profit margin is operating in an industry where sales are divided among thousands of customers with average unit sales of $25 to $500. The credit department has received an application for credit with a limit up to $2,500. The potential customer is expected to purchase goods worth $15,000 annually if the credit is approved. Calculate the 1st-year profit and cash at risk. Should credit be extended to this customer?
19. A firm has received a credit application from Hi-Score, Inc. Over the years, Hi-Score has remained a strong company in its industry. What is the maximum amount of credit that can be extended to Hi-Score, assuming this firm has a $10,000 credit limit on any one account? Further assume a limit of 10 percent of net worth and 20 percent of net working capital. Following is the balance sheet of Hi-Score, Inc. (000s).

| Current assets | 750 | Current liabilities | 250 |
|---|---|---|---|
| Fixed assets | 1,500 | Long-term debt | 500 |
| Total assets | 2,250 | Total liabilities | 750 |
| | | Equity | 1,500 |
| | | Total liabilities & equity | 2,250 |

# ELKHART SUPPLY AND HARDWARE COMPANY CASE
## Management of Receivables

*This case exposes the reader to the concept of the management of receivables in terms of different credit policies.*

The Elkhart Supply and Hardware Company has operated from offices in Elkhart, Indiana, since 1923. The company was founded by Gregory Daniels and ran as a one-man business until his death in 1967. Since 1970, Nancy Daniels Marsden, the daughter of the founder, has been running the business with the title of president.

Shortly after taking over the management of Elkhart Supply, Nancy began to question a number of practices. She experimented with the distribution channels and discovered that she could eliminate many dealers' complaints while increasing her sales. By 1975, she felt comfortable with the firm's production activities and sales efforts. Nancy then began to work on cash-flow and credit problems. In 1978, Elkhart Supply sold most of its west coast accounts to a subsidiary of Inland Steel Company. The resulting cash from the sale of the accounts was used to modernize the firm's machinery for manufacturing plumbing supplies. Some of the funds were used to purchase new trucks for delivering supplies.

These actions brought about a considerable improvement in the service for midwest and east coast customers and produced strong increases in sales. The 1985 net sales are being forecast at $98 million if the firm continues to market its product aggressively.

At the end of 1984, Nancy began to analyze the impact of high interest costs on the firm's debt. She began with the firm's 1984 and 1983 balance sheets as prepared by the accounting department. She did not request a pro forma income statement because she liked to prepare her own. In addition to knowing the forecast sales figure, Nancy knew that the firm's cost of goods sold historically ran about 60 percent of sales. Of this 60 percent, labor accounted for 45 percent; raw materials, 25 percent; depreciation, 17 percent; and miscellaneous expenses, 13 percent of the cost of goods sold. She expected these percentages to continue into 1985.

Nancy looked through the forecast expenses for general and administrative items. The firm was budgeting three relatively stable items for 1985: office and marketing salaries, $4.5 million; sales expenses and promotion, $7 million; and miscellaneous overhead, 2.2 million. Nancy knew that if the firm did not borrow any additional funds, Elkhart would be facing a likely interest expense of approximately 4.5 million in 1985.

Having gathered these data, Nancy needed to look at collection costs and bad-debt losses not included in the general and administrative expenses. She decided to forecast these items using data from the firm's risk-class approach to receivables management. All accounts were assigned to a risk-class category, which was reviewed on a regular basis. The credit manager normally prepared an estimate of the collection costs and bad-debt losses to be allocated to each category of customer. These estimates were compared against actual data at the end of each year; for the past 5 years, the estimates proved to be fairly accurate. The bad-debt losses were based on actual losses over the past 6 years, and the collection costs were allocated based on the routine expenses and the special collection efforts required for each category of customer. The following table resulted from this process.

**ELKHART SUPPLY AND HARDWARE COMPANY**—Collection Costs and Bad-Debt Losses by Category of Customer

| Risk Category | Collection Costs as a Percentage of Sales | Actual Bad-Debt Losses as a Percentage of Sales |
|---|---|---|
| 1 | 1.0% | 0.5% |
| 2 | 1.5% | 1.0% |
| 3 | 2.0% | 2.0% |
| 4 | 5.0% | 3.0% |

During the period 1978 to 1984, Elkhart Supply Company sold on terms of 2/10 net 30. With these terms in 1985, the company could expect $30 million in sales to category 1 customers, $42 million in sales to category 2 customers, $24 million in sales to category 3 customers, and $2 million in sales to category 4 customers. Based on past data, 30 percent of the total customers would take the 2 percent discount while the others would pay in 35 to 40 days.

After giving some thought to the data, Nancy spoke with Fred Morris, the firm's sales manager. Two months earlier, Fred had suggested that the firm increase its terms of trade to 2/10 net 60. This would increase receivables, collection costs, and bad-debt losses but would provide additional sales and profits to the firm, according to Fred. Fred estimated that selling expenses would rise by approximately $2 million and the level of receivables would also rise. If the additional profits were high enough, it would make sense to borrow money at an average cost of 16 percent to finance these receivables. Nancy asked Fred whether the firm should also check out changing the terms of trade to net 15. This would reduce receivables and allow the firm to pay off a portion of the variable rate percent notes owed to Manufacturer's National Bank. These notes would probably average 16 percent a year, just like new debt. Fred indicated that selling expenses would probably drop by half a million dollars, but this savings would probably be more than offset by the loss of sales and profits. From this discussion, it appeared that Fred was willing to make an honest appraisal of both alternatives and he indicated that he would get back to Nancy with the effect of each alternative on sales.

## ELKHART SUPPLY AND HARDWARE CO.

### —Balance Sheet (December 31, 1984; 000s)

|  | 1984 | 1983 |  | 1984 | 1983 |
|---|---|---|---|---|---|
| Cash | $ 3,000 | $ 2,800 | Accounts payable | $ 5,000 | $ 5,500 |
| Marketable securities | 2,000 | 2,000 | Notes due (current) | 400 | 200 |
| Accounts receivable | 7,700 | 6,800 | Notes (noncurrent) | 1,200 | 1,400 |
| Inventories | 13,000 | 11,000 | Mortgage (14.2%) | 18,000 | 19,200 |
| Other current assets | 3,000 | 2,500 | Bank note | 14,000 | 14,000 |
| Plant and equipment | 79,900 | 82,000 | Common stock ($1 par) | 10,000 | 10,000 |
| (Accumulated deprec.) | (22,000) | (23,000) | Premium | 13,000 | 13,000 |
| Total assets | $86,600 | $84,100 | Retained earnings | 25,000 | 20,800 |
|  |  |  | Total | $86,600 | $84,100 |

Two weeks later, Fred sent Nancy the forecast for 1985 sales with each alternative.

A quick check of Fred's calculations indicated to Nancy that they were in agreement on the 2/10 net 30 alternative. Since this was the case, she felt that she could rely on his estimates for the net 15 and 2/10 net 60 alternatives. Nancy knew that the cost of goods sold would be approximately 73 percent at $98 million in sales; she estimated that they would run 75 percent at $81 million in sales and 70 percent at $120 million. The general and administrative expenses, with the exception of the collection costs, bad-debt losses, and selling expenses, were, in effect, fixed for 1985. Using these assumptions, she was prepared to develop the data and reach a decision on the appropriate credit policy for Elkhart Supply and Hardware Company. She decided in advance that she would not change policies unless the new policy gave either an increase in sales of 20 percent or an increase in profits of 10 percent. She preferred both but would accept a decline in sales of 25 percent or less as long as profits rose by 10 percent or more.

**ELKHART SUPPLY AND HARDWARE COMPANY—1985 Sales Estimate with Different Terms of Trade (000s)**

|  | Net 15 | 2/10 Net 30 | 2/10 Net 60 |
|---|---|---|---|
| Gross sales | 84,000 | 102,000 | 125,000 |
| Less returns | 3,000 | 3,400 | 4,700 |
| Less discounts | — | 600 | 300 |
| Net credit sales | 81,000 | 98,000 | 120,000 |
| by credit category: | | | |
| 1 | 26,000 | 30,000 | 30,000 |
| 2 | 37,000 | 42,000 | 48,000 |
| 3 | 18,000 | 24,000 | 24,000 |
| 4 | — | 2,000 | 18,000 |

**Required**

1. Prepare a separate schedule of collection costs and bad-debt losses with each policy. (Use Table 9–3 to determine average collection period.)
2. Using Fred Morris's estimates, what percentage of customers will take the discounts with each credit policy?
3. What is the likely size of the accounts receivable with each policy if the firm has relatively steady sales over the course of a year?
4. Prepare a 1985 pro forma income statement for Elkhart Supply with each of the three credit policies (use a 40 percent tax rate).
5. Using Fred Morris's estimates, what reaction do you think Fred expects from Elkart's competition if the new policies are adopted? what reaction from its customers?
6. (Optional) What is the likely size of the accounts receivable with each policy if the firm does 13 percent of its sales in each month from October to February and 5 percent per month from March to September?

# Credit Limits

*This case tests on skills in evaluating a credit request and reaching a credit decision.*

Dynatronics International is a large manufacturer of petroleum and rubber-based products used in a variety of commercial applications in the fields of transportation, electronics, and heavy manufacturing. In the southwestern United States, many of the Dynatronics products are marketed by a wholly owned subsidiary, Texas Electronics Company. Operating from a headquarters and warehouse facility in San Antonio, Texas Electronics has 850 employees and handles a volume of $75 million in sales annually. All but $5 million of the sales represents items manufactured by Dynatronics.

Arnold Holmstead is the credit manager at Texas Electronics. He supervises six employees who handle credit applications and collections on 4,500 accounts. The accounts range in size from $100 to $75,000. The firm sells on varied terms, with 2/10 net 30 as the most common of terms. Sales fluctuate seasonally and the average collection period tends to run 42 days. Bad-debt losses are less than 0.5 percent of sales.

Arnold is evaluating a credit application from Booth Plastics Incorporated, a wholesale supply dealer serving the oil industry. The company was founded in 1972 by Leland A. Booth and has grown steadily since that time. Texas Electronics is not selling any products to Booth Plastics and had no previous contact with Leland Booth.

Texas Electronics purchased goods from Dynatronics International under the same terms and conditions as Dynatronics used when it sold to independent customers. Although Texas Electronics generally followed Dynatronics in setting its prices, the subsidiary operated independently and could adjust price levels to meet its own marketing strategies. The Dynatronic's cost-accounting department estimated a 22 percent markup as the average for items sold to Texas Electronics. Texas Electronics, in turn, resold the items to yield a 15 percent markup. It appeared that these percentages would hold on any sales to Booth Plastics.

Texas Electronics incurred out-of-pocket expenses that were not considered in calculating the 15 percent markup on its items. For example, the contact with Booth Plastics had been made by Ron Sanders, the salesman who handled the Galveston area. Ron would receive a 2 percent commission on all sales made to Booth Plastics, a commission that would be paid whether or not the receivable was collected. Ron would, of course, be willing to assist in collecting on any accounts that he had sold. In addition to the sales commission, the company would incur variable costs as a result of handling the merchandise for the new account. As a general guideline, warehousing and other administrative variable costs would run 2 percent of sales.

Arnold Holmstead approached all credit decisions in basically the same manner. First of all, he considered the potential profit from the account. Ron Sanders had estimated 1st-year sales to Booth Plastics of $55,000. Assuming that Leland Booth took the 2 percent discount, Texas Electronics would realize a 15 percent markup on these sales since the average markup was calculated on the basis of the customer taking the discount. If Leland Booth did not take the discount, the markup would be slightly higher, as would the cost of financing the receivable for the additional period of time. In addition to the potential profit from the account, Arnold was concerned about his company's exposure. He knew that weak customers could become bad debts at any time and therefore required a vigorous collection effort whenever their accounts were overdue. His department probably spent three times as much money and effort managing a marginal account as compared to a strong account. He also figured that overdue and uncollected funds had to be financed by Texas Electronics at a 16 percent rate. All in all, slow-paying or marginal accounts were very costly to Texas Electronics.

With these considerations in mind, Arnold began to review the credit application for Booth Plastics.

## Required

1. What is the potential profit to Texas Electronics on the 1st year of sales to Booth Plastics?
2. If Arnold Holmstead approves a $10,000 credit limit, what is the maximum cash exposure at any one time for Texas Electronics?
3. Should the credit limit be approved? If not, how much credit should Texas Electronics give to Booth Plastics?

## SOUTHWESTERN CREDIT AGENCY Report on Booth Plastics Inc.

*March 10*

**Requested by:**  Credit Department, Texas Electronics.
**Requested on:**  Booth Plastics, Highway 6 Industrial Park,
Galveston, Texas.

**Business:**        Sale and service of plastic and metal supplies and components, primarily to Oil Industry. 1982 sales of $1.8 million, 16 employees.

**Market area:**     Texas Gulf.

**Number of accounts:**   Unknown, estimate perhaps 250.

**Management:**      Leland A. Booth, 96 percent owner and company president. No other significant shareholders.

**Background:**      Leland Booth started the business as a sole proprietorship in June 1972 with an estimated $60,000 in capital. Business was incorporated on June 30, 1980. Firm appears to be growing rapidly from estimated 1980 sales of $1.5 million.

### Dun and Bradstreet Report

Booth Plastics Inc.
12 Waterford Drive
Galveston, Texas
Tel: (713)446-2235
Leland A. Booth, Pres.
No other officers

Rating:  EE2
Payments discount—prompt
Sales:  $1,745,360
Worth:  $155,000
Employs:  14–16
Record:  Clear
Condition:  Good
Trend:  Steady to up

| Payments | High Credit | Owes | Term | Payment |
|----------|-------------|-------|-------------|-------------|
|          | $72,345     | 17,000 | 2/10 net 30 | discount |
|          | 27,200      | 4,500 | net 30 | discount |
|          | 2,432       | 2,432 | net 30 | net + 10 |
|          | 17,525      | 7,450 | 2/10 net 30 | net discount |

Financial statements not available. Booth (president) estimates current balance sheet as follows:

| | | | |
|------|------|------|------|
| Cash | $ 27,500 | Trade payables | 125,000 |
| Receivables | 225,000 | Notes due bank | 40,000 |
| Inventory | 175,000 | Taxes due | 12,000 |
| Fixtures | 25,000 | 3-year note | 110,000 |
| | | Equity | 165,500 |
| Total assets | $452,500 | Total | 452,500 |

Booth reports steady improvement in business for past 3 years: From $1,525,312 to $1,745,360. Current income statement is:

| Sales | $1,745,360 |
|---|---|
| Expenses | 1,374,000 |
| Commissions | 115,000 |
| Net income | 256,360 |
| To owner | 150,000 |
| To taxes | 85,000 |
| Retained | 21,360 |

History

Founded by Leland Booth in 1972. Largely borrowed funds. Has been increasing equity holdings on regular basis each year. Has expanded storage twice (1979 and 1982).

Wholesale supply dealer to energy industry, principally oil. Handles assorted plastic and rubber-related items for medium to heavy industrial use. Sixteen major customers; 200–300 small accounts. Facilities seem adequate for storage.

Financial position seems sound. First National Bank of Galveston offers secured line in five figures. No adverse reports.

# NORTH JERSEY CARPET COMPANY CASE

# Credit Decision

*This case is designed to test the reader's skills in evaluating a credit request and reaching a credit decision.*

On July 30, 1983, the North Jersey Carpet Company applied for a $50,000 loan from the main office of the National Bank of New Jersey. The application (Exhibit A) was forwarded to the bank's commercial loan department.

Harry Bernard, the president and principal stockholder of North Jersey Carpet, applied for the loan in person. He told the loan officer that he had been in business since February 1982 but he had considerable experience in flooring and carpets; he had worked as an individual contractor for the past 14 years. Most of this time, he had worked in Ohio, Indiana, and Michigan. He finally decided to "work for himself"; he formed the company with John Walters, a former co-worker. This information seemed to be consistent with the Dun and Bradstreet report obtained by the bank (Exhibit B).

According to Harry Bernard, the purpose of the loan was to assist him in carrying his receivables until they could be collected. He explained that a flooring business required him to expend considerable cash to purchase materials but his customers would not pay until the job was done. Since he was relatively new in the business, he did not feel that he could compete if he had to require a sizable deposit or payment in advance. Instead, he could quote for higher profits if he were willing to wait until completion of the job for payment. To show that his operation was sound, he included a list of customers and projects with his loan application (Exhibit C). He also included a list of current receivables (Exhibit D).

Harry told the loan officer that he had closely monitored his firm's financial status and that he had financial reports prepared every 6 months. He said that he would send a copy to the bank (Exhibit E). In addition, he was willing to file a personal financial statement with the bank (Exhibit F).

## Required

Prepare your recommendation on North Jersey Carpet Company.

## EXHIBIT A: Loan Application

NATIONAL BANK OF NEW JERSEY
211 Sinclair Lane
Morristown, New Jersey 07931

DATE 7/30/83

The undersigned hereby make application for a loan of _$50,000_ net repayable in __60__ monthly installments on the _5th_ day of each month beginning __SEPT. 1983__. The purpose of the loan is:

TO FINANCE RECEIVABLES

The collateral offered is:

LIEN ON RECEIVABLES; LIEN ON FIXED ASSETS

Business form:   CORPORATION      Kind of business:   COMMERCIAL
CARPETING/
FLOORING

Business address: 502 Main Street, Morristown, N.J. 07960 Tel: (201)762-4410

Previous loans with NBNJ?____Yes _X_ No. Year established _Feb. 1982_

Checking account at NBNJ? _X_ Yes____No.

Landlord: DANNEMANN REALTY Lease expires: 8.1.79 Annual rent: _$1,200_

Name of partners, officers,
   or stockholders

|                        | Title | Shares owned | Percent owned |
|------------------------|-------|--------------|---------------|
| 1. HARRY BERNARD       | Pres. | 998          | 99.8          |
| 2. ESTELLE BERNARD     | Wife  | 1            | .1            |
| 3. JOHN WALTERS        | V.P.  | 1            | .1            |

The undersigned represents, warrants, and affirms that the statements made in this application are true and correct and have been made to induce you to grant a loan to the undersigned with knowledge that you will rely thereon. The undersigned also affirms that no obligations exist by undersigned or company except as disclosed with this application.

   You are authorized to obtain any information you may require to verify this application. Any status changes by undersigned with respect to items furnished herein will be reported promptly to the bank.

*NORTH JERSEY CARPET CO., INC.*

*Name of Applicant*

*by: (s) Harry Bernard, Pres.*

## EXHIBIT B: Dun and Bradstreet Report

SIC 57 13 D-U-N-S 06-279-4140 May 9, 1983 Started: Feb. 82 Rating: EE2

| North Jersey Carpet Co., Inc.<br>502 Main Street<br>Morristown, N.J. 07960<br>Tel: (201) 762-4410<br>Harry Bernard, pres.<br>No other officers | SUMMARY | |
|---|---|---|
| | Payments | disc—ppt |
| | Sales | $349,340 |
| | Worth | $25,514 |
| | Employs | 4-10 |
| | Record | Clear |
| | Condition | Good |
| | Trend | Up |

| Payments | HC | Owes | Terms |
|---|---|---|---|
| | 2,000 | 800 | 15 |

Finance

On this date, Bernard, pres., submitted following statement dated March 31, 1983

| Cash | $ 7,236 | Accts. pay. | $128,058 |
|---|---|---|---|
| Accts. rec. | 120,553 | Notes pay. | 1,800 |
| Inventory | 22,140 | Taxes | 5,851 |
| Notes rec. | 7,924 | Current | 135,709 |
| Ppd. expenses | 720 | | |
| Current | 158,573 | | |
| Fix. & equip. | 4,900 | L-T liab.—other | 2,500 |
| Deposits | 250 | Capital stock | 1,000 |
| | | Retained earnings | 24,514 |
| Total assets | $163,723 | Total | $163,723 |

1982 annual sales $349,340; cost of goods sold $270,840; gross profit $78,500; operating expenses $26,446; net income $52,054. Prepared from statements by Lawrence and Whitlow, CPA. Prepared from books without audit.

Financial statement indicates a good condition exists. Majority of current assets centered in accounts receivable, sufficient to finance operations. Suppliers report a good account.

History

Incorporated N.J. Feb. 1982. Business started Feb. 1982 by Harry Bernard and John Walters. Relocated Aug. 1982 from 6545 Orange Avenue, East Orange. Starting capital $6,000 derived from $6,000 savings.

Walters, former partner, left business in 1982. No reason given. No compensation given to Walters.

H. Bernard born 1930, married. Prior to 1982 not residing in N.J.

Operation

Retails and installs carpets and floor coverings. Terms net 30. Sells to industrial concerns. Territory N.J. Rents 250 sq. ft. on 2nd floor of 2-story bldg. Premises are neat. Maintains 1,000-sq.-ft. warehouse space at 12 Seney Rd., East Orange.

### EXHIBIT C: Customers and Projects, North Jersey Carpet Co., Inc.

July 25, 1983

| *Completed and Billed* | *Job Location* | |
|---|---|---|
| Hankins Bros. | Singelton Storage | $9,249.28 |
| Hankins Bros. | Locklin Hardware Supply | 325.87 |
| G&R Construc. | Diesel Fuel Marketers | 1,666.00 |
| Saddle Brook | Town Hall Tile | 470.28 |
| Armine Inc. | Flooring | 685.30 |
| Dynamic Industries | Central Processing | 850.00 |
| Garbaldi Corp. | Whalen Products | 5,309.90 |
| John Reynolds | Lighting of Central Jersey | 2,350.00 |
| Central Processors | Carpeting and tile | 840.75 |
| Petroci Bros. | Bullock Interiors | 4,387.00 |

**In Process**

| *Contractor* | *Project* | *Amount* | *Billed* | *Receivable* |
|---|---|---|---|---|
| Lyons Bros. | Main office | $96,050.00 | $19,500 | $19,500 |
| Jannell Corp. | Pub. School 12 | 16,422.75 | 6,500 | 2,400 |
| Shoemaker Co. | Reception area | 4,860.00 | 4,860 | 4,860 |
| Midway Constr. | E. Orange Recreation | 41,876.23 | 27,420 | 16,510 |
| Hankins Bros. | Warehouse tile | 13,900.00 | 13,900 | 13,900 |

**Summary**

| | |
|---|---|
| Completed and billed, 1983 | $ 26,134.38 |
| In process, billed, 1983 | 72,180.00 |
| Accounts receivable, current but not shown in schedule above | 37,284.12 |
| Contracts not started | 358,847.90 |
| Contracts in process, not billed | 100,928.98 |
| Total | $595,375.38 |

## EXHIBIT D: Current Receivables, North Jersey Carpet Co., Inc.

July 15, 1983

| | | |
|---|---|---|
| Hankins Bros. | 7/15/83 | $ 22,150.37 |
| G&R Constr. | 7/02/83 | 1,666.00 |
| Saddle Brook | 6/29/83 | 470.28 |
| Lyons Bros. | 6/29/83 | 19,500.00 |
| Jannell Corp. | 6/29/83 | 6,500.00 |
| Armine Inc. | 6/29/83 | 685.30 |
| Dynamic | 6/17/83 | 850.00 |
| Shoemaker Co. | 6/17/83 | 4,860.00 |
| Garbaldi | 6/07/83 | 5,309.90 |
| Midway Constr. | 6/01/83 | 27,420.00 |
| John Reynolds | 5/24/83 | 2,350.00 |
| Central Processors | 5/18/83 | 2,600.00 |
| Fleming Realty | 5/04/83 | 14,350.00 |
| High Ridge Inc. | 4/23/83 | 6,421.60 |
| Roundtop Co. | 4/17/83 | 781.46 |
| Benjamin Bros. | 3/27/83 | 11,414.28 |
| Total | | $127,329.19 |

*Aging Schedule*

| | |
|---|---|
| 1–30 days | $ 56,681.95 |
| 31–60 days | 37,679.90 |
| 61–90 days | 21,553.06 |
| Over 90 days | 11,414.28 |
| | $127,329.19 |

## EXHIBIT E: Financial Statements, North Jersey Carpet Co., Inc.

Lawrence and Whitlow
CPAs
160 E. Linden Avenue
S. Orange, N.J. 07079

Ronald Lawrence, CPA                                    Tel: (201) 487-8560
Gilbert Whitlow, CPA

North Jersey Carpet Company, Inc.
502 Main Street
Morristown, New Jersey 07960

Dear Mr. Bernard:

In accordance with your request, we have prepared the following financial statements from the books, records, and inventories furnished without verification.

The financial statements submitted herein were not audited by us according to generally accepted auditing standards; therefore, we do not express an opinion on them.

Respectfully submitted,

(s) Ronald Lawrence, CPA

| Balance Sheet, North Jersey Carpet Company, March 31, 1983 | | |
|---|---|---|
| | As of March 31, 1983 | As of September 30, 1982 |
| Current assets | | |
| Cash | $ 7,236.00 | $ 3,523.00 |
| Accounts receivable-trade | 120,553.00 | 35,396.00 |
| Inventory at cost | 22,140.00 | 8,723.00 |
| Loans receivable | 7,924.00 | 0 |
| Prepaid expenses | 720.00 | 835.00 |
| Total current assets | $158,573.00 | $48,477.00 |
| Other assets | | |
| Auto equipment | $ 4,200.00 | $ 4,200.00 |
| Office equipment | 700.00 | 900.00 |
| Deposits | 250.00 | 220.00 |
| Total other assets | $ 5,150.00 | $ 5,320.00 |
| Total assets | $163,723.00 | $53,797.00 |

| Current liabilities | | |
|---|---|---|
| Notes payable—due in one year | $ 1,800.00 | $ 1,800.00 |
| Accounts payable | 128,058.00 | 32,080.00 |
| Payroll taxes payable | 5,851.00 | 1,518.00 |
| Total current liabilities | $135,709.00 | $35,398.00 |
| Long-term liabilities | | |
| Notes payable—due after 1 year | $ 2,500.00 | $ 3,000.00 |
| Equity | | |
| Capital | $ 1,000.00 | $ 1,000.00 |
| Retained earnings | 24,514.00 | 14,399.00 |
| Total equity | $ 25,514.00 | $15,399.00 |
| Total liabilities and equity | $163,723.00 | $53,797.00 |

### Statement of Profit and Loss
### North Jersey Carpet Company, Inc., March 31, 1983

| | 12 Months Ending March 31, 1983 | 6 Months Ending Sept. 13, 1982 |
|---|---|---|
| Sales | | |
| Gross sales | $350,090.00 | $119,048.00 |
| Less returns and allowances | 750.00 | 750.00 |
| | $349,340.00 | $118,298.00 |
| Net sales | | |
| Cost of sales | | |
| Beginning inventory | 450.00 | 450.00 |
| Purchases | 227,900.00 | 69,752.00 |
| Salaries and wages | 47,350.00 | 19,381.00 |
| Subcontractors | 14,500.00 | 4,600.00 |
| General and administrative—direct | 2,780.00 | 952.00 |
| Less ending inventory | (22,140.00) | (8,723.00) |
| Cost of goods sold | $270,840.00 | $ 86,412.00 |
| Gross profit on sales | $ 78,500.00 | $ 31,886.00 |
| Operating expenses | | |
| Payroll taxes and assessments | 12,045.00 | 7,443.00 |
| Union fees and insurance | 6,981.00 | 3,723.00 |
| General and administrative—indirect | 7,420.00 | 3,800.00 |
| Total operating expenses | $ 26,446.00 | $ 14,966.00 |
| Net profit for period | $ 52,054.00 | $ 16,920.00 |

## EXHIBIT F: Personal Financial Statement, Harry Bernard

As of July 31, 1983

Harry and Estelle Bernard, 206 Morris Avenue, Morristown, N.J. 07960
Occupation: Self-Employed
Business Address: 502 Main Street, Morristown, N.J. 07960

I/we make the following statement of all my/our assets and liabilities at the close of business on the date above:

| Assets | | Liabilities | |
|---|---|---|---|
| Cash on hand | $    850.00 | Notes to banks—secured | |
| Cash in banks (itemize) | 4,500.00 | Notes to banks—unsecured | |
| Securities—marketable | | Notes to others— | |
| Securities—not readily | | secured | $ 7,200.00 |
| marketable | 25,000.00 | Notes to others—unsecured | |
| Real estate | 58,000.00 | Mortgage payable | 37,500.00 |
| Automobile(s) | 5,000.00 | Other liabilities | None |
| Other assets | | | |
| Jewelry, furs, antiques, | | | |
| household, misc. | 25,000.00 | | |
| Total assets | $118,350.00 | Total liabilities | $44,700.00 |
| | | Net worth | $73,650.00 |

1. Banking relations: None in N.J.
2. Detail of notes: N/A
3. Life insurance: Self—$10,000 with Mutual of Omaha, term
                          Wife—$75,000 with Liberty Mutual, whole life
4. Securities: $25,000 face value of worth in North Jersey Carpet Co.
5. Real estate: Own home $58,000 value; mortgage $37,500, purchased in 1982 for $47,500
6. Age: 48 years; dependents: 3
7. Pledged assets: None
   Contingent liabilities: None
   Legal Actions: None
   Insurance coverage: Sufficient

I certify that the statements above are true and give a correct showing of my financial condition as of the date indicated. In the event of material change in my financial condition, I agree to notify the NATIONAL BANK OF NEW JERSEY immediately in writing.

signed this 31st day of JULY, 1983 (s)

## WESTERN OUTFITTERS CASE
# Management of Inventories

*This case requires the reader to analyze a firm's methods of inventory management using the appropriate tools.*

Western Outfitters had a good year in 1981 as it benefited from a period of high demand for western-style clothing throughout the United States. Bob Jordan, the operating vice-president, was particularly pleased to note that the firm had its best year ever. It was the largest distributor of western-style clothing in the Northeast, with substantial sales in New York and Pennsylvania. The warehouse in Suffern, New York, had shipped over $40 million worth of items in the 1981 fiscal year, and Bob hoped that the firm would do even better in 1982.

In late 1981, Bob was working on refinements to the 1982 budget. In looking at the figures, he decided that he would have to take steps to provide more warehousing in the New York area. The existing warehouse was overflowing; increasingly, there were bottlenecks when items were being moved in and out of the warehouse. The situation became acute on days when the firm was loading or unloading railroad cars. Boxes were piled in the aisles, a procedure that greatly slowed the loading or unloading. Since the railroad cars were leased on a daily basis, the company was experiencing costly charges for the use of the cars as storage facilities.

Bob Jordan was not certain that the company was handling its inventories most efficiently. He decided to focus on a single item to analyze whether the firm was overstocking or understocking inventory. He selected the Plainsman X13, a suede, broad-brimmed cowboy hat. Western Outfitters manufactured and distributed the Plainsman X13, which was its largest-selling cowboy hat. Some 9,000 of these hats were sold in 1981. These sales were fairly evenly distributed over the course of the year, which is the case with most of Western's line of headgear. The hat is carried on the firm's cost of goods sold at $30 and sold by Western at $42.

The Plainsman X13 is manufactured in production runs only when ordered by the warehouse. An average of 22 days is required from the time the hat is ordered until it is available at the warehouse. To guard against shortages, the warehouse supervisor maintains a 15-day safety level of the hat.

The firm's cost accounting department had additional information on the Plainsman hat. It costs the firm approximately 6 percent of the hat's cost to store it in the warehouse. This includes an insurance premium for protection against damage or theft of the product. Ordering the hat, including confirmation that the supply is actually running low in the warehouse, costs the firm about $50 per order. The average inventory of the hat in 1981 was 2,000 units and this level seemed to work fairly well.

In considering the inventory level and annual sales, Bob Jordan thought that the firm might be stocking too many units of the hat. He decided to analyze the situation. He knew that the average inventory should be calculated by the formula:

$$\text{average inventory} = \frac{\text{EOQ}}{2} + \text{safety stock level}$$

If this formula produced an inventory level lower than 2,000 units, it would be an indication that Western may be overstocking its overall inventory in its Suffern warehouse. If this were the case, a reduction of the inventory might be attainable which would allow the existing warehouse to handle all the items without slowdowns and costly delays. If the formula indicated that the firm was not overstocked, Bob would have the support that he needed to gain an approval for additional warehouse space.

### Required

1. What is the economic order quantity for the hat?
2. What is the safety stock level?
3. What is the reorder point?
4. Does Western Outfitters overstock or understock the hat? How many units should it stock on the average?

# 10

# Economics of Working Capital

As we saw in the previous chapter, it costs money when the firm ties up its resources in working capital. Usually the firm pays for raw materials, labor, and overhead items before the goods are sold. Similarly, funds tied up in receivables are not available for investment. The cost of financing working capital can be a significant financial expense of a business. In this chapter, we will develop techniques to measure the cost of financing receivables and inventory.

The decision to invest in receivables and inventory is basically a matter of risk and return analysis. By tying up money, the firm has an opportunity to earn profits. Will the investment in working capital pay off? This topic is covered in the chapter on capital budgeting. What does it cost to finance receivables and inventories? This topic is covered in this chapter. We will begin with the foundations of the time value of money. Then we will look at the effective costs of different working capital decisions. Finally we will calculate the effective cost of short-term debt financing for receivables and inventory.

## TIME VALUE OF MONEY

If given a choice between having a dollar today or a dollar next year, most firms and financial organizations would choose the dollar today. This is because money has a time value. If the firm had the dollar today, it could be invested so that the firm had more than a dollar in one year. This decision would not be so easy if the amount offered were larger next year than this year. As an example, if a firm could accept $10,000 today or $11,000 in 1 year, the firm would have to consider the time value of the two offers. If money had a 10 percent time value, the firm would be indifferent to the two alternatives. If the $10,000 were accepted, it could be invested to earn 10 percent so that the firm would have $11,000 in 1 year. If the $11,000 were accepted, the firm could borrow against it today and receive $10,000. When the money actually arrived, it would repay the loan plus $1,000 interest. This example assumes that the firm's borrowing and lending rates are the same, an assumption that may not be true. But the example shows that, at a 10 percent time value of money, a receipt of $10,000 today is worth exactly the same as a receipt of $11,000 in one year. This may be diagrammed:

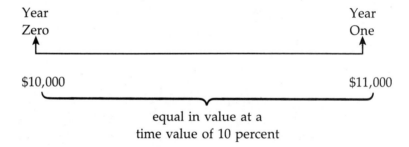

Year
Zero

Year
One

$10,000

$11,000

equal in value at a
time value of 10 percent

### COMPOUND VALUE AND PRESENT VALUE

*Compounding* is the mathematical process of calculating a future value of a payment or series of payments when interest is earned on the original principal and on the interest accumulated from prior periods. It differs from simple interest calculations, which occur only when interest is earned on the original principal. *Compound interest* calculations are used to determine the future value of money invested at a moment or moments in time.

The *present value* of a fixed sum of money or stream of money over a period of time is defined as today's value. It is calculated by discounting future payments or receipts by an appropriate discount factor. The process of finding present values is the inverse of compounding and is, once again, a recognition of the time value of money.

An *annuity* is a series of payments of a given amount for a specified number of years. As an example, if an installment loan requires the payment of $125.33 a month for 2 years, a 24-month annuity would exist. The compound value or present value of an annuity is calculated using the same conceptual basis as the compound or present value of single dollar amounts.

## FORMULAS FOR TIME VALUE OF MONEY

The following formula is used to calculate compound interest on a single investment when interest is compounded annually:

$$\text{prin}_n = \text{prin}_0(1+i)^n$$

where

$\text{prin}_n$ = future value of the investment at the end of $n$ periods;

$\text{prin}_0$ = original principal invested in year zero (at the start of the 1st year);

$i$ = interest rate as an annual percentage.

**Example:** A person deposits $5,000 in a commercial bank that pays 13 percent interest compounded annually. What will it be at the end of 1 year? 5 years?

**Answer:** $5,650 at the end of 1 year; $9,212 at the end of 5 years, as follows:

| Year | Principal | × | (1+i) | = | Ending Amount |
|------|-----------|---|-------|---|---------------|
| 0 | $5,000 | | | | |
| 1 | 5,000 | × | 1.13 | = | $5,650 |
| 2 | 5,650 | × | 1.13 | = | 6,385 |
| 3 | 6,385 | × | 1.13 | = | 7,215 |
| 4 | 7,215 | × | 1.13 | = | 8,152 |
| 5 | 8,152 | × | 1.13 | = | 9,212 |

Using the formula for each case, we get the same results:

1 year  . . . . $\text{prin}_1 = 5,000 \ (1.13)^1 = 5,650$

5 years . . . . $\text{prin}_5 = 5,000 \ (1.13)^5 = 9,212$

The formula for calculating the present value of a future dollar amount is the same formula as for compounding; the only difference is that we solve for a different value in the formula. The present value formula begins with the compound value formula

$$\text{prin}_n = \text{prin}_0(1+i)^n$$

and is changed to read

$$\text{prin}_0 = \frac{\text{prin}_n}{(1+i)^n}$$

which is commonly written

$$\text{prin}_0 = \text{prin}_n \left[ \frac{1}{(1+i)^n} \right]$$

**Example:** A borrower has agreed to retire a note that will mature in 4 years; $60,000 will be needed to retire the note. If money has a time value of 17 percent, what is the present value of the $60,000 that will be needed? (Stated differently, how much must be invested today at 17 percent compounded annually to have $60,000 in 4 years?)

**Answer:** $32,019, as follows:

$$\text{prin}_0 = \$60,000 \left( \frac{1}{(1+.17)^4} \right) = 60,000 \left( \frac{1}{1.8739} \right) = 32,019$$

The compound or present value of an annuity is calculated on the same conceptual basis as single receipts or payments. We have a series of "principals" and must reach a single beginning or ending value. As an example, suppose an individual deposits $1,000 a year for 5 years in a savings account. What would be the ending value of the deposits if interest were earned and compounded annually at 8 percent? The first question that we would ask is when the first deposit was made. If it occurred at the end of the first year, we would have a *deferred* or *regular annuity*. The first deposit occurs at the end of the first year (and thus draws no interest the 1st year) and the last deposit occurs at the end of the 5th year (and draws no interest at all). If, on the other hand, the first deposit occurred at the start of the 1st year (year zero), the last deposit would be made at the start of the 5th year (year 4). This would be called an *immediate annuity*. The two types of annuities have differing future values because the immediate annuity will earn more interest than the regular annuity. The two compound values are $5,866 and $6,335, as follows:

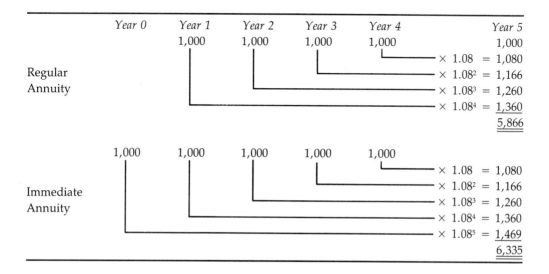

| | Year 0 | Year 1 | Year 2 | Year 3 | Year 4 | Year 5 |
|---|---|---|---|---|---|---|
| | | 1,000 | 1,000 | 1,000 | 1,000 | 1,000 |
| Regular Annuity | | | | | | $\times 1.08 = 1,080$ |
| | | | | | | $\times 1.08^2 = 1,166$ |
| | | | | | | $\times 1.08^3 = 1,260$ |
| | | | | | | $\times 1.08^4 = \underline{1,360}$ |
| | | | | | | 5,866 |
| | 1,000 | 1,000 | 1,000 | 1,000 | 1,000 | |
| Immediate Annuity | | | | | | $\times 1.08 = 1,080$ |
| | | | | | | $\times 1.08^2 = 1,166$ |
| | | | | | | $\times 1.08^3 = 1,260$ |
| | | | | | | $\times 1.08^4 = 1,360$ |
| | | | | | | $\times 1.08^5 = \underline{1,469}$ |
| | | | | | | 6,335 |

Calculating the present value of annuity is the reverse process to compounding. Each deposit would be divided by the appropriate factor $[(1+i)^n]$ to bring it to a present value. The present values of all the deposits are then added to get a total present value for the annuity.

The compound and present value of immediate and regular annuities can be calculated with a specific formula. The formula is more complex than the formula for single principals and is illustrated in Chapter 17. If desired, the reader may cover the formula in Chapter 17. The concept of the formula, however, is as shown. Each payment or receipt is adjusted, using a time value of money factor to a present or future value.

## COMPOUND OR PRESENT VALUE TABLES

One method of determining the present or future value of a payment or receipt of cash employs compound or present value tables. Tables 10–1 to 10–4 can be used to calculate the compound or present value of single receipts or annuities. To illustrate this process, let us consider an example of $100,000 invested at 14 percent compounded annually for 5 years. We will be seeking the future value of a single sum, so we use Table 10–1. With this table, the *compound value factor (CVF)* will replace $(1+i)^n$ in the formula for compound interest. At the 5-period row and the 14-percent column in Table 10–1, the CVF is 1.925. Substituting this for $(1+i)^5$ in the formula, we get

$$prin_5 = 100,000(1.925) = \$192,500$$

the same value as given by the formula.

Tables 10–2 through 10–4 are used in a similar fashion to Table 10–1. Note that the present value tables are set up so that all factors are multiplied times the principal amounts. It is not necessary to divide values when using compound or present value tables.

**Example:** A company wants to set aside $15,000 a year beginning at the end of the 1st year in an account that earns 12 percent compounded annually for a 6-year period. What is the present value of this annuity at a 12 percent cost of money? the compound value in 6 years?

**Answer:** Using Table 10–4, the present value is $61,665, as follows:

15,000 (4.111) = 61,665

Using Table 10–2, the compound value is
15,000 (8.115) = 121,725

**Example:** A receipt of cash is due in 4 years in the amount of $7,000. Money has a time value of 16 percent. What is the present value of the cash?

**Answer:** Using Table 10–3, the present value is $3,864: 7,000 (.552) = 3,864.

## PRESENT AND COMPOUND VALUE CALCULATORS

Once the credit analyst or loan officer has mastered the concept of present and compound value and the appropriate tables, it should be noted that most time value of money calculations in business are actually done with calculators containing built-in time-value-of-money formulas. These machines speed up the process of determining the present value of future cash flows and the future value of earlier cash flows.

Although there are variations in format, a time value calculator generally has five buttons, as follows:

where

$n$ = the number of periods in a financial transaction

$i$ = the interest rate or discount factor per period

PMT = payment or receipt amount per period; assumes equal payments

PV = present value or amount of money at the start of the financial time period

FV = future value or amount received or paid at the end of the financial time period

Since the formulas for present value and compound value are built into the calculators, the analyst can work solely with the calculator. The general rule is that three buttons must be pushed (including either $n$ or $i$) with values given by the analyst, and the calculator will determine the value of a fourth button. As an example, suppose a bank is due to receive a $20,000 payment on a note in 5 years. The current interest rates on similar notes is 18 percent. The analyst enters [$20,000 FV], [5 $n$], and [18 $i$] without using percents for the $i$ entry and then pushes the PV button to get the present value of the future receipt. The answer is $8,742.

ENTER      5                    18                                                                    20,000
ANSWER
                                                                        [8,742]

**Example:** A credit sale offers a $4,000 annual payment for 4 years when money is worth 16 percent. What is the future value of this stream at the end of the 4 years?
**Answer:** $20,266 is the FV when we enter [4 $n$], [16 $i$], and [4,000 PMT].

**TABLE 10-1.** Compound Value of $1 [($1) (CVF)].

| Period | 2.00% | 4.00% | 6.00% | 8.00% | 10.00% | 12.00% | 14.00% | 16.00% | 18.00% | 20.00% |
|---|---|---|---|---|---|---|---|---|---|---|
| 1 | 1.020 | 1.040 | 1.060 | 1.080 | 1.100 | 1.120 | 1.140 | 1.160 | 1.180 | 1.200 |
| 2 | 1.040 | 1.082 | 1.124 | 1.166 | 1.210 | 1.254 | 1.300 | 1.346 | 1.392 | 1.440 |
| 3 | 1.061 | 1.125 | 1.191 | 1.260 | 1.331 | 1.405 | 1.482 | 1.561 | 1.643 | 1.728 |
| 4 | 1.082 | 1.170 | 1.262 | 1.360 | 1.464 | 1.574 | 1.689 | 1.811 | 1.939 | 2.074 |
| 5 | 1.104 | 1.217 | 1.338 | 1.469 | 1.611 | 1.762 | 1.925 | 2.100 | 2.288 | 2.488 |
| 6 | 1.126 | 1.265 | 1.419 | 1.587 | 1.772 | 1.974 | 2.195 | 2.436 | 2.700 | 2.986 |
| 7 | 1.149 | 1.316 | 1.504 | 1.714 | 1.949 | 2.211 | 2.502 | 2.826 | 3.185 | 3.583 |
| 8 | 1.172 | 1.369 | 1.594 | 1.851 | 2.144 | 2.476 | 2.853 | 3.278 | 3.759 | 4.300 |
| 9 | 1.195 | 1.423 | 1.689 | 1.999 | 2.358 | 2.773 | 3.252 | 3.803 | 4.435 | 5.160 |
| 10 | 1.219 | 1.480 | 1.791 | 2.159 | 2.594 | 3.106 | 3.707 | 4.411 | 5.234 | 6.192 |
| 11 | 1.243 | 1.539 | 1.898 | 2.332 | 2.853 | 3.479 | 4.226 | 5.117 | 6.176 | 7.430 |
| 12 | 1.268 | 1.601 | 2.012 | 2.518 | 3.138 | 3.896 | 4.818 | 5.936 | 7.288 | 8.916 |
| 13 | 1.294 | 1.665 | 2.133 | 2.720 | 3.452 | 4.363 | 5.492 | 6.886 | 8.599 | 10.699 |
| 14 | 1.319 | 1.732 | 2.261 | 2.937 | 3.797 | 4.887 | 6.261 | 7.987 | 10.147 | 12.839 |
| 15 | 1.346 | 1.801 | 2.397 | 3.172 | 4.177 | 5.474 | 7.138 | 9.265 | 11.974 | 15.407 |
| 16 | 1.373 | 1.873 | 2.540 | 3.426 | 4.595 | 6.130 | 8.137 | 10.748 | 14.129 | 18.488 |
| 17 | 1.400 | 1.948 | 2.693 | 3.700 | 5.054 | 6.866 | 9.276 | 12.468 | 16.672 | 22.186 |
| 18 | 1.428 | 2.026 | 2.854 | 3.996 | 5.560 | 7.690 | 10.575 | 14.462 | 19.673 | 26.623 |
| 19 | 1.457 | 2.107 | 3.026 | 4.316 | 6.116 | 8.613 | 12.055 | 16.776 | 23.214 | 31.948 |
| 20 | 1.486 | 2.191 | 3.207 | 4.661 | 6.727 | 9.646 | 13.743 | 19.461 | 27.393 | 38.337 |
| 21 | 1.516 | 2.279 | 3.399 | 5.034 | 7.400 | 10.804 | 15.667 | 22.574 | 32.323 | 46.005 |
| 22 | 1.546 | 2.370 | 3.603 | 5.436 | 8.140 | 12.100 | 17.861 | 26.186 | 38.141 | 55.205 |
| 23 | 1.577 | 2.465 | 3.820 | 5.871 | 8.954 | 13.552 | 20.361 | 30.376 | 45.007 | 66.247 |
| 24 | 1.608 | 2.563 | 4.049 | 6.341 | 9.850 | 15.178 | 23.212 | 35.236 | 53.108 | 79.496 |
| 25 | 1.641 | 2.666 | 4.292 | 6.848 | 10.834 | 17.000 | 26.461 | 40.874 | 62.667 | 95.395 |
| 30 | 1.811 | 3.243 | 5.743 | 10.062 | 17.449 | 29.960 | 50.949 | 85.849 | 143.367 | 237.373 |

**TABLE 10–2.** Compound Value of an Annuity (Regular) of $1 [($1) (CVF$_a$)].

| Period | 2.00% | 4.00% | 6.00% | 8.00% | 10.00% | 12.00% | 14.00% | 16.00% | 18.00% | 20.00% |
|---|---|---|---|---|---|---|---|---|---|---|
| 1 | 1.000 | 1.000 | 1.000 | 1.000 | 1.000 | 1.000 | 1.000 | 1.000 | 1.000 | 1.000 |
| 2 | 2.020 | 2.040 | 2.060 | 2.080 | 2.100 | 2.120 | 2.140 | 2.160 | 2.180 | 2.200 |
| 3 | 3.060 | 3.122 | 3.184 | 3.246 | 3.310 | 3.374 | 3.440 | 3.506 | 3.572 | 3.640 |
| 4 | 4.122 | 4.246 | 4.375 | 4.506 | 4.641 | 4.779 | 4.921 | 5.066 | 5.215 | 5.368 |
| 5 | 5.204 | 5.416 | 5.637 | 5.867 | 6.105 | 6.353 | 6.610 | 6.877 | 7.154 | 7.442 |
| 6 | 6.308 | 6.633 | 6.975 | 7.336 | 7.716 | 8.115 | 8.535 | 8.977 | 9.442 | 9.930 |
| 7 | 7.434 | 7.898 | 8.394 | 8.923 | 9.487 | 10.089 | 10.730 | 11.414 | 12.141 | 12.916 |
| 8 | 8.583 | 9.214 | 9.897 | 10.637 | 11.436 | 12.300 | 13.233 | 14.240 | 15.327 | 16.499 |
| 9 | 9.755 | 10.583 | 11.491 | 12.488 | 13.579 | 14.776 | 16.085 | 17.518 | 19.086 | 20.799 |
| 10 | 10.950 | 12.006 | 13.181 | 14.487 | 15.937 | 17.549 | 19.337 | 21.321 | 23.521 | 25.959 |
| 11 | 12.169 | 13.486 | 14.972 | 16.645 | 18.531 | 20.655 | 23.044 | 25.733 | 28.755 | 32.150 |
| 12 | 13.412 | 15.026 | 16.870 | 18.977 | 21.384 | 24.133 | 27.271 | 30.850 | 34.931 | 39.580 |
| 13 | 14.680 | 16.627 | 18.882 | 21.495 | 24.523 | 28.029 | 32.088 | 36.786 | 42.218 | 48.496 |
| 14 | 15.974 | 18.292 | 21.015 | 24.215 | 27.975 | 32.392 | 37.581 | 43.672 | 50.818 | 59.196 |
| 15 | 17.293 | 20.023 | 23.276 | 27.152 | 31.772 | 37.280 | 43.842 | 51.659 | 60.965 | 72.035 |
| 16 | 18.639 | 21.824 | 25.672 | 30.324 | 35.949 | 42.753 | 50.980 | 60.925 | 72.938 | 87.442 |
| 17 | 20.012 | 23.697 | 28.213 | 33.750 | 40.544 | 48.883 | 59.117 | 71.673 | 87.067 | |
| 18 | 21.412 | 25.645 | 30.905 | 37.450 | 45.599 | 55.749 | 68.393 | 84.140 | | |
| 19 | 22.840 | 27.671 | 33.760 | 41.446 | 51.158 | 63.439 | 78.968 | 98.603 | | |
| 20 | 24.297 | 29.778 | 36.785 | 45.762 | 57.274 | 72.052 | 91.024 | | | |
| 21 | 25.783 | 31.969 | 39.992 | 50.422 | 64.002 | 81.698 | | | | |
| 22 | 27.299 | 34.248 | 43.392 | 55.456 | 71.402 | 92.502 | | | | |
| 23 | 28.845 | 36.618 | 46.995 | 60.893 | 79.542 | | | | | |
| 24 | 30.421 | 39.082 | 50.815 | 66.764 | 88.496 | | | | | |
| 25 | 32.030 | 41.645 | 54.864 | 73.105 | 98.346 | | | | | |
| 30 | 40.567 | 56.084 | 79.057 | 113.282 | | | | | | |

313

**TABLE 10–3.** Present Value of $1 [($1) (PVF)].

| Period | 2.00% | 4.00% | 6.00% | 8.00% | 10.00% | 12.00% | 14.00% | 16.00% | 18.00% | 20.00% |
|---|---|---|---|---|---|---|---|---|---|---|
| 1 | .980 | .962 | .943 | .926 | .909 | .983 | .877 | .862 | .847 | .833 |
| 2 | .961 | .925 | .890 | .857 | .826 | .797 | .769 | .743 | .718 | .694 |
| 3 | .942 | .889 | .840 | .794 | .751 | .712 | .675 | .641 | .609 | .579 |
| 4 | .924 | .855 | .792 | .735 | .683 | .636 | .592 | .552 | .516 | .482 |
| 5 | .906 | .822 | .747 | .681 | .621 | .567 | .519 | .476 | .437 | .402 |
| 6 | .888 | .790 | .705 | .630 | .564 | .507 | .456 | .410 | .370 | .335 |
| 7 | .871 | .760 | .665 | .583 | .513 | .452 | .400 | .354 | .314 | .279 |
| 8 | .853 | .731 | .627 | .540 | .467 | .404 | .351 | .305 | .266 | .233 |
| 9 | .837 | .703 | .592 | .500 | .424 | .361 | .308 | .263 | .225 | .194 |
| 10 | .820 | .676 | .558 | .463 | .386 | .322 | .270 | .227 | .191 | .162 |
| 11 | .804 | .650 | .527 | .429 | .350 | .287 | .237 | .195 | .162 | .135 |
| 12 | .789 | .625 | .497 | .397 | .319 | .257 | .208 | .168 | .137 | .112 |
| 13 | .773 | .601 | .469 | .368 | .290 | .229 | .182 | .145 | .116 | .093 |
| 14 | .758 | .577 | .442 | .340 | .263 | .205 | .160 | .125 | .099 | .078 |
| 15 | .743 | .555 | .417 | .315 | .239 | .183 | .140 | .108 | .084 | .065 |
| 16 | .728 | .534 | .394 | .292 | .218 | .163 | .123 | .093 | .071 | .054 |
| 17 | .714 | .513 | .371 | .270 | .198 | .146 | .108 | .080 | .060 | .045 |
| 18 | .700 | .494 | .350 | .250 | .180 | .130 | .095 | .069 | .051 | .038 |
| 19 | .686 | .475 | .331 | .232 | .164 | .116 | .083 | .060 | .043 | .031 |
| 20 | .673 | .456 | .312 | .215 | .149 | .104 | .073 | .051 | .037 | .026 |
| 21 | .660 | .439 | .294 | .199 | .135 | .093 | .064 | .044 | .031 | .022 |
| 22 | .647 | .422 | .278 | .184 | .123 | .083 | .056 | .038 | .026 | .018 |
| 23 | .634 | .406 | .262 | .170 | .112 | .074 | .049 | .033 | .022 | .015 |
| 24 | .622 | .390 | .247 | .158 | .102 | .066 | .043 | .028 | .019 | .013 |
| 25 | .610 | .375 | .233 | .146 | .092 | .059 | .038 | .024 | .016 | .010 |
| 30 | .552 | .308 | .174 | .099 | .057 | .033 | .020 | .012 | .007 | .004 |
| 35 | .500 | .253 | .130 | .068 | .036 | .019 | .010 | .006 | .003 | .002 |
| 40 | .453 | .208 | .097 | .046 | .022 | .011 | .005 | .003 | .001 | .001 |
| 45 | .410 | .171 | .073 | .031 | .014 | .006 | .003 | .001 | .001 | .000 |
| 50 | .372 | .141 | .054 | .021 | .009 | .003 | .001 | .001 | .000 | .000 |

**TABLE 10-4.**  Present Value of Annuity (Regular) of $1 [($1) (PFV$_a$)].

| Period | 2.00% | 4.00% | 6.00% | 8.00% | 10.00% | 12.00% | 14.00% | 16.00% | 18.00% | 20.00% |
|---|---|---|---|---|---|---|---|---|---|---|
| 1 | .980 | .962 | .943 | .926 | .909 | .893 | .877 | .862 | .847 | .833 |
| 2 | 1.942 | 1.886 | 1.833 | 1.783 | 1.736 | 1.690 | 1.647 | 1.605 | 1.566 | 1.528 |
| 3 | 2.884 | 2.775 | 2.673 | 2.577 | 2.487 | 2.402 | 2.322 | 2.246 | 2.174 | 2.106 |
| 4 | 3.808 | 3.630 | 3.465 | 3.312 | 3.170 | 3.037 | 2.914 | 2.798 | 2.690 | 2.589 |
| 5 | 4.713 | 4.452 | 4.212 | 3.993 | 3.791 | 3.605 | 3.433 | 3.274 | 3.127 | 2.991 |
| 6 | 5.601 | 5.242 | 4.917 | 4.623 | 4.355 | 4.111 | 3.889 | 3.685 | 3.498 | 3.326 |
| 7 | 6.472 | 6.002 | 5.582 | 5.206 | 4.868 | 4.564 | 4.288 | 4.039 | 3.812 | 3.605 |
| 8 | 7.326 | 6.733 | 6.210 | 5.747 | 5.335 | 4.968 | 4.639 | 4.344 | 4.078 | 3.837 |
| 9 | 8.162 | 7.435 | 6.802 | 6.247 | 5.759 | 5.328 | 4.946 | 4.607 | 4.303 | 4.031 |
| 10 | 8.983 | 8.111 | 7.360 | 6.710 | 6.145 | 5.650 | 5.216 | 4.833 | 4.094 | 4.192 |
| 11 | 9.787 | 8.760 | 7.887 | 7.139 | 6.495 | 5.938 | 5.453 | 5.029 | 4.656 | 4.327 |
| 12 | 10.575 | 9.385 | 8.384 | 7.536 | 6.814 | 6.194 | 5.660 | 5.197 | 4.793 | 4.439 |
| 13 | 11.384 | 9.986 | 8.853 | 7.904 | 7.103 | 6.424 | 5.842 | 5.342 | 4.910 | 4.533 |
| 14 | 12.106 | 10.563 | 9.295 | 8.244 | 7.367 | 6.628 | 6.002 | 5.468 | 5.008 | 4.611 |
| 15 | 12.849 | 11.118 | 9.712 | 8.560 | 7.606 | 6.811 | 6.142 | 5.575 | 5.092 | 4.675 |
| 16 | 13.578 | 11.652 | 10.106 | 8.851 | 7.824 | 6.974 | 6.265 | 5.669 | 5.162 | 4.730 |
| 17 | 14.292 | 12.166 | 10.477 | 9.122 | 8.022 | 7.120 | 6.373 | 5.749 | 5.222 | 4.775 |
| 18 | 14.992 | 12.659 | 10.828 | 9.372 | 8.201 | 7.250 | 6.467 | 5.818 | 5.273 | 4.812 |
| 19 | 15.679 | 13.134 | 11.158 | 9.604 | 8.365 | 7.366 | 6.550 | 5.877 | 5.316 | 4.843 |
| 20 | 16.352 | 13.590 | 11.470 | 9.818 | 8.514 | 7.469 | 6.623 | 5.929 | 5.353 | 4.870 |
| 21 | 17.011 | 14.029 | 11.764 | 10.017 | 8.649 | 7.562 | 6.687 | 5.973 | 5.384 | 4.891 |
| 22 | 17.658 | 14.451 | 12.042 | 10.201 | 8.772 | 7.645 | 6.743 | 6.011 | 5.410 | 4.909 |
| 23 | 18.292 | 14.857 | 12.303 | 10.371 | 8.883 | 7.718 | 6.792 | 6.044 | 5.432 | 4.925 |
| 24 | 18.914 | 15.247 | 12.550 | 10.529 | 8.985 | 7.784 | 6.835 | 6.073 | 5.451 | 4.937 |
| 25 | 19.524 | 15.622 | 12.783 | 10.675 | 9.077 | 7.843 | 6.873 | 6.097 | 5.467 | 4.948 |
| 30 | 22.397 | 17.292 | 13.765 | 11.258 | 9.427 | 8.055 | 7.003 | 6.177 | 5.517 | 4.979 |
| 35 | 24.999 | 18.665 | 14.498 | 11.655 | 9.644 | 8.176 | 7.070 | 6.215 | 5.539 | 4.992 |
| 40 | 27.306 | 19.793 | 15.046 | 11.925 | 9.779 | 8.244 | 7.105 | 6.233 | 5.548 | 4.997 |
| 45 | 29.490 | 20.720 | 15.456 | 12.108 | 9.863 | 8.283 | 7.123 | 6.242 | 5.552 | 4.999 |
| 50 | 31.424 | 21.482 | 15.762 | 12.234 | 9.915 | 8.305 | 7.133 | 6.246 | 5.554 | 4.999 |

315

When using time-value-of-money calculators, several considerations should be noted. First, there are variations in the different calculators available. Some machines allow the entering of values in any order; others may require that $n$ be entered before $i$ and so forth. Also, calculator answers usually differ slightly from answers achieved from tables. This is true because the calculators' built-in formulas may go to 8 or 10 decimal places, while printed tables have only 3 to 5 decimal places. Finally, the calculators offer more flexibility than tables. A printed table usually is limited to full percentages (.10, .11, .12, and so on), while the calculator can handle interest or discount factors between full percentages (.1254, .1382, and so on).

## EFFECTIVE COST OF WORKING-CAPITAL DECISIONS

Once we have established the concept of the time value of money, we can examine a number of specific applications dealing with working-capital management. In this section, we will discuss the effective cost or actual return from selected cash, inventory and receivable decisions. In this context, *effective cost* will be defined as the actual gain or loss to each party in a transaction as a result of the time value of money or administrative expenses.

### EFFECT OF DELAYED PAYMENTS

A selling company loses money when its customers are slow to pay. The loss results from two factors: (1) the company has a cost of funds tied up in receivables, and (2) the company must incur collection costs. The effective cost of delayed payments is the sum of the cost of funds and cost of collections.

To illustrate the effective cost of a later payment, let us consider a textile manufacturer that is entitled to receive a cash payment of $1,500 from a department store. The money is received 38 days late. The manufacturer has a cost of money of 18 percent annually, and collection costs on late payments are estimated at $15 on the average. What is the effective cost to the manufacturer of this late payment?

To answer this question, we must consider two effects: (a) the time value of not having the money for 38 days, and (b) the additional collection costs. The lost opportunity cost on the funds may be calculated by the formula:

$$\begin{array}{c}\text{dollar}\\\text{amount}\end{array} \times \begin{array}{c}\text{annual}\\\text{cost of}\\\text{money}\end{array} \times \frac{\text{days in period}}{\text{360 days}} = \begin{array}{c}\text{lost}\\\text{opportunity}\\\text{cost}\end{array}$$

For our example, the cost is $28.50, as follows

$$1,500 \times .18 \times \frac{38}{360} = \$28.50$$

On a time value calculator, we get the same answer as follows:

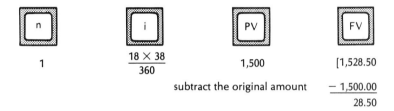

| n | i | PV | FV |
|---|---|----|----|
| 1 | $\dfrac{18 \times 38}{360}$ | 1,500 | [1,528.50 |

subtract the original amount    − 1,500.00

28.50

Subtract the original amount  −  1,500

$28.50

In addition to the lost opportunity cost, the firm has collection costs of $15. The effective cost of the late payment is $43.50 (28.50 + 15).

Two items should be noted in this example. First, compound or present value tables cannot be used to solve the problem because the 38-day period does not match the values in the table. Second, we used 360 days instead of 365 days. The use of 365 days gives a more accurate estimate of the effective cost. Still, financial institutions commonly use 360 days. At present, there is no uniformity on time value calculations, and we must be prepared to use either 360 or 365 days.

> **Example:** A firm sells $15,000 of goods on terms of net 30 to a customer that pays on the 157th day after the invoice date. The company's cost of funds is 18 percent annually, and its collection costs are $25 a month on its outstanding receivables. What is the effective cost of the late payment?

**Answer:** $1,059, as follows.
The $15,000 was not due until 30 days after the sale, so the lateness is 157 − 30, or 127 days. The financing cost is

$$15{,}000 \times .18 \times \frac{127}{360} = \$953$$

Collection costs are $25 a month, or

$$25 \times \frac{127}{30} = \$106$$

The effective cost of the late payment is $1,059 (953 + 106).

On the time value calculator, we have

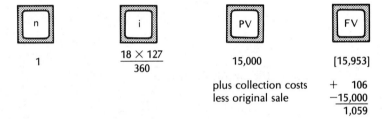

| n | i | PV | FV |
|---|---|---|---|
| 1 | $\dfrac{18 \times 127}{360}$ | 15,000 | [15,953] |

plus collection costs    +    106
less original sale    −15,000
     1,059

## INSTALLMENT FINANCING FOR CUSTOMERS

When goods are sold on extended credit terms, the analyst must determine the monthly payments needed to pay off the debt. This is a process of converting from a present value to an annuity at a given interest level.

**Example:** A car dealer extends a 36-month loan to a customer to finance the purchase of a car. The face amount of the loan is $7,500, and the annual percentage rate on the loan is 16 percent compounded monthly. What are the monthly payments?

**Answer:** $263.68, as follows:

| n | i | PMT | PV |
|---|---|---|---|
| 36 | 16/12 | [263.68] | 7,500 |

$$\frac{7500}{(1/.0133)(1-1/(1.0133)^{36})} = 263.68$$

In some cases, the creditor may extend credit and then may sell the credit instrument to a bank or finance company. Multiple calculations may be needed to determine the effects of such transactions.

**Example:** A company sells three trucks at a selling price of $110,000 total. The company agrees to finance the vehicles over a 60-month period at an effective cost of 18 percent compounded monthly. Once the agreement is signed, the company sells the agreement to a bank, which purchases it to yield an effective rate of 15.5 percent compounded monthly. How much does the company receive for the agreement?

**Answer:** $116,129 is received by the company. The agreement calls for the customer to pay $2,793.28 per month for 60 months.

$$\frac{110,000}{(1/.015)(1-1/(1.015)^{60})} = 2,793.28$$

| n | i | PMT | PV |
|---|---|---|---|
| 60 | 18/12 | [2,793.28] | 110,000 |

Then the company sells the stream of $2,793.28 to the bank at 15.5 percent to net $116,129.

| n | i | PMT | PV |
|---|---|---|---|
| 60 | 15.5/12 | 2,793.28 | [116,129] |

$$(2793.28)(1/.0129)(1-1/(1.0129)^{60}) = 116.129$$

In this example, the selling company has increased its profit on the sale of the vehicles by arranging for the financing.

EFFECTIVE COST OF NOT TAKING DISCOUNTS

Normally, cash discounts are designed so that it is attractive to pay for purchases within the discount period. The purchasing firm's accounts payable is, after all, the selling firm's accounts receivable. One way for a seller to minimize outstanding receivables is to offer large cash discounts for prompt payment.

In deciding whether to take a discount, a purchasing firm should calculate the effective cost of passing up the discount and paying the full invoice amount at the end of the net period. A formula for this calculation is:

$$\text{effective cost} = \frac{365 \text{ days}}{\text{net period} - \text{discount period}} \times \text{discount amount}$$

For terms of 2/10 net 30, the annual cost of passing up the discount would be:

$$\text{effective cost} = \frac{365}{30 - 10} \times .02 = .365$$

This is a high cost of money; most firms would take the discount rather than pay 36.5 percent effective interest to delay payment 20 days.

**Example:** A firm can borrow money at 12 percent interest. It has purchased goods with terms of 1/10 net 60. Should the firm take the discount if it is short of cash?

**Answer:** No. The effective cost of passing up the discount is only 7.3 percent, which is less costly than borrowing at 12 percent.

$$\text{effective cost} = \frac{365}{60 - 10} \times .01 = .073$$

KEY TERMS

| | | |
|---|---|---|
| *annuity* | *compound value factor* | *immediate annuity* |
| *compounding* | *deferred annuity* | *present value* |
| *compound interest* | *effective cost* | *regular annuity* |

STUDY QUESTIONS

1. How does compounding interest differ from simple interest?
2. Why do an immediate and a deferred annuity have different future values?
3. What two factors result in a loss to a firm due to slow-paying customers?
4. What is the effective cost of delayed payments?

PROBLEMS

1. An individual deposits $10,000 in a bank account that offers 12 percent interest compounded annually. How much will the person have in 6 years?
2. An individual deposits $10,000 in an account that offers 12 percent compounded semiannually. How much will the person have in 6 years?
3. A borrower has signed a note that will mature in 3 years; $15,000 will be needed to retire the note. The borrower has $10,000 that can be invested at 10 percent per year compounded annually. If the $10,000 is invested, will it produce a sufficient amount of money to retire the note? If not, how much must be invested today to have $15,000 in 3 years?
4. A company decides to set aside $8,000 a year for 8 years. The money can be invested to yield 14 percent compounded annually. What is the present value of this annuity? the future value in 8 years?
5. A firm wants to retire a long-term note that has a maturity value of $60,000 in 7 years. It can make annual investments at 14 percent compounded annually. How much would the firm have to set aside each year in order to have $60,000 in 7 years?
6. A firm has a credit sale of $200,000 on terms of net 30. The customer pays on the 120th day. The firm's cost of funds is 2 percent a month and the collection costs are $15 a month. What is the effective cost of the late payment?
7. A company sells a boiler at $150,000 and agrees to finance the equipment at 1 percent a month over a period of 24 months. After the sale, the company sells the note to a financing company at a rate of 1.5 percent a month. How much does the company receive on this sale? If the boiler cost $80,000 to manufacturer, what is the company's profit on this transaction?
8. A firm can purchase goods on terms of 2/10 net 45. The firm can borrow money short term at 18 percent. Should the firm borrow to take the discount?

# LARSON MANUFACTURING CASE I
## Economics of Credit

*This case is designed to test the reader's ability to calculate the costs of financing receivables and inventories using the time value of money concept to calculate effective costs.*

The Larson Manufacturing Company produces a wide variety of display items for the home and office. The firm sells picture frames, trophy cases, gun racks, and related items to department stores throughout the country. In addition, the firm has sales to some 200 independent distributors or sales representatives who make sales to variety stores, furniture stores, and gift shops. Larson's accounts receivable range in size from $200, which represents the minimum order that it will accept, to $25,000–30,000 for its five largest distributors and 10 to 15 of its large department store accounts.

The president of Larson Manufacturing Company is Craig Larson, the youngest son of the firm's founder. The company is privately owned with the majority of the shares held by members of the Larson family and former employees of the firm. Craig follows the firm's traditional policy of, as his father used to say, "a sound product line and a sound balance sheet." By stressing new technology and a complete product line, the firm has shown strong profits with minimum cyclical downturns. By emphasizing a sound balance sheet, the firm has avoided borrowing to finance capital purchases. The firm has retained a portion of its earnings each year to finance expansion. Last year, as an example, the firm retained almost $100,000 after declaring a dividend of $530 a share. The firm's most recent balance sheet and income statement are attached.

Craig Larson typically selects one area of the company for detailed review each spring. This year he has become concerned with his staff's knowledge of the fundamental economics of credit. He recently attended a seminar where a speaker advocated a greater usage of handheld calculators and minicomputers in business problem solving. The speaker, a vice-president of a large California bank, claimed that "nothing beats the $25 time-value-of-money calculator for helping you understand what's happening when you borrow or invest money."

One day, during a routine meeting with Anna Gibson, his account representative at City Central Bank, Craig mentioned the seminar. Anna agreed that a basic knowledge of small business calculators was an essential part of managing the firm. Anna indicated that she was familiar with the machines, since her bank held a training session on the use of calculators as a tool for working with customers. After some discussion, Anna agreed to bring some of the bank's training materials to Craig so that he could use them with his own staff.

Two weeks later, Craig sent the following memorandum to his department heads:

*TO:*      Department Heads
*FROM:*    C. LARSON
*SUBJ.:*   Executive Development


We are a sufficiently large company that all managers should know about borrowing and investing.

The following problems have been given to us by City Central State Bank. They can be solved on small business calculators with time-value-of-money formulas built in for them.

I request each department head to individually solve each problem as our spring program for management development.

Please send me a copy of your results.


**1.** A company has approached the bank to borrow $275,000 to be repaid in 12 quarterly installments. The effective annual rate on the loan is 13.5 percent, compounded quarterly. What is the quarterly payment that would be required on the loan?

**Answer:**

**2.** A customer has asked for a $275,000 loan but does not want to make any repayments for the first 18 months. Beginning at the end of the 19th month, the customer will repay the loan in 60 monthly payments. The rate is 13.5 percent. What is the monthly payment with monthly compounding of the rate?

**Answer:**

**3.** One of the bank's customers is late making a payment. A check is received 67 days after the money was due. The check is for $16,272. The bank has a 17 percent late charge, calculated on an annual basis. How much does the customer owe?

**Answer:**

**4.** A company finances the sale of $175,000 of goods for one of its customers. It charges 18 percent interest with monthly payments over 3 years. The bank has agreed to buy the contract without recourse at a 14.5 percent rate. How much will the bank pay the company?

**Answer:**

**5.** A customer wants to borrow $500,000 with monthly payments over a 4-year period. The rate will be 12.25 percent. The customer has requested a maximum monthly payment of $10,000 or so, and will accept a balloon payment to be refinanced. If the bank agrees, how much will the customer have to refinance at the end of 4 years?

**Answer:**

**6.** A customer has approached the bank for the purpose of investing some excess cash. The bank has located a corporate bond with a face value of $25,000 and 262 days to maturity. The bond pays semiannual interest based on a coupon of 7.25 percent. Yields on similar issues are averaging 8.43 percent. How much should the customer pay for the bond if the bank charges a service fee of $25?

**Answer:**

7. From problem 1, if the first quarterly installment were payable on the date the loan was made, an immediate annuity would be created. What quarterly payment would be required if the loan were repaid as an immediate annuity?

**Answer:**

# Investing Excess Cash

An important aspect of working-capital management involves investing excess cash. Basically, this is a task of balancing liquidity and profitability needs. The firm purchases marketable securities that can easily be converted to cash with a minimum of difficulty or transactions costs. At the same time, the firm seeks a reasonable return at an acceptable risk level. In this chapter, we will examine the major marketable securities available to the firm and will develop techniques for calculating the rates of return on each.

## RETURN ON TREASURY BILLS

A *treasury bill* is an unconditional promise by the U.S. Treasury to pay to the holder of the bill a specified amount at maturity. Treasury bills are issued for short periods of time, normally 3, 6, or 12 months. The U.S. Treasury sells 91- and 182-day bills at weekly auctions, while 1-year bills are offered every 4 weeks. Prospective buyers submit written bids to a Federal Reserve District Bank, offering to purchase a given amount of bills. Two types of bids may be submitted. A *competitive bid*, or tender, is an offer to buy provided the bills have a specified yield. As an example, a firm may offer to purchase $1 million of treasury bills at maturity value for $980,000, with a maturity in 91 days. If the bid is accepted in full, the yield will be 8.07 percent, as follows:

$$980,000 \times \text{yield} \times 91/360 = 1,000,000 - 980,000$$

$$\text{yield} = \frac{20,000}{980,000} \times \frac{360}{91} = .0807$$

| n | i | PV | FV |
|---|---|---|---|
| 1 | [2.04] | 980,000 | 1,000,000 |

$$2.04 \times 360/91 = 8.07$$

This competitive bid would be submitted on a standard form provided by the Federal Reserve Bank, and the purchase price would be specified as 98.000, that is, on the basis of 100 with 3 decimal places. The Treasury will accept the highest bids, since the higher the bid, the lower the interest rate paid by the government. The second type of bid is the *noncompetitive bid*. Once the competitive bids have been accepted, the noncompetitive bids up to $200,000 each will be filled at the weighted average of the competitive bids. If too many bids are received, the bills are prorated among the bidders.

Treasury bills are the most secure and liquid investment for the firm's excess cash. With respect to security, the U.S. government has the direct obligation to redeem the bills. With respect to liquidity, there is a large, active market for the bills. They can be quickly and easily sold prior to maturity if the firm runs short on cash. The large secondary market also allows the firm to purchase bills without submitting a formal bid to the U.S. Treasury. The bills can be bought or sold in denominations of $10,000, $50,000, $100,000, $500,000, or $1 million from securities dealers or commercial banks. To determine the current *yields*, or rates of return, for different maturities, the analyst can check the *Wall Street Journal* or most daily papers for quotations.

We are now ready to calculate the rate of return on treasury bills. To begin, we check the quotes in the local papers, as given in Table 11–1.

According to the data in the table, treasury bills with maturity dates are yielding 11.32 to 12.76 percent annually, with the highest yields on bills with maturities of 3 to 7 months. These yields are given in the column marked "yield." We can also determine how much we can get if we buy or sell a bill. If the firm buys a bill on January 22, and holds it to maturity, it will earn the yield in the "ask" column. If the firm sells a bill

**TABLE 11–1.**   Treasury Bill Yields, January 22.

| Date | Bid | Ask | Yield | Date | Bid | Ask | Yield |
|---|---|---|---|---|---|---|---|
| Jan. | | | | May | | | |
| 24 | 11.86 | 11.16 | 11.32 | 1 | 12.14 | 12.00 | 12.62 |
| 31 | 11.86 | 11.16 | 11.34 | 15 | 12.12 | 12.00 | 12.68 |
| | | | | 27 | 12.12 | 11.94 | 12.66 |
| Feb. | | | | | | | |
| 5 | 11.70 | 11.22 | 11.42 | June | 12.07 | 11.93 | 12.69 |
| 7 | 11.70 | 11.22 | 11.43 | 5 | 12.03 | 11.89 | 12.71 |
| 14 | 11.70 | 11.26 | 11.50 | 19 | 12.03 | 11.89 | 12.73 |
| 21 | 11.73 | 11.33 | 11.59 | 24 | | | |
| 28 | 11.76 | 11.36 | 11.65 | July | | | |
| Mar. | | | | 3 | 12.01 | 11.89 | 12.70 |
| 4 | 11.75 | 11.69 | 12.05 | 22 | 11.94 | 11.78 | 12.73 |
| 6 | 11.95 | 11.73 | 12.10 | Aug. | | | |
| 13 | 11.99 | 11.73 | 12.12 | 19 | 11.77 | 11.61 | 12.56 |
| 20 | 12.09 | 11.91 | 12.39 | Sept. | | | |
| 27 | 12.13 | 11.95 | 12.37 | 16 | 11.44 | 11.24 | 12.17 |
| Apr. | | | | Oct. | | | |
| 1 | 12.15 | 11.95 | 12.43 | 14 | 11.30 | 11.14 | 12.11 |
| 3 | 12.13 | 11.95 | 12.44 | Nov. | | | |
| 10 | 12.16 | 11.98 | 12.50 | 6 | 11.23 | 11.09 | 12.10 |
| 17 | 12.23 | 12.19 | 12.76 | Dec. | | | |
| 24 | 12.23 | 12.15 | 12.75 | 4 | 11.06 | 10.94 | 12.00 |
| 29 | 12.14 | 11.96 | 12.56 | | | | |

on January 22, the securities dealer will pay a price reflecting the yield in the "bid" column. All the values in the table reflect annual yields.

Now let us see if we can calculate the buying or selling price for a $10,000 treasury bill based on the quotations in the table. Suppose we want to buy or sell a bill that matures on July 3. Since treasury bills bear no interest, today's price must be below $10,000 if the bearer is to earn a return on the investment. The formula used to calculate most yields quoted for treasury bills in the financial press is

$$\frac{\text{present}}{\text{value}} = \frac{\text{future}}{\text{value}} - \frac{\text{yield in basis pts.} \times \text{days to maturity}}{360 \text{ days}}$$

where yield in = the quoted yield where a *basis point* is 1/100 of
basis pts.      a percentage point, or .0001. Therefore, 1
                percent equals 100 basis points.

days to    = the number of days beginning with tomorrow
maturity     and including the maturity date of the bill

In our example, the July 3 bill has a bid yield of 12.01 percent and an ask yield of 11.89 percent. The purchase or sale price respectively would be $9,464.95 or $9,459.55 for a $10,000 bill, as follows:

Buy a $10,000 Bill Maturing on July 3:

$$\text{present value} = 10,000 - \frac{1,189 \times 162}{360} = \$9,464.95$$

Sell a $10,000 Bill Maturing on July 3:

$$\text{present value} = 10,000 - \frac{1,201 \times 162}{360} = \$9,459.55$$

Once we have determined the price that the firm must pay for a $10,000 bill, we can determine the effective yield to the firm. The 11.89 percent ask value in the table is a quote that reflects a discounting from the maturity value. To get the effective yield, we must take the interest earned, divide it by the money paid, and then multiply it by a factor that annualizes it. The formula is

$$\text{effective yield} = \frac{FV - PV}{PV} \times \frac{360 \text{ days}}{\text{days to maturity}}$$

In our example, the effective yield is 12.56 percent, as follows:

$$\text{effective yield} = \frac{10,000 - 9,464.95}{9,464.95} \times \frac{360}{162} = \underline{.1256}$$

This is the yield that is of most interest to the firm. It is the effective return from investing $9,464.95 in a security that will mature in 162 days.

This calculation can also be performed on the time-value-of-money calculator, as follows:

$$5.65 \times 360/162 = 12.56$$

**Example:** A dealer offers a firm a $100,000 treasury bill with 187 days to maturity for $95,292 at a time when yields are reported at 9.07 percent. What is the actual annual yield?

**Answer:** 9.51 percent, as follows:

$$\frac{\text{effective}}{\text{yield}} = \frac{100,000 - 95,292}{95,292} \times \frac{360}{187} = .0951$$

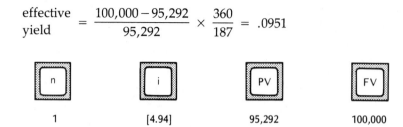

$$4.94 \times 360/187 = 9.51$$

## RATES OF RETURN ON INTEREST-BEARING BONDS

The calculation of the rate of return on an interest-bearing bond is a similar, if a little bit more complicated, analysis. The U.S. government issues interest-bearing securities. A *treasury note* is an issue that ranges in maturity from 1 to 7 years, is available in registered or bearer form, and can be purchased in denominations from $1,000 to $1 million. A *treasury bond* is similar to the note but may be issued for maturities over 7 years. The notes and bonds trade activity in secondary markets with other fixed return securities.

In addition to direct treasury obligations, a firm may purchase the securities of federal agencies. Over 40 government bodies are empowered to raise money in capital markets, and many of them carry government guarantees or other sponsorship. Two groupings of government entities may be identified. The first group consists of *federal agencies* that issue obligations that generally have a direct government guarantee. Some of these agencies are the Government National Mortgage Association (Ginnie Mae), U.S. Postal Service, Federal Housing Administration (FHA), and Export-Import Bank (Exim Bank). The second group consists of *government-sponsored agencies* whose securities are issued without an express government guarantee. These are generally publicly owned and include the Federal National Mortgage Association (Fannie Mae), Federal Home Loan Mortgage Association (Freddie Mac), and Federal Land Banks. Government agencies are very active in the money markets, and their securities are generally regarded almost as highly as direct Treasury securities.

A variety of other interest-bearing bonds are available for purchase by firms with excess cash. These bonds are evaluated with the same techniques as for government notes, bonds, and agency obligations.

To illustrate the method for determining the rate of return from interest-bearing bonds, let us consider a firm that has been offered $250,000 of bonds at face value with a maturity in 294 days. The coupon rate is 8.75 percent with semiannual interest payments. The bonds are offered at a purchase price of $251,000. The firm has checked similar bonds and determined that they offer a 10.2 percent yield. Do the bonds in the new offer represent an improvement over the earlier offers?

To solve this problem, we must recognize that two interest payments are involved—one in 294 days and the other in 294 minus 182.5 days, or 111.5 days. Each interest payment will be $250,000 × .04375, which equals $10,937.50. To evaluate the rate of return, we discount each future receipt of interest and the future return of principal to a present value of $251,000. The yield that sets the future receipts equal to $251,000 is the rate of return.

First, we might try 10.2 percent to see if the new bonds are competitive. We can use the formula for treasury bills, namely:

$$\frac{\text{effective}}{\text{yield}} = \frac{FV - PV}{PV} \times \frac{360}{\text{days}}$$

where we solve for the present value. Letting $i$ replace effective yield and rearranging the formula, we get:

$$PV = \frac{FV}{1 + (i)\,(\text{days}/360)}$$

Since we have two future values, we must perform two calculations, one for each future receipt of cash. Then we add the two values together to see if they total $251,000. The calculations are:

$$PV = \frac{260{,}937.50}{1+(.102)\,(294/360)} = \frac{260{,}937.50}{1.0833} = 240{,}873$$

$$PV = \frac{10{,}937.50}{1+(.102)\,(111.5/360)} = \frac{10{,}937.50}{1.0316} = \underline{10{,}603}$$

present value   251,476

With the calculator, we get the same answer as follows:

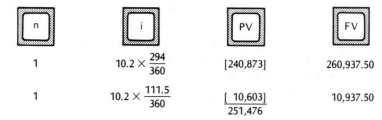

| n | i | PV | FV |
|---|---|---|---|
| 1 | $10.2 \times \frac{294}{360}$ | [240,873] | 260,937.50 |
| 1 | $10.2 \times \frac{111.5}{360}$ | [ 10,603]<br>251,476 | 10,937.50 |

The value of $251,476 is a little high; therefore, the bond offers a return in excess of 10.2 percent. If we repeat the process with 10.5 percent as the discount factor, we get a present value of $250,922, which approximates the $251,000 offering price. This means that the return is approximately 10.5 percent and the new bond is a better alternative than similar bonds returning 10.2 percent.

## CERTIFICATES OF DEPOSIT VERSUS COMMERCIAL PAPER

The first investment decision will distinguish between two instruments offered for short-term investments. A *certificate of deposit* is an instrument evidencing a time deposit at a commercial bank or other financial institution. CDs are generally negotiable, usually have minimum maturities of at least 30 days, and are sold in denominations of $100,000 or more. The certificates of the nation's largest and strongest banks—the so-called prime banks—have been very popular because they are secure investments that offer relatively high yields. In addition, a CD can be sold prior to maturity in a large and well-developed secondary market.

Commercial paper is a short-term, unsecured promissory note issued by a large nonfinancial corporation. It is called *finance paper* when issued by a financial corporation. These notes are issued by firms needing cash for periods of 30 to 270 days, may be sold through dealers or directly to the investing firm, and have historically offered higher yields than other short-term money market instruments. A limited secondary market exists for commercial and finance paper, so it is generally viewed as being less liquid than many other short-term investments.

The degree of risk offered by certificates of deposit and commercial paper can be approximated by examining the credit ratings of the issuing organizations. Table 11–2 gives the Moody's ratings for corporate debentures, a system that is used to rate bank-holding companies that issue debt securities.

As an example of applying the Moody's rating scale to the debentures of bank-holding companies, Table 11–3 shows the ratings of selected issues.

Similarly, the Moody's ratings can be applied to corporations issuing commercial paper. A separate Moody's rating is often available for

**TABLE 11–2.**  Key to Moody's Bond Ratings.

| Category | Meaning |
| --- | --- |
| Aaa | Bonds that are rated Aaa are judged of the best quality. Interest payments are protected by a large or exceptionally stable margin, and principal is secure. |
| Aa | Bonds that are rated Aa are judged of high quality by all standards. They are rated lower than the best bonds because margins of protection may not be as large as in Aaa securities, fluctuation of protective elements may be of greater amplitude, or there may be other elements present. |
| A | Bonds that are rated A possess many favorable investment attributes and are considered upper-medium-grade obligations. The designation A1 is used to identify the strongest bonds in the A class. |
| Baa | Bonds that are rated Baa are considered medium-grade obligations; that is, they are neither highly protected nor poorly secured. Baa1 designates the best bonds in this class. |
| Ba | Bonds that are rated Ba are judged to have speculative elements; their future cannot be considered as well assured. |
| B | Bonds that are rated B generally lack characteristics of the desirable investment. |
| Caa | Bonds that are rated Caa are of poor standing and may be in default. |
| Ca | Bonds that are rated Ca represent obligations that are speculative in a high degree. |
| C | Bonds that are rated C are the lowest rated class. |

**TABLE 11–3.**   Recent Ratings of Bank Debentures.

| Rating | Organization | Coupon | Maturity |
|--------|--------------|--------|----------|
| Aaa | BankAmerica | 8.350% | 2007 |
| Aaa | Manufacturers Hanover | 8.125 | 2007 |
| Aa | Bankers Trust | 8.125 | 1999 |
| Aa | Wells Fargo | 8.60 | 2002 |
| A | Republic New York | 9.00 | 2001 |
| A | Shawmut | 8.625 | 1999 |
| A | New England Merchants | 8.85 | 1999 |

the commercial paper of the company. Moody's uses its commercial paper scale to rate selected issues with maturities of less than 9 months. The ratings are:

Prime-1   P-1   highest quality
Prime-2   P-2   higher quality
Prime-3   P-3   high quality

Table 11–4 shows the ratings on commercial paper and finance paper for selected organizations.

Once we acknowledge the existence of a number of services to assist in evaluating the risk from purchasing CDs or commercial paper, we are ready to compare the expected returns. Table 11–5 gives some yields on 3-month investments that might be considered by the firm.

In evaluating the alternatives in the table, the real issue becomes the spread between the yields when two securities are compared. As an example, in November 1981 the spread between treasury bills and prime

**TABLE 11–4.**   Recent Commercial Paper Ratings.

| Rating | Organization |
|--------|--------------|
| P-1 | Bankers Trust Company |
| P-1 | Barclays American Corp. |
| P-3 | Appalachian Power Company |
| P-1 | American Express Credit Crop. |
| P-1 | Chase Manhattan |
| P-2 | Continental Telephone Company |
| P-2 | GATX Leasing Corporation |
| P-2 | Detroit Edison Company |
| P-1 | Commercial Credit Corporation |
| P-2 | Firestone Tire and Rubber Company |

**TABLE 11–5.**   Yields on Treasury Bills, Certificates of Deposit, and Commercial Paper.

| Date | Prime Commercial Paper, 90-119–Day Maturities | Certificates of Deposit, Secondary Market, 90-Day Maturities | Treasury Bills, 3 Months, Secondary Market |
|------|------|------|------|
| Nov. 1981 | 12.16 | 12.48 | 10.86 |
| Dec. 1980 | 12.66 | 13.07 | 11.43 |
| Dec. 1979 | 10.97 | 11.22 | 10.07 |
| Dec. 1978 | 7.94 | 8.22 | 7.19 |
| Dec. 1977 | 5.54 | 5.48 | 5.27 |

Source: *Federal Reserve Bulletin,* December 1981.

commercial paper is 130 basis points (.1216 − .1086). For some treasurers, the lower liquidity and greater risk of commercial paper would be more than justified by the spread. These same treasurers may have felt quite different in December 1977, when the spread was only 27 basis points (.0554 − .0527). This kind of analysis must be continually done as relative yields fluctuate so that the analyst can find the best risk-return trade-off when investing excess cash. The same analysis would, of course, apply when comparing commercial paper and certificates of deposit and even when comparing the CDs of prime and regional banks.

## IDENTIFYING SOURCES OF RISK

An important skill for the manager investing the firm's excess cash is the ability to determine the real risk features offered by an investment. We will illustrate this process by comparing certificates of deposit with banker's acceptances.

A *banker's acceptance* is a time draft whose payment is guaranteed by a commercial bank or similar entity. The acceptance is used in short-term financing of goods traded by two or more parties. Most acceptances arise from international transactions, but there is an increasingly large business conducted in domestic acceptances.

Two kinds of acceptances are generally identifiable. One finances the fabrication of goods for later shipment; the second finances the transportation of the goods. Figure 11–1 shows the creation of an acceptance when acceptances yield 14 percent to the holder if a 90-day maturity is specified. In this case, a foreign firm has ordered $200,000 of goods from a U.S. firm, and its bank has sent a letter of credit for the $200,000. The

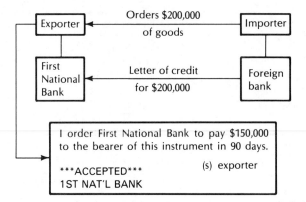

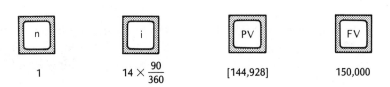

Figure 11–1    Banker's Acceptance to Finance Construction of Goods.

U.S. firm's bank has agreed to provide acceptance financing up to $150,000 for the purchase of materials and hiring of labor to construct the goods. The firm orders its bank to pay $150,000 to the bearer of a draft in 90 days, and the bank stamps its approval on it. The draft can be sold as an acceptance to yield 14 percent annually. A treasurer investing excess cash will be paid $144,928 for the acceptance, as shown in the calculation:

$$PV = \frac{150,000}{1 + (.14)\,(90/360)} = 144,928$$

or

| n | i | PV | FV |
|---|---|---|---|
| 1 | $14 \times \dfrac{90}{360}$ | [144,928] | 150,000 |

Before beginning the risk analysis of the acceptance, we might examine yields on acceptances and CDs. Table 11–6 shows the yields for prime banks, as taken from the *Federal Reserve Bulletin*.

What are the sources of risk in each instrument? For both, the primary source of repayment is the bank, and this represents the primary exposure, usually a slight exposure at worst. But what would happen if the bank defaulted? For the CD, the first $100,000 of any time deposit by an individual or company is insured by the government at most institutions. If the treasurer has no other time deposits with the bank, the first

**TABLE 11–6.**   Yields for Prime Bank COs and Acceptances

| Date | Certificates of Deposit, Secondary Market, 90-Day Maturities | Prime Bankers' Acceptances, 90-Day Maturities, Domestic Issues |
|------|-------------------------------------------------|-------------------------------------------------|
| Dec. 1978 | 8.22% | 8.11% |
| Dec. 1979 | 11.22 | 11.04 |
| Dec. 1980 | 13.07 | 12.78 |
| Nov. 1981 | 12.48 | 12.00 |

**Source:** *Federal Reserve Bulletin,* December 1981.

$100,000 is safe even if the bank defaults. The balance is at risk. What happens to the acceptance? It is not insured by the government, but there is a secondary source of payment. The holder can go to the maker of the draft, the exporter in our preceding example, and demand payment. This provides quite a bit of additional protection. Which is riskier? The analyst can decide after considering these facts and current economic conditions. This is the process of determining the source of risk and then estimating the likelihood of default from each source.

**DISTINGUISHING SECONDARY RISK SOURCES**

A number of investments offer a secondary collateral to a primary agreement, as in the case of government insurance backing a time deposit in a bank. One of these investments is a *repurchase agreement,* or REPO, an agreement that a bank or security dealer sells specific marketable securities to another party and agrees to repurchase the securities at a fixed price on some future date. As an example, $1 million worth of treasury bills may be sold on Thursday for $999,622, and the dealer agrees to buy them back on Friday for $1 million. A repurchase agreement is used by the bank or security dealer to finance a portion of its securities inventory and is a short-term instrument, most commonly used overnight, over a weekend, or for periods less than a week.

The primary source of repayment on a repurchase agreement is the credit of the bank or dealer. Still, the secondary collateral is deemed important. If treasury or agency securities are used as collateral, the return to the investor will be lower than arrangements where municipal bonds are the collateral. In some cases, the spread may be as much as 50 basis points. Is such a spread justified? Each investor must answer this question individually, but it should be recognized that the marketable securities are the secondary source of risk. The primary analysis should involve the credit of the bank or securities dealer.

> **Example:** A securities dealer agrees to sell a portfolio of corporate bonds for $1.5 million on Friday and will repurchase them on Monday for $1,501,700. What is the effective return to the investor who holds this instrument?
>
> **Answer:** 13.6 percent, as follows:
>
> $$\frac{\text{effective}}{\text{yield}} = \frac{1,501,700 - 1,500,000}{1,500,000} \times \frac{360}{3} = .136$$
>
> or

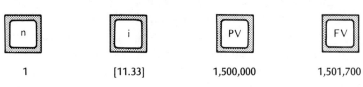

| n | i | PV | FV |
|---|---|---|---|
| 1 | [11.33] | 1,500,000 | 1,501,700 |

$$.1133 \times \frac{360}{3} = 13.6\%$$

When evaluating investments for the firm's excess cash, the treasurer is not limited to investments in the United States. A number of foreign opportunities can be considered if the firm has funds in excess of $100,000 to be invested at any one time. In this section, we will discuss these possibilities.

A *eurodollar* may be defined as a dollar deposited outside the United States, either in the foreign branch of a U.S. bank of in a foreign bank. The term is used to describe dollars held in Europe, the Bahamas, Bahrain, Cayman Islands, Panama, Canada, Japan, Hong Kong, Singapore, and possibly other countries. The market grew rapidly in the 1970s, as shown in Table 11–7, and provides liquidity to finance world trade as well as offering an investment haven for individuals and companies seeking to hold and invest U.S. dollars.

Funds may be invested in the eurodollar market to meet the maturity requirements of the firm's operations. Table 11–8 shows the yields available, depending upon the maturity of the deposit, from 1974 to 1981.

When evaluating eurodollar deposits, the firm does not face any

**TABLE 11–7.**  Eurodollar Market Size (Billions of Dollars at End of Year, except June 1981).

| Year | Eurodollars | Year | Eurodollars |
|------|-------------|------|-------------|
| 1972 | 163.8 | 1977 | 562.4 |
| 1973 | 233.1 | 1978 | 703.0 |
| 1974 | 300.2 | 1979 | 878.4 |
| 1975 | 378.3 | 1980 | 1,121.1 |
| 1976 | 476.0 | 1981 | 1,212.7 |

**Source:** Morgan Guaranty Trust Company of New York, *World Financial Markets,* February 1982.

currency exposure since the funds are held in U.S. dollars. Therefore, the real comparisons must deal with yields on competing investments. Suppose, for example, that the treasurer has $2 million to invest for 90 days in relatively secure instruments. One might compare U.S. treasury bills, prime certificates of deposit, and prime bank eurodollar deposits. Table 11–9 gives some yields for comparison purposes from 1974 to 1981.

When considering foreign investments, the firm has the opportunity to accept exposure to exchange rate fluctuations. If a firm is holding a currency whose value increases during the holding period, the firm receives both the interest and appreciation in value. On the other hand, a currency that declines in value during the investment period can wipe out the interest and produce a loss of principal. Table 11–10 shows index numbers when four major currencies were plotted against a weighted average of the currencies of 15 major countries. The period is January 1981

**TABLE 11–8.**  Eurodollar Deposit Rates (Prime Banks' Bid Rates in London, at or near end of month).

|  | Overnight | 7-day Fixed | 1 Month | 3 Months | 6 Months | 12 Months |
|------|-----------|-------------|---------|----------|----------|-----------|
| December 1974 | 8.00 | 9.38 | 9.75 | 10.19 | 10.19 | 9.75 |
| 1975 | 5.13 | 5.19 | 5.38 | 5.81 | 6.63 | 7.19 |
| 1976 | 4.63 | 4.75 | 5.13 | 5.00 | 5.38 | 5.56 |
| 1977 | 7.12 | 6.31 | 6.87 | 7.19 | 7.50 | 7.67 |
| 1978 | 10.62 | 10.62 | 11.00 | 11.69 | 12.31 | 12.00 |
| 1979 | 14.00 | 14.00 | 14.37 | 14.44 | 14.44 | 12.87 |
| 1980 | 19.25 | 19.75 | 19.12 | 17.62 | 16.75 | 14.87 |
| 1981 | 12.87 | 13.00 | 13.31 | 13.75 | 14.81 | 14.75 |

**Source:** *World Financial Markets,* February 1982.

**TABLE 11–9.**   Yields on Three 90-Day Investments.

|              |      | Treasury Bills | Certificates of Deposit | Eurodollar Deposits |
|--------------|------|----------------|-------------------------|---------------------|
| December     | 1974 | 7.28           | 9.25                    | 10.19               |
|              | 1975 | 5.27           | 5.50                    | 5.81                |
|              | 1976 | 4.41           | 4.70                    | 5.00                |
|              | 1977 | 6.33           | 6.80                    | 7.19                |
|              | 1978 | 7.19           | 8.22                    | 8.78                |
|              | 1979 | 10.07          | 11.22                   | 11.96               |
|              | 1980 | 11.43          | 13.07                   | 14.00               |
| November     | 1981 | 10.86          | 12.48                   | 13.33               |

**Source:** *Federal Reserve Bulletin,* December 1981.

**TABLE 11–10.**   Effective Exchange Rates, Selected Currencies, January 1981 to January 1982.

|                             | U.S. Dollar | Japan Yen | U.K. Pound | German Mark |
|-----------------------------|-------------|-----------|------------|-------------|
| January 1981                | 99.4        | 126.7     | 87.8       | 132.8       |
| February                    | 102.3       | 127.3     | 87.7       | 131.7       |
| March                       | 102.5       | 125.4     | 85.1       | 134.0       |
| April                       | 104.2       | 123.0     | 84.8       | 133.8       |
| May                         | 107.3       | 122.0     | 84.8       | 132.6       |
| June                        | 109.3       | 121.9     | 82.1       | 131.9       |
| July                        | 111.6       | 118.8     | 79.5       | 131.6       |
| August                      | 113.3       | 119.4     | 78.7       | 131.3       |
| September                   | 110.3       | 119.4     | 75.4       | 133.8       |
| October                     | 109.7       | 117.4     | 75.3       | 137.4       |
| November                    | 107.6       | 121.1     | 76.9       | 137.2       |
| December                    | 107.7       | 124.1     | 77.6       | 137.1       |
| January 1982                | 109.4       | 123.9     | 78.0       | 137.0       |
| Average                     | 107.3       | 122.34    | 81.05      | 134.02      |
| Maximum movement in any month | +3.1      | +3.7      | −3.3       | +3.6        |

**Note:** Index numbers, March 1973 = 100. The index for a currency is a measure against 15 other major currencies.
**Source:** *World Financial Markets,* January 1982.

to January 1982, a relatively stable period in terms of currency movements. Still, an investor holding pounds for 30 days could have suffered sizable losses while an investor holding yen could have made sizable gains.

Once the firm recognizes the possible currency exposure, it can compare yields on different investments to see if they are attractive. The firm's bank can advise on any restrictions in foreign investing and can facilitate the transfer of funds and make other arrangements. Table 11–11 shows some representative yields on foreign currency investments in December 1981.

**INTEREST RATE RISK**

A major risk to investing in marketable securities is the possible loss of principal from selling the security prior to maturity. This could occur, for example, if a 6-month treasury security were purchased and then sold in 30 days. *Interest rate risk* is defined as the possible loss of principal of a fixed return security that is sold prior to maturity. Two factors involved with this risk are particularly important.

1. *Market Value Fluctuates in Opposite Direction of Interest Rates.* The market value of outstanding securities fluctuates in the opposite direction of the yield on new securities entering the marketplace. When interest rates rise, the value of outstanding securities drops, and vice versa.

**TABLE 11–11.**  Yields on Selected Foreign Currency Investments, December 1981.

| Country | Treasury Bills, 90 Days | Bond Yields, 90 Days | Daily Money Rates | Bank Deposits, 90 Days |
|---|---|---|---|---|
| United States | 11.90 | 15.50 | 12.37 | 12.62 |
| Canada | 14.41 | 16.48 | 14.53 | 15.20 |
| Japan | 5.42 | 7.70 | 6.70 | 6.50 |
| United Kingdom | 15.31 | 16.55 | 9.13 | 15.69 |
| Belgium | 16.00 | — | 12.78 | 15.50 |
| France | — | 17.33 | 15.46 | 9.16 |
| Germany | — | 10.50 | 10.65 | 9.50 |
| Switzerland | — | 6.60 | 3.38 | 8.75 |

**Source:** *World Financial Markets,* February 1982.

2. *Time to Maturity Is Key Factor.* The degree of interest rate risk is directly related to the length of time to maturity for a security. If the asset is held to maturity, there is no loss of principal as a result of interest rate fluctuations. Thus, if the term to maturity is fairly short, the market value fluctuates within a relatively narrow range. If the term to maturity is long, market value fluctuates widely.

To illustrate the concept of interest rate risk, let us assume that a firm has invested its excess cash in commercial paper of medium-grade firms, a Moody's rating of P-3. Further assume that a number of uncertainties drive up the yields on P-3 paper, and the firm must sell its holding 60 days before maturity. Originally, the firm purchased $500,000 of paper on a discount basis to yield 13 percent annually in a period of 182 days. Sixty days prior to maturity, the yields have risen to 17 percent on 60-day paper, and the firm sells its holdings. Let us see what happens. The firm purchases the paper for $469,165 and will receive $500,000 at maturity, as follows:

$$PV = \frac{500,000}{1 + (.13 \times 182/360)} = 469,165$$

or

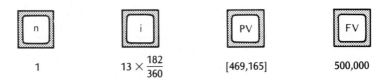

| n | i | PV | FV |
|---|---|---|---|
| 1 | $13 \times \frac{182}{360}$ | [469,165] | 500,000 |

When the firm finds a buyer 60 days prior to maturity, the paper will be sold to reflect the new yield of 17 percent. The firm will receive $486,224 for it, as follows:

$$PV = \frac{500,000}{1 + (.17)(60/360)} = 486,224$$

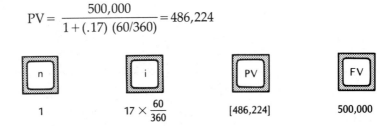

| n | i | PV | FV |
|---|---|---|---|
| 1 | $17 \times \frac{60}{360}$ | [486,224] | 500,000 |

What has been the yield to the firm for the 4 months it held the paper? The answer is 10.7 percent as follows:

$$\frac{\text{effective}}{\text{yield}} = \frac{486{,}224 - 469{,}165}{469{,}165} \times \frac{360}{122} = .107$$

| n | i | PV | FV |
|---|---|----|----|
| 1 | [3.64] | 469,165 | 486,224 |

3.64 × 360/122 = 10.7  percent

The difference between the expected return of 13 percent and the actual return of 10.7 percent is the result of interest rate risk.

## KEY TERMS

| | | |
|---|---|---|
| banker's acceptance | finance paper | repurchase agreement |
| certificate of deposit | government-sponsored | treasury bill |
| commercial paper | agencies | treasury bond |
| competitive bid | interest rate risk | treasury note |
| eurodollar | noncompetitive bid | yields |
| federal agencies | prime banks | |

## STUDY QUESTIONS

1. What is the most secure and liquid investment for a firm's excess cash?
2. What is the major difference between a treasury note and a treasury bond?
3. What are the two groups of government entities empowered to raise money in capital markets? How are they different?
4. What is the major issue to be concerned with when evaluating the alternatives from the Moody's ratings? Why is it important?
5. What are the two uses of banker's acceptances?
6. What should a firm be concerned with when considering foreign investments?
7. What are the two factors involved in interest rate risk?

## PROBLEMS

1. A firm submits a competitive bid to purchase $500,000 of treasury bills at maturity value for $475,000, with maturity in 182 days. What is the yield?

2. An investor wants to buy a treasury bill worth $10,000 on its maturity date of May 31, 1982. On December 31, 1981, *The Wall Street Journal* had a bid yield of 13.43 percent and an ask yield of 12.75 percent. What would be the purchase and sale prices?

3. What is the effective yield on the treasury bill in problem 2?

4. A firm has been offered $375,000 of bonds at face value with a maturity of 362 days. The purchase price is $378,000. The coupon rate is 7.96 percent, with semiannual interest payments. Similar bonds offer an 11.5 percent yield. Should the firm accept this offer?

5. A foreign firm buys $500,000 worth of goods from a domestic firm. The domestic firm's bank offers a banker's acceptance for the full amount, with a 13.5 percent yield, payable in 60 days. How much will a treasurer be paid for the acceptance?

6. A bank agrees to sell a portfolio of marketable securities for $3.2 million on Tuesday and rebuy the securities for $3,201,300 on Wednesday. What is the effective return to the bank that holds this instrument?

7. A firm purchases $1 million of paper rated P-2 by Moody's. The paper is to yield 14.7 percent annually in a period of 91 days. Sixty days prior to maturity, yields have risen to 16.8 percent on 60-day paper, and the firm sells its paper. How much will the firm receive at maturity?

8. For the preceding firm, what has been the yield for the 30 days that it has held the paper?

# DUNN INDUSTRIES CASE
# Short-Term Investing

*This case requires the reader to have knowledge concerning the major marketable securities and the techniques for calculating the rate of return on each.*

Ken Flanagan is the treasurer of Dunn Industries, a manufacturing company located in Montreal with primary operations in the Canadian and U.S. markets. Eighty percent of the firm's sales are to the steel and automobile industries, although a small portion of the company's output is exported to customers in Europe. To a certain degree, the business is seasonal, and Ken recognizes that his cash needs are higher in the summer and early fall. To meet any contingencies, he keeps $3 to $4 million in U.S. currency at the Bank of Montreal and has lines of credit with the same bank and with Mellon Bank in Pittsburgh.

Ken is preparing a tentative investing strategy for the next 6 months. In the next quarter, he expects an average of $3 million to invest. This will take him through March. Then, in the second quarter he will have $4.5 million. He pursues a simple strategy of achieving the highest return consistent with four investing rules:

1. Investments will be limited to U.S. treasury issues, Canadian or U.S. bank certificates of deposit or time deposits (U.S. dollar denominated), bank acceptances, commercial paper, or overnight money market funds, with all investments in U.S. dollar instruments.
2. The maturities of the short-term portfolio will be 30 percent under 3 weeks, 40 percent from 3 weeks to 3 months, and the balance in instruments that offer the highest yields with maturities of 1 year or less.
3. Not more than 25 percent of the portfolio will be invested in one kind of instrument or at one time to maturity.
4. At least 20 percent each will be invested in treasury securities and certificates of deposit or time deposits.

Ken has been working on a forecast of interest rates and yields in different markets. Using bank estimates, government data, and the forecasts of U.S. and Canadian investment bankers, he has established some predictions as follows:

| Investment | Forecasted Average Quarterly Yields | |
| --- | --- | --- |
| | First Quarter | Second Quarter |
| 1-week treasuries | 11.5% | 11.0% |
| 1-month treasuries | 12.0 | 10.5 |
| 3-month treasuries | 13.5 | 10.0 |
| 2-week bank CDs | 13.0 | 12.0 |
| 1-month bank CDs | 13.5 | 11.5 |
| 3-month bank CDs | 14.5 | 11.0 |
| 6-month bank CDs | 15.5 | 10.5 |
| 3-month acceptances | 15.0 | 10.5 |
| 3-month commercial paper | 16.0 | 13.0 |
| 6-month commercial paper | 16.5 | 12.0 |
| 9-month commercial paper | 18.0 | 11.0 |
| Overnight money market fund | 13.0 | 11.5 |

**Required**

Assume that Ken's forecasts are correct and that he has $3 million to invest in the first quarter and $4.5 million in the second quarter. Further assume that he follows his strategy and the rules that accompany it. What will be his average return in the first quarter? in the second quarter?

PART IV

# Investment Policy

Capital Budgeting
Risk and Required Return
Valuation of the Firm
Mergers and Acquisitions

# 12

# Capital Budgeting

For the first 11 chapters of this book, we have been examining the management of the firm's ongoing operations. Our focus has been on the environment of the firm; the firm's assets, liabilities, and equity; and methods of evaluating next period's profits and financial position. We have studied decision-making techniques for analyzing the firm's liquidity and profitability; managing its cash, receivables, and inventory; and forecasting results when we consider factors such as the firm's break-even point, the degree of leverage in its operations or financing, and the impact of inflation.

In this chapter, we begin a completely new emphasis. For the remainder of the book, we will deal with the investment and financing decisions that must be made before the firm can successfully conduct operations. We will develop techniques for forecasting the return from proposals and determining the required level of return before an investment is acceptable. We will evaluate factors that affect the value of the firm's common stock. Finally, we will cover the management of funds by examining the differing sources of financing and how the firm's policies on dividends or leasing can affect these sources.

One way to view the shift in emphasis is in terms of the two different budgets that most firms prepare each year. The *operating budget* is developed for the short term, commonly 1 year, and is concerned with revenues and expenses related to the firm's daily operations. In Chapters 1 through 11, we dealt primarily with issues that pertain to the operating

budget. The *capital budget* deals exclusively with major investment proposals and is used to help the firm invest its funds over the long term.
Decisions in the area of the capital budget will be the emphasis of the
remaining chapters.

## NATURE OF CAPITAL BUDGETING

*Capital budgeting* may be defined as the decision-making process by which
firms evaluate the purchase of major fixed assets, including buildings,
machinery, and equipment. It also covers decisions to acquire other
firms, either through the purchase of their common stock or groups of
assets that can be used to conduct an ongoing business. Capital budgeting describes the firm's formal planning process for the acquisition and
investment of capital and results in a capital budget that is the firm's formal plan for the expenditure of money to purchase fixed assets.

A capital-budgeting decision is a two-sided process. First, the analyst must evaluate a proposed project to forecast the likely or *expected return from the project* (E $(Rtn)_{proj}$). This calculation generally begins with an
expenditure of cash at the beginning of the project's service life and a
stream of cash flowing to the firm over the life of the project. The calculation of forecast return may be done by two methods: (a) *internal rate of
return* or (b) *net present value*. These two methods are discussed in this
chapter.

The second side of a capital-budgeting decision is to determine the
required return from a project (E $(Rtn)_{req}$). We may calculate the forecast
return to be 12 percent, but the question is whether this is good enough
for the proposal to be accepted. In order to determine whether the return
is adequate, the analyst must evaluate the degree of risk in the project
and then must calculate the required return for the given risk level. Techniques for determining requiring return are developed in Chapter 13.

The two sides of the capital-budgeting process are shown in Figure
12–1.

### SIGNIFICANCE OF CAPITAL BUDGETING

The preparation of the firm's capital budget is highly significant for a
number of reasons:

1. *Substantial Expenditures.* Capital expenditures may range from
   pieces of equipment costing thousands of dollars to complete factories and other physical facilities costing millions of dollars. A
   $25 million factory or oceangoing vessel has become common-

| Likely Return Side | | Required Return Side | |
|---|---|---|---|
| Goal: | To calculate the likely or forecasted return from a proposal $[E(Rtn)_{proj}]$ | Goal: | To select a required return that a project must achieve before it is acceptable. $[E(Rtn)_{req}]$ |
| Focus: | The cash flows over the life of the investment proposal. | Focus: | The relationship between risk and return. |
| Methods: | Internal rate of return and net present value. | Methods: | Are covered in Chapter 13. |

**Decision Rule:**   The two sides come together in a single decision rule as follows: If $E(Rtn)_{proj}$ exceeds $E(Rtn)_{req}$, then accept project. If not, reject it.

**Figure 12–1**   Comparison of the Two Sides of the Capital-Budgeting Decision.

place and a $300 million oil refinery is an occasional investment. The very size of these items in terms of dollars underlies their importance to the firm.

2. *Long Time Periods.* The effects of capital-spending decisions will be felt by the firm over extended periods of time. Once a multi-million dollar building is begun, the firm cannot easily withdraw from the construction. When a firm forecasts the need for additional manufacturing space, it may begin constructing a factory. If changes in the marketplace eliminate the need for the extra capacity, the firm faces a serious problem. Does it keep the facility, incurring heavy fixed costs with no revenues, in the hope that conditions will improve and the capacity will be needed? Does it sell the plant at a potentially large loss? The long-term commitment adds considerable risk to the firm's capital-budgeting decisions.

3. *Implied Sales Forecasts.* The spending of funds for fixed assets represents an implied forecast of future sales. If machinery or a building is not purchased, the firm may not be able to meet the demand in the future. If too much is purchased, the firm is stuck with unneeded capacity. An important part of the capital-budgeting process is forecasting sales, possibly 10 or 15 years into the future.

4. *Over- and Undercapacity.* If the budget is carefully drawn, it usually improves the timing and quality of asset acquisition. If done poorly, it costs the firm large sums of money because of overcapacity or undercapacity—sometimes at the same time. The firm

may have idle assets to produce a product that is not in demand while it has a shortage of the machinery and facilities to produce a much-demanded, high-profit product.

## KINDS OF PROPOSALS

A firm may include several different kinds of proposals in its capital-budgeting process. One classification identifies five kinds of proposals:

1. *Replacements.* As fixed assets are used, they wear out or become outdated by new technology. Money may be budgeted to replace wornout or obsolete equipment.
2. *Expansion.* Successful firms tend to experience growth in the sales of primary products. If a firm is experiencing shortages or delays in high-demand products due to inadequate production facilities, it will consider proposals to add capacity to existing product lines.
3. *Diversification.* A business can reduce the risk of failure by operating in several markets rather than a single market. Diversification allows the firm to protect itself against the collapse of sales in a single product. Firms seeking the facilities to enter new markets will consider proposals for the purchase of new machinery and facilities to handle the new products.
4. *Research and Development.* Firms in industries where technology is rapidly changing will expend large sums of money for researching and developing new products. If large sums of money are needed for equipment, these proposals will normally be included in the capital budget.
5. *Miscellaneous.* A firm frequently has proposals that do not directly help achieve profit-oriented goals. The proposal to install pollution-control equipment on a factory's smokestacks is an example. Safety items, such as automatic sprinkling systems to protect against fire, may involve considerable expenditures. These types of proposals may be included in the firm's capital-budgeting process.

## CAPITAL-BUDGETING POLICIES

Because of the importance of capital-budgeting decisions, firms usually have detailed policies for administering the budget. We will identify several major issues facing firms and outline some guidelines for policies dealing with each issue.

1. *Estimating Needs.* The amount of funds needed for a project should be estimated by using a combination of past performance and historical data, future expectations, and the recommendations of all interested departments in the firm. By including all three sources of information, the firm reduces the possibility of omitting a major factor. It takes a special skill to bring together the estimates of data, check the different items for accuracy, and resolve the differences. This is an important part of the financial manager's ability to develop a realistic and accurate capital budget.

2. *Approval for Proposals.* Approvals for expenditures are usually linked to the size of the investment proposal. Larger dollar amounts normally must be approved at higher levels in the corporation than smaller dollar amounts. The purchase of a small piece of machinery may be approved by a plant manager without further discussion. A major purchase, such as one involved in the installation of a new computer system, may be discussed by top management and may require the approval of the board of directors.

3. *Planning Horizon.* The capital budget is prepared at least 1 year in advance and may extend 5, 10, or even 15 years into the future. Five to 7 years is common. The most important factor affecting the planning horizon is the rate of change in technology in the industry. If a firm is in an industry with relatively few advancements in technology, a capital investment will be useful for many years. The firm can plan for 10, 15, or more years of service life from an asset. This is not the case for a firm facing rapid technological change. In this situation, the firm must plan for an early return on investments so that funds will be available to replace obsolete equipment. Firms dealing with costly or complex technologies may establish two planning horizons. First, a specific set of proposals will be considered for the next 5 to 7 years. Second, a different set of expectations will be prepared for the long-term period beyond 7 years. Although the long-term predictions will be subject to continuous review, the long-term plan helps the firm analyze its needs and direction into the distant future and encourages management to prepare for technological changes.

**RANKING OF PROPOSALS**

Once the capital budget is nearing completion and a variety of different projects has been identified, the firm must select the projects it will finance. Among problems that arise are the following:

1. *Mutually Exclusive Projects.* If the firm accepts one project, it may rule out the need for another. These are called *mutually exclusive projects.* An example of this kind of project would be the need to transport supplies from a loading dock to the warehouse. The firm may be considering two proposals—forklifts to pick up the goods and move them, or a conveyor belt connecting the dock and warehouse. If the firm accepts one proposal, it eliminates the need for the other.

2. *Contingent Projects.* The utility of some proposals is contingent upon the acceptance of others. For example, a firm may be considering the construction of a new headquarters building and a new employee parking lot. If it decides not to build the headquarters, the need for the lot is gone. At the same time, if the firm builds the headquarters and not the lot, the employees will have no place to park. These are *contingent policies.*

3. *Capital Rationing.* Firms normally have more proposals than can be funded properly. In this case, only the most desirable projects receive approval. *Capital rationing* occurs when the firm has more acceptable proposals than it can finance. In this situation, the firm should rank the projects from highest to lowest priority. Then a *cutoff point* is selected. Proposals above the cutoff will be funded; those below will be rejected or delayed. The cutoff point is selected after carefully considering the number of projects, the goals of the firm, and the availability of capital to finance the capital budget.

## CASH FLOWS

*Cash flow* is an essential concept in capital budgeting. The accounting approach to calculating return is not appropriate in making the decision to invest funds in new investments. Accounting techniques should be limited to two areas:

1. *Calculating Tax Effects.* The firm pays its taxes on the basis of accounting data and reported profits. Depreciation and noncash

expenses are a tax shield. These tax effects are included in capital budgeting because they affect the cash flow.

2. *Calculating Future Earnings per Share.* This is in addition to the capital-budgeting process; it is not part of it. Along with the return on a cash-flow basis, the firm may want to check the effect of an investment on future earnings per share. As a general rule, a high return on a cash-flow basis also yields a high future EPS. Still, the firm may want to ensure that this is the case, and it should use accounting data to determine future EPS.

Capital budgets should carefully forecast the timing and amounts of cash flowing to and from the firm as a result of capital expenditures. The rate of return is calculated on money being expended or tied up at one point in time and being available at another point in time.

## DIFFERENTIAL AFTERTAX CASH FLOW

In considering an expenditure of cash for an investment project, only *differential aftertax cash flows* are included in the analysis. The term *differential* refers to a comparison of what will be received and spent on a proposal *compared* with what would be received and spent in the absence of the proposal. The term *aftertax* refers to the fact that all calculations are evaluated after considering the effects of corporate income taxes.

A *cash-flow stream* is a series of cash expenditures or receipts written so that their timing can be seen. The cash-flow stream in Table 12–1 will be used to illustrate the differential aftertax flow for a proposed project. In the first column, the years are listed beginning with year 0. As a matter of standard form, cash-flow streams begin with the investment decision that occurs in year 0. This is normally a cash outlay on the new proposal, which is indicated by a minus sign in front of the dollar amount.

**TABLE 12–1.**   Differential Aftertax Cash-Flow Stream.

| Year | With Proposal | Without Proposal | Differential Aftertax Flow |
|------|---------------|------------------|----------------------------|
| 0 | $-100,000 | $     0 | $-100,000 |
| 1 | + 60,000 | +40,000 | + 20,000 |
| 2 | + 67,000 | +45,000 | + 22,000 |
| 3 | + 74,000 | +51,000 | + 23,000 |
| 4 | + 82,000 | +58,000 | + 24,000 |
| 5 | +122,000 | +66,000 | + 56,000 |

The outlay in Table 12–1 is $100,000. Since the firm incurs no outlay if it does not invest in the project, the differential column shows the difference between 0 and $100,000.

In year 1, without the proposed project, the firm forecasts that its cash inflows will exceed its cash outlays on existing operations by $40,000. The net inflow is indicated by a plus sign. If the firm accepts the new proposal, inflows will increase from $40,000 to $60,000, a differential of $20,000, which is recorded in the differential column. This process continues for the life of the new proposal.

## TWO SIDES TO A CASH INFLOW

To be a worthwhile investment, a firm must receive differential aftertax cash inflows from a proposed project. This inflow can occur by two means:

1. *Additional Revenues.* If a firm is entering a market that will increase sales, the excess of cash revenues over cash expenses provides a net cash inflow. As an example, a firm forecasting $120,000 in additional sales and $90,000 in additional cash expenditures will have a $30,000 net cash inflow.
2. *Cash Savings on Operations.* Sometimes a proposal is intended to reduce operating costs. A firm may be expending $50,000 for the operation of a large machine. A new machine would cost $80,000 but would reduce the need for one operator, thus reducing costs to $40,000. This is a net cash inflow of $50,000 minus $40,000, or $10,000.

In either case, the inflow is shown in the stream preceded by a plus sign. In the first case, the inflow is additional revenue; in the second, a reduction of a cash outflow.

## DEPRECIATION AS A TAX SHIELD

A firm's noncash expenses offer a tax shield on income and will reduce the amount of tax paid. When making capital-budgeting decisions, an important noncash expense is the depreciation on equipment or other fixed assets. *Depreciation* is an accounting device that allows a firm to charge off a portion of the original cost of equipment as an expense over some period during the service life of the equipment. This depreciation appears as an expense (but does not involve any cash) on the firm's income statement. Since expenses reduce reported profits, they also reduce taxable income.

Since depreciation acts as a tax shield and allows the firm to keep cash that would otherwise flow out to the government, depreciation increases the firm's cash flow. This effect is shown in Table 12–2. In this example, the firm with depreciation pays $160,000 less taxes than the firm without depreciation and is able to keep $760,000 in cash compared to $600,000 in cash.

## TAX EFFECTS FROM DEPRECIATION

In making capital-budgeting decisions, the tax effects from depreciation are considered in the calculations of cash flows. Two methods of determining the rate of depreciation are permitted in the United States:

1. Accelerated Cost Recovery System (ACRS). Since 1981, firms have been able to recover the cost of capital assets following an accelerated cost recovery system. This replaced earlier approaches that also used forms of accelerated depreciation. Under these rules, the cost of tangible depreciation assets can be recovered over different periods, depending upon the category of assets being considered. The classes of assets are:
   a. 3-Year Property. Cars, light-duty trucks, research equipment, and certain other shortlived assets are in this class.
   b. 5-Year Property. This consists of most machinery and equipment not specifically identified in one of the other classes.

**TABLE 12–2.**   Effect of Depreciation on Aftertax Cash Flow.

|  | *With* *$400,000* *Depreciation* | *Without* *$400,000* *Depreciation* |
|---|---|---|
| Revenues | $1,600,000 | $1,600,000 |
| Less cash expenses | − 600,000 | − 600,000 |
| Less depreciation | − 400,000 | −         0 |
| Taxable revenues | 600,000 | 1,000,000 |
| Taxes at 40% rate | − 240,000 | − 400,000 |
| Aftertax income | 360,000 | 600,000 |
| Plus revenue shielded | + 400,000 | 0 |
| Aftertax cash flow | $   760,000 | $   600,000 |

   c. 10-Year Property. Theme-park structures, railroad tank cars, mobile homes, and certain utility property are in this class.
   d. 15-Year Property. Buildings, other permanent real estate structures, and much public utility property are in this class.
2. Straight-Line Depreciation. Using this method, the cost of a fixed asset is spread equally over its expected service life. As an example, suppose a machine cost $3 million, has a life expectancy of 12 years, and will have a scrap value estimated at $600,000 at the end of the 12 years. Using the straight-line method, the *depreciable cost* is $2.4 million (the difference between the original cost and the scrap value) and this amount is recovered over the 12-year service life of the asset. The annual depreciation in this example is $200,000 as follows:

$$\frac{\text{annual}}{\text{depreciation}} = \frac{\text{original cost} - \text{salvage value}}{\text{years of service life}}$$

$$\frac{\text{annual}}{\text{depreciation}} = \frac{3,000,000 - 600,000}{12 \text{ years}} = 200,000$$

Because of the increased cash flow with the accelerated cost recovery system, most firms use it in determining the depreciation schedule for capital assets. Since most general business assets fall in the 5-year category, we will use this class of investment for all examples in this book. The recovery percentages for assets depreciable over 5 years will be:

| Year | Annual Depreciation |
|------|---------------------|
| 1 | 20% |
| 2 | 32 |
| 3 | 24 |
| 4 | 16 |
| 5 | 8 |
|   | 100% |

Note that the depreciation schedule of 20/32/24/16/8 totals 100 percent. Under the accelerated cost recovery system, it is not necessary to consider any scrap or salvage value. When the asset is eventually sold by the firm, any gain on the sale is treated as ordinary income up to the amount of the total depreciation taken. Any gain above the original purchase price is treated as a capital gain and may qualify for a lower tax rate. The amount of gain up the original purchase price is called a *depreciation recapture;* the amount of gain above the original purchase price is called a *capital gain.*

**Example:** A firm has purchased an asset for $5 million. The asset can be depreciated over 5 years on a schedule of 20/32/24/16/8. What is the annual depreciation on the asset?

| **Answer:** | *Year* | *Percentage* | *Annual Depreciation* |
|---|---|---|---|
| | 1 | .20 | 1,000,000 |
| | 2 | .32 | 1,600,000 |
| | 3 | .24 | 1,200,000 |
| | 4 | .16 | 800,000 |
| | 5 | .08 | 400,000 |

**Example:** For the firm in the preceding example, assume that the asset value rises quickly. At the end of one year, it is sold for $7.5 million. What is the amount of the depreciation recapture? the capital gain?

**Answer:** Depreciation recapture is the difference between the original cost of $5 million and the remaining book value of the asset. Since $1 million is the 1st year depreciation, the remaining book value is $4 million; $1 million is the depreciation recapture taxable as ordinary income; $2.5 million is the capital gain.

## TAX EFFECTS FROM INVESTMENT TAX CREDIT

An *investment tax credit* is a tax benefit allowed to businesses purchasing capital assets. The firm may claim a specified percentage of new capital investments as credit against income tax in the current year. The credit is granted under legislation designed to encourage firms to invest in assets and thus help create jobs. As an example, legislation may authorize a 10 percent investment tax credit for an investment of $4 million in printing equipment. Suppose that a firm is making such an investment in a year when it would otherwise pay $1.5 million in federal income taxes. If no restriction exists against taking the entire 10 percent in the current year, the firm would only pay $1.1 million in taxes, as follows:

| | |
|---|---|
| Taxes originally due | $1,500,000 |
| Investment tax credit ($4,000,000 × .10) | 400,000 |
| Taxes due | $1,100,000 |

Investment tax credits have the effect of reducing the amount of money that must be spent by the firm at the start of an investment project (that is, the money spent on the project, not on taxes). An investment tax credit is considered in the net cash flows when making a capital-budgeting decision.

### WORKING CAPITAL TIED UP

In capital budgeting, the timing of cash movements is the prime concern. *Cash flowing* out in one year and returning in a later year is recorded as an outlay initially and an inflow later. It does not matter that the money was not actually given away permanently. It only matters that it was tied up and not available to the firm.

We will use working capital as an example of funds tied up during the life of a capital-budgeting proposal. A firm may be considering the purchase of a machine that is capable of faster production than the old machine. This will allow the firm to process more inventory and to sell more items, thus increasing receivables. The cash tied up in year 0 to increase inventories and receivables is treated as an outflow. After the new machine ends its production in a number of years, the inventories may be liquidated and the receivables collected. The funds tied up in working capital would be treated as an inflow in the final year of the cash-flow system.

It may be argued that the working capital does not return to cash at the end of the machine's service life. Rather, a new machine will be purchased and the funds remain tied up. This does not matter. By handling working capital as an outflow in year 0 and inflow in the final year, we make a mathematical adjustment that will be important when we consider the time value of money. The outflow will have a higher present value than the inflow, and the tying up of funds will reduce the rate of return from the project. This is correct, since the more we expend or tie up, the lower the return.

Sometimes a proposal will free working capital. For example, a new machine may be so efficient that we do not have to store large volumes of inventory of finished goods; the machine can produce them as needed. If a proposal frees working capital, it is treated as an inflow in year 0 and an outlay in the final year. This recognizes that the freed working capital is not really a revenue but does mathematically adjust the value of freeing the funds when the time value of money is considered. Table 12–2 shows both effects.

TABLE 12–2.   Effect of Tying Up Funds or Freeing Them.

| If Working Capital Increases | If Working Capital Decreases |
| --- | --- |
| an outlay in year zero | an inflow in year zero |
| an inflow in final year | an outflow in final year |

BOOK AND CASH RESIDUAL VALUES

When a firm purchases a fixed asset, it records the value at cost and pre-pares a *depreciation schedule*, as shown in Table 12–3. In this schedule, the machine is depreciated, using a 5-year schedule of 20/32/24/16/8. The *book residual value*, which is defined as the estimated value of the machine at the completion of its service life, is 0 in this example. The machine may actually be worth more than this amount in 5 years, but the accounting records will record it at a 0 book value. This means that the machine will be *fully depreciated* at the end of 1991.

The *cash residual value* is defined as the amount of money received by the firm when the machine is finally sold. If the machine is sold for $40,000 in June 1991 and the firm must pay $5,000 to remove it from the plant and transport it to the purchaser, the firm receives a net of $40,000 minus $5,000, or $35,000 cash residual value.

A problem arises when the book and cash residual values are com-pared. Three situations are possible.

TABLE 12–3.   Simplified Depreciation Schedule.

Stone crusher, serial no. 224715, purchased June 23, 1986
    Cost: $115,000 + 17,000 installation
    Book residual value: $0, June 1991

| Year | Book Value | − | Rate | Annual Depreciation Dollars | = | Ending Book Value |
| --- | --- | --- | --- | --- | --- | --- |
| 0 | $132,000 | − | 0 | $ 0 | = | $132,000 |
| 1 | 132,000 | − | .20 | 26,400 | = | 105,600 |
| 2 | 105,600 | − | .32 | 42,240 | = | 63,360 |
| 3 | 63,360 | − | .24 | 31,680 | = | 31,680 |
| 4 | 31,680 | − | .16 | 21,120 | = | 10,560 |
| 5 | 10,560 | − | .08 | 10,560 | = | 0 |

1. *Cash Exceeds Book Value.* If the firm receives $35,000 from the sale of a machine carried at 0 book value, the firm has a $35,000 gain and must pay taxes on the gain. In effect, this means that the depreciation schedule allowed too much in tax credits for the wearing out of the machine. When the machine is sold, the firm must show the gain, normally as ordinary income, which is taxable at the corporate rate.

2. *Book Exceeds Cash Value.* In some cases, the firm will plan to sell the asset while it still has a positive book value. If, for example, the firm only received $12,000 from the sale of a $25,000 book value machine, it would have a loss of $13,000. The depreciation schedule underestimated the wearing out of the machine. The loss is normally treated as a tax credit against ordinary income.

3. *Book Equals Cash Value.* If this occurs or if the machine is traded in on a new machine, no tax effects normally need to be considered.

#### DIFFERENT BOOK AND CASH RESIDUAL VALUES

Because of the difficulties of forecasting value into the distant future, the firm expects to have different book and cash values at the end of an asset's service life. In many cases, a difference is expected before the machine is even purchased. This is true because of two characteristics of the book salvage value.

1. *Firm Seeks the Smallest Possible Book Residual Value.* Normally, the firm is interested in gaining maximum depreciation and a minimum book residual value so that it may gain greater tax shields and cash inflows. Thus, the firm will usually set up a depreciation schedule with a book value of zero, if permitted by the tax laws.

2. *Book Residual Value Must Comply with IRS Guidelines.* The book residual value is determined in accordance with guidelines from the Internal Revenue Service. This may result in a higher or lower book value than expected.

Because book values and cash values of assets may differ when the firm expects to sell the assets, the decision to invest in fixed assets must consider the tax effects on the sale of the old assets. When the book value is less than the cash value, the firm must pay additional taxes. When the book value exceeds the cash value, the firm receives a tax shield from the sale of the asset, and a tax saving results. Table 12–4 shows the calculations when a $100,000 book value machine is sold for either $160,000 or $60,000. The calculations assume ordinary tax rate for the firm although, in some cases, the firm may qualify for a capital-gains rate.

**TABLE 12–4.** Additional Taxes to Be Paid or Tax Saving When an Asset Is Sold at a Different Value than the Book Value.

| Additional Taxes—When Book Value Is Less than Cash Value | | Tax Savings—When Book Value Is Greater than Cash Value | |
|---|---|---|---|
| Book value, existing asset | $100,000 | | $100,000 |
| Cash received | 160,000 | | 60,000 |
| Gain on sale | 60,000 | Loss on sale | 40,000 |
| Times tax rate | × .40 | | × .40 |
| Additional taxes | 24,000 | Tax savings | 16,000 |

## TIME VALUE OF MONEY

If given a choice between having a dollar today or a dollar next year, the firm would choose the dollar today. This is because money has a time value. We have already covered this concept in some detail in Chapters 10 and 11. In capital budgeting, we recognize that money has a time value. If two projects were identical in every way except that one gave a return of $500,000 at the end of 2 years and the other gave $500,000 at the end of 3 years, we would choose the one with the earlier return.

It becomes more difficult to decide between projects when we are dealing with different returns and different time periods. If the second project gave us $550,000 at the end of 3 years, how would we compare it with $500,000 at the end of 2 years? The answer is, we would adjust the dollar amount and express the future value of each project in terms of today's dollars. This is called *discounting*. We discount both dollar amounts to the present at an appropriate discount rate and compare the *present value* of each. The one with the higher present value has the higher return.

At 10 percent, these two projects would be worth the same approximate amount. If the discount factor is less than 10 percent, the $550,000 project would have a higher present value. If the discount factor is greater than 10 percent, the $500,000 project would have the higher value. These effects are illustrated in Table 12–5.

From the table, note the relationship between the discount factor

**TABLE 12–5.**   Putting Future Dollar Amounts in Present Values.

| Present Value | | Year 1 | | Year 2 | | Year 3 |
|---|---|---|---|---|---|---|
| Discounting by 5% | | | | | | |
| $453,515 | ⟵ | $476,190 | ⟵ | $500,000 | | |
| 475,110 | ⟵ | 498,865 | ⟵ | 523,808 | ⟵ | $550,000 |
| Discounting by 10% | | | | | | |
| 413,223 | ⟵ | 454,545 | ⟵ | 500,000 | | |
| 413,223 | ⟵ | 454,545 | ⟵ | 500,000 | ⟵ | 550,000 |
| Discounting by 15% | | | | | | |
| 378,072 | ⟵ | 434,783 | ⟵ | 500,000 | | |
| 361,634 | ⟵ | 415,879 | ⟵ | 478,261 | ⟵ | 550,000 |

and the present value of the future returns: the higher the discount factor, the lower the present value. Stated differently, with high interest rates, less money is needed today to achieve a stated goal. At 5 percent, we need $453,515 to have $500,000 in 2 years. At 15 percent, only $378,072 is needed to have $500,000 in 2 years.

### PRESENT VALUE OF STEADY STREAMS

A difference occurs when projects are forecast to provide a steady stream of annual returns. An *annuity* exists when a project offers a series of equal cash inflows that occur at the end of successive periods of equal duration. As an example, a firm is considering two projects. Project A will return $500,000 annually for 2 years; project B will return $400,000 annually for 3 years. At a 10 percent discount factor, the present value of each project is:

| Project A | | | | Project B | | |
|---|---|---|---|---|---|---|
| Year | Cash Flow | PV | | Year | Cash Flow | PV |
| 1 | $500,000 | | | 1 | $400,000 | |
| 2 | 500,000 | $867,769 | | 2 | 400,000 | |
| | | | | 3 | 400,000 | $994,741 |

In this example, project B is worth more to the firm because the present value of its future receipts is higher than the present value of the receipts from project A.

CALCULATING THE PRESENT VALUE

Two formulas are used to discount future cash flows from capital budgeting projects.

**1.** *Present Value of Single Future Amount.* The formula is:

$$PV = \frac{FV}{(1 + int)^n}$$

where *PV* and *FV* are the present value and future value respectively, *int* is the discount factor, and *n* is the number of periods. If the firm is due to receive $550,000 in 2 years at a time when money is worth 10 percent, the present value is $454,545 as follows:

$$PV = \frac{550,000}{(1.10)^2} = 454,545$$

**2.** *Present Value of an Annuity.* The formula is:

$$PV = (PMT)\left(\frac{1}{int}\right)\left(1 - \frac{1}{(1 + int)^{12}}\right)$$

where *PMT* equals the dollar amount of each periodic cash flow. If the firm is due to receive $400,000 annually for 3 years, when money is worth 10 percent, the present value of the annuity is $994,741:

$$PV = (400,000)\left(\frac{1}{.10}\right)\left(1 - \frac{1}{(1.10)^3}\right) = \$994,741$$

Alternatively, the present values can be determined with the time-value-of-money calculators. For our two examples, we get:

| n | i | FV | PV |
|---|---|---|---|
| 2 | 10 | 550,000 | [454,545] |

and

| n | i | PMT | PV |
|---|---|-----|----|
| 3 | 10 | 400,000 | [994,741] |

**Example:** What is the present value of a $600,000 cash inflow due in 7 years when money has a time value of 13.5 percent?

**Answer:** $247,275, as follows:

$$PV = \frac{600,000}{(1.135)^7} = 247,275$$

or

| n | i | FV | PV |
|---|---|----|----|
| 7 | 13.5 | 600,000 | [247,275] |

**Example:** A project offers a $2.5 million annual aftertax return for 4 years when money is worth 15 percent. What is the present value of this project?

**Answer:** $7,137,446, as follows:

$$PV = 2,500,000\left(\frac{1}{.15}\right)\left(1 - \frac{1}{(1.15)^4}\right) = 7,137,446$$

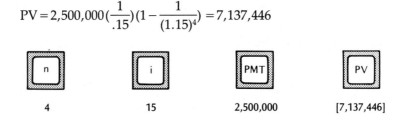

| n | i | PMT | PV |
|---|---|-----|----|
| 4 | 15 | 2,500,000 | [7,137,446] |

The present value of future receipts can also be calculated using present value tables, such as those in Chapter 11. If the reader desires to use these tables, they are accompanied by directions for their use. Because most tables are limited to even percents, we will not use them in this chapter. All of our calculations will assume the use of the formulas or time-value-of-money calculators.

## CALCULATING THE CASH-FLOW STREAM

A number of techniques exist for the detailed calculation of the cash flows projected from an investment of capital. In this section, we will outline one procedure that uses a step-by-step approach. This will increase the chances that the final stream will include all factors resulting from the proposal that may affect cash flow. Before developing the step-by-step procedures, it is important to understand the kind of stream that we are seeking.

### DIFFERENTIAL AFTERTAX STREAM

The differential stream results from taking the difference between a cash-flow stream without the new proposal and a stream with the new proposal. Let us use the following stream as an example:

| Year | Differential Aftertax Cash Flow |
|------|--------------------------------|
| 0 | $-4,000,000 |
| 1 | + 700,000 |
| 2 | + 900,000 |
| 3 | +1,100,000 |
| 4 | +1,600,000 |

An important general characteristic of a capital-budgeting cash-flow stream is that it normally begins with an outlay. This reflects the fact that we are dealing with a decision to commit funds today to get a project underway. This is the *net cash outlay (NCO)* represented by the −$4 million in year 0 in our cash-flow stream.

Once the money is invested, the firm expects a project to bring a return to the firm in the form of inflows after the initial expenditure. These are called the *net cash benefits* and are represented by the +$700,000 through the +$1.6 million in our stream. The inflows may begin in year 1 or 2 or later, but they normally are sustained once the project begins to produce a return.

### DUAL CASH-FLOW STREAMS

The conceptual framework for our differential stream is that we really must evaluate two streams. To illustrate this, assume that the firm is considering the purchase of a new machine to replace an existing machine. If the new machine is purchased, a cash-flow stream can be developed to reflect its purchase and the return from it. If the existing machine is kept, a similar cash-flow stream can be developed for it. The differential stream must consider the effects of both streams.

Let us begin with the stream for the new machine. Assume that the installation price of the new machine is $1.2 million and the aftertax return from the machine will be $500,000 a year for 3 years. At the end of 3 years, the new machine can be sold for $200,000 in cash. If the new machine is purchased, the existing machine can be sold immediately for $200,000. The existing machine costs nothing today since it already is operational, but it brings in a return of $100,000 a year and can last for 3 more years. Then it must be scrapped for $50,000. The two streams are

| Year | Purchase of New Machine | Continue Existing Machine |
|------|------------------------|---------------------------|
| 0 | $ − 1,200,000 | $        0 |
|   | +   200,000 |  |
| 1 | +   500,000 | + 100,000 |
| 2 | +   500,000 | + 100,000 |
| 3 | +   500,000 | + 100,000 |
|   | +   200,000 | +  50,000 |

What exactly is the conceptual decision facing the firm? Stated simply, should the firm invest the $1.2 million shown as an outlay in year 0 in the first stream to receive the differential benefits when the two streams are compared. After all, the firm will earn $100,000 a year if it does nothing; any new investment must be judged against an incremental benefit. Therefore, the decision to invest should be based on the differential stream, as follows:

| Year | New Machine | | Existing Machine | | Differential Stream |
|------|-------------|---|------------------|---|---------------------|
| 0 | $ − 1,000,000 | − | $        0 | = | $ − 1,000,000 |
| 1 | +   500,000 | − | + 100,000 | = | +   400,000 |
| 2 | +   500,000 | − | + 100,000 | = | +   400,000 |
| 3 | +   700,000 | − | + 150,000 | = | +   550,000 |

Note that the net cash outlay is not the $1.2 million purchase price of the new machine but rather the difference between the cost of the new machine and the cash from selling the existing machine. Also, the final year's inflows consider selling both machines.

In calculating differential streams, some actions appear to be counted twice. In our stream, the existing machine is sold in year 0 in the new machine column and in year 3 in the existing machine column. This is not double counting. If the new machine is purchased, the cash effects of selling the existing machine need to be shown in year 0. If it is not purchased, the sale occurs at the end of year 3. Both effects show up in the differential stream, but it is because the actions occur at different times, not because the same action is counted twice.

In our example, the differential stream is determined by subtracting values in the existing machine column from values in the new machine column. It is possible to develop two separate cash-flow streams and then subtract one from the other to get the differential. We will use this approach in the next section.

## FINANCIAL DATA FOR SAMPLE PROBLEM

To illustrate the process of calculating differential cash-flow streams, consider a firm that has an existing machine and is considering the purchase of a new machine. The relevant data follow.

1. The new machine is more efficient than the existing machine. It can produce additional output and can lower costs. This will increase the firm's revenues from products made by the machine from $4 million to $4.5 million and will lower costs from $2.1 million to $1.7 million. These numbers recognize factors such as the selling prices for the additional output and the relative maintenance and operating costs of the two machines.
2. The new machine will cost $2.2 million. Transportation and installation of the machine will cost $200,000. The firm will receive a $240,000 investment tax credit as a result of the purchase and installation of the machine.
3. The new machine will have a service life of 15 years, but the likely service life of the existing machine is only 4 years. Therefore, the decision will be based on a 4-year period.
4. The new machine processes raw materials more quickly and works more efficiently on long production runs. Thus, the firm

must tie up an additional $200,000 of goods in inventories to support the new machine.

5. At present, the book value of the existing machine is $800,000; it is being depreciated at $200,000 per year to a 0 book value. If the existing machine were sold today, its cash value would be $400,000. If it continues to operate for 4 more years, its cash value would be $100,000.

6. The new machine will be depreciated using a 5-year rate of 20/32/24/16/8. It will have a 0 book value in 5 years. In 4 years, it will have a $300,000 cash value.

## Step 1. Calculate the Net Cash Outlay

The net cash outlay is the differential amount of money that will be spent when the investment is made in year 0. It may be calculated by

$$NCO = -TC_{new} + ITC \pm workcap + cash_{exist} \pm taxes$$

where $TC_{new}$ = total cash paid for the new investment including purchase price, transportation, installation, and any related charges.

   $ITC$ = tax savings from investment tax credit.

   $workcap$ = changes in working-capital requirements; any cash to be tied up (an outlay) or freed (inflow) during service life of new machine.

   $cash_{exist}$ = net cash received from replacing existing machine. This could be the selling price or money received less any costs of removing the asset.

   $taxes$ = either the taxes saved or additional taxes to be paid as a result of purchasing the new asset.

In our example, the $TC_{new}$ is the $2.2 million purchase price plus $200,000 for transportation and installation. The investment tax credit produces a tax savings of $240,000. The working capital tied up is $200,000, which is treated as an outlay in year 0. It will be an inflow in year 4. The cash for the existing machine is $400,000. The tax effect is a savings that occurs because the firm sells an $800,000 book value machine for $400,000, producing a noncash or book loss. At a 40 percent tax rate, the loss of $400,000 on the sale produces a $160,000 tax savings.

Substituting into the formula, the net cash outlay is:

$$NCO = TC_{new} + ITC \pm workcap + cash_{exist} \pm taxes$$

$$= -2,400,000 + 240,000 - 200,000 + 400,000 + 160,000$$

$$= \underline{-1,800,000}$$

## Step 2. Calculate the Depreciation Schedule

Using the indicated 5-year depreciation rates, the depreciation each year is:

| Year | Rate | Annual Depreciation | Book Value |
|------|------|---------------------|------------|
| 0 | 0 | $ 0 | $2,400,000 |
| 1 | .20 | 480,000 | 1,920,000 |
| 2 | .32 | 768,000 | 1,152,000 |
| 3 | .24 | 576,000 | 576,000 |
| 4 | .16 | 384,000 | 192,000 |
| 5 | .08 | 192,000 | 0 |

The depreciation on the existing machine is given at $200,000 per year, down to a 0 book value. Since the current book value is $800,000, the annual depreciation of $200,000 will be realized for the 4-year planning period of the analysis.

## Step 3. Calculate Annual Aftertax Cash Flows

In our example, the annual cash flows will differ each year since the depreciation differs each year. To solve for each year's tax cash flows from the operation or employment of the asset, we begin with revenues, deduct cash expenses and noncash expenses, calculate taxes and deduct them, and then add back depreciation. This is done for our example in Table 12–6.

When examining the numbers in the table, the reader may wonder why we add back depreciation to get the aftertax cash flow. This can be illustrated by the first year of the cash flow from the proposed machine. What are the cash effects? The answer is $4.5 million in revenues, $1.7 million in costs, and $928,000 in taxes. The cash flow is $1,872,000 as follows:

| Revenues | $4,500,000 |
|---|---|
| Less costs | 1,700,000 |
| Less taxes | 928,000 |
| Aftertax cash flows | $1,872,000 |

We get the same answer when adding depreciation back to net income.

Another question from the table might ask why we do not include interest from debt in the calculation. The answer is that any financing costs are deliberately omitted. They are handled as part of the required return from a project and are not covered in capital budgeting. This is a traditional practice to avoid double counting the financing effects.

## Step 4. Calculate Additional Effects in Final Year

In this step, we incorporate any other effects into the individual cash-flow streams. We focus on the final year because the two most common miscellaneous effects occur here. The first is the return of the working capital tied up in year 0. The $200,000 in our example is treated as an

**TABLE 12–6.**  Calculating Differential Annual Aftertax Cash Flows.

| New Machine | Year 1 | Year 2 | Year 3 | Year 4 |
|---|---|---|---|---|
| Annual revenues | $4,500,000 | $4,500,000 | $4,500,000 | $4,500,000 |
| Less annual costs | 1,700,000 | 1,700,000 | 1,700,000 | 1,700,000 |
| Beforetax cash flow | 2,800,000 | 2,800,000 | 2,800,000 | 2,800,000 |
| Less annual depreciation | 480,000 | 768,000 | 576,000 | 384,000 |
| Taxable income | 2,320,000 | 2,032,000 | 2,224,000 | 2,416,000 |
| Less taxes (.40) | 928,000 | 812,800 | 889,600 | 966,400 |
| Net income | 1,392,000 | 1,219,200 | 1,334,400 | 1,449,600 |
| Add back depreciation | 480,000 | 768,000 | 576,000 | 384,000 |
| Aftertax cash flow | 1,872,000 | 1,987,200 | 1,910,400 | 1,833,600 |

| Existing Machine | Each Year |
|---|---|
| Annual revenues | $4,000,000 |
| Less annual costs | 2,100,000 |
| Beforetax cash flow | 1,900,000 |
| Less annual depreciation | 200,000 |
| Taxable income | 1,700,000 |
| Less taxes (.40) | 680,000 |
| Net income | 1,020,000 |
| Add back depreciation | 200,000 |
| Aftertax cash flow | $1,220,000 |

inflow in the final year. If working capital had been freed in year 0, it is treated as an outflow in the final year. This is conceptually correct even though the firm may not plan on tying up working capital when the machine is salvaged. Let us consider why. If the firm frees working capital by installation of a more efficient machine, it should recognize the benefit as an inflow in year 0. But this inflow is not the same as when the firm earns money. What is really happening is that the money is freed for other uses during the life of the new asset. By returning the working capital in the final year, we recognize, in effect, the time value of freeing the working capital. This is why we would treat it as an outflow in the final year.

The second major effect in the final year is that each machine is assumed sold in its respective cash-flow stream. To get the aftertax effect, we must estimate the book and cash values and compute the net cash value from the sale of each asset. Table 12–7 shows the calculation for both machines in our example.

Thus, we have a final year cash flow as follows:

|  | New Machine | Existing Machine |
| --- | --- | --- |
| Annual inflow from step 3 | $1,833,600 | $1,220,000 |
| Return of working capital | +   200,000 |  |
| Sale of machine | +   256,800 | 60,000 |
| Final year cash flow | 2,290,400 | 1,280,000 |

## Step 5. Calculate the Differential Aftertax Stream

To calculate the different stream, we subtract the existing machine stream from the new machine stream as follows:

| Year | New Machine | − | Existing Machine | = | Differential |
| --- | --- | --- | --- | --- | --- |
| 0 | $− 1,800,000 | − | $          0 | = | $− 1,800,000 |
| 1 | 1,872,000 | − | 1,220,000 | = | +   652,000 |
| 2 | 1,987,200 | − | 1,220,000 | = | +   767,200 |
| 3 | 1,910,400 | − | 1,220,000 | = | +   690,400 |
| 4 | 2,290,400 | − | 1,280,000 | = | + 1,010,400 |

This stream shows both the timing and amount of the net cash outlay and net cash benefits over the 4-year planning period. All cash that is re-

**TABLE 12–7.**   Net Cash Values from Sale of Machines in Final Year.

|  | New Machine | Existing Machine |
|---|---|---|
| Book value in 4 years | $ 192,000 | $        0 |
| Cash value in 4 years | 300,000 | 100,000 |
| Gain (loss) on sale in 4 years | 108,000 | 100,000 |
| Tax savings (additional taxes) (.40) | (43,200) | (40,000) |
| Plus cash received | 300,000 | 100,000 |
| Net cash value | 256,800 | 60,000 |

ceived, spent, or otherwise tied up during the life of the project is included in the stream. All effects are differential—the difference between having the investment and not having it. This is the correct basis for computing streams that can be evaluated with time-value-of-money techniques, as in the next section.

### A SOLVED PROBLEM

To illustrate the step-by-step approach to calculating a differential aftertax cash-flow stream, Figure 12–2 contains a solved problem.

### CONCLUSION TO CALCULATING A CASH-FLOW STREAM

The calculation of a differential aftertax cash-flow stream is a detailed process based on estimates of future returns from a current investment. Actual streams can be considerably more complicated than those illustrated in this chapter, but the principles are the same. The analyst must bring together all possible effects on cash flow into two streams: (1) one stream if the firm accepts the investment, and (2) another if the firm does not accept the investment. The net cash outlay required by the investment is included in the early year or years; the net cash benefits are derived downstream. Only the differential effects of both outlay and benefits should be considered in the analysis.

## EVALUATION OF INVESTMENT RETURNS

Once the cash-flow streams for competing capital-budgeting proposals have been developed over the service lives of the different assets, we are ready to evaluate each proposal. We call them *competing* proposals be-

**Given:**

| | |
|---|---|
| Purchase price of the new asset .......... | $10 million |
| Investment tax credit .................... | $ 1 million |
| Installation costs........................ | $ 2 million |
| Increase in working capital in year zero ... | $ 2.5 million |
| Book residual value of the new asset in 4 years .......................... | $960,000 |
| Cash residual value of the new asset in 4 years .......................... | $ 3.5 million |
| Revenues from new asset ................ | $21.5 million annually |
| Cash expenses on new asset ............. | $ 9.5 million annually |
| Book value, existing asset, today .......... | $ 4 million |
| Cash value, existing asset, today .......... | $ 5 million |
| Cash value, existing asset, in 4 years ....... | $ 1 million |
| Revenues from existing asset ............. | $19.25 million annually |
| Cash expenses on existing asset .......... | $11.25 million annually |

Planning period, 4 years.
Depreciation on new asset is 20/32/24/16/8.
Existing asset to be depreciated at a rate of $1 million a year
   for 4 more years.
Tax rate is 40 percent.

---

**Step 1.** Calculate the Net Cash Outlay

| | | | |
|---|---|---|---|
| Purchase price | $−10,000,000 | Today's book value | |
| Installation costs | − 2,000,000 | existing machine | $4,000,000 |
| Investment tax credit | + 1,000,000 | Cash from sale | 5,000,000 |
| Working capital tied up | − 2,500,000 | Gain | 1,000,000 |
| Sale of existing asset | + 5,000,000 | Additional taxes (.40) | −400,000 |
| Taxes on sale (.40) | − 400,000 | | |
| NET CASH OUTLAY | − 8,900,000 | | |

**Step 2.** Calculate the Depreciation Schedules

*New Machine*

| Year | Rate | Annual Depreciation | Book Value |
|---|---|---|---|
| 0 | — | — | $12,000,000 |
| 1 | 20 | $2,400,000 | 9,600,000 |
| 2 | 32 | 3,840,000 | 5,760,000 |
| 3 | 24 | 2,880,000 | 2,880,000 |
| 4 | 16 | 1,920,000 | 960,000 |
| 5 | 8 | 960,000 | 0 |

*Existing Machine*

$1 million a year for 4 years to a zero book value.

**Figure 12–2**   A Solved Cash-Flow Stream Problem.

**Step 3.** Calculate Annual Aftertax Cash Flows

| New Machine | Year 1 | Year 2 | Year 3 | Year 4 |
|---|---|---|---|---|
| Annual revenues (000s) | $21,500 | $21,500 | $21,500 | $21,500 |
| Annual cash expenses | 9,500 | 9,500 | 9,500 | 9,500 |
| Beforetax cash flow | 12,000 | 12,000 | 12,000 | 12,000 |
| Less annual depreciation | 2,400 | 3,840 | 2,880 | 1,920 |
| Taxable income | 9,600 | 8,160 | 9,120 | 10,080 |
| Less taxes (.40) | 3,840 | 3,264 | 3,648 | 4,032 |
| Net income | 5,760 | 4,896 | 5,472 | 6,048 |
| Add back depreciation | 2,400 | 3,840 | 2,880 | 1,920 |
| Aftertax cash flow | 8,160 | 8,736 | 8,352 | 7,968 |

| Old Machine | Each Year |
|---|---|
| Annual revenues (000s) | $19,250 |
| Annual cash expenses | 11,250 |
| Beforetax cash flow | 8,000 |
| Less annual depreciation | 1,000 |
| Taxable income | 7,000 |
| Less taxes (.40) | 2,800 |
| Net income | 4,200 |
| Add back depreciation | 1,000 |
| Aftertax cash flow | 5,200 |

**Step 4.** Calculate the Effects in Final Year (000s)

|  | New Asset | Existing Asset |
|---|---|---|
| Book salvage value | $   960 | $    0 |
| Cash salvage value | 3,500 | 1,000 |
| Gain (loss) on sale | 2,540 | 1,000 |
| Tax savings (additional taxes) (.40) | (1,016) | (400) |
| Plus cash received | 3,500 | 1,000 |
| Net cash value | 2,484 | 600 |
| + return of working capital | +2,500 | 0 |
| + annual inflow from step 3 | +7,968 | +5,200 |
| Final year cash flow | 12,952 | 5,800 |

**Step 5.** Calculate the Differential Aftertax Stream (000s)

| Year | New Asset | − | Existing Asset | = | Differential |
|---|---|---|---|---|---|
| 0 | $− 8,900 | − | $    0 | = | $−8,900 |
| 1 | + 8,160 | − | +5,200 | = | +2,960 |
| 2 | + 8,736 | − | +5,200 | = | +3,536 |
| 3 | + 8,352 | − | +5,200 | = | +3,152 |
| 4 | +12,952 | − | +5,800 | = | +7,152 |

**Figure 12–2**   *(continued)*

cause most firms have more investment opportunities than financial resources. Therefore, the acceptance of one project may rule out the acceptance of others. To distinguish among the competing proposals, the firm must develop a ranking procedure that will determine the method of allocation of capital funds.

This section covers the evaluation of capital investments under conditions of certainty. We will begin with one traditional approach to evaluating proposals, even as we recognize that it is limited in usefulness. Then we will examine in detail the two present-value approaches that are considerably stronger tools for evaluating capital budgeting proposals.

## PAYBACK METHOD

One traditional approach to evaluating capital-budgeting proposals is the payback method. The *payback period* is the length of time needed to regain an original cash outlay from an investment proposal. The calculations are in dollars and not adjusted for the time value of money. As an example, Table 12–8 shows cash-flow streams for projects A and B. The outlays are given in year 0; the payback periods are indicated at 3 years and 3⅓ years.

The payback method is the easiest and least precise of the cash-flow methods and has been widely used for a long time. Its primary role is as a supplemental tool in the evaluation of capital investments. Although it should not be used alone, it has the distinct benefit of highlighting the liquidity aspects of a proposal. It shows, in effect, how quickly cash will return to the firm. This information can be useful if the firm might be short on cash in the near future and is seeking early returns to finance future proposals. Also, if the firm is operating in a highly uncertain environment, early cash return can be important. As an example, consider a firm that is entering a new field where competitors are expected in a

**TABLE 12–8.**   Payback Periods for Two Cash-Flow Streams.

| Year | Project A | | | | Project B |
|---|---|---|---|---|---|
| 0 | $ − 18,000 | | | | $ − 26,000 |
| 1 | + 6,000 | | | | + 7,500 |
| 2 | + 6,000 | → 3 years | Payback | 3⅓ years ← | + 7,500 |
| 3 | + 6,000 | | Period | | + 7,500 |
| 4 | + 10,000 | | | | + 18,000 |

few years. The uncertainty of who will enter and how successful they will be places a premium on early returns. In this situation, payback is a valid concept.

Although it has utility as a supplemental tool, the payback method suffers from some weaknesses. One problem is that it places too much emphasis on liquidity. If payback is the main criterion for project selection, liquidity would receive priority over profitability. This would not be correct for most long-term investments. Another problem is that payback does not recognize variations in cash flow. As an example, one project may have cash inflows of $300,000 year 1, $400,000 year 2, and $500,000 year 3. A second project may have $500,000, $400,000, and $300,000 for years 1 to 3, respectively. If both projects involved net cash outlays of $1.2 million, the payback would be 3 years for each. But the second project would give more cash earlier and would be more valuable. This kind of situation cannot be adequately handled by payback.

Perhaps the major difficulty in using payback is that it cannot properly handle investments of differing economic lives. If two projects cost $2.5 million and have a $500,000 annual cash inflow after taxes, the payback period would be 5 years for each. If one project had an estimated life of 7 years and the other a 10-year life, the additional cash-flow in years 8 to 10 would not be reflected in the payback method. But the cash flow makes the longer project more valuable.

### PRESENT VALUE APPROACHES TO EVALUATING INVESTMENTS

Given the weaknesses and limitations of the payback method, most investment analysis is performed with one of the two present value approaches to calculating return. These are the *internal rate of return* and *net present value methods*. We shall discuss each in turn.

### Internal Rate of Return (IRR)

The *internal rate of return* method calculates the actual rate of return provided by a specific stream of net cash benefits compared to a specific net cash outlay. It uses a trial-and-error approach to find the discount factor that equates the original investment to the net cash benefits. The discount factor, then, is the actual rate of return.

We are solving for *int*, which is the discount factor and rate of return. If, for example, we find that the 10 percent factor sets the benefits equal to the outlay, the internal rate of return for the investment is 10 percent.

As an example of this technique, we will calculate the internal rate of return for a 4-year stream, as shown.

| Year | Differential Flows (000s) | |
|------|------|------|
| 0 | $ −1,800 | net cash outlay |
| 1 | + 600 | |
| 2 | + 600 | net cash |
| 3 | + 600 | benefits |
| 4 | +1,000 | |

We set the net cash outlay equal to the net cash benefits times the appropriate discount factors. The stream has an annuity of $600,000 for 3 years and a single payment of $1 million in year 4.

We must estimate the rate of return and select a discount factor. This is essentially a trial-and-error process that is helped by experience. Let us try 10 percent as a factor.

| Present Value at 10 Percent | |
|------|------|
| Year | Present Value |
| 0 | $ −1,800 |
| 1 | |
| 2 | |
| 3 | +1,492 |
| 4 | + 683 |
| | + 375   net present value |

In this example, we have solved for the *net present value*, which is the difference between the present value of the net cash benefits and present value of the net cash outlay. A positive net present value of $375,000 is not very close to the 0 that we need. We must now try another factor; the question is, "Do we go up or down?" The rule is this:

**In using present value tables, raising the discount factor lowers the present value.**

**Lowering the discount factor raises the present value.**

Thus, the discount factor of 10 percent is too low. Let us raise it to 18 percent in order to lower the present value of the benefits.

| Present Value at 18 Percent | |
| --- | --- |
| Year | Present Value |
| 0 | $-1,800 |
| 1 | |
| 2 | |
| 3 | +1,305 |
| 4 | + 516 |
| | + 21  net present value |

This is much closer but still a little high. Try 20 percent to see if we can achieve a negative net present value.

| Present Value at 20 Percent | |
| --- | --- |
| Year | Present Value |
| 0 | $-1,800 |
| 1 | |
| 2 | |
| 3 | +1,264 |
| 4 | + 482 |
| | - 54  net present value |

We did it. We now know that the rate of return for the stream is 18 to 20 percent, since we bracketed a 0 net present value with these numbers. Since the $21,000 net present value at 18 percent is closer than the $54,000 at 20 percent, we know that the rate of return is closer to 18 percent than 20 percent. We can repeat our calculation at, say, 18.5 percent if we want more accuracy. For our purposes, we will not seek more accuracy. We recognize that the rate of return is between 18 and 19 percent, probably around 18.5 percent.

### Acceptance Criterion—The Required Return

Once the internal rate of return has been forecast for a proposal, the firm must determine whether the project is acceptable. At this point, the firm usually considers return as a single input into the final decision. In addition to profits, the firm evaluates liquidity, growth, diversification, company image, and other factors that affect the goal of maximizing wealth. Perhaps the most important single factor in evaluating proposals is the level of risk inherent in the project. If a project offers high risk that the return will not be achieved, the required return on the project will also be high. The trading off of risk and return is the process that the firm should use in determining the acceptability of its proposals.

Once the risk level of a proposal has been determined, the firm will select a *cutoff point* for that risk level. This is defined as the boundary between accepted and rejected investment proposals. The proposal's *required return* for the level of risk will be the cutoff point for the proposal. Because of the difficulty in calculating required return, we will cover this topic separately in the next chapter. In the meantime, we will assume a required return for all proposals in this chapter. As an example, we might state that the aftertax required return for a project is 12 percent, and we will accept the proposal only if the forecast return is 12 percent or greater.

Bringing together the forecast or internal rate of return and the required return, we have an *acceptance criterion* for the proposal. Subject to the availability of capital, the firm will accept projects that offer a return at or above the required return. Proposals that fail to meet this acceptance criterion would be rejected.

### Net Present Value (NPV) Method

The *net present value method* is the second time-value-of-money approach to evaluating the return from an investment proposal. It differs from the trial-and-error approach of the internal rate of return method. With the NPV method, we discount a project using the required return as the discount factor. If the net present value is positive, the proposal's forecast return exceeds the required return and the proposal is acceptable. If the net present value is negative, the forecast return is less than the required return and the proposal is not acceptable.

To illustrate the net present value method, let us consider the preceding project and assume that the required return on it is 15 percent.

When we discount the cash flows at 15 percent, we get a net present value of:

| Year | Cash-Flow Stream | Present Value at 18 Percent |
|---|---|---|
| 0 | $ − 1,800 | $ − 1,800 |
| 1 | + 600 | |
| 2 | + 600 | |
| 3 | + 600 | + 1,370 |
| 4 | + 1,000 | + 572 |
| | net present value | + 142 |

When discounted at the 15 percent required return, this proposal has a positive net present value. This would be expected, since we have already determined the forecast rate of return to be over 18 percent. Under the net present value method, proposals with positive net present values are acceptable since they have higher forecast returns than the required return; negative NPV proposals are not acceptable.

### Difference Between the IRR and NPV Methods

The internal rate of return and net present value methods can give different results in the ranking of proposals. This is the case because conceptually at least, the two methods make different assumptions on the reinvestment of proceeds. In effect, the IRR method assumes that future cash receipts are invested at the rate of return forecast for the project. The net present value method assumes that proceeds are invested at the required return. If the forecast return on the project exceeds the required return, the two methods can give a different ranking of proposals.

To understand what is happening with the two methods, let us compare the results when projects A and B are being evaluated. Proposal A involves a $1 million net cash outlay and has only one future receipt of cash, $1.2 million in 1 year. Proposal B also involves a $1 million outlay and also has a single future receipt of cash, $1.5 million in 3 years. The internal rate of return on these two proposals is 20 percent for A and 14.47 percent for B, as follows:

|       | Proposal A | | | Proposal B | | |
|-------|------------|---------|--|------------|-----------|--|
| Year  | Cash Flow | PV (.20) | | Cash Flow | PV (.1447) | |
| 0     | $ – 1,000  | $ – 1,000 | | $ – 1,000 | $ – 1,000 | |
| 1     | + 1,200    | + 1,000   | | 0         |           | |
| 2     | 0          |           | | 0         |           | |
| 3     | 0          |           | | + 1,500   | + 1,000   | |
|       |            | NPV   0   | |           | NPV    0  | |

Using the internal rate of return method, proposal A would be more desirable than proposal B, since a 20 percent return is higher than a 15 percent return. But what would happen if the aftertax required return were only 8 percent? Using the net present value method, we get a higher net present value with proposal B, as follows:

|       | Proposal A | | | Proposal B | | |
|-------|------------|---------|--|------------|-----------|--|
| Year  | Cash Flow | PV (.08) | | Cash Flow | PV (.08) | |
| 0     | $ – 1,000  | $ – 1,000 | | $ – 1,000 | $ – 1,000 | |
| 1     | + 1,200    | + 1,111   | | 0         |           | |
| 2     | 0          |           | | 0         |           | |
| 3     | 0          |           | | + 1,500   | + 1,191   | |
|       |            | NPV  +  111 | |           | NPV  +  191 | |

With the net present value method, proposal B is more desirable than proposal A.

Which is correct? The answer is that it depends on what happens to the $1.2 million that proposal A will return at the end of year 1. If this $1.2 million can be invested so that it produces more than $1.5 million by the end of year 3, proposal A should be more desirable. If it cannot achieve $1.5 million, proposal B is more desirable. In other words, the firm would be better off receiving just under 15 percent for 3 years rather than 20 percent for 1 year and a lower percent for the next 2 years.

Most financial analysts correctly argue that the net present value method is more accurate for most capital-budgeting proposals. It assumes the investment of future cash flows at the required return, not at the potentially higher forecast return for a single proposal. Generally, it would be a rare case for a forecast return to be much higher than a required return. Thus, assuming investment of future cash flows at the required return is more accurate in most cases. But, should the firm have the rare case when proceeds can be invested at the internal rate of return, the IRR method is more accurate.

## KEY TERMS

| | | |
|---|---|---|
| *acceptance criterion* | *contingent projects* | *net cash benefits* |
| *annuity* | *cutoff point* | *net cash outlay* |
| *book residual value* | *discounting* | *net present value* |
| *capital budgeting* | *internal rate of return* | *operating budget* |
| *capital rationing* | *investment tax credit* | *payback period* |
| *cash-flow stream* | *mutually exclusive projects* | *required return* |
| *cash residual value* | | |

## STUDY QUESTIONS

1. What is capital budgeting? What are the two sides to the capital-budgeting decision?
2. Why is capital budgeting significant to the firm?
3. What kinds of proposals are found in a firm's capital budget?
4. How does a firm estimate needs for the capital budget?
5. What is the general guideline with respect to approval for proposals?
6. How long is an industrial firm's planning horizon?
7. What is meant by mutually exclusive projects? contingent projects?
8. What does capital rationing mean to the person preparing the capital budget?
9. What role do accounting techniques play in capital budgeting?
10. What kind of cash-flow stream is used in capital budgeting?
11. How does a firm realize a cash flow?
12. How is depreciation included in capital budgeting? How are investment tax credits included? working capital? What roles do cash and book salvage values play?
13. What are the two methods of depreciation permitted in the United States? Which one do most firms use for capital asset depreciation?
14. What is depreciation recapture? capital gain?
15. What is the relationship between the discount factor and the present value?
16. From what does a differential stream result?
17. What is an important general characteristic of a cash-flow stream? What does it reflect?
18. In what circumstances is the payback period a useful technique? What are its weaknesses?
19. What is the major difference between internal rate of return and net present value techniques?

## PROBLEMS

1. A machine costs $500,000 and has a life expectancy of 10 years and a scrap value of $4,000. What is the depreciable cost? the annual depreciation?
2. A firm buys heavy equipment for $3 million. It is depreciated over 5 years on a schedule of 20/32/24/16/8. What is the annual depreciation?
3. A firm buys a computer for $800,000. One year later, its value has appreciated to $950,000, and the firms sells it for this amount. What is the capital gain?
4. What is the present value of a $200,000 payment due in 5 years at 6 percent?
5. If a firm is due to receive seven annual payments of $150,000, what is the present value of the stream when money is worth 10 percent?
6. A firm is due to receive $50,000 a year for the next 4 years and $70,000 at the end of the 5th year. Money is worth 4 percent. What is the present value of the stream?
7. A firm is due to receive $80,000 next year, $100,000 in 2 years, $120,000 in 3 years, and $150,000 at the end of 4 years. What is the present value of the stream if money has a time value of 12 percent?
8. A firm is purchasing an asset to replace an existing asset. The purchase price is $300,000 plus an additional $40,000 to transport and install it. It will operate much more quickly than the asset that it replaces and therefore will tie up additional inventory worth $60,000. The asset qualifies the firm for a $45,000 investment tax credit. The firm has an existing asset that can be sold for $45,000; it will cost $15,000 to remove it so that it can be delivered to the buyer. The book value on the existing asset is $40,000. What is the net cash outlay for the new asset?
9. The installed cost of a new piece of equipment is $600,000. The machine will have a 10-year service life, at which time it will have a book value of $60,000. Using the straight-line method, what is the depreciable cost of the machine? the annual depreciation?
10. A firm has an asset that generates annual revenue of $850,000 and incurs annual costs of $350,000. These costs do not include $60,000 of depreciation. If a replacement machine is purchased, the revenues would rise to $950,000, the costs would drop to $320,000, but the depreciation on the new machine would be $80,000 per year. What are the annual aftertax cash flows on each machine?
11. In the final year of a new asset's service life, the firm expects to liquidate $400,000 of working capital and receive an aftertax cash flow of $260,000. This does not count the cash from the sale of the new asset, which should bring $120,000, a figure that is higher than the book salvage value at the same time, which will be $90,000. Had the new asset not been purchased, an existing machine would have lasted until the same year, when it would have had a book value of $40,000 and a cash value of $30,000. The existing machine would have had an aftertax cash inflow of $110,000. What are the final-year effects for the old and new assets?
12. A firm is considering purchasing a replacement machine. The existing machine can run for 5 more years, producing annual revenues of $60,000 with

cash expenses of $30,000. Its book value is $20,000 and it is being depreciated at $4,000 a year down to a 0 book value. The machine could be sold today to net $8,000 or it could be sold in 5 years to net $5,000. The replacement machine will cost $50,000 plus an additional $20,000 to transport it to the factory and install it. It will generate revenues of $90,000 but will have cash expenses of $40,000. It will be depreciated using the straight-line method over a 5-year period, at which time it will have a book value of $20,000 and a cash salvage value of $25,000. The replacement machine will require additional working capital of $5,000 to be tied up permanently. What is the differential aftertax cash-flow stream?

13. A firm is having difficulties with an automated grinding machine. Even though the machine has 4 more years of service life, its operating costs are fairly sizable compared to its revenues. For the next 4 years, the revenues generated will be $1.3 million annually but the annual cash expenses will be $950,000. In addition, it must take depreciation of $200,000 per year until the machine reaches 0 book value. The machine could be sold today to a foreign manufacturing firm for net cash of $200,000, which is less than its current book value of $400,000. This is not good since, if the machine were held for 4 years, it could probably be sold for $200,000 net cash. The firm's alternative is to invest in a new grinding machine costing $1 million, not counting the $200,000 needed to transport and install it. The new machine would generate revenues of $2.3 million with cash expenses of $1,450,000. It would be depreciated over a 4-year period to a book value of $400,000, at which time it could be sold for $350,000 net cash. Depreciation would be by the straight-line method. The new machine would require tying up an additional $500,000 of inventory and receivables over the 4-year period. What is the differential aftertax cash-flow stream for this proposal?

14. An investment of $650,000 will yield returns of $150,000 the 1st year, $250,000 the 2nd year, $300,000 the 3rd year, and $450,000 the 4th and 5th years. What is the payback period?

15. What are the rate of return and the net present value for the following proposal if the firm's cost of capital is 10 percent?

| Cash Flow | |
| --- | --- |
| 0 | − 12,000 |
| 1 | + 4,000 |
| 2 | + 4,000 |
| 3 | + 6,000 |

16. What are the rate of return and the net present value of the following proposal at a 10 percent cost of capital?

| Cash Flow | |
| --- | --- |
| 0 | − 27,000 |
| 1 | + 10,000 |
| 2 | + 15,000 |
| 3 | + 15,000 |

17. A firm is evaluating an investment of $17 million to build a small refinery to process lube oils and specialty products. The terms of the construction agreement would require an initial payment of $6 million on January 1, another $6 million payment one year later, and a final $5 million one year after the second payment. The firm's required return is 12 percent. After the third payment, the refinery would be operational and should produce cash inflows of $2 million per year after taxes for 15 years. What is the rate of return on this investment? the net present value?

18. A firm receives $9 million a year after taxes from an investment in a steel-processing plant that has 12 more years of service life. The firm's required return is 12 percent. The firm can make improvements to the plant to raise its service life to 20 years and its annual aftertax cash flow to $32 million per year. These investments would cost $140 million. With the improvements, the plant's aftertax value at the end of 12 years would rise from $5 million to $50 million. Would the improvements produce a return satisfactory to the firm?

# Capital Budgeting

*This case requires the reader to evaluate a project by forecasting its rate of return and by calculating its net present value at an effective interest rate.*

Darnell Inc. is a small California bottling company, founded by Jacob Darnell at the turn of the century. It was founded at the site of a mineral spring 40 miles from San Francisco and still ships bottled water throughout a six-state area. Its cash sales have stabilized at $9 million compared to cash expenses of $5 million on its bottled-water operations.

There is considerable excitement in the office of Jerry Darnell, the president and grandson of the founder. The company has been offered a 5-year lease on a well-known mineral spring near the Nevada-California line. The water from this spring has certain medicinal properties that make it valuable to physicians nationwide. Ralph Walton, the company's financial manager, has just worked up figures on the possibility of taking over the lease.

Ralph estimates that an operation at the new mineral spring would increase the firm's sales from $9 to $15 million each year over the 5-year period. He also estimates an increase in cash expenses from $5 to $9 million.

Walton's plan is to move the water by tank truck from the spring to the company's main facilities for bottling. The problem is capacity. At the present level of sales, the firm cannot handle the additional bottling needs of the new spring. A check with a machinery foundry indicates that it will cost approximately $6.5 million to purchase, transport, and install new bottling machinery capable of handling the new spring. This machinery will replace the existing machinery and will have a 25-year service life. After 4 years, the machinery will have a cash value of $800,000. It will be depreciated at 20/32/24/16/8 over a 5-year period.

The company's existing machinery has been working fairly well. It is carried on the books at a $1 million value, although it could be sold for only $500,000. In 4 years, its cash value will be $300,000. The firm uses straight-line depreciation on the existing machinery, with 2 more years at $500,000 a year remaining on its schedule.

Ralph Walton has mentioned that the new operation would tie up an additional $300,000 in inventories and $400,000 in receivables during the life of the project. The firm has the funds to finance these amounts, particularly since a 10 percent investment tax credit is available.

Ralph Walton thinks the firm should seriously consider the new project and Jerry is also favorably inclined. But as Ralph left the office, Jerry was heard to call out, "I want to know our rate of return on the project first. If we're not making our normal 12 percent after taxes, forget it!" The firm's tax rate is 40 percent.

## Questions

1.  What is the rate of return on this project?
2.  What is the net present value at 12 percent?

# BALMOR CORPORATION CASE
## Capital Budgeting

*This case tests the reader's knowledge of capital-budgeting in requiring the reader to pull conflicting information into the capital-budgeting decision.*[1]

The Balmor Corporation is a medium-sized cable manufacturing company in northern Indiana, approximately 40 miles from Chicago. Founded in 1923, the company has expanded steadily and has developed solid contacts with utilities in a number of midwestern states. The company has several long-term contracts with firms, including subsidiaries of American Telephone and Telegraph.

Balmor's management has been particularly interested in taking advantage of the demand for soft, fully annealed copper wire that is used in insulated conductors in communication and power systems. The executive committee of the firm has been discussing an expansion of wire-drawing facilities to meet anticipated demand.

To gain the most recent information, Joe Halli, the firm's controller, went to the 1984 Wire Association Convention to review the various types of machines available. He paid particular attention to manufacturers with machinery that promised high production and consistent quality. After 3 days of discussion with a variety of production and industry experts, Joe called George Gray, a representative for a milling and machinery firm in Cincinnati. Joe asked George to send him some of the details on the machinery that they had discussed and George agreed to do so. Two weeks later, Joe received the following letter:

> Dear Mr. Halli:
>
> In response to your inquiry, I am pleased to suggest two possible machines that would amply meet your needs for high-quality fully annealed copper wire.
>
> Our first machine, the MX900 model, is proba-

---

[1]This case is based on data developed by Linda R. Tassi.

bly the finest full-production wire-drawing machine on the market today. The wire-drawing machine and annealer are an integral unit with special electronic controls that allow the annealer to work during start-up procedures. Your production manager will well understand how this excellent machine offers lower operating costs due to less scrap and simplified operating procedures.

Our second machine, the MX700, is also a very fine machine and may well meet your needs. The wire-drawing machine and annealer are an integral unit, but the annealer does not start up until operating speed is reached. This causes some scrap wire during start-up since, without the annealer operating, the first reel of output would contain hard wire. But this may be the perfect machine for long production runs.

If you order one of these machines by January 1, 1985, and make the required deposit, I will personally guarantee that the machine will be set up and operating by January 1, 1986. And I will be further able to guarantee that you will receive our 1984 price less a 10 percent discount, an attractive offer indeed! The pricing is as follows:

|                            | MX900       | MX700       |
|----------------------------|-------------|-------------|
| 1984 price                 | $1,666,667  | $1,333,333  |
| Less 10% discount          | 166,667     | 133,333     |
| Net full price             | $1,500,000  | $1,200,000  |
| +shipping and installing   | 300,000     | 200,000     |
| Fully installed price      | $1,800,000  | $1,400,000  |
|                            |             |             |
| Deposit (Jan. 1, 1985)     | 750,000     | 600,000     |
| Balance due (Jan. 1, 1986) | $1,050,000  | $  800,000  |

As an item of interest, you should know that our prices have already risen by 5 percent on these machines and will rise another 8 percent on January 1. By ordering and paying your deposit prior to January 1, you in effect will be saving 23 percent compared to an order placed in 1985, when I probably will not be able to offer any discount.

If you need any additional information,
please do not hesitate to call me. I look forward
to hearing from you in the near future.
                        Sincerely yours,
                        George Gray

After reading the letter carefully and making some notes on it, Joe sent a memoranda to Nick Schafer, the firm's production manager, and Lew Wallis, the firm's senior production accountant. He asked both men to respond to the letter from George Gray and to answer some questions related to other aspects of the investment decision. Three days later, Joe received Nick's reply.

TO:     Joe Halli
FROM:   Nick Schafer

We should seriously consider both machines. We
could buy one of these and get rid of an old MX430,
which we bought 2 years ago from the same firm. The
MX430 works fine and I'd bet that we could get
$400,000 if we sold it in January 1986—pretty good
since we only paid $600,000 for it and its book
value on January 1, 1986 will only be $300,000
(we're depreciating it at $100,000 a year down to
a 0 book value). According to what I've heard
there is one difference between these machines.
The MX900 is so efficient that we could probably
eliminate some $80,000 of inventory around here
once the machine was fully operational. The other
machine needs longer production runs and we would
have to increase inventory, probably by about
$20,000. This is important; but more importantly,
the machines will save us money. So I think it
would make sense to make a replacement and my personal choice would be the MX900.

Two days after receiving Nick's memorandum, Joe received a reply from Lew Wallis.

TO:     Joe Halli
FROM:   Lew Wallis

I got a copy of Nick's memo and we had better think
twice on these new machines. By 1989, I'd bet
either of these new machines would be a piece of

junk. I made a couple of phone calls and learned
that these new machines are just too sophisticated
for long-term use. Our MX430 will probably be
worth $250,000 at the end of 1985. Do you know what
my ''experts'' estimate the new machines would be
worth? $150,000 for the almost $2 million MX900,
and about $110,000 for the MX700. Some cash value
in 4 years, heh? But that's the price of buying
fancy equipment. And everybody knows this. Even
with a 20/32/24/16/8 depreciation schedule (20
percent the first year, and so on) over 5 years to
a 0 book value, these machines are not reasonable.
And the MX900 for $1.8 million? You'll never con-
vince me that it makes sense. I think Nick's just
not thinking and I STRONGLY urge you to stay with
our existing machine.

Before Joe had a chance to consider either of the positions, he got a second memorandum from Nick Schafer.

TO:      Joe Halli
FROM:    Nick Schafer

Hold it! Stop! Wait! Whatever happened to production efficiency? Lew's memo does not even touch on
the rather impressive economies offered by each
machine. I have done some quick figures and the
MX900 will save us a bundle. Even the MX700, which
requires a little more maintenance and has slower
production capabilities, is better than the
MX430. I've figured in a few probabilities and
just look at the annual cash savings-operating
savings that we could get with these machines:

| MX900 | MX700 |
|---|---|
| 20% chance of $850,000 | 20% of $500,000 |
| 60% chance of $800,000 | 50% of $430,000 |
| 20% chance of $500,000 | 30% of $350,000 |

These are savings compared to the MX430-big savings.
Even if we only got them for 4 years, we would be
ahead with any of the machines. Don't give up the
ship.

After receiving the final memorandum, Joe called Lew Wallis. Lew said that he helped Nick work out the figures on the annual savings and Lew indicated that the percentages and dollar savings figures were logical and probably correct. But Lew insisted that the purchase of new machinery still did not make sense because the machinery was simply too expensive.

That night, Joe took the memorandums home to decide whether either of the pieces of machinery would provide a return equal to or greater than the firm's 14 percent aftertax required return.

## Questions

1. What are the net cash outlays (2 years) for each of the new machines?
2. Prepare a cash-flow stream for each new machine, assuming that each machine would become operational on January 1, 1986.
3. What is the rate of return for each machine?
4. What are the net present values for each machine?
5. Which machines are acceptable?

# 13

# Risk and Required Return

The conceptual basis for examining the relationship between risk and return is developed in a framework called the *capital asset pricing model.* The model offers a theory and methodology for evaluating any investment decision where capital is committed for the purpose of earning future profits. The model was first proposed and developed by Sharpe, Lintner, Miller and Modigliani, and others in the l960s[*] and is fully developed today. It has modified cost of capital analysis and the approach to capital budgeting in the firm.

In this chapter, we will develop a capital asset approach to the required return. We will tie the model in to the traditional cost of capital theory. Then we will reconcile the concepts of required return and cost of capital. We will do this without deriving the elements of the capital asset theory, which is, in itself, highly mathematical and complex. The underlying truth of the theory and its application in capital-budgeting situations can be seen without the quantitative proof of relationships.

---

[*]William F. Sharpe, "Capital Asset Prices: A Theory of Market Equilibrium under Condition of Risk," *Journal of Finance,* September 1964; John Lintner, "Dividends, Earnings, Leverage, Stock Prices, and the Supply of Capital to Corporations," *Review of Economics and Statistics,* August 1962; and Franco Modigliani and Merton Miller, "The Cost of Capital, Corporation Finance, and the Theory of Investment," *The American Economic Review,* June 1958.

## CAPITAL ASSET THEORY

In its purest form, the capital asset pricing model is a comprehensive theory of risk and return relationships in perfect markets. It makes such assumptions as rational behavior on the part of all investors; a highly competitive environment for investing, where all investors know risks and expected returns; no fees, commissions or taxes; and no risk of bankruptcy. Within the confines of these highly restrictive assumptions, a risk-return relationship is developed in considerable detail. In perfect markets, such as those assumed by the model, there is no quarreling with capital asset theory. It is a conceptually correct approach to risk and return.

For our purposes, we are seeking the required return in imperfect markets. All information is not known. All investors are not rational. Bankruptcy is a daily possibility and occurrence. How does the capital asset theory hold up under such circumstances? The answer is remarkably well. In this section, we will develop a modified capital asset theory for imperfect markets.

### MEANING OF RISK

In evaluating a capital-budgeting proposal, the firm should recognize that the forecast return may or may not be achieved. This is the element of risk in the decision-making process. *Risk* may be defined as the likelihood that the actual return from an investment will be less than the forecast return. Stated differently, it is the *variability of return* from an investment.

There are many ways to measure risk. Three methods are commonly used:

1. *Beta Coefficient.* This is a mathematical value that measures the risk of one asset in terms of its effects on the risk of a group of assets, called a *portfolio.* It is concerned solely with *market-related risk,* as would be the concern for an investor holding stocks and bonds. It is derived mathematically so that a high beta indicates a high level of risk; a low beta represents a low level of risk.
2. *Standard Deviation.* This is a measure of the dispersion of forecast returns when such returns approximate a normal probability distribution. It is a statistical concept and is widely used to measure risk from holding a single asset. The standard deviation is derived so that a high standard deviation represents a large disper-

sion of return and is a high risk; a low deviation is a small dispersion and represents a low risk.

3. *Subjective Estimates.* A subjective risk measure occurs when qualitative rather than quantitative estimates are used to measure dispersion. As an example, an analyst may estimate that a proposal offers a "low" level of risk. This means that, in the analyst's view, the dispersion of returns will not be very wide. Similarly, a "high" risk level will accompany a project whose forecast returns may vary a great deal.

We will use the definition of risk that deals with dispersion of return. We will also note the fact that mathematical approaches can be used to estimate such dispersions. In this chapter, we will confine our examples to subjective estimates of the level of risk in proposals.

## MEANING OF RETURN

The rate of return from a capital investment is a concept that has different meanings to different investors. Some companies seek near-term cash inflows and give less value to more distant returns. Such a firm might purchase the stock of other firms that pay large cash dividends. Other investors are concerned primarily with growth. They would seek projects that offer the promise of long-term, higher-than-average growth of sales and earnings. Still others measure return using financial ratios. They might seek to invest in a company that has a high return on investment or equity.

In this chapter, we will use a discounted cash-flow measure of return, using the internal rate of return or net present value methods from Chapter 12. We will assume that any investment requires an outlay of cash and involves a forecast series of inflows in future periods. Since the concept of return was thoroughly developed in the last chapter, it will not be repeated here.

## RISK AND RETURN RELATIONSHIP

The expected return from any investment proposal will be linked in a fundamental relationship to the degree of risk in the proposal. In order to be acceptable, a higher-risk proposal must offer a higher forecast return than a lower-risk proposal. This relationship is shown in Figure 13–1.

EXPECTED RETURN

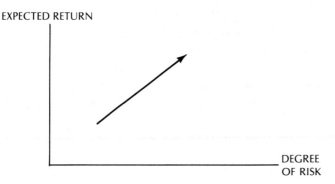

Figure 13–1 General Pattern of Risk and Return.

A *market line* may be defined as the general pattern of risk and return in an investing market. Such a line is shown in Figure 13–2. With respect to this diagram, we might note some characteristics of the line, namely:

1. *Upward Sloping.* The line slopes upward from the left axis of the diagram. This reflects the general pattern of more risk, more return.
2. *Risk on X Axis.* The horizonal, or *x*, axis takes the independent variable. The vertical, or *y*, axis takes the dependent variable. From this diagram, we can see that the rate of return is dependent upon the degree of risk in a proposal. Thus, risk is an independent variable; return, a dependent variable.
3. *Riskless Rate of Return.* Note that the market line touches the *y* axis at 8 percent. This is identified as the *riskless rate of return* and is the return on government securities. If such securities are held to maturity, it is widely felt that they offer no risk of default on either principal or interest. Thus, the investor can achieve a return at a zero risk level. For a rational company, this is the minimum acceptable return from any investment.
4. *Market Portfolio.* This is defined as a group of assets weighted at the same dollar value as all assets in the market. It is the average return, if you will, on all the assets traded in the market. The *market rate of return* is the expected return on the market portfolio. For example, suppose the New York Stock Exchange securities in total experienced an 11 percent annual return last year. An investor holding a portfolio with 2 percent of every stock on the exchange would also receive an 11 percent return.

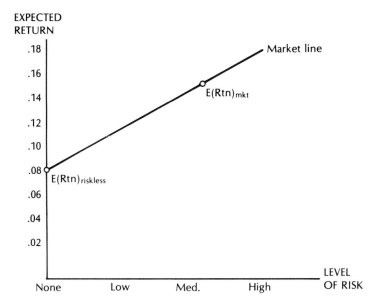

**Figure 13–2**   The Market Line.

## TWO COMPONENTS OF RISK

Within the overall definition of risk as dispersion of return, two components may be identified:

1. *Business Risk.* This is defined as the chance that the firm will not have the ability to compete successfully with the assets that it purchases. As an example, the firm may acquire a machine that may not operate properly, that may not produce salable products, or that may face other operating or market difficulties that cause losses. Any operational problems are classed as business risk.

2. *Financial Risk.* This is the chance that an investment will not generate sufficient cash flows either to cover interest payments on money borrowed to finance it or principal repayments on the debt or to provide profits to the firm. If the firm falls short of its return goal, it may be able to cover operating expenses but not the financing costs of the original investment.

The two components of risk are implied in the market line. The market portfolio offers both business and financial risk. Figure 13–3 shows an

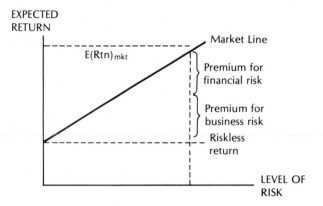

**Figure 13–3**   Business and Financial Risk.

assumed identification of business and financial risk in the capital asset framework.

### MARKET LINE IN AN INEFFICIENT MARKET

In an *efficient market,* all assets are traded in the proper relationship of risk and return. Therefore, all stocks, bonds, and capital assets would be located somewhere on the market line. In an inefficient market, some assets offer a better return than others at a given risk level. Not all of the assets would be found on the market line. Figure 13–4 shows a market line and individual assets in a market that is not efficient.

### INVESTOR INDIFFERENCE CURVES

In Figure 13–4, we can see the investments available in the marketplace. They are only one-half of the investment decision. The other half involves the firm's attitude toward risk; that is, which investment will be selected from all the available choices. Conceptually, we can formalize the investor's view of risk through the use of indifference curves. An *indifference curve* is a graphic representation of the tradeoffs in value between two variables—in our case, risk and return. As an example, suppose a firm wants no risk if it can achieve an 11 percent return. If it accepts low risk in a proposal, it wants a 13 percent return. Medium-low risk commands 15 percent and medium risk a 17 percent return. Medium-high or high risk is not acceptable. Since risk is the independent variable, we place it on the horizontal axis and draw the indifference curve for this firm as shown in Figure 13–5.

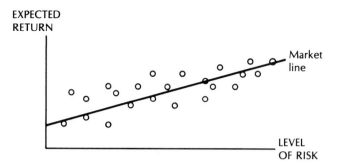

**Figure 13–4**  Market Line with Inefficiencies.

The investing firm will trade off risk and return as shown by the curve. Suppose, for example, the firm can accept a medium-low proposal with a 15 percent return but can only get 9 percent on government securities. Which investment would be undertaken? The answer is the 15 percent alternative because this has a greater utility than a 9 percent no-risk investment. But if a 12 percent no-risk bond had been available, it would have been chosen over the 15 percent alternative. If both an 11 percent no-risk bond or 15 percent medium-low risk proposal had been available, the firm would be indifferent to which one was acceptable.

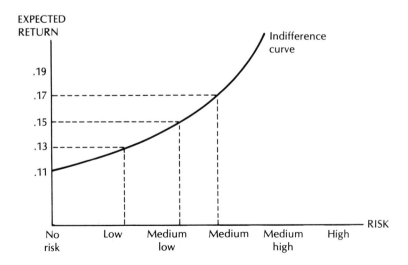

**Figure 13–5**  Investor Indifference Curve.

RISK AND REQUIRED RETURN

To complete the conceptual relationship between risk and return, we join the concepts of the market line and indifference curve. The optimal investment will be found at the point where the indifference curve touches an investment alternative. This is shown for an imperfect market in Figure 13–6. Several indifference curves are shown, as the firm moves down toward the investments available in the market. When an indifference curve reaches a proposal, we have a risk level satisfactory to the firm. We also have an investment that offers an appropriate return for that risk level. This is an acceptable investment.

## WEIGHTED AVERAGE REQUIRED RETURN

We have now established a theoretical basis for viewing the required return from a capital investment. First, we measure the level of risk; then, the level of return. Finally, we bring them together so that higher risk investments offer a higher return. This approach is used for capital-budgeting projects, the purchase of bonds or other creditor securities, the purchase of common stock, and any readily identifiable capital or financial investments.

The capital asset approach is not the traditional methodology for determining the firm's required return on new proposals. Many firms still use a weighted average of debt costs and equity returns to develop an

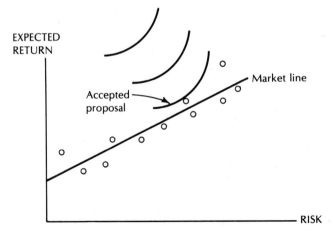

**Figure 13–6** Indifference Curves and the Market Line to Produce an Acceptable Investment.

overall required return. In this section, we will examine this method and compare it to the capital asset approach.

## CAPITAL STRUCTURE AND COST OF CAPITAL

A firm's *capital structure* may be defined as the mixture of debt and equity that comprises the financing of its assets. In some writings, short-term debt is omitted in the discussion of capital structure. If, however, short-term debt is used as a source of permanent financing over a period of time, it should be included in capital structure analyses. Since such debt is commonly rolled over and is therefore a form of permanent financing, we will include it in our examples.

The term *cost of capital* is the rate of return required on a capital investment. It is synonymous with the term *required return*. The *weighted average cost of capital* is a technique that measures required return in terms of the individual components of the firm's capital structure. The cost of each debt component and the return on each equity component are separately identified with a weighted value. By adding together each weighted component, we can determine an overall required return; that is, a sufficient return to cover interest payments on the firm's debt and dividends for preferred shareholders and still to provide an adequate return to common shareholders for the risk that they accept.

The term *cost of capital* is often confusing when it is used in discussions of required return. Debt may have a cost that can clearly be identified in the interest paid by the firm. A required return to be earned for common shareholders is less clearly a "cost" of the business. To avoid possible problems with semantics, we will use the term *weighted average required return* in our discussion of the weighted average method.

## WEIGHTED AVERAGE FORMULA

The weighted average required return can be expressed by the formula:

$$E\,(\text{rtn})_{\text{req}} = (\%D_{\text{mkt}})\,(K_i)\,(1-\text{tr}) + (\%PS_{\text{mkt}})\,(K_{\text{ps}}) + (\%CS_{\text{mkt}})\,(K_e)$$

where

$$E\,(\text{rtn})_{\text{req}} = \text{overall required return for the firm}$$

$$K_i = \text{beforetax cost of debt}$$

$$1-\text{tr} = 1 \text{ minus the firm's corporate tax rate}$$

$K_{ps}$ = required return on preferred stock

$K_e$ = required return on common stock

$\%D_{mkt}$, $\%PS_{mkt}$, and $\%CS_{mkt}$ = percentages in the capital structure of debt, preferred stock, and common stock, respectively

As an example of the use of this formula, consider a firm with $15 million of debt at 14 percent, $10 million of preferred stock at 15 percent, and 4.5 million shares of common stock with a current market price of $20 per share. The current rate of return on the common stock is 17 percent and the firm's tax rate is 40 percent. What is the weighted average required return?

In order to get the percentages of debt and equity, we must know the total value of the firm. This can be determined by adding each component as follows:

$$V_{mkt} = D_{mkt} + PS_{mkt} + CS_{mkt}$$

where $V_{mkt}$ is the total value of the firm in the marketplace. In our example, the total value is

$$V_{mkt} = 15,000,000 + 10,000,000 + (4,500,000)\ (20)$$

$$= \$115,000,000$$

The weighted average required return would be:

$$E\ (rtn)_{req} = \frac{15,000}{115,000}(.14)\ (1-.40) + \frac{10,000}{115,000}(.15) \ + \ \frac{90,000}{115,000}(.17)$$

$$= .0110 + .0130 + .1330 = \underline{\underline{.157}}$$

The weighted average formula gives us the overall required return when the costs or returns on the individual components are known. We must perform separate steps to calculate the costs and returns on debt, preferred stock, and common stock. These steps will be illustrated in turn.

**COST OF DEBT**

In most cases, the cost of a firm's debt is known. By using such reference materials as the *Wall Street Journal*, the firm can learn the cost of debt for similar firms. The company can check its borrowing agreements with banks and others to determine what it pays for borrowed money. It can total its payables and learn how much low-cost or no-cost short-term liabilities it has. In a required return calculation, we seek the *effective cost of debt*, which is defined as the actual cost when all relevant factors are considered. Essentially, this involves two adjustments to simple interest or return calculations:

1. *Market, Not Book, Values.* For outstanding debt, the market value might differ from the face or par value. On the balance sheet, the debt is shown at face value. Prior to maturity, fixed return debt fluctuates in value depending upon the yields in the market for all debt securities. To be accurate, the firm should use market values in all required return calculations.
2. *Net Proceeds.* For new issues of debt, the amount of money actually received (the *net proceeds*) differs from the face value because of the costs of issuing the new debt. This means that new debt is more costly than existing debt with the same interest rate. To get an effective cost, the net proceeds should be used.

To solve for the beforetax cost of debt, we use the formula:

$$K_i = \frac{\text{interest}}{D_{mkt}}$$

where *interest* is the dollar value of interest paid annually on the debt. To illustrate the use of this formula, let us consider a firm that has four debt items:

| Item | Annual Cost | Book Value | Market Value or Net Proceeds |
|------|------|------|------|
| Payables | 0 | $ 8,500,000 | $ 8,500,000 |
| Short-term notes | .150 | 4,000,000 | 4,000,000 |
| Long-term bonds | .145 | 15,000,000 | 13,000,000 |
| New long-term debt | .162* | | |
| | | 6,000,000 | 5,500,000 |
| | | | $31,000,000 |

*The annual cost for new debt is calculated using a formula that amortizes the issuance fees over the life of the loan. We will not cover this technique, but the reader should be aware that the cost of new debt must recognize issuance costs.

If the firm maintained exactly these debt balances for 1 year, it would pay $3,747,000 of annual interest:

$$\text{interest} = (8{,}500{,}000)\,(0) + (4{,}000{,}000)\,(.150)$$
$$+ (15{,}000{,}000)\,(.145) + (6{,}000{,}000)\,(.162)$$
$$= \$3{,}747{,}000$$

Dividing the interest by the market value of the debt, we get a beforetax cost of debt of 12.1 percent:

$$K_i = \frac{3{,}747{,}000}{31{,}000{,}000} = .121$$

## REQUIRED RETURN ON PREFERRED STOCK

The required return on preferred stock is calculated in a similar manner to the cost of debt. The relationship is dividends to the market value of the stock. In this calculation, we assume that the firm intends to declare and pay dividends to the preferred shareholders. Since such dividends do not offer the firm a tax shield, as the case with interest payments, we solve directly for the aftertax required return on preferred stock. The formula is simply:

$$K_{ps} = \frac{\text{dividends}_{ps}}{PS_{mkt}}$$

As an example, a $100 par preferred stock is selling for $120. The firm declares dividends at the 14 percent stated rate for the preferred stock issue. The required return on the stock is

$$K_{ps} = \frac{(\$100)\,(.14)}{120} = \underline{\underline{.117}}$$

## REQUIRED RETURN ON COMMON STOCK

Determining the required return on common stock presents greater difficulties than the known values for preferred stock. The common shareholder does not expect to receive any fixed, predetermined return. Rather, the shareholder receives the right to participate in sharing future earnings and cash dividends. To recognize these rights, the return on equity capital must note factors such as earnings, dividends, growth rate, and market price of the common stock. Let us consider a number of separate problems in developing the correct relationships.

First, we must identify the viewpoint for valuation. A *going concern value* assumes that the firm will continue to operate successfully for an indefinite period of time. This differs from a *liquidation value* that would be received if the firm's assets were sold, its liabilities paid, and the remaining funds distributed among the shareholders. The implication of a going concern approach is that the value of the common stock depends upon future net cash inflows to the shareholder. The weighted average approach assumes a going concern foundation and uses cash flows as the measure of return on common stock.

Using a cash-flow approach, we might then ask what cash flows accrue to the shareholder? From the simplest point of view, the shareholder has claims against the firm's earnings. All of the net income can, in theory at least, be paid out to the shareholders in the form of cash dividends. Therefore, the required return on equity could be:

$$K_e = \frac{EPS}{MktPr}$$

One apparent objection to this formula is that all earnings are not paid out in cash dividends and, therefore, we are not using a cash-flow approach. To determine the market value of common stock correctly, we should discount all future dividends at the required return to some present value. The current stock value might be written:

$$MktPr = PV \text{ of } [div_1 + div_2 + div_3 + \ldots + div_\infty]$$

where the market value is being expressed as the present value of a dividend stream that begins in year 1 and runs to infinity.

In taking this approach, there is the practical matter of performing the calculation. How can we determine the value of dividends in a perpetual stream? One technique is to assume a constant growth rate of dividends. If we assume that all future growth results from the retention of earnings, the growth rate of dividends can be calculated by the formula

$$g = \frac{EPS}{MktPr}(\%RE)$$

where

%RE = percentage of future earnings likely to be retained by
the firm

This measure of growth does not consider funds raised by additional borrowings or by the sale of common stock. It uses only retained earnings to finance working capital, plant and equipment, and other assets that would be needed by the firm as it grows. This is conceptually correct in a required return context. Only the retention of earnings will produce growth in dividends for the firm's existing shareholders without a change in the financial risk from debt or a dilution of ownership from the sale of more common stock.

Now that we have defined the growth rate, we can return to our formula that discounts an infinite stream of dividends. With a constant growth rate, the formula can be rewritten so that we solve easily for the market value of the stock. It can also be rearranged so that we can solve for the required return on common stock. The two variations of the formula, which is known as the Gordon model,* are:

$$\text{MktPr} = \frac{\text{div}_{\text{curr}}}{K_e - g} \qquad \text{and} \qquad K_e = \frac{\text{div}_{\text{curr}}}{\text{MktPr}} + g$$

where

$\text{div}_{\text{curr}}$ = the current cash dividend indicated for the next year

With the Gordon model, we have a cash-flow stream in the required return analysis. Either the shareholder receives a cash dividend, or the firm will grow by retaining earnings and the shareholder's stock value will grow. Since the stock can be sold at any time, the shareholder either receives a cash dividend or an increased common-stock value—in either case, a cash claim. Thus, the cash flow is the total of the cash dividend and future ability to sell the common stock for more than was paid.

Two items should be noted at this point. First, the determination of required return under the weighted average approach implies a long-term viewpoint. The board of directors does not expect shares to go up in value exactly by the percentage of retained earnings. Second, earnings per share over the long term will approximate cash flow for most firms.

---

*Myron J. Gordon, *The Investment, Financing, and Valuation of the Corporation* (Homewood, Ill.: Richard D. Irwin, Inc., 1962).

To illustrate this, let us consider a firm with an EPS of $4 and a market price of $30 per share. With earnings formula for required return, we get

$$K_e = \frac{4}{30} = .1333$$

Now, let us consider two possible dividend policies. First, the firm could pay out $1 per share (dividend payout $= \$1/\$4 = .25$). It could declare dividends of $2.50. Since the percentage of retained earnings is 1 minus the dividend payout, the two growth rates would be:

$$g = \frac{4}{30}(.75) = .10 \qquad\qquad g = \frac{4}{30}(.375) = .05$$

Substituting the Gordon model, we get required returns of 13.33 percent with either dividend policy:

$$K_e = \frac{1}{30} + .10 = .1333 \qquad\qquad K_e = \frac{2.50}{30} + .05 = .1333$$

To solve for the required return on equity under the weighted average method, we can use either the earnings formula or Gordon model since they give the same result and both come to grips with the future cash flows as the basis for required return.

**Example:** A firm has a current dividend of $10 per share, an EPS of $25, and an actual market price of $150. What is the required return on equity?

**Answer:** 16.7 percent. Using the earnings formula,

$$K_e = 25/150 = .167$$

Using the Gordon model, the growth rate is (25/150) (.60), or 10 percent. The required return is

$$K_e = 10/150 + .10 = .167$$

When a firm is considering the financing of a new project, it may have plans to issue new common stock. The new issue can be considered in the required return calculation. To do this, net proceeds are used in the formulas instead of market price. For the new stock, the formulas become:

$$K_e = \frac{EPS}{NP} \qquad \text{or} \qquad K_e = \frac{div_{curr}}{NP} + g$$

where

NP = issue price less flotation costs, or net proceeds, from the new issue

**Example:** A firm has a $2.50 EPS and a 5 percent growth rate. Its stock sells for $20 per share. After commissions, fees, and other expenses, a new issue would have net proceeds of $18. The current dividend is $1.50. What is the required return on common stock without the new issue? with the new issue?

**Answer:** Without the new issue, the required return is 12.5 percent:

$$K_e = \frac{2.50}{20} = .125 \qquad\qquad K_e = \frac{1.50}{20} + \frac{2.50}{20}(.40) = .125$$

For the new issue, the required return is 13.9 percent:

$$K_e = \frac{2.50}{18} = .139 \qquad\qquad K_e = \frac{1.50}{18} + \frac{2.50}{18}(.40) = .139$$

## CALCULATION OF OVERALL REQUIRED RETURN

With the weighted average approach, we use a three-step process to determine overall required return. First we determine the cost or return on each component, using the formulas already presented. Then we multiply each aftertax cost or return by the percentage of the component in the capital structure. Finally we add the weighted values to get an overall required return. An overview of this process is given in Figure 13–7.

To illustrate the process of determining overall required return under the weighted average model, consider a firm with the following capital structure.

| | |
|---|---|
| Accounts payable | $ 3,000,000 |
| Bank loan (.145 variable rate) | 9,000,000 |

New bond issue (.152 effective cost after
    amortization of fees)                                            25,000,000
Preferred stock (.11 indicated dividend)
    Par value                                                         4,000,000
    Market value                                                      2,600,000
Common stock (800,000 shares at $22)                                 17,600,000
New issue of common stock (100,000 shares at $20
    net proceeds)                                                     2,000,000

In addition to capital structure information, we know that the firm has an earnings per share of $3.50, a current dividend of $2.10, and a 40 percent corporate tax rate. What is the overall required return?

To solve for the overall required return in this example, we follow a three-step process:

**Step 1. Cost of Each Component**

The total interest for this firm will vary, depending upon the varying level of interest rates and the amount of debt outstanding during different times of the year. Let us assume steady interest rates and debt levels. We then get annual interest of $5,105,000:

$$\text{interest} = (9,000)\,(.145) + (25,000)\,(.152) = 5,105$$

| **Cost of Debt**<br>(After tax basis) | **Cost of Preferred Stock** | **Cost of Common Stock** |
|---|---|---|
| $K_i = \dfrac{\text{interest}}{D_{mkt}}(1 - tr)$ | $K_{ps} = \dfrac{\text{Dividends}_{ps}}{PS_{mkt}}$ | $K_e = \dfrac{\text{EPS}}{\text{MktPr}}$ |
| | | or |
| | | $= \dfrac{\text{Div}_{curr}}{\text{MktPr}} + g$ |

| **After Tax Cost** | **Percentage of Total Capital Structure** | **After Tax Cost of Each Component** |
|---|---|---|
| $K_i$ (after tax) | $\times\ \%D_{mkt}$ | = |
| $K_{ps}$ | $\times\ \%PS_{mkt}$ | = |
| $K_e$ | $\times\ \%CS_{mkt}$ | = _____ |
| | Overall required return | |

**Figure 13–7**  Overview of Overall Required Return.

The overall debt component of the structure totals \$37 million:

$$D_{mkt} = 3,000 + 9,000 + 25,000 = 37,000$$

The aftertax cost of debt is 8.3 percent:

$$K_{i(aftertax)} = \frac{5,105}{37,000}(1 - .40) = .083$$

To calculate the required return on preferred stock, we determine annual indicated cash dividends of \$440,000:

$$dividends_{ps} = 4,000 \times .11 = 440$$

The required return on preferred stock is 16.9 percent:

$$K_{ps} = \frac{440}{2,600} = .169$$

To calculate the required return on common stock, we begin with the determination of the percentage of retained earnings. It is 40 percent:

$$\%RE = \frac{3.50 - 2.10}{3.50} = .40$$

The growth rate is 6.4 percent:

$$g = \frac{3.50}{22}(.40) = .064$$

The market value of common stock must consider both the existing and newly issued stock. First we determine the overall common stock value to be \$19.6 million:

$$CS_{mkt} = (800)(22) + (100)(20) = 19,600$$

Dividing this by the number of existing and new shares gives us a market price of \$21.78:

$$MktPr = 19,600/900 = \$21.78$$

The overall required return on equity is 16 percent:

$$K_e = \frac{2.10}{21.78} + .064 = .160$$

## Step 2. Multiply Each Cost or Return by Percent of Structure

In this step, we calculate the weighted values for each component. First we determine the total capital structure at market value:

| | |
|---|---:|
| Accounts payable | $ 3,000,000 |
| Bank loan | 9,000,000 |
| New bond issue | 25,000,000 |
| Preferred stock | 2,600,000 |
| Common stock | 19,600,000 |
| Total structure | $59,200,000 |

Next we determine the percentage of each component:

| | | |
|---|---|---|
| Debt | 37,000/59,200 = | .625 |
| Preferred stock | 2,600/59,200 = | .044 |
| Common stock | 19,600/59,200 = | .331 |
| | | 1.000 |

Finally we calculate the weighted values:

| | Aftertax Cost | | Percent of Structure | | Weighted Value |
|---|---|---|---|---|---|
| Debt | .083 | × | .625 | = | .052 |
| Pref. stock | .169 | × | .044 | = | .007 |
| Com. stock | .160 | × | .331 | = | .053 |

## Step 3. Add the Weighted Values

The final step is to add the weighted values to get the required return. In our example, the overall required return is 11.2 percent after taxes:

$$.052 + .007 + .053 = .112 \text{ overall required return}$$

UTILITY OF WEIGHTED AVERAGE METHOD

The weighted average cost of capital is still a widely used approach to determining the required return on a firm's investments. It offers a number of strengths, including:

1. *Straightforwardness.* It is a logical and direct method for tackling a difficult problem. The weighted average approach constructs an overall required return by building upon the components of capital structure. It solves for a cost or return on each component; the overall return is the sum of the individual costs or returns. This is an easily understood methodology.
2. *Responsiveness to Changing Conditions.* Since it builds upon individual debt and equity components, the weighted average approach reflects each element in the capital structure. Small changes in the structure, in the cost of debt, or in earnings will be reflected by small changes in the overall required return. Large changes will be similarly reflected.
3. *Reasonable Results when Normal Profits.* When the firm is achieving a satisfactory or efficient return on its investments, the weighted average model provides a reasonable estimate of the required return for the firm. In periods of normal profits, the firm will have a higher cost of equity capital than debt capital. The weighted average method recognizes the relatively low debt costs and the need to continue to achieve the higher returns on the portion of assets financed by equity.
4. *Reasonable Results when Reasonable Debt.* The use of debt in the weighted average approach has the effect of lowering the required return. But what if the debt level is excessive in areas such as payables, which have a 0 or low cost. Financing with short-term payables can be a risky business, requiring a high return. But the low-cost payables will actually drop the required return. This can produce serious errors in selecting the required return for a proposal. But if debt levels are low to moderate, the weighted average method produces acceptable results.

In spite of these strengths, the weighted average model is not recommended for determining a firm's required return. Two reasons may be given:

1. *Failure to Consider Proposal Risk.* The weighted average model makes no provision for the level of risk in an investment proposal. It assumes that all proposals offer the same degree of risk that the firm faces in its existing investments. Obviously, this is not always the case. Some proposals are not very risky at all. Others might have considerably more risk than existing activities.

2. *Possible Errors.* If the firm is not making satisfactory profits or if it has excessive short-term debt, the weighted average model gives incorrect answers. In our preceding example, the preferred stock had a 16.9 percent required return while the common stock had only a 16 percent required return. But the common stock is always riskier than the preferred stock. Most investors would require a higher common stock return as compared to preferred stock. The real possibility of errors limits the utility of the weighted average model.

## HOW SHOULD WE DETERMINE REQUIRED RETURN?

The process of determining required return involves the calculation of the appropriate level of return to compensate the firm for the risk undertaken. If a firm is considering a high-risk proposal, it should get a high return. A low-risk proposal would offer a lower return in most situations. This is the correct basis for determining the required return on an investment.

Under the capital asset approach, the distinction between different sources of funds is eliminated. Proposals are not accepted because they meet or exceed a weighted average required return. Rather, they are accepted because they are efficient in terms of risk and return and also meet the firm's desires with respect to risk and return tradeoffs. Figure 13–8 shows the difference between the weighted average and capital asset approaches. With the weighted average example, the firm can accept any proposals above the overall required return. With the capital asset model, proposals on or above the line are efficient in risk-return terms; they are acceptable only if they meet the firm's risk-return requirements, as expressed with indifference curves in the figure.

### ROLE OF THE WEIGHTED AVERAGE MODEL

In light of this discussion, we can see that the weighted average model has historically been used incorrectly. Is there a role for it? The answer is

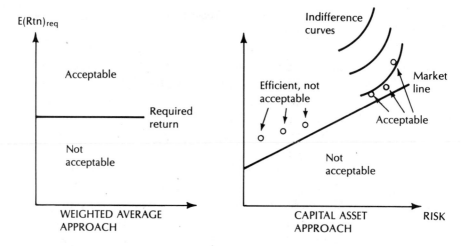

**Figure 13–8**  Acceptable Proposals Under Weighted Average and Capital Asset Approaches to Required Return.

yes, but not the traditional role. To prove this point, let us look at the formula and determine what is known and what must be calculated. The formula is:

$$E(rtn)_{req} = (\%D_{mkt})\,(K_i)\,(1-tr) + (\%PS_{mkt})\,(K_{ps}) + (\%CS_{mkt})\,(K_e)$$

Do we know the overall required return? The answer is yes. Any new project must earn an adequate return for its risk level. Without new projects, the firm must earn an adequate return for level of risk of its activities. First we measure risk. Then we can estimate required return. As an example, suppose we investigate opportunities for investment and determine that a low-risk project offers an 11 percent return, medium-risk offers a 15 percent return, and high-risk offers a 23 percent return. We can draw a market line (as shown in Figure 13–9), plot individual proposals A, B, and C against the line, and determine whether they offer an adequate return for the risk involved. In the example, A and B are low-risk proposals and C is a medium-risk proposal. A and C are efficient; C is also acceptable to a firm willing to accept medium-risk proposals.

In addition to knowing the overall return, we also know the cost of debt and required return on preferred stock. General interest levels in the market and preferred stock yields give us these. What we do not really know is the required return on common stock. We know the actual re-

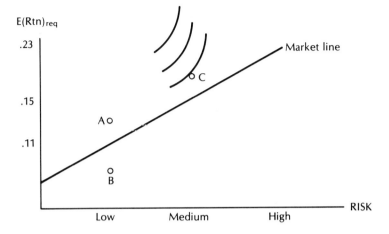

**Figure 13–9**   Efficient and Acceptable Proposals Under Capital Asset Theory.

turn based on the cash dividends, growth rate, and market price. But is this also the required return in an inefficient market? The answer is not necessarily. If the firm has low profits or its stock is not in vogue in the stock market, the required return will not equal the actual return. This means that we must solve for the required return that gives the shareholder a fair return for the level of risk assumed. Now we have reached the correct usage for the weighted average model. It should be used to solve for the required return on the common stock, not the overall required return. Then the investor can compare the actual return with the required return. If the firm is earning less than required, the stock is not efficiently priced in the market. If it is earning as much as or more than required, the stock itself is a good investment.

In this chapter, we have examined the concept of required return. Building upon capital asset theory, we developed a market line that shows the relationship between risk and return. Then the firm must identify investments that offer an appropriate return for the level of risk assumed. The weighted average method, although traditionally and still employed, should not be used to determine the overall required return. It cannot adequately handle low profits or excessive short-term debt. Nor can it determine whether the stock is efficiently priced in the market. Instead, it should be used to determine the required return on the common stock.

STUDY QUESTIONS

1. What is the meaning of risk? What are three ways to measure risk?
2. What is the meaning of return? What is the general relationship of risk and return? How is the relationship shown?
3. What are two components of risk? What does each mean?
4. What is an efficient market?
5. What is an investor indifference curve? How is it used?
6. What is the meaning of capital structure? cost of capital?
7. What is the effective cost of debt? What adjustments must be made to convert simple interest to effective cost?
8. What is the viewpoint for valuing common stock? How does the weighted average method apply this viewpoint?
9. Why is the weighted average method a widely used technique for calculating required return?
10. What are the drawbacks to the weighted average method?
11. How should the firm calculate required return? What role does the weighted average model play in this determination?

PROBLEMS

1. A firm has $5.6 million in debt at 12.5 percent, $3 million of preferred stock at 14 percent, and 800,000 shares of common stock at a market price of $40 per share. The current rate of return is 16 percent and the firm's tax rate is 40 percent. What is the weighted average required return?
2. A firm has $2 million of payables, short-term inventory financing of $3.5 million at 13 percent, and long-term debt of $7 million at 12 percent. The tax rate is 40 percent. What is the beforetax cost of debt? the aftertax cost?
3. A firm has preferred stock with a market value of $6 million and a book value of $8 million. The indicated dividend rate is 15 percent. What is the required return on the stock?
4. A firm has an earnings per share of $2.50 and a market price of common stock of $13 per share. The dividend payout is 56 percent. What is the firm's annual dividend? growth rate? required return with the earnings and dividends plus growth rate methods?
5. If the firm in problem 4 issued new stock with a net proceeds of $11.50, what happens to the required return?
6. A firm has short-term noninterest-bearing debt of $2.1 million, other short-term debt of $700,000 at 16 percent, and long-term debt of $4.3 million at 14.6 percent. The firm's tax rate is 40 percent. What is the firm's effective cost of debt on an aftertax basis?
7. A firm has $5.7 million in short-term debt at an average cost of 4.3 percent. It also has a 3-year bank loan with a variable rate of interest. The average rate for the next 3 years is estimated at 16 percent and the loan will probably average $2.5 million. The firm has long-term bonds of $10 million at 13.5 percent,

with a current market value of $8.6 million. It has preferred stock of $4 million at a 12 percent indicated dividend and market value of $2.8 million. It has 2 million outstanding shares of common stock selling at $9 per share. The firm's earnings per share are $1.90 and the tax rate is 40 percent. Using the weighted average method, what is the required return on new projects for this firm?

8. An analyst knows that a firm's overall required return based on the risk of its activities should be 12 percent. Data for the firm are given in problem 7. With this additional information, what should be the current market price of the common stock for the firm in problem 7?

9. A firm uses the beta coefficient as a measure of risk. It has developed a market line where the following relationships hold:

| Beta | Forecast Return (before Taxes) | Investment |
|------|--------------------------------|------------|
| 0    | .095                           | treasury securities |
| 1.0  | .160                           | portfolio of common stocks |
| 2.0  | .225                           | typical capital budgeting proposals |

Four proposals have been identified for this firm:

| Proposal | Beta | Likely Return |
|----------|------|---------------|
| A        | 0.8  | .152          |
| B        | 1.3  | .165          |
| C        | 1.5  | .196          |
| D        | 2.3  | .246          |

The firm's indifference curves towards risk are:

|                  | Indifference Curves |      |      |
|------------------|------|------|------|
|                  | #1   | #2   | #3   |
| First position   |      |      |      |
| Beta             | 0.7  | 0.7  | 0.7  |
| Required return   | .20  | .18  | .16  |
| Second position  |      |      |      |
| Beta             | 1.4  | 1.4  | 1.4  |
| Required return   | .22  | .20  | .18  |
| Third position   |      |      |      |
| Beta             | 2.1  | 2.1  | 2.1  |
| Required return   | .25  | .23  | .21  |

With this data, which proposal is acceptable to the firm?

# ARNOLD ATHLETIC SUPPLIES CASE
## Required Return

*This case requires the reader to analyze the efficiency of a firm in terms of risk and return. It also requests that the reader evaluate the acceptability of projects.*

Arnold Athletic Supplies, Inc. is a small, publicly held company located between Dallas and Fort Worth. Arnold manufactures a variety of supplies and small equipment used by players and coaches around the country. Over the past 15 years, Arnold has had particular success in the high school and junior college markets; its products can be found in most dressing rooms of football, baseball, and basketball teams throughout the Southwest and Midwest.

Arnold is considering expanding into product lines. Its well-established sales force would be able to handle supplies and equipment for sports such as swimming, golf, and track through its current activities in high schools and junior colleges. The marketing manager and director of finance have begun working on figures related to the profitability of different athletic supplies and equipment. At this time, five possible markets have been identified and the likely return on a cash-flow basis has been determined for each. Specific proposals have been drafted and will soon be available for internal distribution in the company. In the meantime, the president has been given the aftertax internal rates of return for each proposal as follows:

1. swimming supplies, 18 percent return, medium risk
2. golf equipment, 22 percent return, medium-high risk
3. golf supplies, 11 percent return, medium-low risk
4. track equipment, 13 percent return, low risk
5. track supplies, 16 percent return, medium risk

At a meeting of the board of directors called to discuss the proposal, the director of finance presented financial data, including the current year's balance sheet and income statement. He reported that the stock was selling for $12 per share and that the firm's sales and earnings were growing at a respectable 7.5 percent annually.

As the discussion shifted from the specific proposals to the need for financing, the director of finance was asked to make a recommendation. He had been studying different possibilities and was prepared to discuss specifics. "I recommend," he began, "that we do not attempt to raise separate funds for a series of small projects. Rather, I suggest that we prepare to raise $6 million to cover whatever proposals are finally accepted by this board. If this seems logical, I have investigated three alternatives that currently seem to be possible:

1. We can borrow $6 million from Commercial Credit Corporation or a similar company. Our investment banker believes that we would be able to place such a financing with a 17 percent coupon to net us the $6 million. If this is done, we will have a debt-equity ratio near 1/1, an acceptable ratio for our firm.
2. We can sell 62,000 shares of preferred stock. Our banker feels that a 14 percent offering would be successful and would net us $6 million as $100 par. Most of the shares would probably be purchased by our existing common shareholders, but a strong market seems to exist generally and I would expect no problems with this alternative.
3. We could issue common stock. Our banker thinks that we could sell 570,000 shares at $11 per share. From this amount, we would have to deduct fees of approximately $270,000 which would leave us with $6 million net.

The next presentation was made by Ed Dawkins, a vice-president with a local consulting firm. He said, "I have been studying the tradeoffs between risk and return using your definitions of risk levels. I suggest that the following holds:

| Project Risk | Required Return before Taxes |
|---|---|
| None (T bills) | .115 |
| Low | .135 |
| Medium-low | .160 |
| Medium | .185 |
| Medium-high | .210 |
| High | .250 |

After the presentation by the director of finance, the board began to discuss the different possibilities. Finally, the board began to discuss the cutoff point for the acceptance of the different proposals. One board member inquired about the firm's present required return, as basically a medium-risk investment. The director of finance agreed to develop data on the required returns and how they would affect the acceptance of each of the five proposals.

## Questions

1. What is the firm's current required return? Is the firm efficient in risk-return terms?
2. Which projects are acceptable?

### ARNOLD ATHLETIC SUPPLIES, INC.—Balance Sheet

| | | | |
|---|---|---|---|
| Cash | $ 600,000 | Accounts payable | $ 500,000 |
| Accounts receivable | 1,400,000 | Notes payable, current (15%) | 600,000 |
| Inventories (at cost) | 3,200,000 | Bonds (13%) | 1,500,000 |
| Plant & equip. | | Mortgage (14%) | 1,400,000 |
| (At cost) | 12,400,000 | Common stock ($1 par) | 1,200,000 |
| (Less acc. depr.) | 4,400,000 | Surplus | 2,400,000 |
| Land | 2,200,000 | Retained earnings | 7,800,000 |
| | $15,400,000 | | $15,400,000 |

### ARNOLD ATHLETIC SUPPLIES, INC.—Income Statement

| | |
|---|---|
| Sales | $13,250,000 |
| Cost of goods sold | 6,400,000 |
| Gross margin | 6,850,000 |
| General and administrative expenses | 1,800,000 |
| Earnings before interest and taxes | $ 5,050,000 |
| Interest charges | 250,000 |
| Federal income taxes | 1,920,000 |
| Net income after taxes | $ 2,880,000 |
| Dividends declared and paid | $1.50 share |

# GENERAL TRANSPORT CASE
## Required Return

*This case exposes the reader to the concept and uses of the required return, specifically in the efficient valuation of stock.*

General Transport Corporation (GTC) is a major transportation and financial holding company operating from home offices in Houston. The company has excellent relationships in the petrochemical complex along the Gulf Coast and works closely with the major oil and chemical companies in the distribution of bulk petroleum, chemicals, petrochemicals, and byproducts.

GTC is organized around five profit centers that conduct relatively autonomous operations. The structure is shown in Exhibit 1. The operating responsibilities of each profit center are:

1. *GTC Terminals, Inc.* This subsidiary is located in Jacksonville, Florida, and is responsible for storing and transhipping bulk liquids. The company owns and operates 12 terminals that store gasoline, chemicals, and other liquids for petroleum and chemical companies, fertilizer manufacturers, and the food-processing industry. The liquids are delivered to GTC terminals by ocean-going tankers, barges, pipelines, railroad cars, and tank trucks.

## EXHIBIT 1
### Organization Chart for General Transport Company

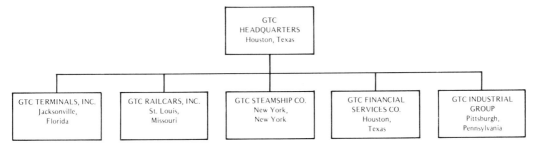

423

They are then either reshipped in bulk or repackaged in smaller volumes for direct shipment to final customers. The total capacity of the GTC terminal system has been growing steadily and is almost 30 million barrels, 24 million in the United States and 5.5 million in Europe.

2. *GTC Railcars, Inc.* This subsidiary operates a fleet of 35,000 railroad tank and boxcars and manufactures both kinds of rail equipment at its own plant in Saint Louis, Missouri. The railcars are leased to major corporations over 7- to 10-year periods. This allows GTC to pay off the railcars on an initial lease while providing modern equipment to companies that do not desire to incur the capital outlay and operating expense involved in establishing and maintaining their own fleets. Since the cars have average service lives of 40 years or more, the business is fairly profitable after the 7- to 10-year period needed to cover the cost of the cars. The size of the tankcar fleet has been growing steadily for 20 years; GTC has cars that carry over 450 different products, including chemicals, poisons, phosphates, flour, starch, and coal.

3. *GTC Steamship Company.* This New York-based subsidiary owns and operates 23 oceangoing tankers and bulk carriers totaling 1.7 million dead-weight tons. For the most part, the vessels are chartered on a medium- to long-term basis to companies in the petroleum, chemical, and steel industries. Some of the ships operate in the spot market when they are subject to wide fluctuations in rates and profits. A depressed shipping market in the early 1980s resulting from high petroleum prices and excess vessels depressed overall GTC earnings from 1980 to 1984.

4. *GTC Financial Services Company.* This subsidiary offers a wide variety of financial services, including lease packaging, mortgage financing, and insurance. Its portfolio of leased capital equipment includes jet aircraft, railroad cars, ships, and a variety of production and mining equipment. The company has shown sustained growth in revenues and profits over the years, although it has had a few wide fluctuations due to difficulties with individual loans or investments.

5. *GTC Industrial Group.* This company designs and manufactures a variety of heavy-equipment products. It produces pneumatic conveying equipment, cooling and heat-regulating equipment, compressors, blowers, pumps, dust and fume control equipment, crushers, mills, and similar items. It has steadily expanded its operation over a 15-year period and has shown consistent, if

**EXHIBIT 2.**   Return on Asset Achieved by General Transport Corporation
Common Shareholders, 1970–1984.

| Year | ROA | Year | ROA | Year | ROA |
|------|-----|------|-----|------|-----|
| 1970 | 12.0% | 1975 | 11.1% | 1980 | 13.5% |
| 1971 | 12.3 | 1976 | 11.8 | 1981 | 11.2 |
| 1972 | − 4.0 | 1977 | 2.4 | 1982 | − 2.4 |
| 1973 | 9.9 | 1978 | 7.9 | 1983 | 16.6 |
| 1974 | 10.7 | 1979 | 14.2 | 1984 | 14.8 |
| Average | 8.2% | | 9.5% | | 10.7 |

not spectacular, profits. Its backing of orders averages 31 months
and has never dropped below 21 months.

The management of General Transport Corporation has been examining the market behavior of the firm's common stock. The stock
trades on the New York Stock Exchange and has been generally favored
by institutional investors. The price fluctuates within a relatively narrow
range and appears to be closely linked to the firm's policy of steady dividend payments. Through the early 1980s, the combination of dividends,
plus rises in market value, produced average returns on asset of 8 to 11
percent annually for common shareholders, as shown in Exhibit 2. This
concerns management since an inadequate return may cause shareholders to sell their stock, seeking better investments. This will depress the
stock price.

The degree of risk inherent in a stock clearly influences how investors perceive the stock's value. To have some basis for comparison,
management hired Ann Barrow and Associates to provide some statistical
data on the stock. These are shown in Exhibit 3. Note that the firm's
standard deviation of return and beta coefficients are given for three periods of 5 years each. Also, Ann Barrow created a market of 16 similar
stocks and calculated a market standard deviation for this group.

**EXHIBIT 3.**   Statistical Data on General Transport That Can Be Used to
Measure and Analyze Dispersion of Returns and Market Correlations.

| | 1970–1974 | 1975–1979 | 1980–1984 |
|------|-----------|-----------|-----------|
| Standard deviation of return on asset | 6.9% | 4.6% | 5.6% |
| Beta coefficient for GTC | .46 | .49 | .56 |
| Standard deviation of market returns | 5.4% | 7.5% | 8.0% |

Along with the statistical measures, Ann Barrow provided an estimate of the market line for the late 1980s. She provided two formulas, depending on whether an investor holds common stock alone or as part of a portfolio. The formulas are:

*if held alone*

$$E(rtn)_{req} = E(rtn)_{riskless} + [E(rtn)_{mkt} - E(rtn)_{riskless}] \left[ \frac{\sigma \ sec}{\sigma \ mkt} \right]$$

*if held in a portfolio*

$$E(rtn)_{req} = E(rtn)_{riskless} + [E(rtn)_{mkt} - E(rtn)_{riskless}] \ [Beta_{sec}]$$

where

$E(rtn)_{req}$ = rate of return required on the investment

$E(rtn)_{riskless}$ = rate of return on government bonds

$E(rtn)_{mkt}$ = rate of return on a diversified portfolio of securities in the market

$Beta_{sec}$ = beta coefficient for a security

According to Ann's comments, the current market price of $19 and required return on GTC common stock could be evaluated in light of the market line developed with either formula. Once this is known, the stock could be checked for likely future market prices. To graph such a merger line, Ann suggested solving for the required return on government bonds and the market portfolio, drawing each point on a graph and connecting the two points with a straight line.

The GTC management is aware that the return to the shareholder involves two factors. The first is the firm's level of dividend payments, which reflects the fundamental operating and financial strength of the company. The second is market activity that causes rises or declines in the firm's stock aside from the company's basic business. Ann Barrow was asked to provide data on these two factors and she produced the items in Exhibit 4.

**REQUIRED:**

1. What is the required return on the GTC common stock for the 1985–1989 period?
2. Is the stock efficiently valued at the present time?

**EXHIBIT 4**

|  | 1970–74 | 1974–79 | 1979–84 | 1985–89 |
|---|---|---|---|---|
| GTC DPS | $1.05 | $1.50 | $1.65 | $2.25 |
| GTC EPS | 1.50 | 2.20 | 2.40 | 3.50 |
| Mkt. rate of rtn. | 13.5% | 12.0% | 14.4% | 17.0% |
| Rtn. on med-term |  |  |  |  |
| U.S. Govt. bonds | 6.8% | 7.9% | 11.8% | 13.4% |

# 14

# Valuation of the Firm

Throughout our study of finance, we have emphasized the goal of maximization of wealth—the maximization of the present value of the firm's common stock. The firm's earnings, dividends, growth rate, and psychological factors contribute to the value of its stock in the marketplace. In this chapter, we will broaden our analysis. We will begin with a valuation of the firm's fixed return securities. Then we will cover common stock value in perfect and imperfect markets. Finally we will examine the issues related to the valuation of the firm in light of the capital asset theory.

## CONCEPT OF VALUE

An important role of the financial manager is to make recommendations concerning the value of different securities. When a firm is considering the purchase of marketable securities—debt, preferred stock, or common stock—it must have some knowledge of investment values. If the firm is evaluating an acquisition, it must have techniques to determine how much to pay for the stock to be acquired. When a firm is considering a public offering to sell its own stock in order to raise additional equity capital, it must establish a price for the issue and time the offering to achieve a maximum benefit to existing shareholders. These are all issues related to the valuation of the firm and its securities.

The *value* of a security may be defined as its worth in money or other securities at a given moment in time. The value is expressed either in terms of a market for the security or in terms of the laws or accounting procedures applicable to the security. Four major concepts of value may be identified:

1. *Going Concern Value.* The value of the securities of a profitable, operating firm with prospects for indefinite future business might be expressed as a *going concern value*. The worth of the firm would be expressed in terms of the future profits, dividends, or growth expected of the business.

2. *Liquidation Value.* If the analyst is dealing with the securities of a firm that is about to go out of business, the net value of its assets, or *liquidation value*, would be of primary concern. After selling the firm's assets and paying its liabilities, how much would be left for the stockholders to divide? If the firm were unable to pay all its debts after the sale of assets, how much can each bondholder or other creditor expect to receive?

3. *Market Value.* If we are examining a firm whose stock or debt is traded in a securities market, we can determine the market value of the security. This is the value of the debt or equity securities as reflected in the bond or stock market's perception of the firm.

4. *Book Value.* This is determined by the use of standardized accounting techniques and is calculated from the financial reports, particularly the balance sheet, prepared by the firm. The book value of debt is usually fairly close to its par or face value. The book value of the common stock is calculated by dividing the firm's equity on the balance sheet by the number of shares outstanding.

**Example:** An analyst forecasts an earnings per share for Union Rubber Products of $4 and says that the stock is worth 8 times this much, or $32. What kind of value is the analyst determining?

**Answer:** Going concern—a value related to future profits.

## INTRINSIC VALUE

A security's *intrinsic value* is the price that is justified for it when the primary factors of value are considered. In other words, it is the *real worth* of the debt or equity instrument as distinguished from the current market price. The financial manager estimates intrinsic value by carefully appraising the following *fundamental factors* that affect security values:

1. *Value of the Firm's Assets.* The physical assets held by the firm have some market value. They can be liquidated if need be to provide funds to repay debt and distribute to shareholders. In techniques of going concern valuation, asset values are usually omitted.

2. *Likely Future Interest and Dividends.* For debt, the firm is committed to pay future interest and repay principal. For preferred and common stock, the firm makes attempts to declare and pay dividends. The likelihood of these payments affects present value.

3. *Likely Future Earnings.* The expected future earnings of the firm are generally viewed as the most important single factor affecting security value. Without a reasonable level of earnings, interest and dividend payments may be in jeopardy.

4. *Likely Future Growth Rate.* A firm's prospects for future growth are carefully evaluated by investors and creditors and are a factor influencing intrinsic value.

## INTRINSIC VALUE ANALYSIS

*Intrinsic value analysis* is the process of comparing the real worth of a security with the current market price or proposed purchase price. The fundamental factors affecting value usually change less rapidly than the market price of a security. In imperfect markets, the analyst can hope to locate variances between intrinsic value and the asking price for a security. The primary goal of intrinsic value analysis is to locate *clearly undervalued* or *clearly overvalued* firms or stocks. In the case of an undervalued security, the market has not discovered that fundamental factors justify a higher market price. That is, the security is worth more than its selling price. As soon as the investing public discovers this situation, such as when management announces higher earnings per share than expected, investors will buy the stock and force a rise in its price. The individuals or firms that purchased the stock when it was undervalued would profit. For overvalued stock, the reverse situation is true. When investors holding the stock discover that it is overvalued, they will sell their shares, causing a drop in market price. It is thus wise to avoid purchasing overvalued stocks.

An overview of intrinsic value and its uses is presented in Figure 14–1.

Intrinsic value analysis will not work in all cases because of three major limitations:

1. *Marketplace Slow to Recognize Real Value.* If the investing public does not discover the intrinsic value of the common stock, the firm's stock may remain undervalued or overvalued for a long time.

2. *Stocks of Highly Speculative Firms.* Firms whose activities are highly speculative in nature are not readily analyzed with intrinsic value analysis. Stocks in oil exploration companies, gold-mining companies, or firms attempting to develop new inventions profitably have a value that depends upon future uncertainties rather than on fundamental financial factors. In these situations, the real value may hinge on a single event, such as the discovery of oil. Intrinsic value analysis has no technique to evaluate this kind of situation.

3. *High-Growth Stocks.* Firms with records of extremely rapid growth will command high prices in the marketplace because investors

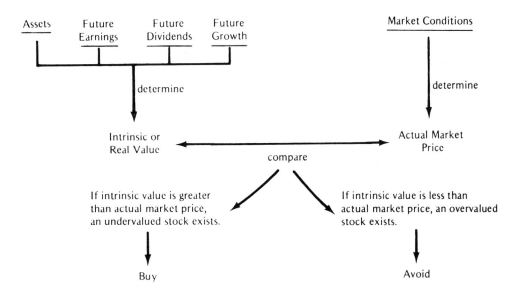

**Figure 14–1**   Comparison of Intrinsic Value and Actual Market Price.

are optimistic with respect to continuing future growth. When a stock has unusually high prospects for future growth in sales and profits, such as Atari and Apple Computer in the 1970s, its intrinsic value is a function of whether and how long growth can be sustained. Because of future uncertainties concerning continuous growth, the intrinsic value approach cannot adequately be used with high growth situations.

**Example:** An insurance company is considering the acquisition of a small manufacturing firm. The firm has had a steady volume of sales and somewhat outdated fixed assets. Its main potential lies in a patented process that it holds for plastic coating on specialty papers used for certain types of printing. The firm can expect booming sales if the expected demand for the process materializes. Can intrinsic value analysis be applied to this situation?

**Answer:** Intrinsic value is of limited use. This is a highly speculative situation that cannot be properly handled by such analysis.

Although most intrinsic value analysis is applied to common stocks, the technique is equally valuable for analyzing bonds and preferred stock. Using interest rate levels or dividend levels, the analyst would find the intrinsic value for the fixed return security. Then this value would be compared to the actual market price of the security in order to determine whether the security was undervalued, properly valued, or overvalued.

## CURRENT MARKET VALUE APPROACH

A second major technique of security valuation considers the price of individual stocks compared to other indicators in the marketplace. If the analyst believes that a security is worth more in terms of market value than the asking price, purchasing it is recommended. The *current market value approach* deals simply with prices in the market, not with issues of intrinsic value. Three short-term factors are of primary concern:

1. *Depressed Overall Market.* An investor can make purchases only when the market appears to be at a low for most stocks. This would occur after a broad-based decline in the level of stock prices, as measured by the New York Stock Exchange Index or some other indicator. The rationale for this technique is that the

current market value of almost all stocks is below a *normal* current market value, and hence prices will soon rise. A similar approach can be used for bonds or preferred stock when investor confidence in these securities drops prices and makes them attractive for short-term gains.

2. *Industry Comparison.* With this approach, a firm or investors will seek purchases that seem to be bargains compared to other firms in the industry. This might occur when similar stocks have risen in price while the stock of one firm has lagged behind for no apparent reason. If the lagging firm can be acquired during a period of rising stock prices, the acquisition may call attention to the low price and the stock may gain in value. This is a case of a single firm's current market price being below its near-term value.

3. *Cyclical Lows.* A number of securities have market prices that follow a cyclical pattern. As an example, a stock may rise to $60 a share, and then institutional and other investors may decide to sell it and accept some profits. The selling pressure may force it down to $40 per share, at which point the investors might again begin to buy shares. From historical data, an analyst can find securities that follow this kind of cyclical pattern. The analyst would then purchase the security near a cyclical low and attempt to sell it near a cyclical high.

The intrinsic and current market value approaches overlap in situations where the current market value seems low compared to the intrinsic value. Both methods are concerned with locating undervalued and overvalued stocks and seeking securities that offer high value for the price paid for them.

**Example:** An investor has plotted the annual high and low stock prices for a specialty steel company as follows. The current price of the common stock in early 1986 is $44. Can a current market value approach be used with this stock?

|      | 1980 | 1981 | 1982 | 1983 | 1984 | 1985 |
|------|------|------|------|------|------|------|
| High | $38  | $37  | $43  | $49  | $55  | $60  |
| Low  | 19   | 17   | 21   | 27   | 36   | 40   |

**Answer:** Yes. This appears to be a cyclical stock with 20 or so points difference between the annual highs and lows. At $44, the stock may be at a cyclical low.

# VALUE OF DEBT OR FIXED RETURN SECURITIES

Most firms finance a portion of their assets with variable rate debt or securities that offer a fixed return to the holders. To determine the value of these securities or loans, we face three separate processes. These are covered in this section.

### VARIABLE RATE DEBT

A firm may sign a note or otherwise borrow funds requiring interest payments that will vary with some index value. The *prime rate* is a widely used measure of interest rates charged by banks. The *London Interbank Offered Rate (LIBOR)* is another indicator used for the cost of money in international financing. With domestic or foreign financing, a firm may have a loan that fluctuates with the prime rate, LIBOR, or another indicator of general interest levels.

The value of such debt is easily obtained. It is the outstanding principal of the loan. No calculation is necessary. If a firm owes, say, $10 million and will pay interest at prevailing rates, the $10 million loan has a market value of $10 million.

### FIXED RATE SECURITY—GIVEN MATURITY

With debt or preferred stock carrying a fixed rate of interest or indicated dividend, it is possible for the market value to fluctuate. If the security has a specified maturity date, its present value must consider all future interest or dividends plus the return of the principal at maturity. To illustrate the valuation process, let us consider a firm that has sold $50 million of 10-year bonds at a coupon rate of 14 percent. The bonds are sold in $10,000 multiples, and interest is paid semiannually. One year after the issuance of the bonds, long-term interest rates have dropped to 10 percent. The debt now carries a different value if bondholders wish to sell securities in the secondary market. Potential purchasers will buy the bonds to yield 10 percent over the remaining 9 years to maturity. Since the interest rate is fixed at 14 percent, the bonds will rise in value above the issuing price of $10,000 a bond. How much will one bond be worth? Let us develop the value.

If the original bond indenture promised to pay 14 percent interest compounded semiannually, the bondholder would receive $700 every 6 months:

$$\text{semiannual interest} = (10{,}000)\left(\frac{.14}{2}\right) = 700$$

After a year, the bond offers 18 more semiannual interest payments of $700 plus $10,000 principal repayment at maturity. Thus, we have a cash-flow stream with 18 semiannual payments of $700 and a final payment of $10,000. The present value of the stream is the intrinsic value of the security and is $12,423.69, as follows:

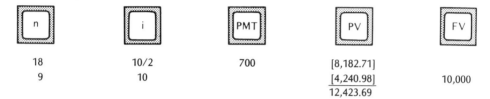

| $n$ | $i$ | PMT | PV | FV |
|---|---|---|---|---|
| 18 | 10/2 | 700 | [8,182.71] | |
| 9 | 10 | | [4,240.98] | 10,000 |
| | | | 12,423.69 | |

Using the formulas for present value, we get the same answer:

$$PV = (700)\left(\frac{1}{.05}\right)\left(1 - \frac{1}{(1.05)^{18}}\right) = 8{,}182.71$$

$$PV = \frac{10{,}000}{(1.10)^{9}} = \frac{4{,}240.98}{12{,}423.69}$$

An investor, evaluating the purchase of this bond 1 year after issuance when interest rates dropped to 10 percent, should be willing to pay $12,423.69 for the bond. This gives the investor a 10 percent return (compounded semiannually for the interest, annually for the principal) on the bond if it is held the remaining 9 years to maturity. Because the return on the bond must reflect other investment opportunities to the purchaser (that is, bonds with this level of risk are now 10 percent bonds), the $12,423.69 value is the intrinsic value or real worth of the bond.

## FIXED RETURN SECURITY—NO SPECIFIED MATURITY

Most issues of preferred stock do not have a stipulated maturity date. Such issues generally have a *call feature*, which allows the issuing firm to retire or convert the preferred stock to common stock at the firm's option. Since the call date is usually unknown, we view the preferred stock as a *perpetuity*, which is defined as a stream of cash to be paid or received indefinitely. The intrinsic value of a perpetuity is given by the formula:

$$PV = \frac{PMT}{i}$$

where PMT = the annual receipt or payment of cash in dollars

i = the appropriate time value of money

As an example of the use of this formula, a firm may have a $100 par preferred stock with an indicated dividend of 14 percent. Similar stocks yield 11.75 percent. The intrinsic value of the stock is:

$$PV = \frac{100 \times .14}{.1175} = 119.15$$

If the preferred stock had a specified or estimated maturity date, it is valued using the same technique as for the preceding fixed return securities. We discount the stream of expected future dividends and the call or maturity value to determine the intrinsic value.

## VALUE OF COMMON STOCK

A *capitalization technique* is a method of converting future cash flows into a single present or intrinsic value for a security. As an example, we *capitalize* dividends when we return them to a present value of stock. For debt and fixed return securities, we have been capitalizing future interest or dividends. The same process is followed for common stock, with a single exception. Common stock offers the potential for growth of future cash flows, and this must be reflected in the intrinsic value analysis. In this section, we will develop approaches to the valuation of common stock.

### SINGLE-PERIOD MODEL

The rate of return on an investment may be expressed solely in terms of the effects for one period, normally a year. It is assumed that the security is purchased at point 0 and sold at point 1. Any cash received during the year plus any increase in value represent the return from the investment. The formula is:

$$E(rtn)_1 = \frac{val_1 - val_0 + cash_1}{val_0}$$

where $E(rtn)_1$ = rate of return earned in period 1

$val_1$ = ending value of the security at the end of period 1

$val_0$ = starting value at point 0

$cash_1$ = any cash received between point 0 and the end of period 1

**Example:** An investor purchases 100 shares of common stock for $4,000 plus a $100 commission. In a single year, he sells the stock for $4,500, less a $100 commission. During the year, he received $250 in dividends. What was the rate of return?

**Answer:** 13.4 percent, as follows:

$$E(rtn)_1 = \frac{4,400 - 4,100 + 250}{4,100} = .134$$

A single-period approach can also be developed on a time value calculator, as follows:

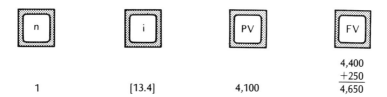

| n | i | PV | FV |
|---|---|---|---|
|   |   |   | 4,400 |
|   |   |   | +250 |
| 1 | [13.4] | 4,100 | 4,650 |

From the viewpoint of an investor holding common stock, the required return is the return on equity, or $K_e$, and we might rewrite the formula:

$$K_{e(req)} = \frac{val_1 - val_0 + div_1}{val_0}$$

To use this formula to solve for the market value, we can rewrite the formula to solve for $val_0$. When we do this algebraically, we get:

$$val_0 = \frac{1}{1+K_{e(req)}} (div_1 + val_1)$$

The formula now expresses the present value of a share of common stock in terms of a single-period model, where dividends represent cash received and an ending value is given or estimated.

> **Example:** In 1 year, 100 shares of common stock will be worth a total of $7,000. During the year, the holder of the shares will receive dividends of $500. Investments in this kind of stock require an 11 percent return before taxes. What is the intrinsic value of the 100 shares?
>
> **Answer:** $6,756.76.

$$val_0 = \frac{1}{1.11} (500 + 7,000) = 6,756.76$$

or

| n | i | PV | FV |
|---|---|---|---|
| 1 | 11 | [6,756.76] | 7,500 |

## PERPETUAL DIVIDENDS, NO GROWTH

A second approach to the valuation of common stock looks at more than one period. It is useful for firms that will perpetually pay dividends but will not grow in terms of earnings or dividends. Even though such firms are rarely, if ever, found, the valuation of such a stock is relatively easy. We use the same formula as used for the valuation of preferred stock, namely:

$$PV = \frac{PMT}{i}$$

which can be rewritten:

$$val_0 = \frac{DPS_1}{K_{e(req)}}$$

since $DPS_1$ = dividends per share in period 1 and every future period if the firm's dividends are not growing.

At this point, the reader should note that dividends equal earnings for a firm that is not growing. In the chapter on required return, we saw that growth may be expressed by the formula

$$g = \frac{EPS}{MktPr}(\%RE)$$

In order for the growth rate to be 0, the percent of retained earnings must be zero. Thus, all EPS is paid out as DPS and the value of the stock can be expressed:

$$val_0 = \frac{DPS_1}{K_{e(req)}} = \frac{EPS_1}{K_{e(req)}}$$

## PERPETUAL DIVIDENDS, CONSTANT GROWTH

A third approach to the valuation of common stock considers a situation where earnings and dividends are growing at a constant rate. In this situation, the firm retains a portion of its earnings to finance growth but maintains a constant *dividend payout,* which is defined as the relationship between dividends and earnings, or

$$\text{dividend payout} = \frac{DPS}{EPS}$$

Under the assumption of a constant growth rate, the intrinsic value is a function of an infinite stream of steadily growing dividends. The valuation formula is:

$$val_0 = \sum_{t=1}^{\infty} \frac{1}{[1+K_{e(req)}t]}[DPS_0(1+g)^t]$$

where $g$ is the constant growth rate of earnings and dividends.

If this formula looks burdensome to solve since it involves an infinite stream of dividends, the problem is not as great as it looks. Algebraically, the formula simplifies very nicely to:

$$val_0 = \frac{DPS_1}{K_{e(req)} - g}$$

which is the Gordon model from the chapter on required return.*

**Example:** A firm has an earnings per share of $5 and a dividend payout of 44 percent. An investor requires a 16 percent return on this kind of stock. The growth rate equals 12 percent. What is the intrinsic value of the stock?

**Answer:** $55.

$$val_0 = \frac{5 \times .44}{.16 - .12} = \$55$$

## THE GORDON MODEL

A number of considerations have been included in the development of the Gordon model. Thus, it can be used to illustrate how a mathematical model comes to grip with issues of intrinsic value. In this section, we will examine the Gordon model closely to see just what is happening.

### FACTORS INCORPORATED IN THE MODEL

Three primary design factors should be noted in terms of the construction of the Gordon model:

1.  *Shareholder's Return—Single Variable.* In the single-period model, the return to the shareholder consisted of dividends and capital gains. This is not the case with the Gordon formula. The return to the shareholder consists solely of future dividends. Earnings retained by the firm are part of the growth factor that will operate to increase dividends, but only future dividends are viewed as a return.
2.  *Normal and Actual Returns.* The Gordon model is built upon a comparison of a normal or required return and an actual return. These are:
    a.  *Required return ($K_e$).* Given the risk and return characteristics

---

*The supporting math can be found in John J. Hampton, *Modern Financial Theory: Perfect and Imperfect Markets* (Reston, Va.: Reston Publishing Company, January 1982), page 373.

| EPS/MktPr Actual | | Retained Earnings as a Percentage | | Amount of Growth | Explanation |
|---|---|---|---|---|---|
| 0 | | 0 | | None | No profits to retain |
| .05 | | 0 | | None | All profits paid out as dividends |
| .05 | × | .50 | = | .025 | |
| .10 | × | .50 | = | .050 | Growth increases owing to higher profits. |
| .10 | × | .60 | = | .060 | Growth increases owing to higher level of retained earnings. |

**Figure 14–2**   Growth Factor in the Gordon Model.

of the stock, the market will require some return on equity. This is expressed by EPS/MktPr as required by investors in similar common stocks. Since this is the reciprocal of the price-earnings ratio, this is commonly expressed in terms of a normal P/E multiple.

b. *Actual return.* This is the actual EPS/MktPr for the individual firm. It is included as part of the growth factor, since *g* equals EPS/MktPr times the percentage of retained earnings.

As we will see shortly, the difference between the required return and actual return has a significant impact on the value of the stock.

3. *Inclusion of a Growth Factor.* In order to take a long-term viewpoint, the model assumes steady growth of dividends and includes a factor to incorporate such growth into the valuation formula. Since we are interested in the growth of value to today's shareholders, growth is restricted to the retention of earnings. The sale of additional stock or growth from increasing the amount of debt or other limited return securities is omitted. The impact of the growth variable can be seen in Figure 14–2.

**A DIFFERENT VIEWPOINT**

Once we understand some of the components of the Gordon model, we can take another look at it. As an example, it can be rewritten:

$$\frac{\text{intrinsic}}{\text{value}} = \frac{\text{div}_1}{K_{e(req)} - [K_{e(act)}][\%RE]}$$

where $\text{div}_1$ = current indicated dividend in dollars (annual basis)

$K_{e(req)}$ = normal or required return on equity demanded by the market for a stock of this risk level

$K_{e(act)}$ = actual return on equity for the firm

%RE = percentage of EPS that the firm is likely to retain in the future

Now we are ready to see what is really happening in the Gordon model. To understand it fully, we must examine the effect of changing the dividend payout under different situations with respect to the returns on equity. As an example, let us consider a company with an EPS of $2 and an actual return on equity of 10 percent. There are three possible situations:

1. *Required Return less than Actual Return.* If this is the case, the stockholder is gaining more earnings by investing in the company than required from this risk level. For example, an 8 percent return may be required, and the firm is actually achieving 10 percent. The shareholder would want the firm to retain the earnings and achieve a 10 percent return on them. If dividends are paid, the investor can probably only earn 8 percent or so from similar investments. Thus, we would expect that raising the dividend payout would lower the intrinsic value, since it lowers the growth rate of a highly profitable firm. Table 14–1 shows that intrinsic value drops from $60 at a 30 percent dividend to $25 at 100 percent payout, confirming our expectation.

2. *Required Return Equal to Actual Return.* In this case, the firm is doing about as well as expected, and the shareholder probably does not care about the level of dividends. If they are declared, they will be reinvested in the firm or in a similar firm. We would expect that intrinsic value would be unaffected by the level of dividend payouts. Table 14–1 shows an intrinsic value of $20 at all payouts when the firm earns what is required.

3. *Required Return Exceeding Actual Return.* In this case, the firm is not doing as well as expected. Overall, the intrinsic value will be less than for a firm doing as well as required. But we would expect the intrinsic value to rise if the firm increased its dividend payout, since the shareholders would like to have cash to invest at a higher return elsewhere. Table 14–1 shows that the intrinsic

**TABLE 14-1.** Comparing Intrinsic Values with the Gordon Model under Different Returns and Dividerd Payouts.

| | Capitalization Rate Required | | |
|---|---|---|---|
| | *8 Percent* | *10 Percent* | *12 Percent* |
| 30% dividend payout | $\dfrac{\$.60}{8\% - (10\% \times 70\%)} = \$60.00$ | $\dfrac{\$.60}{10\% - (10\% \times 70\%)} = \$20.00$ | $\dfrac{\$.60}{12\% - (10\% \times 70\%)} = \$12.00$ |
| 50% dividend payout | $\dfrac{\$1.00}{8\% - (10\% \times 50\%)} = \$33.33$ | $\dfrac{\$1.00}{10\% - (10\% \times 50\%)} = \$20.00$ | $\dfrac{\$1.00}{12\% - (10\% \times 50\%)} = \$14.29$ |
| 70% dividend payout | $\dfrac{\$1.40}{8\% - (10\% \times 30\%)} = \$28.00$ | $\dfrac{\$1.40}{10\% - (10\% \times 30\%)} = \$20.00$ | $\dfrac{\$1.40}{12\% - (10\% \times 30\%)} = \$15.56$ |
| 100% dividend payout | $\dfrac{\$2.00}{8\% - (10\% \times 0\%)} = \$25.00$ | $\dfrac{\$2.00}{10\% - (10\% \times 0\%)} = \$20.00$ | $\dfrac{\$2.00}{12\% - (10\% \times 0\%)} = \$16.67$ |

**Note:** All data are for a firm with $2 EPS and a 10 percent actual return on equity.

value increases from \$12 to \$16.67 when the dividend payout is raised from 30 to 100 percent.

The validity of the Gordon model is supported by the data in Table 14–1. Changing the dividend payout has different results, depending upon the relationship between actual and required return. A firm that is doing better than required has a higher intrinsic value than a firm doing worse. The firm is encouraged to retain its earnings and reinvest them at the actual rates that are higher than required for the given risk level.

In actual practice, of course, some other factors come into play. When investors receive cash dividends, they must incur brokerage fees and other costs before they can reinvest the money. In most cases, the cash dividends present tax effects that differ from the tax impacts of retained earnings. These considerations modify the basic intrinsic values calculated by the Gordon model. But they do not destroy the validity of the concepts. As a valuation tool, the Gordon approach provides an approximate intrinsic value. Firms that are more profitable than required should be encouraged to reinvest dividends so long as they continue to have projects that offer a high return for the level of risk undertaken.

## COMPARATIVE APPROACHES TO VALUATION

In many cases, the financial analyst will seek the intrinsic value by comparing one firm with others. It can be argued that firms with similar operating characteristics and risk have similar intrinsic values. In this section, we will examine three comparative approaches to determining intrinsic value.

### COMPARING PRICE EARNINGS MULTIPLES

Many analysts rely heavily on the price earnings multiple as a determinant of value. In effect, they seek to capitalize earnings using the formula

$$\text{intrinsic value} = \frac{\text{EPS}}{K_{e(req)}}$$

which is a variation of the formula

$$K_e = \frac{\text{EPS}}{\text{MktPr}}$$

where intrinsic value replaces the market price. Once this formula is accepted, the analyst can observe the reciprocal of EPS/MktPr, or the price earnings multiple for stocks of publicly traded stocks in order to determine the value of privately held securities.

Is this a valid method? The answer is yes within a very restricted scope. Suppose an analyst is valuing privately traded common stock. Further suppose that the private company is similar to a publicly traded company in terms of risk, profitability, and growth rate. In this situation, the publicly traded stock's price earnings multiple could be used as a proxy for the intrinsic value of the privately held stock.

To illustrate this process, let us consider firm A, which is privately owned and has a $4 earnings per share. Firms B and C are similar in risk and return, and they trade publicly at a 7/1 price earnings multiple. What is the value of firm A? If the reciprocal of the price earnings multiple (1/7) is used as the required return, the intrinsic value is $28 as follows:

$$K_{e(req)} = 1/7 = .1429$$

$$\text{intrinsic value} = \$4/.1429 = 28$$

The same answer can be obtained by multiplying the observed price earnings multiple by the EPS, or $7 \times 4 = \$28$.

> **Example:** Companies X, Y, and Z are similar firms. Company X is the strongest of the three and trades at a 11/1 price earnings multiple. Company Y is less strong and trades at 9/1. Company Z is still less strong, is not publicly traded, but has an EPS of $2. What is the intrinsic value of company Z?
>
> **Answer:** If the strongest trades at 11/1 and the next strongest trades at 9/1, the least strong would trade at less than 9/1. At 7.5/1, company Z would have an intrinsic value of $7.5 \times 2 = \$15$.

## COMPARING VALUE WITH GORDON MODEL

The Gordon model can be used to compare values if we make a single important assumption. We must assume that the market price of similar firms is also the intrinsic value of the firms. When this is done, the formula becomes

$$\text{market price} = \frac{\text{div}_1}{K_{e(req)} - [K_{e(act)}] \, [\%\,RE]}$$

This formula has four components: market price, current dividend, growth rate, and the required return on equity. For similar, publicly traded firms, the first three of these components are known. We can modify the formula to solve for the required return on equity:

$$K_{e(req)} = \frac{div_1}{market\ price} + [K_{e(act)}]\ [\%RE]$$

Once we have the required return on equity for similar firms, we can apply it to the firm being valued. Since privately owned firms frequently pay dividends, we can use the dividend, growth rate (actual $K_e$ times percent retained earnings), and required return on equity to determine the probable market price if the stock were traded. Then we can assume that this would probably be close to the intrinsic value.

In an example of the use of this technique, a privately held firm has a 5 percent growth rate and pays a $6 dividend. A similar firm is publicly traded at $80 per share, pays a $4 dividend, and has an 8 percent growth rate. What is the value of the privately held firm? The required return on equity is

$$K_{e(req)} = 4/80 + .08 = .13$$

The expected market price, and intrinsic value, of the privately held firm is

$$market\ price = \frac{\$6}{.13 - .05} = \$75$$

**Example:** Companies Q, R, and S are in the same basic industry and offer similar risk and return. Company Q sells for $18 per share, pays a $1.50 dividend, and has a 5 percent growth rate. Company R sells for $36 per share, pays a $2.50 dividend, and has a 7 percent growth rate. Company S is privately owned, pays an $8 dividend, and has a 9 percent growth rate. What is the value of company S?

**Answer:** The required returns on equity for Q and R can be calculated:

$$For\ Q: K_{e(req)} = \frac{1.50}{18} + .05 = .13$$

$$\text{For R: } K_{e(req)} = \frac{2.50}{36} + .07 = .14$$

Since company S is similar, we might use the average required return, or 13.5 percent. The value of S is thus:

$$\text{intrinsic value} = \frac{8}{.135 - .09} = 178$$

### RELATIONSHIP OF BOOK VALUE AND MARKET PRICE

Although the book value of a firm cannot be used directly to determine the market or intrinsic value of a going concern, similar firms may have similar ratios of market value to book value. That is, if two similar firms have a 40 percent ratio of book to market value, this knowledge may be helpful in estimating the market value of a third similar firm that is privately held. For example, a publicly traded firm has a book value of $30 per share and a market price of $45 per share. What is the intrinsic value of a similar firm with a $10 book value per share? Since one firm has a 30/45, or 2/3 ratio of book value to market price, the second firm might be worth $10/.667, or $15.

> **Example:** Companies A, B, and C are similar in risk and return. Company C is privately held. Company A has a market price of $80 and a book value of $60. Company B has a market price of $20 and a book value of $14. Company C has a book value of $40. What is the possible value of C?
>
> **Answer:** For company A, the ratio of book to market value is 60/80, or 75 percent. For company B, the ratio is 14/20, or 70 percent. For company C, dividing the $40 book value by .70 and .75, we get a range of value from $53 to $57.

### KEY TERMS

| | | |
|---|---|---|
| book value | dividend payout | liquidation value |
| call feature | going concern value | market value |
| capitalization technique | intrinsic value | perpetuity |
| current market value | intrinsic value analysis | prime rate |
| approach | LIBOR | value |

## STUDY QUESTIONS

1. What are the four major concepts of value? In what terms are they expressed?
2. What is intrinsic value? the four factors used to estimate it? the most important factor?
3. What is the goal of intrinsic value analysis? the three limitations?
4. What are the three primary concerns of the current market value approach?
5. What are the three situations for the valuation of debt or fixed return securities?
6. How is the value of a variable-rate loan calculated?
7. If a security has a given maturity date, what considerations are included in its present value?
8. What are the three approaches for valuing common stock? In what situation is each used?
9. What is a capitalization technique? How is it modified in the valuation of common stock?
10. What are the three factors incorporated into the Gordon model?
11. With the Gordon model, does a change in dividend payout cause the intrinsic value to change?
12. What are the three comparative approaches to determining intrinsic value?
13. What assumption must be made to compare securities using the Gordon model?

## PROBLEMS

1. A financial analyst uses the current balance sheet to determine the value of the common stock of Sorino Pianos Inc. What kind of value is being determined?
2. An analyst has determined that the real worth of a security is $24 per share. The going market price is $30. Should the investor buy or sell?
3. A large manufacturing firm wants to diversify and is looking at a small firm formed 4 years ago. The firm has an average growth rate of 40 percent per year. Can intrinsic value analysis be used in this situation?
4. Delta Incorporated has a loan whose interest rate varies with the prime rate. The outstanding principal on the loan is $5 million. What is the loan's current market value?
5. A firm has sold $10 million of 15-year bonds at a coupon rate of 18 percent. The bonds were sold in multiples of $1,000 and interest is paid semiannually. After one year, interest rates in the market dropped to 12 percent for this kind of bond. What is the value of one bond at the end of the 1st year?
6. A corporation has $150 preferred stock with an indicated dividend rate of 10 percent. Similar stock yields 8.5 percent. What is the intrinsic value of the stock?
7. In one period, 150 shares of common stock will be worth $6,000. The investor will receive $200 in dividends during the year. This investment has a 15 percent required return before taxes. What is the intrinsic value of the stock?

8. An investor purchases 200 shares of common stock for $8,000, not including a $125 commission. In one year, the investor sells the stock for $10,000, less a $150 commission. During the year he received $250 in dividends. What was the rate of return on this investment?

9. An investor can purchase a stock that will be worth $60 per share in 3 years. It is expected to pay dividends of $8 per share each year for the next 3 years. The investor requires a 15 percent beforetax return on the stock. What is the intrinsic value of the stock?

10. A firm has earnings per share of $7.50 and a dividend payout of 35 percent. An investor requires a 14 percent beforetax return on this kind of investment. The firm's growth rate is 7 percent annually. What is the intrinsic value of the stock?

11. An analyst is valuing the privately traded stock of firm A, which has an earnings per share of $5. Firm B is a similar firm with an EPS of $1.20 and common stock price of $6 per share. What is the intrinsic value of one share of stock in firm A?

12. Companies A, B, and C are similar but C is privately owned. A has a 3 percent growth rate, a $1 dividend, and stock at $10 per share. B has a 5 percent growth rate, a $1.25 dividend, and stock at $12 per share. C has a $4 dividend and 10 percent growth rate. What is the likely value of company C's stock?

13. Company A has a market price of $50 per share and a book value of $30. B has a market price of $90 per share and book value of $59. Both are publicly held. Company C has a book value of $45 and is privately held. All three companies offer similar risk to investors. What is a supportable market value for the stock of company C?

# Valuation

*This case tests the reader's ability to determine the reasonable value of a firm and the minimum and maximum prices for use in negotiations.*

The Panama Printing Company was founded by Charlie Daniels in 1946 in a small town just outside of Panama City, Florida. Starting with a single printing press in his basement, Charlie has built the business from scratch. The business has sales of almost $300,000 annually and a book value of assets of approximately $200,000. The firm's unaudited balance sheet and record of sales and earnings before taxes are given here.

| PANAMA PRINTING COMPANY—Balance Sheet, December 31, 1984 | | | |
|---|---|---|---|
| Cash | $ 16,000 | Accounts payable | $ 5,000 |
| Accounts receivable | 40,000 | Misc. current liabilities | 1,000 |
| Inventories | 55,000 | Owner's equity | 198,000 |
| Machinery | 110,000 | | |
| (Less acc. deprc.) | (42,000) | | |
| Buildings and land | 44,000 | | |
| (Less acc. deprc.) | (19,000) | | |
| Total assets | $ 204,000 | | $204,000 |

Charlie has decided to sell Panama and retire. The problems of managing the business have become too much for him. Two problems have been particularly important in his decision. His two largest customers are paper mills located just outside Panama City. Although these firms account for 40 percent of his sales volume, they are both quick to complain about errors or delays in shipments. Charlie is frequently working in the evening to proof the written copy submitted by the paper mills, to check on the accuracy of the printed materials, and to ensure that shipments will be delivered promptly the next day.

The firm's second problem involves the need for a part-time salesman to secure new business. In his earlier days, Charlie was able to get out and call on prospective customers. Now he is tired by midafternoon and hardly ever visits potential customers. Charlie is convinced that sales visits would greatly increase his revenues. When he was canvassing firms, his revenues increased by 15 percent annually (the period 1961 to 1971). But recently he has relied on the two paper mills; about 15 other commercial customers, which account for 40 percent of sales; and a walk-in trade for the remaining 20 percent of volume. Charlie has been unable to find a salesman and he has decided not to begin selling by himself.

After considerable thought, Charlie placed the following advertisement in newspapers in Miami, Atlanta, and Philadelphia:

> PRINTING BUSINESS—FOR SALE. Multiline commercial printing firm available on Gulf Coast of Florida. Owner retiring after 35+ years of operation. Sales $300,000 annually. Turn-key operation for person with printing knowledge. Asking $170,000. Contact Charles Daniels, Panama Printing Co., Panama City, Fla.

In Philadelphia Jim Wilson read the advertisement with considerable interest. Jim had been working with his dad in the father's printing business just across the Delaware River from Philadelphia. A year earlier, the father had sold the business with the intention of retiring. Jim had been managing a print shop for another firm for about 8 months when his father unexpectedly passed away. Jim has inherited about $250,000 after taxes and would like to establish himself in a printing business in a growing area. Panama City would be suitable for his purposes.

After talking to Charlie Daniels on the telephone, Jim flew to Panama City to evaluate the situation firsthand. The local chamber of commerce provided him with information on the rapid growth of Panama City and forecast continued growth. He also learned that most of the printing in Panama City and surrounding areas was done in either of two ways. The extremely large jobs were sent to other cities and the completed jobs were shipped by truck, train, or ship. The medium and small jobs were taken care of by a variety of printing shops such as Panama. No one firm had a stranglehold on the market, although the city newspaper was becoming increasingly interested in using its presses for commercial jobs.

On his visit to Panama Printing, Jim had the following observations:

1. The physical facility was greatly underutilized. The building had considerable room for additional presses and equipment, but the existing machinery was only being used 6 to 8 hours a day. The machinery appeared to be in good shape.
2. The firm was doing virtually no advertising. The advertisement in the yellow pages represented the only money spent to promote the business. Charlie knew that most printing shops in Panama City were growing at an 8 to 10 percent rate in sales but

explained that the paper mills demanded his time and he could not be too concerned about new accounts until he got some sales help.

3. The chief printer working for Charlie was a young man who was totally competent in running the shop. Jim and the chief printer hit it off well and the printer complained that Charlie was spending too much time in the shop. "I can handle the production end of this business," the printer told Jim. "The boss just duplicates what I've already done."

When he got home, Jim sat down and gave similar risk investments offered a careful thought to purchasing Panama Printing. He decided that, since common stock offered a 16 to 18 percent return without requiring his personal time and attention to a business, an investment like a printing company should return approximately 22 percent as a minimum. With this in mind, he would begin negotiations with Charlie's lawyer.

## Questions

1. What offering price should Jim use to begin negotiations? What is the maximum that he should pay for Panama Printing?
2. What is the minimum that Charlie should accept?
3. What is a reasonable value of the business?

### PANAMA PRINTING COMPANY

#### Sales and Earning Before Taxes (1978–1984)

| Year | Annual Sales | Earnings Before Taxes |
|------|------|------|
| 1978 | $270,000 | $58,000 |
| 1979 | 283,000 | 54,000 |
| 1980 | 294,000 | 55,000 |
| 1981 | 297,000 | 49,000 |
| 1982 | 281,000 | 43,000 |
| 1983 | 294,000 | 39,000 |
| 1984 | 290,000 | 42,000 |

Note: As a sole proprietorship, Panama Printing pays no corporate taxes.

## LIQUIDATION STATISTICS—Small Businesses

When a small business liquidates its assets and ceases operations, it can expect to convert its assets into cash at approximately the following percentages:

| | |
|---|---|
| Cash | 100% |
| Accounts receivable | 90% |
| Inventories | 50–60% |
| Fixed assets | 50–60% |
| Real estate | At market value |

## REPORT FROM COUNTY ASSESSMENT OFFICE ON VALUE OF PANAMA PRINTING BUILDING AND LAND

Property is assessed at 40 percent of market value.

| | |
|---|---|
| Land | $40,000 assessed value |
| Building | $45,000 assessed value |
| Total assessment | $85,000 |

# Security Valuation

*This case provides the reader with several investment alternatives, of which the most favorable must be selected.*

Three months after learning of the death of his uncle, Fred Marshall got a letter from Armes, Gettings, and Wasson, attornies at law, that read in part:

. . . and therefore, you will receive from your uncle's estate the following securities:

20  Atlantic Industry bonds
     Par value: $1,000
     Coupon: 11.5 percent, compounded
               semiannually
     Maturity: December 31, 1987
     Current yield: 13.8 percent

25  Atlantic Industry bonds
     Par value: $1,000
     Coupon: 12 percent, compounded
               semiannually
     Maturity: June 30, 1986
     Current yield: 13 percent

300  shares, Atlantic Industry preferred stock
     Par value: $100
     Indicated dividend: 11 percent
     Maturity: None
     Current yield: 15 percent

These securities may be picked up by you or your representative at our office at any time after December 31, 1984.

Fred was very pleased to be remembered in his uncle's will but was less than pleased with a portfolio consisting solely of fixed income securities from Atlantic Industries. Being a young man with family responsibilities, Fred decided that he was more interested in capital growth than fixed income. He called Charlie Dyne, his broker, and asked for some advice. In response, Charlie wrote the following letter:

> I am delighted to hear of your good fortune and of your desire to invest in high quality equity securities. May I suggest that you investigate Wayburn International and Phillips Electronics, two fine companies with excellent prospects for their common stocks. I enclosed our recent writeups on each company. If you decide to invest in common stock, let me know and I would be pleased to liquidate your fixed income holdings.

After looking over the prospects for the two companies, Fred has decided that either company would suit his needs, provided it offered an 18 percent beforetax return on his investment in the common stock. He has decided to liquidate his current portfolio and invest in the firm whose stock is most realistically priced, if the stock also offers a return of at least 18 percent.

## Required

1. What is the current value of Fred's portfolio?
2. What are the intrinsic values of the common stock of Wayburn and Phillips?
3. Which stock is the best buy?
4. Does the stock offer an 18 percent return?

### Wayburn International

|  | 1983 | 1984 | Projected 1985 | Projected 1986 |
|---|---|---|---|---|
| Revenues (millions) | 41.1 | 45.3 | 50.0 | 55.0 |
| Net income (millions) | 7.3 | 8.0 | 8.8 | 9.7 |
| Earnings per share | $1.22 | $1.30 | $1.47 | $1.62 |
| Dividends per share | $ .50 | $ .55 | $ .60 | $ .65 |
| Market price |  |  |  |  |
| Average for year | $ 8 | $ 9 |  |  |
| High for year | $13 | $14 |  |  |
| Low for year | $ 6 | $ 7 |  |  |

10-year growth rate:
    1975–1984   11 percent annually
    1985–1994    9 percent annually
Shares outstanding, September 30, 1984: 6,150,000 shares
Market price, December 31, 1984: $8.50

**Phillips Electronics**

| | 1983 | 1984 | Projected 1985 | Projected 1986 |
|---|---|---|---|---|
| Revenues (millions) | 89.7 | 102.2 | 116.5 | 133.0 |
| Net income (millions) | 17.9 | 20.4 | 23.3 | 26.6 |
| Earnings per share | $1.79 | $2.04 | $2.33 | $2.66 |
| Dividends per share | $ .70 | .80 | .95 | 1.10 |
| Market price | | | | |
| Average for year | $18 | $21 | | |
| High for year | $27 | $31 | | |
| Low for year | $11 | $15 | | |

10-year growth rate:
  1975–1984   12 percent annually
  1985–1994   10 percent annually
Shares outstanding, September 30, 1984: 10 million
Market price, December 31, 1984: $16

# 15

# Mergers and Acquisitions

## MEASURES OF CORPORATE GROWTH

Financial managers use the term *growth* to mean increases in the size and activities of a firm over the long run. Three measures of corporate growth are commonly used:

1. *Increases in Sales.* This widely accepted measure gives an indication that a firm is able to maintain its competitive position, increase either the size or number of its primary markets for goods and services, and achieve the stability that usually accompanies a large volume of sales. Increase in sales is a direct indicator of growth in a firm's operating areas.
2. *Increases in Profits.* This measure is frequently used by the financial community and stockholders of a firm. It shows the firm's ability to convert growth in sales and operations into increasing returns to shareholders. The growth in profits is normally measured through increases in the firm's earnings per share.
3. *Increases in Assets.* Steady increases in a firm's operating resources may also be viewed as an indication of growth. This is the least desirable method of measuring growth. Although most firms must increase their assets to increase capacity for production and sales, a firm's assets may increase without a corre-

sponding increase in sales or earnings per share, an indication of inefficiencies rather than growth. Because of this possibility, increases in assets should not be used by itself as an indicator of growth.

## INTERNAL GROWTH

A firm is said to be growing *internally* when it increases sales and profits by expanding its own operations. It may purchase new machinery to increase its capacity to produce existing products, or it may purchase machinery and train its sales force to produce and sell a new product. In either case, management is committing itself to an expansion of existing activities. In one case, the firm seeks a larger volume of sales with current products. In the other, the firm begins to expand into new product areas and markets.

Internal growth may be funded from sources inside or outside the firm. Internal sources include retained earnings and the funds shielded by depreciation and other noncash expenses. If outside funds are sought, the firm may offer debt or equity securities to raise money. Even though the firm receives funds from external sources, the firm is experiencing internal growth, since the money is used to expand existing operations.

## EXTERNAL GROWTH

*External growth* occurs when a firm takes over the operations of another firm. The acquiring firm may purchase the assets or stock or may combine with the second firm. Since the second company has sales and assets of its own, the first company does not have to generate the new business from scratch. The term *acquisition* is generally used to refer to the taking over of assets in the process of external growth.

External growth offers a number of advantages over internal growth:

1. *Rapid Expansion.* Taking over the operations of another firm is the quickest path to growth. The acquiring firm eliminates the lead time for ordering and installing machinery, producing the product, and achieving sales in the marketplace.
2. *Immediate Cash Inflows.* Since the firm is taking over an operating business, it will realize almost immediate inflows as customers receive their goods and pay for them. These inflows would not

be received if the firm had to begin new construction of facilities and then the production of goods.

3. *Reduction of Risk*. Whenever a firm enters a new market, it takes a calculated risk. Will the new products sell in sufficient volume to be profitable? Will the firm's managers be able to make the proper decisions in the new operating environment? The acquired firm will be operating, perhaps successfully, in an environment familiar to its managers. By entering a field through an established and experienced management, we reduce the chances for failure.

4. *Economies*. Entering a new market involves a number of start-up costs. A *start-up cost* is an initial expense incurred when a firm begins a new operation. It may be the cost of training a new sales force or paying the legal fees required for the new activity. Frequently, these costs can be held to a minimum by purchasing an operating firm. For example, it would be less expensive to take over a firm with a strong marketing force than to have to compete with the marketing force by building one's own marketing department. The reduction of start-up costs offers economies from external growth.

## REASONS FOR SEEKING GROWTH

A number of reasons may be offered as to why firm's seek to grow. Among the more important ones are the following:

1. *Diversification*. Most firms recognize that diversifying their operations reduces the risk of failure. If a firm produces a single product, it is subject to the market pressures on the product. If demand diminishes rapidly, the firm will experience an unsettling cutback in its production. If a competitor introduces an improved version of the product or a substitute for it, the firm may no longer be able to compete in the marketplace. Since demand and competitive factors are difficult to predict, the only certain safeguard against a market disaster is diversification. If the firm is operating in a variety of markets with many products, it can cope better with a cutback in a single product or market.

2. *Stability*. When a firm is able to achieve a large volume of sales, it becomes more stable than firms with smaller volumes of sales. The high level of revenues allows production economies and

other cost-saving techniques, which allow a high margin of profit on sales. Also, the high sales level allows a deep penetration of most of the firm's markets. If a firm dominates a market, it is better able to withstand pressures and problems in the market.

3. *Operating Economies.* Large firms are able to achieve economies not available to small firms. As an example, Procter and Gamble is a large producer and seller of nondurable consumer products such as soaps, paper products, and food items. Because of its size, the firm is able to purchase large blocs of television advertising time at lower rates than firms purchasing fewer blocs of time. The reduced advertising rates are an economy that would not have been available if Procter and Gamble had not grown to its present size.

4. *Profits from Turnaround Situations.* When a firm is operating below its potential profit levels, a new management could remove inefficiencies and solve problems, resulting in a dramatic rise in profits. Such a firm offers a *turnaround situation.* When a firm is doing poorly but has strong potential for improvement, the firm will become the target of acquiring firms. The stock of the poorly managed firm will be *depressed,* or selling at a low price in the market. It will offer a bargain to an acquiring firm because, if profits can be restored to higher levels, the stock price will rise correspondingly.

## FORMS OF BUSINESS COMBINATIONS

External growth may be achieved by the purchase of the assets or common stock of another firm, paid for with cash or the issuance of securities. In this section, we will discuss the basic forms of organizing for external growth and some characteristics of each form.

### MERGERS

A *merger* is a combination of two or more businesses in which only one of the corporations survives. The other corporation ceases to exist, and its assets and, possibly, debts are taken over by the surviving corporation. In a merger of companies X and Y, company X may continue while Y ceases to exist.

The merger may occur in four ways:

1. *Purchase of Assets.* The assets of company Y may be sold to company X. Once this is done, company Y is a *corporate shell* with a capital structure but no resources. The company is then legally terminated; company X survives in the asset merger.
2. *Purchase of Common Stock.* The common stock of company Y may be purchased. When company X holds the stock of company Y, company Y is dissolved.
3. *Exchange of Stock for Assets.* Company X may give shares of X common stock to the shareholders of Y for the assets of Y. Then Y is terminated by a vote of its shareholders, who now hold X stock.
4. *Exchange of Stock for Stock.* Company X gives its shares to the shareholders of Y. Then Y is terminated.

State laws govern the merger of firms into a single economic unit. In most cases, the merger must be recommended by the boards of directors of both firms and must be approved by a majority to three-fourths of the shareholders in accordance with the applicable state laws.

## CONSOLIDATIONS

A *consolidation* is a combination of two or more businesses into a third, entirely new corporation. The new corporation absorbs the assets, and possibly liabilities, of both original corporations, which cease to exist. The legal and financial characteristics of a consolidation are basically the same as those for a merger.

When is a consolidation preferable to a merger? Possible situations are the following:

1. *For Firms of Equal Size.* When a large and small firm combine, normally the small firm is merged into the large firm. For firms of equal size, however, it may be difficult to get either of the boards of directors to agree that their company should terminate by being merged into the other company. In these cases, a new company is the better choice.
2. *When a New Charter Is Desired.* Companies receive their corporate charters at the beginning of their existence from an individual state. In many cases, the charters contain undesirable features that restrict the firm as it reaches maturity. A consolidation rep-

resents an opportunity to obtain a new corporate charter with more favorable features than in either of the charters of the existing companies.

Because mergers and consolidations involve the combining of two or more firms into a single firm, the term *merger* is commonly used to refer to both forms of external growth. We will follow this convention in the following discussions; only *merger* will be used, even though the item also refers to consolidations.

## KINDS OF MERGERS

Three major types of mergers have been important in the development of large American corporations:

1. *Horizontal Merger.* This is the joining of two firms in the same area of business. Examples would be the combining of two book publishers or two manufacturers of toys.
2. *Vertical Merger.* This is the joining of two firms involved in different stages of the production or distribution of the same product. Examples would be the combining of a coal company and a railroad that carries the coal or the joining of a typewriter manufacturer and a chain of office supply stores.
3. *Conglomerate Merger.* A *conglomerate* is a firm that has external growth through a number of mergers of companies whose businesses were not related either vertically or horizontally. A typical conglomerate might have operating areas in manufacturing, electronics, insurance, and other unrelated businesses.

## HOLDING COMPANIES

A *holding company* is a corporation that owns a controlling interest in the voting stock of one or more other corporations called *subsidiaries*. In some cases, as little as 10 to 15 percent of a firm's stock may be sufficient ownership to control the firm. In this kind of business combination, both firms continue to exist even if the holding company has 100 percent of the voting stock of the subsidiary. If the holding company actively engages itself in the management of the subsidiary, the holding company is also called a *parent company*.

The holding company form of business combination is desirable to firms for a number of reasons:

1. *Ease of Ownership.* The holding company can purchase the common stock of publicly traded firms without difficulty. No formal approval is required by either firm's stockholders.

2. *Lower Cost.* If the common stock is purchased in small installments over a period of time, the price of the stock may not be affected. If the shareholders of the soon-to-be subsidiary knew that another firm were seeking control, the price of the stock would probably rise.

3. *Leverage and Control.* Because a firm in many cases can be controlled with only 10 percent of the voting stock (assuming the rest is widely held), a holding company allows the control of a large amount of assets with a small investment.

4. *Diversification.* Since control is possible with a small investment, the holding company can purchase the stock of different firms, thus diversifying its investments.

5. *Avoiding Foreign Corporation Status.* A *domestic corporation* is chartered by the state in which it operates. A *foreign corporation* is chartered outside the state. Since many states favor domestic corporations with lower taxes and other privileges, a large corporation may establish a domestic holding company to conduct its operations in these states. If the parent operated directly in the state, it would lose the benefits of the domestic status.

## NONTAXABLE REORGANIZATION

Tax considerations affect the form of external growth. In an acquisition of stock for cash, the seller will be required to pay taxes on any gain in value resulting from the sale. For example, suppose a stockholder paid $100,000 for 5,000 shares of stock and is now selling the stock for $500,000. The seller will be required to pay capital gains taxes on the $400,000 difference between the original cost of the stock and the selling price today. The requirement to pay taxes on the gain may affect willingness to sell the common stock.

To avoid the payment of these taxes immediately, a business combination must qualify as a nontaxable reorganization under the terms of the Internal Revenue Service code. A *reorganization* is defined as a readjustment of corporate structure or ownership and may occur either when one corporation acquires the stock of another or when an existing corporation changes its capital structure or name, place, or form of organization. The following conditions generally apply to all nontaxable reorganizations:

1. The reorganization must be a sound business purpose, as opposed to being a scheme to avoid taxes.
2. There must be a continuity of ownership interest by the former stockholders of the acquired corporation.
3. The combination must comply with both the technical form and the intention of the law and Internal Revenue regulations.

## FACTORS AFFECTING EXTERNAL GROWTH

As firms seek the advantages found in external growth situations, they must deal with and analyze a variety of environmental factors, including the following.

### ANTITRUST CONSIDERATIONS

The United States has laws that forbid business combinations that have the effect of substantially lessening competition or which tend to create a monopoly. Three statutes provide the framework for antitrust legislation:

1. *Sherman Act (1890)*. The stated goal of the Sherman Act is to protect trade and commerce against unlawful restraints and monopolies. Two sections are noteworthy with respect to business combinations:

   Section 1. Every contract, combination in the form of trust or otherwise, or conspiracy, in restraint of trade or commerce among the several States, or with foreign nations, is hereby declared to be illegal. . . .

   Section 2. Every person who shall monopolize, or attempt to monopolize, or combine or conspire . . . to monopolize any part of the trade or commerce among the several States, or with foreign nations, shall be deemed guilty of a misdemeanor. . . .

2. *Clayton Act (1914)*. The Clayton Act forbids restrictive or monopolistic practices whose effect may be to *lessen competition substantially*. With respect to business combinations, the major restrictions are the following:

   a. Section 7 prohibits stock acquisitions that lessen competition between competitors. It does not forbid acquisitions of suppliers, customers, or others in the production or distribution channels of a single market.

   b. Section 8 forbids interlocking directorates that have the effect of lessening competition.

**3.** *Celler-Kefauver Amendment (1950).* This amendment to the Clayton Act resulted in a major change in government antitrust policy. It has three major impacts:

   **a.** Section 7 of the Clayton Act forbids the acquisition of *stock* when competition was lessened. The amendment broadens the prohibition to stock or assets. This prevents a monopoly created when one firm sells the assets of an operating division without selling any corporate stock.

   **b.** The amendment applies the Clayton Act to *individual markets,* a narrower scope than the previous lessening of competition between competitors. It does this by amending Section 7 so that it applies *in any line of commerce in any section of the country.* This allows government intervention to prevent monopolistic practices in major metropolitan areas or regional markets. It also prevents many combinations whereby one firm can control the supply and distribution channels and thereby make it difficult for its competitors to operate successfully.

   **c.** The amendment authorizes *divestment of assets or stock* acquired in violation of section 7 of the Clayton Act. This is highly significant because it allows the government to apply an after-the-fact remedy to business combinations that tend to lessen competition.

The antitrust laws are enforced through the combined efforts of the Department of Justice, Antitrust Division, and the Federal Trade Commission. Their major responsibilities are as follows:

**1.** *Federal Trade Commission (FTC).* Created by the Federal Trade Commission Act (1914), the FTC is:

   **a.** Empowered and directed to prevent unfair methods of competition in commerce (within the scope of the laws).

   **b.** Authorized to enforce compliance with the provisions of the Clayton Act.

   **c.** Authorized to order divestment of assets and stock acquired in violation of the Clayton Act.

**2.** *Antitrust Division, Department of Justice*

   **a.** Enforcement of the Sherman and Clayton Acts, which allow criminal penalties for violation. The act provides for fines, prison terms, or both.

   **b.** Instituting civil proceedings to prevent and restrain violations of the law. In recent years, this has been a highly significant power since it allows the Justice Department to seek injunctions against future combinations that would violate antitrust laws.

The enforcement measures used by the Antitrust Division of the Justice Department and the Federal Trade Commission have major impacts on firms that are considering external growth. For this reason, firms considering combinations with other firms must hire expert legal counsel and must be aware of any antitrust aspects of the proposed combinations. If a firm has questions on possible government intervention in a combination, it may deal directly with the Justice Department and Federal Trade Commission to receive advice and even formal opinions on combinations under the scope of the Clayton Act.

If favorable opinions are received on a proposed combination, the firm may proceed with some confidence. It is still possible, but not likely, that the government will attempt to block or divest a combination that has been favorably reviewed in advance. If a negative opinion is received, the firm may still proceed, but it must be prepared for lengthy and costly legal battles to resist the civil proceedings of the Justice Department or to overturn the orders of the Federal Trade Commission.

### AVAILABILITY OF FINANCING

In preparing to take over the operations of another firm, the acquiring firm must locate adequate and reasonable financing. Two major courses of action are possible:

1.  *Pay Cash.* To make the purchase for cash, the firm must either have the cash available or must be willing to raise it through debt or equity sources. The level of interest rates and the activity in the markets for equity securities strongly influence the kinds of financing and the availability of funds to finance the proposed acquisition.
2.  *Issue Corporate Stock.* The sellers may be willing to accept preferred or common stock of the acquiring corporation. This offers the advantage of reducing the amount of cash needed. It may also allow the sellers to avoid the immediate payment of capital-gains taxes on the sale of the assets.

The antitrust and financing factors affecting external growth are illustrated as part of an overview of external growth in Figure 15–1.

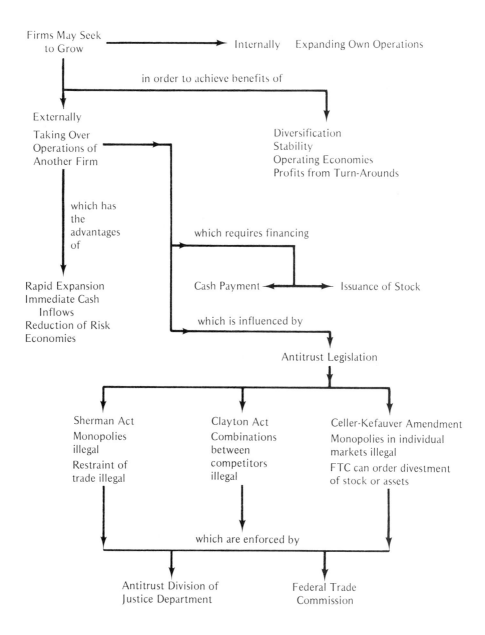

**Figure 15–1**  Overview of External Growth.

TAXATION

An important factor affecting external growth is the level of taxation and the tax regulations. A number of studies have been conducted since World War II; these indicate that tax considerations have played a major role in mergers and acquisitions. Two kinds of tax effects are particularly important as factors in business combinations:

1. *Tax-Loss Credits.* When a corporation sustains an ordinary operating loss, the loss may be averaged over an 18-year period. This is designed to allow a firm with widely fluctuating income to gain the full tax benefits from its losses. The law requires the firm to carry a loss back 3 years and forward 15 years. The loss is first carried back to the earliest year. If the loss exceeds the earnings before taxes, it is used to reduce EBT to 0; the balance is used to reduce earnings in the next year; and so on. If the loss *carry-back* exceeds the earnings for the 3 prior years, a loss *carry-forward* allows the firm to gain a tax credit in the future years up to 15 years ahead.

   **Example:** A firm has a loss of $4 million in 1984. It had an EBT of $500,000 in 1981, $1.2 million in 1982, $300,000 in 1983, $1.5 million in 1985, $3 million in 1986, and $2 million in 1987. How is the loss applied to reduce the firm's taxes?

   **Answer:** The loss is applied as follows (figures are in millions of dollars):

| Year | Old EBT | Loss–Carry-Back | Carry-Forward | New EBT | Tax Saving or Tax Refund (40 percent) |
|------|---------|-----------------|---------------|---------|----------------------------------------|
| 1981 | $ 500   | $ 500           |               | 0       | $200 |
| 1982 | 1,200   | 1,200           |               | 0       | 480 |
| 1983 | 300     | 300             |               | 0       | 120 |
| 1985 | 1,500   |                 | $1,500        | 0       | 600 |
| 1986 | 3,000   |                 | 500           | $2,500  | 200 |
|      |         | 2,000           | 2,000         |         |      |

When two corporations merge, the privilege of applying the tax carry-back or carry-forward can be gained by the new corporation. Thus, a profitable firm can benefit from tax breaks that cannot be used by an unprofitable firm. A corporation can acquire a firm with a tax loss, operate it as a subsidiary, and combine the tax returns to gain the tax refund or savings. A combination would be especially attractive if the acquiring firm can *turn around* the unprofitable firm at the same time it is benefiting from the tax shelter.

2. *Converting Ordinary Income to Capital Gains.* Shareholders receive dividends as their primary income from common-stock investments. The first $100 of dividends ($200 if jointly owned by husband and wife) is excluded from taxable income. All dividend income above $100 is taxed as ordinary income.

   When a shareholder sells common stock for more than the purchase price, the profit is taxed by either of two methods. If the stock were held for 12 months or less, the gain is taxed as ordinary income. If the stock were held for a period in excess of 12 months, the profit is taxed as a *capital gain*. The tax rate for the long-term gain is the same as for ordinary income, but only 40 percent of the gain is included in the tax calculation. This has the effect of cutting the tax on the capital gain to a maximum of 20 percent (for stockholders in the 50 percent bracket).

   Rather than continue to pay 50 percent tax on dividends, a shareholder might decide to sell out and accept the capital gain with its 20 percent tax rate. Evidence indicates that this is a motive in many business combinations.

**MONEY-MARKET FACTORS**

The overall levels of activity in the capital and money markets are factors that affect a firm's ability to grow externally. If the markets are depressed, the firm cannot sell or exchange common stock to finance acquisitions. If interest rates are high or if financing is not available, external financing is costly or prohibitive. If the acquiring firm's stockholders view a potential acquisition with alarm, the firm experiences a drop in the market price of its stock, a factor that will affect management's decision to acquire. Any firm planning for acquisitions must analyze investor confidence and the availability of money prior to final decisions.

# PYRAMIDING

Through the use of a technique called *pyramiding*, parent-subsidiary relationships may be used to allow one firm to control a number of other firms. *Pyramiding* may be defined as controlling several or many firms with a relatively small investment in each. We have already noted that as little as 10 percent of a firm's stock may be sufficient to control the firm. This fact facilitates pyramiding.

Actual pyramids in American business are highly complicated structures that are put together and managed through complex legal, financial, and communications arrangements. For our purposes, we will examine a model of a pyramid rather than an actual operating structure.

**SAMPLE PYRAMID**

As an example of the pyramid structure, consider a firm that has $500,000 in cash and is able to borrow another $500,000. It may use its $1 million cash to buy all the stock in two intermediary companies, 1 and 2. Once it owns these companies, they may be instructed to borrow $500,000 each. This will give the original firm, now a parent company, control of assets valued at $2 million. Each intermediary firm uses its cash to buy the equity in subsidiary firms 3, 4, 5, and 6. If these firms borrow $500,000 each, the parent will be controlling firms with $4 million in assets as a result of its initial $500,000 in equity investment. The pyramid structure is shown in Figure 15–2.

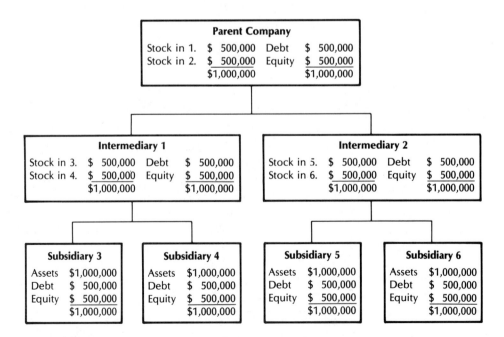

**Figure 15–2**  Corporate Structure Using Pyramiding.

In the pyramid in the figure, the subsidiaries are operating companies that own assets and produce revenues. The intermediaries are holding companies with no assets other than the stock in other companies. The revenues earned by the operating companies are passed on to the holding companies and then on to the parent company.

## TAXATION IN PYRAMIDS

The U.S. corporate tax regulations are a critical element in pyramiding. The tax rate applied to dividends paid by one corporation to another vary with the degree of ownership by the parent or holding company. Two situations are possible:

1. *Less than 80 Percent Owned.* To minimize corporate taxes on dividends, the subsidiary must be 80 percent or more owned by the parent company. If the subsidiary is not 80 percent owned, 15 percent of the subsidiary's dividends to the parent are treated as ordinary income and are subject to taxation at the parent's corporate income tax rate. The computation is (dividends) × (15%) × (corporate tax rate) = additional taxes.
2. *At Least 80 Percent Owned.* When the parent company owns at least 80 percent of the subsidiary's common stock, two possible savings occur.
   a. No part of the dividends is taxed. The entire amount of the dividends from the subsidiary is considered to be additional net income after taxes.
   b. A consolidated return may be filed. A *consolidated return* is a single tax return that combines the parent's and subsidiary's revenues and expenses. It saves the parent money in a situation where the parent has a loss while the subsidiary has a profit. Through the use of a consolidated return, the parent's loss can be used as a tax shield for a portion or all of the subsidiary's profit. This has the effect of reducing the taxes paid in the pyramid.

**Example:** A company receives $800,000 in dividends from a subsidiary that is 60 percent owned. How much additional tax must the company pay on the dividends at a 40 percent tax rate?

**Answer:** $48,000. The calculation for taxes on subsidiaries that are less than 80 percent owned is (dividends) (.15) (corporate tax rate) = ($800,000) (.15) (.40) = $48,000.

**Example:** A company declares $1 million in dividends. Eighty-five percent of the dividends are paid to its parent company; the remaining 15 percent are distributed to other shareholders. How much of the dividends are received by the parent and how much taxes are paid on the dividends?

**Answer:** $850,000 is received and none of it is subject to additional tax since the parent owns more than 80 percent of the subsidiary.

## RISKS AND LEVERAGE IN PYRAMIDS

Significant financial leverage may be achieved through the use of a pyramid structure. In the pyramid in Figure 15–2, a $500,000 equity is used to borrow $3.5 million and thus finance $4 million in assets. This will work fine as long as the firm's return on investment exceeds its interest rate. In Table 15–1, for example, the pyramid is shown with a 10 percent

**TABLE 15–1.**   Comparing Profits with Favorable and Unfavorable Financial Leverage in Corporate Pyramid of Figure 15–2.

| | *Favorable Financial Leverage* *No Consolidated Return* *15% ROI and 10% Interest* | | | | | *Unfavorable Financial Leverage* *No Consolidated Return* *8% ROI and 10% Interest* | | | |
|---|---|---|---|---|---|---|---|---|---|
| | *Subsidiaries* | | | | | *Subsidiaries* | | | |
| | 3 | 4 | 5 | 6 | | 3 | 4 | 5 | 6 |
| EBIT (000s) | 150 | 150 | 150 | 150 | EBIT (000s) | 80 | 80 | 80 | 80 |
| Interest | 50 | 50 | 50 | 50 | Interest | 50 | 50 | 50 | 50 |
| EBT | 100 | 100 | 100 | 100 | EBT | 30 | 30 | 30 | 30 |
| Net income | 60 | 60 | 60 | 60 | Net income | 18 | 18 | 18 | 18 |
| | *Intermediaries* | | | | | *Intermediaries* | | | |
| | 1 | 2 | | | | 1 | 2 | | |
| 100% dividends to intermediaries | 120 | 120 | | | 100% dividends to intermediaries | 36 | 36 | | |
| Interest | 50 | 50 | | | Interest | 50 | 50 | | |
| Aftertax income | 70 | 70 | | | Loss | (14) | (14) | | |

| *Favorable* | | *Unfavorable* | |
|---|---|---|---|
| 100% dividends to parent: | 140 | No dividend to parent: | |
| Interest | 50 | interest = | |
| Aftertax income | 90 | loss | (50) |
| Return on equity = 90/500 = .18 | | No return on equity. Intermediaries lose $14,000 each; parent loses $50,000 | |

**Note:** Figures based on pyramid in Figure 15–2.

interest rate on $3.5 million. The first structure has a 15 percent ROI in the operating subsidiaries. The profit is sufficient to cover the interest payments of the intermediaries and the parent, leaving a $90,000 parent aftertax income. The second structure shows an 8 percent ROI, which is not sufficient to cover the interest payments. The result is a loss of $78,000—$14,000 in each intermediary and $50,000 in the parent.

The data in Table 15–1 are compiled without the use of a consolidated income tax return at the parent level. In these examples, the intermediary and parent companies have interest payments but no operating income. Thus, these companies are unable to gain a tax credit for the interest payments. If the parent were eligible to file a consolidated return, as it actually is since it owns 100 percent of the subsidiaries and intermediaries, the interest payments at the parent and intermediary levels could be used to shield a portion of the operating revenues from the subsidiaries. The effect, shown in Table 15–2, is to increase the net income after taxes in the example with favorable financial leverage and reduce the loss in the example with unfavorable financial leverage.

As these examples illustrate, the opportunities for leverage are high in pyramids, but so are the risks. Slight improvements in profit margins or asset turnover can be converted into large rises in the earnings per share of the parent company. Similarly, small decreases in the operating profits can create a situation where the parent or intermediary cannot meet its interest payments. Since the pyramid is already highly levered, it is unlikely that the firm would be able to borrow to meet its fixed charges. The result may be a collapse of the pyramid and possible bankruptcy.

---

**TABLE 15–2.**   How Consolidated Returns Improve Profits or Reduce Losses.

| Favorable Financial Leverage Consolidated Return 15% ROI and 10% Interest | | | Unfavorable Financial Leverage Consolidated Return 8% ROI and 10% Interest | | |
|---|---|---|---|---|---|
| EBIT | 600 | $(15\% \times 4,000)$ | EBIT | 320 | $(8\% \times 4,000)$ |
| Interest | 350 | $(10\% \times 3,500)$ | Interest | 350 | $(10\% \times 3,500)$ |
| EBT | 250 | | EBT | (30) | |
| Net income | 150 | | | | |
| ROE = 150/500 = .30 | | | | | |
| With a consolidated return, ROE increases from .18 to .30 due to tax shield on interest of intermediaries and parent. | | | With a consolidated return, the loss decreases from a total of $78,000 to $30,000 | | |

**Note:** Figures based on pyramid in Figure 15–2. No consolidated return shown in Table 15–1.

**PROFIT CENTERS—TECHNIQUE FOR MANAGING THE PYRAMID**

The management of subsidiaries in a pyramid poses many problems for parent firms. A commonly used technique is to designate the subsidiary as a profit center. A *profit center* is any operating unit of a firm or any subsidiary that is given a profit goal and is held accountable for achieving that goal. The following are important characteristics of a profit center:

1. *Profit Goal Defined in Advance.* The parent organization and the profit-center manager work out a profit goal in advance of the operating period. The goal may be stated in dollars (for example, $500,000), as a ratio (for example, a 30 percent ROE), or in some other manner. But both the parent and subsidiary know the goal in advance.

2. *Control over Revenues and Costs.* In the decentralized structure of profit centers, each one must have control over its own costs and ability to earn revenues. The parent should not place restrictions on the size of the sales force or the use of the company plane. As long as the profit center is charged for all expenses, the profit-center manager should have authority to incur the costs as deemed necessary. The subsidiary must also be allowed to set its own prices and take steps needed to bring in revenues without interference.

Although the profit-center structure frequently results in a high level of profits, it poses several problems for the parent company:

1. *Allocation of Headquarters Services.* A subsidiary occasionally requires the services of the parent or headquarters staff. A lawyer may be needed for a patent search for a new product. Specialized tax expertise and advice may be helpful to the subsidiary's accounting department. The pyramid must make arrangements to account for the costs of these and similar services. A problem arises when the subsidiary does not want the services and does not want to be charged for them. As an example, how does the parent allocate the cost of printing the annual report if a profit center objects to paying part of it?

2. *Interdivisional Pricing.* When one profit center sells a product to another, a price must be established. Should the selling unit make its regular profit? Should the buying unit get the product at cost or near cost?

3. *Research and Development.* The parent may have a department that is working on technology for future products. Since the profit centers will eventually benefit, should they not pay a part of the cost? how much? Which center will benefit the most?

4. *Inherited Costs.* Management will frequently commit itself to projects that involve continuing costs over a long period of time, or that involve mistakes that will be costly in the future. If the management changes, must the new manager of a profit center be accountable for long-term costs that resulted from the decisions of the old manager?

5. *Performance Measurement.* One of the most difficult jobs is determining which profit centers are doing good jobs. Different operations face different conditions, market factors, and cost factors. A factory in an urban area will have high labor costs; a rural factory will have lower costs. The parent company must set goals that are realistic in light of existing conditions and measure performance against the goals, not against other profit centers.

## TAKEOVER STRATEGIES

The successful identification and takeover of another corporation involves complex legal and financial actions on the part of the acquiring firm. In this section, we will discuss some strategic considerations in mergers and acquisitions.

### FINDING A SUITABLE ACQUISITION

When a firm decides to seek external growth, it begins to search for suitable candidates for acquisition. This usually involves a team approach, since it is conducted by the firm's top management, legal staff, bankers, and even outside consultants who specialize in recommending workable corporate unions. When a consultant's recommendation is accepted and the merger is completed, the new firm pays a *finder's fee* to the consultant. This may be very sizable, up to 5 percent of the assets of the acquired firm.

The search process may focus on a number of key characteristics, including the following:

1. *Candidates with Net Operating Losses.* To be in a position to make acquisitions, a firm is normally highly profitable. If the acquired firm has a recent history of operating at a loss, the loss may be

applied as a tax carry-back or carry-forward to reduce the taxes of the acquiring firm. This can be a key factor in the desirability of a combination.

2. *Candidates That Must Avoid Improper Profit Accumulation.* Corporations are not allowed to retain earnings in excess of the reasonable needs of the business. The Internal Revenue code provides for stiff penalties for firms that retain earnings for the purpose of allowing stockholders to avoid paying personal income tax on the distributed dividends. A firm accumulating cash that represents improper retained earnings may be a takeover target. The cash would be useful to the acquiring firm since it can help finance additional growth. The takeover might be desirable to the shareholders of the firm with excess profits since they can avoid paying ordinary income taxes on dividends by paying capital-gains taxes on the sale of the company (at the lower capital-gains rate).

3. *Candidates That Offer Synergistic Prospects. Synergism* is the concept that some combinations have a total greater than the sum of the parts; that is, $2 + 2 = 5$. If we combine two firms with the proper operating characteristics, it may be possible to realize synergistic effects. One firm may have a strong research and development capability while the other has a strong marketing force. Together they would be able to develop new products and bring them forcefully to the customer, resulting in profits that neither could achieve alone. This would be an example of synergism.

4. *Candidates with Low Price-Earnings Multiples.* External growth can be particularly beneficial in the short run if the acquired firm is selling at bargain prices in the market. In most cases, the price-earnings ratio is used as the indicator of value in a business combination. A low price-earnings ratio indicates good value. This concept is discussed further in the following section.

5. *Candidates with Turnaround Prospects.* A prime takeover candidate is the firm with low operating profits due to poor management or other controllable factors. The profit prospects from a turn-around situation are illustrated later.

## AVOIDING A DILUTION OF EARNINGS

In making an acquisition, a firm must be aware of its own P/E ratio, the ratio of the to-be-acquired firm, and the general condition of the stock market. Two factors are particularly important.

1. *Market Value Largely Determines the Exchange Ratio.* The *exchange ratio* is the factor that determines how much common stock is issued or sold in making an acquisition. For example, a firm whose stock sells for $30 is planning to acquire a firm whose stock sells for $20. A logical exchange ratio might be 20/30, or two-thirds. This means that the acquiring firm must give up two-thirds of a share of stock for every full share acquired.

**Example:** Firm X's stock sells for $75; Y's sells for $25. If X takes over Y, what might be the exchange ratio?

**Answer:** 1/3. X must exchange 1 share of stock for every 3 of Y.

In actual practice, the exchange ratio usually includes a *premium* to encourage the shareholders of the to-be-acquired firm to surrender their stock. The premium normally ranges between 20 to 50 percent above the expected exchange ratio, which is normally based on market price. For example, in the preceding example, where X takes over Y, whose stock sells for $25, if X decided to offer a 20 percent premium to encourage Y's shareholders to sell their stock, the Y stock would be revalued ($25) (1.20), or $30. The new exchange ratio would be 30/75, or 40 percent, rather than 33⅓ percent.

**Example:** Firm R's stock sells for $60. S's stock sells for $100. R wants to take over S and plans to offer a premium of 25 percent. What is the exchange ratio?

**Answer:** 125/60, or 208 percent. The premium is $100 times .25, or $25. The exchange price of the S stock is $100 + $25, or $125. The exchange ratio is 125/60, or 2.08 shares of R stock for every share of S stock.

**Example:** Firm J's stock sells for $25; K's sells for $15. J wants to take over K and plans to offer a premium of 20 percent. What is the exchange ratio?

**Answer:** 18/25, or 72 percent. The premium is $15 times .20, or $3. The exchange price of the K stock is $15 + $3, or $18. The exchange ratio is 18/25, or .72 of a share of J stock for every share of K stock.

Note that the concept of the exchange ratio is valid even if the firm must sell its stock in the market and then use the proceeds to purchase another firm's stock. The acquiring firm must sell a bloc of shares at some price near the prevailing market price and then must pay a price at or above the current market price of the to-be-acquired firm. The transaction involves cash in a manner similar to a direct exchange of stock.

2. *Price-Earnings Multiple Largely Determines Whether a Dilution of Earnings Occurs.* A *dilution of earnings* is a decrease in earnings per share as a result of paying a high price for an acquisition. It occurs when a firm acquires another firm at a higher P/E multiple (after the premium is considered). To illustrate this concept, we will use the data in Table 15–3. Three situations are shown. In each case, firm A is planning to take over B. In situation 1, the exchange ratio is based on the same P/E multiple. When this happens, firm A has a $2 EPS before and after the acquisition—no dilution of earnings occurs. In situation 2, the exchange price is determined using different exchange P/E ratios. A's price reflects a 5/1 ratio; B's reflects 10/1. When this happens, the new firm A experiences a decrease in EPS to $1.50. In situation 3, the

**TABLE 15–3.**   Sample Acquisition Illustrating the Concept of Dilution of Earnings.

| 1. *Exchange Ratio Based on Same P/E. No Dilution of Earnings Occurs.* | | | 2. *To-Be-Acquired Firm Has Higher P/E. A Dilution of Earnings Occurs.* | | | 3. *To-Be-Acquired Firm Has Lower P/E. An Increase in Earnings Occurs.* | | |
|---|---|---|---|---|---|---|---|---|
| | *A* | *B* | | *A* | *B* | | *A* | *B* |
| Net income | $200 | $100 | Net income | $200 | $100 | Net income | $200 | $100 |
| Shares out. | 100 | 100 | Shares out. | 100 | 100 | Shares out. | 100 | 100 |
| EPS | $ 2 | $ 1 | EPS | $ 2 | $ 1 | EPS | $ 2 | $ 1 |
| Exch. P/E | 10/1 | 10/1 | Exch. P.E | 5/1 | 10/1 | Exch. P/E | 10/1 | 5/1 |
| Exch. price | $ 20 | $ 10 | Exch. price | $ 10 | $ 10 | Exch. price | $ 20 | $ 5 |
| Exch. ratio | 1/2 | | Exch. ratio | 1/1 | | Exch. ratio | 1/4 | |

| *Firm A Issues 50 New Shares* | | *Firm A Issues 100 New Shares* | | *Firm A Issues 25 New Shares* | |
|---|---|---|---|---|---|
| | *New Firm A* | | *New Firm A* | | *New Firm A* |
| Net income | $300 | Net income | $300 | Net income | $300 |
| Shares out. | 150 | Shares out. | 200 | Shares out. | 125 |
| EPS | $ 2 | EPS | $1.50 | EPS | $2.40 |

**Note:** In the three situations, firm A is taking over firm B.

exchange price reflects a 10/1 ratio for A but only a 5/1 ratio for B. In this case, B is a relative bargain in terms of its profits, and A experiences an increase in EPS after the acquisition. Of the three situations, it should be obvious that situation 3 is preferred since it raises the reported earnings of the firm after the acquisition. As a minimum, the firm must achieve situation 1—the same P/E factor—if a dilution of earnings is to be avoided.

## POSTMERGER PRICE-EARNINGS MULTIPLE

After the two firms are merged, the stock market must establish a single P/E multiple to apply to the two firms. If the multiple will be low, the acquiring firm should avoid a merger and should operate the acquired firm as a subsidiary with its own common stock. If the multiple will be high, the two firms should probably be merged to gain the benefit of the high multiple on the combined earnings. Table 15–4 continues the examples in Table 15–3 and assumes that the market will probably give a merged firm a P/E multiple of the old firm A, the old firm B, or an average of the two. Note the importance of the new P/E multiple with respect to the price of the stock.

**TABLE 15–4.**   Different Common Stock Prices, Depending on Which Price-Earnings Multiple Is Given by the Stock Market.

| 1. Originally Firms A and B Had Same P/E. | | 2. Originally Firms A and B Had Different P/Es. New P/E Can Be High, Low, or Average of Old P/Es. | | | | 3. Originally Firms A and B Had Different P/Es. New P/E Can Be High, Low, or Average of Old P/Es. | | | |
|---|---|---|---|---|---|---|---|---|---|
| EPS | $ 2 | EPS | $1.50 | | | EPS | $2.40 | | |
| P/E | 10/1 | P/E | High 10/1 | Avg. 7.5/1 | Low 5/1 | P/E | High 10/1 | Avg. 7.5/1 | Low 5/1 |
| New mkt. price | $20 | New mkt. price | $15 | $11.25 | $7.50 | New mkt. price | $24 | $18 | $12 |
| Old mkt. price | $20 | Old mkt. price | $10 | $10 | $10 | Old mkt. price | $20 | $20 | $20 |
| Gain (loss) | 0 | Gain (loss) | $5 | $1.25 | ($2.50) | Gain (loss) | $4 | ($2) | ($8) |

**Note:** All data continued from the final EPS figures in Table 15–3.

1. When both firms have the same P/E, no gain or loss in market value occurs.
2. When the acquiring firm has the lower P/E (the dilution of earnings situation), the acquiring firm can gain from either an average or high P/E multiple after the merger. The rise in P/E multiple offsets the dilution of earnings in these cases. But if the P/E multiple remains low (the acquiring firm's multiple), the dilution of earnings is translated into a reduced market price of the stock.
3. When the acquiring firm has the higher P/E (situation 3), any reduction in the P/E multiple can be very harmful. If the new firm takes the high P/E ratio, the stock value gains. But either an average or a low multiple causes a loss. In these cases, the lower P/E multiple offsets the higher earnings per share to reduce the price of the stock.

The different possibilities for EPS and P/E ratios and the effect on the future price of the stock are illustrated in Table 15–5.

It is one thing to recognize the different effects of possible dilutions of earnings and reduction of P/E multiples. It is another thing to predict exactly which P/E multiple will be given to the new company by investors in the stock market. As long as we know the preceding relationships, we can take steps to avoid diluting our earnings and encourage conditions and mergers that hold the prospect of increasing or maintaining our firm's P/E multiple.

**TABLE 15–5.** Changes in Earnings per Share and Price-Earnings and Their Effect on the Future Market Price of the Acquiring Firm's Stock.

| Situation | Future EPS | Future P/E | Effect on Market Price of Stock |
|---|---|---|---|
| 1 | ↑ | ↑ | The stock will increase in value. |
| 2 | ↓ | ↓ | The stock will decrease in value. |
| 3 | ↔ | ↔ | The stock's value will not change. |
| 4 | ↑ | ↔ | Value will increase. |
| 5 | ↓ | ↔ | Value will decrease. |
| 6 | ↔ | ↑ | Value will increase. |
| 7 | ↔ | ↓ | Value will decrease. |
| 8 | ↑ | ↓ | Offsetting effects. Value may increase, decrease, or remain the same. |
| 9 | ↓ | ↑ | Offsetting effects. Value may increase, decrease, or remain the same. |

**SPOTTING A TURNAROUND SITUATION**

Firms seeking acquisition candidates usually pay particular attention to possible turnaround situations. A number of guidelines may be offered to help a firm identify a company with low profits but high prospects for improvement if acquired:

1.  *Recent Drop in Profits for Individual Firms but Not Industry.* If a firm is experiencing internal problems, it may suffer a drop in operating profits. When the firm's overall industry does not suffer such a drop, it is a good sign that the profit decline results from an internal, and thus possibly controllable, factor. A check of industry profits frequently reveals this kind of situation, which can be investigated further.

2.  *Industries to Be Affected Favorably by Forecast Economic Changes.* At any time, but particularly in the fall, the nation's economists predict future levels of economic activity. Included in these forecasts are shifts in demand and changes in production for major industries. Each year brings forecasts of reduced production in some industries and increases in others. By analyzing these forecasts, a firm can identify industries with growth prospects in the short- to medium-term and can seek turnaround candidates in these industries. In recent years, economists have made favorable predictions for leisure-oriented industries, transportation industries, and many service industries.

3.  *Break in Management Ranks.* Normally, a firm's top management works together and presents a united front to the outside world. Occasionally, some members of the management team break away and do not want to participate in moving the firm on its current course. This may indicate that these managers see a better way to run the firm but are blocked by the controlling managers. If the firm is not profitable, the new ideas of the minority managers may be able to increase profits greatly. These situations call for further investigation.

4.  *Laggard Firm in the Industry.* Most industries have a range of firms from the most successful to the relatively unsuccessful. If the less profitable firms have the same machinery and as much experience as the more profitable firms, their problems may result from weak management. Taking over a laggard firm and replacing its management may bring a rapid increase in profits.

5.  *Poorly Performing Firm with Complementary Strength to One's Own*

*Strength.* The acquiring firm may have great strength in marketing consumer products through its sales force and excellent advertising and research departments. This firm may begin to review other firms in the consumer products market, looking for low profits and a solid production capability. By merging with these firms, the combined firm would have both the production and marketing expertise and might be able to achieve solid increases in profits in a short period of time.

## DETERMINING THE PURCHASE PRICE FOR A TURNAROUND CANDIDATE

The technique of estimating future earnings per share can be very useful in arriving at a purchase price for a company that is not performing up to its potential. To illustrate the use of this technique, we will consider the acquisition of Lenox Products, Inc. The financial data are given in Table 15–6.

At present, the operating and financial characteristics indicate the following about Lenox.

1.  *Its P/E Value Is Only $2 per Share.* Its current market price of $10 is thus based more on the value of its assets than on its profits.

**TABLE 15–6.**   Lenox Products, Inc. Financial Data at Present and After Acquisition.

| *Present Balance Sheet* | | *Projected Balance Sheet If Acquired* | |
|---|---|---|---|
| Cash | $10,000,000 | Cash | $ 2,000,000 |
| Other assets | 10,000,000 | Other assets | 28,000,000 |
| Total | $20,000,000 | Total | $30,000,000 |
| | | | |
| Debt | $ 1,000,000 | Debt | $11,000,000 |
| Equity | 19,000,000 | Equity | 19,000,000 |
| Total | $20,000,000 | Total | $30,000,000 |

| *Other Financial Data* | *Present* | *Future* |
|---|---|---|
| Sales | $20,000,000 | $60,000,000 |
| Net income after taxes | 400,000 | 6,000,000 |
| Shares outstanding | 2,000,000 | 2,000,000 |
| Earnings per share | $     .20 | $     3.00 |
| Market value of one share of stock at 10/1 P/E | $    2.00 | $    30.00 |
| Present market price of stock | $   10.00 | |

2. *It Has Excess Cash.* At present it could pay a $5-dividend per share ($10 million/2 million shares). Half its assets are cash, an excessive amount for operations.

3. *It Has Very Small Profits.* Its EPS are only $.20. Its return on equity is 2.1 percent (400/19,000).

If our firm acquires Lenox, we would take the following actions. The results of our actions are considered in the projected and future data in Table 15–6.

1. We would eliminate the excess cash and invest it in other assets. At the same time, we would take advantage of favorable financial leverage by borrowing $10 million and increasing our debt-equity ratio to an acceptable .58/1.

2. We would use the additional capital to purchase new equipment, which could increase production and provide more units to sell.

3. We would use our own excellent marketing team to sell the products of Lenox, a step that would dramatically increase sales from $20 to $60 million.

4. The new equipment and larger sales volume would result in more acceptable profit levels, as reflected in the $3 EPS and the 32 percent return on equity ($6 million/$19 million).

In the case of Lenox, the current market price of $10 would make the stock seem overpriced on the basis of profits. But considering future earnings if the firm were acquired, we would be willing to pay $10 or more per share for the firm. How much should be paid for one share? The answer is some price below $30, depending upon the degree of risk that we shall not be able to effect the turnaround. At $12 to $15 per share, the firm offers a chance for a sizable increase in the value of common stock if projected figures can be attained.

## TAKEOVER APPROACH

Once we have selected a firm to become the target of a takeover, we must decide how the takeover will occur. Basically, we have three major choices:

1. *Negotiations.* Frequently, we can approach the management or large shareholders of the target firm and discuss a possible merger or purchase with them. If they are interested, our ac-

counting and legal departments with their counterparts in the to-be-acquired firm can work out details and develop the data needed to determine a purchase price or exchange ratio. With the approval of both companies, the combination can take place.

2. *Solicit Tenders.* A *tender* is an offer to sell a definite number of shares at a specific price. When a firm selects this method of obtaining voting control, it will solicit tenders from the stockholders. This is done by placing a public notice or by sending letters to all shareholders announcing that the acquiring firm will pay a certain price for shares of stock tendered by the shareholders of the target firm. Normally, a limit is placed on the number of shares and a deadline is specified. For example, the notice may state that:

*Roberts, Inc. will pay $14 per share for up to 1.2 million shares of Lenox Products, Inc. common stock. Tenders should be sent to Roberts, Inc., in care of the Chase Manhattan Bank, postmarked not later than April 1.*

If enough shares are tendered, the acquiring firm will be able to purchase voting control.

3. *Solicit Proxies.* A *proxy* is a written power of attorney allowing one person to vote the specific shares of a corporation's stock held by another person. Normally, proxies are issued prior to stockholders' meetings to allow stockholders to have their interest represented without their personal presence at the annual meeting. Most companies routinely mail proxies to shareholders asking permission for management to vote the shares of stock at the meeting. If the stockholders return enough proxies, management can decide to accept or reject a takeover. If an outside company solicits proxies for the purpose of voting for a takeover, a proxy fight can result between the management and the acquiring firm. If the acquiring firm receives sufficient proxies, it will have enough votes to effect the takeover.

## RESISTING AN ACQUISITION

In many cases, the management of a firm decides that the firm should not be acquired by another firm. Many reasons may be given to explain the management's feelings:

1. *Failure to Understand Target Firm's Problems.* The management may feel that the acquiring firm does not understand the real dif-

ficulties being faced by the existing management. This lack of understanding may cause even greater problems once the acquisition has been completed.

2. *Future Plans Not in the Interest of Target Firm's Shareholders.* The acquiring firm may be planning to operate the target firm as a subsidiary in a new or restricted role. The target firm's operations may be modified or partially eliminated to fit in with the parent firm's other activities. This reduction of growth in production and sales might be viewed as harmful to the remaining shareholders of the target firm.

3. *Tender Price or Exchange Ratio Too Low.* We have already noted that a firm that is about to be acquired is normally not realizing its full potential. If it were, the price of its stock would be too high for another firm to attempt a takeover. The target firm's management may feel that conditions will soon be improving and the target firm's stock will soon be rising rapidly. Thus, they may object to a takeover at the bargain price implied in the tender offer or exchange ratio.

4. *Acquiring Firm's Plan for New Management.* Perhaps the most common objection of the existing management is that a new management will be installed after the takeover. The acquiring firm usually makes a major effort to identify the deadwood in the old management and may even replace it entirely. If the old management were strong, the firm would be doing better. This reasoning is commonly used to replace the old management.

A firm may employ a number of tactics to avoid being taken over by another firm. Perhaps the classic defense against an attempted takeover occurred in the late 1960s, when B.F. Goodrich successfully resisted the efforts of Northwest Industries. Some of the major features of that case were the following:

1. *Get Stockholders to Vote against the Takeover.* The B.F. Goodrich management sent notices to all shareholders, recommending that they refuse to sign proxies for the Northwest Industries group. This blocked the possibility that the takeover could be achieved through a merger approved by both companies' stockholders.

2. *Block Efforts to Solicit Tenders.* The B.F. Goodrich management refused to release the mailing list of its stockholders, thus making it difficult for Northwest to solicit tenders. This action forces the acquiring firm to use indirect means, such as advertisements in

newspapers, to solicit tenders and reduces the effectiveness of the tender campaign.

3. *Get a Government Agency Involved.* If a government agency shows interest in the acquisition, it will make the effort more difficult. The Justice Department could investigate antitrust considerations, or some other agency could step in. In the B.F. Goodrich case, Goodrich purchased a trucking company during the acquisition campaign. Since Northwest already owned a railroad and since the Interstate Commerce Commission normally objects to one company owning both a railroad and a trucking company, the action was designed to get the ICC involved in the merger. To avoid this, Northwest was forced to go to court to try to block the purchase of the trucking company, an additional problem for Northwest.

4. *Get Controlling Stock into Friendly Hands.* The firm resisting the takeover may issue stock in return for assets to a corporation that will vote the stock on the side of management. The additional outstanding stock will make it more difficult for an unfriendly company to gain voting control. In the B.F. Goodrich case, stock was issued to the Gulf Oil Company in return for the assets of a chemical subsidiary of Gulf. The additional stock would be voted by Gulf on the side of management if the merger came to a vote.

5. *Begin an Unfavorable Publicity Campaign.* The very fact that management is openly willing to fight the acquisition in the newspapers will have a detrimental effect on the acquisition. The acquiring firm may feel that the unfavorable publicity is more harmful than the beneficial effects expected from the successful takeover. Frequently, the publicity hurts the stock price of the acquiring firm, as it did the price of Northwest Industries stock. This drop in the stock price makes it difficult to raise additional money through the sale of stock, reduces the desirability of a stock for stock exchange, and generally is harmful to the management of the acquiring firm.

## ACCOUNTING FOR MERGERS AND ACQUISITIONS

The prospects for a business combination may be affected by the accounting techniques used to record the merger. These techniques can have important effects on the balance sheet and reported earnings of the surviving firm. Two accounting techniques are generally accepted under the regulations of the Securities and Exchange Commission. These are the

(1) pooling-of-interests and (2) purchase methods of accounting; they will be covered in this section.

## POOLING-OF-INTERESTS VERSUS PURCHASE METHODS OF ACCOUNTING

The pooling-of-interests method of accounting for a business combination assumes a continuity of both the asset values and the ownership of the combined firms. In effect, we combine the balance sheets of the merged firms and report their combined earnings to our shareholders. The *purchase* method assumes a new ownership and a need to reappraise the assets of the acquired firm in light of current market value. The balance sheet is restated to reflect the current values as the combination is completed. If a firm is acquired for a price in excess of its book value, the excess is recorded either as an increase in value on specific depreciable assets or in an account titled "good will."

The pooling-of-interests method is generally preferred by corporations considering a business combination. To see why this is so, let us examine some of the differences between the two methods of accounting.

1. *Treatment of Good Will. Good will* is the account used to report the excess paid for a firm over the book value of the depreciable assets. It is used only in the purchase method of accounting. Good will is an intangible-asset account carried on the balance sheet of the surviving or parent corporation. Two characteristics of good will are especially important in merger accounting.
   a. It must be written off over some reasonable period not longer than 40 years. If the full 40 years is used, a writeoff of 2.5 percent annually of the good will must be taken as a *reduction of reported profits*. This is not desirable, because it causes the combined firm to report lower profits than would be reported in the absence of good will.
   b. Good will is not deductible for tax purposes. Whereas other writeoffs such as depreciation are deductible, good will is not. Thus, good will has the disadvantage of reducing reported earnings while not allowing the benefit of lowered income taxes.

   Good will is not recorded with the pooling-of-interests method of accounting; earnings are therefore not reduced by a required writeoff.
2. *Sale of Assets Acquired at Depreciated Book Values.* Since pooling involves a combination of the balance sheets of the two firms, it

does not provide for adjusting the value of undervalued depreciable assets. For example, a machine may have a market value of $100,000 and a book value of only $20,000. Under the purchase method, the machine would be revalued to $100,000, and a new depreciation schedule would be established. If the machine were sold for $100,000, no gain or loss would be reported. Under pooling, the machine would retain its $20,000 book value. If it were sold for $100,000, a profit of $80,000 could be recorded as a profit on the sale of assets on the combined income statement. When this is done, the combination could be used to create the appearance of a growth in profits. This, of course, would be misleading but nonetheless is an advantage to pooling.

3. *Difference in the Asset Base.* When purchase accounting is used, the new balance sheet is increased by the amount of good will. For example, if a firm pays $50 million for a company with a book value of $20 million, the $30 million in good will is shown on the balance sheet. With pooling of interests, only the $20 million in assets would be shown. This has the effect of reporting a lower asset base, which results in higher ratios, such as return on investment and return on equity. It also reduces the amount of equity for the debt-asset and debt-equity ratios.

## CONDITIONS REQUIRING THE POOLING-OF-INTERESTS METHOD

Accounting Principles Board Opinion No. 16 specifies 12 conditions that must be met in order to classify the combination as a pooling of interests. If 1 or more of these conditions are not met, the purchase method must be used for the purpose of combining the companies. These 12 specifications fall under these three categories:

1. *Attributes of the Combining Companies.* Each company must not have been a subsidiary of any corporation within the past 2 years nor had intercompany investments of voting common stock in excess of 10 percent.

2. *Manner of Combining Interests.* The combination must be the result of a single transaction or a plan that is completed within 1 year after being initiated. The corporation must issue only common stock with identical rights of the majority of its outstanding voting common stock, in exchange for at least 90 percent of the voting common stock of the other company. Each common stockholder who exchanges stock must receive a voting common stock

interest exactly in the same proportion to the relative voting common stock interest prior to the combination.

3. *Absence of Planned Transactions.* The combined corporation must not enter into other financial arrangements for the benefit of the former stockholders of a combining company and must not agree, directly or indirectly, to retire or reacquire all or part of the common stock issued to effect the combination. Also, the combined corporation must not intend to dispose of a significant part of the assets of the combining companies within 2 years after the combination.

## MERGER ACCOUNTING WITH PURCHASE AND POOLING

As an example of the differences in recording assets between the pooling and purchase methods of accounting, Table 15–7 shows a simplified balance sheet when firm X purchases firm Y and receives $1.2 million in equity for $2 million. With respect to the purchase method, note the following:

1. *Good Will Account.* This is the difference between the purchase price and the book value of the equity, as follows:

good will = purchase price − equity
$800,000 = $2,000,000 − $1,200,000

2. *Increase in Accounting Value of Total Assets.* With increases in the good will account on the asset side and the equity account on the financing side, the balance sheet shows an increase of $800,000

---

**TABLE 15–7.** Accounting under the Pooling-of-Interests and Purchase Methods of Accounting (in Millions of Dollars).

| Account | X Alone | Y Alone | X + Y Purchase Method[a] | X + Y Pooling Method[a] |
|---|---|---|---|---|
| Assets | 14 | 1.6 | 15.6 | 15.6 |
| Good will | 0 | 0 | .8 | 0 |
| Total | 14 | 1.6 | 16.4 | 15.6 |
| Debt | 6 | .4 | 6.4 | 6.4 |
| Equity | 8 | 1.2 | 10.0[b] | 9.2 |
| Total | 14 | 1.6 | 16.4 | 15.6 |

[a] Y is purchased for $2 million and X receives 100 percent of stock.
[b] Includes the $800,000 difference between $1.2 million book value and $2 million purchase price.

on each side. Prior to the merger, the combined total assets had a book value of $14 million and $1.6 million, or $15.6 million. Afterward, this increases by $800,000 to $16.4 million.

**Example:** Company Q offers $12 million for $4 million of R's stock at book value. R has a $1 million debt. How much good will arises? If Q has $20 million in equity and a $5 million debt itself, what is the combined balance sheet using the purchase method? the pooling method?

**Answer:** $8 million in good will ($12 million − 4 million). Balance sheets (in millions of dollars) are as follows:

| *Purchase Method* | | | | *Pooling-of-Interests Method* | | | |
|---|---|---|---|---|---|---|---|
| Assets | 30 | Debt | 6 | Assets | 30 | Debt | 6 |
| Good will | 8 | Equity | 32 | Good will | 0 | Equity | 24 |
| Total | 38 | Total | 38 | Total | 30 | Total | 30 |

## PURCHASE AND POOLING WITH DEBT USED FOR TAKEOVER

In Table 15–7, company X is taking over company Y by selling or exchanging X's own stock. The company may plan to issue shares of stock directly to the shareholders of Y, in which case it might qualify for pooling. It may sell the stock in the market to outside investors and use the cash to purchase Y, in which case the purchase method would be required. If company X had decided to borrow money to purchase Y, the final balance sheet would be changed as follows.

1. *Debt Would Increase.* The $2 million from the sale of debt securities would be added to the debt of each individual firm on the new balance sheet.
2. *Equity Would Not Increase.* Company X would add the stock of company Y as an asset on one side of the balance sheet, but no new equity would be created on the other side. In an exchange of stock, the issuance of new stock causes an increase in the equity. When debt is used, no additional equity is created.

Table 15–8 shows the accounting for the takeover using the purchase method (since pooling is not allowed with a purchase for cash).

**TABLE 15–8.**   Accounting Using Purchase Method When Takeover Involves Borrowed Funds (in Millions of Dollars).

| Account | X Alone | X after Borrowing | Y Alone | X + Y Purchase Method |
|---|---|---|---|---|
| Assets | 14 | 16 | 1.6 | 15.6 |
| Good will | 0 | 0 | 0 | .8 |
| Total | 14 | 16 | 1.6 | 16.4 |
| Debt | 6 | 8 | .4 | 8.4 |
| Equity | 8 | 8 | 1.2 | 8.0 |
| Total | 14 | 16 | 1.6 | 16.4 |

**Example:** Company J offers $6 million for $4 million of K's stock at book value. K has $2.5 million debt. How much good will arises? If J had $30 million in equity and a $9 million debt before it borrowed the $6 million for the takeover, what would be the combined balance sheet?

**Answer:** $2 million good will ($6 million − 4 million). Balance sheets (in millions of dollars) are as follows:

| | J Before | J after Borrowing | K Before | J + K Combined |
|---|---|---|---|---|
| Assets | 39 | 45 | 6.5 | 45.5 |
| Good will | 0 | 0 | 0 | 2.0 |
| Total | 39 | 45 | 6.5 | 47.5 |
| Debt | 9 | 15 | 2.5 | 17.5 |
| Equity | 30 | 30 | 4.0 | 30.0 |
| Total | 39 | 45 | 6.5 | 47.5 |

## KEY TERMS

acquisition
Antitrust Division,
    Department of Justice
capital gain
carry-back
carry-forward
Celler-Kefauver Amendment
Clayton Act

conglomerate
consolidated return
consolidation
corporate shell
dilution of earnings
domestic corporation
exchange ratio
external growth

Federal Trade Commission
finder's fee
foreign corporation
good will
growth
holding company
horizontal merger
internal growth

*merger*     *proxy fight*    *statutory merger*
*parent company*  *purchase method*  *subsidiary*
*pooling-of-interests method* *pyramiding*   *synergism*
*premium*    *reorganization*  *tender*
*profit center*   *Sherman Act*   *turnaround situation*
*proxy*     *start-up cost*   *vertical merger*

## STUDY QUESTIONS

1. What are some different meanings of the word *growth*? Which is the least useful meaning and why?
2. What is the difference between internal and external growth? Why is external growth frequently preferred by large firms?
3. Why do firms seek to grow?
4. What is the difference between a merger and a consolidation? How many ways can each occur? When is a consolidation preferable to a merger?
5. What is the meaning of *horizontal merger*? *vertical merger*? *conglomerate merger*?
6. What is a holding company and what are some reasons for its use?
7. What is a nontaxable reorganization? Why is it desirable? How does one qualify for it?
8. What are some of the major laws affecting business combinations? some characteristics of each? Who enforces them?
9. What are two tax effects that influence business combinations?
10. What is pyramiding? How are dividends taxed in a pyramid?
11. How is leverage gained in a pyramid?
12. What is a profit center? some characteristics of one? some problems with it?
13. When searching for a suitable acquisition, what are some factors to look for?
14. How does the price-earnings ratio affect a dilution of earnings in an acquisition? How does it affect market price?
15. What are some signs of a potential turnaround situation? How do we arrive at an offering price for a turnaround candidate?
16. What are some ways to approach the takeover of another firm? How may a firm resist a takeover attempt? Why would management want to resist?
17. What are three important differences between pooling-of-interests and the purchase methods of recording a business combination? Which is preferred in most cases and why?

## PROBLEMS

1. Company J receives $50,000 in dividends from company K. J owns 50,000 of the 75,000 outstanding shares of K. How much must J pay in taxes on the K dividends?
2. Company M receives $300,000 in dividends from company N. M owns 150,000 of the 175,000 shares of N. How much must M pay in taxes on the N dividends?

3. Firm D's stock sells for $30; E's stock sells for $50. D wants to take over E and plans to offer a premium of 10 percent. What is the exchange ratio?

4. Firm G's stock sells for $125; H's stock sells for $20. G wants to take over H and plans to offer a premium of 20 percent. What is the exchange ratio?

5. Company X expects a net income of $300,000 on sales of $2.5 million. X has 100,000 shares of stock outstanding. Company Y expects a net income of $100,000 on sales of $1.2 million. Y has 50,000 shares of stock outstanding. X plans to make a tender offer for Y so that a premium of 20 percent is given on the basis of earnings. How many shares would X have to offer to gain 100 percent of Y? What would X's net income be after the acquisition if it were successful? What would be the future EPS for X after the acquisition? Were the earnings diluted; why or why not?

6. Company R expects a net income of $1 million on sales of $4 million. R has 200,000 shares of stock outstanding. Company S expects a net income of $200,000 on sales of $2 million. S has 400,000 shares of stock outstanding. R can sell shares of stock to yield a 12/1 P/E ratio. S is selling for $7.50 per share. R plans to purchase S by selling stock and using the proceeds to make a tender offer with a 25 percent premium. What would R's net income be after the acquisition if it were successful? How many shares would R have to sell? What would be the future EPS for R after acquiring S? Was the EPS diluted; why or why not?

7. For problem 5, assume that company X after the merger will have either the same P/E as before the merger, the same P/E as the old company Y, or an average of the two. Assume also that X sold at a 20/1 ratio and Y sold at 12/1. What are the three possible market prices for X after the merger?

8. For problem 6, assume that R will have either its old P/E ratio, S's ratio, or an average. What are the three possible market prices for R after the merger?

9. Company M expects sales of $6 million and a net income of $300,000 next period. It has 500,000 shares of stock outstanding and is selling at a 15/1 P/E multiple (calculated on its future earnings). If we take over the company, we can increase sales to $9 million and the net income to $700,000. The stock will probably sell at a 12/1 P/E multiple. If we want to offer a 10 percent premium for 50 percent of the stock of company M, how much cash will we need? What will be the value of our investment if we are successful in turning the company around?

10. Company A wants to acquire 2 million shares of B's common stock at a time when B's book value per share is $6. Company A will exchange 1 million shares with a book value of $9 and a market value of $25 per share. Company A has $7 million in debt and $16 million in equity. Company B has $2 million in debt. What is the combined balance sheet with the purchase method? with pooling?

11. Company D offers $9 million for $4 million of E's common stock at book value. Company D has $11 million in debt and $22 million in equity. Company E has $4 million in debt. Company D's book value per share is $18 and company E's is $10. If company D borrows the money to finance the acquisition, what would the combined balance sheet be?

# INTERNATIONAL TELECOMMUNICATIONS CASE

# Acquisition

*This case tests the readers skills in analyzing a proposed acquisition. The reader must develop cash-flow streams to determine the effect of the acquisition on earnings per share under different methods of financing.*

International Telecommunications Inc. (ITI) is one of the world's largest international conglomerates and is an active participant in the following industries: telecommunication equipment and operations, electronic data processing, industrial and consumer products, consumer and business services, natural resources, and defense-space manufacturing. The firm has a strong and capable management and has experienced substantial internal growth. Even during the period of high interest rates and limited economic growth in the early 1980s, ITI was able to sustain a reasonably strong position in terms of sales and earnings.

As a result of a large number of international activities and commitments, ITI pays careful attention to the political ramifications of its actions. The U.S. government has been a frequent observer of the growth and diversification of the corporation. In the early 1980s, the French government considered the nationalization of ITI's French telecommunications company. After ITI reached a compromise with the French government, it established new guidelines for the acquisition of new companies. One major guideline was that potential acquisitions would not attract the attention of U.S. or foreign regulatory agencies.

In the summer of 1984, ITI was evaluating a possible acquisition that seemed to meet all the guidelines. Food Services Inc. was a Chicago-based firm engaged primarily in the operation of vending machines, catering, restaurant management, and the operation of concessions. Its customers ranged from airlines to universities; it also had a chain of 27 restaurants. Its revenues had been increasing steadily through the 1980s but net earnings had been somewhat erratic. The management of Food Services had endorsed the idea of being acquired by ITI, largely because Food Services needed capital for expansion. The proposed acquisition was in the hands of ITI corporate planning department.

Once the proposed acquisition met the overall guidelines, it also had to pass three financial tests:

1. *Cash-Flow Rate of Return.* ITI followed a policy of identifying all cash flows over a 7-year period. These cash flows were then discounted to a net present value, using either a 12, 14, 16, or 18 percent time value factor. When aftertax cash flows were used, the acquisition had to hurdle the rate of return appropriate for its risk level. The company decided that Food Services had a moderate degree of risk and should show a positive net present value when a 14 percent hurdle rate was used.

2. *Next Year's Earnings per Share.* ITI followed a policy that acquisitions should not dilute the earnings per share reported in the year following the acquisition. That is, if Food Services were acquired toward the end of 1984, the 1985 EPS of ITI should not be adversely affected as a result of the acquisition. In some instances, management had waived this requirement if the project were otherwise sufficiently attractive.

3. *Next Year's Balance Sheet.* If debt were used for an acquisition, ITI checked carefully to measure the impact on the balance sheet. As a corporate policy, a 40 percent debt-asset ratio was viewed as appropriate. Any acquisition that might endanger this ratio would be viewed unfavorably in most cases.

To assist in a detailed analysis of the financial impact of acquiring Food Services Inc., ITI's corporate staff developed a variety of financial data. By October 1984, it had pro forma balance sheets and income statements for ITI and Food Services. It also had some historical data on each company, as shown in the financial statements. Working from these data, ITI began to make some assumptions about the future of Food Services. It appeared that the firm would recover from its earnings slump, as shown by the pro forma forecast on the statement of earnings. With additional capital from ITI, the firm might actually realize a very significant gain in revenues and earnings. Any such earnings gain would probably pass through as an increase in the market value of the firm's stock. The stock was trading at a 6/1 price-earnings multiple. This appeared to be a reasonable level after considering the risk offered by the stock and the price-earnings multiples of other stocks. This would probably also be the multiple in 7 years if ITI decided to sell the Food Services stock at that time.

In developing its forecast of Food Services earnings, the ITI staff decided to assume a 6 percent growth rate in earnings per share after 1987. Included in this assumption was an annual dividend payout of 50 percent of the firm's earnings. This approximated the 1984 indicated payout but was somewhat higher than earlier payouts.

The ITI analysis made the assumption that 100 percent of the Food Services stock would be sought in a tender offer. The tender price would be set at a price-earnings multiple of 7 times the indicated 1984 earnings for Food Services. Or, if ITI decided to offer an exchange of common stock, the exchange ratio would allow a 20 percent premium based on earnings per share. In either case, ITI would incur legal expenses and fees equal to about 3 percent of the total value of the deal.

If ITI decided to make a cash tender offer, it would have to raise almost $500 million. The ITI treasurer had already alerted the financial markets to the possibility of a bond offering with a 10-year maturity. Smith Barney had indicated a willingness to place the offering with effective interest costs to ITI of 16.2 percent before taxes. With an effective tax rate of 40 percent, the aftertax cost would be considerably lower.

The only remaining item of information dealt with the value of ITI's own common stock. Trading in a 1981–1984 range of $13 to $19, the company figured its real value to be $18 per share. This value should be used in the analysis of the Food Services acquisition.

In developing its recommendation, the staff decided to analyze:

1. the cash-flow return as though no debt were used to make a cash purchase
2. the cash-flow return considering the effects of the debt
3. a cash-flow return with an exchange of stock
4. the effect on 1985 earnings per share with a debt-financed purchase
5. the effect on 1985 earnings per share with an exchange of stock
6. the 1984 debt-asset ratio if debt were used to finance the acquisition

### Required

Complete the analysis and prepare the recommendation for ITI's management.

## INTERNATIONAL TELECOMMUNICATIONS INC.—
### Consolidated Balance Sheet (000s)

| | 1984 Pro forma | 1983 Actual | 1982 Actual |
|---|---|---|---|
| **Current Assets** | | | |
| Cash and short-term investments | $ 296,839 | $ 271,334 | $ 274,339 |
| Receivables | 638,172 | 621,445 | 597,421 |
| Inventories | 705,851 | 721,438 | 674,933 |
| Other current assets | 120,269 | 111,565 | 103,228 |
| | | | |
| **Capital Assets** | | | |
| Investments and securities at cost | 166,817 | 153,418 | 155,627 |
| Receivables, noncurrent | 59,564 | 57,420 | 51,380 |
| Property and equipment | 2,882,438 | 2,731,887 | 2,744,790 |
| Less accumulated depreciation | (1,046,645) | (993,451) | (987,766) |
| Other assets | 199,095 | 204,569 | 191,777 |
| | | | |
| Total Assets | $4,022,400 | $3,879,625 | $3,805,729 |

## INTERNATIONAL TELECOMMUNICATIONS INC.—
### Balance Sheet (continued)

| | 1984 Pro forma | 1983 Actual | 1982 Actual |
|---|---|---|---|
| **Current Liabilities** | | | |
| Accounts payable | $ 563,215 | $ 544,272 | $ 553,885 |
| Loans and long-term debt due in one year | 376,169 | 356,773 | 311,890 |
| Income taxes payable | 149,180 | 137,603 | 135,411 |
| **Long-Term Debt** | | | |
| Deferred liabilities | 202,641 | 186,660 | 179,432 |
| Def. income taxes | 69,340 | 63,439 | 58,666 |
| Long-term debt | 931,772 | 929,934 | 959,142 |
| Other | 77,991 | 75,401 | 74,333 |
| **Equity** | | | |
| Preferred stock | 372,637 | 372,637 | 372,637 |
| Common stock ($1 par) | 59,059 | 59,131 | 59,003 |
| Capital in excess of par value | 388,613 | 388,904 | 388,045 |
| Retained earnings | 831,783 | 764,871 | 713,285 |
| | | | |
| Total Liabilities and Equity | $4,022,400 | $3,879,625 | $3,805,729 |

## INTERNATIONAL TELECOMMUNICATIONS INC.—
### Income Statement (millions)

| | Pro forma | | | | Actual | |
|---|---|---|---|---|---|---|
| | 1987 | 1986 | 1985 | 1984 | 1983 | 1982 |
| Revenues | $3,950 | $3,670 | $3,430 | $3,204 | $3,160 | $3,071 |
| Cost of products and services | 2,490 | 2,330 | 2,180 | 2,034 | 2,051 | 1,978 |
| Selling and administrative | 720 | 700 | 665 | 605 | 587 | 581 |
| Income from operations | 740 | 640 | 585 | 565 | 522 | 512 |
| Interest expenses | 240 | 235 | 230 | 228 | 215 | 210 |
| Earnings before taxes | 500 | 405 | 355 | 337 | 307 | 302 |
| Federal income taxes (40%) | 200 | 162 | 142 | 135 | 123 | 121 |
| Earnings after taxes | 300 | 243 | 213 | 202 | 184 | 181 |
| Preferred stock dividends | 31 | 31 | 31 | 31 | 31 | 31 |
| Net income | 269 | 212 | 182 | 171 | 153 | 150 |
| Earnings per share | $4.56 | $3.59 | $3.08 | $2.91 | $2.59 | $2.54 |
| Cash dividends | — | — | — | 94 | 99 | 80 |
| Dividends per share | — | — | — | $1.60 | $1.68 | $1.36 |

## FOOD SERVICES INC.—Consolidated Balance Sheet (000s)

| | 1984 Pro forma | 1983 Actual | 1982 Actual |
|---|---|---|---|
| Current Assets | | | |
| Cash including time deposits | $  58,084 | $  53,752 | $ 14,617 |
| Marketable securities at cost, which approximates market | 10,807 | 17,399 | 21,352 |
| Net receivables | 311,671 | 297,896 | 243,258 |
| Inventories | 390,393 | 453,925 | 344,329 |
| Prepaid expenses | 17,199 | 17,912 | 14,186 |
| Total Current Assets | 788,154 | 840,884 | 637,742 |
| Property, plant, and equipment | 337,925 | 300,787 | 234,551 |
| Other assets | 38,693 | 41,548 | 38,172 |
| **Total Assets** | $1,164,772 | $1,183,219 | $910,465 |

| Current Liabilities | | | |
|---|---|---|---|
| Accounts payable | $  79,890 | $  92,914 | $ 90,445 |
| Short-term borrowings | 35,007 | 92,267 | 49,668 |
| Accrued liabilities | 89,570 | 95,146 | 79,097 |
| Income taxes payable | 24,180 | 48,412 | 51,772 |
| Total | 228,647 | 328,739 | 270,982 |
| Long-term debt | 269,032 | 225,608 | 90,749 |
| Deferred income taxes | 41,516 | 39,290 | 24,663 |
| Other long-term debts | 17,596 | 15,981 | 10,286 |
| Total | 328,144 | 280,879 | 125,698 |
| Common stock | | | |
| ($.50 par) | 21,054 | 21,032 | 21,005 |
| Capital in excess of par | 197,639 | 196,961 | 196,130 |
| Retained earnings | 389,288 | 355,608 | 296,650 |
| Total | 607,981 | 573,601 | 513,785 |
| **Liabilities & Equity** | $1,164,772 | $1,183,219 | $910,465 |

### FOOD SERVICES INC.—Statement of Earnings (millions)

| | Pro forma | | | | Actual | |
|---|---|---|---|---|---|---|
| | *1987* | *1986* | *1985* | *1984* | *1983* | *1982* |
| Net sales | $1,725 | $1,620 | $1,530 | $1,431 | $1,438 | $1,205 |
| Cost of | | | | | | |
| products sold | 1,060 | 990 | 940 | 890 | 884 | 737 |
| G&A | 470 | 445 | 420 | 394 | 377 | 303 |
| Operating | | | | | | |
| income | 195 | 185 | 170 | 147 | 177 | 165 |
| Interest | | | | | | |
| expense | 55 | 55 | 50 | 49 | 24 | 10 |
| Earnings | | | | | | |
| before taxes | 140 | 130 | 120 | 98 | 153 | 155 |
| Taxes on | | | | | | |
| income (40%) | 56 | 52 | 48 | 39 | 61 | 62 |
| Net | | | | | | |
| earnings | 84 | 78 | 72 | 59 | 92 | 93 |
| Earnings | | | | | | |
| per share | $2.00 | $1.85 | $1.71 | $1.39 | $2.19 | $2.23 |

PART V

# Financing Decisions

Sources of Short- and Intermediate-Term Financing
Long-Term Financing Decisions
Lease-Buy Decisions
Dividend Policies and Decisions

# 16

# Sources of Short- and Intermediate-Term Financing

In the conduct of its business, a firm obtains its funds from a variety of sources. Some capital is provided by suppliers, creditors, and owners, while other funds arise from earnings retained in the business. In this chapter, we will examine the sources of short- and intermediate-term funds supplied by creditors. In the following chapters, other sources of funds will be covered.

## SHORT-TERM FINANCING

A major portion of a firm's financing normally is derived from short-term sources, that is, from sources that require repayment in a year or less. Several characteristics of short-term financing are important:

1. *Cost of Funds.* Short-term financing can provide both the highest and lowest cost funds in the firm's capital structure. Some forms of short-term financing are more costly than intermediate- or long-term funds. On the other hand, some short-term sources provide funds at no cost at all to the firm. Payables and accruals fall into this category.

2. *Rollover Effect.* This occurs when short-term liabilities are continually refinanced from period to period. Even though short-term financing must, by definition, be repaid in less than 1 year, some sources provide funds that are continuously rolled over. The

funds provided by payables, for example, may remain relatively constant because, as some accounts are paid, other accounts are created.

3. *Clean-up.* This occurs when commercial banks or other lenders require the firm to pay off its short-term obligation. Just as some sources are rolled over, some must be reduced to 0, or *cleaned up,* at one point in the year. This is frequently a requirement of bank credit where the clean-up offers proof that the short-term financing is being used to meet short-term or cyclical needs only.

## GOALS OF SHORT-TERM FINANCING

The firm can use short-term sources to achieve a number of goals, including flexibility. Some firms have widely fluctuating needs for funds over a given cycle, commonly 1 year. Funds are needed to finance inventories during a production period; excessive funds are on hand once the inventories are sold. Short-term financing allows the firm to match its funds against its needs over an annual, seasonal, or other cyclical period.

A second goal is to achieve low-cost financing. The interest-free sources provide low-cost financing for the firm by reducing its borrowing need from interest-bearing sources.

A third goal is to secure additional funds. In some cases, a firm may not be able to issue equity and may be nearing its borrowing capacity from intermediate- or long-term lenders. Short-term sources may be the only means for raising additional funds to finance inventories of receivables during a peak period.

## INTEREST-FREE SOURCES

Two major sources of short-term financing arise spontaneously from the daily activities of the firm and have no interest charges associated with them. These are accounts payable and accruals.

### Accounts Payable

Accounts payable are created when the firm purchases raw materials, supplies, or goods for resale on credit terms without signing a formal note for the liability. These purchases on "open account" are, for most firms, the largest single source of short-term financing. Payables represent an unsecured form of financing since no specific assets are pledged as collateral for the liability.

Even though no formal note is signed, an accounts payable is a le-

| Example of Credit Terms | Meaning |
|---|---|
| 1. 2/10 net 30 | A 2 percent discount from the invoice price may be taken if payment is made within 10 days; otherwise, the net invoice amount is due within 30 days. |
| 2. net 45 | The invoice amount is due within 45 days; no cash discount is given. |
| 3. 1/10 net 45 EOM | A 1 percent discount may be taken for payment within 10 days following the last day of the current month (EOM or end of month); otherwise, the invoice amount is due within 45 days following the current month. |
| 4. net 10 ROG | The net amount is due 10 days after receipt of the goods (ROG). |

**Figure 16–1**   Sample Credit Terms.

gally binding obligation of a firm. By accepting the merchandise, the purchaser agrees to pay the supplier the invoice amount under the terms of trade required by the supplier. This obligation is as binding as if a note had been signed. The only advantage of a note would be in a case where the purchaser denied having received the goods. The existence of a note would eliminate the need to prove delivery of the goods. Most business transactions are made on open account, but occasionally notes are required if a seller does not know the purchaser or if the purchaser's character is questionable.

Sales on open account are accompanied by credit terms that spell out the credit period; the cash discount, if any; and the cash discount period. Credit terms are stipulated in a concise, shorthand language, such as shown in Figure 16–1.

Figure 16–2 graphically displays credit terms of 2/10 net 30 EOM.

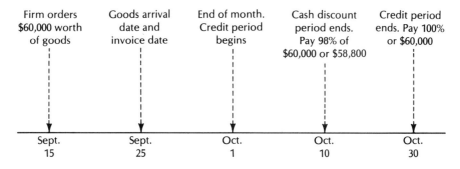

**Figure 16–2**   Credit Terms of 2/10 Net 30 EOM.

**Example:** A company has made four purchases as follows:

| Invoice Number | Invoice Date | Invoice Amount | Credit Terms |
|---|---|---|---|
| 639 | Sept. 1 | $6,800 | 1/10 net 20 EOM |
| 640 | Sept. 3 | $4,500 | 1/10 net 20 |
| 641 | Sept. 6 | $2,300 | 2/10 net 30 |
| 642 | Sept. 11 | $9,100 | net 30 |

If the firm takes all discounts, what is the amount paid and last date for payment for each purchase? If discounts are not taken, what are the amounts and last dates of payment?

**Answer:** The dates and amounts of payment are:

| Invoice Number | With Discount | | Without Discount | |
|---|---|---|---|---|
| 639 | Oct. 10, | $6,732 | Oct. 20, | $6,800 |
| 640 | Sept. 13, | $4,455 | Sept. 23, | $4,500 |
| 641 | Sept. 16, | $2,254 | Oct. 6, | $2,300 |
| 642 | Oct. 11, | $9,100 | Oct. 11, | $9,100 |

## Accruals

*Accruals* are short-term liabilities that arise when services are received but payment has not yet been made. The two primary accruals are wages payable and taxes payable. Employees work for a week, 2 weeks, or even a month before receiving a paycheck. The salaries or wages, plus the taxes paid by the firm on those wages, offer a form of unsecured short-term financing for the firm.

The government provides strict rules and procedures for the payment of withholding and social security taxes, so that the accrual of taxes cannot be readily manipulated. It is, however, possible to change the frequency of paydays to increase or decrease the amount of financing through wages accrual. The effect of such a change is shown in the following example.

**Example:** A firm has a weekly payroll of $600,000. The firm is considering changing to a biweekly payroll to reduce the cost of writing checks and similar expenses by $300 per payroll. The firm has a 14 percent cost of money. What would be the total annual savings if wages were paid every 2 weeks instead of weekly?

**Answer:** $49,800, as follows. If the firm owes $600,000 at the end of a week and 0 at the beginning, the average wage accrual is half of the $600,000, or $300,000. On a biweekly payroll, this doubles; the firm receives an additional $300,000 of interest-free financing on the average. The additional accruals can be invested elsewhere at 14 percent; the benefit is $42,000 per year ($300,000 × .14). In addition, a $300 payroll expense can be saved 26 times a year for another $7,800 in savings. The total benefit is $42,000 plus $7,800, or $49,800.

## UNSECURED INTEREST-BEARING SOURCES

A stable and profitable firm can borrow funds from short-term sources at competitive rates of interest. This section covers some of the unsecured sources of interest-bearing loans.

### Self-Liquidating Bank Loans

The most common commercial bank borrowing for a firm is the unsecured, self-liquidating short-term loan. *Self-liquidating* means that the bank is providing funds for a seasonal or cyclic business peak and the money will be used to finance an activity that will generate cash to pay off the loan. An example of a self-liquidating loan is money borrowed to finance inventory just before the peak seasonal sales period. The inventories that are being financed by the bank loan will be converted first to receivables, then into cash, which will be used to pay off the loan.

Short-term bank loans are generally tied into the *prime rate,* which is defined as a reported level of interest charged on business loans. The prime rate fluctuates with supply and demand for short-term funds. The rate on any individual bank loan is a combination of the prime rate plus a premium to reflect the degree to which a borrower has operating or financial risk greater than the bank's strongest customers. The premium generally runs from 0 to 2 or 3 percent. Firms possessing higher levels of risk generally do not qualify for unsecured short-term bank financing.

Three kinds of unsecured short-term bank loans are commonly used. The first is a *single-payment note.* A commercial bank will lend a strong business customer a lump sum repayable with interest in a single payment and at a specified maturity, usually 30 to 90 days. A *note* is a legal instrument that is signed, evidencing the debt.

> **Example:** A firm applies to Citibank to borrow $100,000 for 60 days at a time when the prime rate is 16.5 percent. Citibank approves the loan at "prime plus 2." How much must be repaid in 60 days?
>
> **Answer:** $103,083.33. The interest rate is 18.5 percent and the interest is ($100,000) (.185) (60/360) = $3,083.33.

The second form of unsecured bank borrowing is the *line of credit,* which is an agreement between a commercial bank and a firm whereby the bank agrees to make available upon demand up to a stipulated amount of unsecured short-term funds, if the bank has the funds available. A line of credit is normally established for 1 year, and the interest rate is expressed as prime plus some fixed percentage. Banks are willing to extend lines of credit to avoid the need to reexamine the creditworthiness of a customer each time a small loan is requested.

The third form is a *revolving credit agreement,* which is, in effect, a guaranteed line of credit; that is, the bank guarantees that the firm can borrow up to a specific limit regardless of the degree of tightness of money. If the revolving credit agreement is made for more than 1 year, as is common, it represents an intermediate-term source of funds rather than a short-term source.

### CHARACTERISTICS OF SHORT-TERM BANK FINANCING

A number of characteristics are frequently found in agreements for unsecured short-term bank financing. This section covers some of these characteristics.

### Maximum Amount Borrowed

Commercial banks closely monitor the amount of the note or line of credit, and a maximum outstanding loan balance is permitted. It is technically possible to borrow more than this maximum in a series of borrowings as long as the outstanding obligations do not exceed the maximum allowed by the bank.

> **Example:** A firm has a $2.4 million line of credit with a large commercial bank. The following transactions occurred during the year. Did the firm exceed its maximum amount allowed by the bank?

| Date | | Borrowed | Repaid | Loan Balance |
|------|----|----------|--------|--------------|
| January | 12 | $1,300,000 | $ — | $1,300,000 |
| March | 4 | 600,000 | — | 1,900,000 |
| April | 9 | — | 400,000 | 1,500,000 |
| June | 6 | 800,000 | — | 2,300,000 |
| August | 27 | — | 600,000 | 1,700,000 |
| October | 15 | — | 700,000 | 1,000,000 |
| November | 10 | — | 400,000 | 600,000 |
| December | 7 | — | 600,000 | 0 |
| | | $2,700,000 | $2,700,000 | |

**Answer:** No. Although the firm borrowed $2.7 million during the year, its loan balance never exceeded the $2.4 million line of credit.

### Annual Clean-up

Short-term bank loans are generally made to assist firms in meeting seasonal or cyclical needs. For long-term needs, the firm should develop intermediate- or long-term sources of funds in order to reduce the risk of liquidity problems. To ensure that short-term funds are not continually rolled over, thus providing, in effect, long-term funds, banks normally require an annual clean-up—a zero loan balance for a specified minimum number of days each year.

### Restrictive Covenants

A line of credit or short-term bank loan normally includes certain requirements or restrictions as part of the agreement. One example would be operating restrictions to limit the firm's ability to change its activities or structure without bank approval. A loan agreement, for example, may give the bank the right to veto any significant changes in the firm's product mix if such changes may weaken the firm's ability to pay its short-term obligations. A second limitation could occur in the form of financial restrictions. A bank may have the right to veto additional borrowings by the firm from other sources.

### Compensating Balance

A *compensating balance* is a requirement to maintain a stipulated portion, normally 5 to 20 percent, of the outstanding loan balance in a checking account at the lending bank. This forces the borrower to be a customer of the bank. It also raises the effective cost of the loan to the customer.

### Effective-Cost Calculations

The actual or effective cost of a loan may be calculated by dividing the interest actually paid by the loan amount available and converting the result to an annual percentage. The formula is:

$$\frac{\text{effective}}{\text{cost}} = \frac{FV - PV}{PV} \times \frac{360}{\text{days of loan}}$$

**Example:** A firm borrowed $100,000 for 90 days and paid back $103,750 at maturity. What was the effective cost?

**Answer:** 15 percent.

$$\frac{3,750}{100,000} \times \frac{360}{90} = .15$$

This may also be calculated

|      n      |      i      |     PV      |     FV      |
| :---------: | :---------: | :---------: | :---------: |
|      1      |   [3.75]    |   100,000   |   103,750   |

$$3.75 \times \frac{360}{90} = 15$$

**Example:** A firm borrowed $100,000 for 90 days and paid $3,750 interest in advance. At maturity, the firm paid back $100,000. What was the effective cost?

**Answer:** 15.6 percent. This is a *discount loan* defined as a borrowing with interest paid in advance. It is more costly than a simple interest loan.

$$\frac{3,750}{96,250} \times \frac{360}{90} = .156$$

On a calculator, we get

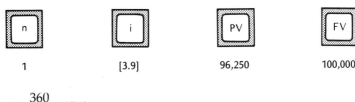

|   n   |   i   |   PV   |   FV    |
|:-----:|:-----:|:------:|:-------:|
|   1   | [3.9] | 96,250 | 100,000 |

$$3.9 \times \frac{360}{90} = 15.6$$

**Example:** A firm borrowed $100,000 for 90 days and paid $103,750 at maturity. During the period, a $20,000 compensating balance was required. What was the effective cost?

**Answer:** 18.8 percent. Since the firm cannot touch the compensating balance, 20 percent of the loan was not really available. This raises the effective cost of the loan.

$$\frac{3,750}{80,000} \times \frac{360}{90} = .188$$

or

|   n   |   i    |   PV   |   FV   |
|:-----:|:------:|:------:|:------:|
|   1   | [4.69] | 80,000 | 83,750 |

$$4.69 \times \frac{360}{90} = 18.8$$

### UNSECURED NONBANK SHORT-TERM SOURCES

Three nonbank sources of short-term financing are commonly used, although they are not available to every business:

1. *Commercial Paper.* These consist of promissory notes with maturities of a few days to 270 days. Commercial paper is usually issued in multiples of $100,000 or more and can only be used by

large well-known corporations because they are unsecured obligations of the firm. Commercial paper is purchased by other firms that are seeking marketable securities to provide a return on temporarily idle funds. Individuals, commercial banks, insurance companies, pension funds, and other institutions also purchase commercial paper.

2. *Private Loans.* A short-term unsecured loan may be obtainable from a wealthy shareholder, a major supplier, or other party interested in assisting the firm through a short-term difficulty. This kind of arrangement generally occurs when a temporary liquidity problem endangers the firm's operations and a shareholder, creditor, or supplier feels that its existing stake in the company is in jeopardy.

3. *Cash Advances for Customers.* A customer may pay for all or a portion of future purchases before receiving the goods. This form of unsecured financing provides funds to purchase the raw materials and produce the final goods. Normally, this form of financing is a special arrangement for expensive or custom-made items that would strain the financial resources of the manufacturing company.

## SECURED SHORT-TERM SOURCES

A *secured loan* occurs when the borrower pledges a specific asset, called *collateral,* to back a loan. The collateral may be securities, receivables, or physical assets. The lender is given a claim to the collateral through the signing of an agreement that may be filed in a public office, normally a county or state agency. This *security agreement* spells out the terms of the loan, the assets pledged as collateral, and provisions affecting the safeguarding of the collateral. By filing the security agreement, the borrower is legally establishing the lender's first claim on the assets in the event of default. The filing also places prospective lenders on notice that certain assets are not available to back additional loans.

Three types of security interests are commonly used in secured short-term financing. These are the warehouse receipt, trust receipt, and floating lien loans. Each is discussed in turn.

### Warehouse Receipt Loan

A *warehouse receipt loan* is a form of short-term financing that is secured by a pledge of inventory controlled by the lender. The lender, which may be a commercial bank or finance company, selects the inventory that is acceptable as collateral for the loan. A warehousing company then takes physical possession of the inventory in one of two ways:

1. *Field Warehouse.* Under this arrangement, a warehousing company establishes a field warehouse on the premises of the borrower. The pledged goods are isolated from other inventory, are counted and listed on a warehouse receipt, and are placed in the possession of a guard or warehouseman who is not allowed to release the goods without authorization from the lender. The *warehouse receipt*, which itemizes the goods along with an estimated value for each item, becomes, in effect, the title for the goods. By holding the warehouse receipt, the lender has complete control over the inventory and the first claim to it over other creditors in the event of default or bankruptcy.

2. *Terminal Warehouse.* Under this arrangement, a central warehouse near the borrower is used to store the inventory. This arrangement generally occurs when the goods are easily and inexpensively transportable. The goods are checked in upon arrival at the warehouse, and a warehouse receipt is issued. Once again, the public warehouse keeps the goods under a 24-hour guard, and only the lender can authorize release of the inventory.

Warehouse receipt loans are generally more costly than unsecured short-term financing. In addition to the financing charges, the borrower must pay the warehousing costs and insurance on the goods. It is not uncommon for warehouse receipt loans to run 3 to 7 percent above prime, a rate that is usually above unsecured commercial bank loans.

## Trust Receipt Loan

A *trust receipt loan* is secured by specific and easily identified collateral that remains in the control or physical possession of the borrower. Pledges of inventories or receivables are common. When automobile dealers use this kind of financing for the cars in their showrooms or in stock, it is called *floor planning*.

As implied by the name, this kind of loan requires a considerable degree of trust in the honesty and integrity of the borrower. As soon as the inventory is sold or the receivable is collected, payment must be remitted to the lender. If this is not done, the loan is said to be secured by *bogus collateral*, and the loan is technically in default.

Trust receipt loans are common when the collateral is easily identified by description or serial number and when each item of collateral has a relatively large dollar value. For automobiles or appliances, it is fairly easy for a lender to make spot checks by visiting the borrower's facilities and confirming that the collateral has not been liquidated. This kind of control would not be feasible for loans secured by numerous small items without distinguishing characteristics.

## Floating Lien Loan

A *lien* is a claim by a lender on the property of a borrower as security or collateral for a debt or obligation. A *floating lien loan* is secured by a group of assets that are not specifically identified by individual items. For example, a loan that is secured by "the hardcover books physically on the premises" would be a floating lien loan. Some books would be sold and some purchased on a continuing basis, but the existing inventory at any one time is the collateral for the borrowing.

From the lender's viewpoint, the floating lien loan is less satisfactory than the trust receipt loan. Thus, floating lien loans typically are made as a lower percentage of value than trust receipt loans. For example, a bank may lend 80 percent of the value of an automobile but only 40 percent of the value of hardcover books. In the event of default, the automobile can be sold quickly and easily at a high percent of its value; it is far more costly to liquidate hundreds or thousands of hardcover books that may have to be sold for only a fraction of their value.

## FINANCING INSTITUTIONS

Primary sources of secured short-term financing are banks and financial institutions, including insurance companies, finance companies, and the financial subsidiaries of major corporations. Usually these organizations have the ability, through economies of size and volume, to set up a department of specialists who know the people and companies in the industry serviced, who can analyze loan applications and determine the degree of risk in each, and who can monitor the loans once they are made. In spite of the specialization by industry or loan type, it is not uncommon for financial institutions to compete aggressively for business. This often allows a company to shop around for financing that best meets its specific needs.

## FINANCING SECURED BY RECEIVABLES

Two techniques of secured short-term financing are commonly employed with accounts receivable as the collateral. The first involves the *pledging of accounts receivable*. An assignment is a transfer of a claim or right in an asset from one party to another. By pledging or assigning an account receivable, a firm gives up the rights to the cash collected on that account. Because receivables are normally quite liquid, they are attractive as collateral to commercial banks or finance companies.

The second technique for borrowing against receivables involves factoring. A *factor* is a financial institution that purchases accounts receivable from business firms. *Factoring receivables* is the outright sale of the accounts receivable to a factor that generally accepts all the credit risks associated with collection of the accounts. Since the accounts are sold, a factoring arrangement does not involve a loan unless the firm takes an advance against the funds, as described shortly.

### PLEDGING RECEIVABLES

The pledging of accounts receivable as collateral for short-term financing involves four steps:

1. *Selecting the Accounts.* The firm can pledge some or all of its accounts as collateral for a loan. Usually accounts are pledged on a *selective basis,* which means that the lender analyzes the payment records of each customer and lends money only against the accounts that represent good credit risks. With careful selection, a lender may be willing to lend as much as 90 percent of the face value of the receivable. If weak accounts were included, the lender might not be willing to lend more than 50 percent of the face value.

2. *Adjusting the Face Values.* Each account receivable has a face value on the books of the borrowing company. But some goods may be returned after being inspected. This lowers the value of the receivable. To allow for returns and to reflect the customers that will take cash discounts for early payment, the lender adjusts the face value of the receivable downward. Thus, a $1,000 receivable may be viewed to be worth $950.

3. *Determining the Percentage.* Next the lender must determine the percentage of the face value that will be lent. For a strong credit

risk, the lender may be willing to advance 90 percent. On a $950 receivable, the loan would be 90 percent of $950, or $855.

4. *Collecting the Payments.* When the customer pays the obligation that created the receivable, the bank or finance company gets its money. This can happen two ways:

   a. *Nonnotification basis.* In most cases, the customer whose account has been pledged is not notified of the pledging. The customer remits payment directly to the firm as though the account had not been pledged as collateral for a loan. As soon as payment is collected by the firm, it must immediately notify the bank or finance company and pay off its loan. On a nonnotification basis, the firm's obligation is a form of trust receipt loan.

   b. *Notification basis.* In these cases, the customer is directed to remit payment directly to the lender. This arrangement is safer from the point of view of the lender. It is less satisfactory to the borrower since the customer may interpret the pledging as a sign that the firm is in financial trouble.

**Example:** Republic National Bank is analyzing the receivables of the Simonson Company in order to identify acceptable collateral for a short-term loan. The company's credit policy is 2/10 net 30. The bank lends 80 percent on accounts where customers are not currently overdue and where the average payment period does not exceed 10 days past the net period. A schedule of Simonson's receivables has been prepared. How much will the bank lend on a pledge of receivables if the bank uses a 10 percent allowance for cash discounts and returns?

| Account | Amount | Days Outstanding | Average Payment Period Historically in Days |
|---------|--------|------------------|---------------------------------------------|
| 74  | $ 25,000 | 15 | 20 |
| 91  | 9,000    | 45 | 60 |
| 107 | 11,500   | 22 | 24 |
| 108 | 2,300    | 9  | 10 |
| 114 | 18,000   | 50 | 45 |
| 116 | 29,000   | 16 | 10 |
| 123 | 14,000   | 27 | 48 |
|     | $108,800 |    |    |

**Answer:** $48,816 as follows:

1. Select accounts. The bank requires that no selected accounts be overdue. Thirty days is the net period, so accounts 91 and 114 are overdue. Eliminate them. The bank requires that the average payment be less than 10 days beyond the net period, or 40 days. Eliminate 123. The selected accounts are 74, 107, 108, and 116.

2. Adjust face values and determine percentage of loan. The bank uses 10 percent adjustment for cash discounts and returns; it lends at 80 percent of adjusted face value. The loan is calculated:

| Account | Original Value | 90 Percent of Original | 80 Percent of Adjusted | |
|---------|---------------|------------------------|------------------------|---|
| 74 | $25,000 | $22,500 | $18,000 | |
| 107 | 11,500 | 10,350 | 8,280 | |
| 108 | 2,300 | 2,070 | 1,656 | |
| 116 | 29,000 | 26,100 | 20,880 | |
| | | | $48,816 | loan value |

## FACTORING RECEIVABLES

A factoring agreement is normally drawn up specifying the charges and procedures for the sale of the receivables. Most factoring arrangements are continuing; that is, all the firm's receivables are sold as they are created. This places the full credit and collection burden on the factor. Some of the key elements of a factoring arrangement are:

1. *Selection of Accounts.* As with pledging, the factor selects the accounts to be purchased. If the factor is accepting all the firm's receivables, the factor then becomes responsible for making the firm's credit decisions. This role of the factor is widely used in the garment and textile industries.

2. *Collection of Accounts.* The factor becomes responsible for the collection of receivables. Normally, the customers are notified and instructed to send their payments directly to the factor. In cases where the firm desires to keep the presence of a factoring agreement secret, the customer is simply forced to send the payment to a new address. At this new address, the factor receives the payment directly even though the customer may not be aware of the factoring agreement.

3. *Recourse on Bad Debts. Recourse* is the right of one party to demand payment from a second party if a third party fails to pay an obligation. Most factoring is done *without recourse*, that is, without the factor having the right to demand payment from the firm if the customer does not pay his bills. In some rare situations, usually with particularly weak credit, the agreement may be made with recourse.

4. *Date of Payment.* The agreement normally stipulates that the firm will be paid when the factor collects the account or on the last day of the net credit period, whichever occurs first. When the date of payment is also the date of collection, no credit is being granted by the factor to the seller.

5. *Advances.* A factor will establish for the firm an account that is similar to a bank account. Payments are made by depositing money in the account. The firm can withdraw the money as needed. The secured short-term credit arises when the factor makes an advance against uncollected, and not due, accounts. An *advance* is a payment prior to the due date or collection of a receivable. To get an advance, the firm simply overdraws the account set up with the factor. Interest is charged on any advances.

6. *Surpluses.* The firm does not have to withdraw funds from the account as they are deposited by the factor. A *surplus* is any money that is left in the account; this draws interest.

7. *Factor's Reserves.* As part of the factoring agreement, a certain percentage of the face value of the receivables is set aside as a *reserve* to protect against returns or cash discounts. The reserves are particularly important when the firm draws advances against accounts that have not yet been collected. If the factor made an advance and then the goods were returned because they were damaged, the factor would, in effect, be extending a partially unsecured loan. The reserve of 5 to 10 percent on all the accounts protects against the possibility of a return by a single customer producing an unsecured advance. Once the customer has paid the factor, the amount of the reserve is returned to the firm if an advance has been taken against an uncollected receivable.

## Factoring Costs

Three kinds of calculations must be considered to measure the cost of factoring:

1. *Factoring Commissions.* These are payments to the factor to cover the administrative costs of verifying credit ratings and collecting receivables. These commissions also cover the risk when accounts are purchased without recourse. As a general rule, the factoring commission runs 2 and 4 percent of the face value of factored accounts.

2. *Interest on Advances.* The factor charges 2 to 5 percent above the prime rate as the annual interest rate on advances. It is paid in advance, as in the case of a discount, and thus raises the effective borrowing costs, as compared to paying interest at the end of the period.

3. *Interest on Surpluses.* The factor pays a much lower interest on surpluses not withdrawn by the firm. The interest is close to that paid by banks on savings accounts.

The factoring reserves do not represent a cost of factoring. The reserve is no more than a percentage of the account that is not included in an advance. The advance is made for, say, 90 percent of the receivable; upon collection or the date of payment, the factor forwards the remaining 10 percent.

**Example:** Pierson Associated Milling has sold four accounts that are due for collection on November 30 to the Houston National Bank, which is acting as a factor. The bank charges a 4 percent commission. The accounts are given with their status on November 30. How much does the Houston National Bank deposit in the Pierson factoring account on November 30?

| Account | Face Value | Status on November 30 |
|---|---|---|
| 23 | $120,000 | collected on Nov. 30 |
| 32 | 70,000 | collected on Nov. 10 |
| 35 | 67,500 | not yet collected |
| 41 | 47,000 | collected on Nov. 30 |

**Answer:** $225,120. Account 32 was collected on November 10 and the money has already been deposited. Of the remaining $234,500, the 4 percent commission is deducted and $225,120 is deposited. The fact that account 35 has not yet been collected does not matter. The factor is liable for the loss if unable to collect the $67,500.

**Example:** A factor has accepted an account wtih a $140,000 face value due on March 30. The factoring agreement requires a 3 percent commission and a 10 percent reserve. The factor charges 15 percent on advances. A maximum advance is given on March 10 and the account is collected on April 10. How much was the advance? What was the total amount of money received by the firm?

**Answer:** The advance was $121,201, as follows: 97 percent of $140,000 is $135,800, of which 90 percent can be given as an advance since the remaining 10 percent is held as a reserve. The 90 percent of $135,800 is $122,220 but 15 percent interest is deducted in advance:

$$122,220 \times .15 \times \frac{20}{360} = \$1,019 \text{ interest}$$

$$122,220 - 1,019 = \$121,201 \text{ advance}$$

$134,781 was the total received by the firm, $121,201 as the advance, and 10 percent of $135,800, or $13,580 on March 30.

## BENEFITS OF PLEDGING AND FACTORING

Pledging and factoring receivables offer a number of advantages to the firm, including flexibility. Receivables financing is an additional source of funds that can be called upon as needed. It also is a rising source of financing as the firm grows since higher levels of sales produce more receivables to sell or pledge.

A second benefit to pledging or factoring is that the firm receives assistance in credit decisions. Receivables financing gives outside help to the firm in analyzing customers that desire credit. With factoring, the outside factor makes the complete decision; in pledging, the outside party comments on the relative strength and weakness of customers by selecting only strong customers as collateral.

Another benefit can be cost savings. By reducing or eliminating the credit department, the firm saves money. With factoring, the collection responsibility is gone—an additional saving. The factor, commercial bank, or finance company charges for providing these services, of course, but the commissions paid may be less than the total of collection and credit costs, delinquency costs, and default costs. As a general rule, it costs more to use receivables financing but it may be close to other financing costs, as shown in Figure 16–3.

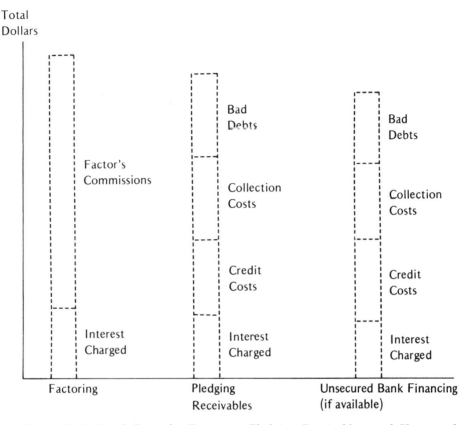

**Figure 16–3**  Total Costs for Factoring, Pledging Receivables, and Unsecured Short-Term Financing Compared.

## DISADVANTAGES TO RECEIVABLES FINANCING

A primary disadvantage commonly associated with receivables financing is that it can be very costly in many cases. Even though receivables financing can be comparable to unsecured financing in some situations, as shown in Figure 16–3, in most cases it is more costly. A large firm with established credit procedures for its customers and continuing contacts with its banks can generally locate less costly financing.

A second disadvantage is that many creditors and customers view receivables financing as a sign of weakness. Receivables are a highly liquid current asset that provide next period's available cash. A firm's customers or creditors may view receivables financing as harmful to next period's cash and may feel that the firm must be experiencing financial difficulties if it must give up future cash and if it must resort to the higher-cost receivables financing. Pledging or factoring receivables is less widely viewed today as a sign of weakness, particularly in the garment and textile industries, where it has been common for many years.

## INTERMEDIATE-TERM FINANCING

*Intermediate-term debt* is defined as borrowings with maturities greater than 1 year and less than 7 to 10 years. Debts with maturities of less than 1 year are classified as short-term; debts with maturities in excess of 7 to 10 years are considered long-term. Many analysts and accountants ignore the distinction between intermediate- and long-term debt. They consider only two kinds of debt: short-term for maturities of 1 year or less; long-term for maturities in excess of 1 year. When intermediate-term debt is identified as a separate category, three types are common:

1. *Revolving Credit Agreement.* As discussed earlier, this is a guaranteed line of credit whereby the bank agrees to lend money on demand in a future period, frequently 2 or 3 years.
2. *Term Loan.* This is a loan from a bank, finance company, insurance company, or other financial institution for a period of 1 to 7 years.
3. *Lease.* This is an agreement that allows the use of assets without ownership of the assets. The owner, or lessor, agrees to allow a user, or lessee, to use the fixed assets in return for a rental payment over a stipulated period of time.

This section focuses on the term loan since the revolving credit agreement has already been discussed under short-term financing and leases are covered in a separate chapter.

### COMMERCIAL BANK LOANS

Commercial banks are primary intermediate-term lenders to business firms. The loans are generally made for periods up to 7 years, although occasionally loans with longer maturities are considered. Some features of commercial bank loans are:

1. *Collateral.* A commercial bank generally requires collateral to secure a term loan. Usually a fixed asset, such as a vehicle, ship, or piece of machinery, is pledged as collateral for the loan.

2. *Participation.* A commercial bank is restricted by law on the amount of money that it may lend to a single customer. For a large loan, the bank may form a group of banks, with each one lending a portion of the money. The act of bringing together a group of lenders to spread the risk of a single large loan is called *participation.*

3. *Fixed versus Floating Rate.* The interest that is due on a term loan with a commercial bank is determined in advance, using one of two methods. A *fixed-rate loan* has a single interest rate for the entire period. Much more common, a floating-rate loan has an interest charge that is tied to current money market rate and will vary or "float" with changes in interest levels. For example, a rate of "1.5 percent above prime each quarter" would vary as the prime rate varied.

**Example:** A firm has two loans with a commercial bank. The first loan has a 19 percent fixed rate on a $100,000 face value. The second has a "2 percent above prime each quarter" floating rate on a $100,000 face value. The prime rate is 15.5 percent on January 1, 17.5 percent on April 1, 18.0 percent on July 1, and 16.5 percent on October 1. How much interest is paid during the year on each loan if interest is paid quarterly and principal is repaid at the end of the year?

**Answer:** $19,000 on the fixed rate loan; $18,875 on the floating loan as follows:

$.19 \times \$100,000 = \$19,000$ for the fixed rate loan

| First | quarter (.155 + .02) | × | 100,000 | × | (90/360) | = | $ 4,375 |
|---|---|---|---|---|---|---|---|
| Second | quarter (.175 + .02) | × | 100,000 | × | (90/360) | = | 4,875 |
| Third | quarter (.180 + .02) | × | 100,000 | × | (90/360) | = | 5,000 |
| Fourth | quarter (.165 + .02) | × | 100,000 | × | (90/360) | = | 4,625 |
| | | | | | | | $18,875 |

Commercial bank loans offer advantages and disadvantages to the firm. The advantages include establishing a working relationship with a bank that can result in advice and financial expertise from the bank's officers. It can also produce introductions to potential customers and information on a variety of credit or business areas. The disadvantages include the need to reveal confidential information and the restrictions that may be imposed as part of the loan agreement.

**INSURANCE COMPANIES**

A number of life insurance companies make term loans to businesses. While commercial banks make loans to firms of varying size and credit risk, insurance companies concentrate on low-risk loans to large and very strong companies. Because of the high credit standing of their customers, insurance companies are willing to offer maturities of 10 or more years, offer loans that are larger than those available from commercial banks, and in some cases even offer unsecured loans.

The major advantages of insurance company term loans are the longer terms and higher amounts of money, as compared to commercial bank financing. The major disadvantages are slightly higher interest rates and the fact that only the most creditworthy businesses can borrow from insurance companies.

**PENSION FUNDS**

A minor source of intermediate-term financing is the employee pension funds that make secured loans to businesses. These loans are frequently secured by mortgages on property and have terms and conditions similar to loans made by life insurance companies.

**FINANCE COMPANIES AND EQUIPMENT MANUFACTURERS**

Commercial finance companies and manufacturers of industrial equipment make loans to assist in the purchase of fixed assets. The loans may require the firm to make a down payment of 10 to 30 percent, and the assets must be pledged or mortgaged to secure the loan. Term loans from finance companies or manufacturers generally mature in less than 10 years and carry interest rates that are higher than bank or insurance company loans.

**CASH-FLOW VERSUS ASSET-VALUE LENDING**

Individual commercial banks and insurance companies tend to fall into two categories with respect to their lending philosophy on intermediate-term loans. The first are *asset lenders*, which seek loans that are fully secured by the asset value of the collateral. As an example, if a new car sells for $6,000 and a 1-year old car sells for $4,500, an asset lender would not lend more than the $4,500 resale value of the auto. Asset lenders may only be willing to lend 50 or 60 percent of an asset's value.

The second category contains *cash-flow lenders*, which seek loans where assets will be employed in a steady and low-risk business to generate cash to pay off the loan. As an example, a bank that is financing an airplane to be used in delivering mail on a fixed contract can view the profits on the contract as a form of collateral on the loan. A cash-flow lender requires a mortgage on the asset, but the primary collateral is viewed as the profits from employing the asset.

### CONCLUSION

This chapter has described the primary forms of secured and unsecured short- and intermediate-term financing available to the firm. The costs and exact features of each type of financing vary with the firm and its individual situation. As a general statement, the fast-moving nature of short-term financing requires considerable skill and flexibility for the firm to choose a proper mix of short- and intermediate-term sources in its total capital structure. The firm should develop a set of procedures and policies for choosing the kinds and amounts of funds from varying sources that best meet its operational and financial needs.

### KEY TERMS

| | | |
|---|---|---|
| accrual | fixed rate loan | prime rate |
| annual clean-up | floating lien loan | receipt of goods (ROG) |
| asset lender | floating rate loan | recourse |
| bogus collateral | floor planning | restrictive covenant |
| cash-flow lender | intermediate-term debt | revolving credit agreement |
| clean-up | lien | reserves |
| collateral | line of credit | rollover |
| commercial paper | note | security agreement |
| compensating balance | notification basis | self-liquidating loan |
| end of month (EOM) | open account | single-payment note |
| factor | participation | trust receipt loan |
| factoring receivables | pledging receivables | warehouse receipt loan |
| field warehouse | | |

### STUDY QUESTIONS

1. What is a rollover effect? a clean-up effect?
2. Why do firms use short-term financing?
3. What are two major sources of interest-free funds? Which is most important to the firm?
4. What are the two major accruals? Which one can be manipulated more easily?

5. What is a self-liquidating bank loan? What is its relationship to the prime rate? What are some kinds of self-liquidating loans?
6. What are two differences between a line of credit and a revolving credit agreement?
7. What are some characteristics of unsecured short-term bank financing?
8. What are three common nonbank unsecured sources of short-term funds?
9. What is collateral? bogus collateral? a security agreement? a warehouse receipt? a trust receipt? floor planning?
10. What are two kinds of warehouse receipt loans?
11. What is a lien? a floating-lien loan?
12. What financial institutions provide secured short-term financing?
13. What is the difference between pledging and factoring accounts receivable?
14. What is an assignment? a factor? selective basis? notification basis? recourse? an advance? a surplus?
15. What are factor's reserves? factoring commissions?
16. Why do firms pledge or factor receivables? What are the disadvantages to receivables financing?
17. What is the difference between a fixed and variable rate loan?

## PROBLEMS

1. A firm has made three purchases. The first is invoice 0174 dated March 7 for $34,500 on terms of 1/10 net 20 EOM; the second is 0175 dated March 11 for $14,000 on terms of 2/10 net 20. The third is 0176 dated March 21 for $22,200 on terms of 1/10 net 30. What are the dates and amounts paid with and without the discounts?
2. A firm has a $4.2 million monthly payroll. Its union has required a 4-times-a-month payroll effective with the next contract. With either system, it costs $2,500 to prepare a payroll. The firm borrows or invests short-term funds at 10 percent. How much would the weekly payroll cost the firm?
3. A firm has a $6.8 million line of credit with a large commercial bank. An auditor at the bank suspects that carelessness allowed the firm to exceed its credit limit. The following transactions occurred during the year. Is the auditor right?

| Date | | Borrowed | Repaid |
|---|---|---|---|
| January | 15 | $2,600,000 | $  — |
| February | 10 | 3,200,000 | — |
| March | 22 | 1,220,000 | — |
| April | 7 | — | 600,000 |
| April | 26 | — | 1,500,000 |
| May | 14 | 1,250,000 | — |
| May | 28 | 1,600,000 | — |
| June | 20 | — | 990,000 |
| September | 4 | — | 4,400,000 |
| November | 15 | — | 2,380,000 |

4. A bank is willing to lend $500,000 for 120 days at 12 percent simple interest or 11 percent on a discount loan. Which one has a lower effective cost to a firm with no compensating balance? What is the effective cost of a 12 percent simple interest loan with a 20 percent compensating balance?

5. A finance company lends 90 percent on receivables that are not overdue, and the customer's average payment period does not exceed the net period. The finance company also uses a 5 percent allowance for cash discounts and returns. A textile manufacturer sells on terms of 1/10 net 30. Its receivables are as follows:

| Account | Amount | Days Outstanding | Average Payment Period Historically |
|---------|--------|------------------|-------------------------------------|
| 212 | $14,500 | 7 | 36 |
| 219 | 26,200 | 14 | 27 |
| 223 | 17,500 | 35 | 41 |
| 227 | 19,000 | 9 | 12 |
| 232 | 32,000 | 27 | 19 |

How much will the finance company lend in this situation?

6. A bank has made a floating rate loan at prime plus 2 percent, with a change in the rate every month. The loan is for 3 months with principal to be repaid at the end of the 3 months. The prime rate is 15 percent at the start of the loan, 16.25 percent one month later, and 16.75 percent at the end of the second month, and 17 percent at the end of the third month. What is the total interest paid on the loan?

# LARSON MANUFACTURING CASE II
## Factoring Decision

*In this case the reader is asked to evaluate the attractiveness of factoring a firm's receivables as compared to retaining them in the company.*

The Larson Manufacturing Company produces a wide variety of display items for the home and office. The firm sells picture frames, trophy cases, gun racks, and related items to department stores throughout the country. In addition, the firm has sales to some 200 independent distributors or sales representatives who make sales to variety stores, furniture stores, and gift shops. Larson's accounts receivable range in size from $200, which represents the minimum order that it will accept, to $25,000–30,000 for its five largest distributors and 10 to 15 of its large department store accounts.

The president of Larson Manufacturing Company is Craig Larson, the youngest son of the firm's founder. The company is privately owned, with the majority of the shares held by members of the Larson family and former employees of the firm. Craig follows the firm's traditional policy of, as his father used to say, "a sound product line and a sound balance sheet." By stressing new technology and a complete product line, the firm has shown strong profits with minimum cyclical downturns. By emphasizing a sound balance sheet, the firm has avoided borrowing to finance capital purchases. The firm has retained a portion of its earnings each year to finance expansion. Last year, as an example, the firm retained almost $100,000 after declaring a dividend of $530 a share. The firm's most recent balance sheet and income statement are attached.

Craig typically selects one area of the company for detailed review each spring. This year he has chosen the firm's credit policy and has begun to collect information so that it may be evaluated. The firm's selling terms are 1/10 net 30 and he does not plan to change them because of competitive factors. But he does want to pay particular attention to bad-debt losses, which seem typically to run some $40,000 to $50,000 a year.

At the beginning of the review, Craig called Anna Gibson, his account representative at City Central Bank. Anna arranged the $245,000 bank note financing that Craig uses to help finance Larson's inventory.

The total line of credit is $350,000 at prime plus 2.8, and the firm finished the year with $245,000 exercised against it. Anna has pointed out the bank's wishes that the line be "cleaned up" by May 4 of the current year and she indicated a willingness to work with Craig on the review of the firm's credit policy.

During the early steps of the review, Anna suggested that Craig consider allowing City Central Bank to factor Larson's receivables. *Factoring receivables*, she explained, is the outright sale of the receivables to a *factor*, who accepts all the credit risks of collecting the accounts. City Central Bank has been in the factoring business for many years and could be very helpful to Larson Manufacturing. Craig indicated interest, so Anna explained the process that the bank would follow. First, the bank would select the accounts that would be purchased. Customers who were excessively slow to pay or who had poor credit records would not be acceptable to the bank. Then all customers would be instructed to send their remittances to Larson Manufacturing Company at a new post office box, the box maintained by the bank's factoring department. The customers would not know that the receivables had been factored. On the date the bank collects the account or on the last day of the 30-day net period, *whichever occurs first*, Larson's account at City Central would be credited with a deposit for the amount collected or the face amount of the receivables, less any reserves. A *reserve* is an amount set aside by the bank to protect against returns, cash discounts or other adjustments.

Craig had some questions on this procedure. First, would the reserve cover bad-debt losses? The answer was no. The accounts would be purchased by the bank *without recourse*, that is, without the bank having the right to demand payment from the company if the customer did not remit payment. In special cases, the bank would be willing to purchase individual accounts—those with a weak credit rating—with recourse, that is, with Larson accepting the risk of nonpayment.

A second question was, who would be responsible for collecting overdue accounts? Anna pointed out that this was the bank's responsibility; Larson would get its money *at the latest* on the last day of the net period.

Craig's final question got to the root of the issue: "How much would it cost?" Anna replied with an example. "Suppose," she said, "the bank purchases a $1,000 receivable on terms of 1/10 net 30 with an invoice dated October 1. On October 30, payment has not arrived at the bank. We deduct our 3.2 percent *commission* and credit your account with $968 on the 30th." At that point, Craig responded, "Isn't a 3.2 percent commission rather steep?" Anna replied that it was needed to cover the administrative costs of verifying credit ratings, collecting the receivables, and accepting the risk of bad-debt losses.

As Craig thought over the proposal, Anna pointed out the benefits of the program. Larson would get its money faster—within 30 days at the maximum—and this would reduce its needs for other financing. Also, the firm would no longer have to perform the differing credit functions. It could reorganize its accounting department and cancel its membership in Dun and Bradstreet's rating service. The headaches of collections would be passed on the bank. The session concluded with Craig expressing a willingness to investigate the matter further.

Craig made an estimate of the possible savings with a factoring arrangement. The accounting department had a manager and three clerical/accounting personnel. The department's salaries and fringe benefits totaled $46,400 and related expenses were $16,000 last year. These numbers included the direct collection costs of $6,450 (long-distance calls and other out-of-pocket expenses). If Craig turned over the credit function to a factor, he would be able to transfer out of accounting one of the clerical/accounting people, at an annual saving of roughly $9,600. This too was attractive.

Another attractive feature would be the reduction in the firm's average collection period or days sales outstanding. Last year, the ACP was almost 53 days; under the factoring arrangement, it would drop to about 25 days according to Craig's calculations of customers that take the firm's discounts.

One thing in which Craig was not interested was borrowing against the receivables. Anna had explained that the bank would advance funds against the receivables purchased. Craig felt that his firm's credit standing at the bank would be hurt over the long term if the bank viewed Larson Manufacturing as a secured borrower. He wanted to continue the existing line of credit arrangement independently of any factoring arrangement.

Craig pursued this matter at his next meeting with Anna. She agreed that the bank would probably accept virtually all of Larson's current accounts without recourse at a 3.2 percent factoring commission. Craig then indicated that he would analyze his situation and give her a firm answer in a few weeks. He said, "I consider our normal borrowing cost to be about 18 percent. By collecting our receivables more quickly, we can reduce this financing cost. If I also cut down my accounting department, and I do need another clerk in shipping, this may be very workable. Let me run the numbers and we'll talk again."

**Required**

Is factoring economically justified for Larson Manufacturing?

## LARSON MANUFACTURING COMPANY—Balance Sheet (December 31)

| | | | |
|---|---:|---|---:|
| Cash (1st Nat. account) | $ 22,441 | Payables | |
| Treasury bills (Apr. 4 | | Trade | $ 143,559 |
| maturity) | 25,000 | Other | 7,272 |
| Receivables | | Notes (1st Nat., 9.75%, | |
| Distributors & reps | 132,415 | May 4 maturity) | 245,000 |
| Others | 232,778 | Mortgage (9.25%) | 51,738 |
| Inventories | | Common stock (no par, | |
| Metals and wood | 43,694 | 520 shares issued) | 520 |
| In process | 157,910 | Retained earnings | 830,167 |
| Finished | 113,124 | | |
| Prepaid items | 3,251 | | |
| Physical facilities | | | |
| Plant | 154,117 | | |
| Equipment | 318,776 | | |
| Land | 75,200 | | |
| **Total assets** | **$1,278,706** | **Total** | **$1,278,706** |

## LARSON MANUFACTURING COMPANY—Income Statement
### (Year Ending Dec. 31)

| | | | |
|---|---:|---:|---:|
| Cash sales | | $ 23,551 | |
| Credit sales | | 2,633,187 | |
| less returns and | | | |
| discounts | | (114,663) | |
| Net sales | | | $2,542,075 |
| Cost of sales | | | |
| Purchases and materials | | $475,631 | |
| Direct salaries and wages | | 515,359 | |
| Overhead and fixed costs | | 229,765 | |
| Selling expenses | | | 1,220,755 |
| Sales force salaries | | 283,774 | |
| Exhibitions and shows | | 43,560 | |
| Administrative and overhead | | 109,738 | 437,072 |
| Management and administrative | | | |
| Data processing | | 55,766 | |
| Salaries and office | | 214,047 | |
| Other | | 33,609 | 303,422 |
| Earnings before taxes | | | 580,826 |
| Reserve for federal taxes (40%) | | | 232,330 |
| Earnings after taxes | | | $ 348,496 |

**Notes:**

1. Depreciation and noncash expenses:
   Depreciation        = $47,850
   Noncash expenses =   4,784
2. Financing charges = $29,853 in other management and administrative expenses

# Intermediate-Term Financing

*This case tests the reader's understanding of the materials presented in the chapter by providing a situation in which the reader must analyze a project to determine whether it is profitable, how much financing would be needed, and what the bank's response to this project would be.*

Dr. Francis Kozinski is a successful surgeon with a practice in the resort areas along the coast of southern New Jersey. With staff privileges at two of South Jersey's larger hospitals, he has built a steady and financially sound business that includes major and minor surgery. In addition to medicine, Dr. Kozinski has one other abiding interest—the development of real estate. His real estate investments offer both a diversion from his main work and a tax shelter for his income.

In the summer of 1983, Francis and his wife Barbara decided to go ahead with the development of Oceanview Condominiums. When they bought the property known as 71 Beach Drive in Cape May, they were not sure what could be done with it. A half-acre parcel with multiunit zoning was too small for most commercial development. For 3 years, a miniature golf course and a small concession stand were operated on the land. In April, Mike Thompson had offered them $85,000 for the property. This started them thinking. Mike owned the adjoining property, approximately an acre and a half. He had been trying to sell the property for some 2 years. He apparently decided that it would be easier to sell if he also owned the neighboring half-acre and could sell both properties as a 2-acre parcel.

In late June, the Kozinskis had outlined a tentative partnership agreement with Mike Thompson. The Kozinskis would develop both pieces of land in residential condominiums and sell the units. They drew up a plan for constructing $200,000 or so, 2-bedroom, 2-bath units that would net $175,000 to $185,000 after selling fees and expenses. The sales would be handled by Pelican Realty in Wildwood; construction would be performed by Jacobs and Sons of Avalon. The Kozinskis had done a similar deal for rental units in Seaside Heights and were experienced in such a construction project.

Frank Kozinski particularly prided himself on creative approaches to financing his real estate activities. The Oceanview project was no exception. By mid-August, he got Mike Thompson to agree to put his land, known as 63 Beach Drive, into a deal at $215,000, which would not be paid until the project was completed. Using his own land and Mike's, he would seek construction financing from a local bank. The land would be the equity in the project; the debt financing would provide the funds to construct units. At the end of the construction, Mike Thompson would get his $215,000 plus accrued interest, and the partners would split the profits, with the Kozinskis getting the lion's share.

To secure the financing, Frank put together a package of materials to present to Marine National Bank, a progressive commercial lender on coastal real estate ventures. Included in the package was his 1982 income tax return along with some supporting schedules and a personal financial statement. He also developed a project cash flow over 2½ years, so the bank could understand his grasp of construction. These materials were provided along with the bank's application form for a loan. A final item was an overview of the partnership agreement prepared by an attorney, so the bank could follow the obligations of each partner.

Frank knew that the bank would require additional documentation, particularly insurance, contractor bonding forms, permits, and other construction items. But first Frank wanted to know something of the bank's reaction to the joint venture proposal and he asked for an indication of interest in financing the project. Thus, in early September he submitted the package and loan request and waited for a response.

### Required

1. Is the project as outlined by the Kozinskis a viable economic activity if the bank's rate would be 2 percent over prime with a 5 percent compensating balance? (Assume an average prime rate of 14 percent.)
2. Prepare the bank's response to the loan application.

Department of the Treasury—Internal Revenue Service
**U.S. Individual Income Tax Return** **1982** (B)

For the year January 1–December 31, 1982, or other tax year beginning , 1982, ending , 19 | OMB No. 1545-0074

| Use IRS label. Other-wise, please print or type. | Your first name and initial (if joint return, also give spouse's name and initial) | Last name | Your social security number |
|---|---|---|---|
| | Francis M. Kozinski     Barbara L. Kozinski | | 265 : 55 : 7109 |
| | Present home address (Number and street, including apartment number, or rural route) | | Spouse's social security no. |
| | 57 Riding Hills Road | | 224 : 71 : 4873 |
| | City, town or post office, State and ZIP code | Your occupation ▶ Surgeon | |
| | Ocean Crest, New Jersey 08037 | Spouse's occupation ▶ Housewife | |

**Presidential Election Campaign**

Do you want $1 to go to this fund? . . . . . . . . . . Yes ▨ No
If joint return, does your spouse want $1 to go to this fund? . . . Yes ▨ No

Note: Checking "Yes" will not increase your tax or reduce your refund.

**Filing Status**

Check only one box.

For Privacy Act and Paperwork Reduction Act Notice, see Instructions.

1 ☐ Single
2 ☒ Married filing joint return (even if only one had income)
3 ☐ Married filing separate return. Enter spouse's social security no. above and full name here ▶
4 ☐ Head of household (with qualifying person). (See page 6 of Instructions.) If he or she is your unmarried child, enter child's name ▶
5 ☐ Qualifying widow(er) with dependent child (Year spouse died ▶ 19 ). (See page 6 of Instructions.)

**Exemptions**

Always check the box labeled Yourself. Check other boxes if they apply.

6a ☒ Yourself    ☐ 65 or over    ☐ Blind
 b ☒ Spouse    ☐ 65 or over    ☐ Blind

Enter number of boxes checked on 6a and b ▶ 2

c First names of your dependent children who lived with you ▶ Linda

Enter number of children listed on 6c ▶ 1

| d Other dependents: (1) Name | (2) Relationship | (3) Number of months lived in your home | (4) Did dependent have income of $1,000 or more? | (5) Did you provide more than one-half of dependent's support? |
|---|---|---|---|---|
| | | | | |
| | | | | |

Enter number of other dependents ▶

e Total number of exemptions claimed . . . . . . . . . . . . . . . . .

Add numbers entered in boxes above ▶ 3

**Income**

Please attach Copy B of your Forms W-2 here.

If you do not have a W-2, see page 5 of Instructions.

| | | | |
|---|---|---|---|
| 7 | Wages, salaries, tips, etc. . . . . . . . . . . . . . | 7 | 6,900 |
| 8a | Interest income (attach Schedule B if over $400 or you have any All-Savers interest) . . . . | 8a | 1,035 |
| b | Dividends (attach Schedule B if over $400) . . . | 8b | |
| c | Total. Add lines 8a and 8b . . . . . . | 8c | |
| d | Exclusion (See page 9 of Instructions) . . . | 8d | |
| e | Subtract line 8d from line 8c (but not less than zero) . . . | 8e | |
| 9 | Refunds of State and local income taxes (do not enter an amount unless you deducted those taxes in an earlier year—see page 9 of Instructions) . . . . . . . | 9 | |
| 10 | Alimony received . . . . . . . . . . . . . . | 10 | |
| 11 | Business income or (loss) (attach Schedule C) . . . . . . . . . . ▶ | 11 | 77,058 |
| 12 | Capital gain or (loss) (attach Schedule D) . . . . . . . . . . . . | 12 | |
| 13 | 40% of capital gain distributions not reported on line 12 (See page 9 of Instructions) . | 13 | |
| 14 | Supplemental gains or (losses) (attach Form 4797) . . . . . . . . . | 14 | |
| 15 | Fully taxable pensions and annuities not reported on line 16 . . . . . . . . | 15 | |
| 16a | Other pensions and annuities. Total received . . . . . 16a | | |
| b | Taxable amount, if any, from worksheet on page 10 of Instructions . . . . . . | 16b | 27,019 |
| 17 | Rents, royalties, partnerships, estates, trusts, etc. (attach Schedule E) . . . . . | 17 | |
| 18 | Farm income or (loss) (attach Schedule F) . . . . . . . . . . . . ▶ | 18 | |
| 19a | Unemployment compensation (insurance). Total received 19a | | |
| b | Taxable amount, if any, from worksheet on page 10 of Instructions . . . . . . | 19b | |
| 20 | Other income (state nature and source—see page 11 of Instructions) ▶ Rental of vacant lot for Xmas tree sales | 20 | 1,058 |
| 21 | Total income. Add amounts in column for lines 7 through 20 . . . . . . . . ▶ | 21 | 113,070 |

**Adjustments to Income**

(See Instructions on page 11)

| | | | |
|---|---|---|---|
| 22 | Moving expense (attach Form 3903 or 3903F) . . . . | 22 | |
| 23 | Employee business expenses (attach Form 2106) . . . | 23 | |
| 24 | Payments to an IRA (enter code from page 11 ........) . | 24 | |
| 25 | Payments to a Keogh (H.R. 10) retirement plan . . . . | 25 | |
| 26 | Interest penalty on early withdrawal of savings . . . . | 26 | |
| 27 | Alimony paid . . . . . . . . . . . . . . | 27 | |
| 28 | Disability income exclusion (attach Form 2440) . . . . | 28 | |
| 29 | Other adjustments—see page 12 ▶ | 29 | |
| 30 | Total adjustments. Add lines 22 through 29 . . . . . . . . . . . . | 30 | |

**Adjusted Gross Income**

31 Adjusted gross income. Subtract line 30 from line 21. If this line is less than $10,000, see "Earned Income Credit" (line 57) on page 15 of Instructions. If you want IRS to figure your tax, see page 3 of Instructions . . . . . . . . ▶ | 31 | 113,070

| | | | |
|---|---|---|---|
| **Tax Compu-tation**<br>See nstruc-ions on age 12) | 32a Amount from line 31 *(adjusted gross income)* . . . . . . . . . . . . . . . . | **32a** | 113,070 |
| | 32b If you do not itemize deductions, enter zero . . . . . . . . . . . . . . . . } | **32b** | 35,840 |
| | If you itemize, complete Schedule A (Form 1040) and enter the amount from Schedule A, line 41 . . . | | |
| | Caution: If you have unearned income and can be claimed as a dependent on your parent's return, check here ▶ ☐ and see page 12 of the Instructions. Also see page 12 of the Instructions if: | | |
| | • You are married filing a separate return and your spouse itemizes deductions, OR | | |
| | • You file Form 4563, OR | | |
| | • You are a dual-status alien. | | 77,230 |
| | 32c Subtract line 32b from line 32a . . . . . . . . . . . . . . . . . . . | **32c** | |
| | 33 Multiply $1,000 by the total number of exemptions claimed on Form 1040, line 6e . . | **33** | 3,000 |
| | 34 Taxable Income. Subtract line 33 from line 32c . . . . . . . . . . . . . | **34** | 74,230 |
| | 35 Tax. Enter tax here and check if from ☐ Tax Table, ☒ Tax Rate Schedule X, Y, or Z, ☐ Schedule D, ☐ Schedule G, or ☐ Form 4726 . . . . . . . . . . . . | **35** | 30,589 |
| | 36 Additional Taxes. (See page 13 of Instructions.) Enter here and check if from ☐ Form 4970, } ☐ Form 4972, ☐ Form 5544, or ☐ Section 72(m)(5) penalty tax . . . . . . . . . | **36** | |
| | 37 Total. Add lines 35 and 36 . . . . . . . . . . . . . . . . . . . . ▶ | **37** | 30,589 |

| | | | | | |
|---|---|---|---|---|---|
| **Credits**<br>See nstruc-ions on age 13) | 38 Credit for contributions to candidates for public office . . . | **38** | | | |
| | 39 Credit for the elderly *(attach Schedules R&RP)* . . . . . | **39** | | | |
| | 40 Credit for child and dependent care expenses ( *attach Form 2441*) . | **40** | | | |
| | 41 Investment credit *(attach Form 3468)* . . . . . . . . . | **41** | | | |
| | 42 Foreign tax credit *(attach Form 1116)* . . . . . . . . | **42** | | | |
| | 43 Work incentive (WIN) credit *(attach Form 4874)* . . . . . | **43** | | | |
| | 44 Jobs credit *(attach Form 5884)* . . . . . . . . . . | **44** | | | |
| | 45 Residential energy credit *(attach Form 5695)* . . . . . | **45** | | | |
| | 46 Total credits. Add lines 38 through 45 . . . . . . . . . . . . . . . | **46** | | |
| | 47 Balance. Subtract line 46 from line 37 and enter difference (but not less than zero) . ▶ | **47** | | |

| | | | |
|---|---|---|---|
| **Other Taxes**<br>(Including Advance EIC Payments)<br><br>06 | 48 Self-employment tax *(attach Schedule SE)* . . . . . . . . . . . . . | **48** | 1,523 |
| | 49a Minimum tax. Attach Form 4625 and check here ▶ ☐ . . . . . . . . . | **49a** | |
| | 49b Alternative minimum tax. Attach Form 6251 and check here ▶ ☐ . . . . . . | **49b** | |
| | 50 Tax from recomputing prior-year investment credit *(attach Form 4255)* . . . . . | **50** | |
| | 51a Social security (FICA) tax on tip income not reported to employer *(attach Form 4137)* . . | **51a** | |
| | 51b Uncollected employee FICA and RRTA tax on tips *(from Form W–2)* . . . . . | **51b** | |
| | 52 Tax on an IRA *(attach Form 5329)* . . . . . . . . . . . . . . . . | **52** | |
| | 53 Advance earned income credit (EIC) payments received *(from Form W–2)* . . . . . | **53** | |
| | 54 Total tax. Add lines 47 through 53 . . . . . . . . . . . . . . . . ▶ | **54** | 32,112 |

| | | | | |
|---|---|---|---|---|
| **Payments**<br>Attach Forms W–2, W–2G, and W–2P to front. | 55 Total Federal income tax withheld . . . . . . . . | **55** | 400 | |
| | 56 1981 estimated tax payments and amount applied from 1980 return . | **56** | 27,425 | |
| | 57 Earned income credit. If line 32a is under $10,000, see page 15 of Instructions . . . . . . . . . . . . | **57** | | |
| | 58 Amount paid with Form 4868 . . . . . . . . . . | **58** | | |
| | 59 Excess FICA and RRTA tax withheld (two or more employers) | **59** | | |
| | 60 Credit for Federal tax on special fuels and oils *(attach Form 4136 or 4136–T)* . . . . . . . . . . . | **60** | | |
| | 61 Regulated Investment Company credit *(attach Form 2439)* | **61** | | |
| | 62 Total. Add lines 55 through 61 . . . . . . . . . . . . . . . . . ▶ | **62** | 27,825 | |

| | | | |
|---|---|---|---|
| **Refund or Balance Due** | 63 If line 62 is larger than line 54, enter amount **OVERPAID** . . . . . . . . . . . . ▶ | **63** | |
| | 64 Amount of line 63 to be **REFUNDED TO YOU** . . . . . . . . . . . . . . ▶ | **64** | |
| | 65 Amount of line 63 to be applied to your 1982 estimated tax . . . ▶ | **65** | |
| | 66 If line 54 is larger than line 62, enter **BALANCE DUE.** Attach check or money order for full amount payable to "Internal Revenue Service." Write your social security number and "1981 Form 1040" on it. ▶ (Check ▶ ☐ if Form 2210 (2210F) is attached. See page 16 of Instructions.) ▶ $ | **66** | 4,287 |

| | |
|---|---|
| **Please Sign Here** | Under penalties of perjury, I declare that I have examined this return, including accompanying schedules and statements, and to the best of my knowledge and belief, it is true, correct, and complete. Declaration of preparer (other than taxpayer) is based on all information of which preparer has any knowledge. |
| | TAXPAYERS COPY |
| | ▶ Your signature                          Date          ▶ Spouse's signature *(if filing jointly, BOTH must sign even if only one had income)* |

| | | | | |
|---|---|---|---|---|
| **Paid Preparer's Use Only** | Preparer's signature ▶ | Date | Check if self-em-ployed ▶ ☐ | Preparer's social security no. |
| | Firm's name (or yours, if self-employed) and address ▶ | | E.I. No. ▶<br>ZIP code ▶ | |

536

# Schedule A—Itemized Deductions
### (Schedule B is on back)
▶ Attach to Form 1040.  ▶ See Instructions for Schedules A and B (Form 1040).

OMB No. 1545-0074

**1982**

Name(s) as shown on Form 1040

Francis M. and Barbara L. Kozinski

Your social security number
265 : 55 : 7109

**Medical and Dental Expenses** (Do not include expenses reimbursed or paid by others.) (See page 17 of Instructions.)

| | |
|---|---|
| 1 One-half (but not more than $150) of insurance premiums you paid for medical care. (Be sure to include in line 10 below.) ▶ | 150 |
| 2 Medicine and drugs . | |
| 3 Enter 1% of Form 1040, line 31 . . . | |
| 4 Subtract line 3 from line 2. If line 3 is more than line 2, enter zero . . . . | |
| 5 Balance of insurance premiums for medical care not entered on line 1 . . . . | |
| 6 Other medical and dental expenses: | |
| a Doctors, dentists, nurses, etc. . . . | |
| b Hospitals . . . . . . . . . | |
| c Transportation . . . . . . | |
| d Other (itemize—include hearing aids, dentures, eyeglasses, etc.) ▶ | |
| 7 Total (add lines 4 through 6d) . . . | |
| 8 Enter 3% of Form 1040, line 31 . . . | |
| 9 Subtract line 8 from line 7. If line 8 is more than line 7, enter zero. . . . . | |
| 10 Total medical and dental expenses (add lines 1 and 9). Enter here and on line 33 . ▶ | 150 |

**Taxes** (See page 18 of Instructions.)

| | |
|---|---|
| 11 State and local income . . . . . | 3,408 |
| 12 Real estate . . . . . . . . . . | 7,153 |
| 13 a General sales (see sales tax tables) . | 1,065 |
| b General sales on motor vehicles . . | |
| 14 Personal property . . . . . . . | |
| 15 Other (itemize) ▶ Personal properties in Cape May and Seaside Heights | 3,115 / 3,340 |
| 16 Total taxes (add lines 11 through 15). Enter here and on line 34 . . . ▶ | 18,081 / 1,081 |

**Interest Expense** (See page 18 of Instructions.)

| | |
|---|---|
| 17 Home mortgage . . . . . . . | 3,792 |
| 18 Credit and charge cards . . . . | 66 |
| 19 Other (itemize) ▶ NJNB Loan | 278 |
| Cape May mortgage | 1,724 |
| Seaside Heights Mortgage | 2,781 |
| Auto loan | 447 |
| Loan from John M. Kozinski(father) | 3,700 |
| 20 Total interest expense (add lines 17 through 19). Enter here and on line 35 ▶ | 12,788 |

**Contributions** (See page 19 of Instructions.)

| | |
|---|---|
| 21 a Cash contributions (If you gave $3,000 or more to any one organization, report those contributions on line 21b). | 975 |
| b Cash contributions totaling $3,000 or more to any one organization (show to whom you gave and how much you gave) ▶ | 132 |
| 22 Other than cash (see page 19 of Instructions for required statement) . . . . | |
| 23 Carryover from prior years . . . . | |
| 24 Total contributions (add lines 21a through 23). Enter here and on line 36 ▶ | 1,107 |

**Casualty or Theft Loss(es)** (You must attach Form 4684 if line 29 is $1,000 or more, OR if certain other situations apply.) (See page 19 of Instructions.)

| | |
|---|---|
| 25 Loss before reimbursement . . . . | 7,214 |
| 26 Insurance or other reimbursement you received or expect to receive . . . | 0 |
| 27 Subtract line 26 from line 25. If line 26 is more than line 25, enter zero . . . | 7,214 |
| 28 Enter $100 or amount from line 27, whichever is smaller. . . . . . . | 100 |
| 29 Total casualty or theft loss(es) (subtract line 28 from line 27). Enter here and on line 37 ▶ | 7,114 |

**Miscellaneous Deductions** (See page 19 of Instructions.)

| | |
|---|---|
| 30 a Union dues . . . . . | |
| b Tax return preparation fee . . . . | |
| 31 Other (itemize) ▶ | |
| 32 Total miscellaneous deductions (add lines 30a through 31). Enter here and on line 38 . . . . . . . . . ▶ | |

**Summary of Itemized Deductions** (See page 20 of Instructions.) **A**

| | |
|---|---|
| 33 Total medical and dental—from line 10 . | 150 |
| 34 Total taxes—from line 16 . . . . . | 18,081 |
| 35 Total interest—from line 20 . . . . | 12,788 |
| 36 Total contributions—from line 24 . . . | 1,107 |
| 37 Total casualty or theft loss(es)—from line 29 . | 7,114 |
| 38 Total miscellaneous—from line 32 . . | |
| 39 Add lines 33 through 38 . . . . . | 39,240 |
| 40 If you checked Form 1040, Filing Status box: 2 or 5, enter $3,400 . . . . 1 or 4, enter $2,300 . . . . 3, enter $1,700 . . . . | 3,400 |
| 41 Subtract line 40 from line 39. Enter here and on Form 1040, line 32b. (If line 40 is more than line 39, see the Instructions for line 41 on page 20.) . . . . . ▶ | 35,840 |

For Paperwork Reduction Act Notice, see Form 1040 Instructions.

# SCHEDULE C
## (Form 1040)
Department of the Treasury
Internal Revenue Service (B)

# Profit or (Loss) From Business or Profession
### (Sole Proprietorship)
Partnerships, Joint Ventures, etc., Must File Form 1065.
► Attach to Form 1040 or Form 1041. ► See Instructions for Schedule C (Form 1040).

OMB. No. 1545–0074

## 1982

| Name of proprietor FRANCIS. M KOZINSKI | Social security number of proprietor 265 55 7109 |
|---|---|

A Main business activity (see Instructions) ► MEDICINE ; product ►

| B Business name ► DR KOZINSKI | C Employer identification number |
|---|---|

D Business address (number and street) ► 57 Riding Hills Rd
City, State and ZIP Code ► OCEAN CREST NJ 6P077

C Employer identification number: 2 2 4 7 8 5 1 0 3

E Accounting method: (1) ☒ Cash (2) ☐ Accrual (3) ☐ Other (specify) ►

F Method(s) used to value closing inventory:
(1) ☐ Cost (2) ☐ Lower of cost or market (3) ☐ Other (if other, attach explanation)

|  | Yes | No |
|---|---|---|
| G Was there any major change in determining quantities, costs, or valuations between opening and closing inventory? . . If "Yes," attach explanation. |  | X |
| H Did you deduct expenses for an office in your home? . . . . . . . . . . . . . ¿ . . . . |  | X |

## Part I  Income

| | | |
|---|---|---|
| 1 a Gross receipts or sales . . . . . . . . . | 1a | 146,435 |
| b Returns and allowances . . . . . . . . . | 1b | 415 |
| c Balance (subtract line 1b from line 1a) . . . . . . . . . . | 1c | 146 020 |
| 2 Cost of goods sold and/or operations (Schedule C–1, line 8) . . . . . . . . | 2 | 2 825 |
| 3 Gross profit (subtract line 2 from line 1c) . . . . . . | 3 | 143 195 |
| 4 a Windfall Profit Tax Credit or Refund received in 1981 (see Instructions) . . . . | 4a | |
| b Other income (attach schedule) . . . . . . . . . | 4b | |
| 5 Total income (add lines 3, 4a, and 4b) . . . . . . . . . . . ► | 5 | 143 195 |

## Part II  Deductions

| | | | | | |
|---|---|---|---|---|---|
| 6 Advertising . . . . . . . | | 29 a Wages . . | 31,438 | | |
| 7 Amortization . . . . . . | | b Jobs credit | | | |
| 8 Bad debts from sales or services . | | c WIN credit | | | |
| 9 Bank service charges . . . . | | d Total credits | | | |
| 10 Car and truck expenses . . . | 1 852 | e Subtract line 29d from 29a . | | 31 438 | |
| 11 Commissions . . . . . . | | 30 Windfall Profit Tax withheld in | | | |
| 12 Depletion . . . . . . . | | 1981 . . . . . . | | | |
| 13 Depreciation (see Instructions) . | 7,024 | 31 Other expenses (specify): | | | |
| 14 Dues and publications . . . | 928 | a DINNERS WHILE WORKING | | 385 | |
| 15 Employee benefit programs . . | | b CONVENTIONS | | 2,052 | |
| 16 Freight (not included on Schedule C–1). | | c Telened service | | 7,004 | |
| 17 Insurance . . . . . . . | 6,447 | d Miscellaneous | | 1,315 | |
| 18 Interest on business indebtedness | 225 | e | | | |
| 19 Laundry and cleaning . . . . | 140 | f | | | |
| 20 Legal and professional services . | 1,455 | g | | | |
| 21 Office supplies and postage . . . | 828 | h | | | |
| 22 Pension and profit-sharing plans . | | i | | | |
| 23 Rent on business property . . . | 7,505 | j | | | |
| 24 Repairs . . . . . . . . | 216 | k | | | |
| 25 Supplies (not included on Schedule C–1) . | | l | | | |
| 26 Taxes (do not include Windfall Profit Tax, see line 30) . . . . | 851 | m | | | |
| | | n | | | |
| 27 Travel and entertainment . . . | 1,742 | o | | | |
| 28 Utilities and telephone . . . . | 3,744 | p | | | |

| | | |
|---|---|---|
| 32 Total deductions (add amounts in columns for lines 6 through 31p) . . . . . . ► | 32 | 66 137 |
| 33 Net profit or (loss) (subtract line 32 from line 5). If a profit, enter on Form 1040, line 11, and on Schedule SE, Part II, line 5a (or Form 1041, line 6). If a loss, go on to line 34 . . . . | 33 | 77 058 |

34 If you have a loss, do you have amounts for which you are not "at risk" in this business (see Instructions)? . . ☐ Yes ☐ No
If you checked "No," enter the loss on Form 1040, line 11, and on Schedule SE, Part II, line 5a (or Form 1041, line 6).

For Paperwork Reduction Act Notice, see Form 1040 Instructions.

# Supplemental Income Schedule

(From rents and royalties, partnerships, estates and trusts, etc.)
▶ Attach to Form 1040. ▶ See Instructions for Schedule E (Form 1040).

OMB No. 1545–0074

**1982**

Name(s) as shown on Form 1040

FRANCIS M KUZINSKI

Your social security number

265 55 7109

## Part I  Rent and Royalty Income or Loss.

1 Are any of the expenses listed below for a vacation home or similar dwelling rented to others (see instructions)? . ☒ Yes ☐ No

2 If you checked "Yes" to question 1, did you or a member of your family occupy the vacation home or similar dwelling for more than 14 days during the tax year? . . . . . . . . . . . . . . . . ☐ Yes ☒ No

| Rental and Royalty Income (describe property in Part V) | | Properties | | | | Totals | |
|---|---|---|---|---|---|---|---|
| | | A | B | C | | | |
| 3 a Rents received . . . . . . . . | | 39993 | 3300 | 2800 | 3 | 46093 | |
| b Royalties received . . . . . . . | | | | | | | |
| **Rental and Royalty Expenses** | | | | | | | |
| 4 Advertising . . . . . . | 4 | | | | | | |
| 5 Auto and travel . . . . . . | 5 | | | | | | |
| 6 Cleaning and maintenance . . . . | 6 | 4966 | 593 | 130 | | | |
| 7 Commissions . . . . . . | 7 | | | | | | |
| 8 Insurance . . . . . . | 8 | 2100 | 480 | | | | |
| 9 Interest . . . . . . | 9 | | | | | | |
| 10 Legal and other professional fees . . | 10 | | | | | | |
| 11 Repairs . . . . . . | 11 | | | | | | |
| 12 Supplies . . . . . . | 12 | | | | | | |
| 13 Taxes (do NOT include Windfall Profit Tax, see Part III, line 35) . . . . . | 13 | | | | | | |
| 14 Utilities . . . . . . | 14 | 4,518 | 327 | 145 | | | |
| 15 Wages and salaries . . . . . | 15 | | | | | | |
| 16 Other (list) ▶ | | | | | | | |

A = Seaside Heights Apts
B = Cape May Property –
Concession Stand
C = Cape May Property –
Miniature golf

| 17 Total deductions (add lines 4 through 16) . . . . . . | 17 | 11584 | 1400 | 275 | 17 | | |
|---|---|---|---|---|---|---|---|
| 18 Depreciation expense (see Instructions), or Depletion (attach computation) . . . . . . | 18 | 5815 | | | 18 | | |
| 19 Total (add lines 17 and 18) . . . . | 19 | 17399 | | | | | |
| 20 Income or (loss) from rental or royalty properties (subtract line 19 from line 3a (rents) or 3b (royalties)) . . . | 20 | 22594 | 1900 | 2525 | | | E |

21 Add properties with profits on line 20, and enter total profits here . . . . . . . . . . . . . . . . 21 | 27019

22 Add properties with losses on line 20, and enter total (losses) here . . . . . . . . . . . . . . . 22 | ( )

23 Combine amounts on lines 21 and 22, and enter net profit or (loss) here . . . . . . . . . . . 23 | 27019

24 Net farm rental profit or (loss) from Form 4835, line 50 . . . . . . . . . . . . . . . . 24

25 Total rental or royalty income or (loss). Combine amounts on lines 23 and 24. Enter here and include in line 37 on page 2 . . . . . . . . . . . . . . . . . . . . . . . . . . . . 25 | 27019

For Paperwork Reduction Act Notice, see Form 1040 Instructions.

```
PERSONAL FINANCIAL STATEMENT SHOWING THE CONDITION OF:

   Francis M. and Barbara L. Kozinski
   SSN 265 55 7109    224 71 4873
   57 Riding Hills Road, Ocean Crest, N.J. 08037
   609 483 5562    609 551 3836
```

| | | |
|---|---|---|
| Cash on hand: | $    200 | |
| Cash in banks: Checking | 6,343 | Marine Bank |
| Savings | 2,002 | Marine Bank |
| Cash value, life insurance: | 78,000 | Aetna & Mutual Benefit |
| Marketable Securiities: | | |
| Receivables: Notes | 5,800 | Dr. Charles Otley |
| Accounts | | |
| Real Estate: Home | 135,000 | 57 Riding Hills |
| Investments | 146,000 | 291 Ocean Blvd, Seaside Hts |
| | | 6 apartment units |
| | 78,000 | Beach Drive, Cape May |
| | | undeveloped land |
| Securities: Not marketable | | |
| Other assets: Automobile | 4,800 | 1981 VW |
| Other | 30,000 | Personal effects |
| **TOTAL ASSETS AT MARKET VALUE** | **$486,145** | |

| | | |
|---|---|---|
| Liabilities: Bank loans | 1,800 | 1981 VW |
| | 35,323 | Loan from father of FMK, |
| | | part financing for Seaside |
| Taxes owed: | | Hts Property |
| Mortgages: | 13,032 | Seaside Heights; 1st State Bank |
| | 42,596 | Home; Ocean Heights S&L |
| | 15,552 | Cape May land; Marine Bank |
| **TOTAL LIABILITIES** | **$108,303** | |
| **NET WORTH** | **$377,842** | |

**Project Cash Flow, 10 Quarters Beginning January 1, 1984, Assuming Sale of 2 Units Each Quarter Starting in 3rd Quarter.**

| Quarter | Sales | Cash Expenses | Net Cash Flow |
|---|---|---|---|
| 1st |  | $    80,850 | $−   80,850 |
| 2nd |  | 161,600 | − 161,600 |
| 3rd | $   330,000 | 185,950 | + 144,050 |
| 4th | 337,000 | 323,400 | +   13,600 |
| 5th | 343,000 | 323,400 | +   19,600 |
| 6th | 350,000 | 204,170 | + 145,830 |
| 7th | 357,000 | 180,590 | + 176,410 |
| 8th | 364,000 | 157,000 | + 207,000 |
| 9th | 371,000 | 25,000 | + 346,000 |
| 10th | 379,000 | 25,000 | + 354,000 |
|  | 2,831,000 | 1,666,960 | 1,164,404 |

## Supporting work flow

1st   quarter—architectural plans, deposits on supplies, some site preparation
2nd quarter—begin construction on 6 units
3rd quarter—complete 2 units; start 2 units
4th quarter—complete 2 units; start 2 units
5th quarter—complete 2 units; start 2 units
6th quarter—complete 2 units; start 2 units
7th quarter—complete 2 units; start 2 units
8th quarter—complete 3 units
9th quarter—complete 3 units
10th quarter—no construction activity

## MARINE NATIONAL BANK
## LOAN APPLICATION REQUEST FORM

*APPLICANT*        Francis M. and Barbara L. Kozinski, 57 Riding Hills Rd., Ocean Crest, N.J. 08037

*GUARANTOR(S)*  None

*AMOUNT*         $1.7 million secured line of credit with guaranteed availability over a 3-year period.

*DISBURSEMENTS*  During the process of construction, disbursements shall be requested, as needed, to finance ongoing cash construction costs for Oceanview Condominiums, a limited partnership between the Kozinskis (general partners) and M. C. Thompson, 280 Park Avenue West, New York, N.Y. 10023 (limited partner).

*INTEREST RATE*   The borrowers agree to pay interest monthly on the unpaid balance at the rate to be determined mutually. As part of the loan, the borrower will establish a reserve under the line in the amount of $250,000, such reserve to be used solely to pay interest automatically as it comes due. The

TERM

bank is authorized to disburse funds from this reserve without prior consent of the borrower. Should the reserve be exhausted prior to repayment of the loan, the borrowers agree to make cash interest payments in a timely fashion.

The line shall mature and all unpaid interest and principal outstanding shall be due and payable on the last day of the 36th month following the initial drawdown, such drawdown likely to occur on or about January 1984.

COLLATERAL

The borrower will pledge the property known as 71 Beach Drive, Cape May, N.J., corner of Beach Drive and Alameda Avenue, building lots 141, 143, and 144 in block 1306.

PROJECT

Proceeds of the loan to be used exclusively for the construction and sale of 16 condominium units on 63-71 Beach Drive, Cape May, N.J. Each unit to contain approximately 1,400 square feet of interior living space with 2 bedrooms and 2 baths.

OTHER

Borrowers to provide title insurance, building permits, flood hazard boundary map, and financial records as requested by the bank.

Date *Sept. 7, 1983*                    Signed *Francis M. Kozinski*

*Partnership Agreement Summarized, M.C. Thompson and the Kozinskis* (prepared by Louis Donlan, Esq., of Kemp and Donlan Associates)

The partners contribute each one parcel of land:

Thompson—63 Beach Drive, 1.4 acres valued at $215,000
Kozinski—71 Beach Drive,  .5 acre valued at $78,000

The Kozinskis will develop the property by constructing 16 luxury condominiums following a budget:

| | |
|---|---:|
| 1st parcel of land | $215,000 |
| 2nd parcel of land | 78,000 |
| Construction costs | 1,666,960 |
| Legal and other fees | 32,000 |
| Contingency | 100,000 |
| Total budget | $2,091,960 |

It is expected that units will be sold over a 2- to 3-year period for:

| | |
|---|---|
| First 2 units | $165,000 each after broker commissions |
| Next 2 units | 168,500 |
| Next 2 units | 171,500 |
| Next 2 units | 175,000 |
| Next 2 units | 178,500 |
| Next 2 units | 182,000 |
| Next 2 units | 185,500 |
| Next 2 units | 189,000 |

Total sales after selling fees: $2,831,000

In return for the contribution of land, M. C. Thompson is to receive $215,000 plus accrued interest at 13 percent from January 1, 1984. In addition, M. C. Thompson is to receive 25 percent of project profits excluding accrued interest. The Kozinskis are to bear all losses, if any, and receive balance of profits. M. C. Thompson is to receive a minimum of $100,000 from the Kozinskis if the project loses money, such money to be paid on January 1, 1987 or on date of sale of last unit, whichever comes first.

Sample profit calculation: 2,831,000 − 2,091,960 = 739,040. $215,000 to Thompson; 524,040 to Kozinski.

# 17

# Long-Term Financing Decisions

In meeting its needs for long-term financing, the firm has a choice between debt and equity sources. The general characteristics of these sources were discussed in Chapter 2. Based upon these characteristics, the financial manager must weigh a number of factors when choosing the mix of long-term debt, preferred stock, and common stock to finance the firm's assets. This process is outlined in this chapter.

The chapter begins with an introduction to specialty securities: convertible bonds and warrants. Then we will examine the characteristics of long-term project financing and the elements of loan structuring between the firm and its primary creditors. We will calculate the effective cost of long-term project financing. The entire process is designed to familiarize the reader with the analytical and decision-making aspects of evaluating long-term sources of financing for the firm.

## CONVERTIBLE SECURITIES

A *convertible security* is a bond or share of preferred stock that can be converted, at the option of the holder, into shares of common stock of the same corporation. Once the conversion option is exercised, the common stock cannot be exchanged later for the bond or preferred stock. The conversion feature on a convertible security may be exercised only under the specified terms and conditions contained in the original offering of the security. Both the conversion price and conversion ratio are established at the time the security is sold. These are:

1. *Conversion Ratio.* This gives the number of shares of common stock to be received in the event the holder surrenders the convertible security to the corporation. For example, a $1,000 bond may be convertible into 25 shares of common stock at any time prior to June 30, 1991. The conversion ratio would be 25 shares to one bond.

2. *Conversion Price.* This is the effective price paid for the common stock when the conversion takes place. It is calculated by the formula:

$$\frac{\text{conversion}}{\text{price}} = \frac{\text{par value}}{\text{shares received}}$$

For the $1,000 bond convertible into 25 shares of common stock, the conversion price would be $1,000/25 = $40 per share.

## CHARACTERISTICS OF CONVERTIBLE SECURITIES

A number of characteristics are generally associated with convertible securities:

1. *Inclusion of a Call Feature.* Most convertible bonds or preferred stocks are callable at the option of the company and at a stipulated price.

2. *Protection against Dilution.* Most convertible offerings contain a provision that protects the holder from dilution as a result of stock splits, stock dividends, or the sale of common stock at low prices. In the event of a stock dividend or stock split, the conversion ratio would automatically be adjusted to prevent dilution. For example, suppose a $100 par preferred stock were convertible into 4 shares of common stock and the company declared a 2-for-1 stock split. After the split, the preferred stock would be convertible into 8 shares of common stock.

3. *Conversion Premium.* The conversion price is normally set 10 to 30 percent above the prevailing market price of the common stock at the time the convertible security is sold. The premium may be calculated by the formula:

$$\frac{\text{conversion}}{\text{premium}} = \frac{\text{conversion price} - \text{market price}}{\text{market price}}$$

Using the example of the $1,000 bond convertible into 25 shares of common stock, let us assume a prevailing market price of $35 per share. The conversion price is $40, so the premium is 14 percent, as follows:

$$\frac{\text{conversion}}{\text{premium}} = \frac{40 - 35}{35} = .14$$

### WHY FIRMS USE CONVERTIBLES

Two primary reasons may be given for the use of a convertible feature on a bond or preferred stock offering. These are:

1. *Lowering the Cost of Financing.* A convertible feature lowers the cost of debt or preferred stock financing. It offers the holder a chance to share in future capital gains if the price of the firm's common stock rises above the conversion price. In the meantime, the security holder receives regular interest or dividends as a fixed income. In return for the capital-gains opportunity, the firm is able to offer the security with a lower interest rate or indicated dividend than required for nonconvertible issues. This lowers the financing costs.

2. *Selling Common Stock at Higher Prices.* A second major reason for the use of a convertible feature is to sell common stock at prices higher than the current market price. When it is seeking long-term financing, the firm may actually prefer to sell common stock rather than add to its debt level. If the price of the common stock is temporarily depressed, an excessive number of common shares would be required to raise the needed funds. By setting the conversion premium 10 to 30 percent higher than the current market price, the firm gives up 10 to 20 percent fewer shares when the security is ultimately converted as compared to a common stock sale at the depressed price.

### FORCING THE CONVERSION

If the price of the common stock rises above the conversion price, the firm can force the security holders to convert into common stock. For example, suppose that the price of common stock has risen to $50 for a company whose $1,000 bonds can be converted into 25 shares of common stock. Also assume that the bond is callable at $1,050. If the bond is called, the bondholder must either surrender it for $1,050 or convert it into 25 shares of common stock worth $50 each, a total value of $1,250. Naturally, the bondholder would convert the bond even if planning to sell the common stock immediately and buy a bond of a different firm. *Forcing the conversion* is the action of calling a bond when the conversion value significantly exceeds the call value.

## WARRANTS

A *warrant* is a security that permits the holder to buy shares of common stock during a stated period and at a given price. When the option is exercised, the holder must surrender the warrant and pay the firm for the common stock purchased at the option price. For many years, warrants were considered speculative instruments rather than investment securities, since the warrant has no value other than as a right to purchase other securities. In the 1970s, major corporations such as American Telephone and Telegraph and Braniff Airways issued securities with warrants attached; a number of actively traded warrants can be found on the New York Stock Exchange, American Stock Exchange, and Chicago Board Options Exchange.

### USE OF WARRANTS

A firm attaches warrants to bond or preferred stock financings as a "sweetener" in an attempt to achieve one or more of the following:

1. *Lower the Cost of the Issue.* A firm can offer a lower yield on a fixed income security if warrants are attached. The warrant offers a promise of sharing in the firm's growth, a favorable feature to the security holder. If the firm's common stock rises in value in the period before the warrant expiration date, the warrants can be exercised and the common stock can be immediately sold at a gain. In return for this possibility, investors accept a lower coupon rate on the fixed income security.

2. *Offset Relatively High Risk.* Some firms issue securities that represent considerable risk to a creditor; such a firm may not be able to borrow without a promise of some equity participation if the firm is extremely successful. In this situation, warrants may be used as an equity "kicker" to make a bond issue more attractive.

3. *Increase Future Equity.* Just as a convertible bond can be viewed as a means of increasing common stock at a future higher price, warrants can accomplish the same effect. The option price is gen-

erally set 10 to 30 percent above the market price of the stock at the time of the bond issue. If the common stock rises in price, the warrants will be surrendered before the expiration date, and the holders of the warrants will buy additional shares of common stock at the option price. The purchase of additional shares will, of course, increase the shares outstanding.

## VALUE OF WARRANTS

Warrants have an intrinsic value that may be calculated by the following formula:

$$\begin{pmatrix} \text{intrinsic} \\ \text{value} \end{pmatrix} = \begin{pmatrix} \text{market} \\ \text{price of} \\ \text{common} \\ \text{stock} \end{pmatrix} - \begin{pmatrix} \text{option} \\ \text{price of} \\ \text{common} \\ \text{stock} \end{pmatrix} \begin{pmatrix} \text{number} \\ \text{of shares} \\ \text{per} \\ \text{warrant} \end{pmatrix}$$

As an example of the use of this formula, consider a firm with a bond offering with attached warrants. Each $1,000 bond has five warrants attached, and each warrant allows the holder to purchase four shares of common stock at $30 per share. The common stock is presently selling for $50 per share. The value of each warrant is $80, as follows:

$$\text{intrinsic value} = (50 - 30)\,(4) = 80 \text{ per warrant}$$

The total value of the five warrants attached to each bond would be $80 times 5, or $400.

Note that the formula for intrinsic value would give a negative value if the market price is less than the option price. In this situation, the value of the warrant is based on future expectations, and the formula cannot be used to calculate intrinsic value. Even when the value is positive, the actual selling price of a warrant usually exceeds the intrinsic value. Once again, speculative factors are at work as warrantholders gamble that the stock will rise further in value and the warrant will be worth more.

## EFFECT OF WARRANTS ON CAPITAL STRUCTURE

The use of warrants in long-term financing has a different effect on the firm's capital structure than the use of convertible securities. If a firm issues a convertible bond and forces conversion, the debt is replaced with equity. This is not the case with a bond offering with warrants. When the warrants are exercised, the firm's bonds are not retired. Instead, the holder of the warrant pays additional money to the firm in return for the common stock. Thus, the exercise of the warrants increases the funds available to the firm while not affecting the fixed income securities outstanding. This characteristic of warrants affects the firm's future earnings per share, as well as the capital structure.

## LONG-TERM PROJECT FINANCING

Commercial banks have been a traditional supplier of short-term funds to corporations. In addition, banks have arranged and participated in long-term financing for large capital projects. In the 1970s and 1980s, insurance companies, pension funds, and other financial institutions joined banks as suppliers of long-term funds for companies. In this section, we will examine long-term financing from banks and similar financial institutions.

### PROJECT FINANCING

The term *project financing* refers to the financing arrangements matched against a specific capital project of the firm. The proceeds from the sale of bonds, preferred stock, or common stock may be used to meet any of the firm's financial needs. Thus, the issuance of these securities does not represent project financing since they fail to match funds against a specific activity of the firm. An example of project financing would occur if a firm purchased a $4.5 million warehouse with a 20 percent cash down payment and 80 percent mortgage on the property. The project financing would consist of $900,000 cash and $3.6 million debt.

### SOURCE OF REPAYMENT

A major concern in any project financing is the source of repayment of the capital. If the firm puts up $900,000 in cash, it seeks to recover its money plus earn a profit on it. If a bank puts up $3.6 million, it wants interest plus a repayment of the principal on the loan. Two sources of payment may be identified in project financing:

1. *Primary Source of Payment.* This is the payment of interest, principal, and profits if all goes well. Both the firm and its creditors are interested in the primary source of payment. For working-

capital loans, the primary source of payment was a conversion of the assets—a self-liquidating loan. Inventory or receivables were sold or collected as the primary source of payment. In project financing, we look to the *cash flow* generated when the capital assets are used. In the case of the $4.5 million warehouse, cash will be generated when the warehouse is used to store goods that are sold at a profit. Cash flow from using the capital asset is the primary source of payment on long-term financing.

2. *Secondary Source of Payment.* This is of interest only to the creditor in a project financing. If the cash flow fails to materialize, how else can the loan be repaid? Two main secondary sources can be identified:

   a. *Collateral.* This may be defined as an asset pledged to secure payment of an obligation. In our example, the warehouse itself is pledged as collateral, which is represented by the mortgage on it. The firm could also pledge other assets as a secondary payment source on the loan.

   b. *Guarantee.* This is a written agreement whereby one party borrows money and a second party agrees to take responsibility for the loan in the event of a default. Suppose the warehouse were purchased by a small subsidiary of a large corporation. In addition to the mortgage, a bank may require a guarantee by the parent corporation. This is an additional secondary source of payment.

## LOAN STRUCTURING FOR PROJECT FINANCING

For the debt portion of any project financing, the company must negotiate the structure of the loan with the lending institution. Some of the major considerations are:

1. *Interest Rate.* A *fixed-rate loan* exists when the stated interest rate does not change during the period of the loan. A *variable- or floating-rate loan* occurs when the interest rate is tied to some money market indicator and changes as the indicator changes. Some key terms for variable-rate loans are:

   a. *Prime.* The *prime rate* is a widely published bank lending rate that is used as a money market indicator. Each bank publishes its own prime rate and ties its loans to that rate.

   b. *LIBOR.* The London Inter-Bank Offered Rate *(LIBOR)* is another money market indicator used by larger banks on loans to large corporations.

c. *Cap.* This is a maximum rate on a loan. As an example, a loan may have a rate of "prime plus 2 with a cap of 20 percent." If, during the life of the loan, the prime rate reached 23 percent, the firm should be paying prime plus 2 percent, or 25 percent. It would not do so, since the cap is 20 percent.

d. *Floor.* This is a minimum rate on a loan. As an example, suppose that the prime plus 2 loan had a floor of 14 percent, yet prime dropped to 9 percent. The loan would never drop below 14 percent.

2. *Time Period.* A capital asset may have a useful service life of 15 years or more. At the same time, the financial institution may not be willing to make a loan for such a long time. In the loan negotiation, the period must be made acceptable to both the company and the creditor. It is rare for financial institutions to make loans for a period longer than 7 years; 3 to 5 years are becoming increasingly common. As a result, many project financing loans require a *balloon payment*, which is defined as a final payment that is significantly larger than other payments.

3. *Fees and Compensating Balances.* The financial institution may receive compensation in forms in addition to the interest paid on the loan. A *fee* is a charge for services performed and may be expressed in dollars or as a percentage of the loan. On a $3.6 million loan with a .5 percent fee, the borrower will pay $18,000 ($3.6 million times .005) to the bank upon approval of the loan. In addition to fees and interest rates, compensating balances may also be required on the loan. The size and amount of fees and balances must be negotiated.

4. *Covenants.* A *convenant* is an agreement contained in a lending situation whereby the borrower makes some formal promise of value to the lender. As an example, a minimum cash convenant requires the borrower to maintain a stipulated minimum amount of cash in the company. Covenants are sought by lenders to increase the likelihood of payment and are negotiated as part of the project financing.

## EFFECTIVE COST OF LONG-TERM DEBT

Whether bonds, mortgages, project financing, or other forms, long-term debt has an expected cost to the firm. For variable-rate debt, the actual cost differs from the forecast cost if interest rates differ from projections of interest rates. Still, the firm should forecast the real or effective cost of each kind of long-term debt. This will be done in this section.

### CALCULATING THE PERIODIC LOAN PAYMENT

An *annuity* exists when a firm has a series of equal cash receipts or payments that occur at the end of successive periods of equal duration. As an example, a loan payment of $500 a month for 24 months is an annuity of $500. In the case of a loan, each periodic payment usually contains some interest as well as an amount to retire the original principal of the loan. When a loan is repaid with an annuity, we have a *steady-payment loan*.

A time-value-of-money formula can be used to examine the relationship between the amount borrowed and the payment needed to retire the loan. The formula is:

$$PV = [PMT] \ \left[\frac{1}{int}\right] \left[1 - \frac{1}{(1+int)^n}\right]$$

where   PV = the amount borrowed (the present value)
   PMT = each repayment on the loan (the payment)
   int = interest rate for each period
   n = number of periods

As an example of the use of this formula, consider a situation where $500 is paid on the last day of each month for 24 months beginning January 31. The interest rate is 1.5 percent a month. What loan as of January 1 would be supported by this repayment schedule? The answer is $10,015.20, as follows:

$$PV = [500] \ \left[\frac{1}{.015}\right] \left[1 - \frac{1}{(1+.015)^{24}}\right] = 10,015.20$$

The calculation can also be performed on a time-value-of-money calculator:

| n | i | PMT | PV |
|---|---|-----|----|
| 24 | 1.5 | 500 | [10,015.20] |

Using the same formula, we can solve for the periodic payment by reorganizing, as follows:

$$PMT = \frac{PV \times int}{1 - 1/(1 + int)^n}$$

For our original example, we get a payment of $500:

$$PMT = \frac{10,015.20 \times .015}{1 - 1/(1.015)^{24}} = 500$$

With the time value calculator, we load in the $n$, $i$, and $PV$ values and solve for $PMT$.

### WHAT HAPPENS WITH VARIABLE-RATE LOANS?

In the preceding calculations, we have determined a loan payment for a fixed-rate loan. With a variable-rate loan, there is no way to know in advance the exact payment each period. However, for planning purposes we can assume an average interest rate for the duration of the loan and perform a calculation similar to the one for a fixed-rate loan. This gives us a likely payment that can be used to compare alternative sources of financing.

**Example:** A firm seeks $1.6 million as the debt portion of a project financing. An insurance company offers it at 17 percent a year with quarterly payments and compounding. The period for the loan is 4 years. What is the quarterly payment on the loan?

**Answer:** $139,856, as follows:
The quarterly interest rate is .17/4, or .0425. The formula is:

$$PMT = \frac{1,600,000 \times .0425}{1 - 1/(1.0425)^{16}} = 139,856$$

or

|       n       |      i       |     PMT      |      PV       |
|---------------|--------------|--------------|---------------|
|      16       |     17/4     |  [139,856]   |  1,600,000    |

**CALCULATING THE BALLOON PAYMENT**

In a period of volatile interest rates, banks and other financial institutions are reluctant to agree to long-term loans. It has become common to see long-term financing on the basis of a 3-year or so loan with a balloon payment. Two terms are important in this kind of lending situation:

1. *Amortization.* This refers to the process of reducing the principal on a loan by a series of periodic payments to the lender. If the entire loan is paid off by the periodic payments, we say the loan is *fully amortizing.* This is not the case with loans that have a balloon payment at the end.
2. *Payout Period.* This is the period over which the loan would be fully amortized. As an example, a firm may be offered a 5-year loan with a 15-year payout. This means that the firm's periodic payments will be calculated as though the loan were made for 15 years; the actual loan will be for 5 years with a balloon payment.

To calculate the amount of a balloon payment, we can follow a four-step process:

1. *Calculate Periodic Payment.* Using the payout period for the loan, we calculate the regular payment that would fully amortize the loan.
2. *Calculate Future Value of Loan with No Payments.* Next we take the original loan and calculate how much it would increase in value if no payments were made. For a 3-year loan, we determine the value in 3 years; for a 5-year loan, in 5 years; and so on.
3. *Calculate Future Value of Payments.* In this step, we take each periodic payment and calculate its value as of the end of the loan period. This is the compound value of an annuity.
4. *Subtract Future Value of Payments from Future Value of Loan Amount.* The difference between steps 2 and 3 is the balloon payment.

The process of determining the amount of the balloon payment is shown in Figure 17–1 for a loan with a 3-year period and a 15 percent cost of funds.

The process of determining the future value of the loan principal and stream of payments involves *compounding,* which is the process of calculating a future value when interest is earned on the original principal and also on the accumulated interest of prior periods. We have two compounding formulas:

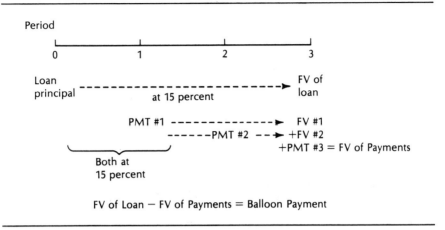

**Figure 17–1**  Calculating a Balloon Payment for a 3-year Loan at a 15 Percent Interest Rate.

For a Single Original Amount     $FV = (prin)(1 + int)^n$

For an Annuity     $FV = [PMT]\left[\dfrac{(1+int)^n - 1)}{i}\right]$

To illustrate the calculation of a balloon payment, let us consider a firm that seeks to purchase a $3 million machine with a 15-year service life. A bank agrees to finance 80 percent of the cost at 18 percent with semiannual payments and compounding. The loan will be for 4 years with a 10-year payout. What is the amount of the semiannual payment? the amount of the balloon payment at the end of 4 years?

The semiannual payment is $262,912:

$$PMT = \frac{2,400,000 \times .09}{1 - 1/(1.09)^{20}} = 262,912$$

or

| n | i | PV | PMT |
|---|---|---|---|
| $10 \times 2$ | $18/2$ | 2,400,000 | [262,912] |

The balloon payment is $1,882,632.

$$FV = (2,400,000)\ (1.09)^8 \quad = \quad 4,782,150$$

$$FV = 262,912\left[\frac{(1.09)^8 - 1}{.09}\right] = -2,899,518$$

$$\overline{\phantom{FV = 262,912}1,882,632}$$

or

| n | i | PMT | PV | FV |
|---|---|---|---|---|
| 8 | 9 | | 2,400,000 | [4,782,150] |
| 8 | 9 | | | −[2,899,518] |
| | | 262,912 | | 1,882,632 |

## EFFECTIVE COST WITH FEES AND BALANCES

When a lending arrangement involves fees or compensating balances, the effective cost analysis must recognize the impact of each item. The formula is:

$$\text{effective cost} = \frac{\left(\begin{array}{c}\text{int.}\\ \text{rate}\end{array}\right)\left(\begin{array}{c}\text{loan}\\ \text{amount}\end{array}\right) + \left(\begin{array}{c}\text{percent}\\ \text{of fee}\end{array}\right)\left(\begin{array}{c}\text{loan}\\ \text{amount}\end{array}\right)}{\begin{array}{c}\text{loan}\\ \text{amount}\end{array} - \begin{array}{c}\text{compensating}\\ \text{balance}\end{array} - \begin{array}{c}\text{fee paid}\\ \text{in advance}\end{array}}$$

To illustrate the use of this formula, let us consider a firm that is borrowing $2 million at prime plus 2 percent. The period is 2 years. A 1 percent fee is payable upon approval of the loan, and a 10 percent compensating balance is required. The prime rate for the 2 years is expected to average 14.5 percent. What is the effective cost of the loan?

Because of the fee, the cost will be higher in year 1. It will be 19.7 percent and 18.3 percent, as follows:

$$\text{effective cost} = \frac{(.165)\ (2,000) + (.01)\ (2,000)}{2,000 - 200 - (2,000)\ (.01)} = .197$$

The fee does not have to be paid in year 2. Also, it is not necessary to subtract it out in the denominator of the formula since, conceptually, we have absorbed the fee in year 1. The calculation for year 2 is:

$$\frac{\text{effective}}{\text{cost}} = \frac{(.165)\ (2,000)}{2,000 - 200} = .183$$

### EFFECTIVE COST OF STANDBY FINANCING

In many cases, a firm arranges financing that it does not really plan to use. Such an agreement is called *standby financing*. It is intended as a backup source of funds for contingency or opportunity purposes. The effective cost of such financing is heavily affected by fees and compensating balances, as we will illustrate with an example. Let us return to our preceding example, where the firm borrowed $2 million, but we will make part of it standby financing. The firm will actually use only 30 percent of the funds in year 1. What is the effective cost if the fee and balances are required on the whole amount for the entire year? In this situation, the interest rate would only apply to 30 percent of $2 million, or $600,000. The effective cost would rise to 31.3 percent:

$$\frac{\text{effective}}{\text{cost}} = \frac{(.165)\ (600) + (.01)\ (2,000)}{600 - 200 - 20} = .313$$

In order to receive standby financing, the firm might be willing to pay a premium over the basic effective cost of the loan. Still, a 31.3 percent effective cost appears excessive. In this example, the compensating balance on the unused portion of the loan is the factor that produces such a high cost. For standby financing, the firm would try to negotiate a different loan pricing to reduce the cost.

In this chapter, we have examined convertibles, warrants, and the cost of long-term financing. The value to this knowledge is the ability to measure cost of different financing sources and prepare a recommendation for management. The problems and cases at the end of this chapter are designed to give some practice in handling long-term financing decisions. As you will see, each situation is different and requires original thought. Still, each decision involves a knowledge of the technical aspects of securities, the analytical techniques for determining effective cost, and some creative thinking. With the material in this and earlier chapters, you should be prepared to tackle even some difficult financing choices.

## KEY TERMS

| | | |
|---|---|---|
| amortization | convertible security | payout period |
| annuity | convenant | primary source of payment |
| balloon payment | fee | prime rate |
| call feature | fixed rate loan | project financing |
| cap | floor | secondary source of payment |
| collateral | forcing the conversion | standby financing |
| compounding | fully amortizing | steady payment loan |
| conversion premium | guarantee | variable- or floating-rate |
| conversion price | LIBOR | loan |
| conversion ratio | | warrant |

## STUDY QUESTIONS

1. What is the difference between a conversion price and conversion ratio?
2. How is the holder of a convertible security protected against dilution?
3. What is a conversion premium?
4. Why do firms use convertibles? How can they ensure that the bonds will be converted while the market price of a stock is high?
5. Why are warrants used?
6. Why do warrants have a different effect on a firm's capital structure than do convertibles?
7. What is meant by project financing? Identify and explain two sources of payment in project financing.
8. What are the major considerations faced by the firm when negotiating a loan with a lending institution?
9. When does an annuity exist?
10. Explain what is meant by amortization and payout period.
11. What is the purpose of standby financing?

## PROBLEMS

1. A $1,000 bond is convertible into 15 shares of common stock. What is the conversion price for the stock?
2. A $1,000 bond is convertible into 20 shares of common stock at a time when the market price of the common stock is $42. What is the conversion premium?
3. A $1,000 bond has three attached warrants, each allowing the holder to buy one share of common stock at $30. The stock is selling for $39. What is the intrinsic value of one warrant?
4. A firm has borrowed $350,000 for 18 months with an interest rate of 1.4 percent per month. What is the monthly payment on this loan?

5. A firm can afford to make monthly payments of $14,000 at a time when American Express will lend it money at 15.6 percent compounded monthly. On a 3-year loan, how much financing would this payment support?

6. A company has arranged $5 million in financing from a credit union. The loan has a 3-year period and a 10-year payout. The interest rate is fixed at 19.2 percent annually compounded quarterly with quarterly payments. What is the quarterly payment? the amount of the balloon payment at the end of 3 years?

7. A company has negotiated a 3-year loan for $6 million at prime plus 1.5 percent. A 1 1/4 percent fee is required upon approval. A 5 percent compensating balance is required on unexercised portions of the loan and 10 percent is required on exercised portions. In the 1st year, the average prime rate is likely to be 13 percent. If the firm borrows 100 percent of the approved amount, what is the first year effective cost? What is the effective cost if it borrows 60 percent?

# LAWRENCE MANUFACTURING COMPANY CASE
## Project Financing

*This case allows the reader to analyze different financing alternatives to determine which is most favorable*

Lawrence Manufacturing Company is a medium-sized producer of subassemblies and components for household appliances. By continuous investments to improve manufacturing productivity, the firm has held its traditional markets while expanding into new lines of business. The company has always sought the lowest unit production costs for the items in its major product lines and has stayed competitive through automation and computerization on fabrication and assembly lines.

The new computerized tool and die project is a good example of modernizing to meet competition. Once installed, the new presses will convert sheet metal or hard plastics into components for lawn mowers and fertilizer spreaders. Coming off the line, each unit will have minimal manual processing as it is punched, assembled, and packaged for shipment. The new process would replace a more costly operation in Nogales, Mexico, and would ensure a market for Lawrence components with a number of new customers.

During the past 6 weeks, Rob Henderson, vice-president, finance, at Lawrence Manufacturing, had been working with banks, insurance companies, and investment bankers to secure financing for the new production operation. The equipment would be set up in an existing company building just north of Milwaukee and most of the equipment would be delivered in the next 3 to 5 months. The major costs to be capitalized totaled just over $9 million, as follows:

| Item | Installed Cost |
|---|---|
| Fabrication machinery | $6,300,000 |
| Packaging and support equipment | 1,600,000 |
| Facility renovation | 1,600,000 |
| | $9,500,000 |

The company had earmarked $2.5 million to finance the project, money that was invested in acceptances and repurchase agreements. Rob intended to borrow the remainder of the capital cost and had narrowed the choices to three proposals, namely:

1. An $8 million bond offering for 7 years. The bond would require semiannual interest payments at a coupon rate of 15.5 percent annually. Investment bankers would receive 2 percent of the offering as a commission. A sinking fund would be required as part of the bond indenture. Semiannual payments would be made to a trustee, beginning 6 months after the bond sale date. An insurance company would hold the sinking fund accumulation and pay 11 percent compounded semiannually on balances in the fund.

2. An $8 million bank loan with fixed rate interest payments at 14 percent annually, compounded quarterly and paid quarterly. The bank would charge a 0.5 percent fee upon approval and Lawrence Manufacturing would have to maintain a 10 percent compensating balance in a transactions account. The period would be 2 years with a 5-year payout.

3. A variable rate loan from a Transamerica financing subsidiary at 3 percent above the 1-year treasury bill rate, compounded and paid monthly. The amount would be $8 million and the loan period would be 8 years. The treasury bill rate for the next year is expected to average 11 to 13 percent.

Rob Henderson decided to prepare a worksheet to compare the three financing alternatives. He took a small microprocessor from his briefcase and began to enter the relevant data on each source of long term financing. Even though the longest choice was for 7 years, he knew he had a project that was viable for 10 or more years. He also knew that he did not want annual payments much in excess of $2 million per year. With these as his constraints, he began to develop the numbers to support a recommendation for the company.

## Required

Compare the financial merits of the three choices. Does any one seem preferable to the others?

# ACORN INDUSTRIAL APPLICATIONS CASE
# Comparing Long-Term Financing

*This case provides the reader with the opportunity to evaluate the debt and equity sources of long-term financing.*

Acorn Industrial Applications provides diversified specialty services in the areas of heavy construction and design contract services. It operates as a holding company with six subsidiaries that operate in the construction of shopping centers, refineries, shipyards, and port facilities. With its headquarters staff in Denver, the company supervises operations on the west and Gulf coasts of the United States, as well as in Mexico.

John Holden is the treasurer and chief financial officer of Acorn Industrial. In addition to long-term planning and bank relations, John is responsible for selecting the specific financing mix for individual projects. Recently, he has been working on financing the equipment needed for the expansion of the Detroit Edison Belle River power plant. Acorn had ordered $40 million worth of pile driving equipment and portable jackup barges to support the project. John had 150 days to locate the permanent financing for this equipment, which would be delivered at the end of the year.

John had been working on this project for over 2 years and was comfortable with his four primary financing possibilities. The choices that survived the process were:

1. Common stock, to be sold at $42 per share and to net $40 per share.
2. 7-year variable-rate financing from Chase Manhattan Bank. The average forecast rate was 17 percent over the 7-year period with no balances required. The initial legal and other fees are included in the rate.
3. Convertible debentures with a 15.5 percent coupon, $980 net, and convertible at $50 per share after 1986.
4. Debentures with warrants, with a 15.5 percent coupon, $980 net, and with each bond have 10 warrants entitling the holder to buy one share of common stock at $50 after 1986.

John is making his plans in the summer of 1984, with the actual funds to be raised in the fourth quarter. Thus, they will be available to start the new year. To check his financial position, John requested the balance sheet and income statement, as shown in the tables. While the financial statements were being prepared, John Holden worked on the assumptions to be used in the analysis. Once he spent $40 million for the new equipment, he would have numerous other projects for the pile drivers and barges. He worked with his operations people to estimate the potential for using the equipment over the long term. After almost a week of talking and refining, he developed the following list of key items for the analysis:

1. Annual beforetax cash flow from using the new equipment. A good planning number would be $8 million per year for 7 years. This would be net cash revenues minus net cash expenses.
2. Depreciation on equipment—20/32/24/16/8 for 5 years to a 0 book value.
3. Residual value of equipment—$21 million if sold in 5 years; $15 million in 7 years.
4. Investment tax credit—5 percent at point 0; 5 percent the 1st year.
5. Tax rate—40 percent seemed reasonable.
6. Growth rate of net income, not considering new equipment. Acorn forecasts 5 percent annual growth of net income for the next 7 to 10 years.

With these assumptions and data, John was ready to prepare a recommendation for management. He knew that the company generally followed three guidelines prior to making an investment:

1. It must increase annual cash flow over the planning period and offer a discounted rate of return of 12 percent after taxes on a cash flow basis.
2. It must increase earnings per share by year 3 and must not cause a significant dilution of earnings in years 1 and 2.
3. The debt-asset ratio for the firm must not exceed 40 percent as a result of the investment.

**Required**

Prepare the recommendation for Acorn's management.

**TABLE 1.**   Income Statement, Acorn Industrial Applications, Consolidated
Operations (for 1984, 6 month's actual, 6 months pro forma) in 000s.

|  | 1984 | 1983 |
|---|---|---|
| Sales and revenues | $420,000 | $382,000 |
| Cost of goods sold | 263,000 | 234,000 |
| Gross margin | 157,000 | 148,000 |
| General & administrative | 35,000 | 32,000 |
| Operating income | 122,000 | 116,000 |
| Interest on debt | 21,000 | 17,800 |
| Earnings before taxes | 101,000 | 98,200 |
| Taxes (40%) | 40,400 | 39,280 |
| Net income | $ 60,600 | $ 58,920 |
| Shares outstanding | 10,000 | 10,000 |
| Earnings per share | $6.06 | $5.89 |

**TABLE 2.**   Balance Sheet (1984 Pro Forma and Actual).

|  | 1984 | 1983 |  | 1984 | 1983 |
|---|---|---|---|---|---|
| Cash & near cash | $ 22,000 | $ 18,000 | Payables | $ 7,000 | $ 6,000 |
| Receivables | 44,000 | 45,000 | Other current liabilities | 11,000 | 10,000 |
| Inventories | 64,000 | 62,000 | Long-term unsecured liabilities | 90,000 | 52,000 |
| Other current assets | 4,000 | 3,000 |  |  |  |
| Capital assets | 252,000 | 231,000 | Secured debt | 30,000 | 55,000 |
| (accum. depr.) | (62,000) | (59,000) | Common stock | 10,000 | 10,000 |
|  |  |  | Capital in excess of par value | 40,000 | 40,000 |
|  |  |  | Retained earnings | 136,000 | 127,000 |
| Totals | $324,000 | $300,000 | Totals | $324,000 | $300,000 |

# 18
# Lease-Buy Decisions

## INTRODUCTION TO LEASING

*Leasing* is an arrangement that provides a firm with the use and control over assets without receiving title to them. A *lease* is the written agreement allowing the use of the assets for a specified period of time. The lease is signed by both the owner of the assets, called the *lessor*, and the user, called the *lessee.*

Leasing has become an increasingly important source of long-term funds for large and small companies. A major impetus was the Economic Recovery Tax Act of 1981, under which the tax advantages to leasing were increased for lessees and lessors. In this chapter, we will cover the basic characteristics of different kinds of leases. Then we will examine some conceptual issues involved with leasing as a source of funds. Next we will compare the major lease forms with purchase choices. Finally we will develop an approach to making the lease-buy decision.

### BASIC TYPES OF LEASES

There are three basic types of leases:

1. *Operating Lease.* The operating lease does not impose any long-term obligation on either the lessor or lessee and may usually be canceled by either the owner or user of the assets after giving a

565

certain stipulated notice. An example of an operating lease would be the rental of office space on a 2-year lease cancelable on 60-day notice. This is a familiar kind of lease to most people but is of limited importance to the financial manager.

2. *Service Lease.* Under this arrangement, the lessor provides both financing and servicing of the asset during the lease period. Computers, copiers, trucks, and other capital assets are leased under contracts that provide maintenance or servicing of the asset during the lease period.

3. *Financial Lease.* This is a long-term lease on fixed assets that may not be canceled by either party. As a source of funds, the financial lease is basically the same kind of alternative as long-term debt financing. This kind of lease is of primary concern to the financial manager.

## CHARACTERISTICS OF SERVICE LEASES

Because modern machinery frequently requires specialized maintenance and support, service leases have been growing in importance. Major characteristics of these leases are the following:

1. *Maintenance Is Included in Lease Cost.* The lessor is responsible for maintaining the equipment and performing all routine servicing and repairs. This feature is considered in the cost of the lease and protects the lessee from having to correct major breakdowns. It also allows the lessor to employ a staff of skilled mechanics who can maintain a large number of leased vehicles, computers, or other equipment.

2. *Equipment May Not Be Fully Amortized.* When a firm *amortizes* an asset, it completely writes it off during a certain period. In service leases, the lease payments may not be sufficient to allow the lessor to recover the original cost of the asset. This means that the lease period is less than the service life of the asset and the lease is not fully amortizing.

3. *Lease May Be Canceled.* In most cases, the service lease may be canceled by the lessee. In return for this option, the lease may contain provisions for the payment of a penalty if the lease is canceled prior to its expiration. In most cases, a stipulated notice for cancellation is required.

4. *Miscellaneous Services May Be Available.* In addition to the equip-

ment and servicing, the service lease may provide for additional services on the part of the lessor. Substitute equipment is provided during breakdowns, and insurance forms may be processed by the lessor as part of the lease agreement.

## CHARACTERISTICS OF FINANCIAL LEASES

Financial leases have assumed a major role in the financing of buildings and equipment for American industry. Some characteristics of financial leases are the following:

1. *Fixed Obligation.* A financial lease imposes a fixed obligation on the firm. The obligation is not cancelable and is similar to the requirement to pay interest on outstanding debt.
2. *Long Time Period.* Financial leases are written to cover a period of at least 1 year and frequently 5 or 10 years. During this period of time, the firm must fulfill the requirements of the lease, even though the asset may become obsolete and no longer useful for business operations.
3. *Fully Amortizing Lease.* The agreement is written so that the lease covers the service life of the asset. If a firm leases a piece of equipment with an expected life of 8 years, the lease period will be approximately 8 years. If an asset has an indefinite life, as in the case of an office building, the lease will be written as though the service life were, say, 20 years. In this case, the building would be fully amortized, even though it may have a residual value at the end of the lease period.
4. *Profit during the Lease Period.* The lease payments total more than the original cost of the asset, which allows the lessor to make a profit on the lease arrangement during the lease period. If the asset has any residual value, this is an additional profit to the lessor.

## ENFORCEMENT OF FINANCIAL LEASES

Leasing offers the firm an alternative to long-term debt financing. The firm borrows an asset, rather than cash, and incurs a fixed obligation to make payments over an extended period of time. This obligation must be met, just as the firm must meet its interest and principal payments on debt. If a firm defaults on its lease, the firm may not return the assets to the lessor and end the obligation. The lessor may bring the lessee to court and request the court to force continued payments on the unpaid portion of the lease. Courts do not usually enforce the lease, but damages may be awarded to the lessor for breach of the lease contract. The very act of bringing the suit to court frequently has detrimental effects on the lessee's credit rating and ability to borrow or lease in the future.

## TYPES OF ASSETS LEASED

A firm can lease almost any kind of asset needed to conduct its business. Firms lease land, buildings, and even factories with all their equipment. Transportation needs can be met by leasing. Railroads lease locomotives; airlines lease large jets; and trucking companies lease all types of vehicles. Manufacturers with a desire to make sales to customers that are short of cash encourage leasing and may even help a customer make arrangements to lease.

## SOURCES OF FUNDS FOR LEASE FINANCING

A number of financial institutions and special leasing companies provide funds for leasing. A firm seeking funds for this purpose will find a variety of institutions competing for its business:

1. *Banks.* Large commercial banks have become increasingly interested in lease financing. Either directly or through the use of a holding company, a bank will make arrangements to purchase equipment and lease it to a customer. This allows the bank to provide an additional service, which helps it to attract the customer for other business and financial services.
2. *Life Insurance Companies.* These firms have become prominent in the long-term leasing of real estate. A life insurance company has large cash inflows that must be invested until needed to make payments on policies. These monies are frequently invested in office buildings or warehouses, which are leased to the occupants under a financial, service, or operating lease.
3. *Financial Service Companies.* Commercial finance companies and leasing companies are important sources of funds for specialized equipment and machinery. These companies usually employ a staff of experts who are thoroughly familiar with the resale market for specialized equipment and who can therefore develop the terms of the lease agreement.

## SALE AND LEASEBACK

One of the most common forms of financing real property involves the use of sale and leaseback. Retail stores, office buildings, multipurpose industrial buildings, and even complete shopping centers are frequently financed with this method.

Under a *sale and leaseback* arrangement, the firm seeking long-term financing purchases or builds the desired building. The firm then sells the building at or near cost to a financial institution, usually a life insurance company or pension fund. Then the firm leases the building on a long-term basis. Thus, the firm has use of the building that it constructed and designed but does not have to tie up its capital in owning the building.

Most leasebacks are on a *net-net* basis, which means that the lessee pays all maintenance expenses, property taxes, insurance, and lease payment.

In some cases, the lease arrangement allows the lessee to repurchase the property at the termination of the lease. The purchase price may be based on economic conditions, for instance, an asset can be purchased at its fair market value at the end of the lease. The lease may specify a fixed price that is independent of market or other values.

# ISSUES RELATED TO LEASING DECISIONS

Many arguments may be offered for a firm to lease rather than borrow, and vice versa. Some points are valid; some are not. We may identify a number of issues that a firm might consider in evaluating the available leasing alternatives. These are discussed in the next sections.

## CASH OUTLAY

When firms purchase assets, they are normally required to make an immediate outlay of cash for a large portion of the purchase price. The balance is financed through debt, as in the case with a mortgage. With leasing, no such outlay is required. Since the asset is being leased, the leasing represents 100 percent financing. Thus, goes the argument, cash-short firms can gain assets more quickly with leasing than with buying.

The avoidance of a cash outlay may or may not be an advantage to leasing over buying. The validity of this argument depends upon the financial position of the firm. If the firm is able to borrow, it might float a bond issue and achieve 100 percent financing with the proceeds from the issue. In this case, leasing offers no advantage with respect to cash out-lay. On the other hand, if the firm is short of cash and is not able to borrow for some reason, the avoidance of the cash outlay would be a valid advantage to leasing as a financing alternative.

## HIGH COST OF LEASING

As a cost of financing, leasing generally is more costly than borrowing for several reasons:

1. *Profit for the Lessor.* The leasing company must pay for its money at rates comparable to other market rates and then must charge a premium to the lessee. This premium represents the profit to the lessor for arranging the financing.
2. *Payment for Expertise.* The leasing company must have employees who are thoroughly knowledgeable on all aspects of the equipment or real estate being leased. The cost of expert advice to help draw up the lease agreement must be included in the lease payments.
3. *Related Services.* Frequently a lease agreement includes services related to the equipment. The lessee must bear the cost of such services in the lease payments.

In spite of the general statement that leasing is more costly, the real cost of leasing versus debt financing can only be determined by an analysis of cash flows, using present-value techniques or some other measurement of cost. In some cases, the specialized knowledge of the leasing company allows a lower lease cost. For example, if the leasing company makes volume purchases of equipment, the company may be able to buy equipment at a lower price than the firm. This would allow the leasing firm to calculate its charges on a lower base than debt calculations and result in a lower cost for leasing.

## ISSUE OF PIECEMEAL FINANCING

One argument in favor of leasing is that it helps the firm avoid the high costs of *piecemeal financing,* which is the process of financing by borrowing in a series of loans or bonds. If a firm is expanding by adding relatively small amounts of fixed assets at regular intervals, the firm must locate a series of funds to finance the growth. In this situation, it has fees, commissions, and administrative costs that are relatively high compared to the dollars borrowed. Leasing, it is argued, eliminates these costs.

The validity of this argument depends upon whether a firm has choices other than expensive small borrowings. In most cases, suitable alternatives are available, such as:

1. *Draw Down a Single Large Line of Credit.* A firm could arrange for a large line of credit or revolving credit arrangement. Then it could finance each small acquisition with funds borrowed against the line. When it has used a substantial portion of the line, it could arrange long-term financing to pay back the line and provide permanent financing.

2. *Larger Long-Term Offering than Needed.* When the firm is facing a small need for funds, the firm has the option of making a large bond offering. A portion of the proceeds could be used for the initial requirement while the balance is invested in marketable securities. As later needs arise, the firm would take a portion of the funds invested in the marketable securities and use the money to finance the assets. Once the large long-term issue is exhausted, the firm could consider floating another large offering for future needs.

## EFFECT ON BORROWING CAPACITY

A firm's *borrowing capacity* may be defined as the additional long-term debt that could be added to its capital structure without seriously damaging the credit rating of the firm and the market price of its common stock. As the firm adds debt without corresponding increases in equity, borrowing capacity is reduced. Conversely, the paying off of debt tends to increase borrowing capacity.

It may be argued that leasing increases a firm's borrowing capacity. The rationale is that the lease obligation does not appear as debt on a firm's balance sheet and thus does not adversely affect the firm's debt-equity ratio. If a firm has borrowing capacity when it leases, it can still borrow after the lease is signed.

Although financial leasing imposes basically the same obligations and risks as debt financing, research indicates that investors and the financial community are more conscious of debt obligations than leasing commitments. Thus, we may conclude that, in many cases, one advantage to leasing is that it provides a firm with more assets than its borrowing capacity might otherwise allow.

**RISK OF OBSOLESCENCE**

When a firm purchases machinery, it undertakes a risk that the machinery will be obsolete before its service life is completed. If this happens, the machinery must be sold or salvaged, possibly at a considerable loss.

An argument in support of leasing is that the lease arrangement shifts to the risk of obsolescence from the user to the owner, that is, from the lessee to the lessor. If a firm owns equipment, it bears the risk. If it leases the equipment, the leasing company bears the risk.

Only rarely is this argument valid. The lessee pays for the services provided by the lessor. If risk taking is one such service, the lessee pays higher leasing payments for this service. Since leasing institutions have specialists in the kinds of equipment that they own, it is likely that they are aware of the dangers of obsolescence and will charge accordingly for bearing any risk.

**RELEASE FROM BAD INVESTMENTS**

When a firm purchases assets, an assumption is made that the assets will be profitable. In some cases the firm discovers that it has entered a business venture that is not profitable and will want to get rid of any assets used in the venture.

An argument for leasing is that it allows a firm to gain a release from assets that cannot be successfully used. If a firm purchases the asset, it undertakes the risk that the asset will not be salable and a loss might be incurred. Under a leasehold, the asset could be returned to the lessor.

This argument is based on the premise that the lease has been written so that the lessor does not cover his investment during the lease period. This is usually not the case. Long-term financial leases are designed so that virtually all the lessor's investment is recovered during the lease period. Should this not be the case, the argument could be valid.

**FREEDOM OF FUNDS FOR MORE PROFITABLE USES**

Some analysts have argued that a distinction should be made between the return on current and fixed assets. Current assets turn over rapidly and bring in a fairly high return each time, for example, inventory is sold. Fixed assets, on the other hand, generate only a limited return because firms have low turnovers compared to the size of their asset base.

An argument for leasing is that it frees funds from financing fixed assets, which have a low turnover, to invest the funds in current assets, which have a high turnover. This is a way to maximize the use of funds to increase a firm's overall profits.

This claimed advantage of leasing is completely invalid. To conduct its business, a firm needs a mix of assets, both current and fixed. Since all the assets are required, it is fallacious to say that some assets earn more than others. If leasing expands borrowing capacity, the firm will realize higher profits. But the freeing of funds to invest in current assets with a higher turnover is incorrect.

## LEASING FORMS

The financial lease is available in two basic forms:

1. *Straight Lease.* This type of lease obligates the firm to pay rental over the expected service life of the asset. No provision is made for any modifications to the basic lease conditions.
2. *Modified Lease.* This type of lease provides several possible options to the lessee during the lease period. As an example, the lease contract may allow the lessee to terminate the lease by returning the asset after some stipulated date. Other options could be permitted.

In this section, we will examine three lease forms: one straight lease and two forms of modified leases.

### LEVEL-RENTAL PLAN

The *level-rental plan* is a straight lease that obligates a firm to make a series of identical payments over the service life of the asset. As an example of this form of lease, consider a lease agreement on a machine costing $100,000. The leasing firm finances the asset under a level-rental plan to yield 10 percent over a 5-year lease period. The amount of the annual payment is solved with the annuity formula or calculator:

$$\text{PMT} = \frac{\text{PV} \times \text{int}}{1 - 1/(1 + \text{int})^n}$$

$$\text{PMT} = \frac{100,000 \times .10}{1 - 1/(1.10)^5} = 26,380$$

or

| n | i | PV | PMT |
|:---:|:---:|:---:|:---:|
| 5 | 10 | 100,000 | [26,380] |

Under this lease agreement, the lessee would have use of the asset for 5 years for an annual payment of $26,380.

## OPTION TO TERMINATE

The *option-to-terminate plan* allows the lessee to gain a release from the lease agreement prior to its expiration date. In return for this option, the rental payments may be affected in either or both of the following ways:

1.  *Increase in Total Rental.* The total amount of renting the asset may be increased as a cost of providing an option to terminate. The extra income from a number of leases helps the lessor make up losses when a percentage of the lessees exercise the option to terminate.
2.  *Acceleration of Payments.* The lease agreement may provide for larger payments in the early years of the lease, which represents an acceleration of cash inflows for the lessor. Receiving more money earlier provides extra income for reinvestment by the lessor. The larger early receipts also help to compensate the lessor for the rapid decrease in the market value of the assets during the first years of service life, if the asset is returned under the termination option.

## OPTION TO PURCHASE

The *option-to-purchase plan* gives the lessee the right to purchase the asset at a declining price after each year of the lease period. It is frequently offered as a joint feature with the level-rental or option-to-terminate forms. In most cases, the rental payments are neither increased nor accelerated. Instead, the option's cost is realized when the lessee exercises it. The longer the lessee waits before exercising the option, the greater the total cash outlay for the asset, because the optional purchase price decreases at a slower rate than the rentals accumulate. An example of an option-to-purchase plan is given in Table 18–1.

**TABLE 18–1.**   Option-to-Purchase Lease Form—$100,000, 5-year, 10% Level-Rental Agreement with Option to Purchase.

| Year | Purchase Price as % of Original Cost | Purchase Price $ | Cumulative Level-Rental Payments $ | Total Capital if Option Is Exercised $ |
|------|------|------|------|------|
| 1 | 85 | 85,000 | 26,380 | 111,380 |
| 2 | 68 | 68,000 | 52,760 | 120,760 |
| 3 | 52 | 52,000 | 79,140 | 131,140 |
| 4 | 36 | 36,000 | 105,520 | 141,520 |
| 5 | 20 | 20,000 | 131,900 | 151,900 |

## INSTALLMENT FINANCING

To make a lease-buy decision correctly, the firm must compare the leasing with purchase alternatives. We have already covered loans for project financing. In this section, we will examine *installment financing,* which occurs when the manufacturer or financial institution lends money to purchase specific items of machinery.

### CHARACTERISTICS OF INSTALLMENT FINANCING

When purchasing a specific piece of machinery on credit supplied by the manufacturer or a bank, the following characteristics will generally apply to the arrangement:

1. *Down Payment Is Required.* The banks, finance companies, or other institutions require the borrower to pay some portion of the purchase price in advance. This is commonly called a *down payment.*
2. *Assets Are Collateral.* The specific assets financed by the loan are pledged to secure the debt. In the event of liquidation, the creditor may take the assets and sell them to compensate for a failure to pay the loan. The creditor has first claim on the proceeds from the sale of the assets compared to the claims of bondholders or other creditors.
3. *Installment Payments Are Made.* The schedule for the repayment of the loan is established so that interest and a portion of the principal are paid in a series of payments.

4. *Assets and Debt Recognized on Firm's Books.* Unlike leasing alternatives, the total cost of the assets is included in the fixed assets reported on the firm's balance sheet. The debt created by the financing is shown in the liabilities section as part of the firm's capital structure.

5. *Assets Possessed by Owner.* During the financing period, the borrower has possession, though not necessarily title, to the assets. Once the final payment is made, the borrower gains the title if it were not transferred at some earlier time.

## STEADY-PRINCIPAL-REDUCTION SCHEDULE

The *steady-principal-reduction method* of repaying a loan requires a payment that reduces the principal in equal amounts during each period. The interest is also paid with each payment. Since interest is calculated on the outstanding balance each period, the interest declines as the principal is paid off. Thus, installment payments decrease each year. Table 18–2 shows a repayment schedule for a $1.3 million machine with steady principal reduction over 5 years. Three hundred thousand dollars is put down and the balance is financed at prime plus 2. The schedule assumes a prime rate of 14 percent. The actual payments would vary each year as the prime rate varied.

## STEADY-PAYMENT SCHEDULE

The second form of long-term installment financing involves a *steady-payment* method of paying principal and interest. We have already discussed this method under long-term financing. The firm borrows money and makes a series of periodic payments of equal amounts (annuities). We

**TABLE 18–2.** Steady Principal Reduction Schedule ($1.3 million asset, prime plus 2 rate, 5-year repayment, $300,000 down payment, with assumed prime of 14 percent).

| Year | Annual Interest | Annual Principal | Total Payment |
|------|-----------------|------------------|---------------|
| 0    |                 | $300,000         | $300,000      |
| 1    | $160,000        | 200,000          | 360,000       |
| 2    | 128,000         | 200,000          | 328,000       |
| 3    | 96,000          | 200,000          | 296,000       |
| 4    | 64,000          | 200,000          | 264,000       |
| 5    | 32,000          | 200,000          | 232,000       |

might note at this point that the term *steady payment* is somewhat misleading for two reasons:

1. *Variable-Rate Interest.* Because most loans are made with interest charges that vary with the prime rate or some other indicator, the payments are not identical. If interest rates do not fluctuate greatly, payments are relatively steady. With widely fluctuating rates, they vary significantly.
2. *Balloon Payments.* Since many loans are for a short period while the service life of a machine is much longer, increasingly we are seeing balloon payments at the end of installment purchases. Even though the dollar amount of the periodic payment may be "steady," the balloon payment at the end is not.

An example of an installment loan with a steady-payment schedule is given in Table 18–3. After putting $300,000 down, the firm finances $1 million at prime plus 2 for 5 years. If the prime rate were to be 14 percent during the loan period, the steady payment would be $305,409.

## CONDITIONAL SALES CONTRACT

One of the most common secured financing forms is the *conditional sales contract*. Under this method, the firm purchasing the equipment is required to make a 20 to 30 percent down payment. The purchaser signs a

**TABLE 18–3.**    Steady-Payment Schedule (Same Data as Table 18–2).

| Year | Annual Interest | Annual Principal | Annual Payment |
|---|---|---|---|
| 0 | | $300,000 | $300,000 |
| 1 | $160,000 | 145,409 | 305,409* |
| 2 | 136,735 | 168,674 | 305,409 |
| 3 | 109,747 | 195,662 | 305,409 |
| 4 | 78,441 | 226,968 | 305,409 |
| 5 | 42,126 | 263,283 | 305,409 |

*Payment is calculated from formula:

$$\text{PMT} = \frac{1,000,000 \times .16}{1 - 1/(1.16)^5} = 305,409$$

or n = 5
  i = 16
 PV = 1,000,000
 PMT = 305,409

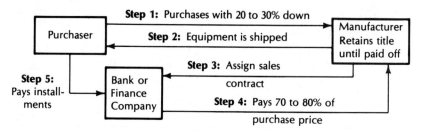

**Figure 18–1**  Conditional Sales Contract.

sales contract that allows the manufacturer to retain the title to the assets until all payments are made. After shipping the equipment, the manufacturer assigns the sales contract to a bank or finance company in return for the remaining 70 to 80 percent of the purchase price. The purchaser makes periodic payments to the financing institution. When all installment payments have been made, the finance company notifies the manufacturer to transfer the title for the equipment to the purchaser.

A purchase under a conditional sales contract is diagrammed in Figure 18–1.

The conditional sales contract can be written with a steady principal reduction or steady-payment method of financing. Balloon payments are also possible. From a lender's point of view, the agreement must be written so that the outstanding debt is less than the net resale value of the assets if repossession were necessary as a result of a default.

### CHATTEL MORTGAGE

A *chattel mortgage* is used less frequently to finance fixed assets than is the conditional sales contract. The chattel mortgage is similar to the conditional sales contract with only two important distinctions:

1.  *Immediate Transfer of Title.* The title to the fixed assets is transferred from the manufacturer to the purchaser when the equipment is sold. With the conditional sales contract, the title is held by the manufacturer until after the last installment payment is received.
2.  *All Money Flows through Financing Institution.* The bank or finance company is involved in all flows of money. The purchaser gives the down payment to the bank and the bank sends the full pur-

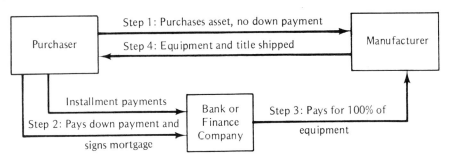

**Figure 18–2**   Chattel Mortgage.

chase price to the manufacturer. An example of a chattel mortgage is shown in Figure 18–2.

## FACTORS IN LEASE-BUY DECISIONS

The decision to lease or buy an asset can only be made after a specific financial analysis that weighs the merits of each choice. In some cases it is advantageous to lease; in others a purchase alternative is less costly. In this section, we will analyze the key factors determining the cost of owning versus the cost of leasing. In the next section, we will develop a process for making the lease-buy decision.

### CASH-FLOW BASIS

The lease-buy comparison correctly uses cash outlays and inflows as a basis for decision making. The accounting effect with respect to earnings per share would be utilized only in cases when the market price of the firm's stock may be adversely affected by leasing the assets. In this case, both a cash-flow analysis and a future-earnings-per-share analysis should be used.

### AFTERTAX CALCULATIONS

The full amount of the lease payments will be deductible for income tax purposes as operating expenses of the firm. If the firm purchases the assets, the interest portion of the borrowing is deductible, but the principal repayment is not. Since the tax payments are directly related to the lease-buy decision and affect the cash-flow stream, all calculations should be made on an aftertax basis.

## OMITTING THE OPERATING COSTS

In a lease-buy decision, it is tempting to include the costs from operating the machine to be financed. This is incorrect. Since we are performing an analysis of marginal costs, we should omit those costs incurred no matter how the asset is financed. Whether we lease or buy, we incur the same operating costs. Thus, they should be omitted from the analysis.

In some cases, a portion of the operating costs must be included in the leasing calculations. This occurs when a service lease covers some of the maintenance or other costs as part of the lease payment. In this case, the estimated costs that are included must be deducted from the amount of the lease payment. As an example, suppose a service lease for $500 a month included $40 worth of maintenance. The real lease cost is $500 minus $40, or $460, and this should be used in the analysis.

## CASH RESIDUAL VALUE

When a firm purchases an asset, it has full rights to the value of the asset at the end of any given period. In the case of assets with large ending cash values, such as real estate or certain kinds of machinery, the cash value affects the cost of purchasing versus leasing. For these fixed assets, the service life is usually much longer than the lease period, and ending cash value is an important consideration.

## COMPARING PRESENT VALUES

Once cash-flow streams have been developed for each alternative, the streams must be compared. This is not a simple matter. In lease-buy comparisons, frequently one alternative is more beneficial in the early years, whereas the other proves to be cheaper in the later years. What is the common denominator to make the comparison?

The answer is that the present value of each alternative is compared. The future streams are discounted to a present value, using the appropriate time value of money. Two time values of money are used in a lease-buy analysis:

1. *Riskless Rate of Return.* This is the firm's required rate of return on assets with no risk of default, such as the return on U.S. or Canadian treasury securities. In choosing between a lease payment

or loan payment, there is no risk to the firm. It should always choose the less expensive financing alternative. Therefore, any benefits from lower cost financing should be computed at a riskless rate of return.

2. *Required Return on Projects.* This is the firm's required return on capital investment projects, such as the one that will employ the asset. This rate is used on the residual value of the asset, if such value is lost under the leasing plan. Under an ownership situation, the firm makes payments for a number of years and eventually owns the asset. This is a benefit to owning. If ownership is not contractually conveyed in the lease agreement, the residual value must be included as a benefit in the owning stream. But will the asset really have the forecast value? This is a business risk, and the required return on projects should be used when discounting this value to the present.

## BENEFITS OF DEPRECIATION

A firm's noncash expenses offer a tax shield on income and reduce the amount of tax paid. In a lease-buy decision, the most important noncash expense is the depreciation on equipment. *Depreciation* is an accounting device that allows a firm to charge off a portion of the original cost of equipment as an expense each year over the service life of the equipment. The depreciation appears as an expense (but does not involve any cash) on the firm's income statement. Since expenses reduce reported profits, they also reduce taxable income.

Since depreciation acts as a tax shield and allows the firm to keep cash that would otherwise flow out to the Internal Revenue Service, depreciation increases the firm's cash flow. This effect was shown in Table 12–2.

The law allows a firm to use a number of methods of depreciating assets. The most widely used is the *accelerated cost recovery system* (ACRS) instituted in the Economic Recovery Tax Act of 1981. Equipment is written off in 3-, 5-, 10-, or 15-year periods, as specified in the law. Most machinery and equipment, with the exception of vehicles, railroad tank cars, public utility property, and selected other items, can be written off over 5 years. The annual depreciation percentages were phased in by the 1981 tax act over a period of 5 years. The rates were changed in 1982. Rather than be concerned with continued changes, we will use the rates shown in Table 18–5. The rates in this table reflect *accelerated depreciation*, a more rapid writeoff of the assets than would be expected by the service life. The use of accelerated depreciation increases the noncash expenses and

**TABLE 18–5.**   Accelerated Cost Recovery Percentages for Equipment and Machinery Qualifying for 5-Year Writeoff.

| Year of Ownership | Depreciation Percentage Each Year |
|:-:|:-:|
| 1 | 20% |
| 2 | 32 |
| 3 | 24 |
| 4 | 16 |
| 5 | 8 |

therefore defers the payment of certain taxes until a future date. The effect when purchasing equipment as compared to leasing is:

1. *Cash Flow Is Speeded Up.* By reducing taxes in the early years of an asset's service life, accelerated depreciation methods speed up cash flow during early years and make more cash available to the firm.
2. *Financing Cost Is Lowered.* The more rapid inflows can be viewed as a benefit to reduce the financing cost. The tax benefits increase the rate of return from using the asset and higher return is an advantage to ownership as compared to leasing.

In examining the effects of depreciation, the analyst must check to see who is actually receiving the tax benefits. In 1981–1982, it was possible for the lessor and lessee to agree to allow the lessee to be treated as the owner of the property for tax purposes. Thus, the depreciation effects must be examined to see if any incremental impact will affect the analysis.

## INVESTMENT TAX CREDITS

For the purchase of certain assets, the law allows the owner to take an *investment tax credit (ITC)* against the firm's federal income taxes. This is a right to reduce taxes by the amount of the credit without affecting the schedule of depreciation on the asset or any other financial aspect of the structure. The credit is designed to encourage firms to invest in capital assets, thus expanding the level of economic activity. In 1981–1982, the credit could have been assigned to either the lessee or lessor. This depended upon which party has sufficient tax liabilities to make use of the ITC. As an example, if a firm has a $200,000 federal tax obligation and a

$1 million ITC, $800,000 of the tax credit is unused that year. In this case, the other party to the lease agreement would probably take the tax credit.

Under the 1981 law, the investment tax credit is 6 percent for qualified assets depreciated over 3 years and 10 percent for all other qualified assets. This was modified in 1982. Rather than become involved with the mechanics of calculating the ITC, the problems in this chapter will assume a 10 percent ITC.

## RECAPTURE

The term *recapture* refers to the paying back to the government of tax benefits from depreciation or the investment tax credit when the firm disposes of the asset. It occurs in two situations:

1. *Excess of Cash Selling Price over Book Value.* If the asset is sold for more than its book value, we have a depreciation recapture. Usually, the excess becomes ordinary income in the year the asset is sold and is taxed at the firm's regular tax rate.
2. *ITC Repayment for Early Sale.* If an asset is sold within 5 years after it is placed in service, a portion of the tax benefits from the investment tax credit may have to be returned to the government. This is an ITC recapture.

# COMPARING LEASING VERSUS BUYING

To calculate the cost of leasing with the cost of buying, we prepare separate aftertax cash-flow streams for each financing alternative. Then we discount the streams to a present value, which is, in effect, the real cost of the asset. The preferred financing method is the one that produces the lowest present value or real cost of the asset. This process is demonstrated in this section.

## DATA FOR A SAMPLE PROBLEM

To illustrate the lease-buy calculations, let us examine a firm that desires to acquire the services of a machine that costs $3.2 million. It can be purchased with financing requiring a 20 percent down payment and 20 semiannual payments, using the steady-payment method. The interest charges are fixed at 16 percent compounded semiannually. The owner of the machine can claim an investment tax credit of 10 percent of the purchase price. Half of the tax credit can be claimed immediately, and the other half can be claimed in the first year of operation. At the end of 10 years, the machine will have a net cash value of $600,000. The firm will use a 5-year depreciation schedule in Table 18–5.

An alternative financing would be to lease the machinery with no initial payments but semiannual payments of $300,000 for 10 years. If this were done, the leasing company would take the tax benefits from depreciation and the investment tax credit. The firm uses 9 percent as the riskless discount factor and 20 percent as the factor for discounting future residual values of assets. Should the firm lease or buy?

## Step 1. Calculate the Loan Payment

The firm will finance 80 percent of $3.2 million, or $2,560,000, for 10 years with semiannual payments at 16 percent annually. The loan payment each 6 months will be $260,742:

$$PMT = \frac{2,560,000 \times .08}{1 - 1/(1.08)^{20}} = 260,742$$

or

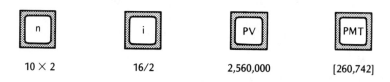

| n | i | PV | PMT |
|:---:|:---:|:---:|:---:|
| 10 × 2 | 16/2 | 2,560,000 | [260,742] |

## Step 2. Calculate ITC and Depreciation Schedule

The investment tax credit is 10 percent of $3.2 million, or $320,000; $160,000 is taken immediately and $160,000 is taken in the first year.

The depreciation schedule down to a book value of 0 is as follows:

| Year | Book Value | Percent | Annual Depreciation |
|:---:|:---:|:---:|:---:|
| 0 | $3,200,000 | 0 | $        0 |
| 1 | 3,200,000 | 20 | 640,000 |
| 2 | 2,560,000 | 32 | 1,024,000 |
| 3 | 1,536,000 | 24 | 768,000 |
| 4 | 768,000 | 16 | 512,000 |
| 5 | 256,000 | 8 | 256,000 |

Note that the applicable percentages are taken of $3.2 million in each case. Also note that the ending residual value of the asset is ignored. If the asset is eventually sold for more than its book value, depreciation recapture occurs.

### Step 3. Determine Aftertax Residual Value

In 10 years, the machine will have a cash value of $600,000. Since it will be fully depreciated in 5 years, the book value in 10 years will be 0. The firm will have a gain of $600,000 and, at a 40 percent tax rate, would pay taxes of $240,000 (600,000 × .40). The aftertax residual value would be:

| | |
|---|---|
| Cash from the sale of the asset | $600,000 |
| Less taxes (600,000 × .40) | − 240,000 |
| Residual value | 360,000 |

### Step 4. Develop an Amortization Schedule

In order to develop eventually a cash-flow stream on an aftertax basis, we must separate each loan payment into a principal and interest component. For our first payment of $260,742, we will have interest at 8 percent on the principal of $2,560,000, or

$$2,560,000 \times .08 = 204,800$$

The remaining $55,942 (260,742 − 204,800) will be used to reduce the outstanding principal. For the second payment, we calculate the new level of interest and the principal reduction. Using the computer terminal to do this for 20 payments, we get the amortization schedule shown in Table 18–6.

### Step 5. Calculate Aftertax Stream for Owning

The aftertax cost of owning is calculated for each year by the formula:

$$- \frac{\text{loan}}{\text{payment}} + \frac{\text{tax}}{\text{savings}} = \frac{\text{aftertax}}{\text{owning cost}}$$

This formula recognizes that any tax shields in the stream help reduce the cost of owning. To get the tax savings, we add together the major tax shields that result from purchasing the asset and multiply them by the

**TABLE 18–6.**   Amortization Schedule for 16 Percent Loan, 20 Semiannual Payments.

| Year | Semiannual Payment | Interest | Principal Reduction | Remaining Principal |
|------|------|------|------|------|
| 0 | | | | $2,560,000 |
| 1 | $260,742 | $204,800 | $ 55,942 | 2,504,058 |
| 2 | 260,742 | 200,325 | 60,417 | 2,443,641 |
| 3 | 260,742 | 195,491 | 65,251 | 2,378,391 |
| 4 | 260,742 | 190,271 | 70,471 | 2,307,921 |
| 5 | 260,742 | 184,634 | 76,108 | 2,231,813 |
| 6 | 260,742 | 178,545 | 82,197 | 2,149,616 |
| 7 | 260,742 | 171,969 | 88,773 | 2,060,844 |
| 8 | 260,742 | 164,867 | 95,875 | 1,964,970 |
| 9 | 260,742 | 157,198 | 103,544 | 1,861,425 |
| 10 | 260,742 | 148,914 | 111,828 | 1,749,598 |
| 11 | 260,742 | 139,968 | 120,774 | 1,628,824 |
| 12 | 260,742 | 130,306 | 130,436 | 1,498,388 |
| 13 | 260,742 | 119,871 | 140,871 | 1,357,518 |
| 14 | 260,742 | 108,601 | 152,141 | 1,205,377 |
| 15 | 260,742 | 96,430 | 164,313 | 1,041,066 |
| 16 | 260,742 | 83,285 | 177,457 | 863,610 |
| 17 | 260,742 | 69,089 | 191,653 | 671,957 |
| 18 | 260,742 | 53,757 | 206,985 | 464,972 |
| 19 | 260,742 | 37,198 | 223,544 | 241,428 |
| 20 | 260,742 | 19,314 | 241,428 | 0 |

tax rate. In our example, the tax shields are the depreciation and interest. When the firm incurs these expenses each year, it reduces its taxes. Thus, the cost of owning is less because of the tax effects of depreciation and interest. This is not true with the repayment of the principal on the loan since the principal is not tax deductible.

In our problem, the first-year depreciation is $640,000 and first-year interest is $405,125 (204,800 + 200,325). At a 40 percent tax rate, these items produce a tax savings of $418,050. The loan payment is $521,484. Thus, the first year aftertax cost of owning is $103,434 (521,484 − 418,050). Using our computer once again, we get the full stream in Table 18–7.

### Step 6. Determine Present Value Cost of Owning

Once we have the cash-flow stream, we can determine its present value by discounting all inflows or outlays at an appropriate rate. The financing

**TABLE 18–7.**   Aftertax Cost of Owning in Sample Problem.

| Year | $-$ | Loan Payment | $+$ | (Depreciation | $+$ | Interest) | $\left(\dfrac{Tax}{Rate}\right)$ | $=$ | Aftertax Owning Cost |
|---|---|---|---|---|---|---|---|---|---|
| 0 | | | | | | | | | $ - 640,000* |
| 0 | | | | | | | | | + 160,000** |
| 1 | | | | | | | | | + 160,000** |
| 1 | $ | − 521,484 | + | (640,000 | + | $405,125) | (.40) | = | − 103,434 |
| 2 | | − 521,484 | + | (1,024,000 | + | 385,762) | (.40) | = | + 42,421 |
| 3 | | − 521,484 | + | (768,000 | + | 363,179) | (.40) | = | − 69,012 |
| 4 | | − 521,484 | + | (512,000 | + | 336,836) | (.40) | = | − 181,950 |
| 5 | | − 521,484 | + | (256,000 | + | 306,112) | (.40) | = | − 296,639 |
| 6 | | − 521,484 | + | (0 | + | 270,274) | (.40) | = | − 413,375 |
| 7 | | − 521,484 | + | (0 | + | 228,472) | (.40) | = | − 430,095 |
| 8 | | − 521,484 | + | (0 | + | 179,715) | (.40) | = | − 449,598 |
| 9 | | − 521,484 | + | (0 | + | 122,846) | (.40) | = | − 472,346 |
| 10 | | − 521,484 | + | (0 | + | 56,512) | (.40) | = | − 498,879 |
| 10 | | | | | | | | | + 360,000*** |

*indicates a down payment.
**indicates an investment tax credit.
***indicates aftertax residual value.
− equals cash outflow.

charges are discounted at a low risk rate, namely, the 9 percent riskless factor. The residual value is discounted at the firm's required rate of return; in our example, this is 20 percent. The present value of the financing stream, considering the benefits of tax shields and a residual value, is the real cost of owning the asset. In our example, it is a $1,844,851 aftertax cost of owning, as shown in Table 18–8.

**Step 7. Determine Annual Aftertax Lease Payment**

After completing the owning cost, we are ready to determine the cost of leasing. The entire lease payment is tax deductible. This means that the aftertax cost of leasing can be determined by the formula:

$$\dfrac{\text{aftertax cost}}{\text{of leasing}} = \dfrac{\text{beforetax}}{\text{lease payment}} \times (1 - \text{tax rate})$$

In our example, we have semiannual payments of $300,000 for 10 years (20 payments). The aftertax lease payment is the same each year and is $180,000 with a 40 percent tax rate:

$$300,000 \times (1 - .40) = \$180,000$$

**TABLE 18–8.**   Calculating the Present Value Cost of Owning.

| Year | Aftertax Owning cost | Present Value at 9% (Residual at 20%) |
|---|---|---|
| 0 | − 640,000* | $ − 640,000 |
| 0 | + 160,000** | + 160,000 |
| 1 | + 160,000** | + 146,789 |
| 1 | − 103,434 | − 94,894 |
| 2 | + 42,421 | + 35,705 |
| 3 | − 69,012 | − 53,290 |
| 4 | − 181,950 | − 128,898 |
| 5 | − 296,639 | − 192,795 |
| 6 | − 413,375 | − 246,482 |
| 7 | − 430,095 | − 235,277 |
| 8 | − 449,598 | − 225,638 |
| 9 | − 472,346 | − 217,481 |
| 10 | − 498,879 | − 210,732 |
| 10 | + 360,000*** | + 58,142 |
| Present value cost of owning | | − 1,844,851 |

*down payment.
**investment tax credit.
***aftertax residual value.
− equals cash outflow.

## Step 8. Determine Present Value Cost of Leasing

This is simply a matter of discounting the aftertax lease stream by the low-cost discount factor. The present value of lease payments is $2,341,429, using the formula:

$$PV = PMT \left[\frac{1}{int}\right] \left[1 - \frac{1}{(1 + int)^n}\right]$$

$$PV = 180,000 \left[\frac{1}{.045}\right] \left[1 - \frac{1}{(1.045)^{20}}\right] = 2,341,429$$

or

| n | i | PMT | PV |
|---|---|---|---|
| 20 | 4.5 | 180,000 | [2,341,429] |

### Step 9. Compare Choices

The firm can own the machine for $1,844,851 for 10 years or lease it for 10 years for a present value cost of $2,341,429. The purchase alternative is less costly than the leasing alternative and should be accepted by the company.

The comparison of lease versus purchase alternatives requires a detailed evaluation of the payments, tax benefits, and time-value considerations in each choice. In most companies, these routines are stored in the computer or are performed with the aid of memory calculators. The analyst must ensure that the routine is current with respect to depreciation and tax calculations. By following the process in this chapter and comparing the answer with the computer solution, the analyst can determine whether the computer formulas are correctly developed and applied.

### KEY TERMS

| | | |
|---|---|---|
| accelerated cost recovery system | investment tax credit | operating lease |
| accelerated depreciation | lease | piecemeal financing |
| balloon payments | leasing | sale and lease agreement |
| borrowing capacity | lessee | service lease |
| chattel mortgage | lessor | steady payment |
| conditional sales contract | modified lease | steady-principal-reduction method |
| depreciation | net-net basis | straight lease |
| financial lease | option-to-purchase plan | variable-rate interest |
| installment financing | option-to-terminate plan | |

### STUDY QUESTIONS

1. What are the three basic types of leases and how do they differ?
2. What does fully amortizing mean? What types of leases are fully amortizing?
3. Who provides the bulk of funds for leasing fixed assets?
4. Why is leasing generally more costly than borrowing to buy a fixed asset?
5. How can a firm avoid the high cost of piecemeal financing?
6. Does leasing increase a firm's borrowing capacity?
7. Does leasing offer a release from bad investments? a protection against obsolescence? a freeing of funds for more profitable uses?

8. Why is the matter of cash residual value important in lease-buy decisions?
9. What is a level rental plan form of lease? How is the lease payment calculated with it?
10. How does the lessor compensate for allowing an option to terminate clause to be included in the lease agreement?
11. How does the lessor compensate for allowing an option to purchase clause to be included in the lease agreement?
12. What are some charactistics of fixed asset financing?
13. What is the difference between a steady principal reduction and steady-payment loan? With which does a balloon payment occur?
14. What are conditional sales contracts and chattel mortgages? How do they differ?
15. What discount factor is used in discounting lease-buy streams?
16. What is an investment tax credit?
17. What is meant by recapture?

## Problems

1. A firm has $14 million in debt and $23 million in equity. The firm can continue borrowing until its debt-asset ratio reaches 50 percent. What is the firm's unused borrowing capacity?
2. A level-rental lease requires a $45,000 lease payment annually for 7 years on an asset valued at $172,000. What is the effective interest rate implied in this lease?
3. A firm wishes to finance a $2 million piece of machinery. It can put $200,000 down and pay the balance using a steady principal reduction schedule over a period of 6 years. What is the payment stream if the interest rate is 14.5 percent?
4. A firm can purchase a crane for $750,000, with one-third down. The balance will be financed with a 2-year loan and 5-year payout at 19 percent, compounded and paid quarterly. What is the amount of the quarterly payment? the balloon payment?
5. A firm can take a 10 percent investment tax credit on $600,000 of printing presses that it purchased. The presses can be depreciated over 5 years at 20/32/24/16/8 to a book value of 0. Calculate the ITC and depreciation schedule.
6. In 7 years, a machine will have a cash value of $1.4 million and a book value of 0. The firm pays taxes at a 40 percent rate. What is the aftertax residual value on this machine?
7. A firm has a 3-year loan with semiannual payments at 15 percent, compounded semiannually. The loan amount is $800,000. Prepare an amortization schedule for the loan.
8. A firm makes a $350,000 down payment on a machine. It receives a $125,000 investment tax credit, half at delivery and half one year later. It makes annual payments of $280,000 for 5 years. Its depreciation and interest are:

| Year | Depreciation | Interest |
|------|-------------|----------|
| 1 | 180,000 | 148,500 |
| 2 | 288,000 | 120,000 |
| 3 | 216,000 | 109,000 |
| 4 | 144,000 | 78,000 |
| 5 | 72,000 | 46,000 |

At the end of 5 years, it sells the machine for $200,000. The firm's tax rate is 40 percent. Prepare the stream for the aftertax cost of owning.

9. A firm discounts its payments at 11 percent and residual values at 19 percent. It has the following stream for the aftertax cost of owning. What is the present value cost of owning?

| Year | Aftertax Cost of Owning |
|------|-------------------------|
| 0 | − 300,000 |
| 0 | +  40,000 |
| 1 | − 120,000 |
| 2 | − 140,000 |
| 3 | − 150,000 |
| 4 | − 175,000 |
| 4 | +  80,000 (residual value) |

# Lease-Buy Decision

*This case requires the reader to analyze leasing and purchasing alternatives by using the techniques in the chapter to develop cash-flow streams for each alternative.*

Levine Shoes Inc. is the owner and operator of a chain of discount shoe stores in the New York–New Jersey metropolitan area. From its headquarters in Garden City, Long Island, the company coordinates the purchases of large lots of name brand shoes that have recently been discontinued by the manufacturer. Jacob Levine founded the company in 1947 with his first shoe store selling traditional lines of shoes. He soon realized a large potential market when manufacturers and large shoe chains seek to unload merchandise that was not in fashion or was left over from a selling season. He converted his store to a discount operation, where he achieved a high volume per square foot of space and per sales person. From that modest start, the business had grown to 6 stores by 1970. During the 1970s, the discount shoe industry emerged fully and Jacob's son pushed the firm aggressively to expand. By the 1980s, the company owned 47 stores and a 100,000-square-foot main warehouse in Hoboken, New Jersey. From Hoboken, the company supplied Levine's own stores as well as the stores of other companies. Every day, thousands of discontinued or otherwise discarded shoes arrived at the warehouse to be transported within a few days to waiting retail stores.

In order to supply shoes to area stores, Levine Shoes used a commercial freight company. The arrangement worked fine in the 1970s but was creating a number of problems in the mid-1980s. Since the deregulation of the trucking industry, a number of marginal truck operators had struggled with inadequate capital and vehicles. Levine had experienced problems with the reliability of deliveries, a factor that upset the sales forecasts in the past 2 years. At a recent meeting of the board of directors, Amos Levine was directed to study the feasibility of the company operating its own fleet of vehicles. Amos was pleased to accept the challenge. After a cursory examination, he decided that the company should operate its own truck fleet and he then developed the numbers to prove his point. The board of directors reviewed his numbers and was in agreement. The decision had been made.

Amos was working on another problem. Should the firm purchase or lease the trucks? Amos determined that 10 medium-sized delivery trucks would be appropriate for handling the distribution of shoes from the warehouse. For the purchase choices, Amos requested competitive bids. The lowest offer came from Secaucus Motor Sales in New Jersey, which would provide 10 trucks for $750,000, including taxes, freight, and preparation. General Electric Financing would provide installment financing for 80 percent of the purchase price. The secured loan would be for 3 years with a 7-year payout and would require annual payments under a steady-payment plan. The annual interest rate would be 13 percent, not including the effects of a $3,000 approval fee to be paid upon signing for the loan. General Electric Financing would retain title to the vehicles until all funds were received under the agreement.

Amos thought the pricing on the General Electric loan was quite competitive. The trucks would have more than a 7-year service life; they would probably be worth $15,000 each in 7 years. Nor was there a real problem with the 3-year period of the loan. At the end of 3 years, the trucks would still be worth about $50,000 each. This was plenty of money so that they could be refinanced at that time.

As an alternative, Exxon Financial was willing to arrange a lease on all 10 trucks. Exxon requires annual payments of $175,000 for 7 years but was willing to go the full period for the lease. The lease was also attractive because it included some maintenance services and insurance that would otherwise cost the firm about $15,000 per year. This was a special deal being offered as a combined deal between Exxon and Mack Trucks.

If the lease arrangement were made, Levine Shoes would lose the tax benefits from the investment tax credit, which would be 5 percent upon purchase and another 5 percent in the first year of operation. Similarly, the tax benefits from depreciation would pass on to Exxon. As medium duty trucks, the 5-year schedule would apply:

| Year | Depreciation Rate |
|------|-------------------|
| 1 | 20% |
| 2 | 32 |
| 3 | 24 |
| 4 | 16 |
| 5 | 8 |

With the lease, Levine would also lose the residual value at the end of 7 years. Exxon's lease contained a clause that the "lessee had the option to purchase the trucks at the fair market value at the end of the lease period."

To compare the lease and purchase alternatives, Amos would use some financial norms for the company. Levine always assumed the low-risk rate of return to be 6 percent after taxes. The required return on projects was 11 percent after taxes. A 40 percent marginal tax rate would apply. With these guidelines, Amos was ready to begin working.

As Amos was sitting down to work out some numbers, he got a call from Steve Monteleone in the company's accounting department. Steve said, "Amos, I know finance is your area but I thought I'd let you in on something that I have discovered. I have been going over this bid from Secaucus and I remembered this shorthand calculation for finding the effective cost of a lease. I had it in college. I applied the formula to the lease arrangement and discovered the effective cost to be 20 percent. Seems to me, we should purchase rather than lease. Anyway, I just thought I might save you some time and trouble."

Amos thought for a moment and then said, "Thanks a lot, Steve. I'll remember your number. But let me run out the cash-flow streams anyway, just to be sure. I'll let you know what I learn."

### Required

Which alternative is more advantageous to the company?

# Lease-Buy Decision

*This case tests the reader's understanding of leases. It requires the reader to compare two different lease agreements, to determine if the lease payments are acceptable and if there is any room to bargain.*

Martin Saunders has always been concerned about his image. This is reflected in the success of his Benning Hotel chain, a collection of 11 hotels and motels located along the interstate highway system in Texas. Even though he only holds 5 percent of the common stock, his management style deserves much of the credit for the firm's rapid growth of profits and cash flow. With gross revenues approaching $12 million this year and $1.7 million in profits, the company is proving to be a wonderful investment for its 7 shareholders.

But first things come first. Marty could hardly be concerned about business this morning. Last night, when the board authorized a new car for President Saunders, Marty knew that his time had come. He must make a decision—which car would it be? He was leaning towards the 4-year-old Rolls Royce offered by Luxury Motors in Dallas. While $150,000 may seem like a lot of money for a "used car," Marty knew that the board was rewarding his efforts. And, as a company car, it could be used to escort key clients who were considering holding business and other meetings in some of the Benning locations. This would be particularly helpful since next year's plans included an expansion into conference centers in the Houston and San Antonio areas.

With respect to the car, Marty had two dilemmas. First, the same dealer also had a new Rolls for $110,000. It was not the same model and had nowhere near the prestige and features. But it was classy and would do the job. The second problem was that he could buy or lease either vehicle. The dealer offered to lease the $150,000 car for 36 months at $3,000 per month lease cost. Or, the $110,000 car could be leased for the same period for $2,400 per month. In each case, Benning Hotels would be signing a financial lease with monthly payments in arrears.

Just before noon, Marty decided that leasing was the better alternative. He had some concern about the psychological impact on the Benning family (four of the seven shareholders) if he went out and bought a company Rolls Royce. But he was not sure whether the $3,000 or $2,400 lease payment made sense. If he leased the car, he was willing to give Luxury a reasonable return on its money, say 18 percent a year with monthly payments and compounding. Did the two quoted payments give this kind of rate?

He did have one helpful bit of information. John Roberts, one of the owners of Luxury Motors, told Marty that each lease choice would also contain the option to buy the car at the end of 36 months. The higher priced car could be purchased at $140,000, a price that reflected the expectation that the car would not be dropping very much in value. The lower priced car could be purchased at $80,000, a much larger percentage drop from the original price. John told Marty that the option prices reflected John's estimate of the fair market value of each car in 3 years.

Before he chose the car that he would lease, Marty decided to calculate the "fair" lease payment for each car. If he found excess profit above the 18 percent financing charge, he would bargain with John Roberts to get a lower lease cost. Then, knowing the lower lease cost, he would make his decision.

### Required

For the car dealer to make 18 percent on the financing of either lease, what should be the monthly payment? Does Marty have any room to bargain on either lease payment?

# 19

# Dividend Policies and Decisions

## NATURE OF DIVIDEND DECISIONS

A firm's dividend policies have the effect of dividing the firm's aftertax profit into two categories:

1. *Funds to Finance Long-Term Growth.* These are represented on the balance sheet by the retained earnings account. Earnings retained by the firm have traditionally accounted for one-half to two-thirds of the firm's long-term financing. The remaining one-third has been provided by debt and by new issues of preferred and common stock.

2. *Funds to Be Distributed to Shareholders.* These are represented by the cash dividends declared by the board of directors and paid to the common shareholders.

### TWO POSSIBLE APPROACHES TO DIVIDEND DECISIONS

Because dividend policies affect both long-term financing and the return distributed to shareholders, the firm may adopt two possible viewpoints on the decision to pay dividends. These are:

1. *As a Long-Term Financing Decision.* With this approach, all the firm's aftertax profits can be viewed as a source of long-term fi-

nancing. The declaration of cash dividends reduces the amount of funds available to finance growth and either restricts growth or forces the firm to find other financing sources. Thus, the firm might accept a guideline to retain earnings as long as either of two conditions exists:

**a.** *Sufficient profitable projects are available.* The acceptance of highly profitable projects represents a worthwhile growth goal for most firms. As long as such projects are available, the firm can retain earnings to finance them.

**b.** *Capital structure needs equity funds.* The firm has a variety of sources of long-term funds. To avoid the high risk associated with excessive debt, the firm must have a balance of debt and equity financing. Because of the costs of floating common stock, retaining earnings are preferable as equity financing. Thus, earnings may be retained as part of a long-term financing decision related to the management of capital structure.

With either of these guidelines, cash dividends are viewed as a remainder. Dividends represent a distribution of earnings that cannot be profitably reinvested by the firm.

**2.** *As a Maximization-of-Wealth Decision.* With this approach, the firm recognizes that the payment of dividends has a strong influence on the market price of the common stock. Higher dividends increase the value of the stock to many investors. Similarly, low dividends decrease the perceived value of the stock. The firm must, in a maximization-of-wealth sense, declare sufficient dividends to meet the expectations of investors and shareholders.

Most firms treat the declaration of dividends as a maximization-of-wealth decision. The validity of this approach depends on whether dividend policies really affect the market price of common stock. Theoretical arguments have been developed that dividends do not affect market price.* On the other hand, other evidence suggests that dividend policies have profound effects on a firm's position in the stock market.** We do not yet have conclusive empirical evidence on whether a maximization-of-wealth approach correctly deals with the dividend decision.

---

*Merton H. Miller and Franco Modigliani, "Dividend Policy, Growth, and the Valuation of Shares," *Journal of Business*, October 1961.

**See, for example, James E. Walter, "Dividend Policy: Its Influence on the Value of the Enterprise," *Journal of Finance*, May 1963, or Myron J. Gordon, "Optimal Investment and Financing Policy," *Journal of Finance*, May 1963.

## FACTORS AFFECTING DIVIDEND DECISIONS

Once we accept the premise that the level of dividends affects the value of a firm's common stock, we need to consider the factors that define the dividend decision. These factors are examined in this section.

### WHY INVESTORS WANT DIVIDENDS

Most investors expect two forms of return from the purchase of common stock. These are:

1. *Capital Gains.* The investor expects an increase in the market value of the common stock over time. If, for example, the stock is purchased at $40 and sold for $60, the investor realizes a *capital gain* of $20. Capital gain may be defined as the profit resulting from the sale of capital investments, in this case common stock.
2. *Dividends.* The investor expects, at some point, a distribution of the firm's earnings. From mature and stable corporations, most investors expect regular dividends to be declared and paid on the common stock. This expectation takes priority over the desire to retain earnings to finance expansion and growth.

A number of factors may be analyzed to help explain the investor's expectation of dividends over capital gains. Perhaps the three major factors are:

1. *Reduction of Uncertainty.* The promise of future capital gains or a future distribution of earnings involves more uncertainty than a distribution of current earnings. A current dividend represents a present-value cash inflow to the investor that cannot be lost if the firm later experiences operating or financing difficulties. This reduction of uncertainty is one factor explaining investor preference for current dividends.
2. *Indication of Strength.* The declaration and payment of cash dividends carry an information content that the firm is reasonably strong and healthy. The dividend declaration reveals liquidity since cash is needed to make the dividend payment, and this cash must be taken away from the firm's operations. The declaration reveals profitability and, more importantly, the expectation of future profitability since the firm would probably con-

serve its cash if the management were preparing for future difficulties.

3. *Need for Current Income.* Many shareholders require income from their investments to pay for their current living expenses. These investors may be reluctant to sell their shares in order to gain cash. Cash dividends provide current income to these investors without affecting their principal or capital.

## CONSTRAINTS ON PAYING DIVIDENDS

While most firms recognize the investor's demand for dividends, several factors may restrict the firm's ability to declare and pay dividends. These are:

1. *Insufficient Cash.* Although a firm may have adequate income to declare dividends, the firm may not have sufficient cash to pay the dividends. The firm's liquid funds may be tied up in receivables or inventory or the firm may be short on liquid funds due to commitments to fixed assets.

2. *Contractual Restrictions.* If a firm is experiencing liquidity or profitability difficulties, creditors may require restrictions on dividends as part of any new loan arrangements. In this situation, the firm agrees as part of a contract with a creditor to restrict dividend payments. As an example, a loan agreement may prohibit dividends as long as the firm's debt-equity ratio exceeds 1.2/1. The firm would be forced to retain earnings to increase equity and thus reduce the debt-equity ratio. A second example would be a loan agreement that restricts the dividend payout to 20 percent of earnings during the life of the loan. The low payout requires the firm to retain cash to reduce the risk of default on interest or principal payments on the loan.

3. *Legal Restrictions.* Occasionally a firm is legally restricted from declaring and paying dividends. The most common example is found in those states where the law requires that all dividends must be paid from current or past income. Firms incorporated in these states must have adequate retained earnings to declare dividends. In the absence of retained earnings, the firms are barred from declaring dividends even though they may have sufficient cash to make the payments.

**IMPORTANCE OF DIVIDEND STABILITY**

The overwhelming majority of mature corporations have dividend policies that emphasize regular and steady dividend declarations. Although earnings may fluctuate from year to year, the dividend does not. The relationship between dividends and earnings is shown in Figure 19-1. Note that the dividends rise with the long-term earnings trend but do not fluctuate on a year-to-year basis.

A number of arguments may be advanced to underline the importance of steady dividend payments, including:

1. *Perception of Stability.* When a firm declares a regular dividend, investors accept the declaration as a sign of continued normal operations. At the same time, a reduction in the declared dividend draws immediate attention and is taken by many as a sign of potential or expected trouble in the future. Many investors will immediately sell their stock without checking further, and this selling pressure will cause a decline in the market price of the stock. Stable dividend declarations avoid this reaction on the part of investors.

2. *Preference of Investors.* The typical shareholders of mature corporations generally prefer to receive steady dividends. They expect to receive an approximate amount of cash each quarter, and they may make advance commitments to invest or spend the money. If a firm fails to declare a dividend, these investors seek to invest in firms that provide a steady cash payment each quarter.

3. *Routinizing of Dividend Decisions.* By establishing a stable dividend

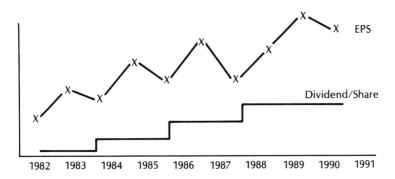

**Figure 19–1**   Relationship Between Dividends and Earnings.

602   Dividend Policies and Decisions

policy, the board of directors avoids a lengthy quarterly discussion on dividend levels. Unless circumstances warrant a possible change, the regular dividend can be declared. This policy avoids wasting the time of the board and allows its members to concentrate on more important matters facing the firm.

4. *Flexibility of the Extra Dividend.* With a steady dividend policy, the firm can flexibly handle a period of temporarily high earnings. This is accomplished by declaring an extra dividend for the quarter. This allows a larger distribution of earnings without raising the expectation of investors.

## ALTERNATIVE FORMS OF DIVIDENDS

In addition to the declaration of cash dividends, the firm has other options for distributing profits to shareholders. These options are the stock dividend, stock split, and stock repurchase.

### STOCK DIVIDEND

A *stock dividend* occurs when the board of directors authorizes a distribution of common stock to existing shareholders.* This has the effect of increasing the number of outstanding shares of the firm's stock. For example, if a shareholder owns 100 shares of common stock at a time when the firm distributes a 5 percent stock dividend, the shareholder receives 5 additional shares.

There are several aspects of a stock dividend:

1. *Conserves Cash.* The stock dividend allows the firm to declare a dividend without using up cash that may be needed for operations or expansion. Rather than seek additional external financing, the firm can retain funds that would otherwise be distributed to shareholders.
2. *Indicates Higher Future Profits.* Normally a stock dividend is an indication of higher future profits. If the profits do not rise, the firm would experience a dilution of earnings as a result of the additional shares outstanding. Since a dilution of earnings is not

---

*This discussion does not cover preferred stock dividends, although they represent another form of stock dividend.

desirable, stock dividends are usually declared only by boards of directors who expect rises in earnings to offset the additional outstanding shares.

3. *Raises Future Dividends for Investors.* If the regular cash dividend is continued after an extra stock dividend is declared, the shareholders receive an increase in future cash dividends. For example, a firm may declare a $1 regular dividend and a 5 percent extra stock dividend. A shareholder with 100 shares receives $100 and 5 additional shares. If the firm continues its $1 dividend, this investor would receive $105, an increase of $5, in the next period.

4. *Has High Psychological Value.* Because of the positive aspects of stock dividends, the dividend declaration is usually received positively by the market. This tends to encourage investment in the stock, thus supporting or raising its market price. Instead of experiencing a drop in value after a stock dividend, the price may actually rise.

5. *Retains Proportional Ownership for Shareholders.* The stock dividend differs from an issue of new common stock. If the existing shareholders do not have the funds to purchase new stock, their proportion of the ownership in the firm will decline as new investors purchase shares. This is avoided by a stock dividend that is, in effect, nothing more than a recapitalization of the firm. Table 19–1 shows a firm's equity before and after a 10 percent stock dividend. In this example, the firm has 200,000 shares of stock outstanding when a 10 percent stock dividend is declared. With a fair market value of $20 per share, the total dividend is worth $20 times 20,000 shares, or $400,000. This amount is removed

**TABLE 19–1.**   Effect of a Stock Dividend on a Firm's Equity.

*Assumes a 10% Stock Dividend When the Fair Market Value Is $20 per Share*

|  | Before the Dividend | After the Dividend |
|---|---|---|
| Common stock ($1 par) | $ 200,000 | $ 220,000  ($1 × 20,000 shares) |
| Additional contributed capital | 600,000 | 980,000 ($19 × 20,000 shares) |
| Retained earnings | 2,000,000 | 1,600,000 ($20 × 20,000 shares) |
| Total equity | $2,800,000 | $2,800,000 |

from retained earnings and distributed among the common stock and contributed capital accounts. The original owners still are credited with the same equity, but the capital structure has been modified slightly with a reduction in retained earnings and an increase in contributed capital. The ownership positions of the existing shareholders are not changed at all.

**Example:** A firm has 200,000 outstanding shares of $2 par common stock, a contributed capital in excess of par account of $3.2 million and retained earnings of $16 million, all before the declaration of dividends. The board of directors declared a $1.50 per-share cash dividend and a 25 percent stock dividend. What are the balances in the equity accounts if the fair market value of the stock is $25 per share?

**Answer:** The cash dividend reduces retained earnings by 200,000 shares $\times$ $1.50 = $300,000. The stock dividend of 50,000 shares increases common stock by $100,000 (50,000 $\times$ $2 par); contributed capital increases by $1,150,000 (50,000 $\times$ $23); retained earnings decreases by $1,250,000 (50,000 $\times$ $25). The changes in equity accounts are:

|  | Before |  | After |
|---|---|---|---|
| Common stock ($2 par) | $ 400,000 | to | $ 500,000 |
| Contributed capital | 3,200,000 | to | 4,350,000 |
| Retained earnings | 16,000,000 | to | 14,450,000 |
| Total equity | $19,600,000 |  | $19,300,000 |

## STOCK SPLITS

A *stock split* is a change in the number of outstanding shares of stock achieved through a proportional reduction or increase in the par value of the stock. Only the par value and number of outstanding shares are affected. The amounts in the common stock contributed capital and retained earnings accounts do not change. This is illustrated in Table 19–2 with a 2-for-1 stock split.

Just as the accounting values in the equity accounts do not change, the market price of the stock will normally adjust immediately to reflect a stock split. As an example, a firm may have 2 million outstanding

**TABLE 19–2.**  Effect of a 2-for-1 Stock Split on a Firm's Equity.

|  | Before the Stock Split | After the Stock Split |
|---|---|---|
| Common stock ($1 par, 200,000 shares) | | |
|              ($.50 par, 400,000 shares) | $  200,000 | $  200,000 |
| Contributed capital | 600,000 | 600,000 |
| Retained earnings | 2,000,000 | 2,000,000 |
|     Total equity | $2,800,000 | $2,800,000 |

shares selling for $20 per share. The firm declares a 2-for-1 stock split. After the split, 4 million shares will be outstanding and will sell for approximately $10 per share. A shareholder with 100 shares worth $2,000 before the split will hold 200 shares worth $2,000 after the split.

### WHY FIRMS DECLARE STOCK SPLITS

Several reasons may be offered for the splitting of a firm's common stock, as follows:

1. *Reduction of Market Price of Stock.* The major goal of most stock splits is to reduce the per-share price of a firm's common stock. A lower price per share makes the stock more affordable in round lots (100 shares) to more investors. It requires $10,000 to buy 100 shares of a stock selling for $100 per share. A 4-for-1 stock split would lower the cost of 100 shares to $2,500. The investor with $10,000 could still buy the stock and would receive 400 shares. The investor with only $2,500 could also afford to buy a round lot of the stock. By reducing the price, the firm encourages more investors to purchase the stock, thus increasing demand and the market price of the stock.

2. *Indication of Growth.* The firm's management may use the stock split to inform the market that continued high growth is forecast. The stock of high-growth companies would soon sell for several hundred dollars per share if it were not split periodically. The split thus might have informational value that the firm wants to avoid future high per-share prices for its stock, which will occur due to growth.

3. *Reverse Split—An Indication of Trouble.* Instead of increasing the number of outstanding shares of stock, the firm may want to re-

duce the number. This can be accomplished through a *reverse split*, which is a reduction of outstanding shares. As an example, a firm may have 200,000 outstanding shares of $1 par common stock. It declares a 1-for-2 reverse split. After the split, it will have 100,000 shares of $2 par stock. The reverse split is normally used to keep the price of the stock from falling below a certain level, frequently around $10 per share. The stock falling below $10 and the need of the company to declare a reverse split to keep the price up are both indicators of financial difficulty. If the firm is not in difficulty, it will expect the market price to rise above $10 due to future earnings, dividends, or growth. With these prospects, it will not declare the reverse split. The declaration of a reverse split is an indication that the firm does not have such prospects.

## REPURCHASE OF STOCK

A *repurchase of stock* occurs when a firm buys back outstanding shares of its own common stock. Firms repurchase stock for three major reasons:

1. *For Stock Options.* A *stock option* is the right to purchase a specified number of shares of common stock during a stated period and at a stipulated price. Stock options are frequently given to senior officers of a company as an incentive to work to raise the value of the firm. As an example, a firm's stock may be selling for $20 a share when the president is given an option to purchase 1,000 shares for $22 at any time in the next 3 years. If the stock value rises to $40, the president can exercise the option, purchase the stock for $22,000 (1,000 times $22), and sell it for $40,000 immediately. The gain on the sale will be a profit for the president as a direct result of the success of the firm. When a firm agrees to such stock options, the firm must have stock available to sell to the officers. Repurchase of stock allows the firm to fulfill options without increasing the total number of shares outstanding.

2. *For Acquisitions.* When a firm is seeking control of another firm, it may be willing to offer its own common stock for the stock of the other firm. In this exchange of stock situation, the firm can repurchase stock to make the acquisition. This allows the takeover without increasing the number of outstanding shares and avoids a dilution of earnings.

3. *For Retiring the Stock, Thus Increasing Earnings per Share.* When a

firm retires a portion of its stock, the retirement increases the firm's earnings per share. The repurchase of stock for the purpose of retiring it is treated as a form of cash dividend by the Internal Revenue Service.

The firm could have distributed dividends with the excess cash. Instead, it chose to reduce the number of shares outstanding so that future dividends could be increased. With this motive, the repurchase decision can be treated similarly to a dividend decision.

## REPURCHASE OF STOCK AS AN ALTERNATIVE TO DIVIDENDS

The Internal Revenue Service does not allow the repurchase of stock to be a regular alternative to the declaration of dividends. Many shareholders would desire such an alternative if it were allowed. This is true because stock repurchases may convert ordinary income from dividends to the capital gains from stock that has risen in value. If the investment qualifies under the tax code, the capital gain is taxed at a lower tax rate than ordinary income.

Table 19–3 shows the situation of an investor who owns $10,000 of a firm's common stock at the beginning of a 5-year period. In one example, the firm declares a $500 annual dividend, and the investor pays taxes at a 40 percent personal tax rate to have total stock and dividends valued

---

**TABLE 19–3.**    Benefit to Shareholder from Repurchase of Stock Rather than Declaration of Dividend.

Investor Holds $10,000 of Common Stock at Beginning of 5-Year Period.

|  | Firm Declares $500 Annual Dividend Payable to Investor | Firm Repurchases Stock Increasing Value of Stock |
|---|---|---|
| Value of stock, beginning of period | $10,000 | $10,000 |
| Total dividends declared, 5 years | 2,500 | 0 |
| Increase in value due to repurchase | 0 | 2,500 |
| Total value to shareholder | $12,500 | $12,500 |
| Tax implied or actually paid on dividends at 40% personal tax rate | 1,000 | |
| Tax implied or actually paid on capital gains at half 40% rate | | 500 |
| Net aftertax value to investor | $11,500 | $12,000 |

at $11,500 at the end of 5 years. In the second example, the firm uses the dividend money to repurchase stock and the value of the stock increases by the amount of the dividends. On the capital gain, the investor has a tax obligation of only half the 40 percent personal tax rate and finishes the 5 years with stock valued at $12,000. The repurchase of stock has resulted in more value to the investor due to the difference in tax treatment between dividends and capital gains.

## DEVELOPING DIVIDEND POLICIES

The dividend decision should reflect the different factors already discussed as well as the firm's present operating and financial position. In this total framework, the firm finds that it has a choice of several dividend policies to follow. These are discussed in this section in the form of specific dividend decisions.

### STEADY DIVIDENDS AT THE PRESENT LEVEL

Perhaps the most common dividend decision is to declare the same dollar dividend as paid last period. This meets the shareholders' expectations for current income and is not likely to affect market price. This policy may result in shortages of funds during years when earnings have declined. For mature firms with unused borrowing capacity, this is not a serious drawback.

### STEADY DIVIDENDS AT A LOWER LEVEL

The decision to reduce dividends would be considered if the firm has high-profit investment opportunities and needs the funds to finance them. This might alienate stockholders seeking current income and affect the market price of the stock. To minimize this impact, the firm might announce that the new level will be maintained in the near future and the board of directors does not anticipate further lowering of dividends. This will reduce some of the uncertainty associated with the reduction of dividends. The firm may also indicate that dividends may be raised if the new investment opportunities are as profitable as expected.

### STEADY DIVIDENDS AT A HIGHER LEVEL

This is a decision to raise the regular dividend declared by the firm. It is warranted when the firm's earnings have risen, when the earnings are stable at the higher level, and when the firm does not need the excess earnings to finance growth. Frequently, the dividend announcement will favorably affect the price of the common stock. In many cases, the higher earnings will already have caused a rise in the stock price, and the dividend declaration will have no effect.

## DIVIDENDS FLUCTUATING WITH EARNINGS

A less desirable policy is to allow the firm's dividend level to fluctuate with its earnings. The advantage to this policy is that it affords management maximum flexibility in retaining funds to finance investments. This advantage is offset by the uncertainty of dividend payments, which results in relatively low prices for the common stock of firms using this approach. The stock price also suffers because this approach emphasizes the fluctuating nature of the firm's earnings.

## LOW REGULAR DIVIDENDS PLUS EXTRA DIVIDENDS

This policy would be appropriate for a firm with cyclical earnings and limited opportunities for growth. In a good earnings year, the firm would declare an extra dividend. This approach offers a great deal of flexibility to a firm that might otherwise have excess funds on hand.

## ELIMINATE THE DIVIDEND ENTIRELY

Usually this is a policy of last resort. There are two reasons for this dividend decision. First, the firm may be experiencing serious financial difficulties and may be unable to pay a dividend. Second, the firm may have extremely attractive investment opportunities and may need to retain earnings to finance them. In this case, the firm can minimize adverse effects on the stock price by carefully explaining the reason for the elimination of the dividend and by indicating that the dividend will be resumed as soon as the funds are no longer needed for expansion.

## KEY TERMS

| | | |
|---|---|---|
| *capital gains* | *repurchase of stock* | *stock option* |
| *dividends* | *reverse split* | *stock split* |

## STUDY QUESTIONS

1. What are the two categories of aftertax profits that result from dividend policies?
2. What two points of view may be adopted with respect to dividend decisions?
3. What returns do investors expect from the purchase of common stock?
4. What is the relationship between dividends and a reduction of uncertainty?
5. What are some constraints on a firm's ability to declare or pay dividends?
6. Why do investors expect firms to declare dividends on a regular basis?
7. Why might a firm declare a stock dividend rather than a cash dividend?
8. What is achieved through a stock split?
9. Why do firm repurchase their own outstanding common stock?
10. How can stock repurchase provide more gain to the shareholder than a cash dividend?
11. What kind of firm would declare low regular dividends plus occasional extra dividends?
12. In what situation might the dividend be eliminated?

## PROBLEMS

1. A firm has 1.2 million outstanding shares of common stock at $1 par, a premium account of $3.3 million, and a retained earnings account of $8.4 million. The firm declares a 20 percent stock dividend at a time when the fair market value of the common stock is $40 per share. Prepare the equity section of the balance sheet before and after the dividend.
2. Assume the firm in problem 1 declared a 100% stock split. Prepare the balance sheet before and after the dividend.
3. A firm has 500,000 shares of $4 par common stock, a premium account of $6.4 million, and retained earnings of $32 million, all before the declaration of dividends. The board of directors declared a $2 per share cash dividend and a 15 percent stock dividend. What are the balances in the equity accounts, assuming that the market value of the stock is $30 per share?

# Dividend Policies

*This case tests the reader's ability to analyze different portfolios in making an investment decision. The reader must work through a careful evaluation of these portfolios to determine what the investment strategy should be.*

Dryden Investing Company has been a rapidly growing force in the investing and pension markets. The firm has its headquarters in Wilmington, Delaware, and has offices in three other east coast cities. It also has an office in Toronto. The firm was founded in 1975 and quickly gained respect as a conservative manager of individual and corporate funds.

In 1983, Dryden's board of directors made a number of high-level changes in management. The new management team made sweeping changes in operating policies as the firm switched its primary areas of emphasis. It began to place less emphasis on the traditional mutual fund sales and stressed tax-sheltered retirement programs for individuals and groups of individuals. The result of some strong innovations in investment counseling and services was a dramatic increase in the funds flowing in to the firm to be invested.

With its substantial cash flows, Dryden had to reconsidered its traditional investing posture. After paying claims and expenses, the firm normally placed its investing funds in very secure investments, largely real estate, fixed return securities of large corporations, and money market instruments. The conservative policy was causing some friction among pension fund managers, who wanted Dryden to seek investments with variable returns and greater liquidity than real estate. Some of the management team members and clients agreed that common stocks deserved more of a presence in the portfolio. After the disastrous 1970s, common stocks had almost disappeared from Dryden's holdings. Now, common stocks may begin to move again, and Dryden wanted to participate in such movement.

Mike Sullivan, the firm's president, met with the three general managers responsible for each of the departments that recommended investments. Ken Holden, Virginia Morris, and Charles Duckett had arrived in Mike's office for the meeting. After some preliminary discussion, Mike said, "All right, it's settled then. Each of your departments will prepare separate recommendations on how to invest October's $22 million net cash inflow. Each recommendation will reflect your department's philosophy of investing that Dryden should follow next year. And each recommendation will be summarized so that I can present it to top management and, possibly, the board."

Each of the general managers realized that this was an invaluable opportunity to influence strongly the firm's investment policies and maybe to impress the president. As a result, the three departments worked diligently for 3 weeks to prepare recommendations. On the day before the meeting of general managers to discuss each proposal, Mike Sullivan received copies of each department's recommendation. He glanced through the summary of each recommendation.

Investment Team A: Department Manager, V. Morris

The attached portfolio contains the common stocks of stable, high-quality companies whose market values slumped throughout most of the 1970s and early 1980s. The firms offer an average dividend payout of 75 percent, thus ensuring steady cash flow to Dryden and its clients. The purchase recommendations are weighted to allow larger purchases of the lowest-priced (undervalued) firms while still providing diversification. A weighted income statement and balance sheet for the portfolio are provided.

### Portfolio A—Weighted Average Income Statement

| Year | Sales | Net Income | EPS | DPS | Market Price per Share |
|------|-------|------------|-----|-----|------------------------|
| | in millions | | | | |
| 1983 | $2,016 | $133.5 | $5.03 | $4.02 | $26.00 |
| 1978 | 1,713 | 113.5 | 4.25 | 3.40 | 26.25 |
| 1973 | 1,373 | 90.8 | 3.41 | 2.72 | 24.60 |
| 1968 | 1,029 | 68.1 | 2.55 | 2.04 | 28.00 |

### Portfolio A—Weighted Average Balance Sheet (millions)

| | 1983 | 1968 | | 1983 | 1968 |
|---|------|------|---|------|------|
| Current assets | $ 511.7 | $213.6 | Current liabilities | $ 352.9 | $135.9 |
| Fixed assets | 1,252.6 | 507.4 | Long-term debt | 958.5 | 332.7 |
| | | | Common stock | 52.0 | 89.3 |
| | | | Retained earnings | 400.9 | 163.1 |
| | $1,764.3 | $721.0 | | $1,764.3 | $721.0 |

Investment Team B: Department Manager, K. Holden

Team B has prepared a portfolio that includes substantial investments in high growth companies. These companies have an average growth rate of 15 percent compounded over the period 1968 to 1983. The average dividend policy for these firms is a 10 percent dividend payout. This team believes that Dryden is not in the business of securing high cash flow from its investments. Our clients already have large cash flows. High dividends compound the problem of selecting high-quality, high-return investments. Our policy should be to seek long-term capital appreciation as a protection against inflation. Thus, we recommend securities that offer a maximum prospect for capital gains with limited prospects for short term dividends. Summary data to support our recommendation are provided.

### Portfolio B—Sales and Other Data

| Year | Sales | Net Income | EPS | DPS | Market Price per Share |
|------|-------|------------|-----|-----|------------------------|
|      | in millions | | | | |
| 1983 | $573.2 | $182.6 | $1.25 | $.13 | $18.00 |
| 1978 | 357.4  | 101.2  | .69   | .07  | 9.50   |
| 1973 | 202.5  | 57.7   | .39   | .03  | 3.00   |

Investment Team C: Department Manager, Charles Duckett

The attached portfolio reflects the kind of securities that have traditionally provided strength to Dryden and its clients. The portfolio is divided evenly between fixed income securities and high-quality corporate stocks. The stocks offer a 50 percent dividend payout and a 7.5 percent dividend yield. The stocks provide a growth element to the portfolio, and we are projecting an average growth rate of 4 percent over the next 5 years for the common stock values. This team sees no advantage to investing in commercial paper, repurchase agreements, low-grade corporate bonds, or other speculative securities, considering our obligation to safeguard the funds entrusted to our management.

After reading the summaries and examining the detailed portfolios that accompanied them, Mike Sullivan decided to run a few calculations on each summary listing. Then he began to write a list of questions to ask each general manager at the meeting the next day.

**Required**

1. Compare the portfolios on the basis of items such as dividend yield and payout, actual return, and growth rates.
2. Develop a summary analysis of each recommendation.
3. Develop some additional questions to ask each general manager.

# Bibliography

## SELECTED FINANCIAL TEXTBOOKS

Aby, Carroll D. Jr., and Donald Vaughn, editors. *Financial Management Classics.* Santa Monica, Cal., Goodyear Publishing Company, 1979.
   Generally readable articles on a variety of subjects, including functions of finance, analysis, control, working capital management, sources of financing, capital budgeting, cost of capital and capital structure, capital markets, and mergers. Suitable for advanced undergraduate or graduate courses. Omits most of the classic quantitative articles.

Archer, Stephen H., and Charles A. D'Ambrosio, editors. *The Theory of Business Finance, A Book of Readings.* New York, Macmillan Publishing Company, 1976.
   Highly quantitative articles on risk and return, capital markets, capital budgeting, cost of capital, and dividend policy. Includes many of the quantitative classics.

Bierman, Harold Jr., and Seymour Smidt. *The Capital Budgeting Decision,* fourth edition. New York, Macmillan Publishing Company, 1975.
   A readable book that covers investment decisions in detail. Topics predate, for the most part, recent developments in capital asset theory. A strong cash flow approach to issues affecting the allocation of capital.

Boudreaux, Kenneth J., and Hugh W. Long. *The Basic Theory of Corporate Finance.* Englewood Cliffs, N.J., Prentice-Hall Inc., 1977.
   Designed for the second-level finance undergraduate or first-level M.B.A. course. Presents theories and describes market economics, corporate valuation, and the relationship between financial decisions and market values. Fairly quantitative with coverage of complex topics. Extensive discussion and application of capital asset theory. A highly developed bibliography.

Brigham, Eugene F., and Ramon E. Johnson, editors. *Issues in Managerial Finance*, second edition. Hinsdale, Ill., The Dryden Press, 1980.

Articles on topics such as financial control, working capital management, long-term financing, and capital structure. Some articles are fairly quantitative. Emphasizes articles published in the mid-1970s; fewer of the classics.

Clark, John J., Margaret T. Clark, and Pieter T. Elgers. *Financial Management, A Capital Market Approach*. Boston, Holbrook Press Inc., 1976.

A quantitative book with considerable detail on capital asset tools for financial decisions. Fairly readable for the level of complexity covered. Does a better job than most texts on providing examples and details to support complex theory.

Copeland, Thomas E., and J. Fred Weston. *Financial Theory and Corporate Policy*. Reading, Mass., Addison-Wesley Publishing Company, 1979.

Highly developed approach to capital asset theory and the ramifications therein. One of the most quantitative textbooks. Closely tied to the mainstream literature in finance theory. Presents numerous models in detail.

Gitman, Lawrence J. *Principles of Managerial Finance*. New York, Harper & Row, Publishers, 1976.

Designed for an introductory course. Not much developed finance theory, but strong practical discussions in easy to read language. A developed bibliography.

Haley, Charles W., and Lawrence D. Schall. *The Theory of Financial Decisions*. New York, McGraw-Hill Book Company, 1973.

A highly theoretical approach to capital asset and other financial theory, summarizing the developments in the 1960s. Designed for advanced graduate course.

Hampton, John J. *Modern Financial Theory: Perfect and Imperfect Markets*. Reston, Virginia, Reston Publishing Company, 1982.

Covers theory and application in areas of investment policy, required return, capital structure management and dividend policy. Mathematical appendices.

Johnson, Keith B., and Donald E. Fischer. *Readings in Contemporary Financial Management*. Glenview, Ill., Scott, Foresman and Company, 1969.

A collection of articles from the 1950s and 1960s that helped shape the finance literature. Major topics are decision tools, asset management, debt and equity financing, capital structure and cost of capital, and valuation. No coverage of capital asset theory. Not highly quantitative.

Kroncke, Charles O., Erwin E. Nemmers, and Alan E. Grunewald. *Managerial Finance: Essentials*, second edition. St. Paul, Minn., West Publishing Company, 1978.

An analytical and theoretical finance book designed for the introductory graduate course. Topics include planning, raising and investing funds, and valuation. Although fairly quantitative, the calculations are not complex. A light treatment of capital asset theory. Developed bibliography.

Levy, Haim, and Marshall Sarnat. *Capital Investment and Financial Decisions*. Englewood Cliffs, N.J., Prentice-Hall International, 1978.

A textbook designed for the second course in finance or a special course on capital budgeting or financial theory. A capital asset approach is used. Covers specific topics such as inflation and the energy crisis in a policy framework. Not highly quantitative.

Myers, Stewart C., editor. *Modern Developments in Financial Management.* New York, Praeger Publishers, 1976.

Articles from the 1960s and early 1970s on financial theory, including capital structure, investment policy, and financial planning. Contains some of the most prominent contributions to the financial literature by theorists such as Lintner, Miller and Modigliani, Black and Scholes, and Myers himself. Highly quantitative articles.

Shuckett, Donald H., and Edward J. Mock. *Decision Strategies in Financial Management.* New York, AMACOM, 1973.

A development of strategies for long-term asset management (treasurer area), short-term asset management (controller area), and mergers. A practitioner's book lacking some of the rigor generally associated with strategy writings. Not quantitative.

Smith, Keith V. *Readings on the Management of Working Capital,* second edition. St. Paul, Minn., West Publishing Company, 1980.

A variety of current articles on cash management, marketable securities management, receivables, inventory, and credit management, and working capital policy. A mixture of quantitative and nonquantitative articles. Probably the best collection of readings available in the area of working capital.

Stevenson, Richard A. *Fundamentals of Finance.* New York, McGraw-Hill Book Company, 1980.

An introductory finance textbook with a general overview of major topical areas. Some quantitative discussions, but not very complex. No coverage of the capital asset pricing model.

Van Horne, James C. *Financial Management and Policy,* fifth edition. Englewood Cliffs, N.J., Prentice-Hall, Inc., 1980.

This 800-page book covers most major topical areas in finance with a capital asset orientation. Designed for the graduate course in finance, it reflects the major financial concepts of the 1960s and 1970s. Most chapters are closely tied to the literature. Not quantitative.

Weston, J. Fred, and Eugene F. Brigham. *Managerial Finance,* sixth edition. Hinsdale, Ill., The Dryden Press, 1978.

Over 1,000 pages, this book joins Van Horne as a classical capital asset textbook. Covers all major areas of financial policy and analysis. Makes extensive use of appendices for more complicated issues. More quantitative than Van Horne, but manageable at the graduate level in most finance courses.

# SELECTED ARTICLES

## INVESTMENT POLICY

1952 Markowitz, Harry. "Portfolio Selection," *Journal of Finance.* March 1952. Rejects hypothesis that investor does or should maximize discounted expected returns. Illustrates relationship between beliefs and choice of portfolio according to the "expected return—variance of return" rule. Fairly quantitative.

1955   Lorie, James H. and Leonard J. Savage. "Three Problems in Rationing Capital," *Journal of Business*. October 1955. Lists problems in budgeting capital and offers solutions to maximize net worth of the firm. Solutions differ in principle from those implied by rate of return method under capital rationing. Not quantitative.

1958   Tobin, J. "Liquidity Preference as Behavior Towards Risk," *The Review of Economic Studies*. February 1958. Covers assumptions put forth by the Keynesian model. Proposes a risk aversion theory of liquidity preference where downward-sloping liquidity preference curves are implausible. Highly quantitative.

Hirshleifer, J. "On the Theory of Optimal Investment Decision," *The Journal of Political Economy*. August 1958. Attempts to solve for optimal investment decision through the use of isoquant analysis. Reviews principles laid down by Irving Fisher regarding interest (See: Fisher, *The Theory of Interest*, N.Y. Macmillan Co., 1930.) building upon earlier work (1907). Shows how Fisher's principles must be adapted for conditions of market imperfection. Shows error in IRR concept and redefines rate of return for higher reliability. Argues that IRR method is generally not correct for multi-period investments. Somewhat quantitative.

1959   Molodovsky, Nicholas. "Valuations of Common Stocks," *Financial Analysts Journal*. February 1959. An empirical study of value and return from common stock investments.

1961   Hirshleifer, J. "Risk, the Discount Rate, and Investment Decisions," *The American Economic Revew*. May 1961. Presents a market theory of risk modeled upon Fisher's treatment of time preference and interest. Attempts to show how criterion of maximization of present value must be modified or generalized when risky investments are considered. Indicates a changing discount rate as method for incorporating different risk levels in projects. Not quantitative.

Holt, Charles C. and John P. Shelton. "The Implications of the Capital Gains Tax for Investment Decisions," *Journal of Finance*. December 1961. Evaluates the effect of the capital gains tax on decisions involving selling or holding stock. Explains roles of capital gains tax when decisions are made. Discusses regulatory workings of the tax in 1950s. Examines possibility of postponement or avoidance of the tax. Somewhat quantitative.

1963   Hillier, Frederick S. "The Derivation of Probabilistic Information for the Evaluation of Risky Investments," *Management Science*. April 1963. Develops a method for determining a probability distribution of returns when appraising a risky investment. Uses standard deviation as risk measure. Somewhat quantitative.

1964   Ahearn, Daniel S. "Investment Management and Economic Research," *Financial Analysts Journal*. January-February 1964. Presents relationships between economics and investment management. Examines role of business forecasting, economic research, and other economic variables.

Hertz, David B. "Risk Analysis in Capital Investment," *Harvard Business Review*. January-February 1964. Examines methods of comparing alternative investments. Develops a probabilistic method of evaluation. Not quantitative.

Hirshleifer, J. "Efficient Allocation of Capital in an Uncertain World," *The American Economic Review*. May 1964. Builds upon Markowitz and Fisher to explain yield divergences. Develops formulation for investment choice considering investor attitude toward risk and uncertainty.

Lerner, Eugene M. and Willard T. Carlton. "The Integration of Capital Budgeting and Stock Valuation," *The American Economic Review*. September 1964. Attacks single-equation capital budgeting and security valuation models. Introduces two-equation model to simultaneously determine IRR, dividend percentage, and price of common stock. Fairly quantitative.

Sharpe, William F. "Capital Asset Prices: A Theory of Market Equilibrium Under Condition of Risk," *Journal of Finance*. September 1964. Discusses relationship between asset price and components of risk. Provides model of investor behavior under conditions of risk. Considers equilibrium conditions in market and derives capital market line. Fairly quantitative with some regression analysis.

Jaedicke, Robert K. and Alexander A. Robichek. "Cash-Volume-Profit Analysis Under Conditions of Uncertainty," *The Accounting Review*. October 1964. Adds probability concepts to CVP analysis in a statistical treatment of risk.

1965 Treynor, Jack L. "How to Rate Management of Investment Funds," *Harvard Business Review*. January-February 1965. Through characteristic lines, security and market returns are related. A performance measure is developed with graphic technique.

Lintner, J. "The Valuation of Risky Assets and the Selection of Risky Investments in Stock Portfolios and Capital Budgets," *The Review of Economics and Statistics*. February 1965. Proves Tobin's separation theorem. Discusses problem of optimal portfolio selection by risk-averse investors. Shows how a set of simultaneous equations can determine optimal portfolio when short sales are permitted. Derives a set of equilibrium market prices. Considers implications of theory in capital-budgeting decisions. Highly quantitative.

Wendt, Paul F. "Current Growth Stock Valuation Methods," *Financial Analysts Journal*. March-April 1965. Analyzes a variety of stock-valuation models, including Walter, Clendenin, Bauman, and Ferguson.

Duvall, Richard M. and James Bulloch. "Adjusting Rate of Return and Present Value for Price-Level Changes," *The Accounting Review*. July 1965. Develops formulas for adjusting return to reflect inflation.

Hespos, Richard F. and Paul A. Strassmann. "Stochastic Decision Trees for the Analysis of Investment Decisions," *Management Science*. August 1965. The title reflects the content. Fairly quantitative.

Lintner, J. "Security Prices, Risk and Maximal Gains from Diversification," *Journal of Finance*. December 1965. One of the major articles contributing to the early development and refinement of capital asset theory.

1966 Mossin, Jan. "Equilibrium in a Capital Asset Market," *Econometrica*. October 1966. Investigates properties of a market for risky assets on the basis of a model of general equilibrium of exchange. Criteria are individual investors seek to maximize preference functions over expected yields and variance of yields on their portfolios. Develops a theory of market risk premiums.

Shows that general equilibrium implies the existence of a market line relating per dollar expected yield and standard deviation. Concept of price of risk is discussed in terms of the shape of the line. Quantitative.

1967 Robichek, Alexander A. and James C. Van Horne. "Abandonment Value and Capital Budgeting," *Journal of Finance*. December 1967. The original article for evaluating the decision to abandon an asset.

1968 Myers, Stewart C. "A Time-State-Preference Model of Security Valuation," *Journal of Financial and Quantitative Analysis*. March 1968. Presents a model of security valuations in which uncertainty takes central role. Quantitative.

Myers, Stewart C. "Procedures for Capital Budgeting Under Uncertainty," *Industrial Management Review*. Spring 1968.

Tuttle, Donald L. and Robert H. Litzenberger. "Leverage, Diversification and Capital Market Effects on a Risk-Adjusted Capital Budgeting Framework," *The Journal of Finance*. June 1968. Attempts to develop a rational and objective basis for making capital-budgeting decisions under conditions of less than perfect knowledge about the future. Quantitative.

1969 Jensen, Michael C. "Risk, the Pricing of Capital Assets, and the Evaluation of Investment Portfolios," *Journal of Business*. April 1969. Examines performance of a portfolio of risky assets in model framework. Includes such areas as rational investor choice under conditions of uncertainty, portfolio analysis through the normative theories of Markowitz and Tobin, market equilibrium under Sharpe, Lintner, and Mossin, efficiency-performance relationships, and others. Includes a quantitative empirical study.

Van Horne, James C. "The Analysis of Uncertainty Resolution in Capital Budgeting for New Products," *Management Science*. April 1969.

Sarnat, Marshall and Haim Levy. "The Relationship of Rules of Thumb to the Internal Rate of Return: A Restatement and Generalization," *Journal of Finance*. June 1969.

Robichek, Alexander A. "Risk and the Value of Securities," *Journal of Financial and Quantitative Analysis*. December 1969.

Mossin, Jan. "Security Pricing and Investment Criteria in Competitive Markets," *American Economic Review*. December 1969. Primarily analyzes the role of the market and its impact on investment decisions. Presents a model of the market, a formula for valuation of the market, and a discussion of the formula's impact on the firm's investment policy.

1970 Hogarty, Thomas F. "The Profit of Corporate Mergers," *Journal of Business*. July 1970. Shows investment performance of merging firms to be generally poorer than average performance. Some firms achieve high returns by merging.

Hagaman, T. Carter. "A Screening Technique for Prospective Acquisitions," *Financial Executive*. December 1970. Outlines a low-cost technique for screening acquisitions without a detailed financial analysis.

Litzenberger, R. H. and Alan P. Budd. "Corporate Investment Criteria and the Valuation of Risk Assets," *Journal of Financial and Quantitative Analysis*. December 1970. A capital asset approach to investing and the valuation of securities. Highly quantitative.

1971 Hakansson, Nils H. "Capital Growth and the Mean-Variance Approach to Portfolio Selection," *Journal of Financial and Quantitative Analysis*. January 1971.

Stapleton, Richard C. "Portfolio Analysis, Stock Valuation and Capital Budgeting Rules for Risky Projects," *Journal of Finance*. March 1971. A capital asset treatment of portfolio investing. Quantitative.

Van Horne, James C. "A Note on Biases in Capital Budgeting Introduced by Inflation," *Journal of Financial and Quantitative Analysis*. March 1971.

Haley, Charles W. "Taxes, the Cost of Capital and the Firm's Investment Decisions," *Journal of Finance. September 1971.*

1972 Schall, Lawrence D. "Asset Valuation, Firm Investment, and Firm Diversification," *Journal of Business.* January 1972.

Lev, Baruch and Gershon Mandelker, "The Microeconomic Consequences of Corporate Mergers," *Journal of Business.* January 1972.

Melicher, Ronald W. and Thomas R. Harter, "Stock Price Movements of Firms Engaging in Large Acquisitions," *Journal of Financial and Quantitative Analysis*. March 1972.

Myers, Stewart C. "A Note on Linear Programming and Capital Budgeting," *Journal of Finance.* March 1972.

Myers, Stewart C. "The Application of Finance Theory to Public Utility Rate Cases," *Bell Journal of Economics.* Spring 1972.

Keeley, Robert and Randolph Westerfield. "A Problem in Probability Distribution Techniques for Capital Budgeting," *Journal of Finance.* June 1972.

Fama, Eugene F. "Components of Investment Performance," *Journal of Finance.* June 1972.

Klammer, Thomas. "Empirical Evidence of the Adoption of Sophisticated Capital Budgeting Techniques," *Journal of Business.* July 1972.

Bierman, Harold Jr. and Warren H. Hausman. "The Resolution of Investment Uncertainty Through Time," *Management Science.* August 1972.

Breen, W. J. and E. M. Lerner. "On the Use of Beta in Regulatory Proceedings," *Bell Journal of Economics.* Autumn 1972.

Jensen, M. C. "Capital Markets: Theory and Evidence," *Bell Journal of Economics.* Autumn 1972.

Kryzanowski, L., Peter Luszlig and B. Schwab. "Monte Carlo Simulation and Capital Expenditure Decisions—A Case Study," *Engineering Economist.* Fall 1972.

Stiglitz, J. E. "Some Aspects of the Pure Theory of Corporate Finance: Bankruptcies and Take-overs," *Bell Journal of Economics.* Autumn 1972.

Van Horne, James C. and William F. Glassmire Jr. "The Impact of Unanticipated Changes in Inflation on the Value of Common Stocks," *Journal of Finance.* December 1972.

1973 Myers, Stewart C. "A Simple Model of Firm Behavior under Regulation and Uncertainty," *Bell Journal of Economics.* Spring 1973.

Weston, J. Fred. "Investment Decisions Using the Capital Asset Pricing Model," *Financial Management.* Spring 1973.

Rubenstein, M. E. "A Mean Variance Synthesis of Corporate Financial Theory," *Journal of Finance.* March 1973.

Lessard, Donald R. and Richard S. Bower. "An Operational Approach to Risk Screening," *Journal of Finance.* May 1973.

Rubenstein, M. E. "Jan Mossin's 'Theory of Financial Markets'," *Bell Journal of Economics.* Autumn 1973.

1974 Melicher, Ronald W. and David E. Rush. "Evidence on the Acquisition-

Related Performance of Conglomerate Firms," *Journal of Finance.* March 1974.

1974   Myers, Stewart C. "Interactions of Corporate Financing and Investment Decisions—Implications for Capital Budgeting," *Journal of Finance.* March 1974.

Modigliani, Franco and Gerald A. Pogue. "An Introduction to Risk and Return," *Financial Analysts Journal.* March-April and May-June 1974.

Ekern, S. and R. Wilson. "On the Theory of the Firm in an Economy with Incomplete Markets," *Bell Journal of Economics.* Spring 1974.

Pettit, R. Richardson and Randolph Westerfield. "Using the Capital Asset Pricing Model and the Market Model to Predict Security Returns," *Journal of Financial and Quantitative Analysis.* September 1974.

Peck, S. C. "Alternative Investment Models for Firms in the Electric Utilities Industry," *Bell Journal of Economics.* Autumn 1974.

Shick, Richard A. and Frank C. Jen. "Merger Benefits to Shareholders of Acquiring Firms," *Financial Management.* Winter 1974.

Hastie, K. Larry. "One Businessman's View of Capital Budgeting," *Financial Management.* Winter 1974.

1975   Petty, J. William, David F. Scott Jr. and Monroe M. Bird. "The Capital Expenditure Decision-Making Process of Large Corporations," *Engineering Economist.* Spring 1975.

Kihlstrom, R. E. and L. J. Mirman. "Information and Market Equilibrium," *Bell Journal of Economics.* Spring 1975.

Lockett, A. Geoffrey and Anthony E. Gear. "Multistage Capital Budgeting under Uncertainty," *Journal of Financial and Quantitative Analysis.* March 1975.

Fewings, David R. "The Impact of Growth on the Risk of Common Stocks," *Journal of Finance.* May 1975.

Ofer, Aharon R. "Investors' Expectations of Earnings Growth, Their Accuracy and Effects on the Structure of Realized Rates of Return," *Journal of Finance.* May 1975.

Litzenberger, Robert H. and O. Maurice Joy. "Decentralized Capital Budgeting Decisions and Shareholder Wealth Maximization," *Journal of Finance.* September 1975.

Stone, B. K. "The Conformity of Stock Values Based on Discounted Dividends to a Fair-Return Process," *Bell Journal of Economics.* Autumn 1975.

Hayes, Robert H. "Incorporating Risk Aversion into Risk Analysis," *Engineering Economist.* Winter 1975.

Robichek, Alexander A. "Interpreting the Results of Risk Analysis," *Journal of Finance.* December 1975.

1976   Thompson, Howard E. "Mathematical Programming, The Capital Asset Pricing Model and Capital Budgeting of Interrelated Projects," *Journal of Finance.* March 1976. Argues that mathematical programming must be tied into market value maximization for interrelated projects. Quantitative.

Mason, R. Hal and Maurice B. Goudzwaard. "Performance of Conglomerate Firms: A Portfolio Approach," *Journal of Finance.* March 1976. Empirical test concluding that conglomerates do not outperform individual assets comprising them. Not very quantitative.

Waters, R. C. and Richard L. Bullock. "Inflation and Replacement Decisions," *Engineering Economist.* Summer 1976.

Nelson, Charles R. "Inflation and Capital Budgeting," *Journal of Finance.* June 1976. Argues that inflation distorts capital-budgeting decisions if inflation is not considered in the analysis. Not very quantitative.

Elton, Edwin J., Martin J. Gruber and Manfred W. Padberg. "Simple Criteria for Optimal Portfolio Selection," *Journal of Finance.* December 1976. Optimization techniques without use of mathematical programming. Highly quantitative.

1977 Bonini, Charles P. "Capital Investment Under Uncertainty with Abandonment Options," *Journal of Financial and Quantitative Analysis.* March 1977.

Roll, R. "A Critique of the Asset Pricing Theory's Tests," *Journal of Financial Economics.* March 1977.

Myers, Stewart C. and S. M. Turnbull. "Capital Budgeting and the Capital Asset Pricing Model: Good News and Bad News," *Journal of Finance.* May 1977.

Fama, E. F. "Risk-Adjusted Discount Rates and Capital Budgeting Under Uncertainty," *Journal of Financial Economics.* August 1977.

1978 Friend, I., R. Westerfield and M. Granito. "New Evidence on the Capital Asset Pricing Model," *Journal of Finance.* June 1978.

Levy, Haim. "Equilibrium in an Imperfect Market: A Constraint on the Number of Securities in the Portfolio," *American Economic Review.* September 1978.

Beranek, W. "Some New Capital Budgeting Theorems," *Journal of Financial and Quantitative Analysis.* December 1978.

1979 Breeden, D. "An Intertemporal Asset Pricing Model with Stochastic Consumption-Investment Opportunities," *Journal of Financial Economics.* September 1979.

Magee, H. Robert and Gordon S. Roberts. "On Portfolio Theory, Holding Period Assumptions, and Bond Maturity Diversification," *Financial Management.* Winter 1979. Discusses limitations of empirical research with respect to selection of holding period for portfolio. Not quantitative.

1980 Schall, Lawrence D. and Gary L. Sundem. "Capital Budgeting Methods and Risk: A Further Analysis." *Financial Management.* Spring 1980.

Van Horne, James C. "An Application of the CAPM to Divisional Required Returns," *Financial Management.* Spring 1980.

Weston, J. Fred and Nai-fu Chen. "A Note on Capital Budgeting and the Three Rs," *Financial Mangement.* Spring 1980.

Blume, Marshall E. "The Relative Efficiency of Various Portfolios: Some Further Evidence," *Journal of Finance.* May 1980. Empirical testing of bond and stock portfolios building upon a Sharpe-Lintner approach. Not quantitative.

Epstein, Larry G. and Stuart M. Turnbull. "Capital Asset Prices and the Temporal Resolution of Uncertainty," *Journal of Finance.* June 1980.

Sunder, Shyam. "Stationarity of Market Risk: Random Coefficients Tests for Individual Stocks," *Journal of Finance.* September 1980. A quantitative testing of hypotheses concerning market risk.

## CAPITAL STRUCTURE AND COST OF CAPITAL

1952 Durand, David. "Costs of Debt and Equity Funds for Business: Trends and Problems of Measurement," *Conference on Research on Business Finance,* 1952, reprinted in *The Theory of Business Finance,* second edition, edited by Archer and D'Ambrosio, New York: Macmillan Publishing Company, 1976. The foundation article on capital structure and cost of capital. Examines problems in measuring capital costs. Develops conceptual problems related to stock financing, retaining earnings, and tax consequences. Quantitative but fairly straightforward and readable.

1958 Modigliani, Franco and Merton H. Miller. "The Cost of Capital, Corporation Finance, and the Theory of Investment," *The American Economic Review.* June 1958. A revised version of a paper delivered at the annual meeting of the Econometric Society in 1956. The classic defense of fixed cost of capital theory. Uses partial equilibrium analysis in developing cost of capital and capital structure theory. Fairly quantitative.

1959 Fisher, Lawrence. "Determinants of Risk Premiums on Corporate Bonds," *Journal of Political Economy.* June 1959. Author develops a hypothesis dealing with the areas of average risk premiums on bonds. Covers risk of default variables and market value of bonds. Incorporates a linear logarithmic equation concerning some variables. Discusses alternatives to main hypothesis. Statistical procedures and charts.

Durand, David. "The Cost of Capital, Corporation Finance, and the Theory of Investment: Comment," *The American Economic Review.* September 1959. Analyzes position of Miller-Modigliani. Indicates difficulties of using their assumptions to support an operational definition of cost of capital and a valuable theory of investment. Regression analysis is used.

Modigliani, Franco and Merton H. Miller. "The Cost of Capital, Corporation Finance, and the Theory of Investment: Reply," *The American Economic Review.* September 1959. Responds to Durand's position in same issue of journal and provides further elaboration of own model.

1962 Donaldson, Gordon. "New Framework for Corporate Debt Policy," *Harvard Business Review.* March-April 1962. Advocates cash flow approach as essential element in capital structure decisions. Suggests improvements in financial risk analysis, including use of probabilities. One of the classic articles in finance.

Malkiel, Burton G. "Expectations, Bond Prices, and the Term Structure of Interest Rates," *Quarterly Journal of Economics.* May 1962. Examines short- and long-term interest rates relating bond prices and yields. Summarizes expectations on the range of interest rates. Highly quantitative.

Lintner, John. "Dividends, Earnings, Leverage, Stock Prices and the Supply of Capital to Corporations, *Review of Economics and Statistics.* August 1962.

Holt, Charles C. "The Influence of Growth Duration on Share Price," *Journal of Finance.* September 1962.

Lintner, John. "The Cost of Capital and Optimal Financing of Corporate Growth," *Journal of Finance.* May 1963. Examines optimal decision rules for financing mix and size of firm's capital budget. Covers optimal growth rates and dividend value. Develops model removing constraint of fixed investment budget. Highly quantitative.

1963 Solomon, Ezra. "Leverage and the Cost of Capital," *Journal of Finance.* May 1963. Shows the effect of changing financial leverage on a company's cost of capital. Addresses position of Miller-Modigliani on fixed cost of capital.

Concludes that the cost of capital rises with increased leverage whenever marginal cost of debt is greater than the cost of capital. Not quantitative.

Modigliani, Franco and Merton H. Miller. "Corporate Income Taxes and the Cost of Capital: A Correction," *American Economic Review*. June 1963. Reexamines effects of tax treatment of interest and dividends and concludes the cost of capital can be lowered and firm value raised by adding debt with favorable leverage. This is the M-M position after taxes. Highly quantitative.

Weston, J. Fred. "A Test of Cost of Capital Propositions," *Southern Economic Journal*. October 1963. Shows that Miller-Modigliani propositions are Dur and's net operating income approach to valuation. Concludes that leverage does influence a firm's cost of capital. Some regression analysis.

Malkiel, Burton G. "Equity Yields, Growth, and the Structure of Share Prices," *American Economic Review*. December 1963.

1964 Boness, A. James. "A Pedagogic Note on the Cost of Capital," *Journal of Finance*. March 1964.

1965 Modigliani, Franco and Merton H. Miller. "The Cost of Capital, Corporation Finance, and the Theory of Investment: Reply," *American Economic Review*. June 1965. Contends that there is no precise definition of risk aversion. Addresses issue of proper measure of the value of debt in world of taxes. Responds to Brewer and Michaelsen.

Brewer, Dawson E. and Jacob B. Michaelsen. "The Cost of Capital, Corporation Finance, and the Theory of Investment: Comment," *American Economic Review*. June 1965. Challenges M-M position that arbitrage operations will make the market value of stock independent of capital structure. Discusses other M-M arguments. Quantitative.

1966 Fisher, Lawrence. "An Algorithm for Finding Exact Rates of Return," *Journal of Business*. January 1966. Presents a method for comparing return when funds are added or subtracted from portfolio. Quantitative.

Baumol, William J. Burton G. Malkiel and Richard E. Quandt. "The Valuation of Convertible Securities," *Quarterly Journal of Economics*. February 1966. Centers on techniques for incorporating convertible debt in capital structure analysis. Includes a valuation model.

Archer, Stephen H. and Leroy G. Faerber. "Firm Size and the Cost of Equity Capital," *Journal of Finance*. March 1966.

Stevenson, Richard. "Corporate Stock Reacquisition," *Accounting Review*. April 1966.

Miller, M. H. and Franco Modigliani. "Cost of Capital to Electric Utility Industry," *American Economic Review*. June 1966. A test and support of M-M's fixed cost of capital theory.

Haley, Charles W. "A Note on the Cost of Debt," *Journal of Financial and Quantitative Analysis*. December 1966.

Wippern, Ronald F. "Financial Structure and the Value of the Firm," *Journal of Finance*. December 1966.

1967 Schwartz, Eli and J. Richard Aronson, "Some Surrogate Evidence in Support of the Concept of Optimal Capital Structure," *Journal of Finance*. March 1967.

Brigham, Eugene F. and K. V. Smith. "The Cost of Capital to the Small Firm," *Engineering Economist*. Fall 1967.

1967   Baxter, Nevins D. "Leverage, Risk of Ruin, and the Cost of Capital," *Journal of Finance*. September 1967.

Kaplan, Seymour, "Computer Algorithms for Finding Exact Rates of Return," *Journal of Business*. October 1967. Presents an improved algorithm (compared to Fisher's) for the examination of exact rates of return. Quantitative.

Baumol, William and Burton G. Malkiel. "The Firm's Optimal Debt-Equity Combination and the Cost of Capital," *Quarterly Journal of Economics*. November 1967.

1968   Elton, E. and Martin Gruber. "The Effect of Share Repurchase on the Value of the Firm," *Journal of Finance*. March 1968.

Fama, Eugene F. "Risk, Return and Equilibrium: Some Clarifying Comments," *Journal of Finance*. March 1968. Brings together Sharpe and Lintner models in CAPM to show that no conflict exists between the two. Discusses risk and return in both models and applies general aspects to market models. Highly quantitative.

Elton, E. and Martin Gruber. "The Cost of Retained Earnings—Implications for Share Repurchase," *Industrial Management Review*. Spring 1968.

Ben-Shahar, Haim. "The Capital Structure and Cost of Capital: A Suggested Exposition," *Journal of Finance*. September 1968.

Smidt, Seymour. "A New Look at the Random-Walk Hypothesis," *Journal of Financial and Quantitative Analysis*. September 1968. Discusses random-walk hypothesis empirically and statistically. Examines Martingale process. Discusses supply and demand for liquidity. Quantitative.

Bierman, Harold Jr. "Risk and the Addition of Debt to the Capital Structure," *Journal of Financial and Quantitative Analysis*. December 1968.

1969   Hamada, Robert S. "Portfolio Analysis, Market Equilibrium and Corporate Finance," *Journal of Finance*. March 1969. Analyzes framework of Sharpe-Lintner-Mossin market equilibrium model as an extension of Markowitz-Tobin model. Quantitative.

Van Horne, James C. "Warrant Valuation in Relation to Volatility and Opportunity Cost," *Industrial Management Review*. Spring 1969. Lightly quantitative study of issues affecting valuation of warrants.

Soldofsky, R. M. and R. L. Miller. "Risk-Premium Curves for Different Classes of Long-Term Securities, 1950–1960," *Journal of Finance*. June 1969. Presents risk-return relationship for long term securities in empirical study. Annual yield profiles are established. Quantitative with tables and charts.

Heims, A. James and Case M. Sprenkle. "A Comment on the Modigliani-Miller Cost of Capital Thesis," *American Economic Review*. September 1969. Repairs an alleged flaw in M-M cost of capital thesis.

Modigliani, Franco and Merton H. Miller. "Reply to Heims and Sprenkle," *American Economic Review*. September 1969.

Sarma, L. V. and K. S. Hanumanta Rao. "Leverage and the Value of the Firm," *Journal of Finance*. September 1969. A presentation of valuation theory in the M-M context. Quantitative.

Bacon, Peter W. and Edward L. Winn, Jr. "The Impact of Forced Conversion on Stock Prices," *Journal of Finance*. December 1969. An empirical study of forced conversion and its effect on the price of common stock.

Stiglitz, Joseph E. "A Re-Examination of the Modigliani-Miller Theorem,"

*American Economic Review*. December 1969. Shows five limitations of M-M position. Covers basic concepts and extensions with bankruptcies and individual borrowing. Quantitative.

1970  Tinsley, P. A. "Capital Structure, Precautionary Balances, and Valuation of the Firm: The Problem of Financial Risk," *Journal of Financial and Quantitative Analysis*. March 1970.

Baldwin, W. L. and T. J. Velk. "Uncertainty of the Income Stream in the Modigliani-Miller Model," *Quantitative Review of Economics and Business*. Spring 1970. Quantitative support of M-M position that capital structure does not affect value of the firm.

Pfahl, John K., D. T. Crary and R. H. Howard. "The Limits of Leverage," *Financial Executive*. May 1970. Explores traditional views of the amount of debt a firm can handle and argues for a high level of leverage. Not quantitative.

Malkiel, Burton G. and John G. Cragg. "Expectations and the Structure of Share Prices," *American Economic Review*. September 1970.

Meinyk, Z. Lew. "Cost of Capital as a Function of Financial Leverage," *Decision Sciences*. July-October 1970.

1971  Hausman, W. H., R. R. West and J. A. Largay. "Stock Splits, Price Changes, and Trading Profits: A Synthesis," *Journal of Business*. January 1971.

Elton, Edwin J. and Martin Gruber. "Valuation and the Cost of Capital for Regulated Industries," *Journal of Finance*. June 1971. An application of M-M theory to regulated industries.

Haugen, R. A. and James L. Pappas. "Equilibrium in the Pricing of Capital Assets, Risk-Bearing Debt Instruments, and the Question of Optimal Capital Structure," *Journal of Financial and Quantitative Analysis*. June 1971.

Robichek, Alexander A. and Marcus C. Bogue. "A Note on the Behavior of Expected Price-Earnings Ratios Over Time," *Journal of Finance*. June 1971. A short analysis of the P/E ratio in the context of a valuation model. Provides theoretical insight into the P/E multiple.

1972  Litzenberger, R. H. and D. P. Rutenberg. "Size and Timing of Corporate Bond Flotations," *Journal of Financial and Quantitative Analysis*. January 1972. Uses analytical model to determine optimal size and timing of debt issues. Appendix on the optimal size of lines of credit.

Litzenberger, R. H. and C. V. Rao. "Portfolio Theory and Industry Cost-of-Capital Estimates," *Journal of Financial and Quantitative Analysis*. March 1972.

Hamada, Robert S. "The Effect of the Firm's Capital Structure on the Systematic Risk of Common Stocks," *Journal of Finance*. May 1972.

Findlay, M. Chapman III and E. E. Williams. "Capital Allocation and the Nature of Ownership Equities," *Financial Management*. Summer 1972.

Boness, A. James, A. H. Chen and S. Jutusipitak. "On Relations Among Stock Price Behavior and Changes in the Capital Structure of the Firm," *Journal of Financial and Quantitative Analysis*. September 1972.

Krouse, C. G. "Optimal Financing and Capital Structure Programs for the Firm," *Journal of Finance*. December 1972.

Stone, B. K. "The Cost of Bank Loans," *Journal of Financial and Quantitative Analysis*. December 1972.

1973  Alberts, W. W. and S. H. Archer. "Some Evidence on the Effects of Company Size on the Cost of Equity Capital," *Journal of Financial and Quantitative Analysis*. March 1973.

1973 Elton, Edwin J. and Martin Gruber. "Asset Selection with Changing Capital Structure," *Journal of Financial and Quantitative Analysis*. June 1973.

Arditti, Fred D. and M. S. Tysseland. "Three Ways to Present the Marginal Cost of Capital," *Financial Management*. Summer 1973.

Ang, James C. "Weighted Average Versus True Cost of Capital," *Financial Management*. Autumn 1973.

Arditti, Fred D. "The Weighted Average Cost of Capital: Some Questions on its Definition, Interpretation and Use," *Journal of Finance*. September 1973.

Kraus, Alan and R. H. Litzenberger. "A State-Preference Model of Optimal Financial Leverage," *Journal of Finance*. September 1973.

1974 Merton, Robert C. "On the Pricing of Corporate Debt: The Risk Structure of Interest Rates," *Journal of Finance*. May 1974.

Johnson, Rodney and R. Klein. "Corporate Motives in Repurchases of Discounted Bonds," *Financial Management*. Autumn 1974.

Keller, T. F. and R. J. Peterson. "Optimal Financial Structure, Cost of Capital, and the Lease-or-Buy Decision," *Journal of Business Finance and Accounting*. Autumn 1974.

Gordon, Myron J. and Paul J. Halpern. "Cost of Capital for a Division of a Firm," *Journal of Finance*. September 1974.

Kumar, P. "Market Equilibrium and Corporation Finance: Some Issues," *Journal of Finance*. September 1974.

Haugen, Robert A. and Prem Kumar. "The Traditional Approach to Valuing Levered-Growth Stocks," *Journal of Financial and Quantitative Analysis*. December 1974.

Kolodny, Richard. "The Refunding Decision in Near Perfect Markets," *Journal of Finance*. December 1974.

1975 Beranek, W. "The Cost of Capital, Capital Budgeting, and the Maximization of Shareholder Wealth," *Journal of Financial and Quantitative Analysis*. March 1975.

Bierman, H., K. Chopra and J. Thomas. "Ruin Considerations: Optimal Working Capital and Capital Structure," *Journal of Financial and Quantitative Analysis*. March 1975.

Kumar, Prem. "Growth Stocks and Corporate Capital Structure Theory," *Journal of Finance*. May 1975.

Brigham, Eugene F. "Hurdle Rates for Screening Capital Expenditure Proposals," *Financial Management*. Autumn 1975.

Lloyd-Davies, Peter R. "Optimal Financial Policy in Imperfect Markets," *Journal of Financial and Quantitative Analysis*. September 1975.

Haugen, R. A. and D. W. Wichern. "The Intricate Relationship Between Financial Leverage and the Stability of Stock Prices," *Journal of Finance*. December 1975.

Nantell, Timothy J. and C. Robert Carlson. "The Cost of Capital as a Weighted Average," *Journal of Finance*. December 1975.

1976 Baron, D. P. "Default Risk and the Modigliani-Miller Theorem: A Synthesis," *American Economic Review*. March 1976.

Inselbag, Isik. "Optimal Financing and Capital Structure Programs for the Firm: Comment," *Journal of Finance*. June 1976. Adds to theory put forward by C. G. Krouse in December 1972 article in same journal.

Ezzell, J. R. and R. B. Porter. "Flotation Costs and the Weighted Average Cost of Capital," *Journal of Financial and Quantitative Analysis*. September 1976.

Jensen, Michael C. and W. H. Meckling. "Theory of the Firm: Managerial Behavior, Agency Costs and Ownership Structure," *Journal of Financial Economics*. October 1976.

Davis, E. W. and K. A. Yeomans. "Market Discount on New Issues of Equity: The Influence of Firm Size, Method of Issue and Market Volatility," *Journal of Business Finance and Accounting*. Winter 1976.

Henderson, Glenn V. Jr. "On Capitalization Rates for Riskless Streams," *Journal of Finance*. December 1976. Disputes Gordon's position on discounting all risk-free cash flows at the pretax interest rate.

1977   Hite, G. L. "Leverage, Output Effects, and the M-M Theorems," *Journal of Financial Economics*. March 1977.

Scott, J. J. "Bankruptcy, Secured Debt, and Optimal Capital Structure," *Journal of Finance*. March 1977.

Gonzalez, N., R. Litzenberger and J. Rolfo. "On Mean Variance Models of Capital Structure and the Absurdity of their Predictions," *Journal of Financial and Quantitative Analysis*. June 1977.

Arditti, Fred D. and Haim Levy. "The Weighted Average Cost of Capital as a Cutoff Rate: A Critical Analysis of the Classical Textbook Weighted Average," *Financial Management*. Fall 1977.

Merton, R. C. "On the Pricing of Contingent Claims and the Modigliani-Miller Theorem," *Journal of Financial Economics*. November 1977.

Myers, Stewart C. "Determinants of Corporate Borrowing," *Journal of Financial Economics*. November 1977.

1978   Arditti, Fred D. and J. M. Pinkerton. "The Valuation and Cost of Capital of the Levered Firm with Growth Opportunities," *Journal of Finance*. March 1978.

Becker, Jack. "General Proof of Modigliani-Miller Propositions I and II Using Parameter-Preference Theory," *Journal of Financial and Quantitative Analysis*. March 1978.

Haugen, R. and L. Senbet. "The Insignificance of Bankruptcy Costs to the Theory of Optimal Capital Structure," *Journal of Finance*. May 1978.

Gordon, M. J. and L. I. Gould. "The Cost of Equity Capital: A Reconsideration," *Journal of Finance*. June 1978.

Brick, J. R. and Howard E. Thompson. "The Economic Life of an Investment and the Appropriate Discount Rate," *Journal of Financial and Quantitative Analysis*. December 1978.

Haley, C. W. and L. D. Schall. "Problems with the Concept of the Cost of Capital," *Journal of Financial and Quantitative Analysis*. December 1978.

1979   Aivazian, V. and J. L. Callen. "Investment, Market Structure, and the Cost of Capital," *Journal of Finance*. March 1979.

Celec, S. E. and R. H. Pettway. "Some Observations on Risk-Adjusted Discount Rates: A Comment," *Journal of Finance*. September 1979.

1979  Gahlon, J. M. and R. D. Stover. "Debt Capacity and the Capital Budgeting Decision," *Financial Management*. Winter 1979. Builds upon the work of Bower and Jenks and Martin and Scott in earlier issues of the same journal

1980  Martin, J. D. and D. F. Scott. "Debt Capacity and the Capital Budgeting Decision: A Revisitation," *Financial Management*. Spring 1980. Incorporates M-M considerations and bankruptcy into debt capacity model.

Litzenberger, R., K. Ramaswamy and H. Sosin. "On the CAPM Approach to the Estimation of a Public Utility's Cost of Equity Capital," *Journal of Finance*. May 1980. Compares traditional, borrowing-constrained, after-tax, three-moment, and other versions of the CAPM to develop risk premiums.

Taggart, R. A. "Taxes and Corporate Capital Structure in an Incomplete Market," *Journal of Finance*. June 1980.

Elliott, J. W. "The Cost of Capital and US Capital Investment: A Test of Alternative Concepts," *Journal of Finance*. September 1980. Empirical testing of different costs of capital concepts with best support for weighted average model.

## DIVIDEND POLICY

1956  Walter, James E. "Dividend Policies and Common Stock Prices," *Journal of Finance*. March 1956. Sets forth the basic Walter model for valuation of a dividend stream.

Lintner, John. "Distribution of Income of Corporations among Dividends, Retained Earnings, and Taxes," *American Economic Review*. May 1956. Lintner's study that corporations behave as though dividends affect value of common stock.

1957  Durand, David. "Growth Stocks and the Petersburg Paradox," *Journal of Finance*. September 1957. Examines dividend yields and probability analysis. Presents limitations for growth stock appraisals. Quantitative.

1959  Gordon, Myron J. "Dividends, Earnings and Stock Prices," *Review of Economics and Statistics*. May 1959. Presents the foundation for the Gordon model.

1961  Modigliani, Franco and Merton H. Miller. "Dividend Policy, Growth, and the Valuation of Shares," *Journal of Business*. October 1961. The M-M proof that dividends are irrelevant. Highly quantitative.

Soldofsky, Robert M. "Growth Yields," *Financial Analysts Journal*. September-October 1961. Examines market prices in terms of future rising dividend streams.

1962  Lintner, John. "Dividends, Earnings, Leverage, Stock Prices and the Supply of Capital to Corporations," *Review of Economics and Statistics*. August 1962.

1963  Baumol, W. J. "On Dividend Policy and Market Imperfection," *Journal of Business*. January 1963.

Gordon, M. J. "Optimal Investment and Financing Policy," *Journal of Finance*. May 1963. Addresses M-M view and suggests that share price and cost of capital are not independent of dividends. Quantitative.

Walter, James E. "Dividend Policy: Its Influence on the Value of the Enterprise," *Journal of Finance*. May 1963. Argues that dividend policies affect value of the firm. Discusses difficulties in empirical testing to link dividend policies and market values. Not quantitative.

1964    Fisher, L. and J. H. Lorie. "Rates of Return on Investments in Common Stocks," *Journal of Business*. January 1964. Presents empirical study on stocks held for varying periods with returns expressed in absence of dividends, dividend retention, or dividend reinvestment.

Lintner, John. "Optimal Dividends and Corporate Growth under Uncertainty," *Quarterly Journal of Economics*. February 1964.

Friend, Irwin and M. Puckett. "Dividends and Stock Prices," *American Economic Review*. September 1964.

1965    Clarkson, Geoffrey P. E. "A Theory of Stock Price Behavior," *Industrial Management Review*. Spring 1965. Empirical study of price movements with implications for future research.

1966    Woods, Donald H. and E. F. Brigham. "Stockholder Distribution Decisions: Share Repurchase or Dividends," *Journal of Financial and Quantitative Analysis*. March 1966.

Modigliani, Franco and Merton H. Miller. "Some Estimates of the Cost of Capital to the Electric Utility Industry," *American Economic Review*. June 1966. Support for a fixed cost of capital in an empirical study.

1968    West, R. R. and H. Bierman Jr. "Corporate Dividend Policy and Preemptive Security Issues," *Journal of Business*. January 1968.

Brigham, Eugene and Myron J. Gordon. "Leverage, Dividend Policy, and the Cost of Capital," *Journal of Finance*. March 1968.

Fama, Eugene F. and Harvey Babiak. "Dividend Policy: An Empirical Analysis," *Journal of the American Statistical Association*. December 1968. Examines dividend policies of firms using Lintner's partial adjustment model. Quantitative.

1970    Mendelson, M. "Leverage, Dividend Policy and the Cost of Capital: A Comment," *Journal of Finance*. September 1970.

1971    Brennan, M. "A Note on Dividend Irrelevance and the Gordon Valuation Model," *Journal of Finance*. December 1971.

1972    Higgins, Robert C. "The Corporate Dividend-Saving Decision," *Journal of Financial and Quantitative Analysis*. March 1972.

Whittington, G. "The Profitability of Retained Earnings," *Review of Economics and Statistics*. May 1972.

Higgins, Robert C. "Dividend Policy and Increasing Discount Rate: A Clarification," *Journal of Financial and Quantitative Analysis*. June 1972.

Pettit, R. R. "Dividend Announcements, Security Performance, and Capital Market Efficiency," *Journal of Finance*. December 1972.

1973    Watts, R. "The Information Content of Dividends," *Journal of Business*. April 1973.

1974    Black, F. and M. Scholes. "The Effects of Dividend Yield and Dividend Policy on Common Stock Prices and Returns," *Journal of Financial Economics*. May 1974.

Fama, Eugene. "The Empirical Relationships Between the Dividend and Investment Decisions of Firms," *American Economic Review*. June 1974.

Higgins, Robert C. "Growth, Dividend Policy and Capital Costs in the Electric Utility Industry," *Journal of Finance*. September 1974.

1975   Ben-Zion, U. and S. S. Shalit. "Size, Leverage, and Dividend Record as Determinants of Equity Risk," *Journal of Finance*. September 1975.

Wrightsman, D. and J. O. Horrigan. "Retention, Risk of Success, and the Price of Stock," *Journal of Finance*. December 1975.

1976   Mehta, Dileep. "The Impact of Outstanding Convertible Bonds on Dividend Policy," *Journal of Finance*. May 1976.

Stewart, S. S. "Should a Corporation Repurchase its Own Stock?" *Journal of Finance*. June 1976.

Lee, Cheng F. "Functional Form and the Dividend Effect in the Electric Utility Industry," *Journal of Finance*. December 1976. Continued work on whether dividends are relevant in a specific industry.

1978   Long, J. "The Market Value of Cash Dividends, A Case to Consider," *Journal of Financial Economics*. June-September 1978.

Miller, M. and M. Scholes. "Dividends and Taxes," *Journal of Financial Economics*. December 1978.

1979   Spraakman, G. P. "The Sensitivity of Earnings Per Share Growth to Some of its Financial Components," *Financial Management*. Winter 1979.

1980   DeAngelo, H. and R. W. Masulis. "Leverage and Dividend Irrelevancy Under Corporate and Personal Taxation," *Journal of Finance*. May 1980.

Mukherjee, T. K. and L. M. Austin. "An Empirical Investigation of Small Bank Stock Valuation and Dividend Policy," *Financial Management*. Spring 1980.

## WORKING CAPITAL MANAGEMENT

1952   Baumol, W. J. "The Transactions Demand for Cash: An Inventory Theoretic Approach," *Quarterly Journal of Economics*. November 1952. Applies an inventory model to the problem of cash inventory. Determines the economic order quantity when cash receipts exceed disbursements, and vice versa.

1956   Magee, J. "Guides to Inventory Policy: Problems of Uncertainty," *Harvard Business Review*. March-April 1956. A series of articles discussing the analysis of inventory policies for use by management in selecting the best inventory system.

1960   Lasher, A. "Managing Your Corporate Cash for Profit," *Dun's Review and Modern Industry*. June 1960. Discusses the management of corporate cash to support higher sales, manage reserves, and minimize short-term borrowing. Uses the spreading of disbursements, the lock-box system, and short-term investing as methods of management.

1961   Lasher, A. "Managing Company Cash," *Studies in Business Policy*. 1961.

1963   Dundas, P. "Cash Flow—A Management Tool," *Credit and Financial Management*. August 1963.

1964   Walker, E. W. "Towards a Theory of Working Capital Management," *Engineering Economist*. January-February 1964. Formulates a theory of working capital management, with the amount of risk as the determinant for the quantity and type of working capital.

Snyder, A. "Principles of Inventory Management," *Financial Executive*. April 1964. Analyzes the development and uses of the principles of inventory control. Presents the theory of the economic order quantity defined as a range of quantities rather than one specific quantity.

Baxter, N. D. and H. T. Shapiro. "Compensating Balance Requirements: Results of a Survey," *Journal of Finance*. September 1964.

Anderson, P. F. and R. D. B. Harman. "The Management of Excess Corporate Cash," *Financial Executive*. October 1964.

1965 Robicheck, A. A., D. Teichroew and D. Jones. "Optimal Short-Term Financing Decisions," *Management Science*. September 1965. Discusses the problem of short-term financing decisions when no alternative is clearly advantageous, and develops a model for use in this situation.

1966 Soldofsky, R. M. "A Model for Accounts Receivables Management," *Management Accounting*. January 1966.

Archer, S. H. "A Model for the Determination of Firm Cash Balances," *Journal of Financial and Quantitative Analysis*. March 1966. A presentation of a structure with which management can subjectively select an optimal cash balance for a point in time.

Miller, M. H. and D. Orr. "A Model of the Demand for Money by Firms," *Quarterly Journal of Economics*. August 1966.

Bean, V. L. and R. Griffith. "Risk and Return in Working Capital Management," *Mississippi Valley Journal of Business and Economics*. Fall 1966.

1967 Barry, J. K. "Cash Management, A Sharper Focus," *Journal of Accountancy*. April 1967.

Mock, E. J. "Investment of Corporate Cash," *Management Science*. September-October 1967.

Greer, C. C. "The Optimal Credit Acceptance Policy," *Journal of Financial and Quantitative Analysis*. December 1967. Identifies the components of credit-related profits that a financial manager should consider when deciding how many credit applicants to accept, and how these components change when a firm accepts riskier applicants.

1968 Mehta, D. "The Formulation of Credit Policy Models," *Management Science*. October 1968. Studies the formulation and efficiency assessment of a credit extension policy for a single account. Focuses on the decision rules for credit extension, incorporating a description of the credit system and an evaluation of its stability.

1969 Wrightsman, D. "Optimal Credit Terms for Accounts Receivable," *Quarterly Review of Economics and Business*. Summer 1969.

Van Horne, J. C. "A Risk-Return Analysis of a Firm's Working Capital Position," *Engineering Economist*. Winter 1969. Outlines a method with which management can evaluate the risk-return trade-off for varying amounts of liquid assets and quantities of debt, and thereby determine its working capital position.

1970 Marrah, G. L. "Managing Receivables," *Financial Executive*. July 1970.

Walter, P. "How to Calculate Savings Possible Through Reduction of Working Capital," *Financial Executive*. October 1970. Presents working capital as the sum of all necessary expenditures made prior to the collection of sales revenue, and formulates the savings from the reduction in working capital in this framework.

1970 Frost, P. A. "Banking Services, Minimum Cash Balances and the Firm's Demand for Money," *Journal of Finance*. December 1970. Theorizes that the firm's two reasons for holding on to its money, minimum cash balance and transaction balance, are interdependent. Formulates a model incorporating Miller and Orr's basic stochastic structure and an explicit demand for banking services.

1971 Abraham, A. B. "Factoring: The New Frontier for Commercial Banking," *Journal of Commercial Bank Lending*. April 1971.

Eiteman, W. J. and J. N. Holtz. "Working Capital Management," *Essay on Business Finance*. Spring 1971.

Glautier, M. W. E. "Towards a Reformulation of the Theory of Working Capital," *Journal of Business Finance*. Spring 1971.

Cossaboom, R. A. "Let's Reassess the Profitability-Liquidity Trade-Off," *Financial Executive*. May 1971. Discusses the profitability-liquidity trade-off in terms of the flexibility and innovativeness of financial managers. Segmental financing is given as an example.

1972 Pogue, G. and R. Bussard. "A Linear Programming Model for Short-Term Financial Planning Under Uncertainty," *Sloan Management Review*. Spring, 1972.

Stone, B. K. "The Cost of Bank Loans," *Journal of Financial and Quantitative Analysis*. December 1972. Focuses on the interdependence of loan cost and tangible bank activity as the cost of bank debt, and establishes the effective cost of bank loans in the presence of compensating balance requirements.

Knight, W. D. "Working Capital Management—Satisficing Versus Optimization," *Financial Management*. Spring 1972.

DeSalvo, A. "Cash Management Converts Dollars Into Working Asset," *Harvard Business Review*. May 1972. Discusses the effective management of cash based on the premise that idle dollars should be kept at a minimum. Examines the role of the treasurer as the coordinator of short-term funds.

1973 Heyman, D. P. "A Model for Cash Balance Management," *Management Science*. August 1973.

Smith, K. V. "An Overview of Working Capital Management," *Financial Management Associates*. October 1973. A presentation of the existing literature on working capital management. Discusses the definitions, goals and decisions involved in the management of working capital. Examines the contrasting approaches to working capital management.

Smith, K. V. "State of the Art of Working Capital Management," *Financial Management*. Autumn 1973.

1974 Ludeman, D. H. "Corporate Liquidity in Perspective," *Financial Executive*. October 1974. Discusses corporate liquidity in the framework of a firm's accessibility to various capital sources. States that "continuous availability" of capital sources and good internal management are the keys to maintaining liquidity.

Mao, J. C. "Controlling Risk in Accounts Receivable Management," *Journal of Business Finance and Accounting*. Autumn 1974.

Mao, J. C. "Accounts Receivable Financing," *Credit and Financial Management*. December 1974.

1975 Murphy, J. F. "Sound Cash Management and Borrowing," *Small Marketers' Aid*. 1975.

Suryanarayanan, S. "Control of Accounts Receivables," *Management Accounting*. February 1975.

Bierman, H., K. Chopra and L. Thomas. "Ruin Considerations: Optimal Working Capital and Capital Structure," *Journal of Financial and Quantitative Analysis*. March 1975. Examines the correlation between working capital and the optimal capital structure. Presents ruin, defined as a given level of equity, in terms of its effects on working capital decisions.

Schiff, M. "Credit Management," *Financial Executive*. November 1975.

1976  Long, M. S. "Credit Screening System Selection," *Journal of Financial and Quantitative Analysis*. June 1976. Focuses on the selection of the best of alternative credit selection systems. The proposed method uses the maximization of the net present value as the basis for selection.

Oh, J. S. "Opportunity Cost in the Evaluation of Investment in Accounts Receivable," *Financial Management*. Summer 1976.

1978  Yardini, E. E. "A Portfolio-Balance Model of Corporate Working Capital," *Journal of Finance*. May 1978.

Mao, J. and C. Sarndal. "Cash Management Theory and Practice," *Journal of Business Finance and Accounting*. Autumn 1978.

Maier, S. and J. Vander Weide. "A Practical Approach to Short-Run Financial Planning," *Financial Management*. Winter 1978. Develops a computerized model for use in evaluating short-term investment financing decisions. Integrates various forecasting and optimization models.

1979  Gitman, L., E. Moses and I. White. "An Assessment of Corporate Cash Management Practices," *Financial Management*. Spring 1979.

Cascino, A. "How to Make More Productive Use of Working Capital," *Management Review*. May 1979. Reviews the business problems of the present economy, and the deep-rooted assumptions that cause managers to overlook the possibilities for cost savings in the area of working capital.

Lambrix, R. J. and S. Singhui. "Managing the Working Capital Cycle," *Financial Executive*. June 1979. Outlines the working capital cycle and the level of investment, and suggests that financial managers should work to achieve a full understanding of working capital so as to optimize the firm's investment.

Gitman, L. and M. Goodwin. "An Assessment of Marketable Securities Practices," *Journal of Financial Research*. Fall 1979.

1980  Smith, K. and S. Bell. "Working Capital Management in Practice," *Readings on the Management of Working Capital*. St. Paul, Minn., West Publishing Co., 1980. A survey of contemporary practices of working capital management, with a discussion of the implications and results.

Kalotay, A. "Optimal Management of Short-Term Debt," *Public Utilities Fortnightly*. November 1980. Analyzes the terms under which it is desirable to invest in a short-term security with a minimum yield rather than to repay a loan with a greater nominal yield, and vice versa.

Dogget, R. "Managing Working Capital," *Management Accounting*. December 1980. Reviews the trade-offs between risk and profitability and presents some approaches to the tracking and control of working capital.

1981  Maier, S., D. Robinson and J. Vander Weide. "A Short-Term Disbursement Forecasting Model," *Financial Management*. Spring 1981. Develops a statistical model for use in forecasting short-term cash flows. Discusses the value of the model in the framework of the selection of short-term portfolios and the timing of short-term borrowing.

1981   Westbrook, W. and C. Rawlins. "Bank Credit Commitments and Cash Management—Are Fees Really Cheaper Than Balances," *Public Utilities Fornightly*. August 1981. Uses a methodology which determines certain basic relationships to estimate the cost of continuing credit agreements under various circumstances, using differing balances and fees.

1982   Johnson, J., D. Campbell and J. Wittenbach. "Identifying and Solving Problems in Corporate Liquidity," *Financial Executive*. May 1982. Presents the results of a survey concerning the signs of illiquidity and the solutions to it. Sites inventory build-up as the most significant monitoring device and reduction in inventories as the major solution to illiquidity.

# Index

Accelerated cost recovery system (ACRS) 357, 581
Acceptance 228
Acceptance criterion 381
Accounts payable 80, 504
Accounts receivable 248
Accounts receivable turn-over 126
Accrual basis 59
Accruals 506
Acid test 125
Acquisition 458
Acquisition, resisting 484
Administrative expenses 252
Aging of accounts receivable 255
American Stock Exchange 48
Amortization 34, 554
Annual clean up 504, 509
Annuity 364
Anti-trust considerations in mergers 464
Asset leverage 195
Asset turnover 134
Assets, defined 17, 60, 88
Assets, intangible 60
Auditing 58
Average collection period 260
Average cost of capital 403

Bad debt losses 251
Balance sheet 62, 87
Balloon payment 551, 577
Balloon payment, calculating 554
Banker's acceptance 228, 335
Beta coefficient 396
Bibliography 615
Billing float 238
Bogus collateral 513
Bond 34
Book residual value 361
Book value 92, 145, 429
Borrowing capacity 571
Bottleneck items 277
Break-even analysis 164
Broker 46
Budget 58, 164
Business risk 399

Call 435
Callable bonds 35, 545
Cap on loan 551
Capital asset pricing model 395
Capital asset theory 396
Capital budgeting 349
    cash flows in 354

kinds of proposals 352
    significance of 350
Capital gain 469, 599
Capital rationing 354
Capital structure 41, 403, 623
    factors affecting 41
    ratios 143
Capitalization approach to intrinsic value 436
Cash 86, 225
    investing excess 326
    safety level 235
Cash flow stream 355, 367
Cash flows 354
    calculating the stream 367
    forecasting 232
    in capital budgeting 354
Cash management 234
Cash residual value 361, 580
Celler–Kefauver Amend-ment 465
Certificate of Deposit 227, 332
Certified Public Accountant (CPA) 5
Charter 31
Chattel mortgage 578
Circulating assets 220
Clayton Act 464

637

Cleanup 504, 509
Closing accounts 69
Collateral 512, 522, 550
Collateral trust bond 34
Collection costs 251
Combined leverage 200
Commercial paper 226, 332, 511
Common stock 38
    required return on 406
    value of 436
Compensating balance 231, 509
Competitive bid 326
Compound value 306
Compound value tables 310
Concentration banking 241
Conditional sales contract 577
Conglomerate 462
Consolidation 461
Constant cost 166
Constant dollars 60
Contingent projects 354
Controller 22
Conversion premium 545
Conversion price 545
Conversion ratio 545
Convertible bond 35
Convertible securities 544
    characteristics of 545
Corporation 31
    foreign 463
Cost accounting 58
Cost control 15
Cost of capital 403, 623
    and capital structure 403
    weighted average
       approach to 403
Covenant 551
Credit limits, establishing 263
Current assets 86, 220
    current dollars 60
    current liabilities 61, 86
    current ratio 125
Cutoff point 381

Data processing 25
Dealer 46
Debenture 34
Debt 29

    cost of 404
    securities 29
    value 434
Debt-asset ratio 144
Debt-equity ratio 143
Default 232
Deficit 236
Depository bank 239
Depository transfer check (DTC) 241
Depreciation 356
    accelerated 357, 581
    benefits in leasing 581
    schedule 361
    straight line 358
Differential cash flows 355
Dilution of earnings 478
    avoiding 476
    and role of P/E 479
Direct costs 273
Direct placement 45
Disbursements 242
Disbursements, managing 237
Disbursing bank 239
Discounting to present value 363
Discounts, effective costs of 320
Diversification 459
Dividend
    alternative forms of 602
    approach to valuation 438
    constraints on paying 600
    decisions 597
    factors affecting 599
    and importance of stability 601
    payout 146, 439
    policies 597, 608, 630
    ratios 146
    three types 39
    yield 146
Dividend-growth model 440
Double entry accounting 63
Dupont chart 136

Earning power 137
Earnings before interest and taxes (EBIT) 98

Earnings before taxes (EBT) 98
Earnings per share (EPS) 142
Earnings per share, future 173
Earnings ratios 141
Economic order quantity (EOQ) 277
Effective cost of debt 510, 556
Efficient market 400
Electronic funds transfer 243
Equity 61, 91
Equity securities 29, 81
Eurodollar 338
Exchange ratio 461, 477
Expected return E(Rtn) 397
Expense 62
External analysis 121
External growth 464

Factor 515
Factoring costs 518
Factoring receivables 517
Factors reserves 518
Favorable financial leverage 204
Federal agency issues 228
Federal Trade Commission (FTC) 465
Field warehouse 513
Finance, fields of 6
    nature of 5
    paper 226, 332
Financial accounting 57
Financial analysis and control 121
Financial decision making 4
Financial leverage 203
Financial management 8
    functions of 14
    goals of 12
    ratios 122
    tool of 18
Financial norms 148
Financial risk 399
Financial security 29
Financial statement 85
    uses of 105
Finders fee 475
Fixed assets 61
Fixed costs 99, 165

Fixed rate loan 523
Float 238
Floating lien loan 513
Floating rate loan 523
Floor, on loan 551
Flow of funds statement 100
    developing 106
Forcing the conversion 546
Forecasting cash flows 232
Funds 86
    from operations 101
Future earnings per share
    173

General and administrative
    expenses 97
Generally accepted account-
    ing principles 59
Goals of financial manage-
    ment 12
Going-concern value 59, 407,
    429
Goodwill in acquisitions 487
Gordon model 408, 440
Gross margin 98
    profit margin 134
Growth external 458
Growth factor in Gordon
    model 441
Growth internal 458
Growth, measures of 457
Growth, reasons for seeking
    459

Holding company 462
Horizontal merger 462

Income statement 95
    defined 62
    management format 98
Indenture 34
Indifference curve 400
Installment financing 318,
    575
Interest 97
Interest charges leverage 199
Interest-rate risk 341
Intermediate-term financing
    522
Internal analysis 121

Internal growth 458
Internal rate of return 378
International finance 6
Intrinsic value 429
Inventory 89
    benefits of holding 271
    costs of 273
    kinds of 271
    management of 275
    turnover 127
Investment banker 46
    policy 617
    tax credit 359, 582

Lead time 280
Lease-buy decisions 565
    factors in 579
    issues related to 569
    sources of funds 568
Leases
    basic types 565
    financial 566
    forms of 573
    service 566
Level-rental plan 573
Leverage 194
    asset 195
    combined 200
    financial 203
    interest-charges 199
    operating 198
    return on investment
        194
Liabilities 61, 90
Lien 514
Line of credit 508
Liquidation value 407, 429
Liquidity, analyzing 130
    functions 14
    ratios 125
Lockbox 240
London Interbank Offered
    Rate (LIBOR) 434, 550
Long-term liabilities 61
Long-term debt, effective
    cost 551

Macroeconomics 6
Mail float 238
Managerial accounting 58
Marginal analysis 170

Marginal leverage concept
    198
Marginal contribution 99
Market line 397
Market portfolio 398
Market rate of return 398
Market value 429
Markets for corporate securi-
    ties 45
Marketable security 88
Material cost 273
Maximization of profits 9
Maximization of wealth 10
Merger 460
    accounting for 486
    horizontal 462
    vertical 462
Microeconomics 6
Microprocessor 25
Money market funds 228
Money market rates 230
Money, time value of 305,
    363
Mortgage bond 34
Mutually exclusive projects
    354

National Association of Se-
    curities Dealers (NASD) 47
Negotiable 34
Net
    cash benefits (NCB) 367
    cash outlay (NCO) 367
    present value (NPV) 381
    proceeds 405
    sales 96
    working capital (NWC)
        219
New York Stock Exchange
    47
Non-linear break-even anal-
    ysis 167
Non-taxable reorganization
    463
Norm, determining 148
Normal price earnings ratio
    175
Note 507

Objectives of the firm 8
Open account 249

Operating budget 349
Operating income (EBIT) 98
Operating leverage 198
Option to purchase 574
Option to terminate 574
Order costs 274
Over-the-counter (OTC)
   market 46
Ownership ratios 141
Ownership rights 41

Parent company 462
Participating preferred stock
   37
Participation 523
Partnership 30
Payback method 377
Payout period 554
Perpetual existence 32, 436
   dividends 438
Piecemeal financing 570
Placements, direct and
   underwritten 45
Planning 161
   benefits of 163
Plant and equipment 108
Pledging of accounts receiv-
   able 514
Pooling of interests 487
   conditions allowing 488
Preemptive right 39
Preferred stock 36
   required return on 406
   value of 435
Premium on common stock
   92
Present value 306
   calculators 314
   tables 312
Price-earnings ratio 142
   normal 175
Price level adjusted state-
   ments 60
Primary markets 45
Prime rate 434, 550
Pro forma financial state-
   ment 58
Profit and loss statement 95
Profit center 474
Profit, defined 161
   margin 133
   planning 161

planning, weaknesses of
   206
Profit-volume analysis 168
Profitability 15
   analyzing 138
   ratios 132
Project financing 549
Proxy 484
Public finance 6
Purchase method, account-
   ing for acquisitions 487
Pyramiding 469
Pyramids
   risks and leverage in
      472
   taxation in 471

Quick ratio 125

Ratios 122
   liquidity 125
   profitability 132
   users of 126
Recapture 583
Receivables
   costs of 251
   nature of 248
   purpose of holding 249
   turnover 126
Recourse 518
Remote disbursing 243
Reorder point 279
Reorganization 463
Repurchase agreement
   (REPO) 229, 337
Repurchase of stock 606
Required return 381, 410,
   581
   how to determine 415
Research and development
   352
Residual value 361
Restrictive covenant 509
Retained earnings 92
Return
   concepts 397
   on equity 136
   on investment 135, 374
Return on investment lever-
   age 195
Revenues 61, 96

Revolving charge plan 249
Revolving credit agreement
   508, 522
Risk 396
   business 399
   class 256
   financial 399
   and required return 395
Riskless rate of return 398,
   580
Rollover effect 503

Safety level 235
   stock level 280
Sale and leaseback 569
Sales 96
Secondary Markets 46
Secured loan 512
Secured versus unsecured
   bonds 34
Securities and investment
   analysis 7
Securities Markets, regula-
   tion of 48
Self-liquidating loan 507
Sherman Act 464
Short term financing 503
   goals 504
Shortage 236
Single payment loan 507
Single period model 436
Sinking fund 34
Sole proprietor 30
Sources and uses statement
   100, 106
Standard deviation 396
Standby financing 557
Steady payment schedule
   576
Stock
   dividend 602
   option 606
   repurchase 606
   split 604
Stock exchanges 47
Stock-level subsystem 281
Storage costs 274
Subsidiary 462
Surplus 236
   or premium on common
      stock 92
Synergism in mergers 476

Takeover approach 483
Takeover strategies 475
Tangible assets 60
Tax loss credits 468
Taxation in mergers 468
Taxation in pyramids 471
Tender 484
Term loan 522
Time value of money 305,
    363
Times interest earned ratio
    137
Trading on the equity 203
Treasurer 22
Treasury bill 226, 326
Treasury note 228, 330
Treasury stock 126
Trust receipt loan 513
Turn-around situation 460
    determining price for
    482

Underwritten placement 46
Unfavorable financial lever-
    age 203
Usage rate 279


Valuation, comparative ap-
    proaches to 444
Valuation, current market
    value approach 432
Valuation of the firm 428
Value 429
    book 92, 145, 429
    going-concern 59, 407,
    429
    intrinsic 429
    liquidation 407, 429
    of common stock 436
    of preferred stock 435
Variable costs 165
Vertical merger 462

Vice president finance 22

Warehouse receipt loan 512
Warrant 35, 547
    effect on capital struc-
    ture 548
    value of 548
Wealth 10
Weighted average cost of
    capital 403
Weighted average required
    return 402
Wire transfer 240
Working capital 86, 219
    management of 219,
    223, 632
    pool 100
    tied up 360
    write off 108

Zero balance account 243